Mushrooms of British Columbia

Also from the Royal BC Museum

Food Plants of Coastal First Peoples
by Nancy J. Turner

Food Plants of Interior First Peoples
by Nancy J. Turner

Trees and Shrubs of British Columbia
by T. Christopher Brayshaw

Plant Technology of First Peoples in British Columbia
by Nancy J. Turner

Saanich Ethnobotany
by Nancy J. Turner and Richard J. Hebda

Royal BC Museum Handbook

MUSHROOMS
OF BRITISH COLUMBIA

ANDY MACKINNON AND KEM LUTHER

ROYAL **BC**
MUSEUM

VICTORIA, CANADA

Mushrooms of British Columbia

Published by the Royal BC Museum, 675 Belleville Street,
Victoria, British Columbia, v8w 9w2, Canada.

The Royal BC Museum is located on the traditional territories of
the Lekwungen (Songhees and Xwsepsum Nations). We extend our
appreciation for the opportunity to live and learn on this territory.

See p. 482 for credits and copyright information for specific elements in the book.

Library and Archives Canada Cataloguing in Publication
Title: Mushrooms of British Columbia / Andy MacKinnon and Kem Luther.
Names: MacKinnon, A. (Andrew), 1956- author. | Luther, Kem, 1946- author. |
    Royal British Columbia Museum, publisher.
Series: Royal British Columbia Museum handbook.
Description: Series statement: Royal BC Museum handbook | Includes
    bibliographical references and index.
Identifiers: Canadiana (print) 2021012587x | Canadiana (ebook) 20210126019 |
    ISBN 9780772679550 (softcover) | ISBN 9780772679567 (EPUB) |
    ISBN 9780772679574 (Kindle) | ISBN 9780772679581 (PDF)
Subjects: LCSH: Mushrooms—British Columbia—Identification. |
    LCGFT: Field guides.
Classification: LCC QK605.7.B8 M33 2021 | DDC 579.609711—dc23

10   9   8   7   6   5   4   3   2

Printed and bound in Canada by Friesens.

Contents

Introduction	**1**
About This Guide	1
What Are Mushrooms?	3
Mushroom Life Cycles	4
Ecological Roles	6
How to Use This Guide	9
Species Descriptions	10
Collecting and Eating Wild Mushrooms	22
Other Ways to Enjoy Mushrooms	25
Other Resources	27
References Cited	29

Guide to Mushroom Groups	**30**

Mushroom Descriptions	
Veined	33
Gilled	43
Pale-spored Gilled	44
Russula	45
Lactarius	61
Hygrophorus and Similar	77
Lepiota and Similar	97
Amanita and Similar	105
Clitocybe and Similar	125
Tricholoma and Similar	145
Mycena and Similar	173
Marasmius and Similar	185
Pleurotus and Similar	207

Pink-spored Gilled	221
Brown-spored Gilled	228
Agaricus	229
Cortinarius	239
Inocybe and Similar	253
Gymnopilus and Pholiota	261
Other Big Brown-spored	271
Other Little Brown-spored	281
Dark-spored Gilled	288
Coprinus and Similar	289
Gomphidius and Similar	295
Other Dark-spored	299
Boletes	317
Toothed	335
Clubs	349
Corals	369
Polypores	378
Jelly Fungi	411
Puffballs	421
Bird's Nest Fungi	431
Morels and Similar	436
Cups	449
Truffles	463
Other Fungi	472

Acknowledgements	**477**
Glossary	**478**
Credits	**482**
Index	**485**

"The individual who desires to engage in the study [of wild mushrooms] must boldly face a good deal of scorn. He is laughed at for his strange taste among the better classes, and is actually regarded as a sort of idiot among the lower orders. No fad or hobby is esteemed so contemptible as that of the 'fungus-hunter' or 'toadstool-eater.'"
—*An Elementary Text-book of British Fungi, 1887*

Fungus Among Us festival in Whistler, 2013. Fungal forays are one of the best ways to learn about mushrooms. Mycological societies, natural history societies, and fungus festivals host numerous forays each year.

Introduction

British Columbia is huge and diverse. Its 94.5 million hectares covers an area larger than Washington, Oregon, and California combined. About 40,000 islands dot BC's 26,000 kilometres of Pacific coastline. Inland, a series of southeast-to-northwest-trending mountain ranges ripple across the province, from the Vancouver Island Ranges and Queen Charlotte Ranges in the west to the Rocky Mountains in the east. The mountains offer a wide array of elevational zones (sea level to alpine) and precipitation zones (wetter on the western, windward side of the mountains, drier on the leeward). All of this physical diversity results in a tremendous variety of ecosystems, from rainforests to near deserts, lush valley bottoms to windswept alpine, southern elements to magnificent boreal forest. There are more types of ecosystems in BC than anywhere else in Canada.

Ecological diversity generates species diversity—the more types of ecosystems in an area, the more species we expect to find there. BC biologists find large numbers of species of almost every group of organisms that they study. BC has more species of plants, animals, and—most relevant for this book—fungi than any other region in Canada. A recent inventory (Kroeger and Berch, 2017) of mushroom species recorded in BC counted just over 3,000 species of macrofungi. (Macrofungi are fungi whose fruiting bodies are visible without a microscope.)

About This Guide

Those who want to know more about BC mushrooms—whether to study them with scientific goals, harvest them for the table, photograph them, or pursue them as a hobby—are not as fortunate as those interested in BC flora and fauna. There are good, up-to-date print guides that focus on BC plants, BC birds, BC mammals, and BC marine life. When asked to recommend a field guide for those beginning the study of BC mushrooms, however, we have had to add qualifications. The only guides that were specific to BC and that covered all of our province were far too dated and hard to find. Print guides that were available were either not comprehensive enough or not specific to BC. (We have provided a brief overview of these other resources at the end of this introduction.)

In light of this, we were delighted when the Royal British Columbia Museum agreed to produce a new field guide to BC's mushrooms. It was appropriate that the museum should take on this task—it had already published, in its widely respected Handbook series, two previous field guides to the mushrooms of our province. Almost 70 years ago, the museum issued *Some Mushrooms and Other Fungi of British Columbia* by George Hardy (1952), with illustrations by Frank Beebe, a small guide of about 90 pages containing 50 mushrooms. In 1964, the museum published *Guide to Common Mushrooms of British Columbia* by Robert Bandoni and Adam Szczawinski. It was larger than the first guide—about 170 pages and about 150 mushrooms. This second guide was revised in 1976 to include some colour photographs. Both guides are long out of print.

This new field guide covers considerably more ground than the earlier handbooks—we know a lot more about BC mushrooms than we did 50 years ago. On these pages you will find main entries for 350 species of mushrooms, each with one or more colour photographs. About 850 species are mentioned somewhere in the book. Yet even these numbers represent only a fraction of the BC species of mushrooms. To decide what should be included in the book and what should be left out, we naturally tapped into our own field experience, but we didn't just rely on our subjective and limited perspectives. We compared records of what had been officially observed in BC and deposited in herbaria. We also collected inventories of mushroom species from different parts of the province, trying to determine which species hikers and foragers would most likely encounter and where they would encounter them. We asked BC mycology specialists from several regions of the province to comment on our list and help us find important species that we might have overlooked. The list that came out of this long process is, we believe, a fairly accurate compendium of BC's most common and more easily identified mushrooms, as well as a sampling of less common but distinctive species.

Our next challenge, once we had a tentative species list, was to decide how to arrange them. A strict taxonomic approach seemed out of step with the book's role as a field guide—closely related mushrooms can look very different, and distantly related mushrooms quite similar. In addition, taxonomic work on the evolutionary history of mushrooms has lagged behind similar research in other fields of biology—there would have been species that had uncertain taxonomic homes. We opted instead for the widely used morphological-group approach, clumping mushrooms by their overall shape. (See the "Guide to Mushroom Groups," p. 30.) Within each of these groups, we have arranged the mushrooms by similarity rather than by alphabetized names. If you find a specimen in the field and locate something like it in this book, you can flip backward and forward a page or two to see if you can find a better fit.

Matching mushrooms with pictures, mycologists will tell you, is not the best way to do field identification. We agree, and for that reason have provided detailed descriptions for the mushrooms covered in this book. However, we have also noticed that most people who are starting to learn mushrooms lean heavily on a visual approach. For that reason, we have sought out the best diagnostic pictures we could find. The works of some 60 photographers are found on these pages (see "Credits," p. 482). Whatever use this book finds in coming years will be due as much to these photos as to the text.

We have attempted to minimize use of technical terminology in this guide. Serious students of mushrooms, we realize, will eventually have to acquire a specialized vocabulary. Technical terms open the door to a larger discipline, allowing students to interact with specialists and the scientific literature at the heart of the discipline. Mycology is not unique in this respect—almost any subject we want to master, from law to literature to science, brings with it large numbers of words and concepts that can be unfamiliar to those outside the discipline. But we are also aware that these special vocabularies, as important as they are, can build a high fence around a subject, making it hard for beginners to get started. The terms that we have employed in this guide can be found in the glossary at the back of the book. (See p. 478.)

We have also de-emphasized the use of Latin and Greek binomials, referring to the mushrooms in our text by their common rather than their scientific names. To become fluent in the world of BC mushrooms, you will eventually have to learn most of the scientific names, but you don't have to *start* with these names.

Our goal in this book is practical—helping people identify mushrooms—but we have also tried to capture some of the fun in fungi. On these pages you will discover two dozen diversions that tie the study of mushrooms into a larger historical and social context. We have also tried, in the descriptions and section introductions, to provide counterpoints to the occasionally dull science of mycology by looking at such topics as name derivations and eating. In short, this guide is meant to be both educational *and* entertaining. We find our curiosity tweaked and our passions provoked by this fascinating and beautiful group of organisms—we hope yours will too.

What Are Mushrooms?

A fungus (plural: fungi) is an organism in the kingdom Fungi. It is one of the three kingdoms in the domain Eukaryota that houses complex multicellular life. The other two hold the plants (kingdom Plantae) and the animals (kingdom Animalia). The fork in the eukaryote road that led to a separate kingdom Fungi happened perhaps a billion years ago. Most theorists who study early evolutionary pathways believe that plants diverged quite a bit sooner than when fungi separated from animals. Fungi, therefore, are more closely related to animals—including us—than they are to plants.

Today scientists believe that there are probably between two and four million species of fungi on earth. The vast majority of them have never been described by mycologists, the scientists who study fungi. Most of these fungi—groups such as yeasts or moulds—are outside the scope of this book. The fungi that produce the fleshy fruiting bodies that we call mushrooms include only a small percentage of the millions of fungal species. Mycologists have put names and descriptions to a few tens of thousands of these mushroom-bearing fungi. Perhaps ten thousand of them are known from North America. Three thousand have been found in BC. It is likely, however, that these numbers do not represent the true diversity of mushrooms—new species are continually being added to the lists of what is known.

When we discuss mushroom-bearing fungi, we usually think of them in terms of their fruiting bodies, the mushrooms. But this is a very partial picture. It would be like describing a berry and thinking that you had described the bush that it grew on. Fungi are masses of long, thin filaments, usually a fraction of the thickness of a human hair, called "hyphae" (singular: hypha). The collection of hyphae belonging to a single fungal specimen is called its "mycelium" (plural: mycelia). When fungi grow, they do it by lengthening and branching the hyphae. Unless these mycelial mats get very dense, they are hard to see, but sometimes a group of hyphae will clump together to form a rhizomorph, which can be visible. The mushroom itself also consists of hyphae, some of them specialized for the fruiting body.

All of the fungi included in this book share one important feature: they produce fleshy reproductive structures, fruiting bodies, with details large enough to be seen with the naked eye. All of these fruiting bodies are mushrooms, though in everyday speech the word "mushroom" (like its less flattering cousin, "toadstool") is usually reserved for the fruiting bodies that possess a stem, a cap, and, underneath the cap, a radial series of plate-like gills. Mushrooms in this narrower sense, however, only account for about 60 per cent of the main entries in this book. Taken in the broader sense, the term mushroom embraces fungal fruiting bodies that have pores or teeth or veins instead of gills. It also includes some even stranger shapes. Some mushrooms resemble blobs of jelly, bird's nests, or tiny clubs. And some fruit underground. For those who want to learn to recognize and name mushrooms, one of the first tasks is to become familiar with the many forms assumed by fungal fruiting bodies. In the rest of this book, when we use the word "mushroom," we will be employing it in this broader sense, as the visible fruiting body of a fungus no matter what shape it assumes.

Mushroom Life Cycles

To understand fungi, especially the fungi that produce mushrooms, we need to understand their life cycles, the way that one generation leads to another. Some fungi specialize in asexual reproduction, often by producing asexual spores, but a lot of fungal reproduction is sexual, just as it is for plants and animals. The fruiting bodies are the places where this reproduction takes place. The reason that most mushrooms only appear in certain seasons is because this is the time that the fungal mycelia have the inclination and the energy to reproduce sexually. Many prefer autumn, some prefer the spring, but some scatter their efforts over the whole growing season.

Understanding the way mushroom-producing fungi reproduce sexually can be difficult for those who think in terms of animal reproductive cycles. Animals spend most of their lives with paired chromosomes in the nuclei of their cells, only producing unpaired chromosomes (in sperm and eggs) when they want to mate. Fungi spend a good part of their cellular life with unpaired genes, only acquiring paired genes for a short period, in order to reproduce. Whatever the cycle, however, the goal is the same—to make a new generation that has a combination of the genes from two parents.

Mushroom-making fungi produce spores that have unpaired chromosomes. These spores are cast into the world where some of them, finding just the right conditions, bud and form a new mycelium. If the stars align, this new mycelium will meet up with another mycelium of the right type and mate. The mating mycelia are not male and female, as they are in most species of plants and animals—they are simply compatible mating types. Some fungi have many mating types.

When two compatible mating types come together, the hyphal threads join up and the nuclei that contain their respective genetic codes are exchanged. For most of the mushroom-making fungi, the fusion of these two nuclei into one does not happen right away. Instead, the two different nuclei, each from a separate mating type, proliferate and spread throughout the two mycelial bodies. When it is time to make offspring, primordia (mycelial clumps) form. These dense clumps of hyphae develop into the fruiting bodies (mushrooms). The mushrooms in this book produce one of two types of microscopic structures for producing sexual spores: basidia (singular: basidium) or asci (singular: ascus). The basidia sprout two, four, or more spores from their tops. Asci are more like small sacs, and the spores form inside the sacs.

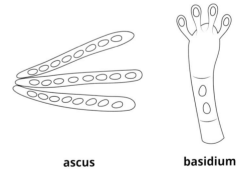

ascus   basidium

So far, the nuclei from the mating types have remained separate in the hyphal tissues. When it is finally time to make the new generation of spores, the two independent nuclei, one from each parent, join up inside the ascus or basidium and, for a brief time, a single nucleus exists with the paired genetic code from the two parents. This nucleus soon undergoes the kind of division that reduces the genetic material—now jumbled so that neither of the paired chromosome sets is exactly like either of the chromosome sets inherited from the two parents—to a single, unpaired set of chromosomes. The nucleus holding this new set of chromosomes migrates into the spores that are contained in the ascus or on the basidium. The spores are released, and the cycle begins again.

Mycologists refer to the various mushroom species as basidiomycetes or ascomycetes, depending on whether they produce basidia or asci. For beginners who have never examined mushrooms under a microscope, this terminology can seem perplexing, since it is only loosely connected to the overall shapes assumed by the mushrooms, but it is an important and fundamental distinction between types of fungi. Most of the mushrooms discussed in this field guide, including all of the mushrooms with gills, spines, and real pores, are basidiomycetes. Some of the club mushrooms, the true truffles, and all of the cups and morels are ascomycetes. One difference between basidiomycetes and ascomycetes can be noticed in the field—basidia, while they can pop their spores a short distance, do not generally give them much of a boost, but asci can literally shoot their spores, propelling them like bullets emerging from the barrel of a gun. Some ascomycetes, when handled or warmed up, can emit a sudden visible cloud of spores from their fertile surfaces.

Ecological Roles

Fungi play a number of important ecological roles in BC ecosystems. Mycorrhizal fungi help plants grow, and decomposer fungi recycle nutrients for reuse by a new generation of plants. Fungi are important predators and prey in soil ecosystems. And the fabulous fleshy fructifications we call mushrooms are food for many animals, from slugs and birds to small and large mammals.

These roles that mushrooms play in our province's ecosystems are often defined by how the fungi obtain their nutrition. Unlike plants, fungi cannot make their own food, so they need to acquire nutrition from sources that ultimately derive from plants. Some fungi derive their nutrition from decaying organic matter (decomposers). Others obtain nutrients by harming a living host (parasites). A few, surprisingly, are predators, capturing and digesting nematodes, bacteria, and protists. And many form partnerships with plants, relying on their plant hosts to supply most of their nutritional needs in exchange for water, mineral elements, and other considerations.

It is the decomposer lifestyle that probably comes to mind when most people think about mushrooms. The impression is not misguided—the majority of mushroom species probably do tap into the organic products of decay. Their hyphae—snaking through both upright and downed trees, through the soil, through dung, and even through decaying corpses (see essay on p. 276)—release enzymes that digest complex organic compounds, converting them to simpler molecules. The digested materials are absorbed into the mycelium and turned into tissues and energy. Without the nutrient-recycling services of decomposer fungi, life on earth would quickly grind to a halt. Decomposer fungi—often called "saprobes"—include many of the polypores, cup fungi, bird's nest fungi, clubs, jelly fungi, crusts, and some of the gilled fungi, especially the smaller ones.

Many of the polypores, some of the clubs, and a few of the jelly fungi and gilled mushrooms are parasites. So are most of the rusts, spots, and galls (such as those listed in the "Other Fungi" section, p. 472). These parasitic fungi grow on, or in, a living host, and a few even kill their hosts. There are many species of parasitic fungi, but most of them are not in this book because they don't produce fleshy fruiting bodies.

A few fungi actively hunt small worms, bacteria, and protists. The hyphae of OYSTER MUSHROOMS (p. 208), for example, release a substance called "ostreatin" that paralyzes very small creatures, giving the hyphae time to surround, digest, and absorb the nutrients contained in the animals. Other fungi produce ingenious microscopic devices for trapping their prey. Some use adhesive hyphae, others use constricting and non-constricting loops, some produce toxins, and some even have sharp, knife-like structures that injure their prey.

The natural world is always more complex than our simple categories, and mushroom species don't always fit neatly in one of these lifestyles. Some combine these roles. For example, a number of our polypores are parasites on living trees, ultimately killing them and then continuing to feed as decomposers on their dead hosts.

One of the more fascinating food-acquiring relationships among the fungi is the plant-fungus symbiosis that we call a "mycorrhiza" (plural: mycorrhizae). The study of mycorrhizae is one of the most exciting and active areas of mycology research. Far from being a rare event, this relationship turns out to be one of the most common ways plants and fungi interact—over 90 per cent of vascular plants take on fungi as mycorrhizal partners. This relationship is so important that without the help of their fungal mycorrhizal partners, many plants would stop growing or die. Without their plant partners, almost all mycorrhizal fungi will die.

In the course of the mycorrhizal relationship, the plant produces sugars through photosynthesis and sends these sugars to its roots for the fungus to use. The fungus absorbs water and minerals from the soil and delivers these to the plant's roots. A single tree can have multiple species of mycorrhizal fungi growing with its roots, and a single mycorrhizal fungus will often attach itself to the roots of numerous trees. In this way the trees in a forest are connected under the ground by their mycorrhizal fungi, in what has been dubbed the "wood-wide web." Water, nutrients, and signalling chemicals pass along the fungal pathways of the web. In some cases, these webs can support plants that don't photosynthesize (see essay on mycoheterotrophs, p. 54). Most of the larger gilled mushrooms (and some of the smaller ones, such as inocybes), the

vast majority of the boletes, corals, and toothed and veined fungi, some clubs, and all of the truffles are the fruiting bodies of mycorrhizal fungi. For more on the mycorrhizal roles of fungi, see p. 74.

Lichens (see essay on p. 138) are another partnership between fungi and plants, involving one or more fungi (the mycobionts) and one or more algae and/or cyanobacteria (the photobionts). The fungus provides the overall structure for the lichen and a safe home for the photobionts. The photobionts photosynthesize, creating the sugars and energy compounds that the fungus needs. The fungi in lichens don't generally form the larger, fleshy fruiting bodies that we would call mushrooms (one major exception, the LICHEN AGARIC, p. 139), so they are not included in the main entries of this guide.

How to Use This Guide

If the goal of the person using this book is to identify a mushroom, then that person will ideally end up on one of the 350 or so pages that contains a mushroom picture and description of the mushroom to be identified. This page will likely be reached by one of three methods.

The first method is simply flipping through the pictures to find something that looks like the mushroom being identified. This is not a systematic method, but for some users it's a good place to start. This method works better in bird guides and plant guides than it does for mushrooms, since mushroom species may look very different in different situations. Because similar mushrooms are clumped together in the book, however, getting close can sometimes be good enough to get the user to the right place.

The second way is more systematic. The user goes to the two-page "Guide to Mushroom Groups" (pp. 30–31) and tries to decide which group the mushroom belongs to. The names of these groups are almost the same as those in other print and online mushroom guides, so those coming to this book from other guides will probably feel at home here. For most of the groups, the procedure is fairly straightforward—for example, if you decide that your mushroom belongs to the cups group, you can turn to the page listed for the cups section and begin to search. The exception is the gilled mushrooms, which are most of the mushrooms in this book. The introduction to gilled mushrooms (p. 43) discusses spore colours, the method we have used to divide the many gilled mushrooms into broad groups. The user will need to determine the spore colour, either by using field clues or by making a spore print (p. 16). There is an introduction page for each of the four spore colours, where users can find further clues to help match specimens to specific sections of the book.

A third portal to the descriptions, the index method, is one that can be employed by more advanced users. The user starts off by making a guess what genus or species the mushroom might be, then tracks down the scientific or common name through the index. We have made an effort to include many of the alternate names for the mushrooms in our descriptions so that the index will contain names the user might be familiar with, even if the name is not the one used in this book.

No matter which method the user employs to arrive at one of the main entries in the book, the search may not be over. We have been able to include only about a tenth of the known BC mushroom species as major entries. On each page is a section (SIMILAR) that compares the entry to other species that might be confused with it. Some of these comparisons will be to other main entries, but most will be mushrooms not mentioned elsewhere in the book. An additional 340 or so mushroom species have been squeezed into the SIMILAR sections. Along with the names of these similar mushrooms, we provide important field-usable clues that will help the user decide if one of these alternatives might be a better match. Users, however, should keep in mind that, even with these other mushrooms included, the coverage in this book is still a fraction of the mushroom species known to be in BC. It is entirely possible that the mushroom being identified is not in the book. At this point, the only recourse is a guide that provides different or more complete coverage. (See the list of resources at the end of this introduction, p. 27; some of the introductions to the different mushroom groups also mention resources with more specific coverage.) BC users in search of the species not listed in this guide are fortunate—a free and continually updated computer program and iPhone app called MycoMatch: Mushrooms of the Pacific Northwest (mycomatch.com) are a perfect complement. Chances are good that any mushroom found in BC is described (and often pictured) in MycoMatch. It is also a valuable source of information for the mushrooms that are only mentioned in passing in this book. However, no matter how exhaustive any mushroom guide is, you must always keep in mind that the specimen being identified may be new to science—it may have no name and may not be described in any resource. Estimates of how many BC mushrooms might be waiting to be named and described vary widely, but it is possible that the 3,000 or so known BC mushrooms may just be the tip of an iceberg that contains 10,000 or more species.

Species Descriptions

Each of the main species descriptions in this guide follows the same pattern. This makes it easier to compare one species to another. It also helps readers focus immediately on the characteristics they want to check. It will be useful, therefore, to review some of the conventions used in the text. We will also use this review to paint a picture of the morphology and habits of the mushrooms covered in this guide.

For each description you will find a photo, the name (common and scientific), and two paragraphs. The first describes the field characteristics of the mushroom, grouped under various categories (CAP, STEM, etc.) in red capitals. The second paragraph steps back to look at some larger perspectives on this species. For almost every mushroom, there will be information about edibility and what other mushrooms most closely resemble the main entry. A final section (COMMENTS) provides background on the taxonomic placement of the species, the derivation of the species names, where and in what regions of BC the species might be found, information on mushroom toxins, and more.

Mushroom names. For each main entry you will find both a common name and the scientific name for the mushroom described on that page.

The official name of any mushroom species is its scientific binomial. We try to provide the most current name used in the technical literature. You may find that some of the names you have been accustomed to using are no longer the official names (*Tricholoma magnivelare*, for example, is now *Tricholoma murrillianum*; *Clitocybe dealbata* is now *Clitocybe rivulosa*). If you delve into the COMMENTS section, you will find explanations for many of these name changes.

Those coming to the study of fungi with a background in biology may find the number of scientific name changes in our volume, when compared to mushroom guides from only 10 or 20 years ago, to be somewhat distressing. It is the common names, we have been told, that change—only the scientific name remains constant. Scientific names, however, are not fixed in stone. They reflect, by necessity, the most recent work by taxonomists, and taxonomists are continually refining and correcting the work of their predecessors.

If you have a sense, though, that scientific names for fungi are more malleable than they used to be, you may be right. Until about 30 years ago, fungal taxonomy was based largely on reactions to chemicals, on detailed studies of fruiting body morphologies—often at the microscopic level—and, in the odd case, on mating studies. To this traditional arsenal of fungal taxonomy has now been added genetic sequencing. Several fungal DNA/RNA regions have been identified that have proved to be fairly reliable indicators of evolutionary relationships between fungal species. To publish an acceptable description of a new mushroom, researchers now find that they must include genomic data. As these data points have accumulated in public repositories such as GenBank, UNITE, and MycoBank, it has become possible to mine these data to do large-scale reorganizations of taxonomic hierarchies.

The mining has produced some surprises. In an ideal world, all the older taxonomies that were based on morphological work would correspond to what genetic sequencing tells us about the same relationships. In the real world, however, morphological characters and genetic data do not always agree—there are morphological expressions (cap colour, gill attachment, etc.) that have been used to define differences that don't exist in the genetic code, and there are genetic differences, sometimes large ones, that have no corresponding morphological features. As mycologists have become more comfortable with the use and interpretation of sequencing tools, there has been a foundational shift in the standards for species identification of mushrooms. It is not unusual to hear researchers say that "this looks like species X, but I can't know for sure without sequencing it."

Some of the scientific names in this volume have the word "group" appended. Mycologists use a number of conventions—"group" is one of them—to indicate that certain species names are not quite correct. In some cases, names are used that the mycological community knows to be incorrect, but the research has not been performed and/or published that would lead to a correct name. This is particularly common where the name applied to our local mushrooms is an existing name from a European species and we're pretty sure that our local species is different. Another problem arises when there are several species with similar descriptions and it is no longer clear which of these names are legitimate and what the real differences are. Genetic sequencing has added a third ambiguity: cryptic species that have been detected by genetic groupings but have not been correlated with morphological data. All this gets quite complex and puzzles beginners, so we have adopted only the one convention, the appended word "group," to represent a number of these ambiguities.

In this book, we have also included a common name for each species that has a main entry. We have used this common name in our cross-references to species that have main entries. Deciding which common name to use was not always easy. In Canada and the United States, many species have come to have, over the years, traditional English-language common names, such as KING BOLETE, OYSTER MUSHROOM, and PINE MUSHROOM. In cases where these traditional common names exist, we adopt them for our guide. About half of the mushrooms that we wanted to include, however, did not have these popular names, leaving us to ferret out less-standard names and, in a few cases, forcing us to invent names. We made this decision to adopt common names for all of the main-entry mushroom species in the guide with some hesitation. Our reason for using the names was that a gateway book designed to be useful to beginners needed to provide names that are signposts rather than stop signs. Birders, mammal watchers, and those who study and forage for many groups of plants have these English-language signposts, we have noted, so why not mushroom hobbyists? Our commitment to the use of common names, though, is not total—beginners who want to leap directly into the use of scientific names will find these as well, in the headings, in the index, and in a few of the cross-references.

Mushroom anatomy. On the next few pages, we will review the various categories used in the first paragraphs of the mushroom descriptions. These categories are based on the overall anatomy of a mushroom. The diagram on the next page shows the main parts of the anatomy.

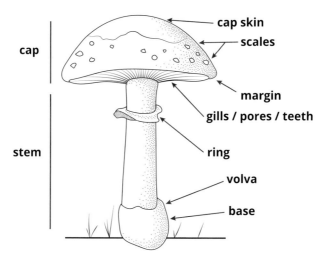

We cover the major morphological features of the mushroom in the first paragraph, except for one. In many mushroom guides, there are separate discussions of microscopic features, such as spore size and spore texture. This book, however, is a field guide, and since these aspects of mushroom identification can only be done in lab conditions, we have mostly omitted them. The exceptions are in the rare cases where microscopic features are the only discernible morphological differences between certain species that we wanted to contrast. Our omission of these details in this guide should not be taken as a judgment on their importance—no serious study of BC mushrooms can get far without considering them. The BC mycologist Oluna Ceska estimates that for every hour she spends in the field, she spends three to four hours in her lab completing the study of the mushrooms she has collected.

Caps. The first category that you will see, at least on the pages for gilled, veined, pored, and toothed mushrooms, is CAP. A mushroom cap has a skin, a protective layer over the top. In some caps, this skin can be peeled off. It can also have a gelatinous layer both in and on the cap skin, giving the cap a glutinous (very slimy) look and feel. Alternately, the protective layer on the top can be slimy/sticky (i.e., slimy when wet, sticky when dry), or it can be dry. The surface of the cap can be smooth (a term we use in this book to mean hairless and not rough to the touch), or it can be covered with small bumps, hairs, scales/fibrils (either pressed down or standing up), and other decorations, such as the warts on some amanitas.

Underneath the skin is the cap flesh. For some caps, this can be quite thick. It is, for mushroom eaters, the meat of the cap. In some mushrooms, the flesh in the cap can change colour when it is cut or bruised. The flesh, like the rest of the mushroom, consists of hyphae that assume special shapes and functions.

Several other features of the mushroom cap are mentioned in the CAP category. We list, for example, the maximum size, measured across the cap from one side to the other in a straight line. (This is the maximum size commonly seen in the field—where caps can occasionally be much larger, we mention this.) Most specimens, of course, will have less than maximum-sized caps. One important feature that is discussed in this category is the cap's colour. The colours can sometimes vary from the centre area of the cap, called the disc, to the outer edges, the margins, and the colour changes can define distinct zones. Also, caps can sometimes change colours when they become wet or dry—when they do this, the caps are described as "hygrophanous." Caps can also have striations on them, especially toward the margins, and when the striations correspond to the underlying gills and show the tops of the gills through a partly transparent cap, they are described as "translucent-striate." Some caps (and stems) can have specific staining reactions to chemical agents. The only agent we mention is KOH, potassium hydroxide.

The shape of the cap can be an important piece of information in identifying mushrooms. The shapes of caps can change over the life of the mushroom, with most caps becoming flatter as they age. Where this shape change is important, we mention it. The chart below shows some of the major shapes and the terms used for these shapes in this book.

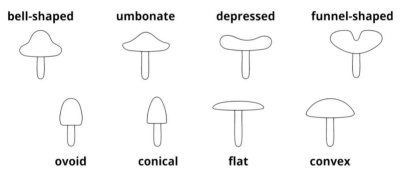

bell-shaped **umbonate** **depressed** **funnel-shaped**

ovoid **conical** **flat** **convex**

Fruiting bodies. Not all mushrooms have distinct caps protecting their fertile layers underneath, nor do all have distinct stems that are separate from the caps. For these mushrooms, a catch-all FRUITING BODY category replaces the individual categories for CAP, STEM, and GILLS/PORES/TEETH/UNDERSIDE.

Gills/pores/teeth/veins. Nestled underneath the cap, protected by the top layer and the cap flesh, is the fertile surface. Since the goal of fungal fruiting bodies is to maximize the area available to hold the spore-producing cells, the fertile surfaces are almost always arranged either as gills (*lamellae*), as pores, as small projections called spines or (in this guide) teeth, or as ridges/veins. A cap that has a surface area of 25 square centimetres might harbour under it an array of fertile surfaces that would cover an area 20 or more times this size. Deep (usually described as "broad" in most guides) gills and deep pore surfaces have a long vertical run from top to bottom; shallow (alternately, "narrow") gills and pore surfaces have a shorter run.

The gills, pores, teeth, or veins attach to the underside of the cap and often to the cap margin. These structures can also attach to the stem. Some of these structures travel down the stem, having what is known as a "decurrent attachment." If they do not travel down the stem but have a wide area of attachment, then we say that they are "broadly attached." If they have a smaller width of attachment, then they are "narrowly attached." In some gill arrangements, the attached gills are "notched"—just before reaching the stem they take a small leap upward and sometimes come slightly back down the stem. And then there are gills that do not attach to the stem at all, known as "free gills." The diagram below illustrates these major types of fertile surface attachment.

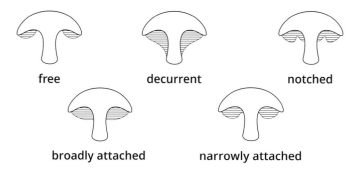

Other characteristics of the fertile surfaces can aid with identification. For gills, edges can be a different colour than the sides (faces) of the gills. Edges can also be irregular in shape, sometimes ragged, scalloped, or sawtoothed. On some gilled mushrooms, the gills are spaced differently (widely spaced, closely spaced, crowded) and may or may not have shortened gills (subgills) between neighbouring full-length gills. Gills may be separate from each other for their full length or they may fork and rejoin. They can also be attached to each other by stubby cross-veins. The length and colour of the teeth in a toothed mushroom can be notable features. For pored mushrooms, the shape of the pores when viewed from above (round, irregular, lengthened) and the pore density can vary from species to species.

Latex. A few mushrooms, almost all of them in the genus *Lactarius*, exude a thick liquid when the gills are cut or torn. If the mushroom being described is one of these, it will have a category called LATEX that discusses the colour, colour changes, and taste of this liquid. For more on this liquid, see the introduction to the genus *Lactarius* species (p. 61).

Odour. Many mushrooms have notable smells. The smell of these mushrooms can be an important clue to their identities. In the ODOUR category, we describe some of these smells. If the smell is not present or is hard to detect under normal conditions, the text will say "not distinctive." Smells, of course, can be difficult to describe, and we have included in this section many comparisons to everyday odours.

In general, the best place to pick up the odour of a mushroom is around the gill, tooth, pore, or vein surfaces (in the caps that have these), though in some cases scratching the stem or crushing a small amount of mushroom tissue can trigger the release of aromatic compounds. Very young mushrooms may not have developed enough of these compounds to be detected by the average nose, and really old mushrooms may acquire a rotten smell that masks the native odours. Cold temperatures can also inhibit the release of aromas, though these odours will often return as the mushrooms warm up.

Taste. Mushrooms can also have distinct tastes. To taste a mushroom, break off a small portion of cap, chew it for a few seconds, and spit it out. In a few cases, licking the cap or stem may be an alternative. Some mushrooms, tasters quickly discover, have bitter tastes, others sweet tastes, and a surprising number of them a hot/peppery taste. As long as the chewed pieces are small, the risk of the tasting leading to toxic effects seems to be minimal, but most people prefer not to taste-test species that have reputations as poisonous mushrooms. We also encourage testers to consider the audience—tasting a mushroom in front of small children may lead them to think that eating raw mushrooms (in general, not a good idea) is acceptable.

Spore print. Mushroom spores, taken individually, are invisible without serious magnification. When the spores pile together, however, they become visible and will often display various hues. These colours can be important in identifying mushrooms. Many mushroom books, this one included, use these colours to divide the gilled species into manageable groups. In the SPORE PRINT category, we provide—for species that could be expected to provide this sort of clue—the colour of the clumped spores for the mushroom being described.

Spore colours can sometimes be detected in the field. Mushrooms that have started to shed their spores can leave clumps of these on caps or on pieces of vegetation that are underneath the fertile surfaces. Also, gill and pore surfaces can, when the spore production becomes heavy, take on the colour of the clumped spores. (Note, though, that really young gills tend to be white, no matter what the spore colour.) If none of the field tricks for determining spore colours work, then it is often possible to make a spore print from a picked mushroom.

It is important to start off with a cap that is producing spores—a mushroom that's not too young to be shedding spores and not so old that it has finished dropping its spores. Separate the cap from the stem, and place the cap on a suitable surface (more on this below) with the gills, veins, teeth, or pores facing downward. Sometimes it helps to cover the cap with a mug or bowl to keep wind currents from blowing the spores around. Leave the cap for a few hours (overnight is best). Spores will pile up on the surface below. Spore prints seem to form best at ambient outside temperature—prints made inside in a warmer room are often sparser. Gilled mushrooms will produce a radial pattern, with the piled-up rows centred below the gaps between the gills.

Many surfaces will work for making spore prints. Paper is popular. If it isn't known whether the spore print will turn out light or dark, then paper that has both white and black sections is best—dark spores show up best on white paper, pale spores on dark paper (though pale spores on white paper can often be seen by tilting the paper to a light). Another alternative is to use a piece of glass or clear plastic. Once the spore mounds have formed, the glass or plastic can be placed on a coloured surface that gives the best contrast. It's best to judge spore-print colour under natural light; incandescent and full-spectrum fluorescent work also.

Spore print of a gilled mushroom with yellow-brown spores.

Regular fluorescent tubes are often deficient in red colours, and red colours in prints may not be as evident.

Spore prints are diagnostic tools. But they can also be pieces of art and wonderful ways to introduce young people to the fun side of mushrooms.

Stem. When mushrooms have them, stems can help in mushroom identification. In the STEM category, we provide maximum stem lengths and widths. For many mushrooms, the shape of the stem—whether it is wider at the top, the middle, or the bottom or an equal diameter throughout, and how the base is shaped (rounded, bulbous, rooting)—are critical features. Some shape features to watch for are illustrated in the diagram below.

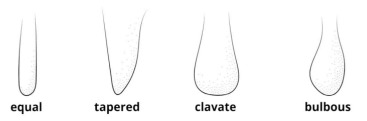

equal   tapered   clavate   bulbous

The overall consistency of the stem also matters—is it rubbery, fragile, brittle, woody? Some stems are solid, some are hollow, and some become hollow as the mushroom matures. We also note how the stem joins to the cap—whether it runs into the centre of the cap, or is off-centre, or is at the side (lateral). The colour, moistness, and surface texture are also important, just as they are with the cap. The flesh in the base can be like the flesh in the cap, or it can have its own character, colour, and colour changes. Two features of the stem area, the ring and volva, can be so important for mushroom identification that we have given them their own category headings.

Ring. The ring is what remains on the stem after the partial veil, which protects the fertile surface of young mushrooms, has broken up. Some parts of the partial veil can hang around on the cap margins—in that case, these remnants are discussed in the CAP category. When, however, they cling to the stem, they are described in the RING category.

Some mushrooms have no partial veils, and therefore no rings. Even in the ones that do have partial veils, the veils can disappear entirely or can end up as just a few wispy strands sticking to the stem. In some mushrooms, however, stem remnants of the partial veil can be persistent, long-lasting features. The diagram shows some shapes the ring might assume.

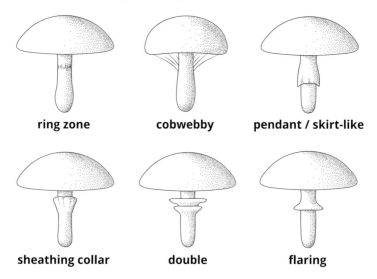

ring zone   cobwebby   pendant / skirt-like

sheathing collar   double   flaring

Rings can be located near the top, middle, or bottom of the stem. Some partial veils (e.g., in the large genus *Cortinarius*) are distinctively cobwebby; others are much more membranous. Ring colour is important, and the persistent rings found on some stems will change colour as spores are dropped, which can provide important field clues to the mushroom's spore colour.

Volva. Mushrooms that have a universal veil—those, for example, in the genus *Amanita*—can leave behind parts of this veil as warts and patches on the cap. The part of the universal veil that surrounds the bottom of the mushroom can persist as a sort of cup that cradles the base of the stem. These cups are called "volvas." The presence of these volvas and the shape of the volvas are important features to note. The diagram below shows some terms that are used in this book to describe how the volvas relate to the stem. The VOLVA category may also discuss volva colours and persistence.

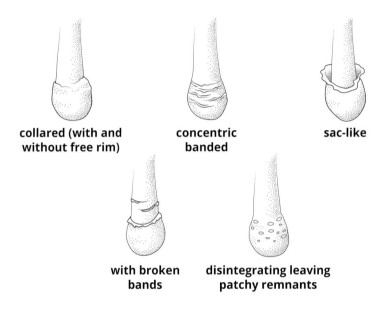

collared (with and without free rim)

concentric banded

sac-like

with broken bands

disintegrating leaving patchy remnants

Fruiting. The late Wilf Schofield, a world-renowned bryologist who taught at the University of British Columbia, used to say about mosses, "Tell me where it grows, and I'll tell you what it is." To a lesser—but still significant—extent, the same is true for mushroom species. When gathering mushrooms that will later be identified, collectors should pay special attention to the habitat in which the mushrooms thrive and to the way groups of mushrooms grow together. In the FRUITING category, we provide short descriptions of growth habits (growing singly, scattered, or in groups; clustered/tufted with joined bases or not), the type of substrate (forest floor, logs, fields, bogs, etc.), the plant associations (growing with conifers, hardwoods, or certain types of trees or bushes), and the seasons in which the mushrooms are generally found (see also "Seasons" in the section "Collecting and Eating Wild Mushrooms," p. 22). We have used the four seasons as fruiting-time indicators, rather than months, because the seasons are not fixed to a rigid timeline—spring in Prince George does not always start in the same month as spring in Victoria.

Edibility. In our experience, most people who take up the study of fungi have plans to forage them as edibles. In the EDIBILITY category we tag the mushrooms with one of six descriptors. In the COMMENTS section we expand on these rankings in the cases where the issue is more subtle than what could be captured with these terms. Here are the six terms we use:

- *Poisonous.* Either the literature contains documented cases of people and/ or animals eating this mushroom and consistently getting sick, or chemical studies have documented the presence of certain known toxins in the fruiting body. See also the section on DEATH CAP mushrooms (p. 112) and the essay on mushroom poisons (p. 256).
- *Unknown.* Not enough experience with edibility of the mushroom species has been accumulated to know whether there are possible adverse reactions.
- *Uncertain.* We have data on edibility, but they are mixed. Some people eat this mushroom and enjoy it; others report unhappy experiences. The unhappy experiences may be due to personal sensitivities or to growing conditions, but they are common enough to raise questions about possible intrinsic toxicity.
- *Not edible.* The mushroom has physical characteristics—toughness, bitterness—that make it an unsuitable food item.
- *Edible.* People widely and consistently eat this mushroom and enjoy it; cases of adverse reactions are rare.
- *Choice.* An edible mushroom that both authors of this book believe provides an exceptional taste experience.

Since we have provided information in this guide that may affect your health and well-being, we must add a standard disclaimer: *The decision to consume any foraged mushroom is ultimately the sole responsibility of the person eating it. Although we have made every effort to provide correct information about edibility, neither the authors nor the publisher can accept liability or responsibility for food and health decisions made as a result of relying on information presented on these pages.*

We provide more information on foraging for mushrooms in the section "Collecting and Eating Wild Mushrooms," p. 22.

Similar. To qualify as a field guide, a printed book that had complete descriptions of every mushroom known to grow in BC would have to come with a free wheelbarrow. The coverage in this portable book is necessarily restricted to common or especially interesting species. This limited coverage, however, is greatly expanded in the SIMILAR category by briefly noting essential field differences between the described species and ones that are similar to it. In addition, we use this category to call attention to simple ways that the described species on one page can be differentiated from the fully treated species on other pages.

First published in 2020 by Massey University Press
Reprinted 2020

Private Bag 102904, North Shore Mail Centre
Auckland 0745, New Zealand
www.masseypress.ac.nz

Extracts published with permission:
Page 48: 'Something Beautiful'. Words and Music by William J.
Gaither & Gloria Gaither. Copyright © 1971 Hanna Street Music
(BMI) (adm. in Australia & New Zealand by SHOUT! Music
Publishing). All rights reserved. Used with permission.
Page 145: Marylyn Plessner, 'Lady Mink: A Sort of Requiem',
in *Vapour Trails*. Montreal: Stephen Jarislowsky, 2000.
Page 157: Emily Long, 'Phantom Child',
http://emilyrlong.com/phantom-child

A catalogue record for this book is available from the National
Library of New Zealand

Printed and bound in China by Everbest Investment Ltd

ISBN: 978-0-9951354-0-6
eISBN: 978-0-9951378-9-9

Collecting and Eating Wild Mushrooms

Among the many ways to enjoy mushrooms, bringing them from the field to the table ranks high. Mushrooms can be both delicious and nutritious. Menus of the finest restaurants and the practices of the best chefs testify to their popularity. In addition, collectors have the added satisfaction of eating something that has been foraged in the wild.

Mycophobia. Warnings about the risks of foraging for and eating wild mushrooms abound. And some mushrooms are truly dangerous. But the actual danger, spread out over the wide variety of mushrooms and the frequency of their consumption, is not as great as is commonly believed (or represented in the media). In British Columbia, we have reliable records of four people dying from mushroom poisoning. These are all tragedies. But the real risks need to be kept in perspective. More mushroom pickers, for example, die from getting lost or seriously injured while picking mushrooms than die from eating them. Also, the risk of being poisoned by a mushroom you have foraged and consumed in BC is about the same—or less—than the risk of being poisoned by eating a foraged plant. And yet people fear mushrooms, not plants. Go figure.

For many people, then, the first step in collecting and eating wild mushrooms may be overcoming an inherent and exaggerated mycophobia (fear of mushrooms). The culture and traditions that dominate BC life derive in large part from customs and attitudes inherited from countries in the United Kingdom. The peoples of the United Kingdom, it turns out, were not a mushroom-loving bunch. When you speak English and live in a province called *British* Columbia, it is all too easy to generalize this attitude and think that mycophobia is a basic human characteristic. It is not—people in other parts of the globe (e.g., Eastern Europe, Asia, and many other places) are mycophiles rather than mycophobes. For them, collecting and eating wild mushrooms, often as a family, is culturally and even ritually important. The author and amateur mycologist William Delisle Hay captured this ancient European divide in a guide to fungi written more than a century ago (*An Elementary Text-book of British Fungi*, 1887):

> The individual who desires to engage in the study [of wild mushrooms] must boldly face a good deal of scorn. He is laughed at for his strange taste among the better classes, and is actually regarded as a sort of idiot among the lower orders. No fad or hobby is esteemed so contemptible as that of the "fungus-hunter" or "toadstool-eater."
>
> This popular sentiment, which we may coin the word "Fungophobia" to express, is very curious. If it were human—that is, universal—one would be inclined to set it down as instinct, and reverence it accordingly. But it is not human—it is merely British. It is so deep and intense a prejudice that it amounts to a national superstition.

Why collect wild edible mushrooms? There is something appealing about free food. But the greatest attraction to foraging for edible mushrooms isn't the monetary savings but the quality of the experience. Many of the choicest mushrooms are the fruiting bodies of the mycorrhizal fungi (see essay on p. 74) that grow attached to the roots of trees. These mushrooms only grow in forests at least 30 to 40 years old, so they are not suited to standard agricultural production. To find these mushrooms, foragers must head into our province's forests, usually in the autumn. Although you can sometimes find them sold in stores, when they show up there, it is because they have been harvested by foraging crews and sold to the retail marketers. The cost of this commercial harvesting (see essay on p. 442) can make them pricey. Plus, the time lag in getting them into retail outlets can mean that they arrive at the store looking old and tired. Bottom line: If you want to eat most of BC's delicious wild mushrooms and you want to eat them in their prime, you will have to collect them in the woods. If you succeed, you will have a feast. If you don't, it will still be a wonderful day in the woods.

Where can I collect? Most of BC is public land—only a small percentage is in private hands. This means that most of our province is available for foraging. But private land is distributed very unevenly. If you live in Vancouver or Victoria, for example, most of the land around you may be private land, and so unavailable (without permission) for mushroom collecting. In addition, some of BC's public land is in various parks and protected areas, and most of these areas prohibit foraging. Still, even with all this taken into account, about three-quarters of BC is available for mushroom foraging, and at this point there are few regulations above and beyond access restrictions that may be imposed by the government or the forestry companies that operate there.

The vast majority of BC public land is forested, so forest mushrooms, especially mycorrhizal mushrooms, can often be found in abundance. But there are also mushrooms of interest in other habitats—fields, pastures, lawns, bogs, alpine, and deserts can have their own fungal treasures. Wherever they find them, collectors make note of places where their favourite edible mushrooms appear and check these sites regularly. Some foragers like to share these spots with other mushroom seekers. Others prefer to keep their spots less widely known.

Collecting safely. Anyone heading out into wild places, whether foraging or not, should take some basic safety precautions. Before departing, make sure that someone knows where you are going and when you are expecting to be back home. It's always best, and usually more fun, to forage with a friend or in a small group. Bring maps and a compass, a GPS unit, and/or a cellphone. Remember that mushroom collecting, with your head down and zigzagging through a forest from one mushroom patch to another, is one of the easiest ways to get lost. Keep in mind also that weather can change quickly and that if you get lost, you may be gone longer than anticipated. This may mean bringing warm and dry clothing and extra food and water. Foray checklists often include such items as whistles, insect repellent, bear deterrents, sunscreen, rain clothes, emergency matches, and waterproof blankets.

Seasons. Where temperatures allow, there are mushrooms over most of BC during every season of the year. But the availability and abundance of the species vary greatly with the seasons. The prime time for mushroom foraging, especially for mycorrhizal mushrooms, is at the end of the summer and into the autumn. As a general rule, the peak of the season comes later in the south of BC than in the north, with the mushrooms in the north rushing to complete their fruiting cycle before snows and freezing weather set in. Mushroom-fruiting times are also responsive to moisture. The warm and dry summer weather of the Interior plateau and the BC southwest suppresses the abundance of the mushroom crop until wetter weather returns in the autumn. South or north, the autumn mushroom season draws to an end whenever hard freezes occur. Ice can put the mush in mushroom.

A minor mushroom fruiting can also occur in the spring. A number of mushrooms appear at the leading edge of the snowmelt line, taking advantage of the fresh flows of water and the renewed photosynthetic activity of the warming trees. People foraging for edible mushrooms in the spring, though, are most often looking for three groups of mushrooms that typically occur well below treeline (the upper elevation at which trees grow): morels, especially burn morels, OYSTER MUSHROOMS (p. 208), and, at higher elevations in the BC Interior, the SPRING KING (*Boletus rex-veris*, p. 318).

Collecting protocols. Most people who collect mushrooms to eat bring along some kind of hard-shelled container, such as a bucket or a basket—floppy bags can jumble up and compress the collected mushrooms. They also carry with them a knife for slicing off the mushrooms (though the whole mushroom should be lifted from the ground when the base is needed for secure identification, such as certain amanitas) and sometimes a brush for cleaning the dirt from the collections. PINE MUSHROOM (p. 146) hunters often carry a stick or other prying device to pop the mushrooms out of the duff. In general, it is best to clean mushrooms as much as possible in the field before putting them into the basket or bucket, to avoid getting dirt or sand worked into the gills.

Mushroom collecting is generally considered to be sustainable, for two reasons. First, mushrooms are the fruiting bodies of fungi, much like the apples on an apple tree. You can pick the apples—or the mushrooms—each year, without reducing the ability of the apple tree—or the fungus—to produce more fruit the following year. Second, a long-term study initiated by the Oregon Mycological Society looked at chanterelle productivity in areas where chanterelles were either plucked out of the ground, cut at the stem base, or not harvested. No statistically significant differences in future productivity were observed. Most collectors that we know, however, try to leave a few mushrooms in a patch, especially the smaller caps, so that there will be plenty of spores for the next generation. Any collecting, however, that disturbs the fungal mycelium itself, such as stripping off the layers of mosses and other vegetation that protect the mycelial networks, should be avoided.

Preparing collected mushrooms. Preparing mushrooms for the table is a bigger topic than we can get into here. Several mushroom cookbooks are available. One of our favourites is Bill Jones's *The Deerholme Mushroom Book: From Foraging to Feasting*. Deerholme Farm is near Duncan on Vancouver Island.

Note that many perfectly edible mushrooms can produce bad effects when eaten raw. And even with those that don't, our digestive systems struggle to derive benefit from mushrooms in their raw state. We recommend that all mushrooms, with perhaps the exception of a small amount of truffle grated onto a dish, be cooked.

Other Ways to Enjoy Mushrooms

Cultivation. Decomposer mushrooms are grown commercially on large mushroom farms and shipped to retail outlets. The most common mushroom grown this way, at least in North America, is the ubiquitous *Agaricus bisporus*, known as the BUTTON MUSHROOM, CREMINI (if it's brown), or PORTOBELLO (if it's brown and large). Also grown commercially and sometimes available in BC grocery stores are the OYSTER MUSHROOM (p. 208), SHIITAKE (*Lentinula edodes*), and ENOKI (*Flammulina velutipes*, p. 202, though the commercially grown versions do not look like the wild VELVET FOOT).

Growing decomposer mushrooms at home as an alternative to purchasing commercially grown mushrooms is quite feasible and is becoming an increasingly popular pastime. If you don't want to bother with the details of cultivation, mushroom kits can be purchased that contain inoculated spawn that has already started to colonize a growth medium, such as compressed sawdust. The kits just need to be kept moist and the mushrooms harvested when they are ready. Many prefer to take this to the next level and prepare their own spawn and growth media. Information on this can be found online. Many mushroom clubs have members who band together to cultivate edible mushrooms.

Citizen science. Many mushroom enthusiasts enjoy mushrooms, as birders do birds—without eating them. The quest to enlarge our own understanding of the natural world can be its own motivation. There is a certain pleasure in keeping lists and puzzling out species. It is also possible for amateurs to make significant contributions to the scientific study of fungi. Indeed, mycology has always been famous as a place where amateurs excel. Mushroom clubs, in our experience, often develop significant centres of gravity around the science of mycology. Members work with each other and with professionals to study in detail certain groups of mushrooms.

Participating in this kind of citizen science demands a higher standard of mushroom collection and study than that practised by the forager or casual hiker. Investigators take notebooks into the field and record the time, places, habitats, and principal characteristics of the mushrooms they find. They take pictures that show the diagnostic features. (Many of the pictures in this book were taken by just these kinds of people.) Mushrooms are collected and wrapped for transport, usually in waxed paper, but for fragile specimens sometimes tinfoil or plastic trays. They are then brought home, dried (usually with a food dehydrator), placed in packets, and labelled. They can be kept and stored in personal herbaria for future reference. Collectors can also, with special arrangements, transfer some of their collections to large public herbaria, such as the Beaty Biodiversity Museum at the University of British Columbia. Many of these citizen scientists keep small labs at home, with microscopes and chemical reagents, so they can study their collections in more detail. Results of their work are usually posted to various online venues, such as mushroomobserver.org and iNaturalist.org, to let others see and comment on their work. In recent years, citizen scientists have even started to acquire the connections and tools needed to have their collections sequenced and to analyze genetic relationships.

Earning money. On a trip around BC forest areas in the autumn mushroom season, you may notice stands, vans, and pickups along the road with the sign "mushroom buyer." You may also see them in the spring in places where there have been forest fires in recent years. These people pay mushroom collectors for certain mushrooms, with the amount paid keyed to the species and the quality of the caps (see essay on p. 442). Thousands of BC residents earn extra cash each year by bringing their mushrooms to these buyers. The buyers make their own money by selling their purchases to wholesale and retail outlets. Mushrooming, it seems, is one of the rare hobbies that can be turned into a (largely unregulated) source of income.

Photographing mushrooms. Taking pictures of mushrooms, often done for scientific reasons, can have an aesthetic side. The autumn mushroom flush in BC is a sort of second spring, a parallel to the season of wildflowers, with mushrooms replacing flowers on the natural canvas and bringing with them the same wide range of colours and smells. These fungal expressions attract photographers, painters, and sculptors.

Psychedelics. Mention "BC" and "mushrooms" to many Canadians, and they immediately jump to the thought of magic mushrooms (see essay on p. 308).

This group of mushrooms—also referred to as "entheogens" (substances that produce a non-ordinary state of consciousness for spiritual purposes)—is widely used in our province. While this is not everyone's cup of reali-tea, it is unquestionably a driver of significant interest in the BC mushroom scene.

Healing. The medicinal aspect of mushrooms (see essay on p. 400) is an area of increasing research. Local mushroom clubs usually harbour a small cadre of people wanting to explore how mushrooms can be used for health and healing.

Dyeing with mushrooms. The popularity of mushrooms as a source of cloth dye is also on the rise in BC and the US Pacific Northwest (see essay on p. 342).

Other Resources

There are many other resources—print, digital, and social—available to those wanting to learn more about BC's mushrooms.

Other things being equal, the value of a mushroom guide increases with its locale proximity and specificity. We know of three self-published guides with significant BC coverage that are available. One of our favourite regional guides is *Mushrooms to Look For in the Kootenays* by Doug McBride and Tyson Ehlers. Doug and Tyson bring valuable insights from southeastern BC to this book, and many of Tyson's excellent photographs appear in its pages (as well as on our own pages). Another excellent BC regional guide is *The Outer Spores: Mushrooms of Haida Gwaii* by Paul Kroeger, Bryce Kendrick, Oluna Ceska, and Christine Roberts—highly recommended, especially if you are travelling to these misty isles. *Common Mushrooms of the Northwest*, by BC author and photographer Duane Sept, covers much of the province.

In addition, there are other useful and entertaining guides for western North America that are published by commercial publishers and are currently in print. They are written by mycologists from California, Oregon, or Washington and so contain some mushroom species that don't make it this far north and omit some northern species that don't make it far enough south. Also, their habitat information—especially where and when mushrooms appear—can be difficult to transfer to a BC setting.

The ones most widely consulted by BC students of mushrooms are David Arora's massive (almost a thousand pages!) and authoritative *Mushrooms Demystified*, first published in 1979, and its smaller field companion, *All That the Rain Promises*, which appeared in 1991. The Arora guides are not only informative—they are immensely fun to read. Another useful guide for our area is Steve Trudell and Joe Ammirati's *Mushrooms of the Pacific Northwest*, especially valuable for its insight into the inner workings of mycology and mycologists. Noah Siegel and Christian Schwarz's masterful *Mushrooms of the*

Redwood Coast focuses on California coastal habitats, but it surveys so many species that its coverage has significant overlap with BC mushrooms. Teresa Marrone and Drew Parker's recently issued *Mushrooms of the Northwest*, a book for smaller pockets, manages to fit into its small dimensions a large number of beautiful diagnostic photographs. Fans of watercolours might also appreciate *Mushrooms of Western Canada* by Alberta-based Helene Schalkwijk-Barendsen. Margaret McKenny and Daniel E. Stuntz's *The New Savory Wild Mushroom* is somewhat dated, but it has been helpfully updated by Joe Ammirati.

In addition to these field guides, there are a number of more technical references available for specific groups of mushrooms. These are mentioned in the introductions to the various species groups.

There are many resources online for mushroom students. Most are not specific to BC, but there are four that are based in BC and have important coverage of provincial mushrooms. We mentioned above the MycoMatch app, created by a committee that includes Ian Gibson and Danny Miller. Ian also maintains a website with identification keys produced by the Pacific Northwest Key Council. The third resource is the extensive mushroom component of E-Flora BC. The fourth resource is the *Mushrooms Up! Edible and Poisonous Species of Coastal BC and the Pacific Northwest* website hosted at the University of British Columbia. In addition to these four BC-based online resources, the databases at MushroomObserver.org and iNaturalist.org list and illustrate many BC fungal species.

Finally, those interested in learning to recognize BC mushrooms can connect to one of the local mushroom clubs. In North America, there are almost a hundred regional clubs, containing a total of about ten thousand members, that are associated through the North American Mycological Association (NAMA). Two NAMA-affiliated clubs in BC, the Vancouver Mycological Society (VMS) and Victoria's South Vancouver Island Mycological Society (SVIMS), each have hundreds of members. Their annual October mushroom shows draw upward of a thousand visitors, and the clubs schedule frequent outings and host speaker series. If there's no mushroom club nearby, your best contacts may be in a local natural history society—check with BC Nature (Federation of BC Naturalists) for your closest club.

References Cited

Arora, David. 1986. *Mushrooms Demystified*. Berkeley, CA: Ten Speed Press.

———. 1991. *All That the Rain Promises, and More… : A Hip Pocket Guide to Western Mushrooms*. 2nd ed. Berkeley, CA: Ten Speed Press.

Bandoni, Robert J., and Adam F. Szczawinski. (1964) 1976. *Guide to Common Mushrooms of British Columbia*. Handbook 24. Victoria, BC: British Columbia Provincial Museum.

E-Flora BC (website). Electronic Atlas of the Flora of British Columbia. Lab for Advanced Spatial Analysis, Department of Geography, University of British Columbia, Vancouver. eflora.bc.ca.

GenBank database. ncbi.nlm.nih.gov/genbank/.

Gibson, Ian, Danny Miller, et al. MycoMatch: Mushrooms of the Pacific Northwest (app and computer program). mycomatch.com.

Hardy, George A. 1946. *Some Mushrooms and Other Fungi of British Columbia*. Handbook no. 4. Victoria, BC: British Columbia Provincial Museum.

Hay, William Delisle. 1887. *An Elementary Text-book of British Fungi*. London, UK: Swan Sonnenschein, Lowrey.

Jones, Bill. 2013. *The Deerholme Mushroom Book: From Foraging to Feasting*. Victoria, BC: Touchwood Editions.

Kroeger, Paul, and Shannon Berch. 2017. *Macrofungus Species of British Columbia*. Technical Report 108. Victoria, BC: BC Ministry of Environment. for.gov.bc.ca /hfd/pubs/Docs/Tr/TR108.htm.

Kroeger, Paul, Bryce Kendrick, Oluna Ceska, and Christine Roberts. 2012. *The Outer Spores: Mushrooms of Haida Gwaii*. Sidney, BC: Mycologue Publications.

Marrone, Teresa, and Drew Parker. 2019. *Mushrooms of the Northwest: A Simple Guide to Common Mushrooms*. Cambridge, MN: Adventure Publications.

McBride, Doug, and Tyson Ehlers. 2015. *Mushrooms to Look For in the Kootenays*. Victoria, BC: First Choice.

McKenny, Margaret, and Daniel E. Stuntz. 1987. *The New Savory Wild Mushroom*. Rev. ed. Revised by Joseph F. Ammirati. Seattle, WA: University of Washington Press.

MycoBank database. mycobank.org.

Schalkwijk-Barendsen, Helene. 1994. *Mushrooms of Western Canada*. Vancouver, BC: Lone Pine.

Sept, J. Duane. 2012. *Common Mushrooms of the Northwest*. Rev. ed. Sechelt, BC: Calypso.

Siegel, Noah, and Christian Schwarz. 2016. *Mushrooms of the Redwood Coast: A Comprehensive Guide to the Fungi of Coastal Northern California*. Berkeley, CA: Ten Speed Press.

South Vancouver Island Mycological Society. "Pacific Northwest Key Council: Keys to Mushrooms of the Pacific Northwest." Updated September 15, 2019. svims.ca/council/.

Trudell, Steve, and Joe Ammirati. 2009. *Mushrooms of the Pacific Northwest*. Portland, OR: Timber Press.

UNITE database. unite.ut.ee.

Vellinga, Else C., Paul Kroeger, Ludovic Le Renard, Adolf Ceska, Oluna Ceska, and Mary Berbee. 2019. *Mushrooms Up! Edible and Poisonous Species of Coastal BC and the Pacific Northwest* (website). Beaty Biodiversity Museum. zoology.ubc.ca/~biodiv /mushroom/.

Guide to Mushroom Groups

 VEINED. Fruiting bodies are caps and stems, or vase-shaped, with low ridges/veins that look like stubby, fat gills often running down the stem and forking and rejoining. Spore prints are white to buff to yellowish. Typical colours are orange, yellow, cream, white, violet, black. Flesh tends to be firm or rubbery or stringy. Usually in forests. **Page 33.**

 GILLED. Fruiting bodies are caps, usually with stems (centrally attached to cap, off-centre, or lateral/at the side). Plate-like gills under the cap. Spore prints can be pale (white or cream or various pastel colours), brown (light brown, cinnamon to rusty brown, or rich chocolate brown), dark (purplish black to black), or pink (pink, pinkish brown, or salmon). Many sizes, colours, odours, tastes. All habitats. **Page 43.**

 BOLETES. Fleshy caps with centrally attached stems. The spores, which typically produce a yellow-brown to pinkish tan spore print, are borne in small tubes in a (usually) spongy and detachable pore layer. Fruiting bodies are short-lived, usually terrestrial, on forest floors. **Page 317.**

 TOOTHED. Fruiting bodies, some of which are vase-shaped, have caps, and most have distinct stems. The fertile surface under the cap is covered with hanging spines/teeth. Spore prints are pale or brown. Some terrestrial, some on wood. Mostly in forests. **Page 335.**

 CLUBS. Fruiting bodies look like upright clubs, unbranched but a few with single branchings near the top. Some cylindrical, others with distinct heads that can be rounded, tongue-like, or irregular. Colours variable. Typically terrestrial. Mostly in forested habitats. Stinkhorns have foul odours. *Mucronella* species hang icicle-like, growing on logs. **Page 349.**

 CORALS. Fruiting bodies shaped like ocean coral, with frequent branching and upward-pointed tips or lobes. Colours white to tan to brighter pinks, reds, oranges, yellows. Forest habitats. **Page 369.**

POLYPORES. Usually with caps, the fertile surfaces under the caps with small pores, the pore layers usually tightly adhering to caps. Usually with tough, woody, or leathery flesh. Spore prints are pale or brown. A few with stems but most without, some crust-like along wood substrates. Some fruiting bodies perennial. **Page 378.**

JELLY FUNGI. Fruiting bodies with jelly-like flesh, appearing as amorphous, blobby clumps or as tongue-shaped, ear-shaped, or cone-shaped. Not many with stems, but sometimes with stem-like bases. Mostly on wood, mostly in forests. Colours yellow, orange, brown, black, or translucent. **Page 411.**

PUFFBALLS. Fruiting bodies spherical or ovoid, the skins often 2-layered, the spores encased inside the fruiting bodies. Fruiting bodies rupture when spores are dry to release spores. In earthstars, the skin splits to form rays. Spore mass usually starts off whitish, often becomes greenish, then finally dark. Terrestrial, some slightly underground. Forests and (commonly) fields. **Page 421.**

BIRD'S NEST FUNGI. Fruiting bodies are small cups, usually a few centimetres or less across, that form nests. The nests (when young) hold whitish to dark brown, egg-like spore packets. The outside of fruiting bodies often hairy or grooved. Colours whitish, grey, brown, or black. Usually on wood. **Page 431.**

MORELS AND SIMILAR. Caps are thimble-shaped, saddle-shaped, or convoluted, and are often honeycombed with pits or vertical ridges. Cap colours are pale, brown, yellow-brown, reddish brown, or blackish. Terrestrial or on wood, in forests and fields. **Page 436.**

CUPS. Cup- or bowl-shaped, with some cups stemmed. Flesh leathery to rubbery to jelly-like to fragile. Usually on wood (sometimes buried), various habitats. **Page 449.**

TRUFFLES. Rounded to irregular underground fruiting bodies, often knobbly, textured, or with convoluted chambers. Spores are inside, with spore masses powdery or gelatinous. **Page 463.**

OTHER FUNGI. A miscellany of parasites and decomposers that go by names such as rusts, spots, knots, and curls. They often alter the tissues of their hosts. **Page 472.**

WOOLLY CHANTERELLE (*Turbinellus floccosus*), p. 40.

Veined

The mushrooms in this section share one major field characteristic: instead of arranging their spore-bearing surfaces on the parallel plates we call gills, they spread them along and between ridges. In mushroom-speak, these ridges are referred to as veins. Some species have quite deep veins that are very gill-like, while on others the veins are little more than raised humps. The veins are often forking and cross-veined.

There are other characteristics shared by the veined mushroom species. Their veins often run from the cap margin far down the stem, sometimes all the way to the soil line. Their caps, which tend to be lobed and irregular, can have such depressed centres that the mushrooms take on the shape of funnels. Their spore surfaces can continue to put out new basidia over a long period of time—chanterelles' fruiting bodies have been known to last for over three months, continuously growing. The veined species are, we think, almost all mycorrhizal and so are typically found in forest environments.

Early mushroom taxonomists assumed that species with similar fruiting surfaces—here, veins—were related. However, microscopic and molecular clues have revealed that veined fruiting surfaces arose more than once in the course of fungal evolution.

Seven of the veined species in this section fall into three distinct groups. First, there are the true chanterelles, represented here by species in *Cantharellus* and *Craterellus*. Worldwide, only about a hundred species call these two genera home, but they are some of the most widely foraged and eaten mushrooms in the world. You know a mushroom is popular if it has a common name: chanterelles are LISITJKA (fox mushroom) in Russia, PFIFFERLING in Germany, GIROLLE in France, LIYOUJUN in China, and KANTARELL in Sweden. They occur from the tropics to the Subarctic. The half dozen or so species that have been found in BC are not only favourites for foragers' tables—they play large economic roles in the edible-mushrooms marketplace (see essay on p. 442).

Second, there are the veined mushrooms represented by *Gomphus* and *Turbinellus*, which are most closely related to club and coral mushrooms. Some species in these two genera are widely appreciated as table mushrooms; others have a tendency to sicken those who eat them.

Finally, we have *Polyozellus*, a genus related to EARTH FANS (p. 408). Most species in this genus appear to be edible. *Polyozellus* species are becoming increasingly important as sources of medicinal compounds.

In addition to these main categories of veined mushrooms, we include in this section an ascomycete parasite, *Hypomyces lactifluorum*, that transforms the russula and lactarius mushrooms that are its hosts into the sought-after edible LOBSTER MUSHROOM (p. 39).

Pacific Golden Chanterelle   *Cantharellus formosus*

CAP To 12 cm across; convex when young, concave and depressed with age, margins often wavy and lobed and at first incurved and then curved down or straight; often with small, slightly darker scales that may lift, especially on the disc, when dry; orange to orange-brown to yellow-brown to yellow and sometimes with greyish tints on disc when dry; dry or moist; smooth or felty; flesh thick (to 1.5 cm), stringy, yellowish white but bruising yellow and then yellow-brown. VEINS Strongly decurrent; to 2 mm deep; forking, cross-veined; usually yellow to light orange-yellow, sometimes slightly paler than the cap and sometimes with a slight pinkish cast, especially near the margin; moderately to closely spaced. ODOUR Not distinctive, or faintly fruity, sometimes described as like apricots. TASTE Not distinctive. SPORE PRINT Yellowish white. STEM To 10 cm tall × 2 cm wide; equal, sometimes narrowing at the base and curved; dense, stringy flesh; solid; surface same colour as cap or slightly paler, bruising darker; dry; smooth. RING Absent. FRUITING Single to small groups or clusters, occasionally in partial arcs; on the ground; under conifers; late summer, autumn.

    EDIBILITY Choice. Some allergic reactions have been reported. SIMILAR CASCADE CHANTERELLE, *Cantharellus cascadensis*, has a cap that is bright, egg-yolk yellow or white-yellow (not yellow-brown), a paler (sometimes white) underside layer, a stouter profile (shorter stem in relation to the cap size), and a stem that is typically wider in the middle or at the base than at the top. The RAINBOW CHANTERELLE (p. 36) has a pinkish, hoary coating on the cap margin of fresh specimens, its cap lacks darker, pressed-down scales, the cap underside is typically at least partly brighter yellow than the cap, and it mainly favours spruce. The WOOLLY CHANTERELLE (p. 40) has a deeply depressed cap with large lifted-up scales, and its cap colour is often more reddish orange. The WOOLLY PINE SPIKE (p. 298) has a rounder, less lobed cap, orange cap flesh, true gills, and purple-black spores. The FALSE CHANTERELLE (p. 129) has true gills that are more crowded and that are typically a darker orange than the cap. COMMENTS PACIFIC GOLDEN CHANTERELLE is the commonest, most widely sought after and commercially important chanterelle in BC. In a multi-year study of typical forest tracts in northern Vancouver Island, plots averaged more than 6 kg of fresh caps per hectare per year (see p. 442 for more on the commercial mushroom harvest in BC). ✎ The PACIFIC GOLDEN CHANTERELLE is ectomycorrhizal with various conifer species, including WESTERN HEMLOCK, DOUGLAS-FIR, and SITKA SPRUCE. It fruits most abundantly in younger and middle-aged stands, preferring fairly well-drained soils, and is found mostly in the western regions of BC. ✎ Until the 1990s, the common golden chanterelle of BC and the US Pacific Northwest was known as *C. cibarius*, the name of its European look-alike. In the early 20th century, however, mycologists realized that our local species was different. E.J.H. Corner, a prolific botanist and mycologist, proposed in the 1960s that the species should be named *C. formosus*, based on a specimen he collected in 1938 in what is now Pacific Rim National Park Reserve—a true BC original! It was only in the 1990s, after genetic sequencing entered the picture and lent its weight to Corner's proposal, that the new name and description caught on. ✎ The yellow chanterelles are an example of how mushroom appearances can deceive. In Oregon, professional mycologists made hundreds of collections of what appeared to be PACIFIC GOLDEN CHANTERELLES. When sequenced, most of the specimens turned out to be *C. formosus*, as they expected, but they were surprised to discover that a small number were CASCADE CHANTERELLE or WHITE CHANTERELLE (p. 37). ✎ "Formosus" means "beautiful."

Rainbow Chanterelle   *Cantharellus roseocanus*

CAP To 12 cm across; convex to flat, becoming depressed in the centre with age, often lumpy, margins initially inrolled and then expanded and wavy; orange to yellow, often with a distinctive hoary pale pink coloration near the edges, especially when young or when moist; moist to dry; smooth; flesh firm, stringy, thick (to 2 cm), and white, bruising slowly (if at all) yellow-brown. **VEINS** Strongly decurrent; shallow (to 5 mm deep); forking and rejoining, sometimes shallowly cross-veined in age; at least partly a bright yellow that is yellower than the cap typically, but also the same colour as the cap (though without pinkish tints); moderately to widely spaced. **ODOUR** Fruity, like apricots. **TASTE** Not distinctive. **SPORE PRINT** Orange-yellow. **STEM** To 5 cm tall × 2.5 cm wide; cylindrical, with an expanded or tapering base, sometimes curved; stringy flesh, easily dividing into vertical strips; solid; surface white to yellow to yellow-brown to orange; dry to finely felted. **RING** Absent. **FRUITING** Single or in groups, sometimes small clusters; on the ground; under conifers (most commonly spruce, but also pine), with a preference for wetter old-growth sites; late summer to autumn.

EDIBILITY Choice. **SIMILAR** The RAINBOW CHANTERELLE can be confused with **PACIFIC GOLDEN CHANTERELLE**—see that entry (p. 34) for comparisons with the RAINBOW CHANTERELLE and other species. **COMMENTS** The ectomycorrhizal RAINBOW CHANTERELLE was for many years cited as a subspecies of *Cantharellus cibarius* (as *C. cibarius* var. *roseocanus*). In the 2010s, molecular data were published that supported its elevation to full species status as *C. roseocanus*. Genetic data suggest that the RAINBOW CHANTERELLE may be the most widely distributed chanterelle species in North America. ☙ "Roseocanus" means "rose-coloured hoary." The "rainbow" in the English name was suggested by the mycologist Scott Redhead because the mushroom "sports an array of colors, it occurs in rainforests, and at its end it is golden."

White Chanterelle   *Cantharellus subalbidus*

CAP To 14 cm across; flat to slightly depressed and funnel-shaped, often lumpy, the margins inrolled or curved down at first and then lifting and becoming wavy and/or lobed; white to cream at first, later buff, bruising orange to orange-brown; generally dry; smooth to finely scaled; flesh under cap dense, stringy, cream-coloured, slowly staining dull yellow in age or when bruised. VEINS Strongly decurrent; forking, joining, and cross-veined; cream-coloured bruising yellowish, sometimes with pink tints; widely spaced. ODOUR Pleasant, fruity. TASTE Not distinctive. SPORE PRINT White. STEM To 7 cm or more tall × 4 cm wide; equal or narrowing downward or with swollen base, sometimes curved; fibrous and stringy flesh; solid; sometimes off-centre; surface cream-coloured, developing yellow or orange stains with age or bruising; dry; smooth. RING Absent. FRUITING Single or in small groups or clusters; on the ground; under conifers; late summer, autumn.

EDIBILITY Choice. SIMILAR Specimens of WHITE CHANTERELLE and PACIFIC GOLDEN CHANTERELLE (p. 34) can sometimes be hard to separate, since WHITE CHANTERELLES become more orange with bruising and PACIFIC GOLDEN CHANTERELLES become paler from growing in shade or from drying. COMMENTS WHITE CHANTERELLES, at this point known only from western North America, are ectomycorrhizal with conifers, especially DOUGLAS-FIR and WESTERN HEMLOCK, and are often found in older stands of these trees. They are the dominant chanterelle in the BC Interior and the BC eastern mountain ranges. ❧ Until the 1940s, the WHITE CHANTERELLE was thought to be a colour phase of *Cantharellus cibarius*. It was first described as a separate species by the mycologists Alexander H. Smith and Elizabeth Morse. ❧ "Subalbidus" means "close to *C. albidus*," a European species that Smith and Morse thought resembled our WHITE CHANTERELLE.

Winter Chanterelle   *Craterellus tubaeformis* group

CAP To 6 cm across; convex to flat to funnel-shaped, wrinkled, with the central depression often continuous with the hollow stem, margins downcurved when young, becoming more uplifted and lobed, scalloped, and ragged with age; brown to dark yellowish brown, margins often paler yellow, fading toward grey in age; generally dry, but somewhat greasy when moist; flesh rubbery and pale yellow. VEINS Decurrent; shallow; forked; yellowish to greyish yellow or pale lilac. ODOUR Not distinctive. TASTE Not distinctive. SPORE PRINT White to cream. STEM To 9 cm tall × 1 cm wide; equal, but usually flattened and/or grooved, sometimes curved; stuffed but then becoming hollow; yellowish, often paler or whitish at the base; dry; smooth. RING Absent. FRUITING Usually in small or large groups or (commonly) clustered; on rotting wood or on the ground; under conifers; autumn, winter.

EDIBILITY Choice. Highly favoured by some, less so by others. SIMILAR Several small yellow-brown mushrooms might be mistaken for the WINTER CHANTERELLE, but they all have true gills, not ridges. GOLDGILL NAVELCAP (p. 141; see that entry for other similar species) is perhaps the most similar of these. COMMENTS This diminutive delectable is also known as YELLOWFOOT in some circles. ❧ Though often fruiting in clumps on well-rotted wood, as a decomposer would, the WINTER CHANTERELLE is known to be ectomycorrhizal with WESTERN HEMLOCK, DOUGLAS-FIR, and SITKA SPRUCE. ❧ The WINTER CHANTERELLE was once placed in the genus *Cantharellus* with other chanterelles. Molecular studies have since established that the WINTER CHANTERELLE belongs in *Craterellus*. These same studies, however, have also shown that the BC and US Pacific Northwest *Craterellus tubaeformis* is not the same as the European species that owns the scientific name. When these mushrooms have been more thoroughly studied, we will probably have other names for the species. ❧ Hedgehogs (pp. 336–337) and WINTER CHANTERELLES often grow in the same habitats and seasons. ❧ "Tubaeformis" means "trumpet-shaped."

Lobster Crust   *Hypomyces lactifluorum*

FRUITING BODY A parasitic ascomycete that spreads out over the host mushroom's stem, gills, and cap, both on the surface and into the interior tissues, assuming the general shape of its gilled host, the host's gills usually transforming into blunt ridges that make it resemble a veined mushroom, the parasitized cap becoming irregular and cracked; sometimes yellowish or whitish, but most commonly bright orange or orange-red, becoming dark red to reddish purple and mottled in age; dry; firm when young, though sometimes infested with insect larvae; covered with often-darker pimples that contain the reproductive bodies. ODOUR Not distinctive. TASTE Not distinctive. SPORE PRINT White. FRUITING Single or in groups; on fruiting bodies of *Russula* and *Lactarius* species, commonly on the SHORT-STEMMED RUSSULA (p. 52); late summer, autumn.

EDIBILITY Choice. Over much of southern BC, *Hypomyces lactifluorum* parasitizes the non-toxic SHORT-STEMMED RUSSULA (p. 52). In central and northern BC, and perhaps elsewhere, the crust can also infect the WOOLLY MILK CAP (p. 69), which is peppery and considered poisonous when not infected and not cooked well. SIMILAR The LOBSTER CRUST and its host—together, the LOBSTER MUSHROOM—is one of our safer edible mushrooms for beginners. There's not much that looks like LOBSTER MUSHROOM. COMMENTS The LOBSTER CRUST, like its host, is a relatively common BC mushroom. ⟫ Research on parasitized russulas has found that, in early stages of colonization, most of the parasitized mushroom, except for the outer crust, is still genetically a russula. By the time the mushroom is fully lobsterized, not much of the host DNA remains. Researchers have discovered that the terpenes and phenolic compounds present in the uninfected russula are greatly reduced and that levels of fatty acids, free amino acids, and monosodium-glutamate-like substances are increased. Somehow this chemical transformation turns a rather blah-tasting mushroom into a delicious one. ⟫ "Lactifluorum" would mean something like "of a flow of milk," perhaps a reference to *Lactarius* hosts.

Woolly Chanterelle   *Turbinellus floccosus*

CAP To 15 cm across; at first cylindrical with a rounded to blunt top, becoming increasingly funnel- or vase-shaped with a hollow centre as the cap expands, the margins wavy to lobed; reddish orange to yellow-orange; moist to sticky; very scaly, the scales on the outer rim pressed down, but upright toward the centre and sometimes curling inward; flesh thick (to 1 cm), firm, fibrous, white. VEINS Decurrent almost to base of stem; shallowly wrinkled; low and splitting/ rejoining; yellowish, fading to cream, brownish where bruised. ODOUR Not distinctive. TASTE Not distinctive. SPORE PRINT Yellow-brown. STEM To 10 cm tall × 5 cm wide, measured below the not-always-distinct decurrent edge of the spore-bearing surface; tapering downward, often buried in the duff; flesh thick, fibrous, white; surface cream to yellowish to yellow-orange, bruising brown; dry; smooth. RING Absent. FRUITING Single, in small groups, or in clusters, sometimes in arcs; on the ground; under conifers; late summer, autumn.

EDIBILITY Uncertain. Some eaters seem to down it with no problems, but others experience serious digestive upset, with symptoms sometimes delayed 12 hours or more. SIMILAR The larger *Turbinellus kauffmanii* (inset photo) has a brown to tan cap that lacks the orange colours of the WOOLLY CHANTERELLE, and its scales are more curved back, sometimes blocking the central cavity. Also, it can have an odour that is described as sharp and pungent. See also the entry for the PACIFIC GOLDEN CHANTERELLE (p. 34). COMMENTS See photo, p. 32. The scientific names of the WOOLLY CHANTERELLE and its *Turbinellus* cousins have been on a long roller-coaster ride through several genera. Before landing (for a second time) in *Turbinellus*, they were listed in *Cantharellus* and then *Gomphus*. ◆ *Turbinellus* species are probably ectomycorrhizal and are abundant throughout much of BC, though they seem to prefer coastal climates. ◆ "Floccosus" means "woolly."

Pig's Ear   *Gomphus clavatus*

CAP To 12 cm across; initially flat with a small depression, the margins lifting, often more on one side than the other, and becoming rough-edged, wavy, and lobed, yielding an irregular funnel shape; light yellow-brown or orange-brown or pale olive, often with violet patches and tones; dry to moist; smooth or finely felt-like, especially over disc; flesh firm, stringy, thick in disc, white to buff to pale rose to purplish. **VEINS** Deeply decurrent, almost to the stem base; shallowly wrinkled; forking, joining, and cross-veined; an arresting lavender colour at first, often a darker lavender near cap margin, gradually fading to a pale lilac or yellow-brown; closely spaced. **ODOUR** Not distinctive. **TASTE** Not distinctive. **SPORE PRINT** Brown to pale yellow-brown. **STEM** To 10 cm tall × 3 cm wide; equal or narrowing downward, but typically fused with neighbouring bases; stringy flesh; solid; sometimes off-centre; often a deeper purple than ridges, extreme base whitish; dry; smooth or felty. **RING** Absent. **FRUITING** In small groups or often fused in clusters; on the ground; under conifers, often associated with old-growth forests; late summer, autumn.

    EDIBILITY Edible. Upset stomachs reported from some eaters. Younger caps are preferred. **SIMILAR** The funnel shape may remind lucky finders of the **WOOLLY CHANTERELLE** (p. 40) or its cousin *Turbinellus kauffmanii* (see inset photo on p. 40), but comparing colours (only PIG'S EAR has violet tones) resolves any confusion. The **BLUE CHANTERELLE** (p. 42) lies a bit closer to PIG'S EAR on the colour spectrum, but it is more persistently blue-black. **COMMENTS** Two different mushrooms have the common name PIG'S EAR: *Gomphus clavatus* and *Gyromitra ancilis* (p. 452). In this book, the latter is called THICK CUP. ⬩ PIG'S EAR, which is ectomycorrhizal with conifers, is found across the Northern Hemisphere, but it is less common than foragers would like. In some European countries it is listed as endangered. ⬩ Genetic analysis places it in close relationship with *Turbinellus* and some *Ramaria* species. ⬩ "Clavatus" means "club-shaped"; it does resemble a club held upright by the narrow end.

Blue Chanterelle   *Polyozellus atrolazulinus*

CAP To 20 cm across; funnel-shaped or spatulate, margins incurved at first, in age wavy, lobed, and often rolled outward; sometimes radially ridged; dark purple to deep blue, often with lighter purple-blue zones, sometimes black in age; dry; surface matte to smooth, margins felty when young; flesh soft, brittle, coloured as the cap. VEINS Deeply decurrent with shallow, meandering ridges, but some regions smooth; forking and joining; coloured like the cap or paler. ODOUR Not distinctive. TASTE Not distinctive. SPORE PRINT White. STEM To 5 cm tall × 2 cm wide; often fused at the base and in mid-portions with other stems in the cluster; same colour as the cap. RING Absent. FRUITING In large, compact clusters; on the ground; under conifers; late summer, autumn.

EDIBILITY Edible. SIMILAR PIG'S EAR (p. 41), though similar in many respects, is a much paler violet. We have occasional BC reports of *Craterellus calicornucopioides*, the famous HORN OF PLENTY, but the species mostly occurs in Oregon and southward. Some BC reports of HORN OF PLENTY are probably BLUE CHANTERELLES. COMMENTS The BLUE CHANTERELLE was known formerly as *Polyozellus multiplex*. *Polyozellus multiplex*, however, is an umbrella concept for at least 5 distinct species, 3 of which occur in the US Pacific Northwest. So far, 2 of these species—*P. atrolazulinus* and *P. marymargaretae*—have turned up in BC. They were first described in 2017. The latter is named after the Washington/Oregon mushrooming legend Maggie (Mary Margaret) Rogers, who died in 2018. ❧ Species in the *P. multiplex* group have chemical compounds that make them of interest to medical research. They can also be used as natural dyes, lending to fabrics blue, green, and violet tints. ❧ The BLUE CHANTERELLE, an ectomycorrhizal species that prefers higher elevations, is uncommon throughout its range, though it can be locally abundant. ❧ "Atrolazulinus" means "dark blue" in Latin, a description of the colour of young fruiting bodies.

Gilled

This section describes mushrooms
whose basidia are arrayed along
gills, thin plate-like or blade-like
structures that hang vertically under a protective cap.

The veined species in the previous section are the mushrooms most likely to
be confused with gilled mushrooms, but with some experience those learning
to identify mushrooms can get the hang (pun intended) of the differences. True
gills are usually quite deep, top to bottom; veins are relatively low relief. True
gills are usually knife-edged; veins are usually blunt-edged.

Mushrooms are the way certain fungi, once they have mated, produce sexual
spores. Gills, like pores or teeth, are a trick that mushrooms use to increase the
surface area that holds the spore-producing basidia without increasing the overall
size of the cap. Over the course of fungal evolution, the gill trick has appeared
more than once, so not all gilled mushrooms are closely related. Most of the
mushrooms described in this section are in the order Agaricales, an order that
is often equated with the gilled mushrooms. But there are Agaricales without
gills (some puffballs, for example), and there are also gilled mushrooms that
belong to other orders. In this guide, for example, we have gilled mushrooms
in Russulales, the russula order (*Russula*, *Lactarius*, and *Lentinellus*). The
Boletales, the bolete order, might be expected to have only pored mushrooms,
but it also has gilled members in such genera as *Chroogomphus*, *Hygrophoropsis*,
and *Phylloporus*.

Almost 60 per cent of the mushrooms covered in this guide are gilled. We
therefore need some way, one that works without having access to a science
lab, to divide up this multitude. The solution in almost all guides, and the one
taken in this book, is to separate mushrooms by spore colour. As a bonus, this
characteristic also has some rough correspondence to evolutionary history.

We group the gilled mushrooms into four spore-colour groups: pale spores
(p. 44), pink spores (p. 221), brown spores (p. 228), and dark spores
(p. 288). You'll need, therefore, to determine the spore colour of the specimen
you want to identify. This sometimes means making a spore print (more on this
technique on p. 16). The pale-spored group includes mushrooms whose spore
prints are white or cream or various pale pastel colours. The pink-spored group
contains species with pink, pinkish brown, and salmon-coloured spore prints.
The brown-spored group contains those whose spore prints are light brown,
cinnamon to rusty brown, or rich chocolate brown. The dark-spored group
have spores that are mostly purplish black to black. There are, unfortunately,
in-betweeners that fall into the gap between the colour groups—in particular,
pale-spored mushrooms that are slightly pinkish and dark-spored mushrooms
that lean toward brown.

Pale-spored Gilled

More than a third of the mushrooms in this book are pale-spored gilled mushrooms. They have gills and pale spores but, beyond that, often little in common. They are sometimes more closely related to gilled mushrooms with other spore colours or to non-gilled mushrooms than they are to other pale-spored gilled mushrooms.

We've divided the mushrooms in this group into 10 sections. Mushrooms in each section share some common, macroscopic field features. Again, this doesn't always mean they're related. This key should help you get to the correct section:

- If your mushroom grows on wood, usually in a forest, and either lacks a stem or has a non-central stem, it's likely in "**Pleurotus and Similar**" (p. 207).
- If your field or forest mushroom has thick, waxy, widely spaced gills and a cap that starts out convex or bell-shaped and flattens in age (but often retains an umbo), look in "**Hygrophorus and Similar**" (p. 77).
- If your woodland mushroom is medium to large, lacks veils and rings, and has a particularly brittle stem that snaps cleanly like a piece of chalk, then cut the gills: if a latex emerges, it's in "**Lactarius**" (p. 61); if not, it's in "**Russula**" (p. 45).
- If your woodland mushroom is medium to large, begins its life looking like an egg, and as it develops it leaves veil remnants as patches on the cap, a ring on the stem, and/or a cup (volva) at the base of the stem, look in "**Amanita and Similar**" (p. 105).
- If your large woodland mushroom lacks a universal veil but often has a partial veil that (sometimes) leaves veil remnants on cap edges, and if it has gills that are notched and have subgills (smaller gills that don't reach all the way to the stem), it's likely in "**Tricholoma and Similar**" (p. 145).
- If your forest-floor mushroom has free gills (or nearly so), a partial veil that often leaves a ring on the stem and tatters on the cap margin, and a scaly cap that's often darker in the centre, look in "**Lepiota and Similar**" (p. 97).
- If your field or forest mushroom is tiny, has a conical or bell-shaped cap less than two centimetres in diameter, has a fragile stem with no ring, and often fruits in large numbers, look in "**Mycena and Similar**" (p. 173).
- If your medium-sized field or forest mushroom has decurrent gills, lacks rings, and (often) has a funnel-shaped cap, look in "**Clitocybe and Similar**" (p. 125).
- Finally, if your small field or forest-floor decomposer mushroom has a flat to convex cap, attached (but not decurrent) gills, thin flesh, and wiry stems, check out "**Marasmius and Similar**" (p. 185).

Russula

Heading out in late summer and early autumn to look at fungi in the BC forests? Expect to encounter a lot of colourful russula mushrooms. With a little practice, you can readily recognize genus *Russula* mushrooms. They generally have a squat stature—stems are often shorter than their caps are wide—and their caps (medium- to large-sized, 5 to 20 centimetres across) typically flatten out and become depressed in the centre as they mature. They are mycorrhizal with many BC conifers and so occur more often on woodland floors than on logs, trees, or lawns. Russulas (our BC ones, at least) do not have universal or partial veils and so have no rings or volvas. Their gills are usually attached to the stem and are rarely decurrent. Spore prints range from white to deep brownish yellow. The most important clue to this genus, however, is often the flesh texture—stems and caps of russulas tend to be both rigid and brittle. The brittleness is due to the widespread presence of globular cells that do not interlace with each other like the drawn-out cells in other types of mushrooms. Stems of fresh specimens will often break cleanly like a piece of chalk; if thrown against a tree or the back of a companion's head, caps and stems can shatter into many pieces.

While recognizing a mushroom as a russula is, with a little practice, rather easy, identifying exactly *which* of the *Russula* species can be a challenge. There are many, many species in the genus—worldwide, nearly a thousand have been acknowledged and half are found in North America. In BC, we probably have more than a hundred. But the sheer number of species is only a part of the problem. A single species, for example, might produce caps that are white, pinkish, red, or purple, sometimes even with yellow, green, and/or brown tints. Add to this that complete identification may require microscopic examination and in some cases genetic testing. Lest all this sounds like the identification of russulas is an impossible task, though, we should emphasize that a few species in the *Russula* genus are easier to identify than others. The dozen species or species groups listed here (11 *Russula* species and one parasite on russulas) are among the easiest to recognize, especially if we accept that getting close to the right identification is often good enough.

Because their texture is crunchy, like celery, russulas attract eaters who are looking for something different than the rubbery texture of other mushrooms. Only one BC russula is seriously sought after as an edible (the SHRIMP RUSSULA, p. 46). Another, SHORT-STEMMED RUSSULA (p. 52), can turn into a choice edible, a LOBSTER MUSHROOM, when infected with the crust fungus *Hypomyces lactifluorum* (p. 39). Some russulas can be nasty, especially when eaten raw, such as THE SICKENER (p. 48).

Mushrooms in the *Lactarius* genus (p. 61) also share the brittle and crunchy texture of russulas, but breaking the cap or gills of a lactarius usually causes a thick latex to ooze out.

Shrimp Russula   *Russula xerampelina* group

CAP To 25 cm across; convex becoming flat or depressed, margins inrolled, often into age; bright red or dark red to purple, often with added greenish yellow or brown colours, and sometimes all greenish or all brown; skin peelable to about half of the radius; somewhat slimy when moist, soon dry and dull and often with captured detritus; smooth; sometimes slightly striate in age; flesh thick (to 2 cm), brittle; white to cream, bruising yellowish at first and later reddish brown. **GILLS** Broadly to narrowly attached; deep; brittle; cream, becoming yellow and yellowish brown, drying brown or grey; somewhat widely spaced to crowded. **ODOUR** Mild when young, like crab shells/seafood in age. **TASTE** Not distinctive. **SPORE PRINT** Pale to dark yellow. **STEM** To 12 cm tall × 4 cm wide; equal or slightly widened below; white, often with flushes the colour of the cap, staining yellowish and then brown; dry; smooth, but often longitudinally striate. **RING** Absent. **FRUITING** Single or in small groups; on the ground, usually in conifer forests; late summer, autumn.

    EDIBILITY Edible. **SIMILAR** Genetic studies indicate that the newly described ***Russula benwooii*** is quite common in the US Pacific Northwest. It differs from the SHRIMP RUSSULA in its more predominately brown to tan cap (but often with other colours mixed in) and its lack of a seafood odour. See also comparisons on the **RED HOT RUSSULA** (p. 50) and the **BITING RUSSULA** (p. 49) pages. ***Russula viridofusca***, a species in the *R. xerampelina* group, has yellow-brown to pinkish brown (and often dark-centred) caps. ***Russula favrei***, also in the group, tends to have browner caps that are sometimes dark-centred. **COMMENTS** The SHRIMP RUSSULA is the only russula widely picked for the table in BC (but see LOBSTER MUSHROOM, p. 39). The gills are often infested with springtails, especially if harvested late. ◄ The SHRIMP RUSSULA is an extremely widespread and common species group in BC, and most beginners can learn to identify it—or at least the more typical members of the group—by paying attention to the field marks highlighted above. ◄ "Xerampelina" means "of dried vine leaves," referring to one of the SHRIMP RUSSULA's many colours.

Violet Russula   *Russula murrillii* group

CAP To 5 cm across; convex becoming flat with depressed centre; violet or greyish violet, darker on disc, sometimes with paler regions where dry; slightly slimy/sticky when moist but soon dry and dull; smooth on the margins, often velvety around the depression; flesh thin, becoming fragile, white. **GILLS** Broadly to narrowly attached; deeper near the margin; brittle and sometimes forked and/or cross-veined; pale yellow becoming darker yellow; somewhat widely spaced. **ODOUR** Not distinctive. **TASTE** Not distinctive. **SPORE PRINT** Pale yellow. **STEM** To 5 cm tall × 3 cm wide; more or less equal; becoming hollow; white; dry; smooth. **RING** Absent. **FRUITING** Single or in small groups; on the ground; in conifer forests; autumn.

    EDIBILITY Unknown. **SIMILAR** *Russula queletii* **group** mushrooms (inset photo) can also have violet to purple caps, but they tend to have green to olive tones on the caps, red flushes on their white stems, and a peppery taste. Species in the *R. zelleri* **group** share most other features with the VIOLET RUSSULA, but they have slimy, shiny caps. **COMMENTS** Genetic analysis of specimens from nearby Washington and Oregon has found at least 3 distinct species in this group, all of which may be endemic to the West Coast of North America. We don't know yet how the names inside this group will sort out or how they will match up with what we have in BC. So far, what we have been calling *R. murrillii* has only been recorded from the southwestern corner of the province. ❧ "Murrillii" derives from the name of the American mycologist William Alphonso Murrill, who collected the type species in Oregon in 1911.

The Sickener   *Russula emetica*

CAP To 8 cm across; convex becoming flat, sometimes umbonate or depressed; reddish orange or deep pink, sometimes with yellowish tones; cap flesh easily peeling back from the margin; slimy when wet, shining when dry; smooth; striate and/or grooved in age; flesh thick, soft, white, sometimes tinged red or pink just under the cap. GILLS Broadly to narrowly attached; deep (3–8 mm); sometimes forked near stem and cross-veined; cream-coloured; closely spaced; with occasional subgills. ODOUR Slightly fruity or not distinctive. TASTE Very peppery. SPORE PRINT White. STEM To 9 cm tall × 2 cm wide; equal, sometimes flared at the top and widened or narrowed at the base; white, occasionally greyish yellow near the base; dry; smooth but sometimes longitudinally striate. RING Absent. FRUITING Single, scattered, or in groups; on the ground; often in swampy conifer and mixedwood forests; late summer, autumn.

EDIBILITY Poisonous. SIMILAR Based on genetic studies, BC russulas with red/pink caps, white stems, a white spore print, and a peppery taste are probably *Russula montana* and *R. emetica*. The important differences between *R. montana* and *R. emetica* are, unfortunately, microscopic ones. Habitat might help—*R. emetica* supposedly grows in bogs and wet areas and *R. montana* grows in forest duff and on wood. Also, *R. montana* specimens are less likely to be pure red. The names *R. silvicola* and *R. bicolor* also occur in BC survey lists, but at least some specimens labelled with these names genetically match *R. montana* and *R. emetica*. See also comparisons under the RED HOT RUSSULA (p. 50). COMMENTS THE SICKENER is widespread in BC. ✎ This species, which often causes vomiting in humans when eaten raw, is enjoyed by squirrels, snails, and slugs. ✎ "Emetica" means "causing vomiting."

Biting Russula

Russula mordax

CAP To 10 cm across; convex becoming flat or depressed, margins inrolled when young and remaining curved down for some time; brick red, reddish brown, to greyish red, sometimes with a yellowish centre; peelable to about half the way from the margins to the centre; slightly slimy/sticky when moist, soon dry and dull; smooth; flesh thick, firm, white. **GILLS** Broadly or narrowly attached; often forking near stem and cross-veined; cream to yellow. **ODOUR** Usually not distinctive, but occasionally floral. **TASTE** Very peppery. **SPORE PRINT** Pale to dark yellow. **STEM** To 8 cm tall × 3 cm wide; more or less equal; white, sometimes with pink or red flushes but remaining pale at the top; dry; smooth. **RING** Absent. **FRUITING** Single or scattered; on the ground; in conifer forests; late summer, autumn.

EDIBILITY Unknown. **SIMILAR** BITING RUSSULAS with caps a brighter red and without yellow tones might resemble **RED HOT RUSSULA** (p.50) specimens, but the latter has a less peelable cap. **SHRIMP RUSSULAS** (p.46) in their red-brown phases might resemble the BITING RUSSULA, but SHRIMP RUSSULAS are larger, have a mild taste, and smell like seafood. **COMMENTS** Students of BC mushrooms have become accustomed, when they find a russula with a brick-red cap, yellow gills, and a peppery taste, to label it with the name *Russula veternosa*, a species originally described from Europe. Recent genetic analysis, however, has pointed toward the name *R. mordax*, a nearly identical mushroom described by Gertrude Burlingham in the 1930s from a type specimen that she collected from under a DOUGLAS-FIR in Seattle, Washington, as the correct name for many of our BC specimens. ❧ The BITING RUSSULA has (so far) been found only in southern BC. ❧ "Mordax" means "biting," presumably a reference to the peppery taste.

Red Hot Russula — *Russula rhodocephala*

CAP To 12 cm across; convex becoming flat or somewhat depressed, in age margins occasionally uplifted and wavy; dark red, brownish red, to bright red; skin peelable at the margin only; somewhat slimy/sticky when moist, then dry and dull; smooth; flesh firm, white. **GILLS** Broadly attached or slightly decurrent; occasionally forking; cream-coloured; closely spaced; subgills common. **ODOUR** Usually not distinctive, but sometimes fruity or of geranium. **TASTE** Quickly and intensely peppery. **SPORE PRINT** Yellowish. **STEM** Typically shorter than cap is wide and thick, giving the mushroom a robust look; equal; white background flushed with red or pink, flesh on lower stem sometimes bruising yellowish; smooth. **RING** Absent. **FRUITING** Scattered or in large groups; on the ground; in conifer forests, especially around pines; autumn.

EDIBILITY Unknown. Too peppery to consider. **SIMILAR THE SICKENER** (p. 48) has creamy gills, a peppery taste, a reddish orange to deep pink cap, a mostly white stem, a white spore print, and a more peelable cap skin. The **SHRIMP RUSSULA** (p. 46) can have a red cap and red flushes on its stem, but its taste is mild and its flesh stains yellow. *Russula americana* is almost identical to the RED HOT RUSSULA, differing mostly by being found in drier areas and under hemlocks and true firs rather than pines. See also comparison notes under **BITING RUSSULA** (p. 49). **COMMENTS** The common BC and US Pacific Northwest russulas with red caps, red flushes on the stems, cream gills, yellowish spore print, and peppery taste have gone by many different names, including *R. rosacea*, *R. sanguinea*, and *R. sanguinaria*. Most of the work on descriptions of mushrooms passing under these names, however, was based on European fungi—what we have in western North America, we have long suspected, is slightly different. Genetic barcoding confirmed these differences at a species level and a new name was created in 2017. ❧ "Rhodocephala" means "red-headed."

Phoenix Russula

Russula phoenicea

CAP To 12 cm across; convex and later flat with depressed centre; colours various and variable, with pinks, greyish pinks, wine red, violet, brown, and green, typically paler in age; skin peelable, sometimes to nearly all the way to the cap centre; slimy/sticky when moist; smooth; weakly striate; flesh white. **GILLS** Broadly attached; white, sometimes cream; closely spaced; none or few subgills. **ODOUR** Not distinctive. **TASTE** Slightly peppery or not distinctive. **SPORE PRINT** White or cream. **STEM** About as tall as the cap is across; equal; smooth or wrinkled. **RING** Absent. **FRUITING** Single or in small groups; on the ground or on rotting wood; in conifer forests with DOUGLAS-FIR; late summer, autumn.

EDIBILITY Uncertain. **SIMILAR** *Russula stuntzii*, usually white or grey-white and sometimes with purplish tints, lacks the rainbow of colours associated with *R. phoenicea*. *Russula versicolor* has a variegated cap, but it grows under birches and it has a yellow-brown spore print. **COMMENTS** For many years, BC and US Pacific Northwest mushroom fans have been accustomed to identifying certain medium-sized, fragile, variable-coloured russulas as the European *R. fragilis*. The genetic signature of *R. fragilis*, however, has not shown up in our area. *Russula fragilis*–like mushrooms, when sequenced, most often end up being one of 2 other species, which were christened in 2017 as *R. phoenicea* and *R. hypofragilis*. The differences between these 2 closely related species are subtle: *R. hypofragilis* tends to have a more peppery taste, to be associated with pines, and to not have green tones. The description above is taken from the published descriptions and from the characters of mushrooms genetically identified as one of these 2 new species. ✦ "Phoenicea" refers to the mythological phoenix, a bird of brilliant, multicoloured plumage.

Short-stemmed Russula   *Russula brevipes* group

CAP To 20 cm across; convex to flat to funnel-shaped, with inrolled margins and often with a depressed centre; dull white, often with yellowish or rusty patches; cap not peelable; dry, but briefly sticky when moist; smooth to finely felty; flesh hard, brittle, white to cream, often staining brown or yellowish. GILLS Narrowly to broadly attached to slightly decurrent; 3–9 mm deep; sometimes forked near stem and/or cross-veined; white to cream, staining yellowish brown; crowded; abundant subgills. ODOUR Not distinctive, or slightly disagreeable. TASTE Not distinctive, or slightly and slowly peppery. SPORE PRINT Usually pale cream. STEM Short (to 6 cm tall) in comparison to the wide cap and stout (to 4 cm wide); equal or tapering downward; solid; white, staining brown; dry; smooth. RING Absent. FRUITING Single, scattered, or in groups, occasionally clustered, often not fully emerging and just showing white caps peeking out from breaks in the duff; on the ground; in conifer forests and near GARRY OAKS; summer, autumn.

EDIBILITY Edible. But lacklustre. SIMILAR *Russula cascadensis* has a rapidly developing peppery taste and a smaller cap (less than 10 cm across). *Hygrophorus subalpinus* has softer flesh and a slimier cap, and prefers high mountain areas near melting snow. COMMENTS The SHORT-STEMMED RUSSULA is one of the most widespread and common large mushrooms in BC. Genetic tests indicate, however, that several species may be hiding under one name. ● When colonized by the crust fungus *Hypomyces lactifluorum*, *R. brevipes* becomes the famous and delicious LOBSTER MUSHROOM (p. 39). ● The SHORT-STEMMED RUSSULA serves as a partner to the mycoheterotrophic plant GHOST PIPE. See p. 54 for more on this relationship. ● "Brevipes" means "short-footed," named for the short stem.

Comb Russula   *Russula cerolens*

CAP To 10 cm across; almost spherical to hemispheric or more shallowly convex becoming flat or broadly depressed, the margins later wavy and uplifted; dark yellow-brown, greyish brown, or dark brown, margins fading in age; slimy when moist; smooth; striate, often with distinct ridged lines; flesh thin except at disc, brittle in age, white. GILLS Broadly to narrowly attached to notched and nearly free; deep; brittle; white, staining olive-brown with age; often closely spaced; few if any subgills. ODOUR Unpleasant, variously described as like burned hair, chemical, spermatic, bleachy; two of the more evocative smell comparisons are like BLACK COTTONWOOD in spring and like a new shower curtain. TASTE Strongly, slowly peppery. SPORE PRINT Pale yellow. STEM To 6 cm tall × 2 cm wide; equal; becoming hollow; white, bruising brownish, staining reddish brown near base; dry; smooth. RING Absent. FRUITING Single or in groups; on the ground; typically in conifer forests or on forest edges, but also in urban areas under beech, birch, lindens, oaks, and hornbeams; summer, autumn, early winter.

EDIBILITY Unknown. Possibly poisonous. SIMILAR The larger mushrooms in the closely related *Russula fragrantissima* **group** have cap discolorations that are more red or orangey and an odour of maraschino cherries or almond extract. COMMENTS BC mushrooms matching this description have traditionally been labelled as the European-defined *R. sororia*. Genetic analysis has confirmed the presence in Washington and Oregon of *R. cerolens*, a western North American species first described in the 1970s, but not, so far, the presence of *R. sororia*. It seems very likely, then, that many or most of COMB RUSSULA mushrooms in BC will turn out to be *R. cerolens*. ◆ "Cerolens" means "smelling of wax."

Mycoheterotrophs

Mycoheterotrophs are a group of distinctively weird vascular plants. They lack chlorophyll, and the missing pigment has two important effects: these plants aren't green (they're usually white or pink), and they can't manufacture their own food through photosynthesis. Many field guides describe these plants as saprophytes, plants that derive their nutrition from decaying organic matter. Plants, however, don't get food this way, and the "myco" at the beginning of the word "mycoheterotroph" explains what is really happening: these odd plants get their nutrition from fungi.

Mycoheterotrophic plants derive their food from fungi second-hand. The fungi, which are attached to the roots of mycoheterotrophs, are also connected to the roots of nearby green, photosynthesizing plants, and the bi-connected fungi transfer food from the green plants to the mycoheterotrophs. Mycoheterotrophs, then, are plants that use an intermediary, a fungus, to aid and abet their food thieving. What the fungi get out of this relationship, if anything, isn't entirely clear.

One of BC's most common mycoheterotrophs is GHOST PIPE (*Monotropa uniflora*), which is widespread and sometimes locally abundant in the southern two-thirds of BC. Its partner in BC is always (as far as we know) the SHORT-STEMMED RUSSULA (p. 52). The russula, which is attached to the roots of nearby conifers, transfers sugars from the conifer to feed the GHOST PIPE. When you spot the spent, clustered

The mycoheterotrophic plant GHOST PIPE and its fungal partner, the SHORT-STEMMED RUSSULA.

fruiting stalks of a GHOST PIPE sticking out of the ground in the autumn, look around and see if you can find the large caps of SHORT-STEMMED RUSSULA heaving out of the ground.

Another interesting mycoheterotrophic plant is CANDYSTICK (*Allotropa virgata*). This plant, which in BC is found only in the extreme southwestern section (Vancouver Island, the Gulf Islands, and around Vancouver as far north as the Whistler-Pemberton area), has as its mycorrhizal partner the fungus whose fruiting body is the PINE MUSHROOM (p. 146). Foragers who find CANDYSTICK blooming at a certain location in the springtime should look around that same place in the autumn for PINE MUSHROOMS.

There are many other BC mycoheterotrophic plants. They are almost all in the orchid family or the heather family. Their basidiomycete fungal associates include several quite different genera: gilled mushrooms in *Russula* and *Tricholoma*, toothed fungi in *Hydnellum*, species in *Thelephora*, and truffles in *Rhizopogon*.

Another interesting group of plants is the heather-family WINTERGREENS (in the genera *Pyrola*, *Moneses*, and *Orthilia*) and PIPSISSEWAS (genus *Chimaphila*). They are often called "mixotrophs" because, while they can steal sugars the same way that full mycoheterotrophs do, they also possess chlorophyll and can make their own food. Whether they choose to make their own food or whether they steal it from neighbours may vary with the time of day or the season.

The mycoheterotrophic plant CANDYSTICK and its fungal partner, the PINE MUSHROOM.

Thick-skinned Russula   *Russula crassotunicata*

CAP To 8 cm across; almost spherical to hemispheric when young, becoming more shallowly convex and eventually flat or centrally depressed, the margins inrolled at first and then uplifted; skin thick, tough, rubbery, translucent; white or cream to pale yellow, often stained yellow-brown in age; peelable from half to all of its radius; somewhat slimy/sticky when moist, soon dry; smooth and then scurfy or felted and finely cracked when dry; flesh moderately thick (to 8 mm), rubbery, firm, white, and staining yellowish brown. GILLS Broadly or narrowly attached; sometimes forking near stem and cross-veined; white to pale yellow, bruising brown; somewhat widely spaced; only occasionally with subgills. ODOUR Sometimes not distinctive, but often coconut-like, or with the smell of inner tubes. TASTE Bitter and/or peppery. SPORE PRINT White. STEM To 5 cm tall × 1.5 cm wide; equal, sometimes widening or narrowing below; hollow in age; white or cream, developing brownish spots; dry; finely roughened, mealy when young, then mostly smooth. RING Absent. FRUITING Single or in small groups; on the ground; in conifer forests, preferring moister habitats; late summer, autumn.

EDIBILITY Unknown. SIMILAR *Russula stuntzii* has a white cap, often with touches of violet, and a thinner skin on the cap that only peels near the margin. Both its cap and stem discolour greyish to buff. See also the SHORT-STEMMED RUSSULA (p. 52) for other look-alikes. COMMENTS The THICK-SKINNED RUSSULA was originally described from the US Pacific Northwest in the 1930s. It seems to be fairly widespread in BC. ☙ A Washington research team proved that it is one of the host species for the not-too-common BRANCHED COLLYBIA (p. 201). ☙ "Crassotunicata" means "thick-shirted," a reference to its thick-skinned cap.

Grass Green Russula
Russula graminea

CAP To 15 cm across; convex becoming flat, the centre often depressed; greenish yellow, often with brown or yellow tints, rarely with touches of red or purple; in age, the skin peelable from the margin to about halfway to the centre; slimy and shiny when moist, dull when dry; striate; flesh white, some greenish tints near cap skin. GILLS To 2.2 cm deep; some forking; cream to pale yellow; closely spaced. ODOUR Not distinctive. TASTE Either not distinctive or slightly peppery. SPORE PRINT Light yellow-brown. STEM To 20 cm tall × 4 cm wide; equal or widening downward; becoming hollow; at first white, later with grey or brown patches. RING Absent. FRUITING In groups; on the ground, in conifer forests; late summer, autumn.

EDIBILITY Unknown. SIMILAR When the GRASS GREEN RUSSULA shades more toward yellow, there are 2 other russulas that could be confused with it. *Russula olivina* has a cap with more olive and brown hues, a yellow spore deposit, and a mild taste. What BC mycologists have been calling *R. lutea* has a mild taste and a yellow, slimy cap with no green colours. COMMENTS A century and a half ago (in *Illustrations of British Mycology*, 1855), Anna Maria Hussey remarked, "If we know of any one, who in the pride of intellect spurned all mental tasks as mere play, we would tame him by insisting on his mastering, classifying, and explaining the synonymes of the genus Russula." Ms. Hussey could have had the variously named green russulas in mind. ❧ In one study, genetic signatures of 14 Pacific Northwest *Russula* specimens with a predominantly green-yellow cap matched *R. graminea*, a green russula found in the Scandinavian countries that was first described in 2013. About as many greenish russulas, with spore prints that were closer to cream, were near (but not exact) matches for the European *R. aeruginea*. ❧ The Latin "gramineus" means "grassy," a reference to the greenish colour.

Blackening Russula *Russula nigricans* group

CAP To 18 cm across; convex becoming flat and sometimes funnel-shaped, often with a depressed centre, margins at first inrolled, then lifting; white or cream becoming brown and eventually black in age; upper skin not (or only slightly) peelable; slightly slimy/sticky when moist, usually dry; finely felted and cracked when dry; flesh thick, hard, brittle, and white, and when cut, changing slowly to brick red and then eventually to black. GILLS Broadly to narrowly attached; deep (to 1.4 cm); brittle, sometimes cross-veined near the stem; pale yellow, bruising black, sometimes with a reddish intermediate stage; closely or somewhat widely spaced; with subgills. ODOUR Not distinctive. TASTE Peppery, or not distinctive. SPORE PRINT White. STEM To 8 cm tall × 4 cm wide, appearing short compared to cap width; more or less equal; white, bruising or aging brown or red and eventually black; smooth. RING Absent. FRUITING Single or in small groups; on the ground; in conifer and mixedwood forests, often along trails; autumn, winter.

EDIBILITY Uncertain. Not recommended. SIMILAR If the mushroom is like the BLACKENING RUSSULA but has a slimier/greasier cream-coloured cap, a more fleeting reddening phase, and a smell like fresh bread, it may be ***Russula adusta***. Caps of ***R. densifolia*** are slimier when wet and shiny when dry. (Up to this point, however, though these names have been applied to BC specimens, neither *R. adusta* or *R. densifolia* have been confirmed in either BC or the US Pacific Northwest by genetic studies.) ***Russula decolorans*** starts off with a cap that is reddish brown, sometimes with green or lilac tones, before turning black, and it is usually associated with birches. Flesh that turns black without a reddish phase may signal ***R. albonigra***, which can also have a menthol-like taste. COMMENTS Another russula in the same group whose flesh turns red and black, *R. dissimulans*, was described in the 1960s, but the differences between it and the BLACKENING RUSSULA are not clear. ● The BLACKENING RUSSULA has only been found in southern BC. ● "Nigricans" means "blackening."

Russula Powdercap *Asterophora lycoperdoides*

CAP To 2 cm across; spherical expanding to hemispheric, with inrolled margins; white, the surface eventually transforming into islands of cinnamon asexual spores; dry; smooth and then powdery; flesh thin, white or cream. GILLS Often absent or rudimentary; broadly attached; blunt-edged; whitish to pale brown; widely spaced. ODOUR Farinaceous and/or rancid. TASTE Not distinctive. SPORE PRINT Technically white, but few sexual spores are produced. STEM To 3 cm tall × 8 mm wide; more or less equal, often curved; becoming hollow; white, then brownish to grey in age; dry; silky to cottony. RING Absent. FRUITING Clustered; on rotting russula and lactarius mushrooms; late summer, autumn, winter.

EDIBILITY Unknown. SIMILAR *Asterophora parasitica*, another russula parasite, has been reported in BC. Its cap does not turn powdery—the asexual bodies are formed in its more fully developed and thick gills. Another possible confusion for RUSSULA POWDERCAP might be with puffballs—when the asexual spores have developed, the cap can resemble a puffball ready to disperse its sexual spores. Puffballs, however, do not parasitize other mushrooms. COMMENTS The RUSSULA POWDERCAP is capable of both sexual reproduction (regular spores on its gills) and asexual reproduction (powdery spores on its cap). The asexual spores are cap cells whose protoplasm withdraws into a ball and whose cell walls thicken—under a microscope they look like irregular 3D asterisks. These dark, thick-walled asexual spores are designed to survive unfavourable conditions such as cold or drought. But they're also probably highly effective in colonizing additional areas of their host's cap (and the caps of other nearby rotting russulas). ☙ RUSSULA POWDERCAP prefers the BLACKENING RUSSULA (p. 58) as its host, and like its host, it is found mainly in southern BC. ☙ "Asterophora" means "star-bearing," an allusion to the small asterisk-like asexual spores. "Lycoperdoides" means "like *Lycoperdon*" (a genus of puffballs).

"*For the rain had ceased at last, and a sickly autumn sun shone upon
a land which was soaked and sodden with water. Wet and rotten leaves
reeked and festered under the foul haze which rose from the woods. The
fields were spotted with monstrous fungi of a size and color never matched
before—scarlet and mauve and liver and black. It was as though the sick
earth had burst into foul pustules; mildew and lichen mottled the walls,
and with that filthy crop Death sprang also from the water-soaked earth.*"
—Arthur Conan Doyle, *Sir Nigel* (1906)

Lactarius

In BC, the original concept of the genus *Lactarius* has held up very well over the last two centuries. Taxonomists have not felt a strong need to remove sections and assign them to new genera. This is not necessarily true outside of western North America—some species previously known as *Lactarius* have been transferred to the genus *Lactifluus*, particularly in the tropics. Additionally, the genus is distinctive—those who write mushroom guides (including the authors of this book) have felt no real need to add to this group some non-*Lactarius* species that might be confused with our lactarius mushrooms.

Lactarius mushrooms in this section have largish caps and substantial stems. The caps start out convex with inrolled rims, and as they mature, they take on flat, depressed, and funnel-shaped profiles. The stems do not have rings, and their flesh contains clusters of round cells, making the stems somewhat brittle—when fresh stems break, they break cleanly, almost snapping. The gills of these mushrooms are broadly attached, sometimes short-decurrent, and they are closely spaced to crowded. The species in the genus have white to pale yellow spores that, viewed under a compound microscope and stained, seem to be covered with warts that are interconnected by tiny ridges. *Lactarius* species are also, one and all, mycorrhizal mushrooms. The sum of these genus characteristics, however, do not uniquely define *Lactarius* species—the same features are found in species belonging to the related genus *Russula* (see p. 45). What makes the lactarius concept persistent and sturdy is the fact that mushrooms of this genus exude a liquid when damaged. The characteristics of this liquid—its initial colour, colour changes, staining effect, and taste—help us to decide which species of *Lactarius* we have found. That little extra help makes all the difference. Russulas, which do not have this exudate, can be quite difficult to identify all the way to the species level.

This helpful exudate, which is easiest to see in younger specimens, is sometimes called milk ("lactarius" is based on "lacto-," the Latin prefix for "milk," and the familiar mammal juice is also the basis for the common name "milk caps"), latex (our choice in this book), or sap, even though the liquid is technically neither milk nor latex nor sap. The easiest way to see this latex is to damage the gills with a knife or fingernail or break off a small piece of the cap. If the cap is fresh, drops of the latex often appear. In some species, the latex stains the gills a certain colour.

Mushrooms in *Lactarius* are good news for mycophagists. In BC, the genus, as far as we know, contains no seriously poisonous mushrooms, though foragers will probably want to avoid the species having latex that stains mushroom tissues purple or yellow and the species that have an especially peppery taste. The most commonly harvested *Lactarius* species in the province are the DELICIOUS MILK CAP (p. 62) and the BLEEDING MILK CAP (p. 63).

Delicious Milk Cap   *Lactarius deliciosus* group

CAP To 15 cm across, sometimes larger; convex with inrolled margins and a depressed centre, becoming shallowly funnel-shaped with age; usually zonate; moist to dry; smooth; orange, ranging from dull orange to carrot orange to orange-brown, often stained with green or even turning all green; flesh thick, grainy, pale yellowish orange. **GILLS** Broadly attached to slightly decurrent; orange to buff, staining green; closely to very closely spaced. **LATEX** Scanty; bright orange, in some forms when older turning red and then variably and slowly (over hours) staining mushroom tissue greenish. **ODOUR** Slightly fruity to some noses. **TASTE** Not distinctive to slightly bitter. **SPORE PRINT** Creamy yellowish. **STEM** To 6 cm tall × 2 cm wide; equal or narrowed at base; rigid; same colour as cap or paler, often green-stained; smooth. **RING** Absent. **FRUITING** Scattered or in groups; on the ground; in conifer forest; autumn, winter.

EDIBILITY Edible. **SIMILAR BLEEDING MILK CAP** (p. 63) is similar in many respects to the DELICIOUS MILK CAP, but the latex of the BLEEDING MILK CAP is blood red from the beginning and does not alter as much with age. *Lactarius olympianus*, often found associated with spruce at higher altitudes, can also have a zonate orange cap, but it has white, unchanging, acrid latex. **COMMENTS** The widespread DELICIOUS MILK CAP is readily colonized by insect larvae, which may add their own poignancy to the taste. ☙ There is a lot we don't know about BC mushrooms in the *Lactarius deliciosus* group. One thing that we have learned, though: they do not include *L. deliciosus*—that name belongs to the European species, which is genetically and morphologically distinct from our western North American DELICIOUS MILK CAPS. A couple of the local varieties have been proposed as species, and others may yet be raised to species status. ☙ "Deliciosus" means, as one might suppose, "delicious"—a bit hyperbolic for this OK-tasting species.

Bleeding Milk Cap
Lactarius rubrilacteus

CAP To 14 cm across; convex with depressed centre and inrolled margins, becoming funnel-shaped with age; sometimes zonate with multiple colours; bright orange to orangish brown to reddish brown to salmon or to buff, often bruised green in older specimens; sticky when wet; smooth but surface can be undulating; flesh thick, firm, grainy, white to dingy yellow or reddish, staining green. **GILLS** Broadly attached to short-decurrent; cinnamon to pinkish cinnamon to purplish red, staining green; closely spaced. **LATEX** Scant; blood red and staining mushroom tissues green, but sometimes orange-red or purple-red in age. **ODOUR** Not distinctive. **TASTE** Not distinctive, though some tasters report a slight bitterness. **SPORE PRINT** Yellowish or buff. **STEM** To 6 cm tall × 2 cm wide; equal, sometimes with a narrower base; hollow in age; coloured like the cap or paler, bruising green; smooth but sometimes pitted. **RING** Absent. **FRUITING** Scattered or in small groups; on the ground; in conifer forests; autumn.

EDIBILITY Edible. **SIMILAR** The cap colours of the DELICIOUS MILK CAP (p. 62) and the BLEEDING MILK CAP can be quite similar and both have latex that stains mushroom tissues green. There are microscopic differences between the 2 species, but the major field indicator (in fresh specimens) will be the red colour of the BLEEDING MILK CAP latex versus the orange colour in the DELICIOUS MILK CAP. Latex in older specimens of the DELICIOUS MILK CAP, however, can turn quite red. **COMMENTS** BLEEDING MILK CAP is common in southern BC, and is likely this region's most widely consumed lactarius. ⚬ Typically the amount of green staining increases with age. At the stem base, small, completely green, and unopened caps can often be found. ⚬ "Rubrilacteus" means "with red milk."

Orange Milk Cap   *Lactarius luculentus*

CAP To 6 cm across; flat to convex, margins inrolled, often wavy in age, centrally depressed when older but sometimes retaining a small bump; bright orange or orange-brown, not zoned but the margin sometimes a little lighter and duller in age; smooth; slightly slippery when moist, soon dry; flesh thin, white to pale yellow. GILLS Broadly attached to slightly decurrent; shallow; cream to pale orange; closely spaced to crowded. LATEX White, unchanging as it dries. ODOUR Not distinctive. TASTE Not distinctive to somewhat bitter. SPORE PRINT White. STEM To 5 cm tall × 1 cm wide; equal; becoming hollow; coloured as cap or gills or slightly paler; somewhat slippery when moist, soon dry; smooth; sometimes with whitish to pale orange mycelial hairs at base. RING Absent. FRUITING Scattered or in large groups; on the ground; in conifer or mixedwood forests; autumn.

EDIBILITY Unknown. SIMILAR *Lactarius subviscidus* has a slimier, more slippery cap that is darker orange-red (becoming brick red to brownish orange) and a slightly peppery taste. Its latex, by some reports, either slowly turns yellow or stains mushroom tissues yellow. The less common *L. subflammeus* and *L. substriatus* (these may end up being the same species) usually start off with scarlet caps that turn reddish orange to brownish orange, and their latex has a peppery taste. The latex of the latter may slowly turn yellow. See also the discussions of similar mushrooms in the entry for the RED HOT MILK CAP (p. 65). COMMENTS The brightest orange lactarius mushrooms are likely to be ORANGE MILK CAP. Further work, however, needs to be done in order to sort out the various varieties and species. ◦ Beginning mushroom foragers have been known to mistake the ORANGE MILK CAP for the delicious CANDY CAP, *L. rubidus*, which occurs in the western and northwestern parts of the United States. Sadly, there has been no credible BC sighting. ◦ "Luculentus" means "full of light, distinguished."

Red Hot Milk Cap   *Lactarius rufus*

CAP To 12 cm across; convex becoming flat, with a depressed centre and sometimes a small umbo, margins inrolled; brick red to reddish brown to orange-brown and not zoned; can be moist, but usually dry; smooth, but occasionally wrinkled; flesh fragile, off-white to dingy orange or reddish. GILLS Broadly attached to short-decurrent; shallow; forking near stem; white when young, developing pink or reddish tints; closely spaced or crowded. LATEX White, unchanging as it dries, not staining mushroom tissues. ODOUR Not distinctive. TASTE Hot and peppery, but often after a delay. SPORE PRINT Cream or pale yellow. STEM To 10 cm tall × 2 cm wide; equal, but sometimes narrowing at base; coloured like the cap, but typically whiter near the base and near the gills; dry; smooth. RING Absent. FRUITING Scattered or in small groups; on the ground; in conifer forests and near bogs; summer, autumn.

EDIBILITY Uncertain. There is little data about the North American version, but the European variety is canned for consumption in Scandinavia and Russia. SIMILAR *Lactarius hepaticus* is slightly smaller, has a cap that is more purple-red (liver-coloured, as "hepaticus" suggests), and sometimes has a velvety stem, especially in younger specimens. It also displays different chemical reactions. *Lactarius occidentalis* caps are small and dull brown, typically displaying tints of olive green, but older caps can have a dark reddish brown colour similar to the RED HOT MILK CAP. However, *L. occidentalis* preferentially associates with alder species, the mature caps are often translucent-striate, and the caps and latex don't have a peppery taste. COMMENTS The RED HOT MILK CAP is more common in Interior BC than along the coast. It's one of the most common *Lactarius* species in the mountains of the southern Interior. ◄ "Rufus" means "reddish."

Coconut Milk Cap — *Lactarius glyciosmus*

CAP To 8 cm across; convex with inrolled margins, then flat, becoming depressed in the centre and slightly funnel-shaped in age, but sometimes retaining a small central bump; grey to pinkish grey or lilac-grey; dry; slightly hairy, a few specimens becoming slightly scaly, sometimes with vaguely defined, clay-coloured zones; flesh thin, pale buff. GILLS Slightly decurrent; shallow (3–4 mm deep); sometimes cross-veined and forking; pinkish buff to darker; crowded; with long and short subgills. LATEX White, unchanging as it dries, not staining mushroom tissues. ODOUR Like coconut. TASTE Slowly peppery. SPORE PRINT Cream to buff. STEM To 6 cm tall × 1.5 cm wide; equal, occasionally flattened; soft and fragile; colour of cap or paler; dry; partly downy above, smooth below. RING Absent. FRUITING Scattered or in small groups; on the ground; primarily with birches, but also with alders; late summer, autumn.

EDIBILITY Uncertain. Consumed by some foragers, apparently. SIMILAR WOOLLY MILK CAP (p. 69) is also found with birch and can sport similar colours, but its cap margins are densely hairy (when young at least), and it has no obvious odour. The PURPLE-STAINING MILK CAP (p. 67), whose cap has more purple tones in it, has colour ranges that overlap with the COCONUT MILK CAP, but the PURPLE-STAINING MILK CAP doesn't smell like coconut. It also has a cap that can be sticky when young, usually grows under conifers, and has a white, unchanging latex that stains mushroom tissues lilac-brown to purple. COMMENTS Certain smells, such as coconut and banana, are often recognized immediately, even by children. It's fun to put the otherwise unremarkable specimen of a COCONUT MILK CAP under someone's nose and watch their eyes widen in recognition. ◆ The mushroom's association with birch trees makes it a rare find on BC's coast, but residents of the southern BC Interior are more fortunate. ◆ "Glyciosmus" means "sweet-smelling."

Purple-staining Milk Cap   *Lactarius montanus*

CAP To 10 cm across; convex with inrolled margins, becoming flat with a depressed centre; pale, becoming pinkish grey, lavender-grey, or purple-brown; sometimes lightly zoned; dry, but sticky when young; smooth; flesh thick, white, staining purple. **GILLS** Broadly attached to short-decurrent; shallow; white to creamy, staining purple; closely spaced. **LATEX** White, unchanging as it dries but staining mushroom tissues purple. **ODOUR** Not distinctive. **TASTE** Resinous, bitter. **SPORE PRINT** Cream or pale yellow. **STEM** To 9 cm tall × 2 cm wide; equal or with expanded lower section; whitish or coloured like the cap, staining purplish overall, sometimes bruising pale orange or yellow near base; dry, but sticky when young; smooth. **RING** Absent. **FRUITING** Single or in small groups; on the ground; in conifer forests, also wet or swampy sections (near willow), usually at montane elevations; autumn.

    EDIBILITY Uncertain. Perhaps poisonous. **SIMILAR** *Lactarius pallescens* closely resembles the PURPLE-STAINING MILK CAP, but it tends to have a paler cap, and both its cap and stem are consistently slimy. **COCONUT MILK CAP** (p. 66) has a distinct coconut odour. **COMMENTS** It's probably safest to avoid eating all purple-staining and yellow-staining milk caps. ◆ *Lactarius montanus* was once known by the name *Lactarius uvidus*, a binomial now properly used for its European and eastern North American relatives. The western North American mushroom was recognized as an *L. uvidus* variety (*L. uvidus* var. *montanus*) in Alexander H. Smith's 1979 treatment of *Lactarius* species, then raised to full species status by another taxonomist in a 2003 study. ◆ "Montanus" means "of the mountains." True to the name, this species occurs most commonly in montane ecosystems.

Pitted Milk Cap

Lactarius scrobiculatus

CAP To 15 cm across; convex with depressed centre, margins at first tightly inrolled, becoming funnel-shaped with age; pale yellow to brownish orange, sometimes darker near disc; slimy when wet; smooth but sometimes finely scaly or matted with age, the margin usually bearded with hairs, young specimens often dotted with small, clear drops; flesh firm, brittle, white turning yellow when exposed. GILLS Broadly attached to short-decurrent; forking near stem; white or pale yellow at first and later staining yellow or orange-brown; closely spaced; with 2–3 tiers of subgills. LATEX White, turning yellow within seconds. ODOUR Like the artificial fruit smell of some cereals or not distinctive. TASTE Not distinctive to slightly peppery. SPORE PRINT White to cream. STEM To 10 cm tall × 4 cm wide; equal or narrowed at the base; hollow with age; same colour as cap, pitted with large, glazed, yellow to honey-coloured spots; dry. RING Absent. FRUITING Single or in groups; on the ground; in conifer forests; autumn.

EDIBILITY Uncertain. SIMILAR WOOLLY MILK CAP (p. 69) is another shaggy milk cap. It has a pinkish cap, and its white latex is unchanging as it dries or, in one variety, dries slowly cream to pale yellow on the gills. *Lactarius repraesentaneus* has a cap that is often a richer yellow, and its latex stains mushroom tissues violet or purple. *Lactarius controversus* has a white cap often with lavender or pink tints or stains. It also has unchanging white latex, a peppery taste, and gills that are coloured pinkish cream, and it lacks the marginal beard of the PITTED MILK CAP. COMMENTS *Lactarius scrobiculatus* was first defined in Europe. Our western North American version of the PITTED MILK CAP, it seems likely, will one day become its own species—some sources already cite it under the name *L. payettensis*. ⚬ "Scrobiculatus," which derives ultimately from a Latin term for "ditch, grave," highlights the pitted stem.

Woolly Milk Cap   *Lactarius torminosus*

CAP To 12 cm across; convex to flat, often depressed, becoming narrowly funnel-shaped, the margins curved under and densely bearded with white hairs when young; pale pink, often a bit zonate, the margin paler, fading to whitish; moist and smooth in centre, at least when young, in age the cap with matted fibrils; flesh firm, aging flaccid, white or tinged with cap colour. GILLS Short-decurrent; shallow; sometimes forked near stem; white becoming cream, often with pale pink tints, and tan in age; close to crowded. LATEX White, unchanging as it dries but in one variety turning yellow and staining gills yellowish. ODOUR Not distinctive. TASTE Immediately peppery. SPORE PRINT Cream. STEM To 7 cm tall × 1.5 cm wide; equal or with narrowed base; cap-coloured or paler, sometimes with yellow-brown spots; dry; smooth or finely hairy. RING Absent. FRUITING Scattered or in groups; on the ground, with birch; late summer, autumn.

EDIBILITY Purportedly poisonous, though prized as a peppery treat in northern Europe following parboiling and/or pickling. SIMILAR The PITTED MILK CAP (p. 68) is another mushroom that is matted in age and bearded with hairs on the margin. It grows under conifers and has a more brownish orange cap, a latex that turns instantly yellow, and a stem that is pitted with yellow to honey-coloured spots. See the PITTED MILK CAP entry for additional species comparisons. COMMENTS In central BC, WOOLLY MILK CAP is sometimes parasitized by the LOBSTER CRUST (p. 39), which turns it into the LOBSTER MUSHROOM. The parasite, in replacing host tissues, transforms this extraordinarily peppery mushroom into a sought-after edible. ✦ WOOLLY MILK CAP can be found anywhere in our province where there are birch trees—both throughout the Interior and on the coast where birches have been planted as ornamentals. ✦ WOOLLY MILK CAP is also sometimes parasitized by the brownish, mould-like *Hypomyces torminosus*. ✦ "Torminosus" means "full of sharpness, causing colic," perhaps a reference to its peppery taste.

Velvety Milk Cap   *Lactarius fallax* group

CAP To 8 cm across; convex to flat with a small umbo when young, often slightly depressed with age, sometimes with a lumpy appearance, the edges becoming scalloped; dark brown to black; dry; velvety; flesh thin, brittle, whitish, slowly staining red to purple with age and/or injury. **GILLS** Broadly attached to slightly decurrent; white becoming cream, edges sometimes with dark pigment; closely spaced to crowded; with subgills, often in several tiers. **LATEX** White and unchanging as it dries, but slowly staining mushroom tissue and gills reddish to pale purple. **ODOUR** Not distinctive. **TASTE** Not distinctive or slightly peppery. **SPORE PRINT** Creamy white to pale yellow. **STEM** To 7 cm tall × 1.5 cm wide; about equal, typically with a curve in the lower half; usually lighter brown than the cap and paler toward the base; dry; unpolished to velvety, sometimes wrinkled and/or furrowed. **RING** Absent. **FRUITING** Scattered or in small groups; on the ground or on rotting wood; in conifer forests; autumn.

    EDIBILITY Uncertain. **SIMILAR** The **SLIMY MILK CAP** (p. 72) shares many characteristics, but its cap and stem are slimy rather than dry and velvety. **COMMENTS** Some foragers report eating VELVETY MILK CAP, though without much joy. ◄ The VELVETY MILK CAP is one of a small number of milk caps that have dark, velvety caps and a white latex that stains mushroom tissues red. It seems likely that further research will reveal more than one species concealed within the *Lactarius fallax* name, with distinctions among them perhaps associated with specific mycorrhizal tree hosts. ◄ "Fallax" means "false," though what is false about this species has been lost in the taxonomic mists.

Kauffman's Milk Cap — *Lactarius kauffmanii*

CAP To 15 cm across; convex with margins inrolled at first, then flat and becoming depressed in the centre and often funnel-shaped; blackish brown, becoming greyish or reddish grey when older and sometimes streaked with darker radial lines; slimy when wet; smooth; flesh 1.5 cm at disc, white to violet-brown to pinkish brown. GILLS Broadly attached to short-decurrent; forking near stem; buff to cinnamon with pinkish tints, often staining orange-brown in age; closely spaced to crowded. LATEX Copious in fresh caps; white, usually unchanging as it dries, slowly staining mushroom tissues olive-brown or orange-brown. ODOUR Not distinctive. TASTE Slowly peppery. SPORE PRINT White to weakly yellowish. STEM To 10 cm tall × 3 cm wide; equal or wider in middle; becoming hollow with age; tan with pink or orange tints; moist to tacky; smooth. RING Absent. FRUITING Scattered and in small troops; on the ground; in coniferous or mixedwood forests; late summer, autumn.

EDIBILITY Unknown. SIMILAR The slightly smaller SLIMY MILK CAP (p. 72) has a slimier, greyer cap. It also has a slimmer (to 1 cm) and slimier stem that is typically cap-coloured (though it may sometimes be lighter in colour). COMMENTS KAUFFMAN'S MILK CAP, like other *Lactarius* species, is consistently mycorrhizal, favouring conifers. ◆ It was first described by Alexander H. Smith, a Michigan mycologist who was active in the middle decades of the 20th century and who published descriptions of several western North American *Lactarius* species, separating them from their European counterparts. ◆ KAUFFMAN'S MILK CAP is named for American mycologist Calvin Henry Kauffman, the same person recognized in the scientific names of KAUFFMAN'S ROOTSHANK (p. 278) and the RAGGED SPRUCE ROT MUSHROOM (p. 216).

Slimy Milk Cap   *Lactarius pseudomucidus*

CAP To 8 cm across; convex to flat, becoming depressed and sometimes funnel-shaped; blackish brown to dark grey; slimy when wet, shiny when dry; smooth; flesh thin, greyish. **GILLS** Broadly attached to slightly decurrent; forking near stem; white, becoming cream or yellow with yellow to brown stains; closely spaced. **LATEX** White, unchanging or becoming yellowish as it dries; staining gills yellow to tan and then brown. **ODOUR** Not distinctive. **TASTE** Slowly peppery. **SPORE PRINT** White. **STEM** To 9 cm tall × 1 cm wide; equal but often widening below, sometimes flattened or with creases; becoming hollow; coloured like the cap or sometimes paler, and sometimes off-white toward the base; slimy when wet, tacky when dry; smooth. **RING** Absent. **FRUITING** Scattered or in small troops; on the ground; in coniferous or mixedwood forests; late summer, autumn, winter.

EDIBILITY Unknown. **SIMILAR KAUFFMAN'S MILK CAP** (p. 71) has a larger cap and a stouter stem that is lighter overall and closer to the colour of the gills. The fruiting body is less slimy. The **GREYLING** (p. 143) has a dry and more steadily grey cap, usually clearly decurrent gills, and sometimes reddening flesh (when cut). **COMMENTS** Literally translated, "pseudomucidus" means "false slimy," which might seem an odd name for the slimiest member of the genus *Lactarius* in this book. The solution to this problem lies in the vagaries of taxonomy. This western North American mushroom was once thought to be the same as the European *L. mucidus*. When our **SLIMY MILK CAP** was defined as a separate species in 1979, it was christened "the false mucidus."

Toadskin Milk Cap   *Lactarius olivaceoumbrinus*

CAP To 12 cm across; convex becoming flat or depressed, the margins inrolled; dark olive to olive-brown, often lighter near the margin, sometimes zoned when young; slimy or sticky when wet, soon dry; smooth, but sometimes with small hairs around the margin; flesh thick, pale olive. GILLS Broadly attached to decurrent; forking near stem; pale, sometimes with orange tints, becoming spotted olive-grey and eventually coloured olive-grey; crowded. LATEX Copious when young; white, slowly changing to greenish grey as it dries, staining gills olive-brown. ODOUR Not distinctive. TASTE Very peppery. SPORE PRINT White to pale buff. STEM To 8 cm tall × 2 cm wide; equal, sometimes broader below; becoming hollow; coloured like the cap or paler, sometimes pitted with darker spots; slimy or sticky when wet, soon dry; smooth. RING Absent. FRUITING Single to scattered; on the ground; under conifers, especially SITKA SPRUCE; late summer, autumn.

EDIBILITY Unknown. The peppery taste does not encourage experimentation. SIMILAR You may come across very similar species, often found on lawns, that associate with introduced birch trees. Some confusion exists about the proper name or names of these birch associates: they are variously noted as *Lactarius turpis*, *L. necator*, or *L. plumbeus*. The cap, gills, and stem of the birch associates can have yellow tints mixed in with the olive-brown colour, and their tops stain magenta when KOH is applied. COMMENTS The TOADSKIN MILK CAP is distinctive but not common in BC. It appears to be a coastal species. ⬥ "Olivaceoumbrinus" refers to the olive-brown (umber) colour.

Mycorrhizae

Mycorrhizae are symbiotic associations between plants and fungi in which the fungi attach themselves to plant roots. (The word "mycorrhiza" is from Greek words for "fungus" and "root.") Fossils from some of the first land plants, 400 million years ago, appear to have mycorrhizal partners, and the partnership continues to be a popular option today: it is estimated that more than 90 per cent of terrestrial vascular plants have mycorrhizal fungi associated with their roots.

More than half a dozen major kinds of mycorrhizae have been recognized, categorized by the plants and fungi involved and the nature of their association. The most common mycorrhizae by far are the ones known as "arbuscular mycorrhizae." GHOST PIPE plants and their *Monotropa* relatives form monotropoid mycorrhizae. Many plant species in the heather family form ericoid mycorrhizae. Plants in the orchid family form orchid mycorrhizae.

We are often not aware of these types of mycorrhizae because the fruiting bodies of the fungi involved are mostly inconspicuous. The mycorrhizae that do have fungi with large fruiting bodies constitute another kind of mycorrhizal association: ectomycorrhizae. "Ecto" means "outside," and they are called this because the fungal hyphae don't penetrate plant root cells, as arbuscular mycorrhizae do. Instead, they form a network in the spaces between the walls of the root's cells. Outside and around the growing root tips they arrange themselves into dense fungal sheaths. From the sheaths, hyphal threads reach out into the surrounding soil.

Fungal mantles on WESTERN HEMLOCK roots.

While only about 2 per cent of earth's plants make ectomycorrhizal connections to fungal networks, this is an extremely important group in BC because they include many of the trees that dominate our western forests. The plants involved are usually woody plants (trees and shrubs) that belong to the pine family (pines, spruces, hemlocks, DOUGLAS-FIRS, larches, and true firs), the birch family (birches, alders, and hazels), the willow family (willows, and poplars such as TREMBLING ASPEN and BLACK COTTONWOOD), and others. The fruiting bodies put up by these fungal networks include many of our large forest mushrooms, including almost all boletes, almost all large (and some smaller) gilled mushrooms, most corals, many toothed fungi, all of our true truffles, and most of our veined mushrooms.

As with other mycorrhizae, ectomycorrhizae are an obligate relationship—without the plant, the fungus would perish, and without the fungus, the plant would perish (or at least be much smaller). The plants photosynthesize and send sugars to their roots, feeding the attached fungi. The fungal mycelium in its turn gathers water and minerals that it shares with the associated plants. Since one tree often hosts a dozen or more species of mycorrhizal fungi on its roots and those fungi can be connected to the roots of multiple trees, the trees and fungi in a BC forest form a common mycorrhizal network through which minerals, sugars, and signalling hormones are exchanged. Forest ecology, once thought of as an arena of competition, may turn out to be more about collaboration and cooperation.

Fungal mantle of POISON PAX (p. 273) on a RED ALDER root.

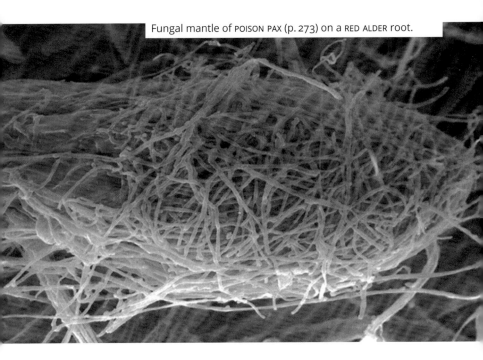

VERMILION WAXY CAP (*Hygrocybe miniata*), p. 82.

Hygrophorus and Similar

The mushroom species in this section are known as waxy caps. The cap tops, though, are not what is waxy—it's the gills underneath the caps that have this texture. The spores of the waxy caps are borne on extra-long basidia, and these structures give the gills a lustrous look and a greasy feel that is similar to that of soft wax. While it takes some practice to learn to recognize this characteristic consistently, once mastered it can be an important clue to the mushroom's identity. Since other types of gilled mushrooms occasionally have waxy gills (those in the genera *Gomphidius* or *Laccaria*, for example), identifiers will also want to look at other characteristics.

The family that contains the waxy caps is quite large—with more than 600 species, one of the largest families of gilled mushrooms—and includes a number of genera treated in other places in this book, such as *Ampulloclitocybe*, *Arrhenia*, *Chromosera*, *Chrysomphalina*, and *Lichenomphalia*. In this section, we describe species in the genera *Hygrophorus* ("moisture-bearing"), *Hygrocybe* ("moisture head"), and *Gliophorus* ("glue-bearing"), all probably named with an eye to the slimy or sticky nature of many of these mushrooms.

The gills of *Hygrophorus* species, besides being more or less waxy, are often thickish and widely spaced. Their caps, typically starting off convex or bell-shaped, flatten in age but often retain umbos. The caps of many of the *Hygrophorus* species are slimy, and the colours on the caps range from white to grey to olive to brown to yellowish orange to red—colourful, but not usually as vibrant as the colours in the species traditionally assigned to *Hygrocybe*. All of the species in *Hygrophorus* form ectomycorrhizal relationships with trees, so they are most often found on the floors of forests. This genus is currently home to about a hundred species of fleshy, medium-sized mushrooms. Nearly half of the world's known *Hygrophorus* species can be found in BC. Here we describe nine of the most common ones.

The modern *Hygrocybe* genus also accounts for about a hundred or so mushroom species and perhaps a quarter of them, we are fairly certain, occur in BC. They are much like *Hygrophorus* species, but they tend to be smaller and to have more brightly coloured, often red or yellow, caps. On some of the *Hygrocybe* mushrooms, tissues stain black with age and handling. *Hygrocybe* species found in BC are generally woodland mushrooms, but worldwide the group is also known as a genus of grasslands and open spaces, which is the reason that *Hygrocybe* species were once thought to be decomposers. More recent evidence, however, points toward *Hygrocybe* mushrooms being symbionts with plants, especially forbs, mosses, and grasses. We will look at only seven of these mushroom species. A pair of them, you will note, have recently moved from the *Hygrocybe* genus to *Gliophorus*.

Witch's Hat — *Hygrocybe singeri* group

CAP To 4 cm across; sharply conical, then broadening, often keeping an umbo, the margins sometimes lobed, and lifting with age; yellow or orange, sometimes red, especially on the disc, and blackening with age or handling, sometimes to the point of being entirely black; slimy, shiny when moist; smooth; translucent-striate; flesh thin, waxy, coloured as surface, blackening with age and bruising. GILLS Narrowly attached or free; deep; thick and waxy; cream or grey to yellowish, bruising black; often closely spaced; typically 2 tiers of subgills. ODOUR Not distinctive. TASTE Not distinctive. SPORE PRINT White. STEM To 6 cm tall × 5 mm wide; equal; stringy and fibrous; hollow; yellow with orange or olive tints; slimy; longitudinally striate. RING Absent. FRUITING Single or in groups; on the ground, in conifer or mixedwood forests, rarely lawns and pastures; usually in autumn to early winter.

EDIBILITY Unknown. Some reports of toxic effects. SIMILAR The ACUTE CONIC WAXY CAP (p. 79) has a yellow to orange cap that does not blacken and retains a more persistently pointed umbo. COMMENTS Once upon a time, we had a world-spanning species known as *Hygrocybe conica*. *Hygrocybe conica* turned out, on closer inspection, to be a group of similar species. Most of the species in this group were based in Europe, but one of them, which went by the name *H. singeri*, was mainly known from western North America, so that became the best name for our local WITCH'S HAT mushroom. We now think that *H. singeri* is itself a species complex, and we await studies that might tell us the right name for our common WITCH'S HAT mushroom. ◆ Elementary students in BC often learn to recognize the widespread and common WITCH'S HAT because of its delightful conical shape, black tones, and appearance at Halloween. Broom and cat not included. ◆ This species group is named after the famous German mycologist Rolf Singer.

Acute Conic Waxy Cap   *Hygrocybe acutoconica* group

CAP To 10 cm across; conical, soon expanding, but often retaining a pointy umbo, the margins sometimes splitting and becoming wavy and uplifted; bright yellow, often with orange tones, especially on the disc and at the margins; slimy/sticky when wet; smooth; finely striate; flesh thin, yellow. **GILLS** Narrowly attached or free; moderately deep; waxy; pale yellow; closely spaced; with subgills. **ODOUR** Not distinctive. **TASTE** Not distinctive. **SPORE PRINT** White. **STEM** To 10 cm tall × 1 cm wide; equal or widened below, sometimes flattened and/ or twisted, easily splitting; coloured as cap, but more whitish in bottom half, base sometimes blackening with age; slightly sticky when wet; fine longitudinal striations. **RING** Absent. **FRUITING** Single or in small groups; on the ground; under conifers or hardwoods; any season.

EDIBILITY Uncertain. It is perhaps edible, but it is too insubstantial and tasteless to consider. **SIMILAR WITCH'S HAT** mushrooms (p. 78) have caps that blacken with age and with handling. Their gills may start off pale yellow but they soon become greyish or black. **YELLOW WAXY CAP** (p. 80) has a rounder cap that is more consistently yellow and does not have an umbo. Its base does not blacken with age. **COMMENTS** "Acutoconica" means "sharply conical."

Yellow Waxy Cap   *Hygrocybe flavescens* group

CAP To 7 cm across; convex to flat and often wavy; yellow, sometimes orange in the centre; slimy/sticky when moist, becoming dry; finely striate when moist; flesh thin, waxy, yellow. GILLS Narrowly attached or free; deep; soft and waxy; yellowish; often closely spaced; numerous subgills. ODOUR Not distinctive. TASTE Not distinctive. SPORE PRINT White. STEM To 8 cm tall × 1 cm wide; equal; hollow; same colour as cap; tacky to dry. RING Absent. FRUITING Single or in small groups; on the ground; in a variety of usually forested habitats; autumn, winter, spring.

EDIBILITY Edible. Or at least suspected to be. Meh. SIMILAR The ACUTE CONIC WAXY CAP (p. 79) is less consistently yellow, has a conical cap with an umbo, and sometimes blackens at the base. ORANGE-BROWN WAXY CAP (p. 90), though its colour varies, tends to have green or grey or brown or pink tones mixed in with the yellow hues on its cap, gills, and stem. It also may have a fishy odour. COMMENTS YELLOW WAXY CAP is a species of southwestern BC. ↝ The scientific name *Hygrocybe flavescens* could change. The differences between it and *H. chlorophana*, for example, are still being investigated. In addition, the genetic signatures of our West Coast species do not match well with European and East Coast versions. ↝ "Flavescens" means "yellowing."

Larch Waxy Cap   *Hygrophorus speciosus*

CAP To 5 cm across; convex expanding to nearly flat, sometimes broadly umbonate; bright red or orange when young, fading to orange-yellow, especially around margins; slimy when wet; smooth; flesh thick, soft, white sometimes with yellow tints. GILLS Broadly attached or decurrent; shallow; waxy; white or pale yellow, edges usually yellow; widely spaced; many subgills. ODOUR Not distinctive. TASTE Not distinctive. SPORE PRINT White. STEM To 10 cm tall × 1 cm wide; equal or widened below, sometimes tapering at base; white, stained dull orange or yellow by the remains of the slimy veil; glutinous when wet on the lower portions at least, the very top sometimes white-powdery. RING Rapidly disappearing slimy outer veil may leave ring-like remnants. FRUITING Scattered or in large groups or clusters; on the ground; under conifers, especially species of larch (*Larix*); autumn.

EDIBILITY Edible. SIMILAR Looking down from head height, the bright red cap invites comparison with some of the red hygrocybes, such as SCARLET WAXY CAP (p. 83), but the glutinous stem and the decurrent white gills of the LARCH WAXY CAP set it apart. *Cuphophyllus pratensis* **group** mushrooms, once classified in *Hygrophorus* but now moved to another genus, have duller orange tints, dry and hygrophanous caps, and (sometimes) gills with light cross-veining. COMMENTS The LARCH WAXY CAP is often noted as *Hygrophorus speciosus* var. *speciosus* to differentiate it from a variety that occurs in eastern North America. ☙ The association with larch means that it is found mostly in the BC Interior. ☙ "Speciosus" means "beautiful" in Latin. The species is well named—the LARCH WAXY CAP is perhaps the most stellar *Hygrophorus* species in BC.

Vermilion Waxy Cap   *Hygrocybe miniata* group

CAP To 4 cm across; convex to flat, sometimes depressed, margins incurved when young and sometimes scalloped; bright red, fading to orange or yellow, often paler at the margin; not slimy; smooth or finely scaly; translucent-striate; flesh thin, waxy, coloured like cap. GILLS Broadly attached to slightly decurrent, but highly variable; deep (to 4 mm); thick and waxy; yellowish or same colour as cap; somewhat widely spaced, 18–35 reaching the stem; usually 3 tiers of subgills. ODOUR Not distinctive. TASTE Not distinctive. SPORE PRINT White. STEM To 5 cm tall × 5 mm wide; equal, sometimes curved; same colour as cap, occasionally lighter toward base; dry; smooth. RING Absent. FRUITING Single or in groups; on the ground or on rotting wood; in deciduous and mixedwood forests and in bogs and pastures; late summer, autumn, winter.

EDIBILITY Edible. Some praise it, some trash it, most don't bother with it. SIMILAR See the comparisons of red hygrocybes in the entry for SCARLET WAXY CAP (p. 83). COMMENTS The VERMILION WAXY CAP is one of a bewildering variety of small red hygrocybes that are largely differentiated by microscopic features. Rest assured, though, that if you find a small red hygrocybe in BC with a dry and minutely scaly cap, chances are good that it will be *Hygrocybe miniata* group. Initial DNA studies, however, suggest that our West Coast species do not include the European *H. miniata*, so the group name is somewhat inappropriate. Expect changes when more complete studies are done. ☙ The word "miniata" looks as if it ought to mean "small," but the word is derived from a Latin term for "cinnabar red."

Scarlet Waxy Cap   *Hygrocybe punicea*

CAP To 10 cm across; bell-shaped becoming convex and then flat or umbonate, margins incurved at first, then sometimes becoming uplifted and/or wavy; deep red when young, fading in streaks to orange; slightly slimy/greasy and shiny when moist; smooth; sometimes translucent-striate in age; flesh thin, fragile, red to yellowish orange. **GILLS** Broadly to narrowly attached or free; deep; waxy and thickish; reddish orange to yellow; somewhat widely spaced; 2–3 tiers of subgills. **ODOUR** Not distinctive. **TASTE** Not distinctive. **SPORE PRINT** White. **STEM** To 10 cm tall × 1.5 cm wide; equal or narrowing toward base; stringy; yellow or reddish fading to orange or yellow, base often lighter, white or sometimes yellowish; dry; longitudinally striate. **RING** Absent. **FRUITING** Scattered or in groups; on the ground; in conifer and mixedwood forests; autumn.

EDIBILITY Uncertain. Often classed as edible, but some eaters report adverse effects. **SIMILAR** *Hygrocybe coccinea* (inset photo) is quite similar to the SCARLET WAXY CAP, but smaller, with a cap less than 5 cm across. The cap of *H. coccinea* is either dry or barely greasy, its stem is not longitudinally striate, and the base of its stem tends to be more deeply coloured. The VERMILION WAXY CAP (p. 82) is also much smaller and has a dry, scaly/bumpy cap. A young LARCH WAXY CAP (p. 81), viewed from the top, has some similarity—see its page for other differences. **COMMENTS** The Latin word "punicea," which means "purple-red," was sometimes used by the Romans as a name for a pomegranate.

Cowboy's Handkerchief   *Hygrophorus eburneus* group

CAP To 8 cm across; convex to flat or slightly umbonate, margins inrolled at first, later sometimes uplifted and wavy; intensely white, in old age occasionally yellowing; extremely slimy; smooth or silky under the slime layer; flesh soft and thick at the disc, thin at the margin, white. GILLS Broadly attached to decurrent; waxy; white, sometimes a bit yellowed with age; widely spaced. ODOUR Not distinctive. TASTE Not distinctive. SPORE PRINT White. STEM To 15 cm tall × 1 cm wide; equal or narrowing downward, often bent; becoming hollow; white, sometimes a bit yellowed with age; slimy; smooth or silky under the slime layer, upper part sometimes scaly. RING Quickly vanishing, leaving slime on stem. FRUITING Scattered or in groups; on the ground; in conifer and mixedwood forests and occasionally in non-forested areas; autumn.

EDIBILITY Edible, but not for the myxophobic mycophagist (slime-hating mushroom eater). SIMILAR The smaller, spruce-loving SPRUCE WAXY CAP (p. 85) is also white, but it does not have the thick, dripping slime of the COWBOY'S HANDKERCHIEF, especially on its stem. DRIPPING SLIMECAP (p. 121) shares the pure sliminess of COWBOY'S HANDKERCHIEF, but its cap is not as white and is often hung with veil remnants, its gills are closely spaced and free or narrowly attached, and its slimy ring is slightly more persistent. The GOLDEN-FRINGED WAXY CAP (p. 86) is less slimy and has golden granules on the cap, especially near the margin. COMMENTS Whoever gave COWBOY'S HANDKERCHIEF its common name was possessed by rare poetic insight. ◆ *Hygrophorus eburneus* is relatively common in BC, both on the coast and inland. ◆ "Eburneus," which means "of ivory," celebrates the essential whiteness of this species.

Spruce Waxy Cap   *Hygrophorus piceae*

CAP To 5 cm across; bell-shaped becoming convex to flat, margins inrolled at first; pure white, but sometimes cream on the disc; slimy when moist; smooth to silky; flesh soft, white. GILLS Broadly attached, becoming decurrent with age; deep; waxy and sometimes forking and cross-veined; white, becoming buff with age; somewhat widely spaced, 25–30 reaching the stem; 3–5 subgills between neighbouring gills. ODOUR Not distinctive. TASTE Not distinctive. SPORE PRINT White. STEM To 5 cm tall × 1 cm wide; narrowing downward; hollow; white; moist to dry, but not slimy; the upper half sometimes with fine cottony hairs. RING Absent. FRUITING Single or in groups; on ground; in wet open areas, often near spruce, often at higher elevations; late summer, autumn. EDIBILITY Unknown. SIMILAR The larger COWBOY'S HANDKERCHIEF (p. 84) is quite similar, but it has a slimier cap and a slimy stem. CEDAR WAXY CAP (*Cuphophyllus russocoriaceus*, once known as *Hygrocybe russocoriacea*) has a somewhat smaller, dry white cap and usually an odour of cedarwood. There are other small, dry white *Cuphophyllus* species with caps under 5 cm across that are more difficult to tell apart. The SPRUCE WAXY CAP bears some resemblance to white clitocybes, such as the SWEAT-PRODUCING CLITOCYBE (p. 135), but the clitocybe has closely spaced gills and often a splotched cap. COMMENTS French mycologist Robert Kühner found the SPRUCE WAXY CAP in the Alps in the 1940s and realized that this small, beautiful shining white mushroom, "d'un beau blanc éclatant," did not fit the descriptions of other white waxy caps. ✺ "Piceae" means "of spruce."

Golden-fringed Waxy Cap   *Hygrophorus chrysodon* group

CAP To 8 cm across; convex becoming flat and often broadly umbonate, the margins inrolled; white with golden yellow granules, especially near the margin; slimy when wet; smooth; flesh thick, soft, white. **GILLS** Decurrent; moderately deep; waxy and cross-veined; white; widely spaced; with subgills. **ODOUR** Not distinctive. **TASTE** Not distinctive. **SPORE PRINT** White. **STEM** To 10 cm tall × 1.5 cm wide; equal; white; slightly slimy when wet; smooth. **RING** Partial ring of golden granules sometimes present on upper stem or dispersed to other parts of the stem. **FRUITING** Single or in small groups; on the ground; under conifers or hardwoods; summer, autumn, winter.

    EDIBILITY Edible. Some eaters apparently have a higher tolerance to slime than others. **SIMILAR** The white **COWBOY'S HANDKERCHIEF** (p. 84) might resemble a **GOLDEN-FRINGED WAXY CAP** whose yellow granules had washed away, but its cap and stem are significantly slimier. The whitish **SPRUCE WAXY CAP** (p. 85) is somewhat smaller and grows near spruce. The similarities between these 2 white *Hygrophorus* species and *H. chrysodon* without yellow granules are quickly resolved with KOH, which turns *H. chrysodon* tissues an immediate yellow. **COMMENTS** The **GOLDEN-FRINGED WAXY CAP** is relatively common in Interior BC. ⚘ "Chrysodon" means "golden-toothed."

Parrot Waxy Cap   *Gliophorus psittacinus*

CAP To 3 cm across; bell-shaped becoming convex or flat, often umbonate; green when young, but the green soon fading from centre outward to yellow, orange, red-brown, or buff; slimy to glutinous when moist, sometimes shiny when dry; smooth; hygrophanous; translucent-striate; flesh thin, coloured like the cap. GILLS Broadly attached to slightly decurrent; thick and waxy; same colour and colour changes as cap; somewhat widely spaced. ODOUR Not distinctive. TASTE Not distinctive. SPORE PRINT White. STEM To 6 cm tall × 5 mm wide; equal or widening downward, often curvy; hollow; same greenish colour as cap and then fading, often to yellow or buff, from the base up; slimy when wet; smooth. RING Absent. FRUITING Single or in small groups; on the ground in wet areas; in forests, pastures, or roadsides; spring, summer, autumn.

EDIBILITY Uncertain. SIMILAR ORANGE-BROWN WAXY CAP (p. 90) can also have touches of green in its gills and at the top of its stem, but it has more decurrent gills and often a rough cap. COMMENTS In this book, we have used the name *Gliophorus psittacinus*, but the mushroom is widely known as *Hygrocybe psittacina*. The genus *Gliophorus* was created in the 1950s to hold the PARROT WAXY CAP and other more marginal members of the *Hygrocybe/Hygrophorus* genera. Scholarly opinion on this division has wavered. Genetic studies in the 2010s, however, have been interpreted as supporting the genus split. ⬥ The range of colour in PARROT WAXY CAP, even in a single specimen over the course of a few days, is paralleled among BC mushrooms only by that of its cousin, the ORANGE-BROWN WAXY CAP. ⬥ "Psittacinus" means "pertaining to a parrot," presumably in reference to the greenish hues found in some parrot plumages.

Brown Almond Waxy Cap   *Hygrophorus bakerensis*

CAP To 15 cm across; convex becoming flat, the margins inrolled and cottony when young; yellow-brown to orange-brown with a pale to white margin that sometimes shows some slight ribbing; somewhat slimy to very slimy when moist; smooth, with pressed-down coloured fibrils sometimes forming streaks; flesh thick, soft, white. GILLS Broadly attached to decurrent; deep in large caps; waxy; white to cream; somewhat widely spaced, 56–88 reaching the stem; 2–3 tiers of subgills. ODOUR Sweet, like almonds. TASTE Not distinctive. SPORE PRINT White. STEM To 15 cm tall × 2.5 cm wide; equal or narrowing downward; solid; whitish, sometimes developing yellowish areas in age or with handling; dry; smooth, but the area near the top can be covered with a cottony powder when young. RING Absent. FRUITING Scattered or in groups; often near rotting wood; under conifers, at elevations above 300 m; autumn, winter.

EDIBILITY Edible, but bland. SIMILAR Other large white-spored species share the almond odour, but they can be easily differentiated by checking other characters of the various species. The smaller *Hygrophorus agathosmus*, for example, has a grey to greyish brown cap. (Note, though, that the name of our western North American *H. agathosmus* may change, depending on the outcome of some studies in progress.) The gills of the aromatic FRAGRANT COLLYBIA (p. 199) are neither waxy nor decurrent. COMMENTS The cap edges, gills, and stems of the BROWN ALMOND WAXY CAP are often covered in clear water droplets. ❧ This species is common and often abundant in our province's southern Interior. ❧ The species is named after Mount Baker, where early specimens were collected.

Olive-brown Waxy Cap   *Hygrophorus boyeri*

CAP To 6 cm across; convex to flat, slightly umbonate or depressed, margins initially inrolled, often uplifted and wavy in age; yellow-brown to greenish yellow, often tinted orange when older, darker brown at the centre; slimy; smooth; flesh thin, soft, white to yellow. GILLS Decurrent; moderately deep; waxy and sometimes cross-veined in age; white becoming pale yellow, sometimes coloured like cap margin; moderately to widely spaced; subgills in 2–3 tiers. ODOUR Not distinctive. TASTE Not distinctive. SPORE PRINT White. STEM To 10 cm tall × 1.2 cm wide; equal or narrowing downward; solid; dry/silky and white at the top, the main section below ring zone coloured like the cap and often slimy, and the base sometimes white and (rarely) developing reddish tints with age. RING Quickly vanishing, leaving slime and sometimes fibrils on stem. FRUITING Scattered or in groups; on the ground; in forest with conifers (especially 2-needle pines); autumn.

EDIBILITY Edible. But bland and gelatinous. SIMILAR The SHEATHED WAXY CAP (p. 93) has a dark brown to blackish cap, gills that remain pure white or grey, and a stem with darkish concentric bands. The HIDEOUS GOMPHIDIUS (p. 297) can be similar, but its spore print is black and its gills separate easily from the cap with a swipe of the thumb. SHEATHED WAXY CAP (p. 93) found mostly around spruce, has a white stem with its lower section sheathed with blackish fibrils. COMMENTS We used to call OLIVE-BROWN WAXY CAP *H. hypothejus*. A recent study reassigns our North American species to the new name *H. boyeri*. ✢ In English-speaking Europe, the common name often used for *H. hypothejus* is HERALD OF WINTER because it shows up, like our OLIVE-BROWN WAXY CAP, about the time of the first frosts.

Orange-brown Waxy Cap *Gliophorus laetus* group

CAP To 3 cm across; convex to flat, sometimes with disc depressed, and margins incurved and often uplifted and wavy in age; the colour variable, shades of orange, pink, yellow, green, purplish, grey, buff, or brown, or sometimes mixtures, often paler at the margin, usually drying pinkish to orange-pink; slimy/sticky when moist; smooth or rugged; hygrophanous; translucent-striate; flesh thin, coloured as the cap or paler, often with shades of grey. GILLS Broadly attached to decurrent; moderately deep; cross-veined; coloured as cap or paler, sometimes with shades of green; somewhat widely spaced. ODOUR If distinctive, then unpleasant—fishy or skunk-like. TASTE Not distinctive. SPORE PRINT White. STEM To 10 cm tall × 6 mm wide; hollow; same colour as cap or paler or yellower, often with a pinkish or greenish tinge at top; slimy. RING Absent. FRUITING Usually in groups; on the ground; in a variety of moist forested and non-forested habitats, including gardens and wetlands; spring, summer, autumn.

EDIBILITY Unknown. SIMILAR The PARROT WAXY CAP (p. 87) tends to have and retain more green hues—the ORANGE-BROWN WAXY CAP, if it displays green, usually only has it on the gills and stem top. The gills of the ORANGE-BROWN WAXY CAP are also more decurrent. Nonetheless, differentiating the 2 species, especially when they are older and the greens have faded, can be a challenge. COMMENTS ORANGE-BROWN WAXY CAP has also been classified with *Hygrophorus* and *Hygrocybe*. ◆ Recent genetic studies indicate that we may have more than one species going by the name *Gliophorus laetus* in our region and that these may not include the European species initially designated by this name. ◆ "Laetus" means "glad."

Blushing Waxy Cap   *Hygrophorus pudorinus*

CAP To 12 cm or more across; bell-shaped or convex to flat, margins inrolled at first; pale tan to pinkish; sticky when moist; smooth; flesh thick, firm, white or tinged with cap colour. GILLS Broadly attached to decurrent; shallow; waxy and thick, sometimes forking and cross-veined; white, often tinged pinkish; with subgills. ODOUR Not distinctive, but some noses detect a pleasant or unpleasant pungency. TASTE Not distinctive. SPORE PRINT White. STEM To 12 cm tall × 3 cm wide; equal or narrowing downward; solid; white or tinged with cap colour, the upper half with scales that darken reddish brown with age or drying. RING Absent. FRUITING Scattered or in groups; on the ground; in wet soils in coniferous forests, with spruce or pine; autumn.

EDIBILITY Edible. Apparently. SIMILAR The slightly smaller *Cuphophyllus pratensis* (once called *Hygrocybe pratensis*) **group** mushrooms are more salmon than pinkish, and the caps are dry. *Hygrophorus erubescens* (inset photo) has darker red highlights on the disc, gills that spot and stain red, and a stem that may be darker in the lower half. *Hygrophorus saxatilis* caps reveal fine, pressed-down hairs when seen under a lens, and the gills are salmon to pinkish brown, contrasting clearly with the whitish fruiting body. COMMENTS A number of varieties of the BLUSHING WAXY CAP have been described, and some attempts have been made to redefine these as species. In one of the varieties/species, the base tends to stain yellow or orange when bruised. ✸ "Pudorinus" means "blushing."

Sooty Brown Waxy Cap   *Hygrophorus camarophyllus*

CAP To 7 cm across; convex, sometimes becoming flat or slightly umbonate, margins inrolled and then uplifted and sometimes downy; brownish grey to brown, streaky along radial lines; sticky when moist, but mostly dry; smooth with pressed-down radial fibres; flesh thick, white. GILLS Broadly attached to short-decurrent; deep; waxy and cross-veined; white or tinged grey; closely spaced; with short subgills. ODOUR Usually not distinctive, but sometimes faintly sulphury. TASTE Not distinctive. SPORE PRINT White. STEM To 12 cm tall × 2 cm wide; equal or narrowing downward; coloured as cap or paler; dry; silky-hairy above, smooth below. RING Absent. FRUITING Scattered or in groups; on the ground; with conifers; autumn, but also spring and summer near melting snowbanks.

    EDIBILITY Edible. But bland. SIMILAR *Hygrophorus calophyllus* has a somewhat slimy to very slimy cap without the radial streaking and gills that are often pink-tinted. *Hygrophorus marzuolus*, another snowbank mushroom, has a slimy, streaked dark grey cap and widely spaced grey to blackish gills. *Hygrophorus agathosmus* has a stature and colour range that is similar to the SOOTY BROWN WAXY CAP, but it has a distinct almond odour. COMMENTS The Swedish mycologist and botanist Elias M. Fries (1794–1878) first published the genus name *Hygrophorus* in 1836. He later recognized subcategories of the genus that he called *Camarophyllus* and *Limacium*, which caused the scientific name of the waxy cap in this entry to do some jumping around. Today, mycologists regard *Camarophyllus* and *Limacium* as synonyms for the genus *Hygrophorus*, which officially makes this mushroom a *Hygrophorus*, since that was the earliest accurate name. ◦ The SOOTY BROWN WAXY CAP is relatively common in BC, especially in the Interior. ◦ "Camarophyllus" means "with arched gills."

Sheathed Waxy Cap   *Hygrophorus olivaceoalbus* group

CAP To 8 cm across; convex or bell-shaped becoming flat, margins incurved at first and sometimes later uplifted; black to dark brown in the centre, grading to green-black or light grey toward the margin; radially streaked with black fibrils; slimy to glutinous; flesh thick, soft, white. GILLS Broadly attached to nearly decurrent; shallow; soft and waxy; white, sometimes tinged grey; with subgills. ODOUR Not distinctive. TASTE Not distinctive. SPORE PRINT White. STEM To 12 cm tall × 3 cm wide; equal or widening downward, sometimes with narrowed base, often bent; sheathed to near top with an inner layer of pressed-down, darkish fibres, often forming broken rings or chevrons, and an outside layer of slime; smooth, silky, and white above sheath. RING Quickly vanishing, often leaving zone of slime and fibrils on the stem. FRUITING Scattered, in groups, and/or clustered; on the ground; in coniferous forests (especially around spruce); late summer, autumn, winter.

EDIBILITY Edible. But bland and slimy. SIMILAR OLIVE-BROWN WAXY CAP (p. 89), another of the slimy brown *Hygrophorus* species, usually has yellow or reddish tones and shows a preference for pines. HIDEOUS GOMPHIDIUS (p. 297) has a black spore print and gills that separate easily from the cap. COMMENTS SHEATHED WAXY CAP is generally classified as a mycorrhizal *Hygrophorus* species, but there is evidence that the relationship to its spruce hosts may include some antagonism. ◦ The SHEATHED WAXY CAP is not a common find in BC. When fresh caps are discovered, however, the stem ornamentation and the contrasting colours of the gills and upper stem with the cap create a strong impression. ◦ "Olivaceoalbus" means "olive-white."

The Mushrooms of Observatory Hill

A mushroom study on Observatory Hill, just outside of Victoria, has become one of the world's largest and longest studies of mushroom species at a given locale. Observatory Hill is a 72-hectare federal government site topped by the Dominion Astrophysical Observatory. The observatory, opened in 1918, had the distinction of possessing, for a few months, the second-largest telescope in the world. The telescope is still in use, and the site has been expanded into an astronomical education and research facility.

Observatory Hill provides three broadly defined ecosystems characteristic of the endangered Coastal Douglas-Fir Biogeoclimatic Zone. On drier upper slopes with south and west aspects, there are rock outcrops and grassy meadows dotted with stands of GARRY OAK and ARBUTUS trees. On drier sites, there are DOUGLAS-FIR-dominated forests. On wetter sites with richer soil, there are WESTERN REDCEDAR forests mixed with DOUGLAS-FIR, GRAND FIR, BIGLEAF MAPLE, and RED ALDER.

Located in a part of our province with extensive suburban development, Observatory Hill was deliberately left undeveloped in order to provide a buffer of darkness for astronomical observation. The absence of site development was turned to another use in November of 2004 when Oluna Ceska, one of BC's most celebrated mycologists, initiated a survey of Observatory Hill fungi, a survey that continues at the time of this writing. Oluna, who is always accompanied by husband Adolf Ceska, a retired botanist and her able field assistant and photographer, employs

Observatory Hill.

what she calls "intuitive controlled survey method" on the hill. She and Adolf walk a variety of paths through the study area, attempting to sample all habitats and spending more time in areas where their considerable field experience suggests there may be a greater variety of species. A day in the field is often followed by long days in the lab.

In the 15 years between 2004 and 2019, Oluna and Adolf documented more than 1,400 mushroom species from Observatory Hill, making nearly 500 research visits. The pair have contributed, largely from their Observatory Hill work, more than 6,000 dried collections to the herbarium at the University of British Columbia's Beaty Biodiversity Museum. These collections have been important in regional studies of *Cortinarius*, *Inocybe*, *Hebeloma*, and other genera. Their contributions to our understanding of BC mushrooms have been recognized by fellow mycologists, who named *Cortinarius ceskae* and *Inocybe ceskae* after them, and by a mycology scholarship in their name at the University of British Columbia.

The Ceskas' Observatory Hill studies have underlined the fact that fungi fruit throughout the year and that some species may fruit one year and then not at all the following years. Even after eight years of studying the same site, for example, the Ceskas were finding that more than 10 per cent of the species that were observed in a calendar year had not been noted previously. Their research has shown that only detailed studies that stretch over all seasons of the year and over many years have any chance of documenting the true fungal diversity of a region.

CONIFER TUFT (*Hypholoma capnoides*), p. 301, on Observatory Hill.

SHEATHED POWDERCAP (*Cystoderma fallax*), p. 101.

Lepiota and Similar

The genus *Lepiota* was initially a catch-all concept for a large group of forest-floor decomposers. These mushrooms had free or narrowly attached pale gills, white spores, partial veils that left rings on the stems, and parasol-like convex caps that often bore scales made out of stretched and broken cap-skin tissue. Elias M. Fries provided the formal definition of the genus in the early 1800s.

The next two centuries were not kind to the original genus concept. Some groups of mushrooms that were once thought to be part of the genus, such as *Cystoderma* (pp. 100–101), were removed to more distant parts of the fungal family tree. Other more closely related species groups that were once inside of *Lepiota* were redefined as new genera, such as *Leucoagaricus* (pp. 122–123) and *Leucocoprinus* (p. 104). The boundaries of all of these species groups, however, are not firmly fixed. DNA work suggests, moreover, that the evolutionary distance between white-spored *Lepiota* species and darker-spored groups in genera such as *Agaricus* and *Coprinus* is not as great as we once thought. In coming decades, we will, in all likelihood, see more rearranging of the lepiotoid furniture.

English common names for mushrooms often reflect the larger groupings that dominated the early days of mushroom taxonomy. *Lepiota* species tended to be called "parasol mushrooms," even when the resemblance to actual parasols was slight, and you can still see this common-name habit at work in the popular names of many of the once-*Lepiota* species. Another collective name heard in BC for *Lepiota* species is "nipple mushrooms," based on the often areolate appearance of the caps.

Only one of the lepiota group of mushrooms is widely appreciated at BC dinner tables: the SHAGGY PARASOL (p. 98). Beginning mushroomers can, with a little practice, learn to recognize and appreciate this large, handsome species. Some of the smaller *Lepiota* and once-*Lepiota* species have been eaten at various times and places. But a few, such as the DEADLY PARASOL (p. 103), have been implicated in serious poisonings and deaths. Foragers are advised to avoid all of the smaller lepiotas.

Shaggy Parasol   *Chlorophyllum brunneum*

CAP To 15 cm across; nearly spherical at emergence, becoming convex and sometimes flat; brown to reddish brown; with the top skin breaking up (except in the centre) into large, difficult-to-detach scales and in the process exposing white flesh that is organized into radial fibres, the fibres sometimes hanging over the margin to form a whitish fringe; dry; smooth when very young, then shaggy; flesh white to beige, becoming orange to red to brown when damaged. GILLS Free; deep; white, becoming beige or brown in age, bruising orange to brown; closely spaced; with multiple tiers of subgills. ODOUR Pleasant when fresh. TASTE Not distinctive. SPORE PRINT White. STEM To 20 cm tall × 2 cm wide at the narrow part; expanding downward to a bulbous base, often with an abrupt, sometimes gutter-like upper edge; hollow centre; white, discolouring reddish brown, especially below the ring; dry; smooth. RING Large, often with frayed edges, but no obvious double edge; white above, sometimes brown patches below; persistent and often movable. FRUITING Single or in fused clumps, sometimes in rings or arcs; in the soil; in forest litter, but usually in gardens or compost heaps; spring, summer, autumn.

EDIBILITY Edible. SIMILAR The OLIVE SHAGGY PARASOL (p. 99) is typically found in forest environments. It is quite similar in most respects to the SHAGGY PARASOL, but it has brown to olive-brown scales on the cap and the exposed flesh that is around its scales is about the same colour as the scales. *Chlorophyllum rhacodes* is very similar to SHAGGY PARASOL, but it has a ring with 2 distinct layers—1 sloped up, 1 sloped down—and the bulb is not abrupt. The poisonous *C. molybdites*, which grows in grass and has green spores that eventually colour the gills green, is probably not present in BC yet, but it is in Washington and may wander north. COMMENTS "Chlorophyllum" means "green-gilled"—a descriptor for *C. molybdites*—and "brunneum" means "brown-coloured."

Olive Shaggy Parasol

Chlorophyllum olivieri

CAP To 15 cm across; nearly spherical at first, becoming convex and sometimes flat; greyish brown, sometimes toned olive-brown; the top skin breaking up (except in the centre) into difficult-to-detach scales and in the process exposing cream- to olive-coloured flesh that is organized into radial fibres, the fibres sometimes hanging over the margin to form a whitish fringe; dry; smooth when very young, then shaggy; flesh white to beige, becoming orange to red to brown when damaged. GILLS Free; deep; white, becoming beige or brown in age, bruising orange to brown; closely spaced; with multiple tiers of subgills. ODOUR Not distinctive, but like raw potatoes to some. TASTE Usually not distinctive, but nutty to some. SPORE PRINT White. STEM To 16 cm tall × 1.5 cm wide; expanding downward to an enlarged base; hollow centre; white, discolouring reddish brown, especially below the ring; dry; smooth. RING Large, often with frayed double edge; white above, sometimes brown patches below; persistent and often movable. FRUITING Single or in small troops, sometimes in rings or arcs; in forests, but often in disturbed areas; late summer, autumn.

EDIBILITY Edible. SIMILAR The SHAGGY PARASOL (p. 98) has larger, coarser cap scales that are a different colour from the flesh underneath (brown on white/cream), and it has a less abrupt base (the base resembles somewhat a chicken drumstick with the meaty side downward). See the SHAGGY PARASOL entry for other similar species. COMMENTS In BC, OLIVE SHAGGY PARASOL has sometimes been found in nutrient-enriched sites, including near a wood-ant nest, in an area where sheep urinate, and in areas of accumulated deciduous leaf litter. ➤ It is known in BC only from the south coast.

Earthy Powdercap
Cystoderma amianthinum group

CAP To 4 cm across; bell-shaped or conical becoming convex to flat to depressed, often keeping a small, broad umbo even if depressed, the margins typically with veil remnants; pale yellow to yellowish brown to orange-yellow, often with a darker disc; covered with mealy granules (but the rain may wash them off) and often radially wrinkled; dry; flesh thin, white. GILLS Attached, becoming narrowly attached; moderately deep; white to yellowish; closely spaced; with 2 tiers of subgills. ODOUR Usually of freshly husked corn or corn silk, but sometimes disagreeable, ammonia-like. TASTE Not distinctive. SPORE PRINT White. STEM To 6 cm tall × 7 mm wide; equal; sometimes lighter (white to pale yellow) above the ring, cap-coloured below the ring; smooth above ring or with white fibrils, covered in granules below; sometimes with white mycelium at the base. RING White above, cap-coloured and granular below; transient, often becoming a ragged zone. FRUITING Single, scattered, or in small troops, sometimes with bases closely attached, sometimes in wide fairy rings and arcs; on the ground; in conifer forest but often in open grassy areas, frequently in moss; late summer, autumn, early winter.

EDIBILITY Unknown. SIMILAR *Cystodermella granulosa* tends to have a reddish brown, non-wrinkled cap and no particular odour. *Cystodermella cinnabarina* has a non-wrinkled, sometimes lobed cap that is coloured coral pink to brick red to rusty orange and a stem that is coloured like the cap. It also has a stouter profile and no distinct smell. SHEATHED POWDERCAP (p. 101) has a darker, rusty brown to yellow-brown cap and a larger, persistent, sheathing ring. The poisonous *Lepiota castanea* has small dark scales on the cap and stem, free gills, and a ring that often disappears. COMMENTS EARTHY POWDERCAP is widespread in BC. ❧ The word "amianthinum," which means "uncontaminated, pure," was used by the ancient Greeks as a name for asbestos, so the reference may be to the striations/wrinkles that characterize mineral asbestos.

Sheathed Powdercap   *Cystoderma fallax*

CAP To 4 cm across; bell-shaped becoming convex to flat and sometimes undulating, at times with a broad umbo, the margins often with veil remnants; covered initially with erect granules that can flatten and wash off; rusty orange, to brown with yellow-brown or olive hues, to darker brown, the disc sometimes darker than the margin; dry; flesh thin, but thicker near centre, white. GILLS Broadly attached to narrowly attached and notched; shallow to moderately deep; pinkish buff to whitish; closely spaced; with 2–3 tiers of subgills. ODOUR Not distinctive. TASTE Not distinctive. SPORE PRINT White. STEM To 6 cm tall × 6 mm wide; equal or widening downward, sometimes curved at base; white to cream to tan above the ring, cap-coloured below ring; smooth above ring but sometimes with close longitudinal fibres, covered in granules below; often with white mycelium at the base. RING Flaring, as though it were an extension of a bumpy sheath over the lower stem; pale on the upper surface, cap-coloured and granular below; persistent. FRUITING Single, scattered, or in small troops; on the ground or on well-rotted wood; in conifer forest; spring, late summer, autumn.

EDIBILITY Unknown. SIMILAR See the comparisons in the entry for the EARTHY POWDERCAP (p. 100). The persistent ring of SHEATHED POWDERCAP sets it apart from other *Cystoderma* species and their look-alikes. COMMENTS This decomposer seems to arrive in unpredictable eruptions—some years it is common, other years hard to find. ◆ SHEATHED POWDERCAP is a western North America species, known from southern BC. ◆ Recent genetic studies suggest that it may be a variety of the white- to pink-capped *C. carcharias*, which is known from Europe and Asia. ◆ "Fallax" means "false."

Yellowfoot Dapperling   *Lepiota magnispora*

CAP To 8 cm across; egg-shaped when very young, then broadly conical to flat, often with an umbo, sometimes with hanging white to yellow veil remnants on the margin; dark brown to reddish brown to orange-brown skin that breaks up as the cap expands, leaving a dark centre with lighter orange-brown skin scales distributed on a whitish brown to yellow-brown background; dry; flesh thin, white. **GILLS** Free; deep; white to cream; crowded, with 3–7 subgills between neighbouring full gills. **ODOUR** Not distinctive. **TASTE** Not distinctive. **SPORE PRINT** White to pale cream. **STEM** To 10 cm tall × 1 cm wide; widening slightly downward and often curved; becoming hollow; white to cream with broken bands of yellow to yellow-brown to orange-brown skin below; dry; section below ring zone shaggy with white to yellow veil remnants. **RING** Indistinct clumps of white or cream cottony tissue that quickly disappear or collapse onto the lower stem. **FRUITING** Single, scattered, or in large clumps; on the ground; in coniferous and mixedwood forests; autumn.

EDIBILITY Uncertain. Best avoided because of similar *Lepiota* species that are known to be poisonous. **SIMILAR** *Lepiota clypeolaria* has a pale brown centre rather than a dark reddish brown centre, and the edges of the dark centre are less defined. Its cap characteristics can overlap with that of the YELLOWFOOT DAPPERLING, however, so microscopic examination of spores may be needed to make a definitive call. In our experience, most of the BC mushrooms fitting the description on this page seem to be, when examined microscopically, the YELLOWFOOT DAPPERLING rather than *L. clypeolaria*. *Lepiota cristata*, besides microscopic differences, has an orange-brown centre and scales and a tan to pinkish tan lower stem that is either smooth or has fine silky fibres. See also the entry for the **DEADLY PARASOL** (p. 103) for other comparisons. **COMMENTS** "Magnispora" means "large-spored," and the YELLOWFOOT DAPPERLING is certainly that, with spores up to a whopping (for spores) 25 microns!

Deadly Parasol   *Lepiota subincarnata*

CAP To 5 cm across; convex becoming flat, at times broadly umbonate and wavy; cinnamon to reddish/pinkish brown, fading to beige, often paler near the margin; dry; matted and felty when young, with the surface (except perhaps the centre) breaking apart into concentric rings of felty scales that dot a creamy background; flesh thin, white. GILLS Free or narrowly attached; deep; white to creamy yellow; closely spaced; with 2–3 tiers of subgills. ODOUR Not always distinct, but also described as fragrant, like burned rubber, musty, sharp, and unpleasant. TASTE Not distinctive. SPORE PRINT White. STEM To 6 cm tall × 1 cm wide; equal or widening downward; white above, cinnamon to pink-brown below; top finely hairy and silky, bottom developing broken, cap-coloured bands; dry. RING Not persistent, but leaving fibrils on stem and sometimes on the cap edge. FRUITING Single or in small groups; on the ground; in gardens and other disturbed sites; usually summer and autumn.

EDIBILITY Poisonous. The DEADLY PARASOL, which has the same toxins as the DEATH CAP (p. 112), has caused a number of fatalities, including a New Westminster man in 1988. SIMILAR Mushrooms in the *Lepiota aspera* **group** (see inset photo), also known as *Echinoderma asperum*, are larger than the DEADLY PARASOL, have stems with a more prominent bulb, and sport a darker brown colour with more erect, pyramidal scales. *Lepiota castanea* has a cap with a background to its scales that is more yellowish than on the DEADLY PARASOL, flesh that is yellowish buff, a slenderer stem, and gills that may become rusty-stained. *Lepiota flammeotincta* has flesh that immediately stains orange-red to pink when bruised. See also comparisons in the entry for YELLOWFOOT DAPPERLING (p. 102). COMMENTS This species is known only from southwestern BC. ☙ *Lepiota subincarnata* may possibly be the same as *L. josserandii*. ☙ The scholar who bestowed the name probably had pinkish flesh, so the name "subincarnata" (literally, "below flesh") was likely a way of saying "approaching pink." It could also have meant "approaching *L. incarnata*."

Flowerpot Parasol

Leucocoprinus birnbaumii

CAP To 5 cm across; egg-shaped at first, becoming bell-shaped to flat, often with a broad umbo, and quickly sagging, margins initially incurved; pleated by radial fibres and covered with powdery scales; bright yellow or greenish yellow, aging to brown, centre sometimes yellowish buff; dry; striate from centre to margin in age; flesh thin, yellow. GILLS Free; white to pale yellow. ODOUR Not distinctive. TASTE Not distinctive, possibly bitter. SPORE PRINT White. STEM To 8 cm tall × 5 mm wide; widening toward base; coloured as the cap; dry; smooth or covered with fine powdery scales. RING Cottony; bright yellow; fleeting. FRUITING Single or in groups; usually in flowerpots and greenhouses, rarely in lawns; any season.

EDIBILITY Uncertain. According to some, poisonous. SIMILAR SUNNY SIDE UP (p. 282) bears a resemblance, but it has a slimy cap and no ring, and it prefers the rustic life of fields and manure to the domesticity of flowerpots. COMMENTS The FLOWERPOT PARASOL excites interest for 2 reasons. First, because of its often vivid yellow colours. Second, because it shows up in homes where the visible fungal repertoire is normally limited to mildews and moulds. ● If the mycelial mats of *Leucocoprinus birnbaumii* have an effect on plants growing in the same pot, it is not apparent. ● The habitat and lack of early records from BC and the US Pacific Northwest suggest that the FLOWERPOT PARASOL may be an introduced tropical decomposer.

Amanita and Similar

Charles McIlvaine (*One Thousand American Fungi*, 1900) writes, "Amanitae are...the aristocrats of fungi. Their noble bearing, their beauty, their power for good or evil, and above all their perfect structure, have placed them first in their realm." His remark "for good or evil" presumably reflects the fact that the genus *Amanita* contains both some of the world's most delicious *and* its most poisonous mushrooms. On the one hand, wild-collected amanita mushrooms are important additions to the table in many countries of the world. On the other hand, most of the world's serious mushroom poisonings are due to just a few species in this genus. In 2018, over a thousand people in Iran were sickened and about 20 died from consuming *A. virosa*, the aptly named DESTROYING ANGEL. In 2016, a three-year-old boy who lived in Victoria, BC, died from eating the DEATH CAP (*A. phalloides*, p. 112).

What makes a mushroom an amanita? One important feature is that the parts of an amanita mushroom are, like a chicken, formed in the egg, in what is called the button stage. Cut vertically into an egg and you can see an outline of what will become the stem and cap and gills. Such slicing is a good practice, because uncut buttons of deadly amanitas can resemble edible puffball mushrooms (p. 421).

Amanitas share a number of other characteristic features. They all have white spores, and nearly all of them have gills that are pale and free, or almost free, from the stem. While they are doing a lot of their development in egg-like buttons, amanitas are protected from the world by a soft shell, the universal veil, which they break when they send up their stems and expand their caps. The universal veil is strong, though, and pieces of it tend to remain behind. On most amanitas, the bottom part of the universal veil becomes a cup-like volva surrounding the stem base. The middle of the veil can hug the top of the stem base and form basal collars. On some amanitas, the universal veil leaves remnants behind on the cap that show up as warts and patches. The gills of most amanitas are at first protected by another kind of veil tissue, the partial veil. When the gills are ready to put out spores, this veil breaks and leaves behind, on many species, a distinct ring around the stem.

In this section we cover about a dozen of BC's most common species of the genus *Amanita* and a few look-alikes. The look-alikes share features with the *Amanita* species that can lead to misidentification, including their overall stature, white gills, white spore deposits, and (sometimes) rings on their stems.

These BC *Amanita* species, like almost all of the others in the genus, negotiate symbiotic mycorrhizal partnerships (p. 74) with plants, especially with trees. This means amanita mushrooms are never found far from their partner trees.

For those interested in learning more about *Amanita* species, we highly recommend Britt Bunyard and Jay Justice's *Amanitas of North America* (The Fungi Press, 2020).

Fly Agaric

Amanita muscaria group

CAP To 30 cm across; nearly spherical at first and then becoming convex to flat; colour variable, most often bright scarlet, even blood red, but also orange to yellow, and (very rarely in our area) white; with whitish to tan or yellowish tan pyramidal warts that sometimes wash off with rain, the warts near the outside edge disappearing first; cap slippery when moist; flesh thick, white, with a layer of yellow-orange flesh below the cap surface in all colour phases. GILLS Free or attached; deep; white to pale cream; closely spaced. ODOUR Not distinctive. TASTE Not distinctive. SPORE PRINT White. STEM To 20 cm tall × 3 cm wide; gradually enlarging downward into an egg-shaped bulb that may taper at the base; white; smooth above ring, smooth or scaly below. RING Skirt-like; white to yellowish; typically more persistent than with some other amanitas, but sometimes disappearing. VOLVA Cottony, often showing as multiple ascending irregular rings or broken bands and patches of crumbly remnants on the lower stem, but sometimes just fragments around the base; white. FRUITING Single or in small to very large groups, sometimes forming interrupted fairy rings; on the ground; found with a variety of different tree species, commonly conifers and birches and BLACK COTTONWOOD; summer, autumn, early winter.

EDIBILITY Poisonous, hallucinogenic. The toxins are water soluble, so some mushroomers eat FLY AGARIC after careful preparation. SIMILAR The 2 mostly spring mushrooms in this genus, SUNSHINE AMANITA (p. 110) and PANTHER CAP (p. 108), might be confused with certain colour phases of the FLY AGARIC if the fruiting seasons have some overlap. But SUNSHINE AMANITA is shorter and smaller, and PANTHER CAP has more brown in the cap and a volva whose top margin tends to be well defined and gutter-like. The most likely confusion for the FLY AGARIC is between the yellow phase of this group and the JONQUIL AMANITA (p. 109), whose volva is more substantial and cup-like.

COMMENTS This is the iconic mushroom featured in *Alice in Wonderland* and in Mario video games. Ask a class of young children to draw a mushroom, and most will produce a picture resembling FLY AGARIC. ❧ The mushroom has a long history as a psychoactive substance and was employed in shamanistic rites in Siberia. Modern psychonauts trying this mushroom, however, seldom try it twice because ingestion without removal of the water-soluble toxins can produce sweating, nausea, vomiting, diarrhea, and neurological symptoms. ❧ Our most common FLY AGARICS on the West Coast have species-level genetic differences from the European *A. muscaria*, so a name change may be in the offing. One thing we do already know is that the exuberant range of colours and presentations in *A. muscaria* are *not* good guides to species boundaries— geographical locales seem to be the controlling variable. In BC, yellow to orange forms (what used to be called var. *formosa*) are most frequently found growing with BLACK COTTONWOOD (throughout the province) and with LODGEPOLE PINE (in the Interior). The scarlet-capped form with yellow colours in its young (button-stage) warts, ring margins, and volval ring patches (which many identify as var. *flavivolvata*) appears to be the most common variety on the coast, especially with birch, and is the most common form in our coastal urban environments. ❧ The FLY AGARIC is widespread throughout BC. In the southern Interior, it can be abundant in BLACK COTTONWOOD forests during the autumn and often grows with KING BOLETES (p. 318). ❧ Both the common name and "muscaria" ("musca" is Latin for "fly") probably echo the belief that the cut-up mushroom mixed with milk could kill barnyard flies.

Panther Cap *Amanita pantherina* group

CAP To 15 cm across; nearly spherical at first, then becoming convex; dark brown, lighter brown, or yellowish brown, darker in centre; with short white to buff warts that readily wash off; somewhat slippery when moist; margins with short striations; flesh white. **GILLS** Free or attached; white, bruising brown; closely spaced; many subgills. **ODOUR** Not distinctive. **TASTE** Not distinctive. **SPORE PRINT** White. **STEM** To 11 cm tall × 2 cm wide; white to buff; often scaly. **RING** Skirt-like, ragged; white, occasionally with tan patches at the edge; often persistent. **VOLVA** Close-fitting on the stem base, appearing as a collar or margin at the top of the basal bulb; white. **FRUITING** Single or in small groups; on the ground; in conifer and mixedwood forests, but also in urban areas; spring, autumn.

EDIBILITY Poisonous. **SIMILAR** Darker specimens of the also-poisonous JONQUIL AMANITA (p. 109) can be difficult to differentiate from lighter specimens of the PANTHER CAP. See JONQUIL AMANITA for discussions of further similar species. **COMMENTS** This common mushroom contains some of the same toxic compounds as the FLY AGARIC (p. 106), sometimes in even greater concentrations, and there may be other differences. It is frequently implicated in human and dog poisonings. Symptoms reported for PANTHER CAP poisonings include nausea, vomiting, drowsiness, confusion, dizziness, uncoordinated movements, delirium, illusions, and muscle twitching. ☙ The name *Amanita pantherina* belongs to a European species. What we have in North America is a complex of similar species, none of which is the European species. One of these, *A. pantherinoides*, first described from near Seattle, Washington, in 1912, may be the correct name for one of our common BC species. ☙ The PANTHER CAP is widespread in BC. ☙ Several large cats with spots (e.g., jaguar and leopard, in the genus *Panthera*) are sometimes called panthers, so "pantherina" ("little panther") probably references the spotted caps.

Jonquil Amanita
Amanita gemmata group

CAP To 10 cm across; nearly spherical when young and becoming convex to flat, centre sometimes depressed when mature; cream to pale yellow to beige, centre darker; with white, randomly scattered felty patches; slippery when moist; cap edges can have minor striations; flesh thick, white. GILLS Ranging from free to directly attached; white; closely spaced. ODOUR Not distinctive. TASTE Not distinctive. SPORE PRINT White. STEM To 12 cm tall × 2 cm wide; widening to a basal bulb; white to pale yellowish; smooth above ring, finely scaly or scurfy below. RING Skirt-like; white to yellowish; sometimes quickly disappearing. VOLVA Cottony, sporting a collar with a free rim at the top of the basal bulb; white; sometimes just fragments remaining on the lower stem. FRUITING Single or in small groups; on the ground; in open forest or adjacent fields, also in urban areas; summer, autumn.

EDIBILITY Poisonous. This group contains some of the same toxins as the FLY AGARIC (p. 106). SIMILAR The beige cap-colour phase of the JONQUIL AMANITA can overlap with PANTHER CAP (p. 108) mushrooms, but the JONQUIL AMANITA tends to be creamy yellow and doesn't have a sharp margin on the basal bulb. A spring fruiting season also helps separate the SUNSHINE AMANITA (p. 110) from the JONQUIL AMANITA, and in addition, the SUNSHINE AMANITA cap colours are brighter and the stem is stockier. The less common yellow phase of the autumn FLY AGARIC (p. 106) can be quite similar to the JONQUIL AMANITA, but the top of the FLY AGARIC's volva has concentric rings. COMMENTS What passes for *A. gemmata* group mushrooms in western North America may be a collection of related mushrooms that does not include the European *A. gemmata*. ➤ The mushroom that ended up as *Amanita gemmata* was originally described as *Agaricus gemmatus* in 1838 by Elias Fries. The description he gave of the specimen, however, looks suspiciously like a FLY AGARIC (p. 106) with a missing ring. Because of this possible error, some taxonomists prefer to trace the species name back to Lucien Quélet's 1877 description of *Amanita junquillea*. ➤ The JONQUIL AMANITA is widespread in BC. ➤ "Gemmata" means "gemmed," probably a reference to the white warts.

Sunshine Amanita   *Amanita aprica*

CAP To 15 cm across; cap spherical at first with inrolled margins, then convex to flat; bright yellow or orange-yellow and fading with age; whitish, frost-like veil remnants on cap as patches (sometimes scattered, sometimes coalesced over the disc) and as tatters on cap margins; sticky in moist conditions; faintly striate in age; flesh up to 2 cm thick at the stem, thinning at the margin, white to pale yellow. GILLS Attached at first, eventually pulling away from stem; white to creamy; closely spaced; subgills present. ODOUR Not distinctive. TASTE Not distinctive. SPORE PRINT White. STEM To 9 cm tall × 3.5 cm wide; sometimes hollowing with age; white to cream, bruising tan where handled; wrinkled to scurfy below ring. RING Skirt-like, often collapsing onto the stem; white to cream; sometimes disappearing entirely. VOLVA Close-fitting, often with a clean collar topped by broken concentric bands; white to cream. FRUITING Single or in groups; in sunny spots (e.g., rock cuts and along trails); near its presumed ectomycorrhizal host, DOUGLAS-FIR, but also found with pines; spring.

EDIBILITY Poisonous. Inducing nausea and cramps. SIMILAR PANTHER CAP (p. 108) mushrooms also fruit in the spring, but their caps are more brown, tan, or dull yellow. JONQUIL AMANITA (p. 109) mushrooms are sometimes pale yellow, but they appear in the late summer and autumn. We tend to picture the FLY AGARIC (p. 106) with a red cap, but yellow caps are also common, and the yellow colours in the FLY AGARIC caps can overlap with SUNSHINE AMANITA colours. FLY AGARICS, however, are not spring mushrooms, have caps with more pyramidal warts, and sport volvas that have stacked concentric rings of veil material. The SUNSHINE AMANITA also tends to be squatter than these other 3 *Amanita* species. COMMENTS In BC, the SUNSHINE AMANITA has only been found in the southwest part of the province. ♦ "Aprica" means "sun-loving," and it also echoes the apricot hues of the cap colour.

Western Yellow-veil Amanita   *Amanita augusta*

CAP To 15 cm across; nearly spherical at first, then convex to flat; yellowish brown to greyish brown; often covered with raised, discrete yellowish to grey warts that tend to wash off in age and that cluster in concentric rings around the outside of the cap and become smaller near the margin; margins not striate; flesh white, tinged yellow. GILLS Free or narrowly attached; deep (9 mm–2 cm); white, sometimes yellow tinged; crowded; subgills present. ODOUR Not distinctive. TASTE Not distinctive. SPORE PRINT White. STEM To 15 cm tall × 3 cm wide; widening toward the bottom, sometimes to a distinct bulb; white to pale yellow above ring, often with reddish brown stains toward base; smooth above ring, fibrillose to scaly below. RING Skirt-like and striate above; on upper part of stem; white to yellowish above, yellow below. VOLVA Rings of tissue and scales at the stem base and in the soil; yellowish; fragile, often falling apart. FRUITING Single or in small groups; on the ground; in older conifer and mixedwood forests; late summer, autumn.

EDIBILITY Poisonous. Bad reactions have been reported in closely related European species. SIMILAR JONQUIL AMANITA (p.109) mushrooms might be confused because of similarities in cap colour, but their veils are whiter and their caps tend to be duller and have whitish warts. PANTHER CAP (p.108) mushrooms can look similar, but *Amanita pantherina* group mushrooms usually show up in spring, their warts are white to buff, the upper side of their rings are not striate, and their cap margins are striate. The SUNSHINE AMANITA (p.110), which also has yellow tones, fruits in the springtime and is shorter and much stockier. COMMENTS In BC, the WESTERN YELLOW-VEIL AMANITA is rarely found in abundance, greeting even serious mushroom foragers only once or twice a year. Look for it in coastal forests. ◦ This mushroom has at times been labelled as *A. aspera* and *A. franchetii* by western North American mycologists. ◦ "Augusta" means "majestic," which this stately stunner certainly is!

Death Cap
Amanita phalloides

CAP To 15 cm across; nearly spherical at first, becoming convex with maturity; colour variable, usually with greenish hues (ranging from light green to olive to greenish yellow), sometimes brown-coloured or almost white, often darker toward the centre and mottled with radial streaks; occasionally with whitish patches of universal veil tissue attached; sticky to the touch when wet, having a metallic lustre in dry weather; smooth; not striate; flesh white, sometimes yellowish green just under the cap. GILLS Free or narrowly attached; deep; white at first, then creamy white with blushes of yellow or green; closely spaced; several tiers of subgills. ODOUR Unpleasant with age, sickeningly sweet to some noses, to others a bit like raw or rotting potatoes. TASTE Not distinctive. SPORE PRINT White. STEM To 15 cm tall × 3 cm wide; widening downward to a bulbous base; white or tinged with the cap colour, often lighter near base; smooth or streaked with small scales or fibrils that sometimes assume chevron patterns. RING Skirt-like; high on stem; white or tinged with the cap colour; sometimes disappearing with age. VOLVA Broad and sac-like, membranous; white; sometimes disintegrating. FRUITING Single, or in small or large groups; in gardens and boulevards near hornbeams, beeches, SWEET CHESTNUT, hazelnut trees, and introduced oaks, also under native GARRY OAK; appearing in mid- to late summer where irrigated, and in autumn.

EDIBILITY Poisonous. SIMILAR Those who consume the DEATH CAP by accident have sometimes confused it with other edible mushrooms. The edible Asian mushroom WHITE CAESAR (*Amanita princeps*), though not found in BC, may contribute to confusions that lead to poisonings of those who are familiar with this species from other places. The PADDY STRAW MUSHROOM, *Volvariella volvacea*, is common in Asia. It can also occur in BC, though it is rare here, mostly popping up in greenhouses, gardens, and sawdust. Unlike the DEATH CAP, the PADDY STRAW MUSHROOM has a brown, velvety cap and pink spores that often, in mature specimens, stain the gills pink. The widely collected and eaten MAN ON HORSEBACK (p. 148) can have a shiny greenish cap when moist, but it has yellowish gills and no ring or volva. The WHITE PARASOL (p. 123) is, in our experience, often mistaken for the DEATH CAP, even though the parasol has no green tints and no volva. There are other deadly poisonous look-alikes on the West Coast that have so far not been documented in BC, such as the 4 species all referred to with the name DESTROYING ANGEL (*Amanita ocreata*, *A. verna*, *A. virosa*, and *A. bisporigera*). COMMENTS The DEATH CAP is seriously poisonous and is currently responsible for about one death a year on the West Coast of North America. All the fleshy parts of the mushroom contain amatoxins, peptides that do not break down with heating or drying and that can damage livers and kidneys. Fatal doses average about 60 g (2 oz.), but 30 g (1 oz.) can be deadly for some, so eating even half a cap can be dangerous. If you think you may have eaten this mushroom, do not wait for symptoms to appear—they are often delayed for 6–24 hours—but seek medical help immediately. ❧ Fruiting bodies are generally found in urban areas, mostly in southwest BC, but they are expected to spread throughout BC. See the essay on recent BC research on DEATH CAP mushrooms (p. 114) for further information. ❧ "Phalloides" means "like a penis" or "like a *Phallus*" (a genus of stinkhorn mushrooms, p. 356).

Sliced-open DEATH CAP "egg" with leaves from hornbeam (*Carpinus*) tree.

Death Caps Arrive in BC

More people in North America have been fatally poisoned by the DEATH CAP mushroom, *Amanita phalloides*, than by all other mushrooms combined. This deadly European species was probably brought to the West Coast of North America on the roots of European tree species that were planted as ornamental and crop trees. They appeared in California as early as the 1930s. By the early 1990s *A. phalloides* was well documented in the US Pacific Northwest as far north as Seattle but was not known to occur in British Columbia, or anywhere else in Canada. Reports in the popular press of DEATH CAP mushrooms' occurrence in Oregon and Washington caused concern that this dangerous mushroom might be present yet undetected in British Columbia.

Members of the Vancouver Mycological Society (VMS) and South Vancouver Island Mycological Society (SVIMS), two of the amateur mushroom clubs in BC, were invited to report and document occurrences of *A. phalloides* in British Columbia.

The first documented occurrence of DEATH CAPS in Canada was in 1997, in a grove of SWEET CHESTNUT trees in Mission, BC. After this initial sighting, reports of this mushroom began to trickle in from other urban areas of southwestern BC. DEATH CAP poisonings were reported in 2003 and 2008. In 2016, the first BC death from DEATH CAPS occurred—a three-year-old child in Victoria. Today, coming across a cluster of DEATH CAP mushrooms in late summer and early autumn is no longer an unusual experience on the streets of Vancouver and Victoria.

Paul Kroeger levitating dried DEATH CAP mushrooms with his mind.

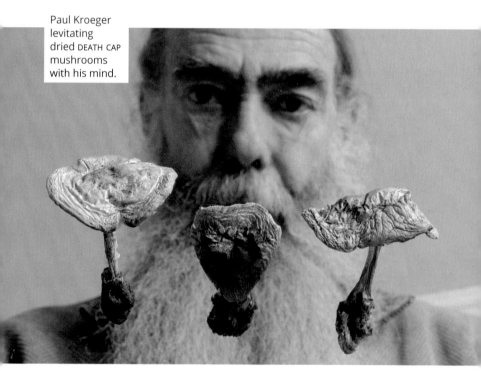

Paul Kroeger, past president of VMS, has watched the range expansion of the DEATH CAP mushroom with great concern. In 2014, VMS volunteers began a survey, originally designed by member Vivian Miao, of DEATH CAP mushrooms near Vancouver street trees. Eventually, VMS members found more than 75 trees around the city that were playing host to the recent fungal arrival. Most of them were European hornbeams that had been planted in the 1960s and 1970s. By correlating house architecture with street foliage, Paul became quite skilled at predicting where DEATH CAPS would be found.

The information collected in this street tree study was a wake-up call to public health officials. Members of VMS and SVIMS were mobilized to spread the word about the new invader. They built websites, put up posters, spoke on TV and radio, and consulted with hospitals.

Once DEATH CAP mushrooms have taken hold, it is almost impossible to eradicate them—they have a wide tolerance for hosts, living symbiotically with many species of European trees found in cities. The greatest worry, though, has always been that they will adapt to trees that are native to BC and start to spread outside the cities. DEATH CAPS did this in California, making a new home with California oaks, TAN OAKS, and pines. Then, in 2016, SVIMS member Dr. Shannon Berch (along with Paul Kroeger and Terrie Finston) discovered that the leap had already happened—a DEATH CAP had set up a symbiotic connection to a native GARRY OAK near Victoria.

Blusher

Amanita novinupta

CAP To 15 cm across; convex becoming flat; white becoming pinkish, reddish, or brownish as the mushroom matures or is bruised or experiences dry weather; often with white warts and patches that are clustered on the centre of the disc, and/or with tatters on the margin; dry; covered with powder when young, aging shiny; flesh white, bruising red or red-brown. **GILLS** Free or nearly so; white, bruising pinkish. **ODOUR** Not distinctive. **TASTE** Not distinctive. **SPORE PRINT** White. **STEM** To 15 cm tall × 4 cm wide; expanding downward, often bulbous at base; white, bruising pink; smooth, cottony, or scaly. **RING** Skirt-like, striate on the upper surface; white, bruising pink or red. **VOLVA** Not well defined, a few rings, warts, and patches on top of the bulbous stem base; white, bruising pink. **FRUITING** Single or in small groups; on the ground under GARRY OAK, DOUGLAS-FIR, and probably other trees; primarily spring, sometimes autumn.

EDIBILITY Uncertain. Some claim this mushroom to be a good edible. The similar European *Amanita rubescens* contains dangerous compounds unless well cooked, though, and our western species may share this trait. **SIMILAR** The BLUSHER might be confused with the **RED-STAINING AGARICUS** (p. 234), the **SHAGGY PARASOL** (p. 98), or the **BLACKENING RUSSULA** (p. 58), based simply on all these mushrooms being large, whitish, and bruising red. Additional characteristics of these mushrooms, however, will readily separate them from the BLUSHER: RED-STAINING AGARICUS has brown spores, the SHAGGY PARASOL has permanent scales on the cap, and the BLACKENING RUSSULA turns black after blushing red. **COMMENTS** At one time, our BLUSHERS were commonly identified in the field as *A. rubescens*, a name now more associated with European and eastern North American species, but *A. rubescens* may also be in the BC species mix. ☙ The BLUSHER appears to be a southwest BC species. ☙ "Novinupta" means "newlywed," a reference to a "blushing bride" in a white dress.

Smith's Amanita   *Amanita smithiana*

CAP To 16 cm across; nearly spherical when young, becoming convex to flat; white, sometimes drying to pale orange-brown in the field; cottony, powdery, or felty patches that are white to pale brown on the cap and sometimes icicle-like tatters on cap margins; young caps slightly slippery when wet; flesh white. GILLS Free or narrowly attached; white to cream; closely spaced. ODOUR Not distinctive for many, for others unpleasant in older specimens, variously described as ham gone bad, ammonia, bleach, or green tomatoes. TASTE Not distinctive. SPORE PRINT White or cream. STEM To 15 cm tall × 4 cm wide; expanding slightly downward, with a spindle-shaped bulb that often roots deeply in the soil; white, bruising pale orange-brown; covered with mealy, easily removable patches of veil tissue when young. RING Cottony and tattered or torn; near the top of the stem; white; often disappearing and leaving behind ragged patches on the stem. VOLVA Concentric rings at the top of the bulb. FRUITING Single or in small groups; on the ground; in coniferous forests; autumn.

EDIBILITY Poisonous. Consuming only a single cap of SMITH'S AMANITA can lead to gastrointestinal distress within a few hours and, after a longer period, kidney damage. SIMILAR Reports of SMITH'S AMANITA, which have been increasing, correlate with the recent popularity in harvesting of the similar-looking PINE MUSHROOMS (p. 146). The characteristic smell of cinnamon (or gym socks) and the absence of cottony warts signals a PINE MUSHROOM. One good way to tell the difference is to grasp the stem near the base and press down hard with your thumb: a PINE MUSHROOM has flesh resembling firm string cheese and resists the pressure with a little bending, but the SMITH'S AMANITA base shatters. COMMENTS In BC, SMITH'S AMANITA appears to be restricted to coastal areas in the southwest. ◦ The species is named after Alexander H. Smith, a University of Michigan mycologist who worked on West Coast mushrooms.

Western Woodland Amanita   *Amanita silvicola*

CAP To 12 cm across; convex becoming flat, margins remaining curved under until later stages; white; with cottony or powdery patches on cap and hanging tatters on cap margin; dry to slightly moist; flesh white. GILLS Free or narrowly attached; gill edges slightly fringed; white; closely spaced; subgills present. ODOUR Usually not distinctive but can be soapy or fishy when older. TASTE Not distinctive. SPORE PRINT White. STEM To 12 cm tall × 2.5 cm wide; overall stocky appearance, with a somewhat ledged bulb up to twice as wide as the central stem; white, sometimes staining brownish; surface powdery. RING Thin, fragile; white; often disappearing and leaving just fibrils. VOLVA White; fragile, leaving cottony white patches at the stem base or in soil. FRUITING Single or in small groups; on the ground; in conifer and mixedwood forests (commonly with DOUGLAS-FIR) and adjacent grassy areas, primarily in southwestern BC; autumn.

EDIBILITY Unknown. Not harvested for the table because of its similarity to the poisonous SMITH'S AMANITA. SIMILAR SMITH'S AMANITA (p. 117) is a close look-alike, but the WESTERN WOODLAND AMANITA can be distinguished by its slightly shorter stature, ledged basal bulb, thinner and less distinct patches on the cap, lack of a deeply rooting stem, and sometimes by its odour. See the SMITH'S AMANITA entry for other similar mushrooms. COMMENTS "Silvicola" means "living in a forest," a good descriptor for all of our amanitas.

Constricted Grisette *Amanita constricta*

CAP To 13 cm across; ovoid or gumdrop-shaped at first emergence, then becoming flat at maturity, sometimes with a small umbo; usually brown to brownish grey; sometimes with white or salmon patches from the universal veil; slightly slippery when moist; conspicuously striate, almost like fanfolds; flesh white to greyish, occasionally pinkish when cut. GILLS Free from the stem or narrowly attached; moderately deep; white becoming grey; crowded; with several tiers of subgills. ODOUR Not distinctive, but sometimes fishy in age. TASTE Not distinctive. SPORE PRINT White. STEM To 16 cm tall × 1.7 cm wide; white to grey; smooth, but often with grey scales that darken when handled. RING Absent. VOLVA Sac-like, the lower part constricted around the stem, the upper part flaring out; white to grey; collapsing with age. FRUITING Single or in small groups; on the ground; in conifer and hardwood forests; autumn.

EDIBILITY Edible. All of the grisettes are reported to be edible and are distinctive enough not to be confused with poisonous amanitas, but beginning mushroomers may be nervous because of the amanita volva that grisettes share with many poisonous amanita species. SIMILAR *Amanita pachycolea* **group** and the *A. vaginata* **group** are remarkably similar to this mushroom, the main difference being in the volva: *A. constricta*, as its name suggests, has a volva that is tightly attached partway up the stem before it flares outward, whereas in the 2 others the volva is usually attached at the bottom of the stem. *Amanita vaginata* caps are dominated by grey tints; caps of *A. pachycolea* group mushrooms tend to be more consistently brown. COMMENTS "Grisette" was once used to describe young working-class French women because of their drab grey ("gris") clothing, and this meaning was presumably transferred to these grey mushrooms.

Purple-brown Amanita
Amanita porphyria

CAP To 12 cm across; convex to flat or slightly umbonate; greyish to grey-brown, often with a violet or purple cast; sometimes with grey, violet, or white warts that readily wash off in the rain; slippery or greasy when moist; sometimes radially streaked; not striate; flesh white. GILLS Free or attached to the stem; deep; white to cream, bruising grey; closely spaced; with numerous subgills. ODOUR Like raw potatoes, radish, or turnips. TASTE Unpleasant, or similar to odour. SPORE PRINT White. STEM To 14 cm tall × 1.5 cm wide; equal or widening downward to a basal bulb that often has a distinct rim or ledge that may be cleft vertically; white or pale grey; smooth above the ring but often with greyish fibrils in a chevron pattern below. RING Skirt-like; high on the stem; white but sometimes underside is violet-tinted or grey; disappearing with age. VOLVA Tightly adhering to the bulbous stem base, flaring as a collar at the top of the bulb; white or grey; sometimes disappearing or just remaining as patches above the bulb. FRUITING Single or in small groups; on the ground; in older conifer or mixedwood forests, especially old-growth forests; late summer or autumn.

EDIBILITY Unknown. SIMILAR The overall stature and cap colour of the PURPLE-BROWN AMANITA can make it resemble grisettes such as the CONSTRICTED GRISETTE (p. 119), but the lack of long striations on the cap and the presence of the ledge on the basal bulb distinguish the PURPLE-BROWN AMANITA from the grisettes. Caps of the browner phases of the PURPLE-BROWN AMANITA can be like those of the JONQUIL AMANITA (p. 109) and the PANTHER CAP (p. 108), but the PURPLE-BROWN AMANITA has a distinctive odour and often has a basal bulb with a prominent ledge. COMMENTS PURPLE-BROWN AMANITA is one of the most common amanita species in BC's southern Interior. "Porphyria" means "purple."

Dripping Slimecap
Zhuliangomyces illinitus

CAP To 8 cm across; almost spherical to hemispheric, becoming more shallowly convex to nearly flat or umbonate, the margins inrolled; white, the disc pale yellow to light brown in some varieties; covered in a clear slime that often drips from the cap edge; flesh thin, white. GILLS Free or nearly so, sometimes notched; white; closely spaced. ODOUR Not distinctive. TASTE Not distinctive. SPORE PRINT White. STEM To 9 cm tall × 1 cm wide; equal or broader at base; white to cream; usually covered in a clear slime. RING At best a fibrillose band, indistinct under the slime layer. VOLVA Absent. FRUITING Single or in small groups; on the ground; in various forested habitats; late summer, autumn.

EDIBILITY Unknown. SIMILAR *Limacella delicata* (part of the *L. glioderma* group) has a reddish brown cast to its cap and stem and a farinaceous or cucumbery odour. Its cap is slimy, but its stem is generally dry unless slime has dripped on it from the cap. Other mushrooms can be slimy and white—some *Hygrophorus* mushrooms, for example, such as the COWBOY'S HANDKERCHIEF (p. 84) and the SPRUCE WAXY CAP (p. 85). These have broad similarities to the DRIPPING SLIMECAP, but their waxy-looking, widely spaced, and often decurrent gills set them apart. COMMENTS Until recently, this species was known as *Limacella illinita*. Species in the genera *Limacella* and *Zhuliangomyces* belong to the same family as the *Amanita* species, but they show significant differences. The most easily observable differences involve slime—limacellas often have slimy coatings on their caps and stems. Amanitas tend to have persistent basal volvas, while the slimy remnants of universal veils at the bases of limacellas blend into the substrate. Amanitas' universal veils often leave behind warts and patches on the caps, and limacellas' universal veils leave behind layers of slime. ● The genus *Zhuliangomyces* was named in honour of Zhu-Liang Yang, an amanita specialist from China. "Illinitus" means "varnished, smeared."

Ruby Parasol
Leucoagaricus rubrotinctus group

CAP To 8 cm across; almost spherical or squarish in profile when young, then becoming convex to flat, occasionally splitting, with a broad umbo; reddish to pinkish brown when young, in age the umbo remaining a deeper red-brown when the margin colour fades; with radial fibres in maturity and with the white flesh between the fibres exposed; flesh thin, white. GILLS Free; white; closely spaced. ODOUR Not distinctive. TASTE Not distinctive. SPORE PRINT White. STEM To 12 cm tall × 1 cm wide; equal or widened toward the base; white, discolouring yellowish with age; mostly smooth. RING A persistent collar with a flared outer edge that may curl downward; white but sometimes tattered and pinkish at the edge. VOLVA Absent. FRUITING Single or scattered; on the ground; in conifer or mixedwood forests or in landscaped areas and compost piles; late summer and autumn.

EDIBILITY Unknown. SIMILAR The uncommon AMERICAN PARASOL, *Leucoagaricus americanus*, has a cap with concentrically arranged scales that darken to a deep burgundy-brown as it dries. Its flesh stains yellow to orange when cut, and its stem is wider in the middle than at the top and bottom. *Lepiota flammeotincta* can also have a red-brown cap that breaks up into radial sections, but the cap skin is composed of concentric circles of small inverted-V fibrils, and the surfaces of both cap and stem stain an intense red when they are touched or bruised. COMMENTS The RUBY PARASOL is one of a complex of several similar species in our area, most of which are still undescribed. The genetic signatures of local specimens are not the same as the European *Leucoagaricus rubrotinctus*. Many of our specimens may be the same as the one described from the West Coast over a century ago as *Lepiota rubrotinctoides* (which should become, when the studies of this group are further along, *Leucoagricus rubrotinctoides*). ◆ RUBY PARASOL is common, especially at the beginning of the autumn mushroom season, but only in southern BC. ◆ "Leucoagaricus" means "white agaricus," and "rubrotinctus" means "red-coloured."

White Parasol

Leucoagaricus leucothites

CAP To 10 cm across; at first, a lumpy marshmallow shape, becoming convex and then sometimes flat or with uplifted margins; white to beige, tinged grey over centre; dry; surface smooth with an almost silky sheen, but sometimes broken up into very fine scales; flesh thick, white. **GILLS** Free; deep; white, aging buff or pinkish, eventually tan; closely spaced. **ODOUR** Not distinctive. **TASTE** Not distinctive. **SPORE PRINT** White. **STEM** To 12 cm tall × 1.5 cm wide; equal or widened toward base; white, sometimes staining pale yellow, pink, or brown when handled, especially around the base; smooth. **RING** Thick, cottony, regularly appearing doubled, with thick, squared-off edges; white; persistent and often movable up and down on mature stems. **VOLVA** Absent. **FRUITING** Single to scattered; on the ground; in lawns, roadsides, open forest; year-round, but most common in autumn.

   EDIBILITY Uncertain. **SIMILAR** While older specimens of the WHITE PARASOL may look a bit like the SHAGGY PARASOL (p. 98) from a distance, the embedded scales on the caps of the SHAGGY PARASOL will always signal the difference. SMITH'S AMANITA (p. 117), when its abundant warts have been washed off, can also be confused with the WHITE PARASOL, but the thicker stem, the fragile ring, and the volva of the amanita set it apart. The DEATH CAP (p. 112) in its white phase and without warts or patches is another confusingly similar mushroom, but the smell (raw or rotten potatoes) and the volva (sac-like) of the DEATH CAP can be important clues. **COMMENTS** Amanitas almost universally form mycorrhizal relationships with trees. The WHITE PARASOL, in contrast, is a decomposer—it lives on decaying vegetable matter such as the dead stems of grasses in lawns. ⚬ WHITE PARASOL is widespread in BC. ⚬ This stately mushroom has been given many common names. One of the more imaginative is WOMAN (MA'AM) ON A MOTORCYCLE, a name probably based on the helmet shape of young caps and the skirt-like ring.

Clitocybe and Similar

The species that became part of the genus *Clitocybe* were first segregated from other mushroom species in the 19th century. The mushrooms that were initially assigned to this genus were wood decomposers that had white to yellow spores, decurrent gills, funnel-shaped caps (the word "clitocybe" means "sloping head"), fleshy stems with a central attachment to the caps, and no rings. For the most part, they were medium-sized mushrooms, but a few were quite large. These characteristics all fit with the CLOUDY CLITOCYBE (p. 133), the type species for the genus.

Other species, however, were lumped into the genus *Clitocybe* that didn't have all the core characteristics of the genus. The BLEWIT (p. 130), for example, had dull pink spores. Some had convex caps and lacked the characteristic decurrent gills. Eventually, the whole *Clitocybe* collection began to seem rather ill-defined. Taxonomists, largely basing their work on microscopic examinations, started to split off certain groups and assign them to new genera, such as *Ampulloclitocybe*, *Clitocybula*, and *Infundibulicybe*. These ambiguities in the overall *Clitocybe* collection became even more pronounced when DNA sequencing became available. Genetic studies made it apparent that many of the macroscopic and microscopic associations among the historical *Clitocybe* species did not correspond to the evolutionary history of mushrooms in the genus. The story is far from finished—the splitting away of historical clitocybes continues apace. One recent analysis of clitocybes in BC and the US Pacific Northwest found that of the 130 species in the region that once belonged to the older genus, only about 80 were still assigned to it.

Overall interest in the genus *Clitocybe* has been muted somewhat by the lack of incredible edibles and perilous poisoners. There are a few exceptions to this. Many foragers treasure BLEWITS for their tables. And some *Clitocybe* species have enough muscarine in them (the SWEAT-PRODUCING CLITOCYBE, p. 135, for example) to poison people.

The clitocybes have always had close associations with the traditional omphalinas, so in this section we have included some species that have historically (though not currently) been considered omphalinas, such as the *Chrysomphalina* species. We have also included several species that, though not historically part of these two groups of mushrooms, have the look of traditional clitocybes and omphalinas.

Amethyst Laccaria — *Laccaria amethysteo-occidentalis*

CAP To 6 cm across; convex to flat, often depressed, the margins inrolled at first, later often wavy; deep rich purple when young, fading to buff; smooth to finely fibrillose or scaly; hygrophanous; translucent-striate in age; flesh thin, fibrous, coloured as cap or paler. GILLS Broadly attached, often notched and with a decurrent tooth; deepest in the middle; sometimes waxy and with shallow cross-veining; dark violet, fading to lavender and then buff, but keeping purple tones longer than the cap; well spaced; with subgills. ODOUR Pleasant, but not particularly distinctive. TASTE Not distinctive. SPORE PRINT White. STEM To 11 cm tall × 1 cm wide; equal or widening downward; purple, often with paler patches; dry; longitudinally striate, sometimes with upturned scales when young; with violet mycelium at the base. RING Absent. FRUITING Scattered or in groups to clustered; on the ground; under conifers; autumn, winter.

EDIBILITY Edible. SIMILAR Some of the more purple *Cortinarius* species might be mistaken for the AMETHYST LACCARIA, but they have a brown spore print. The lilac tones in the TWO-COLOURED LACCARIA (p. 127) are limited to the gills and basal mycelium. The LILAC BONNET (p. 177) is usually smaller (to 5 cm), has gills that are more closely spaced, has a smoother stem with no longitudinal striations, and sometimes gives off a radish-like odour. COMMENTS AMETHYST LACCARIA, a mycorrhizal mushroom like all the other laccarias, is common in BC, especially along the coast. ◦ It has an unusual (and sometimes off-putting) sweet taste when cooked. Many foragers recommend eating only laccaria caps and disposing of the tough-textured stems. ◦ "Amethysteo" means "coloured like amethyst (violet-blue)," and "occidentalis" means "western."

Two-coloured Laccaria
Laccaria bicolor

CAP To 5 cm across; convex to flat, often depressed, the margins inrolled at first, then uplifted, wavy, and eroded in age; pinkish brown when young, fading to buff; finely fibrillose or scaly; hygrophanous, often turning quite pale when dry; flesh thin, whitish with orange-brown or purple tints. GILLS Broadly attached to short-decurrent; deep; sometimes waxy, well spaced; purplish when young, fading to pinkish. ODOUR Pleasant, but not particularly distinctive. TASTE Not distinctive. SPORE PRINT White. STEM To 12 cm tall × 1 cm wide; equal or widening downward; coloured as cap, but sometimes with purple toward the bottom of the base; dry; longitudinally striate and often fibrillose or finely hairy; with mycelium at the base that is violet fading to white. RING Absent. FRUITING Scattered or in large troops; on the ground; usually under conifers, often in moss; late summer, autumn, winter.

EDIBILITY Edible. SIMILAR The AMETHYST LACCARIA (p. 126) has a purple cap as well as a purple stem and gills. The LACKLUSTRE LACCARIA (p. 128) has reddish brown tones and no lilac or purple in the gills, stem, or mycelium, while the TWO-COLOURED LACCARIA has purple tones, mostly in its gills and basal mycelium. When, however, the TWO-COLOURED LACCARIA ages, it is not unusual for it to lose *all* of its purple tones. COMMENTS The TWO-COLOURED LACCARIA is widely used in studies of plant and fungus symbioses. It was the first mycorrhizal fungus to have its full genome sequenced. ✦ Interestingly, the TWO-COLOURED LACCARIA has also been shown to be a carnivore—springtails feeding around the mushroom are killed, perhaps by a fungal-secreted toxin, and their nitrogen is absorbed into the mushroom and into the plant partners of the mushroom.

Lacklustre Laccaria · *Laccaria laccata* group

CAP To 5 cm across; convex to flat, often depressed, the margins inrolled at first, then uplifted, wavy, and eroded in age; orange-brown to pinkish brown when young, fading to buff, centre often darker; finely fibrillose or scaly; hygrophanous, often turning quite pale when dry; somewhat striate when moist; flesh thin, cap-coloured. GILLS Broadly attached to short-decurrent; deep; sometimes waxy; pinkish to buff; well spaced. ODOUR Pleasant, but not particularly distinctive. TASTE Not distinctive. SPORE PRINT White. STEM To 10 cm tall × 1 cm wide; equal to widening downward; coloured like the cap; dry; longitudinally striate and often fibrillose or finely hairy; typically with a white basal mycelium. RING Absent. FRUITING Scattered or in large troops; on the ground; usually under conifers; late summer, autumn, winter.

EDIBILITY Edible. SIMILAR See remarks under TWO-COLOURED LACCARIA (p. 127). SCURFY TWIGLET (p. 284), though it can resemble the LACKLUSTRE LACCARIA in colour and stature, is a brown-spored decomposer with closely spaced gills that grows on wood chips and other decaying materials. COMMENTS The LACKLUSTRE LACCARIA is quite common throughout BC. It has the reputation of a weedy species, seeming to pop up everywhere, sometimes quite far from its mycorrhizal associates. ▸ A number of species and varieties are probably encompassed in the current *Laccaria laccata* concept. ▸ In some parts of the world, *L. laccata* is known as THE DECEIVER because it has such a wide range of appearances that mushroom beginners often fail to recognize it. ▸ "Laccaria" refers to lacquer, and "laccata" means "lacquered," though what the connection is between this doubly emphasized concept and the mushroom's appearance is anyone's guess.

False Chanterelle
Hygrophoropsis aurantiaca group

CAP To 8 cm across; convex to flat and then often slightly funnel-shaped, margins inrolled when young; brownish orange, becoming brighter orange and then paler at maturity, but often retaining a darker centre; dry; velvety at first, hairless or matted in age; flesh thin, white to cap-coloured but paler. GILLS Decurrent; not deep; repeatedly forking from stem to margin, sometimes wrinkled, easily peeled from the cap; orange, often brighter than the cap colour; closely spaced. ODOUR Not distinctive. TASTE Not distinctive. SPORE PRINT White. STEM To 8 cm tall × 1 cm wide; more or less equal, often curved; sometimes off-centre; same colour as the cap, but often darker near the base; dry; at times a little hairy. RING Absent. FRUITING Single or in groups, sometimes clumped; on wood or on the ground; usually under conifers, but also on wood chips in urban areas; late summer, autumn.

EDIBILITY Once widely considered poisonous, the FALSE CHANTERELLE is now consumed by some, but there are reports of stomach upsets and no one seems to rave about its taste. SIMILAR The FALSE CHANTERELLE gets its common name from its similarity to the PACIFIC GOLDEN CHANTERELLE (p. 34), but a brief comparison shows that the similarities are superficial. True chanterelles have stringy flesh and blunt ridges instead of gills. The usually smaller GOLDGILL NAVELCAP (p. 141) has a yellowish brown cap and unforked yellow gills. COMMENTS The FALSE CHANTERELLE, a brown-rot mushroom, can be quite common throughout BC. ☙ At one time, it was considered a single species with a number of subspecies. Some of the European varieties have been raised to species status, and it seems likely that some western North American varieties will also be recognized at the species level. ☙ "Hygrophoropsis" means "looking like *Hygrophorus*" (a mushroom genus). "Aurantiaca" means "orange-coloured."

Blewit

Lepista nuda

CAP To 14 cm across; convex becoming flat or broadly umbonate, often with wavy edges, margins inrolled in young (and sometimes even in older) caps; a shade of purple, lilac, or violet when young, fading to brown, buff, or tan, but often retaining purple tints near the margin; dry, a bit greasy; smooth, can appear shiny; flesh thick, a soft, marbled purple, sometimes aging tan. GILLS Attaching directly to stem, sometimes with a notch, in some cases slightly decurrent; purple, with the colour often persisting longer than on the cap, but eventually fading to buff; closely spaced. ODOUR Sweetly fragrant, citrusy, often compared to the smell of frozen orange juice. TASTE Not distinctive. SPORE PRINT Pink to pinkish buff. STEM To 7 cm tall × 2.5 cm wide; base often swollen and curved; coloured as gills; dry; smooth or fibrillose, sometimes scurfy or mealy near the top; often with lilac-coloured mycelium attached to base. RING Absent. FRUITING Single or in groups, often in fairy rings; on the ground; in various habitats (forests, woodlands, pastures, compost) and wherever soils are rich in organic matter; spring, summer, autumn.

EDIBILITY Choice. Widely eaten and even cultivated. SIMILAR Colour alone is not a secure guide to the BLEWIT—several species of *Cortinarius* (pp. 240, 241, and 249, for example) sport bluish tints. To rule out *Cortinarius* species, look for the fine webbed veil that signal *Cortinarius* species, and check whether the spore print is the characteristic rusty brown of cortinariuses. *Lepista tarda* has lilac colours that are more muted, a thinner stem (usually less than 1 cm wide), and a mild or slightly fragrant smell. COMMENTS The scientific name is often reported as *Clitocybe nuda*, but the debate about whether to roll the genus *Lepista* into *Clitocybe* is still going on. ❧ "Blewit" is probably from the Old French "bleuet," referring to the purple or bluish colours. "Nuda" highlights the cap's smooth surface.

Snowmelt Clitocybe   *Clitocybe albirhiza*

CAP To 10 cm across; convex becoming flat and sometimes funnel-shaped, can be umbonate and/or depressed, margins incurved at first and then uplifted and wavy; pale or pinkish buff with a whitish, sometimes zoned bloom when young, becoming pale brown in age; dry; smooth when older; hygrophanous; flesh thin, soft, greyish to cap-coloured. GILLS Broadly attached and notched, sometimes short-decurrent; deep (to 9 mm); often forking and cross-veined; white, becoming buff or cap-coloured; closely spaced; with subgills. ODOUR Not distinctive, sometimes unpleasant. TASTE Usually not distinctive, occasionally bitter. SPORE PRINT White. STEM To 8 cm tall × 2 cm wide; equal or slightly tapered at top and bottom; tough and fibrous; coloured as cap, including an initial whitish bloom; bald, sometimes with longitudinal striations; with a dense mat of white rhizomorphs at the base that are usually matted with conifer needles. RING Absent. FRUITING Scattered or in small or large groups, often in fairy rings; on the ground; under conifers at higher elevations, often near the snowmelt line; spring and early summer.

EDIBILITY Unknown. SIMILAR *Clitocybe glacialis*, another snowmelt mushroom, has a thicker stem in relation to the cap size, a cap that is not zoned, and a stem base that has a white mycelium rather than white rhizomorphs. COMMENTS The SNOWMELT CLITOCYBE was first described in the 1960s from a specimen collected in a high snowfall area of the Rocky Mountains. ⚬ "Albirhiza" means "white root."

Anise Clitocybe   *Clitocybe deceptiva*

CAP To 6 cm across; convex becoming flat or depressed when old, the margins curved under at first; pale brown fading to buff or almost white, often with a darker centre; dry, but often with a slightly greasy feel; smooth; at times translucent and striate; somewhat hygrophanous; flesh coloured as cap, thin. GILLS Directly attached or somewhat decurrent; whitish or coloured like cap; somewhat closely spaced; with subgills. ODOUR Sweet, like anise or licorice. TASTE Not distinctive. SPORE PRINT Pale pinkish buff. STEM To 6 cm tall × 5 mm wide; often bent and the base slightly enlarged; hollow and compressed in age; coloured like cap; smooth, sometimes finely fibrillose. RING Absent. FRUITING Single or in groups; on the ground; under conifers, also in lawns; autumn, winter.

EDIBILITY Edible. SIMILAR Mushroom hunters can also encounter, often in the same area, mushrooms lacking the anise odour that look very much like the ANISE CLITOCYBE. It is possible that some of these may be specimens of the odourless *Clitocybe elegantula* that was described by the mycologist Jules Favre in his posthumous 1960 work on the mushrooms of the subalpine zones in Swiss national parks, but further genetic work needs to be carried out. The less common *C. odora* does have the anise odour, but the cap and gills are blue-green to blue and the stem is more robust. COMMENTS The ANISE CLITOCYBE is referred to in some sources as *C. fragrans*, though others distinguish the 2 by saying that *C. deceptiva* has not an anise smell but a generic sweet smell, like cheap motel soap. The volatile compounds in ANISE CLITOCYBE are potent. When atmospheric conditions are right, hikers in the autumn woods can encounter an almost palpable wall of anise across their trail that signals the presence of nearby caps.

Cloudy Clitocybe   *Clitocybe nebularis*

CAP To 20 cm across; convex becoming flat to depressed, surface sometimes with waves and lobes, margins often inrolled; greyish white to pale brownish grey, sometimes with a white-hairy bloom and what look like water spots; moist; finely fibrillose, sometimes shiny; flesh thick, white. GILLS Directly attached or slightly decurrent; deep; forked; white, aging tan or yellowish; closely spaced. ODOUR Often strongly unpleasant, described as rotten and skunky. TASTE Unpleasant, sour. SPORE PRINT Pale yellow. STEM To 15 cm tall × 4 cm wide; can be curved and compressed and enlarged at the base; sometimes off-centre; white with light brown fibrils; white mycelium at the base. RING Absent. FRUITING Single, scattered, or in small groups; on the ground; under conifers; autumn, winter.

EDIBILITY This tasty mushroom, widespread in North America and Europe, has been historically collected for the table. However, people have reported stomach upsets and allergic reactions, and its sale is now restricted in certain regions. SIMILAR CLUB-FOOT (p. 137), which lacks the skunky odour, is usually smaller and has long-decurrent gills. The LARGE WHITE LEUCOPAX (p. 168) is another large white mushroom that also has yellowish spores, but it is more consistently white and is overall firmer and heavier. *Aspropaxillus giganteus* (also called *Leucopaxillus giganteus* and *Clitocybe gigantea*), which has been reported a few times in BC, has a cap that is similarly whitish but with more tannish tones and a darker centre that may shade toward a rusty brown colour. *Lepista irina* has a more perfumy odour, a shorter (to 8 cm) scaly/scurfy stem, and a pinkish creamy spore colour. COMMENTS CLOUDY CLITOCYBE has been investigated by medical researchers for its strong antifungal compounds, which may contribute to the mushroom's inconsistent reputation as an edible. ⚬ Both "nebularis" and the common name refer to clouds—a large drift of *Clitocybe nebularis* caps can look like miniature cumulus clouds gathered over a fairy realm.

Crowded White Clitocybe　　　　　　　*Clitocybe dilatata*

CAP To 15 cm across; convex becoming flat, sometimes umbonate, often irregular in shape, margins inrolled when young and tending to remain somewhat downcurved but wavy in age; grey fading to whitish, sometimes with buff patches; dry; smooth, but can be very finely fibrillose under a lens; flesh thick, firm, grey or whitish. GILLS Broadly attached to short-decurrent; to 1 cm deep; sometimes forking; white or pale buff; closely spaced. ODOUR Not distinctive. TASTE Unpleasant, sour. SPORE PRINT White. STEM To 12 cm tall × 3 cm wide; equal or widened below with bases joining, usually flattened and often curved; sometimes off-centre; coloured as cap but often stained darker at base; with fine longitudinal striations, sometimes minutely scaly at the base. RING Absent. FRUITING In large groups or clusters; on bare soil; along the edges of roads or trails; summer to early autumn.

EDIBILITY Probably poisonous—it may contain the toxin muscarine. SIMILAR The FRIED CHICKEN MUSHROOM (p. 170) is another clustered mushroom that also grows along paths. Its caps are browner, however, and they do not have the unpleasant taste of CROWDED WHITE CLITOCYBE caps. Caps of the SWEAT-PRODUCING CLITOCYBE (p. 135) are also white, but the mushroom is typically much smaller (caps to 4 cm across, stems to 3 cm tall) and grows singly rather than in clusters. COMMENTS The *Clitocybe* genus has been a transitional place over the last couple of decades, and the CROWDED WHITE CLITOCYBE has been in the middle of the changes. You may see this mushroom (or something almost exactly like it) listed in some sources as *C. connata* or *Leucocybe connata.* ◦ "Dilatata" means "dilated, spread out."

Sweat-producing Clitocybe *Clitocybe rivulosa*

CAP To 4 cm across; initially convex with inrolled edges, becoming flat and sometimes with uplifted margins; white to cream with greyish to pinkish tinges, sometimes also with grey to tan splotches and concentric rings and radial lines; dry; smooth, but can be covered with a fine white down; flesh thin, white, sometimes with a buff to grey tinge. GILLS Directly attached to stem or slightly decurrent; white to buff; crowded; with subgills. ODOUR Not distinctive. TASTE Not distinctive. SPORE PRINT White. STEM To 3 cm tall × 5 mm wide; often wider at the base and slightly expanded where the gills meet the stem; older stems becoming hollow and compressed; coloured like cap; with fibrils when young, smooth in age; sometimes with white mycelium at the base. RING Absent. FRUITING Scattered or in groups of few to many, often in fairy rings; on the ground; in grassy areas (e.g., lawns, pastures); summer, autumn.

EDIBILITY A poisonous and potentially fatal meal—the SWEAT-PRODUCING CLITOCYBE contains the alkaloid muscarine, which can drive liquid out of every orifice of the body. Victims may experience sweating, tearing, salivation, vomiting, and diarrhea. SIMILAR The FAIRY RING MUSHROOM (p. 186) has a cap with an umbo and more widely spaced gills. The SWEETBREAD MUSHROOM (p. 223), which also grows in grassy areas, has pink spores and a distinct farinaceous odour, like fresh bread dough. The CROWDED WHITE CLITOCYBE (p. 134) is much larger (to 15 cm wide), has an unpleasant (sour) taste, and often grows in clusters. COMMENTS The SWEAT-PRODUCING CLITOCYBE is still widely known as *Clitocybe dealbata*, but scientific consensus seems to be leaning toward the mushroom's earlier epithet, *C. rivulosa*. ⚬ The "rivulosa" of the current name comes from a Latin word for "river, channel" and may refer to the colour accents on the cap.

Pink Bubble Gum Mushroom   *Aphroditeola olida*

CAP To 3 cm across; convex at first and with inrolled margins, becoming flat with a depressed centre and a wavy or lobed margin; pink to brownish orange, occasionally with darker splotches, sometimes buff in dry weather; sticky at first, then dry; appearing smooth, but finely hairy under a hand lens; flesh thin, white. GILLS Long-decurrent; often thickened, forked, and sometimes wavy and with connecting veins; cap-coloured or paler, even to white; closely spaced. ODOUR Strongly sweet and fruity, reminiscent of root beer or bubble gum. TASTE Not distinctive. SPORE PRINT White. STEM To 3 cm tall × 4 mm wide; usually narrower at base and reaching far into the soil; sometimes off-centre; same colour as cap, but occasionally with darker splotches; dry; finely hairy or scaly; sometimes with a pink mycelium clinging to the base. RING Absent. FRUITING Single or in small groups; on the ground; in conifer forest; summer, autumn.

EDIBILITY Unknown. SIMILAR The coloured, decurrent gills might suggest the more common and much larger FALSE CHANTERELLE (p. 129), but the FALSE CHANTERELLE lacks the distinctive bubble gum smell and its caps and gills are much more orangey yellow. COMMENTS PINK BUBBLE GUM MUSHROOM is listed as rare in California and is not all that common in BC. ❧ The genus name *Aphroditeola*, which was assigned in 2013 to this mushroom (and no other), refers to the Greek goddess of love, Aphrodite. The name was presumably bestowed because of the mushroom's pink colour and strong perfume. Aphrodite, however, was also one of the contentious goddesses who started the Trojan War, and attempts by taxonomists to unite this mushroom with existing genera have been equally contentious. "Olida" means "with an odour" in Latin.

Club-foot — *Ampulloclitocybe clavipes*

CAP To 10 cm across; convex, becoming depressed or funnel-shaped with age, margins occasionally wavy; greyish brown, sometimes lightly olive-tinted, usually darker in the centre; moist or dry; smooth or finely fibrillose or scaly; flesh thick, whitish, sometimes pale yellow in the base. GILLS Decurrent; brittle when dry, sometimes forked; off-white to cream or yellowish; often with subgills. ODOUR Not distinctive, but sometimes sweet, described variously as similar to orange blossom, grape soda, or grape bubble gum. TASTE Not distinctive. SPORE PRINT White. STEM To 6 cm tall × 1 cm wide; widening downward, with the basal bulb in some specimens up to 3 times the width of the upper stem; whitish with brown fibrils; often with white mycelium sticking to the base. RING Absent. FRUITING Single or in small or large groups; on the ground; in conifer and mixedwood forest; late summer, autumn.

EDIBILITY Possibly edible, but interactions with alcohol, similar to that of INKY CAP (p. 292) mushrooms, have been reported. SIMILAR *Ampulloclitocybe avellaneialba* is very similar, but tends to have a darker olive-brown to brown cap and stem, no odour, and darker radial lines near the cap margin, and to grow on decaying wood/logs. Overlap of colour and habitat between the 2 species of *Ampulloclitocybe* means that a microscopic examination of spore shapes (spores of *A. avellaneialba* are spindle-shaped, spores of CLUB-FOOT are ovoid) may be needed. *Gerronema atrialbum* (inset photo), which was *Clitocybula atrialba*, has a blackish brown cap that is streaked with lighter brown, a mild odour, and a base not much wider than the stem. *Bonomyces sinopicus* (was *Clitocybe sinopica*) has an orange-brown cap and stem and a farinaceous odour, and often grows along the sides of pathways and road shoulders. COMMENTS CLUB-FOOT can be common in areas of southern BC. Almost all reports come from coastal areas. ⌐ "Ampulloclitocybe" means "flask-like *Clitocybe*," and "clavipes" means "club foot," referring respectively to CLUB-FOOT's funnel-shaped cap and basal bulb.

Lichens

A lichen is a remarkable partnership that includes one or more fungi (the mycobiont) and one or more algae and/or cyanobacteria (the photobiont). Lichens are fascinating, beautiful, ecologically important organisms. And they are widespread and diverse.

The fungal hyphae that make up most of a lichen provide a home for their photosynthesizing partners. Lichen fungi feature many adaptations that support the work of their photobionts, including structural features that allow light to reach the interior of the lichen tissues and allow photobionts to receive carbon dioxide and release oxygen, all the while protecting them from the elements. BC lichenologist Trevor Goward once described lichens as "fungi that have discovered agriculture."

Approximately 20 per cent of known fungal species form lichens. Almost all these fungi are ascomycetes, partners in what are called "ascolichens." A few are basidiomycetes, forming basidiolichens. While there are many species of mycobionts, there are only about a hundred species of photobionts. Of these, most are green algae, some are cyanobacteria, and few are brown algae.

Lichen reproduction is mostly asexual (vegetative). This is accomplished through fragmentation—pieces of the lichen break off that contain both the mycobiont(s) and the photobiont(s) and find a new place to grow. Lichen reproduction that is sexual is more complicated. The photobionts, so far as we know, do not reproduce sexually. Since almost all fungi involved in the lichen symbiosis are ascomycetes, lichen fruiting bodies are almost all ascomycete fruiting bodies. The most common of these is an apothecium, a cup with asci arrayed across its surface—miniature lichen versions of cup fungi (p. 449). For basidiolichens, the sexual fruiting structures resemble mushrooms—see the page on the LICHEN AGARIC (p. 139). The mycobiont partner that sprouts from the spores must acquire their algal or cyanobacterial partners from the environments in which they grow.

METHUSELAH'S BEARD LICHEN (*Usnea longissima*).

BC lichens are ecologically important for the roles they play in primary succession—in breaking bedrock surfaces into soils. But they are also important in nitrogen cycles. Cyanobacteria (sometimes called blue-green algae) can fix nitrogen, pulling free nitrogen out of the air and turning it into biologically available nitrogen compounds. The cyanolichens that include these cyanobacteria are important in nitrogen regulation in many of BC's forested ecosystems, especially in stands of old-growth forest.

Lichens have other useful roles. Lichen species are exquisite indicators of air quality—the cleaner the air, the more lichens. For species such as MOUNTAIN CARIBOU, lichens are critically important food. A number of BC lichens, like their macrofungal cousins, are used in dyeing fabric (see essay on p. 342).

Lichen Agaric
Lichenomphalia umbellifera

CAP To 2 cm across; flat, becoming depressed and funnel-shaped, the margins initially curved down or under, eventually flat or uplifted, often wavy or scalloped or pleated; pale brownish fading to yellowish or straw-coloured, with darker areas in the centre and along the bottoms of the pleats; moist; smooth; striate; somewhat hygrophanous; flesh thin, coloured like the cap. GILLS Decurrent; deep compared to the small cap size; sometimes with cross-veins; pale yellow; widely spaced; with short subgills. ODOUR Not distinctive. TASTE Not distinctive. SPORE PRINT White to yellowish. STEM To 3 cm tall × 2 mm wide; equal or widened at base, often curved and hollow; sometimes with plum hues at top, a muted yellow-brown below, fading paler; moist to dry; smooth; sometimes with white mycelium at the base. RING Absent. FRUITING Scattered or in groups; on decaying conifer logs or on soil; typically in forests; year-round.

EDIBILITY Unknown. SIMILAR The ORANGE MOSSCAP (p. 183) and *Rickenella swartzii* both have longer stems in relation to their cap size and preferentially grow in moss. The former usually has distinct orange highlights and overall coloration; the latter has violet tones on the cap. *Hodophilus paupertinus* has the stature of LICHEN AGARIC, but it has a greyish tan cap that darkens to brown in age and gives off the distinct smell of mothballs. The DARK FUNNEL (p. 142) has a greyish brown cap, gills, and stem. COMMENTS The mushroom described here is the reproductive stage of a lichen. Look with a hand lens for the clumps of extremely small green balls at the bases of the stems—the green in the balls is from the lichen's photosynthesizer, an alga in the genus *Coccomyxa*. ✦ "Umbellifera" means "bearing a parasol."

Lilac-gilled Umbrella
Chromosera cyanophylla

CAP To 2 cm across; convex, sometimes helmet-shaped, eventually with a depressed disc, the margins incurved when young, sometimes scalloped with age; yellow, paler near the margins; slimy or sticky; smooth; translucent-striate when moist, sometimes to almost the centre of the cap; hygrophanous; flesh thin, pale yellow. GILLS Broadly attached, sometimes decurrent; about 2 mm deep; lilac to purple to rosy when young, fading to beige or light yellow; often with several rows of subgills. ODOUR Not distinctive. TASTE. Not distinctive. SPORE PRINT White. STEM To 3 cm tall × 2 mm wide; equal but often enlarged at the base; cartilaginous; coloured as the gills near the top, fading to yellowish, but usually keeping some lilac tint; slimy or sticky to the touch; smooth; usually with lilac mycelium at base. RING Absent. FRUITING Scattered, in groups, or in clusters; on conifer wood, sometimes on cut ends of logs; usually in conifer forests; spring, autumn.

EDIBILITY Unknown. Too small to care about. SIMILAR *Chrysomphalina aurantiaca* (see inset photo on p. 141) might be confused with the LILAC-GILLED UMBRELLA, but the *Chrysomphalina*'s cap is not as slimy/sticky, lacks the lilac tints and the long striations, and often has small hairs around the edge of the cap. YELLOWLEG BONNET (p. 178) does have the striations and the slimy/sticky cap, but the cap usually has an umbo rather than being depressed and its gills do not have lilac tones. COMMENTS The LILAC-GILLED UMBRELLA is a coastal species more overlooked than uncommon. The young fruiting bodies with their lilac gills make excellent photographic subjects when posed against their dull, rotting substrates, especially when backlit. ◦ The genetic signature of our LILAC-GILLED UMBRELLA differs significantly from the European material on which the name is based, so we may get a new scientific name at some point. ◦ "Chromosera" is a word blend of "chromo," meaning "coloured," and "mosera," a term recognizing the work of the Austrian mycologist Meinhard Moser (1924–2002). Besides his fine research, Moser was renowned for his homemade chanterelle schnapps. "Cyanophylla," meaning "blue-gilled," refers to the mushroom's lilac gills.

Goldgill Navelcap
Chrysomphalina chrysophylla

CAP To 4 cm across; convex to flat, sometimes with uplifted margins, often depressed in the centre, the margins initially inrolled; red-brown to yellowish brown to golden yellow when moist, sometimes with a browner disc; bald in some specimens, very finely scaly in others; somewhat hygrophanous; flesh thin, orange. GILLS Decurrent; moderately deep; yellow, often with orange tints; widely spaced. ODOUR Not distinctive. TASTE Not distinctive. SPORE PRINT Yellow to salmon. STEM To 5 cm tall × 3 mm wide; equal or slightly wider at base and often curved; becoming hollow; yellow to golden yellow; moist; hairless or slightly fibrillose; sometimes with white mycelium at base. RING Absent. FRUITING Scattered or in groups; most commonly on decaying conifer logs, but also on the ground; in forests; spring, autumn, winter.

EDIBILITY Unknown. SIMILAR *Chrysomphalina aurantiaca* (inset photo), a close cousin to GOLDGILL NAVELCAP, is typically smaller and has a more orange cap. Its newly opened caps sometimes have fine hairs around the margins. The less common *Pseudoarmillariella ectypoides* has a yellowish brown cap with darker radial fibres that is dotted, when young, with small reddish brown to black pointy scales. The WINTER CHANTERELLE (p. 38) can be distinguished by its gills, which are more like blunt ridges. FUZZYFOOT (p. 144), which has colour phases that overlap the cap and gill colours of GOLDGILL NAVELCAP, has a darker, brownish stem (especially in the lower half), striate margins on the cap, and gills that are forked and cross-connected. COMMENTS The GOLDGILL NAVELCAP, a small and often overlooked decomposer that likes well-decayed logs, is as pleasing to the eye as its common name is pleasing to the mouth. The "navelcap" part of the common name will make more sense to those with innies. ◆ "Chrysomphalina" means "golden *Omphalina*"—*Omphalina* is a mushroom genus whose name is based on the Greek word for "little bellybutton." "Chrysophylla" means, as its common name suggests, "golden-gilled."

Dark Funnel   *Arrhenia epichysium*

CAP To 3 cm across; convex, becoming depressed and eventually funnel-shaped, the margins initially inrolled; grey-brown to almost black, fading in age; dry; smooth, but sometimes finely scaly/scurfy at the centre of the disc; translucent-striate; hygrophanous; flesh thin, greyish to cap-coloured. GILLS Decurrent; shallow to somewhat deep (to 4 mm); often forking and cross-veined, sometimes forming a sharp margin where they meet the stem; greyish brown, usually lighter than the cap; often somewhat widely spaced; with multiple tiers of subgills. ODOUR Not distinctive. TASTE Not distinctive. SPORE PRINT White. STEM To 3 cm tall × 4 mm wide; equal or slightly widened below, sometimes curved; coloured as cap but sometimes darker in age; smooth; often with grey to white mycelium at the base. RING Absent. FRUITING Scattered or in small groups; on decaying wood; in conifer or hardwood forests; winter, spring.

EDIBILITY Unknown. SIMILAR The larger *Pseudoclitocybe cyathiformis*, THE GOBLET, is similar in shape and coloration, but it often grows on the ground instead of on decaying wood. The LICHEN AGARIC (p. 139) shares the shape and habitat of the DARK FUNNEL, but the cap of the former is coloured pale brownish to pale yellowish. *Arrhenia chlorocyanea* (inset photo) resembles the DARK FUNNEL except that its cap is blue-green or a dark blackish green (fading in age) and the flesh just under the cap can take on the same colours. COMMENTS DARK FUNNEL spent time in *Lepiota*, *Omphalia/Omphalina*, and *Clitocybe* before being moved to the genus *Arrhenia*. ◆ It appears to be relatively rare in BC. ◆ "Arrhenia" honours Swedish botanist Johan Peter Arrhenius (1811–89). "Epichysis" is the word for a Greek earthenware jug used for pouring oil and wine, so "epichysium" is possibly a comparison of this funnel-shaped mushroom to the ancient serving implement.

Greyling
Cantharellula umbonata

CAP To 5 cm across; convex at first with margins curved under, then flat to shallowly funnel-shaped, often having a small, pointed umbo and, with age, fine radial wrinkles; smoky grey, sometimes buff with purplish or yellowish tinges, the outer edges of the cap sometimes lighter; dry; smooth to minutely hairy; flesh white to pale grey, sometimes slowly reddening where cut. **GILLS** Decurrent; shallow; forking; white, bruising or staining yellowish or reddish in small patches; crowded. **ODOUR** Not distinctive or with a faint cucumber smell. **TASTE** Not distinctive. **SPORE PRINT** White. **STEM** To 8 cm tall × 8 mm wide; sometimes becoming flattened and twisted; white to grey and silky in the upper part, sometimes bruising reddish below; with white mycelium at the base. **RING** Absent. **FRUITING** Scattered or in small groups, sometimes in fairy rings; on the ground, especially mossy outcrops; in open sites with *Polytrichum* or *Dicranum* mosses; summer, autumn.

EDIBILITY Edible. **SIMILAR THE GOBLET** (*Pseudoclitocybe cyathiformis*) is also grey and funnel-shaped, but its gills are less decurrent and they turn a greyish brown as they age. **SLIMY MILK CAP** (p. 72) has a grey-brown cap and white gills, but its cap is slimy, its gills are barely decurrent (if at all), and its flesh does not stain reddish. **COMMENTS** The GREYLING, a world-ranging species of colder areas, is fairly common, at least in southern BC. In places where it is abundant, it is sometimes collected for the table. ❧ "Umbonata" means "with an umbo."

Fuzzyfoot   *Xeromphalina campanella* group

CAP To 2.5 cm across; convex, even bell-shaped when very young, margins curved down, becoming depressed in the centre as the edges spread and lift; orange-brown to yellow-brown to cinnamon brown, typically a lighter yellow on the margin; usually moist; smooth, often shiny; striate when moist; somewhat hygrophanous; flesh thin, yellowish. **GILLS** Short-decurrent; with shallow cross-veins; cream or yellowish, becoming dull orange; moderately spaced, with 12–15 reaching the stem; with 1–3 subgills. **ODOUR** Not distinctive. **TASTE** Not distinctive. **SPORE PRINT** White to buff. **STEM** To 4 cm tall × 3 mm wide; equal or slightly widened at base, often curved; tough, cartilaginous; yellow above, reddish brown below; moist to dry; smooth or finely fibrillose, often with a polished look; usually with orange-brown mycelium at base. **RING** Absent. **FRUITING** In small groups to densely clumped; on decomposed and almost always coniferous twigs, logs, and stumps; summer, autumn, winter.

EDIBILITY Unknown. **SIMILAR** Our area has several genus *Xeromphalina* species. The ones that occur most frequently, besides FUZZYFOOT, are *X. fulvipes* (inset photo, cited by some as *Heimiomyces fulvipes*), *X. cornui*, and *X. cauticinalis*. The *X. fulvipes* cousin often grows on twigs or on debris on the forest floor. It has a nondecurrent gill attachment and a bitter taste. The other 2 xeromphalinas can have short-decurrent gills, as FUZZYFOOT does, but *X. cornui* has a thread-like (under 1 mm wide) dark brown to black stem and grows singly or in small, scattered troops, while *X. cauticinalis* has a red-brown stem base (often with yellow tones at the top) and a bitter taste and grows in tight clusters. **COMMENTS** FUZZYFOOT is an extremely common decomposer throughout BC, especially in mid-autumn. Clusters of it sometimes cover large sections of the rotting stumps on which its mycelium feeds. ❧ Molecular and mating studies suggest that FUZZYFOOT is more than one species. ❧ "Xeromphalina" means "dry *Omphalina*" (a mushroom genus) or "little dry navel," and "campanella" means "small bell."

Tricholoma and Similar

Most species in this section belong to the genus *Tricholoma*. The trichs (some people say the word as "tricks," some say "trykes") share several important features. People who are learning to recognize mushrooms can quickly catch on to the "trich look" and are often able to pick out mushrooms that belong to this genus, even when they can't identify them to species.

What makes a mushroom a trich? *Tricholoma* species are large, fleshy, fibrous mushrooms whose caps start off conical or rounded. As they mature, the caps expand and flatten out, though many trich caps never completely lose their roundness above the stem, resulting in a broad umbo. All trichs have white spores. The gills of trichs tend to be white or at least a bit lighter than the cap colour, and subgills—the smaller gills that don't reach all the way to the stem—are common. The gills that *are* attached to the stem often take a little hop upward, toward the cap, just before they join the stem—they are, we say, "notched." The stems of the trichs are mostly cylindrical, but can be wider at the top, middle, or bottom. Trichs don't have universal veils, so they don't have volvas at the stem base or warts of universal veil material sticking to tops of the caps, as the amanitas do. Many trichs do, however, have partial veils, and these can sometimes hang around as fringes on the cap and occasionally form a more or less membranous ring or a ring zone. Investigators with good sniffers are kept busy when they find trichs, with smells ranging from a gentle farinaceous to various shades of nice and not nice. Finally, all trichs are, we believe, mycorrhizal, forming symbiotic connections to trees, shrubs, and a few of the non-woody plants.

The edible status of many of the trichs is unknown. There are at least three good table mushrooms in the group—the PINE MUSHROOM (p. 146), the STREAKED TRICH (p. 157), and the POPLAR TRICH (p. 152). Members of some groups—the RED-BROWN TRICH (p. 151)—are known to be poisonous. Shuttling between these extremes is the MAN ON HORSEBACK (p. 148), which has gone from being a good edible to being a suspected poisoner in only two decades.

At present, there are about a hundred North American species still in the genus *Tricholoma*. About 50 of them have been found in BC, and the most common ones—15 or so—are discussed on these pages. In addition to *Tricholoma* species, we have included some of the larger white-spored mushrooms that can be mistaken for trichs—mushroom species from the genera *Leucopaxillus*, *Lyophyllum*, *Melanoleuca*, *Catathelasma*, and *Tricholomopsis*. Also here is *Armillaria*, which has had a long association with *Tricholoma*.

Readers wanting to work further on tricholomas should consult *Tricholomas of North America* (University of Texas Press, 2013) by Alan E. Bessette and others.

Pine Mushroom — *Tricholoma murrillianum*

CAP To 20 cm across; convex becoming flat, with an inrolled, somewhat wavy margin when young that often has cottony veil remnants; white, with cinnamon stains and fibrils in age; dry or slightly sticky when moist; smooth or developing scales; flesh thick, firm, white. **GILLS** Broadly attached to narrowly attached and notched; 8 mm–1.2 cm deep; white to cream, spotting or staining reddish brown or orange-brown; closely spaced to crowded. **ODOUR** Distinctively sweet and spicy, of cinnamon, though some detect a more rank smell, similar to that of old gym socks (also called "fungal funk"). **TASTE** Not distinctive. **SPORE PRINT** White. **STEM** To 15 cm tall × 4 cm wide; equal or narrowing toward base; hard; solid; white and cottony above ring, scaly and cap-coloured below. **RING** Cottony and thick, and flaring when young, then collapsing against stem; white; persistent. **FRUITING** Scattered or in groups; on the ground; in conifer, sometimes mixedwood, forests; autumn.

EDIBILITY Choice. **SIMILAR** Anyone collecting PINE MUSHROOMS needs to be sure that they can tell the difference between PINE MUSHROOM and the seriously poisonous SMITH'S AMANITA (p. 117), which often grows in the same areas and sometimes even grows intermixed with PINE MUSHROOMS—see the page for SMITH'S AMANITA for comparison details. *Tricholoma dulciolens* (formerly called *T. caligatum*) is not as stocky as the PINE MUSHROOM, has darker fibrils on its cap and stem, and tends to be less aromatic and have a less pleasing taste than PINE MUSHROOM. The BIG BROWN CAT (p. 163) and *Catathelasma ventricosum* are 2 other large white mushrooms that some people mistake for PINE MUSHROOMS, but they lack the signature spicy odour. Beginners also have a tendency to mistake the SHORT-STEMMED RUSSULA (p. 52), LARGE WHITE LEUCOPAX (p. 168), LEOPARD TRICH (p. 159), and VEILED ORANGE TRICH (p. 154) for PINE MUSHROOMS—see their species descriptions for further details. **COMMENTS** PINE MUSHROOMS have a strong taste and are often cooked alone or in dishes that put their unique taste (and smell) on display. The PINE MUSHROOM (also called MATSUTAKE, the name used in Japan) is an important commercial mushroom that in some years fetches high prices. They are picked commercially in BC primarily for export to Japan, where they can fetch $95 per kilogram. BC PINE MUSHROOMS are picked commercially primarily in the Kootenays, Vancouver Island, northwestern BC (especially Nass valley), and the south Coast Mountains. ➤ There is much debate about the correct scientific name for our BC PINE MUSHROOMS. We side with mycologist and author Steve Trudell and his colleagues, who recognize 3 PINE MUSHROOM species in North America: one in Mexico; one mainly in eastern North America (*T. magnivelare*); and *T. murrillianum* in western North America. ➤ PINE MUSHROOMS are mycorrhizal partners with several kinds of conifers and with a few hardwoods, and not just, as the common name suggests, with trees in the genus *Pinus*. ➤ In BC, *T. murrillianum* seems to prefer thin, well-drained, often sandy soils that have covers of mosses and lichens. The grouped caps often stay partly submerged in the forest duff, forming hard-to-see humps when the caps are small. Since the young caps (see photo below) have the highest commercial value, those who harvest the fruiting bodies of PINE MUSHROOMS prefer to take them at the humps-under-the-soil stage. Pickers looking for these emerging caps should take extra care not to disturb, more than is necessary, the soils containing the mycelial mats that are the body of the mushroom. ➤ One interesting aspect of our western North American PINE MUSHROOM is its association with a non-photosynthesizing herbaceous plant, CANDYSTICK (*Allotropa virgata*). See p. 55 for further discussion. ➤ "Murrillianum" honours William Alphonso Murrill (1869–1957), the first mycologist to collect and describe our western North American PINE MUSHROOMS as a distinct species.

Man on Horseback *Tricholoma equestre* group

CAP To 12 cm across; convex becoming flat, with margins initially inrolled, then uplifted and sometimes wavy and lobed; entirely yellow or sometimes greenish yellow, but disc may have brownish areas; sticky when moist; smooth, but when young has minute fibres at the centre that break up into scales; flesh firm, white to pale yellow near cap skin. **GILLS** Narrowly attached and notched, almost free; deep (1 cm); yellow to greenish yellow, paler in age; closely spaced; subgills present. **ODOUR** Slightly farinaceous. **TASTE** Not distinctive. **SPORE PRINT** White. **STEM** To 10 cm tall × 2.5 cm wide; equal or base a bit bulbous; white to pale yellow; dry; fibrillose. **RING** Absent. **FRUITING** Scattered or in large groups; on the ground; usually with conifers but occasionally with hardwoods; late summer, autumn.

EDIBILITY Uncertain. **SIMILAR** Three other tricholomas with yellow caps may cause some confusion. The cap of the **SEPARATING TRICH** (p. 149) is more of a greenish yellow with dark streaks in it. **THE STINKER** (p. 150) has a dry yellowish cap and smells sulphury, like the telltale smell of mercaptan added to gas. *Tricholoma intermedium* often has eroded white gills under its yellowish cap. Care should also be taken to distinguish the MAN ON HORSEBACK from the poisonous **DEATH CAP** (p. 112), which can also have a yellow-green cap. The DEATH CAP, however, may display a volva and may have a ring or ring remnants. **COMMENTS** *Tricholoma equestre* was considered a good edible in Europe for centuries, at times even a delicacy reserved for nobility, but in the 1990s reports began to be published of poisonings, even deaths, from consuming large amounts of the mushroom. In Europe, an intense debate continues over its edibility. ◆ Genetic studies reveal that *T. equestre* is the name of a group of several species and subspecies, with specimens from North America differing from European species. Many authorities cite this common mushroom under the name *T. flavovirens*. ◆ "Equestre" means "pertaining to a horseman or knight."

Separating Trich

Tricholoma sejunctum group

CAP To 8 cm across; convex becoming flat or broadly umbonate, margins slightly inrolled when young, often becoming wavy and uplifted and radially split in age; yellow or greenish yellow, with a blackish centre and radially streaked with dark brown or black fibrils; slightly slimy to sticky, becoming dry; flesh thin, whitish, sometimes tinged yellow or grey. GILLS Broadly or narrowly attached and notched; shallow to deep (5 mm–1.5 cm); cream becoming yellow, especially near the cap margin; often closely spaced; with subgills. ODOUR Faintly to strongly farinaceous. TASTE Bitter or not distinctive. SPORE PRINT White. STEM To 10 cm tall × 2 cm wide; equal or widening downward; white, sometimes becoming yellow in part or entirely; dry; smooth, sometimes silky with fine longitudinal fibres. RING Absent. FRUITING Single, scattered, or in dense groups; on the ground in conifer and mixedwood forests; autumn, early winter.

EDIBILITY Uncertain. SIMILAR MAN ON HORSEBACK (p. 148) has a non-streaked yellow or greenish yellow cap that sometimes has a brown centre. Also, its gills tend to be more consistently yellow. *Tricholoma davisiae* has green and yellow hues in its cap and may even have some streaking, especially on young specimens, but it has a dry cap and it often displays pink tints on the surface and in the flesh of the stem base. *Tricholoma intermedium*, another yellowish trich in our area, does not have radially arranged streaks on its cap, and its gills are white. The STREAKED TRICH (p. 157), though it may have pale yellow hues in its gills and on its stem, is much less likely to have yellow or greenish yellow in the cap. COMMENTS The *T. sejunctum* species that was originally defined by European mycologists is a mycorrhizal associate with hardwoods. In western North America, we find it also with conifers, suggesting that *T. sejunctum* is not the right name for our mushroom. • "Sejunctum" means "separated," which may refer either to the deeply notched and almost free gills or to the tendency of the cap to split.

The Stinker   *Tricholoma sulphureum* group

CAP To 8 cm across; convex becoming flat or umbonate; yellow, sometimes pale yellow with tan disc; dry; smooth; flesh thin, pale yellow. **GILLS** Narrowly attached or notched; 2–5 mm deep; yellow; somewhat widely spaced, with 32–38 reaching the stem; 3–7 subgills. **ODOUR** Strong and obnoxious, but hard to describe, sometimes compared to coal tar or to the sulphury telltale smell of mercaptan that is added to natural gas, though some report the smell as intensely floral. **TASTE** Variable, ranging from not distinctive to unpleasant, sometimes described as bitter or peppery. **SPORE PRINT** White. **STEM** To 8 cm tall × 1.5 cm wide; equal or widening downward; solid; yellow, sometimes with darker fibrils; dry. **RING** Absent. **FRUITING** Scattered or in groups; on the ground; in conifer forests; autumn.

EDIBILITY Uncertain. Perhaps poisonous, but to test this we would have to find people willing to introduce this obnoxious-smelling mushroom into their digestive systems. **SIMILAR** Identifiers who lack senses of smell and taste might be tempted to confuse THE STINKER with the MAN ON HORSEBACK (p. 148), which some consider a good edible (but see the discussion on its edibility). In this case, the sticky-when-moist cap and more closely spaced gills of the (usually larger) MAN ON HORSEBACK might provide clues. In contrast, identifiers relying too much on taste and smell might be tempted to think that THE STINKER is the SMELLY TRICH (p. 162) or one of the other sulphur-smelling mushrooms listed in that entry. **COMMENTS** Canadian specimens of this mushroom do not fall securely within the European genotype behind the original species definition, so our BC species may someday have different species names. ☙ THE STINKER is fairly common in the coastal areas of southwestern BC, less so in the Interior.

Red-brown Trich *Tricholoma pessundatum* group

CAP To 14 cm across; convex becoming flat, often umbonate, sometimes wavy and/or lobed; reddish brown, paler at the margins; slimy or sticky when moist; smooth, but sometimes with tiny, flat fibrils at the centre; margins may be ribbed or striate; flesh thick, firm, white. GILLS Usually broadly attached and notched, but sometimes narrowly attached or even free; white, with red-brown spots or stains in age; closely spaced. ODOUR Farinaceous, but one report says it smells like linseed oil. TASTE Not distinctive. SPORE PRINT White. STEM To 10 cm tall × 3 cm wide; usually equal; solid; white, often with red-brown stains near the base; silky. RING Absent. FRUITING Scattered or in groups; on the ground; in forests; autumn.

EDIBILITY Poisonous. SIMILAR POPLAR TRICH (p. 152), which can also have a reddish brown, slimy/sticky cap, grows in sandy soils along riverbanks, almost always in association with BLACK COTTONWOOD and other poplars. *Tricholoma imbricatum* and FUZZTOP (p. 153) both have dry caps that are covered with flattened fibres, with FUZZTOP differing from *T. imbricatum* by having a more radial arrangement of the cap fibres and often having veil remnants hanging from the cap margin. COMMENTS The name and original species description of the RED-BROWN TRICH are based on European studies. North American populations may be several different closely related species… stay tuned. ⟿ "Pessundatum" means "low on the ground, sunken."

Poplar Trich   *Tricholoma populinum*

CAP To 14 cm across; convex with inrolled margins, becoming flat and often wavy; cinnamon to reddish brown, the margins paler and sometimes with watery spots; cap somewhat peelable; slimy or sticky when moist, then soon dry; smooth; flesh thick, firm, white. GILLS Broadly attached and often notched; white, discolouring reddish brown in age; closely spaced. ODOUR Strongly farinaceous. TASTE Not distinctive. SPORE PRINT White. STEM To 7 cm tall × 2 cm wide; equal or widening downward; solid; whitish, discolouring reddish brown with age or handling; smooth, but sometimes with small hairs at the top and sometimes dotted with dark fibrils. RING Absent. FRUITING Scattered or in dense troops or in clumps, sometimes in large fairy rings; in sandy locations and often nestled deeply in the soil; in association with poplars (TREMBLING ASPEN, BLACK COTTONWOOD, or BALSAM POPLAR); summer, autumn.

EDIBILITY Edible. SIMILAR The most important fungal comparison with the edible POPLAR TRICH is with the toxic **RED-BROWN TRICH** (p. 151). The RED-BROWN TRICH has a darker cap and ribbing on the margins. The most important clue that you have found the POPLAR TRICH, however, may be habitat: the RED-BROWN TRICH associates with many types of trees, and the POPLAR TRICH associates only with hardwoods, usually those in the genus *Populus*. See the entry on RED-BROWN TRICH for comparison with other species. COMMENTS The POPLAR TRICH is uncommon, but where it occurs it can fruit in abundance, especially along riverbanks and gravel roads that edge BLACK COTTONWOOD stands. The POPLAR TRICH is an exception to the light usage made of edible mushrooms by First Nations in BC—see the essay on First Nations fungi use for more detail (p. 471). ❧ "Populinum" means "of poplar."

Fuzztop
Tricholoma vaccinum

CAP To 10 cm across; conical or convex becoming umbonate or flat, margins inrolled at first and often hung with veil tatters and splitting in age; buff background with reddish brown fibrils or scales that often separate radially in age, the disc darker; dry; matted or felty on the fibril-covered areas; flesh white to light buff. GILLS Usually broadly attached, but often deeply notched; 2–8 mm deep; cream or buff or light cinnamon, developing darker stains in age; often closely spaced; subgills numerous. ODOUR Usually farinaceous. TASTE Not distinctive to somewhat bitter. SPORE PRINT White. STEM To 8 cm tall × 2 cm wide; equal, sometimes widening downward and tapering to base; often hollow; with a buff background and, on the bottom two-thirds, longitudinal reddish brown fibrils; dry; silky, matted. RING Cobwebby partial veil; disappearing. FRUITING Single or in small groups or clumps; on the ground, occasionally on logs; in conifer forests, especially around spruce; autumn.

EDIBILITY Uncertain. Possibly poisonous. SIMILAR The less common *Tricholoma imbricatum* has a darker and duller cap without a lighter background colour showing through, no cobwebby veil to leave remnants on the cap margin, and a solid stem. The larger RED-BROWN TRICH (p. 151) has a slimy, more evenly brown cap. PANCAKE MUSHROOMS (p. 169) have white gills, a white stem, and an intensely bitter taste. COMMENTS FUZZTOP, one of the real gems of the trichs, is frequently encountered by hikers in BC forests. The relationship between this mycorrhizal fungus and its hosts has been widely studied. ☙ "Vaccinum" means "of the cow," pertaining perhaps to the cap texture and colour (admittedly, owners of HOLSTEIN, BLACK ANGUS, and CHAROLAIS cattle could be excused for not making the colour connection).

Veiled Orange Trich   *Tricholoma focale* group

CAP To 12 cm across; convex becoming flat or umbonate, often with veil remnants on the margin when young; coppery orange, sometimes brown or with olive-green highlighting, sometimes with radial pattern of fibrils or of scales, margins often whitish; dry or greasy, or slimy/sticky when moist; smooth and typically shiny/metallic; flesh thick, white, sometimes slowly bruising orange-brown. GILLS Attached but notched, sometimes with a decurrent tooth; moderately deep (8 mm); white, bruising rusty brown; crowded; 2–3 tiers of subgills. ODOUR Farinaceous or metallic, the smell of raw potatoes or green corn also sometimes detected. TASTE Not distinctive, or sometimes bitter. SPORE PRINT White. STEM To 13 cm tall × 2 cm wide; tapered downward; white to cream above ring with rust-brown scales or fibrils below. RING Ragged; white above, orange below; sometimes disappearing in age. FRUITING Single or scattered; on the ground; under conifers; autumn.

EDIBILITY Not edible. SIMILAR See PINE MUSHROOM (p. 146) for relevant comparisons. COMMENTS *Tricholoma zelleri* and *T. robustum* are other species names associated with this group. *Tricholoma focale* and *T. robustum* are European species that are likely to occur in North America; *T. zelleri* was described in 1949 from Olympic National Park in Washington. Initial genetic analysis indicates that we have at least 2 species-level groups in BC and the US Pacific Northwest, but it is not yet clear how these groups sort with the current names. Vancouver-based mycologist Paul Kroeger, who has studied the species group in Manning Park, has found differences that suggest all 3 may be present in BC. ◆ The 2 tricholomas in this book that have rings, PINE MUSHROOM (p. 146) and this one, spent many years in the *Armillaria* genus before the evolving notion of what constituted a tricholoma allowed them into the *Tricholoma* genus. ◆ "Focale" is a Latin term for a scarf worn around the neck, probably a reference to the ragged ring zone.

Soapy Trich   *Tricholoma saponaceum* group

CAP To 14 cm across; convex becoming flat, sometimes with a low umbo, often with an uplifted, wavy margin in age; the cap splitting and developing cracks in dry weather; colour variable, but often including olive-yellow to greyish brown to rusty brown hues and often paler toward the margin; dry to slightly moist; smooth, sometimes with flattened fibres, sometimes greasy-looking; flesh white. **GILLS** Narrowly to broadly attached, usually notched; 3 mm–1 cm deep; white, often with tints as in cap; ranging from close to moderately well spaced; with subgills. **ODOUR** Soapy, with sweet and sometimes rancid overtones, reminding some people of the powdered soap used in gas station bathrooms. **TASTE** Soapy. **SPORE PRINT** White. **STEM** To 12 cm tall × 2.5 cm wide; often widest in middle and partially rooting; coloured as the gills, typically with a pink or pinkish orange tint in the flesh of the base that may also be visible on the surface; mostly bald, sometimes with longitudinal striations. **RING** Absent. **FRUITING** Single or in groups or clumps; on the ground; in conifer and mixedwood forests; spring, summer, autumn.

EDIBILITY Probably not poisonous, but the phrase "wash your mouth out with soap" comes to mind. **SIMILAR** A common confusion, in our experience, is mistaking a SOAPY TRICH for a *Hygrophorus* species (p. 77)—the soft, often widely spaced gills and greasy-looking cap suggest this. See also the entry for LEOPARD TRICH (p. 159) for other possible confusions. **COMMENTS** This common mycorrhizal species may be the mockingbird of mushrooms— misidentifying a mushroom that turns out to be a SOAPY TRICH is almost a rite of passage in mushroom clubs. The 3 most important clues (none or all of which may be present in a given specimen) are the soapy smell, the pink flesh in the stem base, and a greenish yellow tint on the cap. ✒ Preliminary genetic analysis hints that the SOAPY TRICHS found in BC may represent multiple species. ✒ "Saponaceum" means "soapy."

Mouse Trich   *Tricholoma terreum* group

CAP To 5 cm across; conical or bell-shaped when young, becoming convex and then umbonate or flat, margins wavy, sometimes splitting, and often inrolled or curved down; mouse grey to brownish grey, occasionally nearly black, sometimes paling in age and lighter toward the margins; dry; covered with a felty layer of small grey to black scales; flesh thin, fragile, white to grey. GILLS Broadly to narrowly attached, with a distinct notch; deep; sometimes forking; white to grey; about 50 reaching the stem; multiple tiers of subgills. ODOUR Not distinctive. TASTE Not distinctive. SPORE PRINT White. STEM To 5 cm tall × 1.5 cm wide; equal or wider below; white to grey; finely hairy/silky, especially near the top. RING Absent or cobwebby and disappearing. FRUITING Scattered or in groups, sometimes in fairy rings; on the ground; in conifer forests; generally autumn.

EDIBILITY Uncertain. The MOUSE TRICH is considered an edible in some places where it grows, but the number of species lumped under the one name should give eaters pause. SIMILAR Larger specimens of the MOUSE TRICH might be confused with the LEOPARD TRICH (p. 159) and the ASHEN TRICH (p. 158). The LEOPARD TRICH tends to have a whiter cap and is not as densely scurfy over the disc. The fibrils on the cap of the ASHEN TRICH are more radially arranged than the scales on the MOUSE TRICH cap. COMMENTS This mushroom is called the MOUSE TRICH because the grey colour and felty cap remind finders of mouse fur. ꞏ Several very similar species cluster inside the *Tricholoma terreum* group, but experts disagree about how many and what to call them. ꞏ "Terreum" means "of the earth," a reference to the colour of this species.

Streaked Trich — *Tricholoma portentosum*

CAP To 12 cm across; convex, becoming flat or umbonate, margins incurved at first, then often uplifted, wavy, and split in age; radially streaked; pale to dark grey (to almost black where the streaks meet at the centre), sometimes lilac, greenish, or yellowish tones present, margins often paler; slimy or sticky when wet, shiny when dry; smooth; flesh white or pale grey. GILLS Broadly attached, but usually notched; deep; white, aging yellowish or greyish; closely spaced; often multiple subgills. ODOUR Slightly farinaceous. TASTE Not distinctive. SPORE PRINT White. STEM To 12 cm tall × 3 cm wide; equal, often twisted; solid; white or pale yellow; dry; silky and sometimes longitudinally striate. RING Absent. FRUITING Scattered or in groups to small clusters, sometimes in fairy rings; on the ground; in forests, most commonly conifer forests; autumn. EDIBILITY Choice. But secure identification can be an issue. SIMILAR Unfortunately, the 3 other genus *Tricholoma* mushrooms that resemble the STREAKED TRICH either are not known to be edible or are poisonous. The ASHEN TRICH (p. 158) has a darker grey (but streaked) cap with a more pointed umbo and it has a peppery or bitter taste. The SEPARATING TRICH (p. 149) has dark streaks as well, but it usually has much more yellow on the cap, gills, and stem. The LEOPARD TRICH (p. 159) has charcoal-coloured scales on its cap rather than streaking, and a white to grey stem whose base bruises brown. The somewhat similar MIDNIGHT ENTOLOMA (p. 224), in contrast, is (with caution) edible. It has a streaked cap, but it has a pinkish spore print (often noted by gills that turn pink in age), usually a blue tint on the cap, and generally a much stockier profile. COMMENTS In Europe, what is called *T. portentosum* is sold in markets. ☙ "Portentosum" means "like an omen" or "monstrous, marvellous."

Ashen Trich   *Tricholoma virgatum*

CAP To 10 cm across; conical becoming flat and usually retaining a pointy umbo; silvery background with radiating dark grey to brownish grey fibrils, darker in centre and light grey or buff toward the margins; dry; smooth when young; flesh thin, white or pale grey. **GILLS** Narrowly attached or notched; 4–8 mm deep; white or pale grey; closely spaced; subgills numerous. **ODOUR** Slightly musty or earthy. **TASTE** Gradually bitter and/or peppery. **SPORE PRINT** White. **STEM** To 12 cm tall × 2 cm wide; equal or with basal bulb; white to pale grey; smooth or with fine, silky fibres. **RING** Absent. **FRUITING** Single or in groups; on the ground; in coniferous and mixedwood forests; late summer, autumn.

EDIBILITY Uncertain. But the **ASHEN TRICH** is bitter/peppery to the tongue and easily confused with mushrooms that may be poisonous, so best not brought to the table. **SIMILAR** None of the other primarily grey tricholomas in BC have such a pointy umbo. In addition, the **STREAKED TRICH** (p. 157) has a slimy or sticky cap, a slightly farinaceous odour, and yellowish tones (typically) on the cap and gills. Caps of the **MOUSE TRICH** (p. 156) species are smaller and felty and do not have the prominent radial lines of fibres. The poisonous **LEOPARD TRICH** (p. 159) has a white cap with greyish brown or charcoal scales that are not radially arranged, a farinaceous odour, and a stem base that bruises rusty brown. **COMMENTS** The Latin word "virga" referred to a rod or twig and by extension to anything with a surface like rods or twigs laid together, so botanists have adopted the term "virgatus" to describe species with features that look like stripes or ribbing.

Leopard Trich   *Tricholoma pardinum*

CAP To 15 cm across; convex becoming flat, sometimes wavy, with margins that tend to be downcurved; white to pale grey with greyish brown or charcoal-coloured scales over the cap that sometimes bend upward; dry; smooth around scales; flesh firm, white to pale grey. GILLS Narrowly attached and notched; up to 1.2 cm deep; sometimes ragged in age; white to cream; closely spaced, with 100–116 reaching the stem; 1–2 tiers of subgills. ODOUR Farinaceous. TASTE Not distinctive. SPORE PRINT White. STEM To 12 cm tall × 2 cm or more wide; equal or widening downward; white to grey, the base bruising pale brown or rusty brown; silky, longitudinally striate. RING Absent. FRUITING Scattered or in groups; on the ground; in conifer and mixedwood forests; autumn.

EDIBILITY Poisonous. SIMILAR The smaller MOUSE TRICH species (p. 156) are similar—see that entry for comparisons. *Tricholoma atroviolaceum* does have the farinaceous odour, but the cap colour is violet-black to grey-brown in the centre and surrounded by a lighter margin. ASHEN TRICH (p. 158) usually has a darker grey, often silvery, dry cap with a pointy umbo and radial streaking. STREAKED TRICH (p. 157) also has darker radial streaking, not scales, on its sticky to slimy grey (and sometimes tinged yellow or lilac) cap. SOAPY TRICH (p. 155) often has some greenish tints on its stem and greasy cap and often has a touch of pink or orange at the base of its stem. COMMENTS This is one of the few tricholomas that can do serious harm. Gastrointestinal symptoms can begin soon after consumption. Unfortunately, the toxic LEOPARD TRICH often grows in the same habitat—and is intermingled with—the wonderfully edible PINE MUSHROOMS (p. 146). ◦ The LEOPARD TRICH is a reasonably common mycorrhizal mushroom. ◦ "Pardinum" means "leopard-like," presumably from the spots (scales) on the cap.

Celery-scented Trich   *Tricholoma apium*

CAP To 12 cm across; convex, usually irregularly shaped and undulating, with the margins unevenly inrolled when young and in age either remaining curved in or becoming almost straight; white when young, soon aging greenish to yellow-brown but remaining paler at the margins; dry; suede-like or felted, often cracked with age; flesh thick, whitish. **GILLS** Broadly attached and sometimes with a decurrent tooth; shallow; white to yellowish; closely spaced, with 100–160 reaching the stem; 5–11 subgills between neighbouring gills. **ODOUR** Strongly of celery or fennel. **TASTE** Not distinctive. **SPORE PRINT** White. **STEM** To 5 cm tall × 2 cm wide; narrowing toward base; white with fine scales that may become yellow to brown with age or handling. **RING** Absent. **FRUITING** Single or in groups; on the ground; in drier conifer forests, often with pine or spruce; autumn.

EDIBILITY Unknown. **SIMILAR** The **PANCAKE MUSHROOM** (p. 169) has an intensely bitter taste and profuse white mycelium around the base that sometimes creeps up the stem. The **PINE MUSHROOM** (p. 146) has either a spicy or a gym socks odour and a sometimes prominent ring—see this entry for other possible confusions. **COMMENTS** In BC, the **CELERY-SCENTED TRICH** is apparently confined to coastal and near-coastal areas. ✚ In including the **CELERY-SCENTED TRICH**, we interrupt the pattern of presenting BC's most common mushrooms. It is included here to encourage people to watch for it. This uncommon species has already played an important conservation role in BC—see the essay on rare mushrooms (p. 161). ✚ "Apium" means "of celery."

Rare Mushrooms and Conservation

In 1997, the mycologist Scott Redhead prepared a list of 65 "rare or notable macrofungi" of BC. In this report, he observes that "less than 1% of the macrofungi flora of British Columbia have been examined in systematic studies; hence, it is not possible to provide more than a rudimentary list of rare species for British Columbia." We're a bit better off today, but we still have an incomplete understanding of what fungal species occur in our province, much less what their conservation status might be.

There is reason for concern. We know that the habitats of some of our mushroom species are being altered rapidly and massively. Consider the case of our alpine-adapted mushrooms. A warming climate is causing the treeline, the upper elevation at which trees grow, to increase across our province. A shrinking and rapidly disappearing alpine means less habitat for the fungi—notably certain ectomycorrhizal species of *Hebeloma*, *Inocybe*, and *Cortinarius*—that are associated with the alpine's dwarf willows (*Salix* spp.) and mountain-avens (*Dryas* spp.). Also, we continue to log BC's remaining old-growth forests at a rapid rate, removing habitat for old-growth-associated mushrooms such as KAUFFMAN'S ROOTSHANK (p. 278). BC remains one of the few provinces without legislation protecting threatened and endangered species (including mushrooms) and their habitats.

One hard-fought mushroom conservation success story does give us hope. It involves the creation of Mount Elphinstone Provincial Park on BC's Sunshine Coast. The Mount Elphinstone area has long been recognized for its high mushroom diversity, with more than 60 species recorded, including five species associated with mature and old forests. Of particular interest was the rare mushroom, CELERY-SCENTED TRICH (p. 160). In the mid-1990s, local residents brought a complaint to the Forest Practices Board and organized protests (pictured below) to halt logging on Mount Elphinstone, citing CELERY-SCENTED TRICH as a particular concern. In 2000, a provincial park of 139 hectares was created in the area, comprising three separate parcels on the southwest slopes of Mount Elphinstone. The primary management goal of the new park is "to protect a mixed old growth and second growth forest and the *very diverse and rich fungi populations* associated with the forest" (emphasis added).

Sunshine Coast protests near Roberts Creek, 1996.

Smelly Trich
Tricholoma inamoenum

CAP To 5 cm across; convex becoming flat, sometimes wavy and slightly umbonate; white to beige or tan, especially toward the centre; dry; smooth; flesh thin, firm, white. GILLS Attached and notched, but can be nearly free; shallow (3–5 mm); white to cream becoming tan; somewhat widely spaced, with 33–35 reaching the stem; 3–5 subgills between neighbouring gills. ODOUR Pungent, but hard to describe, sometimes compared to coal tar or to the sulphury telltale scent of mercaptan added to natural gas, though some report it as intensely floral. TASTE Unpleasant. SPORE PRINT White. STEM To 8 cm tall × 7 mm wide; equal or widening downward and often tapering at the bottom of the base; white, sometimes developing brownish or pinkish discolorations at the base; dry; silky. RING Absent. FRUITING Single or in groups; on the ground; in conifer forests, often with spruce; autumn.

EDIBILITY Not edible. Gagging interferes with swallowing. SIMILAR We have 3 tricholomas in BC notable for their sulphurish smell. In addition to the SMELLY TRICH, we have **THE STINKER** (p. 150), which has a yellowish stem, gills, and cap. There is also *Tricholoma sulphurescens* (or whatever name the BC species actually ends up with). Though whitish overall, it develops yellow spotting when it is damaged and its cap is somewhat greasy and silky. COMMENTS A 2004 study of the SMELLY TRICH revealed that size *does* matter—a cap 4 cm across released 25 times the amount of the odiferous chemical as a 2 cm cap. Crushing the cap cells also increases the release of the volatile chemical—which explains why some foragers find this common mycorrhizal mushroom when they step on it. ◦ "Inamoenum" means "unpleasant."

Big Brown Cat   *Catathelasma imperiale* group

CAP Large, to 40 cm across; when young, like a huge spike, with thick veil covering the gills and the margins tightly inrolled, then convex, sometimes with veil remnants at the margin, and finally becoming flat, wavy, and with uplifted margins; dingy brown, reddish brown, or yellowish brown, often mottled with white; smooth or cracked into scales and/or flat fibrils; sticky at first, then dry; flesh white, hard, thick (often more than 10 cm under the centre of the cap). GILLS Short- to long-decurrent; shallow in comparison to the thick flesh; often forked; white to cream, aging yellowish to buff to grey; closely spaced to crowded. ODOUR Farinaceous. TASTE Not distinctive. SPORE PRINT White. STEM To 18 cm tall × 8 cm wide; narrowing downward to a rooting, pointed base; hard-fleshed; whitish above the ring, below the ring coloured as the cap or pinkish buff; dry. RING A double ring, the top ring (derived from the partial veil) striate and flaring, the bottom ring (from the universal veil) indistinct or gelatinous, adhering to stem, and collecting dirt. FRUITING Single or in small groups; on the forest floor; in conifer forests; autumn.

EDIBILITY Edible. But apparently a royal chew. SIMILAR SMITH'S AMANITA (p. 117) has a bulbous base (though sometimes rooting), felted patches on the cap, and a single ring. In our experience, beginners are likely to think they have found a PINE MUSHROOM (p. 146) the first time that they encounter a BIG BROWN CAT. The dirty socks/cinnamon odour and the nondecurrent gills of the PINE MUSHROOM should be enough to separate them. In the Interior montane areas of BC, the shorter *Catathelasma ventricosum* is a more likely find. It has a paler, drier cap and (when viewed under a microscope) longer spores. COMMENTS The names *C. imperiale* and *C. ventricosum* are catch-all concepts for an understudied group of western North American *Catathelasma* species. ◈ The size and heft of the BIG BROWN CAT can be simply stupefying, which probably accounts for the "imperial" in the name (think Henry VIII).

Honey Mushroom
Armillaria ostoyae

CAP To 20 cm across; bell-shaped, then convex to flat and wavy in age, margins inrolled when young, often with white veil remnants attached; yellowish brown to caramel-coloured to darker shades of brown; with abundant dark reddish brown to nearly black scales; dry; lightly striate in age; flesh firm, thick (1–2 cm near stem), white. GILLS Broadly attached, notched, sometimes with decurrent lines; cream becoming cinnamon with age; closely spaced. ODOUR Not distinctive. TASTE Mostly not distinctive, but some say slightly bitter. SPORE PRINT Cream. STEM To 20 cm tall × 1.5 cm wide; often broader at the bottom when young, then later equal and sometimes tapering at the extreme base where it joins the fused cluster; creamy or pinkish tan, staining dark brown to black where handled; dry; smooth or longitudinally striate, surface often dotted with orange to orange-brown or reddish brown fibrils; often with yellowish mycelium and with flattened, branching-like-a-tree black rhizomorphs at the base. RING Thick, membranous, often horizontal, and looking as though it were a standing wave; on the upper part of stem; white, often with brownish edges and darker scales. FRUITING Usually in large clusters, occasionally single or in groups; at the base of trees or stumps; usually on conifers, occasionally on hardwoods; late summer or autumn; southern BC.

EDIBILITY Choice. Some initial caution advised, since eaters have reported reactions. SIMILAR Only 2 BC *Armillaria* species are common and widespread. HONEY MUSHROOM is one, distributed throughout the southern half of BC. The other, found throughout all of BC, is *A. sinapina* (see photo on the next page). Like *A. ostoyae*, *A. sinapina* seems to prefer to feed on conifers in our region. It grows singly or in small clusters of 2 or 3, has a thin ring and black rhizomorphs that send branches out from a central runner rather than repeatedly branching like a tree, and can have remnants of a golden yellow universal veil persisting on the cap, ring, and stem. FRIED CHICKEN MUSHROOMS (p. 170) also grow in clumps of large light brown caps, but they are found on disturbed ground and their stems lack rings. SHEATHED WOODTUFT (p. 270) has a brown spore print and a more translucent-striate and hygrophanous cap. COMMENTS HONEY MUSHROOMS in our province have gone by many names over the years, but mating matches and DNA analysis suggest that we have at least 6 species in BC: *A. ostoyae* and *A. sinapina*, widespread and often common, which are described above; *A. nabsnona* and *A. gallica*, growing with hardwoods and seemingly restricted to southwestern BC; a rarer *A. cepistipes*, also with hardwoods; and *A. altimontana*, seemingly rare and in the mountains of southeastern BC, often with SUBALPINE FIR. ◆ *Armillaria* species are white-rot decomposers. Many armillarias are also pathogens on living trees. A cluster of them have been busy killing 880 hectares of forest in eastern Oregon for several millennia. As a conifer pathogen, this mushroom has received a lot of attention from BC's foresters, who call it ARMILLARIA ROOT DISEASE (see essay on p. 394). The pathogen produces white mycelial fans under the bark of infected trees. It also produces mycelial cords called rhizomorphs, aggregations of parallel hyphae with a protective tough black outer coating that the fungus uses as major arterial highways within and between trees. The handsome black rhizomorphs explain another common name for HONEY MUSHROOM: the BOOT-LACE FUNGUS. ◆ The mycelial fans of *Armillaria* species are bioluminescent. ◆ "Armillaria," related to a Latin term for "bracelet," is perhaps a reference to the thick ring in some members of the species.

Prunes and Custard

Tricholomopsis decora

CAP To 6 cm across; convex becoming flat; with a golden yellow background that is overlaid by brown to almost blackish scales, darker toward the centre; smooth on the background area; sometimes slightly translucent-striate; flesh firm, yellow. GILLS Broadly attached or notched; 5–7 mm deep; golden yellow, sometimes with orange hues in age; crowded, with 50–55 reaching the stem; multiple tiers of subgills. ODOUR Not distinctive. TASTE Not distinctive. SPORE PRINT White. STEM To 6 cm tall × 1 cm wide; equal; sometimes curved and/or off-centre; pale yellow; finely hairy toward top when young, later smooth or with fine longitudinal fibres. RING Absent. FRUITING Single or in groups; on rotting conifer logs; autumn.

EDIBILITY Unknown. SIMILAR MAN ON HORSEBACK (p. 148) also has yellow tones on its cap, gills, and stem, but it has a farinaceous odour, lacks the tiny cap scales, and grows on the ground near its mycorrhizal host (usually conifers, sometimes hardwoods). Two other small yellow decomposers, GOLDGILL NAVELCAP (p. 141) and OLIVE-GOLD LOGLOVER (p. 203), also grow on wood. GOLDGILL NAVELCAP has a yellow-coloured to salmon-coloured spore print and somewhat decurrent, widely spaced gills. OLIVE-GOLD LOGLOVER lacks the tiny cap scales, has a bitter taste, may have a sweet/fruity odour, and may have a lightly wrinkled cap that develops deep red stains when dried. The OLIVE WEBCAP (p. 251) has also been confused with PRUNES AND CUSTARD. The former has brown spores and greenish yellow fibrils on the lower part of the stem and fruits in forest soils rather than on rotting logs. COMMENTS PRUNES AND CUSTARD is frequently found on BC forays. The common name is a wordplay on PLUMS AND CUSTARD (p. 167), the traditional name of its *Tricholomopsis rutilans* cousin. ❧ "Decora" means "beautiful," certainly appropriate for this little charmer.

Plums and Custard
Tricholomopsis rutilans

CAP To 10 cm across; convex becoming flat, often umbonate; golden yellow background overlaid with dark red or (more rarely) purple scales, sometimes fading in age to pink, margins often pale; dry; velvety; flesh thick, pale yellow. GILLS Broadly attached or notched; shallow (under 1 cm); yellow; crowded; 3–4 tiers of subgills. ODOUR Not distinctive. TASTE Not distinctive. SPORE PRINT White. STEM To 10 cm tall × 2 cm wide; equal or widening slightly downward, often curved; yellow with dark red or purple scales, sometimes with a light band at the very top. RING Absent. FRUITING Single or in groups; on rotting conifer logs, on stumps or tree bases, or in soils rich in rotting wood; late summer, autumn, early winter.

EDIBILITY Edible. But so is cardboard. SIMILAR The brown-spored YELLOW-GILLED GYM (p. 264) has a bitter taste, caps that are more cracked than scaly, and (often) a ring or ring zone. The red on the cap, yellow gills, and stems with red and yellow tones may call to mind the GILLED BOLETE (p. 274). COMMENTS The large, striking PLUMS AND CUSTARD, which is relatively common in BC, has made the day of more than one photographer. ✸ Though PLUMS AND CUSTARD has the overall tricholoma look (thus the genus name *Tricholomopsis*, which means "looking like *Tricholoma*"), it has a career as a decomposer rather than as a mycorrhizal associate and does not seem to be closely related on the fungal family tree. The official description of *Tricholomopsis rutilans* is based on European research, and, though the North American and European specimens show no obvious differences in form, a 2015 genetic study found that there may be species-level differences. ✸ "Rutilans" means "reddening."

Large White Leucopax   *Leucopaxillus albissimus* group

CAP To 20 cm or larger across; convex to flat, with inrolled margins when young, often undulate and wavy at the margin in age; white, sometimes aging off-white, buff, or yellowish; dry; smooth but unpolished, the surface sometimes developing cracks; flesh thick, tough and rubbery, white. GILLS Broadly attached or with decurrent lines going down stem; deep (to 6 mm); occasionally forking near stem; easily separable from cap; white to cream, sometimes pale yellow in age; crowded; with subgills. ODOUR Variable, unpleasant to sweet. TASTE Bitter or not distinctive. SPORE PRINT White. STEM To 20 cm tall × 3 cm or more wide; equal or expanding downward, but extreme base often narrowed; tough; solid; colour of the cap; smooth, but often finely scaly in part; often with a dense white mycelium at the base. RING Absent. FRUITING Single or in large groups, sometimes in fairy rings; on the ground; in coniferous or mixedwood forests; autumn.

EDIBILITY Uncertain. Probably not poisonous, but difficult to chew and digest, especially if bitter. SIMILAR CLOUDY CLITOCYBE (p. 133) can have the same overall presentation, but it usually has more grey in the caps, a rotten or skunky smell, and no basal mycelial mat. See the entry for CLOUDY CLITOCYBE for similar mushrooms. The LEOPARD TRICH (p. 159) has small grey scales toward the centre of its white cap, and its gills are broadly attached and notched, never decurrent. See the PINE MUSHROOM (p. 146) for other possible look-alikes. COMMENTS Perhaps the best way to think about the LARGE WHITE LEUCOPAX is as a tricholoma imitating a clitocybe. ☙ Specimens of this mushroom are not only some of our largest decomposers, but also some of our most persistent—the dense caps can remain in top shape for *weeks*. Their gills, like those of most other *Leucopaxillus* species and unlike most gilled mushrooms, can be easily separated from the caps with a firm swipe of the thumb. ☙ "Albissimus" means "very white."

Pancake Mushroom — *Leucopaxillus gentianeus*

CAP To 12 cm across; convex to flat and lumpy, with inrolled margins when young that sometimes become uplifted and wavy in age; brown or reddish brown, often close to the colour of a pecan or a pancake, occasionally paler at the margin than in the centre; dry; velvety at first, then smooth and unpolished, sometimes developing cracks when dry; striations sometimes emerging as distinct ribs in older specimens; flesh thick, firm but often infested with insect larvae, white. GILLS Broadly attached, sometimes notched and/or decurrent by raised lines on stem; shallow to deep (3–8 mm); white to cream; crowded, with 85–110 reaching the stem; with subgills. ODOUR Farinaceous, but often unpleasant. TASTE Quickly and extremely bitter. SPORE PRINT White. STEM To 8 cm tall × 3 cm wide; equal, or base enlarged or bulbous; white, lower part bruising brownish; dry; smooth; base in a dense white to grey mycelium mat. RING Absent. FRUITING Single or in large groups, sometimes in fairy rings; on the ground; in coniferous or mixedwood forests; late summer, autumn.

EDIBILITY Not edible. A bitter batter that deserves no better butter. SIMILAR PANCAKE MUSHROOM resembles somewhat the red-brown tricholomas, such as FUZZTOP (p. 153) and *Tricholoma imbricatum*, but the dense mycelium at the base, the consistently white to cream gills, and the bitter taste make this species distinct. The PANCAKE MUSHROOM can also resemble the CELERY-SCENTED TRICH (p. 160)—see that species for comparison details. COMMENTS Certain regions of Europe where the PANCAKE MUSHROOM occurs list it as a rare species, but western North America seems to be a friendlier habitat for it. ❧ *Leucopaxillus gentianeus* is still known in some circles as *L. amarus*, an apt name ("amarus" means "bitter") but one with taxonomic problems.

Fried Chicken Mushroom — *Lyophyllum decastes* group

CAP To 12 cm across; convex becoming flat and wavy, the margins inrolled when young, often lobed, and uplifted with age; dark brown, or greyish or yellowish brown, sometimes streaked or mottled with darker areas, often paler toward the margin; cap skin peelable when wet; slippery/soapy when moist; smooth; flesh thick in centre, firm, white. GILLS Narrowly to broadly attached, sometimes notched or decurrent; fairly deep; sometimes forking; whitish, at times aging straw-coloured; closely spaced; a large number (up to 15) subgills between neighbouring main gills. ODOUR Not distinctive. TASTE Not distinctive. SPORE PRINT White. STEM To 10 cm tall × 2.5 cm wide; equal or narrowing downward, typically curved; often off-centre; white, discolouring brownish; dry; smooth, longitudinally striate. RING Absent. FRUITING Large troops in compact, fused clumps; on the ground; usually in disturbed areas (typically trailsides); summer, autumn.

EDIBILITY Edible. Despite the common name, not everyone agrees that the FRIED CHICKEN MUSHROOM tastes like fried chicken. There are reports of individual bad reactions, so caution is advised. SIMILAR BLACKENING LYOPHYLLUM (p. 171) is smaller, has a more consistently brown cap, does not usually grow in large clusters, and blackens with age or bruising. The CROWDED WHITE CLITOCYBE (p. 134) also grows in large clusters by pathways. It can resemble a chalky-white FRIED CHICKEN MUSHROOM, but the clitocybe has a sour taste. From the top, a cluster of HONEY MUSHROOMS (p. 164) might be mistaken for FRIED CHICKEN MUSHROOM, but HONEY MUSHROOMS grow on wood (sometimes hidden) and have more reddish brown to orangish to golden colours, scaly caps, and (usually) stems with rings. COMMENTS The *Lyophyllum decastes* group is sometimes divided into separate species on the basis of cap colour. ✦ "Decastes" means "by tens," probably a reference to its clustered growth habit.

Blackening Lyophyllum   *Lyophyllum semitale*

CAP To 8 cm across; convex becoming depressed or broadly umbonate, the margins inrolled when young, uplifted and wavy in age; grey-brown when moist, drying grey, staining dark grey to black where bruised, becoming mostly black; slippery/soapy when moist; smooth; hygrophanous; translucent-striate; flesh thin, white to grey-brown and blackening. GILLS Broadly attached to slightly decurrent; fairly deep; sometimes forking; grey or cream, blackening where handled or with age; closely spaced, with 65–72 reaching the stem; up to 3 subgills between neighbouring gills. ODOUR Unpleasant or farinaceous. TASTE Not distinctive. SPORE PRINT White. STEM To 8 cm tall × 1.5 cm wide; equal, sometimes widening toward base and then narrowing; often off-centre; pale grey, blackening in age; longitudinally striate. RING Absent. FRUITING Single or in groups; on the ground; in conifer or mixedwood forests; late summer, autumn.

EDIBILITY Unknown. SIMILAR FRIED CHICKEN MUSHROOMS (p. 170) are typically larger, do not have the extensive blackening reaction, and almost always grow in fused clusters. COMMENTS *Lyophyllum semitale* and *L. decastes* are 2 closely related species, both morphologically (as we have known for some time) and genetically (as more recent studies have shown). They are part of a group of one or two dozen tricholoma-like *Lyophyllum* species whose exact boundaries require further study. Many species in this group show the tissue-blackening reaction; unfortunately, the black colours can be slow to manifest themselves, especially in prime specimens. ◆ BLACKENING LYOPHYLLUM is a good indicator of PINE MUSHROOM habitat. ◆ "Semitale" means "related to a road or footpath."

Dark Melanoleuca

Melanoleuca melaleuca group

CAP To 8 cm across; convex to flat and then shallowly depressed, but sometimes keeping a broad umbo; dark brown or greyish brown, fading to tan, centre often darker; dry to moist; smooth; hygrophanous; flesh thin, firm, white. GILLS Broadly attached, notched; shallow; whitish to red-brown or cinnamon; crowded to closely spaced. ODOUR Not distinctive. TASTE Not distinctive. SPORE PRINT White. STEM To 8 cm tall × 1.5 cm wide; equal with a slightly bulbous base; sometimes slightly off-centre; paler at the top, darker below; with longitudinal dark brown hairs/fibrils. RING Absent. FRUITING Single or in small groups; on the ground; in forests or non-forested areas (meadows, gardens, disturbed areas); spring, early autumn.

EDIBILITY Edible. But lack of clear species boundaries suggests a cautious approach. SIMILAR *Megacollybia fallax*, which tends to grow on logs, has broadly attached gills and a dry cap streaked with grey fibrils that tends to split as it dries, exposing white flesh. *Melanoleuca cognata* is also found in BC. It tends to have a more tawny/golden cap, whitish to red-brown gills, a slightly fruity or slightly unpleasant smell, and white mycelium at the base. Another BC *Melanoleuca* species, **M. verrucipes**, favours wood chips and buried wood. It is an introduced and weedy mushroom, recently becoming more common in BC, that differs from the other 2 melanoleucas in being all whitish except for blackish scales scattered over the stem, reminiscent of the leccinums. COMMENTS A study of the many species placed in *Melanoleuca* called it a "character-poor genus with many species... differing only in very subtle features... and a morphology strongly influenced by environmental factors." Most BC people in the business of identifying mushrooms resort to calling our most common melanoleuca *M. melaleuca* without trying to tease apart the differences. ◆ "Melaleuca" means "black and white" in Greek, a reference to the cap and gill contrast. "Melanoleuca" means the same thing.

Mycena and Similar

Mushrooms in the genus *Mycena* usually have caps that are two centimetres or less across. Though individually small, mycenas often fruit in mighty troops, contributing their delicate charms to our fields and forests any time of year when there is enough moisture around. Traditionally considered decomposer species, there is evidence emerging that at least some mycenas can form mycorrhizal associations with nearby plants.

More than a hundred species of mycenas have been reported for BC; only 11 species and relatives are given full entries here. Mycenas have white spores, striate conical or bell-shaped caps, and thin, fragile stems that have no rings. Most of them, with only a handful of notable exceptions, wear greys and browns. What they lack in the light of day, however, they make up for at night—more than two-thirds of the species of fungi that are known to bioluminesce are found in the genus *Mycena*. Among these are YELLOWLEG BONNET (p. 178), BLEEDING MYCENA (p. 176), and LILAC BONNET (p. 177). Also, watch for the presence of the mould *Spinellus fusiger* on the caps of mycenas—it will look like a mass of translucent white pins.

Genetic studies indicate that the species that have been clumped as mycenas are a ragtag bunch. New genera have been created (*Atheniella*, for example) to hold former members of *Mycena*, and more new ones will probably emerge.

The mycenas are too small to attract gastronomic attention, but are ecologically important decomposers in forested ecosystems. Diehards who pursue mycenas with taxonomic goals require long hours with eyes at a microscope, heads in the technical literature, and an almost monomaniacal passion for small stuff. Mycologists without this overweening passion content themselves with learning to recognize only a dozen or so mycenas in the field.

GOLDEN EDGE BONNET (*Mycena aurantiomarginata*)

Scarlet Bonnet   *Atheniella adonis*

CAP To 2 cm across; conical becoming broadly bell-shaped; scarlet or bright pink fading to pale orange or salmon; slippery when moist; smooth; translucent-striate when moist; hygrophanous; flesh thin, fragile, coloured as cap or paler. GILLS Narrowly attached, sometimes by a decurrent tooth; pink or creamy or whitish, with a white edge; 12–20 reaching the stem; with 2–3 rows of subgills. ODOUR Not distinctive. TASTE Not distinctive. SPORE PRINT White. STEM To 4 cm tall × 2 mm wide; equal and curved near the base; fragile; hollow; pink or orange, fading to yellow or white, base usually lighter; downy, becoming smooth; the base with whitish fibrils. RING Absent. FRUITING Single or in troops; on the ground or on twigs or decaying wood; generally in conifer forests, sometimes at higher elevations; typically autumn and winter, but at any time of year when conditions are wet enough.

EDIBILITY Unknown. SIMILAR *Mycena monticola* has a more purplish red cap and grows under pines at altitudes over 1,000 m. *Mycena rosella* also exhibits bright pink and salmon pink in its range of cap colours, but its pink gills have a darker red colour along the edges. *Mycena strobilinoidea* (inset photo) has a red cap that quickly fades to orange and/or yellow, but it has yellow, pinkish orange, or pale orange gills that have scarlet edges, at least when young. Its stem can have a covering of small orange hairs (which may disappear, but the base retains orange fibrils). See also the species comparisons on the ORANGE-YELLOW BONNET page (p. 175). COMMENTS "Atheniella" is a reference to the Greek goddess of wisdom and warfare, a nod to her beauty and also to the fact that she's usually portrayed carrying a spear, a good model for these spear-shaped mushrooms. Athena was prominent in Mycenaean culture, and this species was previously in *Mycena*. "Adonis" refers to the handsome mortal who was the lover of the goddess Aphrodite, sister of Athena.

Orange-yellow Bonnet
Atheniella aurantiidisca

CAP To 2 cm across; conical to bell-shaped, the margins tight on the stem when young and upturned in age; bright orange, fading to yellowish on disc and whitish near the margins; smooth; translucent-striate when moist; flesh thin, fragile, orange or yellow. GILLS Narrowly attached or attached by a decurrent tooth; 1–2 mm deep; white, yellowing with age, edges similar to faces; 20–24 reaching the stem. ODOUR Not distinctive. TASTE Not distinctive. SPORE PRINT White. STEM To 3 cm tall × 1 mm wide; equal; fragile; hollow; sometimes more yellow below, white or translucent above; the base often with white fibres. RING Absent. FRUITING Scattered or in dense groups; in conifer forests, especially with DOUGLAS-FIR and pines; any time of year when conditions are wet enough.

EDIBILITY Unknown. SIMILAR The smaller *Mycena acicula* (which is not actually a *Mycena*, but has not yet been definitively reclassified) has a stem that has yellow tones and a cap that is coral-red and that fades along its margins to an orange-yellow or to yellow. The GOLDEN EDGE BONNET (*Mycena aurantiomarginata*, p. 173) has an olive-brown to grey-brown to yellow-brown cap, sometimes with an orange margin, and yellow-orange gills with orange edges. *Mycena citrinomarginata* has a cap that is highly variable, ranging from bright yellow to greyish yellow to olive-yellow to grey. The gills, which are whitish or grey, sometimes have shallow cross-veins and often have edges that are the colour of the cap. See other species comparisons on the page for SCARLET BONNET (p. 174). COMMENTS It is often possible to find patches of the ORANGE-YELLOW BONNET with caps in all stages of the colour transitions. ◆ ORANGE-YELLOW BONNET is primarily a mushroom of southwestern BC. ◆ "Aurantiidisca" means "with orange disc."

Bleeding Mycena   *Mycena haematopus*

CAP To 3.5 cm across; conical to bell-shaped, and often flat, umbonate, and with uplifted margins in age, the margin edge extending beyond the gills and fraying, resulting in a ragged, scalloped, or fringed look (see also the BLEEDING MYCENA photo on the front cover of the book); reddish brown or pinkish brown or dull red, paler toward the margin; covered with minute hairs or granules when young, becoming smooth; translucent-striate; hygrophanous; flesh thin, fragile. GILLS Narrowly attached, sometimes with a decurrent tooth; to 3 mm deep; white, becoming pinkish or pale purple, with darker purple stains in age, margins sometimes reddish; 18–28 reaching the stem; 2–3 rows of subgills. LATEX Blood red, found in flesh and stem tissue when crushed or cut. ODOUR Like radishes, or not distinctive. TASTE Not distinctive. SPORE PRINT White. STEM To 8 cm tall × 3 mm wide; equal; fragile, producing a blood-red liquid when broken or cut; hollow; coloured as cap; slightly hairy, becoming smooth at the top with long hairs at the base. RING Absent. FRUITING Single or clustered; on decaying wood, especially on hardwoods but also on conifers; in coniferous or mixedwood forests; spring, summer, or autumn.

EDIBILITY Uncertain. SIMILAR The slightly smaller and less common *Mycena sanguinolenta* (inset photo) also has a dark red latex, but its gills have dark reddish brown edges and it tends to grow on leaf mould rather than on rotting wood. The greyish brown cap of *M. maculata* (see inset photo on p. 179) can develop reddish stains and blotches, but it does not have a red-orange latex and the gills do not fray. COMMENTS Because of the blood-red latex, this may be the easiest of the widespread mycenas for beginners to recognize. The best way to see the latex is to pick the mushroom and squeeze the base over a lighter surface. Recent research has identified the chemical in BLEEDING MYCENA that is responsible for its colour. It is an alkaloid that is common in marine species such as sponges but rare in terrestrial organisms and that was found to have significant antibacterial properties. ◆ "Haematopus" means "bloody foot."

Lilac Bonnet   *Mycena pura* group

CAP To 5 cm across; convex becoming bell-shaped to flat, often broadly umbonate, sometimes with a wavy and upturned margin; the colouring generally one or more of pink, lilac, purple, blue, grey, and buff, tending to grey or whitish in age; smooth, feeling slightly greasy and sometimes looking shiny when moist, often grooved; translucent-striate; hygrophanous; flesh thin, bluish or lilac and becoming white. **GILLS** Broadly to narrowly attached or slightly decurrent; to 8 mm deep; cross-veined in age; white to pale pink or lilac; 20–25 reaching the stem; several tiers of subgills. **ODOUR** Radish-like. **TASTE** Radish-like. **SPORE PRINT** White. **STEM** To 8 cm tall × 7 mm wide; equal or widening downward; cartilaginous; hollow; cap-coloured, but often paler; small hairs on upper part, becoming smooth, base with long whitish hairs. **RING** Absent. **FRUITING** Single or in troops; on the ground; in coniferous or mixedwood forests; spring, summer, autumn.

    EDIBILITY Uncertain. Chemical studies say that it contains small amounts of the toxin muscarine. **SIMILAR** Among the mycenas, *Mycena purpureofusca* (inset photo) might be a possible confusion. *Mycena purpureofusca*, though, grows on logs, it has a thinner stem, and the edges of its pale gills are lined with dark purple. **BLUEFOOT BONNET** (p. 182), when it wears a bluish hue, is more blue-green. The cap is 2-toned and conical, and it also has a much thinner stem. **WESTERN LILAC FIBREHEAD** (p. 255) has brown spores and a dry, silky cap with radial fibres. The **AMETHYST LACCARIA** (p. 126) is generally a bit larger (stem to more than 10 cm tall), has more widely spaced gills, and has a stem that splits up into fibres when broken. **COMMENTS** The LILAC BONNET, with its thicker stem and wider cap, can seem un-mycena-like. In spite of this, DNA studies have consistently underlined the membership of this widespread mushroom in the genus *Mycena*, though probably as a group that includes a number of cryptic species.

Yellowleg Bonnet — *Mycena epipterygia*

CAP To 2.5 cm across; conical to bell-shaped, sometimes with a small umbo, later becoming flat, the margins minutely scalloped; a range of colours, including mustard yellow, greenish yellow, grey, brown, and white, and sometimes a mixture of these, with possible tints of pink and olive; top skin can be peeled; sometimes appearing dusted at first, becoming smooth; slippery to slimy when moist; translucent-striate; flesh thin, same colour as cap. GILLS Narrowly attached, often with a decurrent tooth; shallow, to 2 mm; white becoming grey, often with pink or yellow tints; 17–23 reaching the stem; the edge sometimes with a separable gelatinous layer. ODOUR Not usually distinctive, but sometimes unpleasant. TASTE Not distinctive or sometimes unpleasant. SPORE PRINT White to pale buff. STEM To 8 cm tall × 2 mm wide; equal; fragile; hollow; a translucent yellow to yellow-green, fading to whitish; sticky/slimy to glutinous; sometimes with fine hairs at top, then smooth, but with more persistent and longer white hairs at the base. RING Absent. FRUITING Scattered or in small troops, sometimes clustered; on the ground; in a variety of habitats, forested land, parkland, and lawns; early autumn to early winter.

EDIBILITY Unknown. SIMILAR The LILAC-GILLED UMBRELLA (p. 140) has a stem that is slightly thicker and often shorter in relation to the cap size, making the fruiting body seem more stout. Also, the cap is depressed rather than having an umbo, and its gills have lilac tints when young. COMMENTS About a dozen different varieties of *Mycena epipterygia* have been described, with differences in colour, smell, habitat, and microscopic characters. Some of these varieties have been put forward as independent species, but consensus is lacking. ◦ The YELLOWLEG BONNET is most often found in southwestern BC coastal areas. ◦ "Epipterygia" means "surmounted by a small wing," perhaps a reference to the protrusions on top of the taller cells separating the spore-bearing basidia.

Toque Mycena   *Mycena galericulata*

CAP To 6 cm across; sometimes conical but usually broadly bell-shaped, umbonate, the margins close to the stem at first but eventually upturned and (sometimes) wavy; radially grooved in maturity; the disc is dark yellowish grey-brown, brown, or grey, then paler toward the margin, often with pinkish tones, and fading to cream or whitish in age; slightly slimy or tacky when moist; smooth; translucent-striate; hygrophanous; flesh thin, pale grey-brown. GILLS Narrowly to broadly attached, often deeply notched with a decurrent tooth; to 8 mm deep; tough, often irregularly shaped, and sometimes forking or shallowly cross-connected; white to greyish white, often with a pink tinge in age; 26–36 reaching the stem; multiple tiers of subgills. ODOUR Variable, from not distinctive to pleasant (like fresh grass, farinaceous, or radishy) to unpleasant. TASTE Not distinctive; or mealy, cucumbery. SPORE PRINT White. STEM To 12 cm tall × 5 mm wide; equal or broader below, sometimes with a twisting groove, often with a rooting base; cartilaginous, tough; hollow; dark grey-brown when young, fading to whitish above, and paler grey-brown (sometimes with yellow tints) below; usually smooth, but with long white hairs at base that reach into the soil or wood. RING Absent. FRUITING Single, scattered, or in small troops, sometimes with bases bundled; usually on decaying wood, but occasionally on the ground; in coniferous or mixedwood forests; commonly in the autumn, but any time of year.

EDIBILITY Uncertain. SIMILAR Smaller caps might be compared to the BLEACH BONNET (p. 180) and the other grey species mentioned on that page. Later autumn and early winter mycenas that resemble the TOQUE MYCENA and that grow on the ground may be *Mycena robusta*. *Mycena maculata* (inset photo) can also have large caps, but it grows in dense clusters on logs/stumps, the caps are usually darker, and the gills and cap develop reddish spots. COMMENTS The TOQUE MYCENA is widespread in BC. "Galericulata" means "helmeted, hooded," a reference to the cap shape. The Canadian equivalent? A toque.

Bleach Bonnet

Mycena leptocephala

CAP To 3 cm across; conical to bell-shaped, often flat with age, the margins pressed to the stem when young, eventually upturned; very dark grey or dark brown, but paler toward the margin, fading somewhat in age to a light grey or grey-brown but retaining darker colours over striations; slightly slimy or tacky when moist; with small hairs when very young, becoming smooth and radially grooved; translucent-striate; hygrophanous; flesh thin, fragile, white to grey. **GILLS** Broadly attached to narrowly attached and notched, sometimes with a decurrent tooth; to 3 mm deep; grey to whitish, the edges sometimes paler; not closely spaced, with 16–26 reaching the stem; 1–2 rows of subgills. **ODOUR** Often of chlorine, bleachy, especially when crushed. **TASTE** Reported as unpleasant, sour. **SPORE PRINT** White. **STEM** To 6 cm tall × 2 mm wide; equal; fragile; hollow; blue-black or purplish black and darker than the cap when young, becoming grey-brown and sometimes paler at the top and darker below; small hairs, becoming smooth at the top and middle and retaining long white hairs at base. **RING** Absent. **FRUITING** Single or in small troops; on decaying wood, most commonly on sticks and cones, or on the ground among needles, mosses, or grass; in coniferous or mixedwood forests; usually autumn.

EDIBILITY Unknown. **SIMILAR** Caps of *Mycena capillaripes*, which can also have a bleach-like odour, are usually lighter than those of the BLEACH BONNET, and the edges of their gills have a slightly darker colour than the gill faces. We probably have at least one other small, dark mycena with a bleach odour in BC. It is usually called *M. alcalina*, and it grows on decaying conifer logs and stumps in the late winter or spring. However, it differs from the BLEACH BONNET in only subtle, microscopic ways, and the relationship of the species description to North American mycenas is under debate. **COMMENTS** BLEACH BONNET is a common decomposer in BC forests. ☙ "Leptocephala" is a Greek compound, with "leptos" meaning "thin, slight," and "kephalos" meaning "head."

Brown Bonnet — *Mycena metata*

CAP To 2 cm across; conical to bell-shaped and flattening, usually broadly umbonate, sometimes splitting in age; fawn brown, pinkish brown, olive-brown, or grey-brown on the disc, buff to grey to whitish toward the margins; with a layer of small hairs when young, then smooth; translucent-striate when moist; flesh thin, fragile, pale to light brown. GILLS Broadly to narrowly attached, sometimes attached by a decurrent tooth; white to cream to pinkish buff; closely spaced; subgills. ODOUR Faint, but sometimes, especially when dry, with a medicinal odour (iodine). TASTE Not always distinctive, can be sour. SPORE PRINT White. STEM To 8 cm tall × 2 mm wide; equal, sometimes curved; fragile; blue-black when young, fading to a pale and sometimes translucent brown; slightly hairy when young, then smooth with a hairy base. RING Absent. FRUITING Scattered or in groups; on the ground; in conifer forests; summer to late autumn.

EDIBILITY Unknown. SIMILAR *Mycena filopes* is difficult to distinguish from *M. metata* in the field, since most of the differences are microscopic. The gills of *M. filopes*, however, do not take on a pinkish tint, the stems are longer in relation to the cap size, and the caps, when young, tend to have a margin that projects beyond the gills and forms a ragged cuff. *Mycena overholtsii* is a grey to brown snowbank mushroom that grows in clumps and clusters at higher elevations and shows profuse conspicuous white hairs at the stem base. Compared to BROWN BONNET, it has a larger cap (to 5 cm across) that is slightly slimy or greasy when moist and a stouter stem (to 6 mm wide) that is reddish in the bottom part. The BLEACH BONNET (p. 180) and the other species mentioned in its entry, and many other mycenas, can have brown phases that cause them to resemble the mycenas in this section. COMMENTS "Metata" means "measured off."

Bluefoot Bonnet
Mycena amicta

CAP To 2.5 cm across; conical to bell-shaped, often with a broad umbo; green-black on the disc to various shades of dark grey, fading to an often 2-toned grey-brown, but there are usually blue or bluish green tints somewhere; with a thick cap skin that can be peeled off; sticky to slimy when moist; with a slightly granular coating when very young, then smooth; flesh thin, white. GILLS Narrowly attached to nearly free; shallow (1–2 mm); white becoming pale greyish brown; closely spaced to crowded; with several tiers of subgills. ODOUR Not distinctive. TASTE Not distinctive. SPORE PRINT White to cream. STEM To 8 cm tall × 2 mm wide; equal, often curved toward base; fragile; hollow; whitish to brownish grey, sometimes with blue tints when young, especially near the base; white to blue hairs, becoming smooth; sometimes with white or blue mycelium at the base. RING Absent. FRUITING Scattered or in small groups; usually on wood, but sometimes on the ground; in conifer or mixedwood forests; spring, summer, or autumn.

EDIBILITY Unknown. SIMILAR While often characterized as a blue mycena, the full-on blue to blue-black versions—typically moist, younger specimens—are the exception, and when encountered, they are usually found on logs. Most typically, the BLUEFOOT BONNET is a grey to brown mycena. See the SIMILAR sections of the BLEACH BONNET (p. 180) and the BROWN BONNET (p. 181) for other small grey to brown mushrooms that might be confused with it. The other mycena in this book with bluish tints, the LILAC BONNET (p. 177), is larger (5 cm wide cap) and has deeper gills, and its stem is cartilaginous and less fragile. COMMENTS The BLUEFOOT BONNET is largely a coastal species in BC. In a 2002 study of second-growth forests on the west side of Vancouver Island, the BLUEFOOT BONNET was one of the most frequently observed decomposer fungi. ◆ "Amicta" means "clothed, covered," perhaps a reference to the layer of cap slime or the fleeting granular coating.

Orange Mosscap   *Rickenella fibula*

CAP To 1.5 cm across; initially marshmallow-shaped, then convex to flat, often deeply depressed in centre, margins usually remaining inrolled or at least downcurved and showing serrations in age; orange to orange-brown and aging buff or pale brown; tacky when moist, but quickly dry; slightly hairy when young, then smooth and often grooved; translucent-striate; flesh thin, pale orange to buff. GILLS Long-decurrent; with cross-veins; whitish; 17–20 reaching the stem; 1–2 rows of subgills. ODOUR Not distinctive. TASTE Not distinctive. SPORE PRINT White. STEM To 5 cm tall × 2 mm wide; equal; fragile; often hollow in age; coloured as cap, sometimes translucent; finely hairy, becoming smooth. RING Absent. FRUITING Single to scattered or in small troops; in lawns, parks, roadsides, most typically in moss; spring, summer, autumn.

EDIBILITY Unknown. SIMILAR *Rickenella swartzii* is similar in size and shape and also favours moss. It is violet-brown to violet-grey at the centre of its cap and pink to light brown on the cap margins, and its stem is darker at the top. There are several small non-*Rickenella* mushrooms with orange tints, depressed caps, and decurrent gills. One of them, *Chrysomphalina aurantiaca* (see inset photo on p. 141), is larger and stouter than ORANGE MOSSCAP, has a moister cap that displays (when young, at least) small hairs on the margin, and has cross-veined gills. It grows on rotting conifers, not in moss beds. LICHEN AGARIC (p. 139) can look quite similar, but it has a shorter stem and is also not closely associated with moss. COMMENTS The ORANGE MOSSCAP and other mushrooms in the genus *Rickenella* typically grow around and sometimes on mosses, though exactly how they interact with mosses—as parasites, symbionts, or decomposers—is not clear. ✦ In BC, ORANGE MOSSCAP appears to be a mushroom of coastal regions. ✦ "Fibula" ultimately derives from a Latin word for "a clasp, buckle, brooch," and the cap can look like a bit of small bronze jewelry dropped on a moss bed.

Slippery Mycena
Roridomyces roridus

CAP To 1 cm across; convex or bell-shaped to flat, becoming depressed in centre; margins often pleated; pale brown on disc, to tan and nearly white at the margins; dry; very finely hairy; striate, becoming radially grooved; flesh thin, fragile, whitish. GILLS Narrowly attached, becoming short-decurrent with age; white to grey or cream; 14–18 reaching the stem. ODOUR Not distinctive. TASTE Not distinctive. SPORE PRINT White. STEM To 3 cm tall × 1 mm wide; equal; elastic; bluish black, then later translucent whitish above, brown below, with a glutinous sheath of slime that sags with age; base hairy. RING Absent. FRUITING In troops; on the ground or on woody debris (e.g., twigs and leaves); in conifer or mixedwood forests; spring, summer, autumn. EDIBILITY Unknown. Only slugs would want to put *this* in their mouth. SIMILAR Beginning in the 1930s, several dozen of the very small whitish decomposers were assigned to the genus *Hemimycena*. The cap of one of the largest of these, *H. delectabilis*, can reach 1 cm, so it could be mistaken for the SLIPPERY MYCENA. However, the *Hemimycena* does not have a slimy stem, it has a bleach-like smell, and its gills develop cross-veining. Another small, dry-stemmed grey-brown to white BC mushroom with a central depression and radial grooves is *Phloeomana speirea*. It grows in wet places, usually in spring, on small twigs, bark, and other wood. The stems of younger specimens sometimes have yellowish greenish tints at the top. A faded-to-white *Mycena aciculata* might resemble the SLIPPERY MYCENA, but *M. aciculata* has larger hairs on the cap and stem (in younger specimens) and a rounded, bulb-like base on the stem. The larger *M. tenax* can also have a slimy stem, but it has a strong farinaceous odour and its gills develop reddish brown spots in age. COMMENTS The genus *Roridomyces* was established in 1994, and the SLIPPERY MYCENA (previously called *Mycena rorida*) was moved into it as the type species. ◄ Spores of the SLIPPERY MYCENA, it is reported, can bioluminesce. ◄ "Roridus" means (appropriately) "dewy."

Marasmius and Similar

Almost all of the mushrooms in this section, no matter what genus they are in now, have spent some time in *Marasmius* or *Collybia*, a pair of often-associated genera of decomposers. The mushrooms in *Marasmius* shared characteristics that taxonomists called "marasmioid." Marasmioid species, they said, were small mushrooms with whitish spores, flat to convex caps, thin flesh, and wiry stems. They were often able to revive successfully after drying out and they shared certain microscopic features. The mushrooms that belonged in *Collybia*, said the taxonomists, had an overall "collybioid" look. Collybioid mushrooms tended to be somewhat fleshy, small to medium-sized mushrooms with whitish spores, convex to flat caps, non-waxy and nondecurrent gills, and slender, ringless, cartilaginous stems.

As the years passed and taxonomists looked in more detail at the microscopic, macroscopic, and genetic features of the collybioid and marasmioid mushrooms, they began to shift them around. Some of the marasmioid mushrooms changed their genus names, but a large number of them managed to stay in *Marasmius*. The ones in *Collybia*, however, did not fare so well. A few of the *Collybia* species went into already-existing genera, but most ended up in a number of new genera that were scooped out of the collybias, such as *Gymnopus* and *Rhodocollybia*. So many species, in fact, were displaced from their home in *Collybia* that only one of the BC mushroom species in this guide, *C. tuberosa*, is still securely in *Collybia*, and it has only kept its place because it is the type species for the genus *Collybia*. (Ironically, this remaining species is not very collybioid, at least in the historical sense of the term—as species were added to *Collybia*, this type species, which grows on dead mushrooms and is really small, turned out to be, well, atypical.) What future studies of DNA and physical characteristics will do with the many mushroom species that used to be in *Collybia* and *Marasmius* is impossible to predict. The same impulse, however, that led the early taxonomists to talk about collybioid and marasmioid motivates us to lump them together in this book.

Those looking in this section with an eye to the dinner table will be disappointed. The FAIRY RING MUSHROOM is tasty, but otherwise there's not much here for a mycophagist to either love or fear. But those looking for easy-to-find mushrooms will be pleasantly surprised—many of the mushrooms in this section are common and abundant in our BC forests.

Fairy Ring Mushroom   *Marasmius oreades*

CAP To 5 cm across; convex to bell-shaped, becoming flat, the top of the bell persisting as a broad umbo, with an initially incurved margin that is often uplifted and wavy in age; light brown to reddish tan to buff and in some cases even to white, the margin fading early to a paler colour; dry; smooth or finely wrinkled; faintly striate when wet; hygrophanous; rehydrating well after drying out; flesh tough, white to buff. GILLS Attachment various, typically narrowly attached or free; white to tan, staining brown with age; fairly widely spaced, 20–28 reaching the stem; with 1–5 tiers of subgills. ODOUR Sweet, sometimes faintly like almonds. TASTE Mild. SPORE PRINT White. STEM To 7 cm tall×5 mm wide; equal and straight; tough; coloured like cap or paler; dry; sometimes finely hairy above, hairier below. RING Absent. FRUITING In groups, often in full or partial fairy rings; in grassy areas, commonly on lawns; spring, summer, autumn.

EDIBILITY Edible. Caution should be exercised about lawn contamination by pesticides. SIMILAR Those harvesting for the table should make sure they know the difference between the FAIRY RING MUSHROOM and the toxic SWEAT-PRODUCING CLITOCYBE (p. 135), since they grow in the same habitat, even side by side. The SWEAT-PRODUCING CLITOCYBE has a white to grey cap, has crowded and decurrent gills, and lacks the pleasant odour of the FAIRY RING MUSHROOM. The BUTTERY COLLYBIA (p. 198), which has a smooth stem and a greasy cap, favours forest environments. COMMENTS This species is a decomposer that frequents lawns and fields throughout BC. ✦ "Marasmius" comes from a Greek word for "drying out," a reference to the ability of some *Marasmius* species to revive when rehydrated. "Oreades" alludes to a Greek myth: an oread is a mountain nymph. The term is perhaps an echo of folk traditions surrounding fairies and fairy rings. (See the essay on fairy rings, p. 188.)

Velvet Pinwheel   *Marasmius plicatulus*

CAP To 4 cm across; bell-shaped or conical, often becoming convex and umbonate and radially furrowed in age, margins downcurved but sometimes uplifted when older; reddish brown, maroon, but also a drabber brown; dry; velvety; faintly striate; flesh thin, buff. GILLS Narrowly attached, sometimes free; deep; cream to buff, sometimes with pinkish tones and developing pinkish brown edges; somewhat widely spaced; with 1–2 tiers of subgills. ODOUR Not distinctive. TASTE Not distinctive. SPORE PRINT White. STEM To 10 cm tall × 3 mm wide; equal; tough, becoming wiry but easily broken; hollow; reddish black, paler at the top, especially when young; smooth, shiny; often with a puff of white mycelium at the base. RING Absent. FRUITING Single or in small groups; in humus and leaf litter; variety of habitats; spring, late summer, autumn, winter.

EDIBILITY Unknown. SIMILAR At first glance, the VELVET PINWHEEL might remind those who find it of a mushroom in the genus *Mycena* (p. 173) because of its small size, habitat, and conical cap, but the velvety surface of the cap (often causing water drops to ball) and glossy red-brown to black stem should quickly lead to the correct identification. Another confusion might be the SUSHI MUSHROOM (p. 190), but the SUSHI MUSHROOM has a fishy cucumber smell, small hairs along the stem, and usually a distinctly paler margin. COMMENTS VELVET PINWHEEL is a fairly common decomposer in BC coastal regions. And a beautiful one—a fresh specimen with beaded water droplets is exquisite. ✦ VELVET PINWHEEL seems to be a West Coast endemic, but it has some equally fetching cousins in eastern North America. ✦ "Plicatulus," derived from the Latin term for "small folds," is a reference to the radially furrowed cap.

Fairy Rings

Ye elves of hills, brooks, standing lakes and groves
. . . .
By moonshine do the green sour ringlets make,
Whereof the ewe not bites, and you whose pastime
Is to make midnight mushrumps, that rejoice
To hear the solemn curfew. . . .
    —Shakespeare, *The Tempest*, act 5, sc. 1

As the Bard notes, fairy rings are rings or partial rings of mushrooms that are formed by the nighttime dancing of fairies or elves. The rings, which often encompass a circle of dead grass (in Shakespeare's words, the sour ringlets where sheep don't feed), can be large—some are 10 metres or more across.

Fairy rings/circles have been well documented at least since the Middle Ages and especially in western Europe. There seems, though, to be some confusion about the ring makers. Some commentators call them elf or pixie rings (or circles). Others attribute them to witches, evidenced by the German name "Hexenringe" and the French phrase "ronds de sorcières." Other accounts highlight the roles of dragons, devils, and vomiting toads.

A man saves his friend from the grip of a fairy ring. *Plucked from the Fairy Circle*, reprinted from *British Goblins: Welsh Folklore, Fairy Mythology, Legends and Traditions* (London, 1880).

One possible source of this confusion is that because they are created at night, few people ever get a good look at the ring makers. And those that do see them, it is reported, often meet a sorry fate. They are forced to join a dance, at times whirling to the point of exhaustion or death (unless rescued by a friend—see woodcut on facing page). And, if they do survive the dance, they sometimes return to the world years later—time spent in the enchanted realm is apparently not equivalent to human time. Should you wish, in spite of the dangers, to investigate a fairy ring under construction, folk wisdom suggests that you should begin by running around it nine times in a clockwise direction.

In our province, fairy rings can be found in both fields and forests. Certain genera and species are more likely to form rings than others. The most common ring-forming mushrooms are puffballs (many species), species in the genera *Tricholoma* and *Agaricus*, and, of course, the edible FAIRY RING MUSHROOM (p. 186) and its poisonous companion, the SWEAT-PRODUCING CLITOCYBE (p. 135). Other species that are known to produce fairy rings are the GREYLING (p. 143), BLUEFOOT WEBCAP (p. 249), BLEWIT (p. 130), POISON PIE (p. 275), and FRIED CHICKEN MUSHROOM (p. 170).

Scientists insist that these rings of mushrooms are the result of the radial growth of a fungal mycelium, producing fruiting bodies at its outer edges and leaving nutrient-poor soil in an expanding centre. This newer explanation seems a bit contrived, in comparison with the extraordinary volume of evidence, accumulated over centuries, attesting to the supernatural origin of fairy rings.

Sushi Mushroom *Macrocystidia cucumis*

CAP To 5 cm across; bell-shaped to conical, umbonate, margins incurved when young, still downcurved in age and sometimes wavy; reddish brown to darker brown or almost black, sometimes yellow-brown, distinctly paler on the margin when wet; moist to dry; smooth (when dry) to silky or velvety (when wet); translucent-striate when moist; hygrophanous; flesh thin, soft, reddish brown to tawny. GILLS Narrowly to broadly attached to almost free, sometimes notched; moderately deep; white to buff, becoming pinkish as spores mature; usually closely spaced; subgills present. ODOUR Usually of raw fish and cucumber together. TASTE Not distinctive. SPORE PRINT Pinkish brown. STEM To 5 cm tall × 3 mm wide; equal or narrowed slightly below, sometimes grooved or flattened; cartilaginous; hollow; coloured as cap, darkening from the bottom up; dry; velvety. RING Absent. FRUITING Single or scattered or small clusters; usually in meadows or gardens, sometimes in openings in woodlands; spring, summer, autumn.

EDIBILITY Unknown. SIMILAR The VELVET PINWHEEL (p. 187) has a smooth rather than velvety stem and more widely spaced gills, lacks the pale band on the cap margin, and does not have a distinctive smell. VELVET FOOT (p. 202) has white spores and grows on stumps or logs. COMMENTS Despite its pinkish brown spores, the SUSHI MUSHROOM belongs to the pale-spored Marasmiaceae family of fungi. ◦ "Macrocystidia" is a reference to the enormous cystidia—sterile cells between the basidia on the gills. It is a feature worth looking at under a compound microscope. ◦ "Cucumis" means "cucumber," a reference to the distinctive smell of this species.

White Marasmius   *Marasmiellus candidus*

CAP To 3 cm across; convex becoming flat to depressed, the margins scalloped or grooved, often all the way to the centre, and sometimes uplifted in age; white, translucent (especially when wet), sometimes becoming buff and/or staining pinkish or reddish with age; smooth or with fine hairs; flesh thin, soft, white. GILLS Broadly attached to stem, often decurrent; many irregular cross-veins; white, staining pinkish or reddish with age; widely spaced; with 1–3 tiers of subgills. ODOUR Not distinctive. TASTE Not distinctive. SPORE PRINT White. STEM Short, to 2 cm tall × 3 mm wide; equal, curved; central or off-centre; tough; white, the base darkening with age from the bottom up to shades of brown or black; dry; smooth or downy; often with a small patch of white mycelium at the point of attachment to the substrate. RING Absent. FRUITING Scattered or in small groups; along wood, berry canes, or ferns; a variety of habitats; year-round.

EDIBILITY Unknown. SIMILAR The smaller *Tetrapyrgos subdendrophora* has a fully lateral stem, stains blue or grey-brown rather than pink, and has a more net-like cross-veining. Some mushrooms in and around the genus *Mycena* (p. 173), especially the white *Hemimycena* species, can look like the WHITE MARASMIUS, but these usually have thinner, straighter stems with a fully central attachment, their stems do not age to a brown colour, and their gills have no cross-veining. From the top, smaller caps of ANGEL WINGS (p. 211) might resemble the WHITE MARASMIUS, but a glance underneath will show the difference: ANGEL WINGS lack stems and have thick gills without cross-veins. COMMENTS The WHITE MARASMIUS, found in BC coastal areas, can be encountered at times of the year when few other mushrooms are around. Hold a cap in front of a light source to see the remarkable beauty of the translucent skin, the thin flesh of the cap, and the meandering veins. ● "Candidus" means, appropriately, "shining white."

Tufted Collybia   *Collybiopsis confluens*

CAP To 5 cm across; convex or bell-shaped becoming flat (though sometimes umbonate), margins turned under at first, later upturned and wavy; reddish brown, especially when moist, fading to pinkish buff or paler, even white, but often retaining darker tones on the central disc; smooth; strongly hygrophanous; flesh thin, white. GILLS Narrowly attached to stem, appearing free in some older caps; shallow (to 1 mm); white or pinkish; closely spaced; with many subgills in multiple tiers. ODOUR Slightly garlic-like in some specimens. TASTE Not distinctive. SPORE PRINT White to cream. STEM To 9 cm tall × 5 mm wide; equal, with stems sometimes fusing at base; fibrous and tough; hollow; coloured as the cap but tending to be paler at top; finely white-hairy; often with white mycelium at base. RING Absent. FRUITING Clustered on the ground; in conifer and mixedwood forests; autumn.

EDIBILITY Edible. But too small and tough to be of much interest. SIMILAR Forest floors in our region sport a number of clustered decomposers with reddish brown to pale caps and stems. CLUSTERED COLLYBIA (p. 200) lacks the white stem hairs, and the basal mycelium tends to crawl up the stems. The OAK-LOVING COLLYBIA (p. 197) is quite similar to the TUFTED COLLYBIA, but also lacks the small white hairs on the stem. WOOD WOOLLYFOOT (p. 193) has long white to yellow-brown lower stem hairs and a peppery taste. The BUTTERY COLLYBIA (p. 198) has a greasier cap (when moist), gills that tend to be finely serrated, and stem bases that often widen downward. COMMENTS Until recently, this mushroom was known as *Gymnopus confluens* and *Marasmiellus confluens*. ➛ TUFTED COLLYBIA is fairly common throughout BC under conifer stands. ➛ "Confluens" means "flowing together," probably a reference to the TUFTED COLLYBIA's clustered habit.

Wood Woollyfoot   *Collybiopsis peronata*

CAP To 5 cm across; convex becoming flat, sometimes umbonate; pale reddish brown, pale yellowish brown, or pale greyish brown with radiating fibrils, the margins downcurved and often lighter than the disc; smooth; somewhat striate when moist; hygrophanous; flesh white to yellow. **GILLS** Free; cream to yellowish to yellowish brown; subgills in multiple tiers. **ODOUR** Can be pleasant, spicy/vinegary. **TASTE** More or less peppery. **SPORE PRINT** Cream. **STEM** To 8 cm tall × 5 mm wide; equal, sometimes with enlarged base; tough; yellowish or coloured as the cap, darker with age; sometimes frosted above and hairy below, and occasionally grooved in age, typically developing conspicuous yellow-brown to white hairs on the lower stem; with white to yellowish mycelium at base. **RING** Absent. **FRUITING** Single or in clusters; on leaves or conifer needles; in forests; summer or autumn.

EDIBILITY Unknown. **SIMILAR** WOOD WOOLLYFOOT is another of the clustered decomposers with reddish brown to pale caps and stems on BC forest floors. See the **SIMILAR** section of the **TUFTED COLLYBIA** (p. 192) for others. **COMMENTS** Until recently, this species was known as *Gymnopus peronatus* and *Marasmiellus peronatus*. ◆ The species has apparently been introduced from Europe, where it is common. WOOD WOOLLYFOOT is primarily found in southwestern BC, and reports of it seem to be increasing in the province. ◆ The caps readily rehydrate after a dry spell. ◆ The mycelial mat can be so dense that large clumps of forest duff come up with a pulled stem. ◆ "Peronatus" means "wearing boots," perhaps a reference to the often enlarged, mycelia-bedecked stem base.

Salal Garlic Mushroom   *Mycetinis salalis*

CAP To 1.5 cm across; convex to almost flat, often radially furrowed and with scalloped margins; pinkish buff, paler in patches and paler at the margins; dry; smooth; translucent-striate, especially when moist; flesh thin, tough; coloured as cap. GILLS Narrowly to broadly attached; white to buff, the margins paler and finely scalloped; moderately spaced; with subgills. ODOUR Strongly of garlic or onions. TASTE Not distinctive. SPORE PRINT White. STEM To 4 cm tall × 3 mm wide; equal to slightly swollen at base; hollow; dark reddish brown to black, but much paler (to almost white) at the top when young; dry; finely to densely hairy (hairier toward base); sometimes with short white rhizomorphs at the base. RING Absent. FRUITING Single or in groups; on dead leaves and stems of SALAL and Oregon-grapes; late summer, autumn.

EDIBILITY Unknown. SIMILAR The almost identical *Mycetinis copelandii*, which grows on the dead leaves of the oak species found in southwest Oregon and California (but may also be in BC), is reported as edible. *Cystolepiota seminuda* **group** mushrooms, which grow on the forest floor but are not confined to dead SALAL and Oregon-grape leaves, have powdery caps that become glistening in age, closely spaced and often pinkish gills, and white to pink stems. COMMENTS This mushroom is listed in some guides as *Marasmius salalis*. ☙ The SALAL GARLIC MUSHROOM is often smelled before it is seen. ☙ Fruiting bodies of this mushroom, like those of many of its marasmioid colleagues, have the ability to dry up and, when rains return, to rehydrate and resume producing spores. ☙ "Salalis" means "of SALAL," an allusion to its habitat.

Tuberous Collybia   *Collybia tuberosa*

CAP To 1 cm across; convex, becoming flat or depressed, sometimes with a small umbo when young, margins curved under when young, later downcurved or flat, and often with pleats; white to cream to buff, the disc often a darker yellowish, brownish, or pink-buff; dry; smooth; flesh whitish. GILLS Directly attached to stem, slightly decurrent in age; white, sometimes with a pink tinge; with subgills. ODOUR Not distinctive. TASTE Not distinctive. SPORE PRINT White. STEM To 4 cm tall × 1 mm wide; equal, sometimes curved; fibrous and flexible; coloured as cap, but often with pale orange tint on the lower part; dry; smooth or with fine fuzz at the bottom from the mycelium; arising from a dark reddish brown or black sclerotium (see below) about 5 mm–1 cm across that resembles a large apple seed. RING Absent. FRUITING Scattered or in troops; on the blackened, rotten remains of larger fungi, or sometimes in soils rich in organic matter; in conifer and mixedwood forests; autumn.

  EDIBILITY Unknown. SIMILAR In our area, there are 3 closely related *Collybia* species that grow on decaying mushrooms. Two of them form sclerotia, which are encased masses of nutrients and mycelia that provide the growing mushroom with food reserves. TUBEROUS COLLYBIA stems have reddish brown or black, apple-seed-like sclerotia at their bases. *Collybia cookei* stems have small, round (but usually irregularly round), yellowish sclerotia at their bases. If you can't find sclerotia after some probing, but you do come across a diffuse mat of white rhizomes, then you probably have found *C. cirrhata*. The BRANCHED COLLYBIA (p. 201) can, when its stems have lost the small branches, resemble TUBEROUS COLLYBIA and the other 2 *Collybia* species, but the grey caps and stems and the persistently black sclerotia (not occasionally reddish, like those of the TUBEROUS COLLYBIA) of the BRANCHED COLLYBIA can still be indicators. COMMENTS "Tuberosa" derives from a Latin term for "swelling, hump," a reference to the sclerotia.

Horsehair Mushroom
Gymnopus androsaceus

CAP To 1 cm across; convex or bell-shaped becoming flat, centre often depressed, radially wrinkled, margins incurved and then downcurving; reddish brown to beige, fading overall with age but the disc often staying darker; smooth; strongly striate; rehydrates after drying out; flesh thin, pale. GILLS Attached to stem, sometimes narrowly; occasionally forked; buff, but sometimes with orange tones; average to widely spaced; subgills in multiple tiers. ODOUR Not distinctive. TASTE Not distinctive. SPORE PRINT White. STEM To 7 cm tall × 1 mm wide; equal, sometimes flattened, twisted; tough and often wiry; pale reddish brown when young, turning to black but often keeping some red-brown at the top; smooth; thin black or dark brown rhizomorphs at the base and in the duff around the bases. RING Absent. FRUITING Scattered or in troops; on leaves, twigs, or conifer needles; in conifer or mixedwood forests, also in boggy areas; autumn or winter.

EDIBILITY Unknown. SIMILAR In habitat and size, HORSEHAIR MUSHROOM can resemble, at first glance, some mushrooms in the *Mycena* genus (p. 173). For those willing to get down on their knees and look closely, the centrally depressed caps, wiry black stems, and black rhizomorphs will readily set the HORSEHAIR MUSHROOM apart. Another look-alike, *Paragymnopus perforans* (until recently called *Gymnopus perforans*), gives off a garlicky odour, does not have the black rhizomorphs around the base, and has a stem with small hairs and a pale or pink apex. *Xeromphalina cornui* can also have a wiry, dark red-brown to black stem, but its cap is more yellow-orange, and its yellowish gills are usually somewhat decurrent. COMMENTS HORSEHAIR MUSHROOM is common in our BC forests but easily overlooked because the small caps shrivel up when they dry out (though rain revives them). ◦ *Gymnopus androsaceus* was previously known as *Marasmius androsaceus*. ◦ Humans may overlook these mushrooms, but birds don't: a 1996 New England study of the nesting materials of 10 different species of birds found that 85 per cent of the nests contained strands of the black rhizomorphs of HORSEHAIR MUSHROOM.

Oak-loving Collybia   *Gymnopus dryophilus*

CAP To 5 cm across; convex becoming flat to a bit depressed, the margins often wavy; a warm yellowish brown or reddish brown when young, in age fading to beige or tan; somewhat slippery when moist; smooth; hygrophanous; flesh white. GILLS Attached and often notched but pulling free and eroding in older specimens; white to pale yellow; closely spaced to crowded. ODOUR Not distinctive. TASTE Not distinctive. SPORE PRINT White or cream. STEM To 6 cm tall × 5 mm wide; equal, but with a noticeable swelling in the base of some specimens; often curved, sometimes becoming flattened; tough and cartilaginous; hollow; cream-coloured to coloured as the cap, but often paler than the cap; smooth; usually with white mycelium at the base. RING Absent. FRUITING Scattered or clustered, sometimes in clumps, on the ground or on well-decayed wood, often in fairy rings; in conifer or mixedwood forests; spring, summer, or autumn.

EDIBILITY Edible. But it causes stomach upset in certain eaters and the stems are tough. SIMILAR Some variations of the widespread OAK-LOVING COLLYBIA can resemble the group of clustered decomposers with reddish brown to pale caps and white spores. See the entry on TUFTED COLLYBIA (p. 192) for comparisons. Other variations of OAK-LOVING COLLYBIA are similar to BUTTERY COLLYBIA (p. 198) and its look-alikes, so see that mushroom's entry for details. The similar *Rhodocybe* (or *Rhodophana*) *nitellina* differs by having a farinaceous odour and pinkish buff spores. COMMENTS "Dryophilus" means "oak-loving," but in our area this species does its decomposing work around many types of trees.

Buttery Collybia · *Rhodocollybia butyracea*

CAP To 6 cm across; smooth, convex becoming flat or with uplifted margins and usually with a broad umbo, margins curved under at early stages; reddish brown becoming light brown or cinnamon with age and sometimes buff, generally darker on the disc; greasy; smooth; hygrophanous; flesh cap-coloured, white, or grey. GILLS Narrowly attached to almost free; edges finely serrated and, especially when older, ragged; white, pink tint in age; closely spaced; with subgills. ODOUR Not distinctive. TASTE Not distinctive. SPORE PRINT Cream to pinkish buff. STEM To 8 cm tall × 1 cm wide; equal, often with an enlarged base; cartilaginous; becoming hollow; pinkish buff when young, cap-coloured with age; sometimes with fine top-to-bottom grooves; lower part usually covered with white mycelium. RING Absent. FRUITING Scattered or in troops; on the ground; in hardwood or conifer forests; autumn.

EDIBILITY Edible. The "butter" in the common name, sadly, refers to the cap texture and not to the taste. SIMILAR The OAK-LOVING COLLYBIA (p. 197) has a less greasy cap (though slippery when moist), and the cap does not have a broad umbo. It also has gills that are less ragged and eroded. The less common *Rhodocollybia badiialba* usually has red-wine tones in its cap and stem, a pungent odour, and a taste that slowly becomes bitter. *Rhodocybe* (or *Rhodophana*) *nitellina* has a drier, less greasy cap, an odour like that of fresh dough, gills with a broad attachment that extend a short way down the stem, and short striations when moist. The FAIRY RING MUSHROOM (p. 186) has gills that are fairly well spaced and a stem with hairs. It also grows in grass, often in fairy rings, and displays rapid rehydration. TUFTED COLLYBIA (p. 192) has non-serrated gills and an equal stem, and typically grows in clusters. *Paralepista flaccida* (also known as *Lepista flaccida* and *L. inversa*) has decurrent gills and a rusty red to tawny cap that often assumes a funnel shape in maturity. COMMENTS The BUTTERY COLLYBIA is a common decomposer in many areas of BC. ✦ "Butyracea" means "pertaining to butter," a reference to the greasy cap texture.

Fragrant Collybia
Rhodocollybia oregonensis

CAP To 10 cm across; convex becoming flat, sometimes with a broad umbo, margins of older specimens wavy and uplifted; red-brown to dark brown at first, fading to pinkish red at the margins, then overall paler; dry, but a bit greasy when moist; smooth; partly hygrophanous; flesh up to 1 cm thick at centre, thin at edges, pale but sometimes with reddish stains. GILLS Broadly to narrowly attached, often deeply notched; edges finely serrated and eroded in age; creamy to buff to pale orange, often with reddish stains in age; closely spaced; with subgills, sometimes in multiple tiers. ODOUR Strongly of almond. TASTE Somewhat bitter. SPORE PRINT White to buff. STEM To 20 cm tall × 2 cm wide; equal above, tapered and curved below, long and often rooting; fibrous, readily splits longitudinally; white but developing reddish stains; dry; smooth, but sometimes grooved in age. RING Absent. FRUITING Single or in small groups; in soil and often near rotting logs; in mixedwood and conifer forests; autumn. EDIBILITY Unknown. The bitterness does not encourage experimentation. SIMILAR *Rhodocollybia badiialba* has a darker red-brown cap that fades more evenly, and it has no almond odour. *Rhodocollybia maculata*, also lacking the almond odour, has a much paler—often cream or white—cap, and perhaps because of the colour contrast, the red-brown spotting on its cap is more obvious. The BROWN ALMOND WAXY CAP (p. 88) shares the almond odour and reddish brown cap of the FRAGRANT COLLYBIA, but the former has waxy gills, a non-bitter taste, and a non-rooting stem. COMMENTS The FRAGRANT COLLYBIA is a West Coast endemic that ranges from California to BC. ☙ "Oregonensis" means "from Oregon."

Clustered Collybia
Connopus acervatus

CAP To 4 cm across; convex becoming flat to a bit depressed, margins incurved at first; reddish brown, fading to brown on the disc and buff on the margin; smooth; strongly hygrophanous; flesh white. GILLS Usually attached and notched, sometimes free in age; white, drying pinkish buff; closely spaced. ODOUR Not distinctive. TASTE Not usually distinctive, but sometimes bitter. SPORE PRINT White. STEM To 12 cm tall × 5 mm wide; equal, usually densely clustered with bases united; fibrous but fragile; hollow; coloured as the cap; smooth, but often with white mycelial threads creeping up from the base; with white mycelium at the base. RING Absent. FRUITING Clustered; on decaying wood, or sometimes on the forest floor; in conifer and mixedwood forests; autumn.

EDIBILITY Uncertain. May be poisonous to some. SIMILAR The TUFTED COLLYBIA (p. 192) is another reddish brown mushroom that can grow in dense clusters, but its stems are covered with small white hairs. *Gymnopus fuscopurpureus* specimens are also clustered and have small stem hairs, but they tend to have deeper purple colours on their stems and caps and stain green with KOH. COMMENTS In older clumps of CLUSTERED COLLYBIA, the buff cap and the red-brown stem can stand in high contrast. ☙ *Connopus acervatus* is also known as *Collybia acervata* and *Gymnopus acervatus*. ☙ The Latin "acervatus," which means "heaped up, together," is probably a reference to the clustered growth habit.

Branched Collybia   *Dendrocollybia racemosa*

CAP To 1 cm across; conical becoming nearly flat or umbonate, sometimes absent; grey to brown, the margins lighter; smooth, silky; flesh extremely thin, coloured as the cap. GILLS Narrowly attached to stem; coloured as cap; subgills present. ODOUR Not distinctive. TASTE Not distinctive. SPORE PRINT White. STEM To 6 cm tall × 1 mm wide; often curved and tapering downward in the lower part; coloured as the cap; covered with tiny white fibrils and, especially on the lower two-thirds, with numerous side branches 2–3 mm long that have enlarged, rounded tips; sometimes arising from a black, wrinkled sclerotium about 5 mm across. RING Absent. FRUITING Clustered; on blackened, rotten remains of other fungi, especially *Russula* and *Lactarius* caps, or sometimes on the forest floor; in conifer forests; autumn.

EDIBILITY Unknown. SIMILAR A mushroom like no other when it has the long side branches sticking out from the stem. These branches, however, can fall off in age, making the mushroom resemble the TUBEROUS COLLYBIA (p. 195) and its relatives. In this case, the BRANCHED COLLYBIA's opaque grey cap and black sclerotia (TUBEROUS COLLYBIA's sclerotia can be reddish brown) may help distinguish them. COMMENTS The BRANCHED COLLYBIA, which appears to be restricted to southern BC, is rare enough to show up on some lists of endangered mushrooms. ◦ The mushroom's numerous side branches are asexual reproductive bodies. ◦ The sclerotia from which the stems arise are not always apparent—some digging may be required to bring them to light. ◦ In Latin, "racemosa" refers to "a cluster of grapes."

Velvet Foot   *Flammulina velutipes*

CAP To 5 cm across; convex becoming flat, sometimes with a gentle umbo; reddish brown to orange-brown to dark brown, often paler near the margins; slimy when moist; smooth; translucent-striate when wet; hygrophanous; flesh white or yellow. GILLS Attached to the stem, often notched; white or yellow-buff; closely spaced; with subgills. ODOUR Not distinctive. TASTE Not distinctive. SPORE PRINT White. STEM To 10 cm tall × 5 mm wide; equal, often curved; tough; sometimes slightly off-centre; orange-brown to yellow-brown, eventually acquiring a dark brown base with a velvet-like layer of dark rusty brown to blackish brown hairs; often with brown rhizomorphs at the base. RING Absent. FRUITING Clustered; on hardwood stumps and logs or sometimes in soils rich in decaying wood, frequently on ornamentals; winter and cooler parts of spring and autumn.

EDIBILITY Edible, but it contains compounds, broken down by heat, that would otherwise destroy red blood cells. Cook well. SIMILAR Though widely harvested and consumed, VELVET FOOT is not a good edible for beginners, since it can resemble seriously poisonous *Galerina* species—the FUNERAL BELL (p. 286), for example, which also grows on logs and has similar coloration. FUNERAL BELL almost never has a slimy cap, however, and it has brown spores and an evanescent ring that often leaves marks on the stem. It also does not have the layer of rusty brown hairs near the base. SHEATHED WOODTUFT (p. 270), another clustered orange-brown log rotter, can sometimes have a semi-slimy cap, but it is brown-spored, has an evanescent ring, and has a spicy, fragrant smell. COMMENTS In its cultivated form, VELVET FOOT is labelled as ENOKI and sold in stores, but the cultivated version, grown in the dark, keeps its white colour and has long stems and small caps. ◆ The fruiting bodies can survive freezing and resume spore production after thawing. Their durability makes them rare winter edibles. ◆ "Flammulina" means "little flame," and "velutipes" means "velvet-footed."

Olive-gold Loglover   *Callistosporium luteo-olivaceum*

CAP To 6 cm across; convex, becoming flat to slightly depressed; dark olive or yellow-brown, becoming more honey yellow with age, occasionally developing deep red stains when dried (or treated with KOH); mostly dry to the touch; smooth or with fine scales when young, sometimes lightly wrinkled; somewhat hygrophanous; flesh thin, pale yellowish or coloured as cap. GILLS Attached to stem, usually notched; yellow to yellow-brown, with reddish marks when dry; closely spaced; with multiple tiers of subgills. ODOUR Mild to sweet/fruity. TASTE Often bitter. SPORE PRINT White. STEM To 7 cm tall × 1 cm wide; equal, often flattening; hollow; coloured as cap but darkening toward the base with age; sometimes weakly dusted with small granules when young, in age bald or streaked with fine fibrils, especially in the lower section; sometimes yellowish mycelium at the base. RING Absent. FRUITING Single, scattered, or in small clusters; on well-rotted conifer wood (logs, stumps), though the wood may be buried; conifer forests; spring, autumn, early winter.

   EDIBILITY Unknown. SIMILAR The brown-spored FIR FLAMECAP (p. 263), another wood decomposer, can have a similar cap coloration, though it does not have olive tints and it usually has a ring or ring remnants. PRUNES AND CUSTARD (p. 166) shares OLIVE-GOLD LOGLOVER's spore colour, but it has gills that are usually a brighter yellow and a cap that is dotted with fine black scales. COMMENTS *Callistosporium luteo-olivaceum* has been collected from many regions of the world. The variation between the collected specimens is large—there may either be more than one species hiding under this name or OLIVE-GOLD LOGLOVER may simply be a species with considerable variation. ◆ "Luteo-olivaceum" means "yellow-olive"—not a bad description of the cap colour.

Douglas-fir Cone Mushroom   *Strobilurus trullisatus*

CAP To 1.5 cm across; convex becoming flat to slightly depressed; white to buff to brownish, but often with pinkish tints, the centre darker with tones of pink, orange, or brown; smooth or wrinkled; faintly translucent-striate at the margin; flesh thin, whitish. GILLS Attached; moderately deep; white to pinkish; usually somewhat crowded; with 2–3 tiers of subgills. ODOUR Not distinctive. TASTE Not distinctive. SPORE PRINT White. STEM To 5 cm tall × 2 mm wide; equal; tough and cartilaginous; whitish above, yellowish orange to brownish orange near base; top hairless, mid-stem downy; rooting base covered in white, yellowish white, to tawny mycelium. RING Absent. FRUITING Scattered or in troops; on decaying cones of DOUGLAS-FIR, rarely on cones of other conifer species; in conifer forests; late summer, autumn, winter.

EDIBILITY Unknown. SIMILAR In BC, the DOUGLAS-FIR CONE MUSHROOM is one of 4 gilled species that we expect to find on decaying cones. *Strobilurus occidentalis* grows on SITKA SPRUCE cones and has a white to grey cap and a stem with more orange tones on the lower half. *Strobilurus albipilatus* has a cap that is greyish brown overall and fades at the margins to a pale yellowish brown. It grows on DOUGLAS-FIR cones and pine cones and on wood, favouring high elevations and often appearing in spring near melting snow. *Baeospora myosura*, found on spruce or DOUGLAS-FIR cones, is a bit larger than the DOUGLAS-FIR CONE MUSHROOM, has a buff to brownish cap with paler margins, a light brown and somewhat hairy stem, whitish mycelial strands at the stem base, and gills that are extremely crowded. See also the comparisons on the SALAL GARLIC MUSHROOM page (p. 194). COMMENTS The first rains of late summer and early autumn can produce a flush of DOUGLAS-FIR CONE MUSHROOMS. They can appear to be growing in the forest duff, but a little digging will usually turn up a (sometimes well-decayed) host cone. ◦ "Trullisatus" means "resembling a small ladle or scoop."

Slime Moulds

Slime moulds, though not fungi, deserve at least a mention in a mushroom guide. They inhabit many of the same environments as fungi, and mushroom foragers often come across them when they are looking for mushrooms. Sometimes these fabulous and fascinating creatures are even mistaken for odd-looking mushrooms.

Like plants, animals, and fungi, slime moulds are eukaryotes—their cells contain a nucleus. They're usually placed in a different eukaryote kingdom, however, with a group of sometimes unrelated, generally unicellular or colony-forming organisms that we call "protists." More than a thousand species of slime moulds have been described worldwide, and doubtless many more remain undescribed.

There are groups of slime moulds that are internal parasites of plants and others that form cool slime nets in the oceans. But most of our commonly encountered BC slime moulds are plasmodial slime moulds, which belong to the class Myxogastria. When their spores germinate, they form a plasmodium, essentially a big bag of cytoplasm containing many nuclei. Even though the plasmodium counts as just one cell (since it has no internal walls), it can grow to one metre across as it moves on or through the soil, wood, and other substrates, eating small organisms (other protists, bacteria, yeasts) and absorbing nutrients. When conditions are right—often involving changes in environmental conditions such as weather or food scarcity—the plasmodium begins to form fruiting bodies. To do this, it moves toward light to find a high, dry, open place in order to better distribute its spores. The plasmodium then transforms itself from the translucent slimy phase to a dry, sometimes brightly coloured fruiting body, which produces large numbers of small spores. The spores, distributed by wind or insects, complete the life cycle.

Laboratory experiments have demonstrated that slime moulds can learn, remember, and transfer information from one organism to another. Scientists had long believed that such functions required complex tissues and organs such as neurons and brains. How these functions are performed at the cellular level is an area of active research.

The SCRAMBLED EGG SLIME MOULD (*Fuligo septica*).

These organisms are important micro-predators and decomposers in forested ecosystems. They're also fascinating and beautiful. If you're wandering our province's fields and forests, seeking mushrooms, keep your eyes open for examples of our marvellous slime moulds.

HYP POP (*Hypsizygus tessulatus*), p. 215.

Pleurotus and Similar

Few of the mushrooms in this "**Pleurotus and Similar**" section are actually in the *Pleurotus* genus, but they have the pleurotus *look*. Mushrooms with this look have gills, but they do not always have stems, and when they do have stems, the stems are usually attached off-centre or at the side of the cap. The caps often grow along vertical surfaces, the reproductive bodies emerging from the wood in stacked rows, one over the other, like rows of shelves. For this reason, we sometimes informally group them with the unrelated polypore shelf mushrooms (p. 378). Like the polypore shelf mushrooms, the mushrooms in this section are all parasites or wood-decay fungi.

In the early days of mushroom taxonomy, naturalists tended to think that mushrooms with the pleurotoid look must be related. We have discovered, however, through careful microscopic studies, chemical work, and DNA analysis, that the gilled shelf mushrooms are really a dog's breakfast of closely and distantly related fungi. In the course of fungal evolution, it seems, many different taxa have learned how to grow in horizontal shelves from the substrate that their mycelium is feeding on, in the same way that many different taxa have learned the trick of living underground and having their spores spread by animals (see the "**Truffles**" section on p. 463).

For the most part, pleurotoid mushrooms excite little interest among gastronomists. While there are no seriously poisonous mushrooms in this section, they are mostly too small, thin-fleshed, and tough to make it to the table. One major exception, of course, is the OYSTER MUSHROOM, which, because it is relatively large and thick-fleshed and fruits in magnificent abundance, is eagerly sought for its savoury umami flavour. OYSTER MUSHROOMS also excite another type of mushroom student—those interested in mycoremediation, the cleaning up of environmental contamination using fungi. Certain species of fungi, researchers have discovered, generate enzymes that can remove persistent organic pollutants, industry byproducts such as textile dyes, and heavy metals from soils and wastewater. The enzymes in the OYSTER MUSHROOM, which is a white-rot fungus that feeds on cellulose and lignin, turn out to be especially useful for mycoremediation projects because they can degrade other long-chain organic compounds such as petroleum (e.g., in oil spills), polychlorinated biphenyls (PCBs), and polycyclic aromatic hydrocarbons.

Oyster Mushroom *Pleurotus ostreatus* group

CAP To 15 cm across; convex at first becoming flat and somewhat depressed, hand-fan-shaped or semicircular or spoon-shaped, margins inrolled when young and becoming wavy and less inrolled in age; white, yellowish, pinkish, or various shades of pale brown; dry, but somewhat greasy when wet; smooth, or finely hairy, especially at the point of stem attachment; flesh thick, firm, tough at the stem, white. GILLS Decurrent if stem is present, and if not, broadly attached to the nub that is at the point of attachment; deep (to 1.5 cm wide); sometimes with cross-veining at the point of attachment to the stem; white to pinkish buff, yellowing in age; crowded; with 2 tiers of subgills. ODOUR Pleasant, sweet, sometimes described as almond. TASTE Not distinctive. SPORE PRINT White or buff or lilac. STEM Absent or, if present, to 3 cm tall × 2 cm wide; equal; firm; solid; lateral or off-centre; white; dry; white-hairy, especially near base. RING Absent. FRUITING Typically in overlapping shelves; on hardwood stumps or logs, but also on wood chips; autumn, winter, spring.

EDIBILITY Choice. Cooked OYSTER MUSHROOMS have the savoury odour and taste of certain broths and cooked meats. They are grown commercially on a variety of rotting media (sawdust, straw, wood chips) and sold in stores, but they can also be grown quite easily at home. Those who seek OYSTER MUSHROOMS in the woods usually look for them in spring, but they can also fruit in the autumn and winter. The caps should be checked for mature beetles in the gills and insect larvae in the flesh. OYSTER MUSHROOMS contain compounds that can damage red blood cells. These compounds can be broken down by heat, so cook the caps before eating. SIMILAR It is important to know how to differentiate the OYSTER MUSHROOM from ANGEL WINGS (p. 211), since ANGEL WINGS have been implicated in some poisoning events and many BC foragers no longer eat them. ANGEL WINGS have smaller, thinner, fully white caps and grow on conifers. The **VEILED OYSTER MUSHROOM** (p. 210) has white to grey fibrils on the cap, a longer stem, and a transient ring. See also the species listed in the **ANGEL WINGS** entry, as well as the ones in the entries for the **WINTER OYSTER** (p. 212) and the brown-spored **FLAT CREP** (p. 214). **COMMENTS** In Interior BC, OYSTER MUSHROOM is typically associated with BLACK COTTONWOOD and TREMBLING ASPEN. It often fruits in the springtime at the same time as morels. In coastal BC, it's found most often around RED ALDER. ❧ The original *Pleurotus ostreatus* species description is based on European specimens. What we have in BC is closer to species descriptions for *P. populinus*, which grows primarily on dead and dying trees in the poplar family, and *P. pulmonarius*, which grows on conifers and other hardwoods, but there is considerable overlap in all of these descriptions, so it is best to think of this as a species group with fuzzy boundaries between the species in it. Fortunately, all species in the group are equally edible and delicious. ❧ OYSTER MUSHROOMS are early-stage decomposers, and there is some concern that they may on occasion act as parasites that kill their host trees. Whether or not they are parasites on wood, they are known carnivores: to obtain extra nitrogen, the mycelium of certain mushrooms in the *Pleurotus* and *Hohenbuehelia* genera paralyze and consume small creatures such as nematodes (roundworms) that try to feed on or near their hyphae. OYSTER MUSHROOMS are the go-to species for mycoremediation, the use of fungi to clean up toxic environments. See the discussion on p. 207. ❧ OYSTER MUSHROOMS are widespread in BC. ❧ "Pleurotus" means "side ear," a reference to the growth habit. "Ostreatus" means "like an oyster."

Veiled Oyster Mushroom   *Pleurotus dryinus*

CAP To 16 cm across, though usually much smaller; in outline round, hand-fan-shaped, or irregular, convex becoming flat and sometimes slightly depressed, margins inrolled when young; white, creamy white, or grey; dry; with fine grey hairs organized into scales when young; flesh thick, firm, rubbery, white. **GILLS** Long-decurrent and cross-veined on stem; white, may yellow with age; closely spaced; with subgills. **ODOUR** Not always distinctive, but sometimes a hint of almond or anise. **TASTE** Not distinctive. **SPORE PRINT** White. **STEM** To 10 cm tall × 3 cm wide, but often much shorter; equal or with narrower base; solid; central or off-centre; whitish, sometimes bruising yellowish; dry. **RING** Membranous; white to cream to grey; disappearing or leaving a ring on the stem and/or tattered remnants on cap margin. **FRUITING** Single or clustered, occasional in shelving groups; emerging horizontally from logs, stumps, or trunks; on living or dead hardwood trees; late summer, autumn, or winter.

EDIBILITY Edible. But sometimes tough. **SIMILAR** The **HYP POP** (p. 215) has nondecurrent gills and always has a central stem, and younger specimens have spots on the cap, not scales. The **SHOEHORN OYSTER** (p. 219) has a brown, moist cap and a downy stem. It grows in mulch and woody debris. VEILED OYSTER MUSHROOMS with very short stems and without rings or ring remnants can resemble lighter-shaded **OYSTER MUSHROOMS** (p. 208). **COMMENTS** The VEILED OYSTER MUSHROOM, while reasonably common in southwestern BC, seldom occurs in large enough flushes to attract table foragers. ❧ Like the related OYSTER MUSHROOM, the mycelium of the VEILED OYSTER MUSHROOM paralyzes and eats small creatures such as nematodes. It is also an early-stage, white-rot decomposer that may play a parasitic role on living trees. ❧ "Dryinus" means "of oaks," and in BC the VEILED OYSTER MUSHROOM is sometimes found on GARRY OAKS.

Angel Wings   *Pleurocybella porrigens*

CAP To 8 cm across; convex becoming flat; tongue-shaped or hand-fan-shaped, margins inrolled and becoming wavy in age; pure white to whitish, sometimes aging cream; dry; smooth; striate when fresh; flesh thin, pliant, white. GILLS If there's a stem, decurrent, and if not, broadly attached to the nub that is at the point of attachment; shallow; white or cream to yellowish; crowded; with subgills. ODOUR Pleasant or not distinctive. TASTE Pleasant or not distinctive. SPORE PRINT White. STEM Generally absent, or as a short, stubby, lateral base. RING Absent. FRUITING Can be solitary, but generally in large groups forming overlapping rows; on conifer stumps or logs; usually autumn.

EDIBILITY Uncertain (see COMMENTS). SIMILAR The OYSTER MUSHROOM (p. 208) has thicker flesh and a darker cap (usually), and it grows on hardwood. *Panellus mitis*, another small, gilled, shelf-forming mushroom, can have the fresh white colour of ANGEL WINGS, but the hygrophanous *Panellus* usually has pink tints on the cap and/or gills and a peelable cap skin. The FLAT CREP (p. 214), when young, can resemble ANGEL WINGS, but the FLAT CREP spore print is brown, and both the cap and gills turn brownish in age. See the FLAT CREP entry for other similar mushrooms. COMMENTS Until the 21st century, ANGEL WINGS were considered a good edible. In 2004, however, they were blamed for 17 deaths in Japan among older people, especially among those with compromised kidney functions. Since then, however, reports of poisonings and deaths have been rare. ANGEL WINGS are common, and commonly consumed, in BC. ❧ What better name than ANGEL WINGS for a heavenly host of brilliant white, often translucent seraphim hovering in a midnight-dark forest? ❧ "Pleurocybella" means "little sideways head," a reference to how the caps grow. "Porrigens" means "stretched out and up."

Winter Oyster

Sarcomyxa serotina

CAP To 10 cm across; flat, hand-fan-shaped, margins inrolled and often wavy and/or lobed when mature; light green to dull green or olive, sometimes with dull violet or bluish tones; slippery when moist, velvety when dry, especially near attachment point; smooth; flesh thick, firm, and rubbery with a gelatinous layer under the skin, whitish. GILLS Broadly attached, sometimes decurrent but usually with a clear line dividing them from the stem region; some forking; often pale orange at first, then cream to pale brownish yellow; crowded, 50–100 reaching the stem; with multiple tiers of subgills. ODOUR Not distinctive. TASTE Not distinctive, or sometimes bitter. SPORE PRINT Cream to yellowish. STEM Absent or, if present, to 2 cm tall × 2 cm wide; lateral attachment; appearing yellow, orange, brown, or cap-coloured; sometimes hairy, with dark scales. RING Absent. FRUITING Single or (more commonly) in overlapping shelves, sometimes clustered; on stumps or logs; typically on hardwoods; late autumn and well into the winter.

EDIBILITY Edible. The WINTER OYSTER can be bitter, and it causes stomach upset in some. SIMILAR As the common name suggests, the WINTER OYSTER bears a vague resemblance to the OYSTER MUSHROOM (p. 208). The OYSTER MUSHROOM, however, does not have green hues on its cap, dark scales on its small stem, or orange tints on its gills. See the OYSTER MUSHROOM entry for other look-alikes. COMMENTS Sightings of the WINTER OYSTER are tinged with both joy and sadness—joy to see its beauty, sadness because its fruiting typically signals the end of another mushroom season. • *Sarcomyxa serotina* was previously known as *Panellus serotinus* and *Hohenbuehelia serotina*. • "Sarcomyxa" means "flesh slime." "Serotinus," a Latin word for "late," refers to the late-season appearance of this species.

Smelly Oyster   *Phyllotopsis nidulans*

CAP To 8 cm along the substrate and projecting out of the substrate up to 5 cm; semicircular or tongue-shaped, convex to flat, margins inrolled when young and often inrolled or downcurved in older specimens, and often wavy and sometimes lobed; pale orange to buff; dry; fuzzy with dense, fine whitish hairs when young; hygrophanous; flesh thin, tough, yellowish. **GILLS** Extending radially from the point of attachment; deep; orange-buff; closely spaced to crowded; with 5–7 subgills between neighbouring gills. **ODOUR** Sometimes mild, but usually unpleasant; described as sulphur-like (rotten eggs), skunky, or sweetish and rancid-oily. **TASTE** Unpleasant, sometimes bitter. **SPORE PRINT** Cream to pinkish orange. **STEM** Lacking, or rudimentary; often with fuzzy hairs where attached to the substrate. **RING** Absent. **FRUITING** Single (rarely), scattered, or in groups, often in rows of overlapping shelves; on decaying wood (logs, fence posts, stumps); spring, summer, autumn.

EDIBILITY Unknown. To paraphrase Jonathan Swift, "He was a bold man that first ate a [Smelly] Oyster." **SIMILAR** The smaller, paler caps of *Panellus longinquus* (also called *Scytinotus longinguus*) may have peach or pink tones that darken to pale orange or pinkish brown in age. It has smooth caps, however, that lack the hairiness and disagreeable smell of the SMELLY OYSTER. *Tapinella panuoides* is another shelf-forming mushroom with orange tones that grows on rotting stumps, but its caps and spore deposit are much browner and its odour is indistinct. **COMMENTS** The stink of this mushroom is a great pity, because the orange colour is due in large part to beta-carotene, the vitamin precursor found in carrots and sweet potatoes. ❧ The SMELLY OYSTER appears to be more common in the BC Interior and is typically found on birch. ❧ "Phyllotopsis" means "looking like a leaf." "Nidulans" means "nesting, lying in a cavity." A leaf nesting in wood is a reasonable description of this mushroom.

Flat Crep   *Crepidotus applanatus*

CAP To 4 cm across; flat, semicircular or irregular in outline, the margins inrolled; white becoming cinnamon; moist; smooth or minutely hairy, especially at the point of attachment; hygrophanous; short-striate when wet; flesh thin, white. GILLS Broadly attached to the point of contact with substrate; shallow; white, becoming brownish as spores mature; closely spaced to crowded. ODOUR Not distinctive. TASTE Not distinctive. SPORE PRINT Brown. STEM Absent, cap attached to substrate by white hair-like strands. RING Absent. FRUITING In rows of overlapping, shingle-like clusters; on decaying wood, more commonly hardwood; spring, summer, autumn.

EDIBILITY Unknown. SIMILAR Both the FLAT CREP and JELLY CREP, *Crepidotus mollis* (inset photo), are common and widespread in our province. The larger JELLY CREP has a cap that, when young, is covered with brown fibrils or small scales, and it is gelatinous in wet conditions (even the gill edges can be gelatinous). The smaller *C. epibryus*, the SNOWY CREP, has a dry, circular, chalk-white (when young) cap. *Panellus stipticus* certainly stands out in the dark: the gills glow greenish white. In the daylight, it differs from the FLAT CREP in having a minutely hairy/scurfy cap, a small, pale stem, a peppery or astringent taste, and whitish spores. *Panellus longinquus* (also called *Scytinotus longinquus*) has peach or pink tones in its pale cap that darken to caramel or pale orange in age, yellow-cream spores, and a strong preference for dead RED ALDER logs and branches. See also the comparisons on the page for ANGEL WINGS (p. 211). COMMENTS The *Crepidotus* species differ from the other mushrooms in this section by having brown, not pale, spores. Before the spore discharge begins to colour the gills, however, they can bear a close resemblance to several of the white-spored shelf mushrooms. ● "Crepidotus" means "slipper ear," and "applanatus" means "flat," both referring to its shelf-like growth habit.

Hyp Pop   *Hypsizygus tessulatus*

CAP To 12 cm across; convex becoming flat, margins inrolled and often remaining downcurved; cream to tan, with pinkish tinges; marbled when young with darker water spots scattered over the cap; dry; smooth; flesh firm, white to pinkish. GILLS Notched at stem juncture, sometimes with a line descending the stem; whitish, with buff to pinkish discolorations; with several tiers of subgills. ODOUR Not distinctive. TASTE Not distinctive. SPORE PRINT Buff. STEM To 20 cm tall × 2 cm wide; equal or narrowed to base, often curved; white; smooth, sometimes with stiff white hairs at the base. RING Absent. FRUITING Typically clustered, several stems sharing a base; on poplars (BLACK COTTONWOOD and TREMBLING ASPEN) and occasionally other hardwoods; autumn.

EDIBILITY Choice. SIMILAR See the comparisons on the page for the VEILED OYSTER MUSHROOM (p. 210). COMMENTS The HYP POP can actually be purchased in supermarkets under the name BUNA-SHIMEJI or BUNAPI-SHIMEJI. It first became available in stores in Japan in the 1970s, and in recent years it has put in an appearance in BC supermarkets. (Be aware, though, that there are a number of different mushroom species that employ the SHIMEJI common name and that product labels are not always helpful.) ⚘ Claims of medicinal effects for the HYP POP have sent chemists in search of unusual compounds that the mushroom might contain, which they have found, though whether these compounds are the effective components and whether the medicinal properties are real are uncertain. ⚘ HYP POP is quite common on BLACK COTTONWOOD in riparian habitats in the Kootenays. ⚘ "Hypsizygus" is a Greek compound for "high yoke," perhaps a reference to clustered growth on vertical tree trunks. "Tessulatus" (which has been spelled in various ways) means "of small square stones, like a mosaic," presumably a metaphor for the spots on the young caps.

Ragged Spruce Rot Mushroom *Neolentinus kauffmanii*

CAP To 8 cm across; convex to flat, margins inrolled when young and then uplifted, sometimes wavy and with irregular lobes; pinkish white, darkening to tan- or wine-coloured with age; dry; with a white cottony sheen of small hairs when young, soon becoming smooth; flesh tough, rubbery, pinkish. GILLS Broadly attached, sometimes decurrent; finely to coarsely sawtoothed; white to pale pink; closely spaced; with subgills. ODOUR Not distinctive. TASTE Slightly peppery. SPORE PRINT White. STEM To 6 cm tall × 1.2 cm wide; equal or somewhat rooting, often curved; central to off-centre or lateral; pinkish white or tan- or wine-coloured; dry; with small white hairs at first, then smooth. RING Absent. FRUITING Single to scattered; on conifer (usually spruce) logs and stumps; in forests; spring, summer, autumn.

EDIBILITY Unknown. SIMILAR Another *Neolentinus* species, TRAIN WRECKER (p. 217), has a whitish to buff to pale yellow cap that is usually studded with darker scales. Its serrated gills bruise brownish or yellowish in age, and its stem has scales and a transient membranous ring. COMMENTS The genus *Neolentinus*, as the name suggests, was hived off from *Lentinus* in the 1980s. More recent genetic analysis suggests that the *Lentinus* and *Neolentinus* mushrooms are not as closely related as the names might indicate. One major difference between the 2 genera is that *Lentinus* species produce a white rot in wood, while *Neolentinus* species are brown-rot fungi. ● In BC, RAGGED SPRUCE ROT MUSHROOM is found in areas close to the Pacific coast, following the range of its usual host, SITKA SPRUCE. ● "Kauffmanii" celebrates University of Michigan mycologist Calvin Henry Kauffman (1869–1931).

Train Wrecker   *Neolentinus lepideus*

CAP To 15 cm across or more; convex to flat, sometimes depressed; whitish or buff to pale yellow, often breaking up into darker brown scales that clump near the centre; sticky when young but soon dry; flesh thick, tough, and dense (almost like a hard rubber ball), whitish and bruising yellow. **GILLS** Usually decurrent, sometimes notched and broadly attached; the edges usually sawtoothed in age; whitish to buff or yellow, bruising yellow or brown or reddish brown; often closely spaced, with about 40 reaching the stem; typically 3 or more subgills between neighbouring gills. **ODOUR** Fragrant, sometimes of anise. **TASTE** Not distinctive. **SPORE PRINT** White. **STEM** To 10 cm tall × 3 cm wide; sometimes narrowed at base; tough; coloured as cap, but bruising reddish brown in age; hairy above, and hairy to scaly below with ridges of darker tissue flaring up and out. **RING** Membranous; on the top third of the stem; whitish; may disappear with age. **FRUITING** Scattered or (more commonly) in large shelving groups; on rotting conifer and occasionally hardwood logs and stumps, but also on milled and treated wood; summer, autumn.

EDIBILITY Edible. Some claim tasty, if picked when young and thoroughly cooked. Any specimens growing on treated wood should be avoided. **SIMILAR** The **RAGGED SPRUCE ROT MUSHROOM** (p. 216) often has a slightly peppery taste and a cap without the large, dark scales and with more red and pink tones. A large **TRAIN WRECKER** might be mistaken for *Neolentinus ponderosus* (previously known as *Lentinus ponderosus*), a higher-elevation, ponderosa pine–preferring relative that has no ring and lacks (except occasionally in old age) the flaring ridges of darker tissue on the lower stem. Before the dark scales have developed, the **TRAIN WRECKER** can also resemble the **VEILED OYSTER MUSHROOM** (p. 210) and the other mushrooms listed on that page. **COMMENTS** The **TRAIN WRECKER**, a brown-rot decomposer, gets its common name from the way it is often found consuming construction timber, including railroad ties and other creosoted wood. ❧ The Greek "lepideus" means "scaly."

Bear Lentinellus
Lentinellus ursinus group

CAP To 8 cm along the substrate × 8 cm projecting from the substrate; semicircular but often lobed and irregular, convex becoming flat or slightly depressed, margins inrolled when young; various shades of brown, often darker where handled or in age, paler near the margin; densely hairy/velvety toward the cap centre, with white and then brown hairs, the margin often with radial wrinkles; flesh thin (to 3 mm), firm, cream to pale brown. GILLS Decurrent if stem base is present, otherwise connected to the point of attachment; medium-deep (to 5 mm); the edges usually finely or coarsely sawtoothed and ragged; buff to pinkish cinnamon; sometimes closely spaced. ODOUR Not always distinctive, but also described as fruity or fragrant. TASTE Usually peppery, sometimes bitter. SPORE PRINT White. STEM Absent or rudimentary and lateral. RING Absent. FRUITING Scattered or (more commonly) in large shelving groups; on rotting and often on debarked conifer and hardwood logs; spring, autumn, winter.

EDIBILITY Not edible. SIMILAR None of the *Lentinellus* species in BC are very common, and those that are found in the province are best distinguished by microscopic analysis. *Lentinellus flabelliformis* tends to have smaller caps than the BEAR LENTINELLUS and a cap surface that is usually smooth (but if hairy, then with whitish hairs). *Lentinellus micheneri* tends to have more developed and longer stems that are often centrally attached to the caps. If the hairy surfaces of BEAR LENTINELLUS caps have been washed away, then the brownish caps can resemble large FLAT CREP (p. 214) and its look-alikes. If the hairy surface has been washed away *and* the caps are lighter, OYSTER MUSHROOMS (p. 208) and ones that look like these might be a source of confusion. COMMENTS In the Kootenays, BEAR LENTINELLUS is typically found on BLACK COTTONWOOD in riparian habitats. ◆ "Lentinellus" means "small *Lentinus*" (a mushroom genus), and "ursinus" means "relating to bears," perhaps a reference to the brown, hairy caps.

Shoehorn Oyster   *Hohenbuehelia petaloides*

CAP To 7 cm across or greater; sometimes hand-fan-shaped when emerging horizontally, when upright more funnel- or shoehorn-shaped, the margins tightly inrolled, usually remaining downcurved in age and often wavy; brown, fading to tan or grey-brown, centre area often darker; moist and often slippery; with a white bloom when young, then smooth and rubbery; flesh tough, pliant, with a gelatinous layer that is most visible when wet, and whitish to grey. GILLS Long-decurrent; shallow, especially near stem attachment; edges sometimes fringed, wavy when dry; white with grey or cream tints; crowded. ODOUR Not distinctive. TASTE Not distinctive. SPORE PRINT White. STEM To 4 cm tall × 2.5 cm wide; off-centre or lateral; white, sometimes with a grey or brownish tinge; with small white hairs and often furrowed or fluted; often with tufts of white mycelium at the base. RING Absent. FRUITING In large groups and clustered; typically on buried, decayed wood, sawdust, mulch, or other built environments, less commonly in natural habitats; autumn.

EDIBILITY Edible. But chewy. SIMILAR The OYSTER MUSHROOM (p. 208) has a paler cap, gills that are deeper and more widely spaced, and a thicker flesh layer. Also, the SHOEHORN OYSTER seldom grows, as the OYSTER MUSHROOM does, shelf-like on logs. For other look-alikes, see the comparisons in the entry for the OYSTER MUSHROOM. The VEILED OYSTER MUSHROOM (p. 210) has a dry, white cap and is usually found on living and dead hardwoods. COMMENTS Like the OYSTER MUSHROOM, the SHOEHORN OYSTER traps and chows down on nematodes in the soil. ➤ The long scientific name is often butchered—in-the-know mushroom people (in BC, at least) usually pronounce it something like *hoe-in-byoo-*HEEL*-ee-uh peta-*LOID*-dees.* ➤ "Hohenbuehelia" honours Ludwig Samuel Joseph David Alexander Heufler zu Rasen und Perdonegg, Freiherr von Hohenbühel, a 19th-century Austrian mycologist in need of a serious name shave, and "petaloides" means "like a leaf."

Split Gill   *Schizophyllum commune* group

CAP To 4 cm across; hand-fan-shaped, margins inrolled, lobed; white to grey; dry; coarsely hairy; flesh thin, leathery, white to grey. **GILLS** Radiating from the point of attachment; grooved lengthwise into a pair of gill-like surfaces that can roll back in dry weather to conserve moisture; white to grey; somewhat widely spaced. **ODOUR** Some say pleasant, others sour. **TASTE** Not distinctive. **SPORE PRINT** White. **STEM** Absent, or short (to 7 mm tall × 3 mm wide); coloured as cap. **RING** Absent. **FRUITING** Scattered, often in clusters or rows; on planks, sticks, logs, hardwood preferentially, but also conifer wood; all seasons.

    EDIBILITY Edible. Too tough, though, to be of much interest. **SIMILAR** See the **FLAT CREP** (p. 214) entries for similar mushrooms. **COMMENTS** There are pockets around the world (Mexico and northeast India, for example) where SPLIT GILL is consumed. This mushroom, unfortunately, also eats us—it has been found, even with fruiting bodies, in people's lungs, nasal cavities, and brain tissue (yecch!). ✎ Thanks to a team at Harvard University, who studied the SPLIT GILL for more than 20 years, we know more about this mushroom, especially about its mating habits, than almost any other fungal species. ✎ A recent study conducted at several sites around the world suggests that, each hour, more than a dozen SPLIT GILL spores rain down on every square metre of land. The same study, however, used DNA analysis to discover that even though these spores came from what appeared to be, based on morphological analysis, a single worldwide species, the SPLIT GILLS around the world were actually divided into several cryptic species. ✎ SPLIT GILL occurs on every continent except Antarctica—perhaps the most widespread mushroom in the world. ✎ "Schizophyllum" means just what the common name says, "split gill." "Commune" means "common."

Pink-spored Gilled

Most pink-spored mushrooms are assigned to the giant *Entoloma* genus. With nearly 1,500 described species, *Entoloma* is second only to *Cortinarius* in the sheer number of mushroom species stuffed into a single genus.

One feature is shared by almost every *Entoloma* species: having pinkish brown, angular spores. Other features are widely shared within the genus but are not as universal. Most of the *Entoloma* species, for example, have smooth caps and have traditionally been considered as ground-dwelling decomposers. (There is, however, mounting evidence that many of them may have symbiotic associations with roots of plants in the rose family.) Other features, however, vary so widely that some taxonomists have tried to separate *Entoloma* into more tightly defined genera. The *Nolanea* and *Leptonia* species found here are a case in point. Though both genus names have long histories of use, many taxonomists, regarding the weak evidence that these genera represent well-defined groups, have chosen to return the species in these two genera to the genus *Entoloma*. Large-scale genetic studies of *Entoloma* species are currently being published, however, and they are helping to clarify the issues. One day, with some shifting around of a few of the traditional *Nolanea* and *Leptonia* species into new genera, it may be possible to justify some of the long-standing genus groups within the larger *Entoloma* collection. In hopes of this outcome, we have chosen in this guide to retain the traditional names.

Not every mushroom species with pinkish brown spores is an *Entoloma*. Of the six main entries in this section, one of them, the DEER MUSHROOM (p. 222), is in the *Pluteus* genus, a group of about 300 smooth-spored species that, though they have pinkish brown spores, are related to species in the white-spored *Amanita* genus. We have also seen other non-*Entoloma* species in this book with some pink hues (usually a lighter pink) in their spore prints: the BLEWIT (p. 130), the BUTTERY COLLYBIA (p. 198), the ANISE CLITOCYBE (p. 132), and the SUSHI MUSHROOM (p. 190).

The *Clitopilus* species listed and mentioned in this section, though technically part of the same family as *Entoloma*, belong to a nicely self-contained and consistent group. Almost all taxonomists describe them as *Clitopilus* rather than *Entoloma*.

There are two harvested edibles in this section, the DEER MUSHROOM (p. 222) and the SWEETBREAD MUSHROOM (p. 223). *Entoloma*, however, has a number of toxic species, so pink-spored mushrooms should be consumed with caution.

Deer Mushroom · *Pluteus cervinus* group

CAP To 12 cm across; hemispheric or bell-shaped becoming more shallowly convex or flat, sometimes with a broad umbo or sometimes depressed, often wrinkled when young; brown to grey-brown, often darker brown when young; dry, but somewhat greasy when wet; smooth or with radial fibrils, occasionally with raised fibrils at centre; flesh thick, soft, white. **GILLS** Free; deep (to 7 mm or more); white, becoming pinkish brown as spores develop, edges sometimes with small white tufts; closely spaced or crowded. **ODOUR** Not distinctive. **TASTE** Not distinctive. **SPORE PRINT** Pinkish brown. **STEM** To 14 cm tall × 2 cm wide; roughly equal or widening downward; whitish; dry; often with longitudinal brown or grey-brown striations. **RING** Absent. **FRUITING** Single to scattered; on decaying wood; year-round, but mostly in autumn.

EDIBILITY Edible but not incredible. **SIMILAR** A few pink-spored, toxic *Entoloma* species can vaguely resemble the DEER MUSHROOM, but they do not grow on wood. ***Pluteus atromarginatus***, which is found on woody debris and wood chips, has a dark brown cap and gills with dark edges. Several other *Pluteus* species have been found in BC, but they are rare compared with the ubiquitous DEER MUSHROOM. **COMMENTS** A 2014 study found that almost all samples of the DEER MUSHROOM from the US Pacific Northwest and southern coastal BC matched perfectly with *P. exilis* (a member of the *P. cervinus* group), a mushroom first described from California in 1989. More recent sequencing work in Washington, however, found the DEER MUSHROOMS to be *Pluteus cervinus* itself. ⚬ "Pluteus" comes from a Latin term for "fence, board, shield." "Exilis" means "slender," a reference to the stem width relative to its height.

Sweetbread Mushroom · *Clitopilus prunulus* group

CAP To 10 cm across; convex becoming flat or depressed, sometimes bumpy, margins inrolled (and often remaining so in age) and often wavy or lobed; white or grey, sometimes with beige tones; dry; smooth but can feel finely felted, like microfibre cloth; flesh thin, white. **GILLS** Usually decurrent, sometimes broadly attached; shallow; white or grey, becoming pinkish as spores develop; closely spaced; subgills in up to 4 tiers. **ODOUR** Strongly farinaceous, some sniffers comparing it to the smell of cucumber or watermelon rind. **TASTE** Not distinctive. **SPORE PRINT** Brownish pink or salmon. **STEM** To 8 cm tall × 2 cm wide; equal, often widening downward and then tapering at base, at times curved; solid; with central or off-centre attachment to cap; coloured as the cap; dry; smooth or finely downy. **RING** Absent. **FRUITING** Single or in groups, sometimes in fairy rings; on the ground; in conifer or hardwood forests or in grass; late summer, autumn.

EDIBILITY Choice. But be certain of identification. **SIMILAR** The SWEETBREAD MUSHROOM is not a mushroom for mycological beginners because it bears a strong resemblance to the toxic **SWEAT-PRODUCING CLITOCYBE** (p. 135). The clitocybe, however, lacks a farinaceous smell and has white spores. **COMMENTS** Genetic sequencing suggests that many of our BC SWEETBREAD MUSHROOMS may actually be *Clitopilus cystidiatus*, which differs from *C. prunulus* in microscopic features. ✷ The chemical causing the strong farinaceous odour in the SWEETBREAD MUSHROOM is one of the odour chemicals in cucumbers. ✷ SWEETBREAD MUSHROOM often shows evidence of small bite marks on cap edges but is rarely consumed, suggesting it has been tasted and rejected. When the cap is broken, it produces a compound that deters feeding by the PACIFIC BANANA SLUG (*Ariolimax columbianus*). ✷ This mushroom is valued even by those who don't eat it because it is considered an indicator species for the delectable KING BOLETE (p. 318).

Midnight Entoloma — *Entoloma medianox* group

CAP To 15 cm across; convex becoming flat or nearly so, often broadly umbonate, margins slightly downcurved but may be upturned in age; bluish grey or purplish blue, sometimes almost black, paler toward the margins and sometimes with blotches, colours fading in age; slimy/sticky when moist; smooth but at times with meandering radial wrinkles; flesh thick, firm, white, sometimes with purplish tints under cap. **GILLS** Broadly attached, usually notched, sometimes so deeply they appear free; moderately deep (4 mm–1 cm); sometimes eroded; whitish or tinged with the cap colour, becoming pinkish as spores mature; closely spaced; frequent subgills. **ODOUR** Farinaceous or not distinctive. **TASTE** Not distinctive. **SPORE PRINT** Pinkish brown. **STEM** To 12 cm tall × 3 cm wide; equal or narrowed to a point at base; solid; upper part is cap-coloured, base is white or stained yellow or orange; dry; smooth or silky from fine longitudinal striations and sometimes with small white fibrils on upper part. **RING** Absent. **FRUITING** Single, scattered, or in groups; on the ground; under conifers or hardwoods; autumn.

EDIBILITY Edible. But the fact that it is an *Entoloma* and that the species definitions are in transition suggests caution. **SIMILAR** This robust *Entoloma*, a species recorded in BC only along the south coast, sometimes reminds those who first encounter it of the **STREAKED TRICH** (p. 157), but the tricholoma has white spores and a white stem. **COMMENTS** You may hear MIDNIGHT ENTOLOMA referred to as *E. bloxamii* or *E. madidum*. Molecular studies, however, have failed to establish the European *E. bloxamii* or *E. madidum* on the West Coast of North America. To date, almost all US West Coast and BC specimens that have been sequenced have turned out to be the single species that was given the name *E. medianox* in 2015. ❧ "Entoloma" means "inner hem"—a reference to the turned-under margin in some entolomas. "Medianox" means "midnight," an allusion to the MIDNIGHT ENTOLOMA's dark blue colour.

Rosy Entoloma   *Entoloma rhodopolium* group

CAP To 12 cm across; convex to bell-shaped, becoming flat to slightly depressed, often broadly umbonate, margins wavy or lobed, sometimes splitting and upturned in age; greyish brown or yellowish brown, paler in age and when dry; dry to slightly sticky; smooth; in some forms the margins translucent-striate; hygrophanous; flesh moderately thick (to 6 mm), firm, coloured as cap. GILLS Broadly to narrowly attached, and notched; shallow to moderately deep (to 8 mm); whitish or tinged with the cap colour, becoming pinkish as spores mature; either closely or somewhat widely spaced. ODOUR Sometimes mildly farinaceous. TASTE Not distinctive. SPORE PRINT Pink or salmon. STEM To 12 cm tall × 1.5 cm wide; equal or sometimes broadened at top, (rarely) middle, or base; becoming hollow; whitish, sometimes tinged grey or pale brown; dry; with fine longitudinal striations; often with a white basal mycelium. RING Absent. FRUITING Single, scattered, or in groups, and sometimes clustered; on the ground; usually under hardwoods; late summer, autumn.

EDIBILITY Poisonous. SIMILAR A large number of *Entoloma* species look like the ROSY ENTOLOMA. One of them, *E. sericatum*, has a darker brown cap and a bleach-like odour when first picked that rapidly becomes farinaceous. COMMENTS In the 1990s, a Washington State mycologist, looking mainly at morphology and habitat, was able to describe 6 distinct forms of the ROSY ENTOLOMA. He stopped short of calling them species, but chances are good that multiple species huddle inside the name *E. rhodopolium*. When the Japanese varieties of the species were subjected to genetic analysis in the 2010s (a more pressing need in Japan, where the ROSY ENTOLOMA is a major poisoner), 3 new species were the result, none of which were the same as the European *E. rhodopolium*. Clearly, the whole BC and US Pacific Northwest group of this *Entoloma* requires further study. ❧ "Rhodopolium" means either "grey-pink" or "shining pink."

Blue-edge Pinkgill   *Leptonia serrulata*

CAP To 3.5 cm across; convex becoming flat or depressed, margins inrolled when young and later becoming flat and sometimes uplifted and wavy; with radial bluish black fibrils and scales that fade to bluish grey, the scales and fibrils set on a background of greyish brown; dry; densely hairy with erect fibrils, remaining so on disc but the rest of cap becoming fine-scaly and the margin eventually becoming bald or with pressed-down fibrils; often striate; slightly hygrophanous; flesh thin, fragile, grey or bluish. GILLS Narrowly attached and notched, often with a slightly decurrent tooth; shallow to moderately deep (3–6 mm); edges finely sawtoothed; dirty white becoming bluish grey, edges a contrasting dark blue-black; closely spaced to widely spaced. ODOUR Sometimes slightly farinaceous. TASTE Not distinctive. SPORE PRINT Pink or pinkish brown. STEM To 7 cm tall × 5 mm wide; equal, usually widened at base; becoming hollow; bluish black, greyer with age; dry; upper part sometimes finely flecked, lower part smooth or longitudinally striate; with white mycelium at the base. RING Absent. FRUITING Single or in groups; on the ground, usually in rich humus; spring (in the mountains), summer, autumn.

EDIBILITY Unknown. SIMILAR There are many blue *Leptonia* species, and they can be relatively easy to identify as a genus. Getting the identification to the species level, however, often means intense work with monographs and microscopes. The BLUE-EDGE PINKGILL has been included in this guide because it has an unusual feature that makes it field-recognizable: the darker blue edges on sawtoothed gills. COMMENTS Some references prefer to call this species *Entoloma serrulatum* because DNA studies do not place the BLUE-EDGE PINKGILL in the same group with other leptonias. ◆ "Leptonia" means "slender"; "serrulata" means "finely toothed," a description of the gill edges.

Nippled Brown Pinkgill   *Nolanea holoconiota*

CAP To 8 cm across; conical to convex with a pointy umbo, expanding to flat but often keeping a sharpish point, margins incurved or downcurved when young and usually eroded and/or cracked with age; pale brown or yellow-brown, becoming pale orange or yellow, often with greyish tints; dry; smooth, sometimes wrinkled or with shiny flecks; translucent-striate except on the disc when moist; hygrophanous with umbo fading faster with drying so that it appears to be bicoloured; flesh thin, fragile, coloured as cap. GILLS Broadly to narrowly attached; moderately deep (to 7 mm); white, becoming pinkish brown as spores develop; closely spaced to somewhat widely spaced; with subgills. ODOUR Not distinctive. TASTE Not distinctive or sometimes slightly bitter. SPORE PRINT Pinkish brown. STEM To 10 cm tall × 1 cm wide; usually equal, sometimes enlarged at base; fragile, easily splitting; becoming hollow; light brown, pale yellow, or orangish; dry; smooth or longitudinally striate, sometimes hairy in the upper half; with abundant white mycelium at base. RING Absent. FRUITING Single to scattered; on the ground; usually under conifers, typically at higher elevations; spring, summer, and early autumn, rarely late autumn.

EDIBILITY Unknown. SIMILAR *Nolanea* species can be difficult to reliably distinguish in the field. Two others that might be recognized in the field: *N. verna*, a spring and early-summer mushroom that also has a pointy umbo and tends to have a darker cap and a uniform colour as it dries; *N. sericea*, which fruits in grassy areas more than in woods and has a broader umbo, a very dark brown cap, greyish brown gills, and a strongly farinaceous odour. COMMENTS *Nolanea holoconiota* is listed in some references as *Entoloma holoconiotum*.

Brown-spored Gilled

BC's brown-spored gilled mushrooms include some fairly distinctive, closely related groups, such as those in the genera *Agaricus* and *Cortinarius*. They also number in their clan a heterogeneous assemblage of the little brown mushrooms (LBMs) that can be damnably difficult to put a name to.

When working with brown-spored gilled mushrooms, it is often important to determine just which shade of brown a spore print is—is it yellow-brown, cinnamon brown, rusty brown, or chocolate brown? Some experience may be required to become familiar with these spore shades.

In this group we've described four reasonably cohesive groups and two catch-all groups to contain the remainder:

- If your large, fleshy field or forest mushroom on the ground has free gills that start out white or pinkish and end up dark brown because of the chocolate-brown spores, and especially if the mushroom has a ring, look for it in "**Agaricus**" (p. 229).
- If your medium to large forest mushroom on the ground has a rusty brown spore print and a cobweb-like partial veil that covers the gills and usually leaves fibrils on the stem that are often rusty-coloured from the spores, and if, especially, it fruits later in the autumn, check out "**Cortinarius**" (p. 239).
- If your small- to medium-sized woodland mushroom grows on the ground, sports muted colours (usually white to yellow-brown to brown), has a cap that is conical when young and flattened in age (though often with an umbo) and that is smooth or (often) has radial fibres, has no ring, and (often) smells of corn silk or semen, scan the "**Inocybe and Similar**" section (p. 253).
- If your medium to large forest mushroom is fruiting on dying trees or logs or on the ground with buried wood, and if it has a dirty brown to rusty brown spore print, look in "**Gymnopilus and Pholiota**" (p. 261).
- And if none of the above descriptions fits your brown-spored gilled mushroom, look in "**Other Big Brown-spored**" (caps are usually more than five centimetres in diameter) (p. 271) or "**Other Little Brown-spored**" (caps are usually less than five centimetres in diameter) (p. 281).

Agaricus

BC species in the *Agaricus* genus tend to be large, fleshy mushrooms that have distinctive chocolate-coloured spores. Agaricus gills, which are generally free from the stems (or nearly so), are usually white or cream-coloured or pink when young, but they turn the same dark chocolate-brown shade when the maturing spores begin to influence the gill colour. Most of the mushrooms in the genus also have a ring, the remnants of a partial veil that covered the gills when the mushrooms were young, though in some agaricuses, such as the MEADOW AGARICUS (p. 236), the ring quickly disappears.

Worldwide, mycologists have identified about 300 different *Agaricus* species. In BC, we have at least 30 of these, but we probably have a number of cryptic species that have not been described or received names. The most definitive study of North American *Agaricus* species, by Richard Kerrigan (*Agaricus of North America*, New York Botanical Garden Press, 2016), notes that "there may be cases where the very best solution presently available will be to say that 'this specimen is very close to…' and if you learn to live with that, I expect that you will be happier while studying *Agaricus*."

Taken as a whole, *Agaricus* features may be more familiar to people in North America than any other genus in this book, for the simple reason that the genus includes the popular store-bought BUTTON MUSHROOMS (*A. bisporus*—a species whose colour and size variations also encompass CREMINI MUSHROOMS and PORTOBELLOS). Mushrooms grown for sale in stores, unless wild-harvested, tend to be decomposers because they are readily grown on available decomposing media, and the BUTTON MUSHROOM is no exception—it is grown at one stage of its life on horse manure. As expected, the agaricuses in this book are, like the BUTTON MUSHROOM, also decomposers.

Many good edibles are found in this genus, but there are also ones to avoid. The nasty ones, which mushroom guides often designate as the "lose-your-lunch bunch," may not be a threat to life, but they can give you a bad night. Applied across the whole range of BC mushrooms, shorthand rules that distinguish edibles from inedibles are notoriously inaccurate, but there is a rule that works fairly well *if* you know that a mushroom is an agaricus: the poisonous ones give off a tarry, creosote- or phenol-like smell, especially when the bases are cut, scratched, or crushed. By contrast, edible ones have more pleasant aromas—many of them an almondy smell.

The Prince   *Agaricus augustus*

CAP To 30 cm across; spherical or marshmallow-shaped, becoming convex (but often flatter around the disc) and eventually flat with uplifted and sometimes wavy margins; background colour is initially white and then yellowish or buff, often described as tawny or golden; covered with pressed-down brown fibrils that darken and become uplifted in age; dry; bruising yellow to orange; flesh thick (up to 3 cm), firm, white, sometimes bruising slightly yellow next to cap. GILLS Free; deep (to 2 cm); white becoming greyish (rarely pinkish grey) and then chocolate brown as spores mature; closely spaced. ODOUR Sweet, like anise or almonds. TASTE Not distinctive. SPORE PRINT Dark chocolate brown. STEM To 25 cm tall × 5 cm wide; usually equal, sometimes widened slightly below; white, with yellow tints in age or with bruising; smooth above ring, scaly below ring. RING Large, flaring, breaking up into cog-like patches; white with yellow hues in age, with white or brownish patches on underside; persistent. FRUITING Single or in groups; on the ground; open areas (e.g., trail edges) in the forest, in deep twiggy duff under RED CEDARS, or disturbed areas such as mulched or composted flower beds; spring, summer, autumn.

EDIBILITY Choice. Negative reactions are rare but have been reported, so first-time eaters should start off slowly. SIMILAR The FLAT-TOP AGARICUS (p. 237) and the FELT-RINGED AGARICUS (p. 231) have smooth stems and a tar- or creosote-like smell, and they lack the tawny, golden cast of mature caps of THE PRINCE. COMMENTS THE PRINCE is a widely sought edible in southern BC, not only for its exquisite taste, but also because a single mushroom can make a whole meal. THE PRINCE can come up in the same location for several years, so pickers regularly check their spots. Since this mushroom is known as an accumulator of heavy metals, the habitat should be taken into account. ◦ "Augustus" means "blessed, majestic, venerable."

Felt-ringed Agaricus   *Agaricus hondensis*

CAP To 15 cm across; hemispheric or more shallowly convex becoming flat; the surface sometimes cracked when dry; white to light tan background with pinkish grey to pinkish brown to lilac-brown to dark reddish brown fibrils that can make the very young caps and the discs of older caps appear darker; dry; smooth around fibrils; flesh thick, white, unchanging as it dries or sometimes staining yellow when cut. GILLS Free; deep (to 1 cm); pale pink, and then dark brown as spores mature; closely spaced. ODOUR Tar- or creosote-like, especially when the flesh is crushed or scratched near the base of stem. TASTE Usually not distinctive, but sometimes described as metallic. SPORE PRINT Dark chocolate brown. STEM To 20 cm tall × 2 cm wide; wider at base; white or pinkish brown, sometimes weakly bruising yellow, especially near base; dry; smooth. RING Thick, felt-like, pendant but sometimes flaring when young; high on the stem; white, smooth above, with cottony patches below. FRUITING Single or in small groups or fairy rings; on the ground; in (usually coniferous) forests; autumn, winter.

EDIBILITY Poisonous. SIMILAR WOODLAND AGARICUS (p. 233) is mild- to sweet-smelling. THE PRINCE (p. 230) has a pleasant almond odour, a different colour and pattern of scales on the cap, and a scaly stem below the ring, and is often found in disturbed or open sites. The FLAT-TOP AGARICUS (p. 237) fruits somewhat earlier, has a different pattern of cap fibrils that are more greyish or blackish, and usually has a stronger yellowing reaction when bruised at the base of the stem. COMMENTS The FELT-RINGED AGARICUS, found only in western North America, is one of southwestern BC's most common woodland agaricuses. ✦ "Hondensis" refers to La Honda, California, where the species was first collected.

Horse Mushroom   *Agaricus arvensis* group

CAP To 15 cm across; but on rare occasions much larger; convex becoming somewhat flat; dry; smooth to finely matted, when dry sometimes cracked into large scales; white or cream to yellowish, bruising yellow; flesh thick, firm, white, sometimes bruising slightly yellow. GILLS Free; deep (to 1.2 cm); white becoming greyish or (rarely) greyish pink and then chocolate brown as spores mature; closely spaced. ODOUR Sweet, like anise or almonds, sometimes musty when old. TASTE Not distinctive. SPORE PRINT Dark chocolate brown. STEM To 15 cm tall × 3 cm wide; equal to slightly bulbous at base; white, with yellow tints in age; smooth above ring, smooth to scaly below ring. RING Large, often breaking up into gear teeth; white with yellow tints in age; persistent. FRUITING Usually in large groups, sometimes clustered; on the ground, occasionally in fairy rings; usually in lawns or meadows, sometimes in openings in woodlands; summer, autumn.

EDIBILITY Edible. SIMILAR The WOODLAND AGARICUS (p. 233) has a thinner ring and a slimmer stature (stem to 1.5 cm broad), and grows in forests. The smaller (to 10 cm) MEADOW AGARICUS (p. 236) does grow in fields, but it lacks the almond odour, has a thin, disappearing ring, and does not bruise yellow. COMMENTS We potentially have 3 or more different species wrapped up in the *Agaricus arvensis* group. These are (in the order of increasing spore size, which is the best way to tell them apart) *A. arvensis*, *A. fissuratus*, and *A. crocodilinus*. *Agaricus arvensis* in this narrow sense is the one described above. *Agaricus fissuratus* is the smallest of the 3 (cap generally to 10 cm diameter). *Agaricus crocodilinus* is the most similar to *A. arvensis*. It sometimes has larger caps (to more than 30 cm diameter) and sometimes has deeply cracked caps, giving its top a crocodile-skin look. ● Like other *Agaricus* species, the HORSE MUSHROOM is a decomposer. ● "Arvensis" means "of the field."

Woodland Agaricus

Agaricus sylvicola group

CAP To 10 cm across; convex, then almost flat; white, bruising weakly yellow; dry; smooth, satiny; flesh moderately thick (to 1.5 cm), firm, white, sometimes yellowing when exposed to air. GILLS Free; moderately deep, especially in the centre; white, becoming pink, and then dark brown as spores mature; crowded. ODOUR Often of almond or anise, but sometimes faintly. TASTE Not distinctive. SPORE PRINT Dark chocolate brown. STEM To 10 cm tall × a slender 1.5 cm wide; equal, sometimes with an abruptly bulbous base; white, sometimes with pink tints above ring, staining yellow with bruising or in age; dry; smooth, but lower part can have woolly patches from the universal veil; sometimes with visible mycelium at base. RING Thin, pendulous, sometimes dividing into a double ring with a broken, scaly underlayer; high on the stem; white. FRUITING Scattered and in groups; on the ground; in conifer forests; late summer, autumn.

EDIBILITY Edible. SIMILAR The HORSE MUSHROOM (p. 232), another white, yellow-staining agaricus, is more robust (stem to 3 cm wide) and prefers fields and meadows. The dangerous DEATH CAP (p. 112) mushroom, if it grows in a woody habitat, if its volva is indistinct, and if its white spores are not noted, might be mistaken for the WOODLAND AGARICUS. COMMENTS WOODLAND AGARICUS occurs throughout BC. ꙮ Although the genetic signature of the European *Agaricus sylvicola* has been confirmed in western North America, many of the white-capped, sweet-smelling agaricus mushrooms in BC woods are probably other, closely related species. Three mushrooms in the *A. sylvicola* group are now recognized as distinct species: *A. albolutescens*, with a variable bulb size up to 4.5 cm across, is larger and more robust, occurs in coastal areas, and emits more intense almond odours; *A. moronii* is similar to *A. albolutescens* but prefers a mountainous habitat; *A. abruptibulbus* (pictured above) is more likely to have a defined bulb at the base of its stem. ꙮ "Sylvicola" means "of the forest."

Red-staining Agaricus *Agaricus sylvaticus* group

CAP To 10 cm across; almost spherical to hemispheric or more shallowly convex and then flat; background white or tan, bruising reddish, with pointed red-brown or dark brown scales; dry; smooth, but sometimes with uplifted scales; flesh thick (to 1 cm), firm, white, staining salmon or red or red-brown when cut. **GILLS** Free; deep (to 1 cm); greyish brown tinged pale pink and then dark brown as spores mature, bruising reddish; crowded. **ODOUR** Not distinctive. **TASTE** Not distinctive. **SPORE PRINT** Dark chocolate brown. **STEM** To 10 cm tall × 2 cm wide; equal or with a bulbous base; white, turning reddish orange to reddish brown when cut or bruised; dry; smooth or finely striate above ring, smooth to finely white-scaly below. **RING** Flaring to pendant, and striate above, finely scaly below; high on stem; white. **FRUITING** Single, scattered, or in groups, sometimes in clusters; on the ground; in conifer forests; late summer, autumn.

EDIBILITY Edible. **SIMILAR** For comparisons with other red-staining mushrooms, see the **BLUSHER** page (p. 116). **COMMENTS** *Agaricus sylvaticus* was once thought to be a single, widespread species. Some of the variants, as is so often the case, have now earned their own species names. We await studies that will tell us which of these variants and species are found in BC. ◆ RED-STAINING AGARICUS seems to be an uncommon species of southwestern BC. A number of different *Agaricus* species—not all of which are closely related—have flesh that turns red or red-brown when exposed to the air. The species in the *A. sylvaticus* group do this in spades (hearts?), with the red colour emerging quickly, sometimes within seconds, but always within a few minutes. One of the best ways to observe this colour change is to slice the mushroom in half vertically. ◆ "Sylvaticus" means "in the forest," a reference to the habitat of the RED-STAINING AGARICUS.

"When I was almost eight and my sister was nearly seven… what a delight it was… to ramble through the clean, fragrant woods, filling our baskets…. We were already proficient mushroom gatherers…. When we were naughty, our mother would punish us by forbidding us to go mushrooming."
 — Valentina Pavlovna Wasson and R. Gordon Wasson,
 Mushrooms, Russia and History (1957), vol. I, p. 3

Young foragers in the Kootenays.

Meadow Agaricus   *Agaricus campestris*

CAP To 10 cm across; deeply convex and eventually becoming shallowly convex or flat, the margin often extending past the gills and hung with veil remnants; dry; smooth or finely fibrillose; white, sometimes with pressed-down grey or brown fibrils; flesh thick, firm, white. GILLS Free; shallow (5–6 mm); pale pink becoming bright pink and then chocolate brown as spores mature; closely spaced. ODOUR With the familiar, faint, pleasant, and earthy aroma of store-bought BUTTON MUSHROOMS. TASTE Not distinctive, can be pleasant. SPORE PRINT Dark chocolate brown. STEM To 6 cm tall × 2 cm wide; cylindrical, usually narrowed at base; dry; smooth above ring, smooth or white silky-fibrillose below; white. RING Thin, membranous; white; sometimes quickly disappearing. FRUITING Single or in groups or clusters, often in fairy rings; on the ground; in grassy areas (e.g., meadows and pastures); any season.

EDIBILITY Choice. But consider the habitat. SIMILAR The MEADOW AGARICUS is the wild mushroom most similar to the widely vended BUTTON MUSHROOM (*Agaricus bisporus*), which occurs in BC only as an escaped species. MEADOW AGARICUS might be confused, because of similarities in colour, habitat, and stature, with the WHITE PARASOL (p. 123), which has white gills and white spores. The HORSE MUSHROOM (p. 232) also grows in fields, but it has a distinct almond/anise odour and is typically larger than the MEADOW AGARICUS. Also, the HORSE MUSHROOM discolours yellow and retains a substantial, cogwheel-like ring. The larger FLAT-TOP AGARICUS (p. 237) can occasionally appear in fields, but it has a tar/creosote odour, and the flesh often stains yellow at the stem base. COMMENTS The MEADOW AGARICUS, widespread in BC, can fruit in magnificent abundance, though it seems less common now than it was several decades ago. ◦ Most North American collections of MEADOW AGARICUS differ genetically from the European *Agaricus campestris*, a problem that may result in future name changes. ◦ "Campestris" means "of the fields or plains."

Flat-top Agaricus   *Agaricus deardorffensis* group

CAP To 10 cm across; marshmallow-shaped when young, then convex and then becoming flat; background white to light grey, usually covered with pressed-down brown to dark grey fibrils that are denser at the cap centre; dry; smooth; flesh moderately thick (6 mm–1 cm), white. **GILLS** Free; deep (to 1 cm); white or grey at first, then pale pink, and then blackish brown; closely spaced. **ODOUR** Creosote/tar (try scratching or crushing the base). **TASTE** Not distinctive. **SPORE PRINT** Dark chocolate brown. **STEM** To 15 cm tall × 2 cm wide; equal or widening downward, base sometimes narrower and rooting; pith-filled to hollow; white, the flesh at first usually staining yellow at the base when cut or bruised, then later darkening to yellow-brown or reddish brown; dry; smooth. **RING** Wedge-shaped to skirt-like and rubbery; white; sometimes becoming free from stem. **FRUITING** Scattered or in groups, sometimes clustered; on the ground; in openings and trail edges in coniferous or mixedwood forests; summer, autumn, winter.

EDIBILITY Poisonous. **SIMILAR** *Agaricus buckmacadooi*, another member of the *A. deardorffensis* group, was described in 2016. It closely resembles the **FLAT-TOP AGARICUS**, but differs mostly in being found in less disturbed forest habitats, having a browner background colour on the cap, and having a pendant ring that remains attached to the stem. Caps of the **FELT-RINGED AGARICUS** (p. 231) have a more pinkish tan background colour, young caps do not have the boxy, marshmallow shape, the stem does not show significant yellow bruising, and the mushroom tends to fruit in forest habitats later in the autumn or winter. **COMMENTS** Several distinct coastal species were once grouped under the misapplied name *A. praeclaresquamosus*, then later under the European name *A. moelleri*, but genetic tests show that North American species differ from *A. moelleri*. *Agaricus deardorffensis* is known to occur in BC, so we have chosen to use its description here. ● "Deardorffensis" comes from Deardorff Road in the California Sierra Nevada mountains, where early specimens were found.

Diminutive Agaricus   *Agaricus diminutivus* group

CAP To 5 cm across but usually 1–3 cm; almost bell-shaped at first, becoming convex and eventually flat (or nearly so), the margins incurved and sometimes extending 1–2 mm beyond the gills; background white, pinkish, or orangish and sometimes staining yellow, sprinkled with pinkish to purplish radial fibrils that make the centre darker than the margins, the cap becoming more brown as it ages; dry; smooth around the pressed-down fibrils; flesh thin, white, sometimes with yellowish tints in age. GILLS Free; rather deep (3 mm); pale becoming grey (sometimes pink), and then blackish brown as spores mature; closely spaced. ODOUR Pleasant, of anise or almonds. TASTE Not distinctive. SPORE PRINT Dark chocolate brown. STEM To 5 cm tall × 4 mm wide, often taller than the cap diameter; equal, sometimes with expanded base; white to cream, bruising yellowish; dry; smooth or longitudinally striate above ring, often with faint fibrils below. RING Thin, membranous, short, pendant, and smooth above, slightly scaly below; near top of stem; white, apricot orange in age. FRUITING Single or in small groups; on the ground; usually in coniferous forests; summer, autumn.

EDIBILITY Uncertain. SIMILAR The larger *Agaricus kerriganii* (previously referred to as *A. semotus*) can also be found in the forest duff, as well as mountain meadows, but it has a slightly wider cap (about 4–7 cm across, almost approaching the length of the stem which is 5–9 cm long). The shorter (with a stem to 3 cm tall) *A. micromegethus* has a 2–4 cm cap, but prefers open, grassy areas and has a smooth stem below the ring. COMMENTS We expect mushrooms in the *Agaricus* genus to be substantial and imposing. We have, however, a number of small species. Most of these small BC agaricuses have a touch of pink to red-brown on their caps, flesh that stains yellow, and an anise odour. ✦ "Diminutivus" means "small."

Cortinarius

The genus *Cortinarius* is huge! Worldwide, there are more than 2,000 described species, and studies hint at more to come. How many of these 2,000 are in BC is impossible to say—a large study of BC genetic sequences looked at almost a thousand specimens and found that it contained at least 180 species. But this number may be just a drop in the bucket.

With this many species to contend with, mycologists find it useful to group *Cortinarius* mushrooms into subgenera. At mushroom shows, you will often see samples labelled by subgenus, such as "*Cortinarius* subg. *Telamonia*" or "*Cortinarius* subg. *Myxacium*." A restricted set of *Cortinarius* subgenera—usually eight or less, depending on which authority you follow—were worked out in the days when we had only macroscopic and microscopic characteristics to work with. When genetic sequencing joined the arsenal of research tools in the late 1990s, these categories were disassembled and the species were redistributed into more than 20 sections. In the description of the dozen *Cortinarius* species on the following pages, we will mention some of the larger subgenus sections because you may see them in other contexts, but we will make almost no attempt here to describe the larger and still-in-transition subgenus picture.

Mushrooms found in the field can be assigned to the genus *Cortinarius* on the basis of a few features. *Cortinarius* species are mycorrhizal mushrooms that grow on the ground, and they all have rusty brown spore prints. Many species fruit later in the autumn mushroom season than species from other forest-based genera. The partial veils that cover the gills are cobweb-like. ("Cortina," the name for this cobwebby veil, which is also the basis for the genus name, comes from a Late Latin word meaning "curtain.") The strands of the web snap apart as the cap opens and often remain behind as fibrils that stick to the stem and pick up the rusty brown colour of the falling spores. Many cortinariuses have violet tints on their caps, stems, or gills, and those that don't tend to sport brown, yellow-brown, and orange colours. Identifying them further, to the subgenus level, usually means paying attention to colour patterns, taste, slime on the caps and stems (the remnants of a glutinous universal veil), and microscopic features. Going beyond the genus and subgenus levels, however, can be a daunting task. On display tables, *Cortinarius* species share with *Russula* and *Ramaria* species the dubious award for "mushrooms most likely to be labelled just with the genus name and 'sp.'"

Cortinariuses are not known as food mushrooms. Indeed, some of them are deadly poisonous. Only two of them are commonly collected by BC mycophagists—GRANNY'S NIGHTCAP (p. 244) and the VIOLET WEBCAP (p. 242). Their utility to humans reaches far beyond the table, however. Because of their close relationship to mycorrhizal partners and their sensitivity to environmental changes, some cortinariuses have been employed as indicator species for Scandinavian ecological zones. The mycelial mats of *Cortinarius* species, we have recently learned, play an important role in carbon cycling in the vast swaths of boreal forests.

Silvery Violet Webcap   *Cortinarius alboviolaceus*

CAP To 9 cm across; bell-shaped becoming convex or nearly flat, broadly umbonate; pale silvery violet when young, silvery white in age, often with yellow-brown blotching; dry; silky, often with a sheen; flesh thick (3 mm–1 cm), whitish to pale lilac. GILLS Broadly to narrowly attached, often notched; moderately deep (to 7 mm); purplish grey, becoming cinnamon brown as spores mature; somewhat closely spaced. ODOUR Not distinctive. TASTE Not distinctive. SPORE PRINT Rusty brown. STEM To 12 cm tall × 2 cm wide; widening downward, often with a swollen base; when sliced in half, the interior showing pale flesh with violet marbling, especially at the top; surface is pale violet, in the lower part overlain with white silky fibrils from the universal veil; dry. RING Cobwebby partial veil; white; disappearing but often leaving a zone of fibrils on the upper stem. FRUITING Scattered or in groups; on the ground; traditionally associated with hardwoods, but also with conifers; late summer, autumn.

EDIBILITY Uncertain. Probably not toxic. SIMILAR Specimens growing with conifers, as in the picture above, and having a (sometimes) slimy stem have been identified as *Cortinarius griseoviolaceus*, though this may not be a different species. *Cortinarius camphoratus* is similar but has a penetrating odour like rotting potatoes. The FRUITY LILAC WEBCAP (p. 241) has brown flesh marbled with cream or beige in the cut stem and a pear-like odour. *Cortinarius occidentalis* **group** (previously known as *C. mutabilis*) species have slimy caps that have darker purple radial streaking, and the cut stems show mostly blue-purple tones. All of these corts might be mistaken for the BLEWIT (p. 130), which has pink spores, a slightly greasy cap with inrolled margins, and a citrusy odour, or with the WESTERN LILAC FIBREHEAD (p. 255), which is smaller, yields a dull brown spore print, and has a semen-like odour. COMMENTS "Alboviolaceus" means "whitish violet."

Fruity Lilac Webcap　　　　　*Cortinarius traganus*

CAP To 12 cm across; hemispheric becoming more shallowly convex to flat, often broadly umbonate, the margin when young hung with remnants of the partial veil and somewhat inrolled, in age sometimes wavy; pale lilac, fading to dirty white, often with yellow-brown stains, sometimes becoming entirely brown; dry; smooth to finely silky, sometimes cracking at the centre and/or with upturned fibrils; flesh thick (to 1.5 cm), firm, yellow-brown to rusty brown, often marbled. GILLS Broadly or narrowly attached, often notched; yellowish brown, becoming rusty brown as spores mature; moderately spaced. ODOUR Sweet, fruity, sometimes described as overripe pears, but the odour can be hard to detect in some specimens. TASTE Not distinctive, or slightly bitter or sour. SPORE PRINT Rusty brown. STEM To 11 cm tall × 2 cm wide; with a swollen base; flesh (slice stem to check) yellow-brown marbled with cream or beige; surface lilac, becoming brown from the base up; dry; surface has silky fibres and belts of white or violet from the universal veil on the lower section. RING Cobwebby; pale violet; leaving a zone of fibres on the stem that soon becomes rusty brown from spores. FRUITING Single or in groups; on the ground; in conifer forests; late summer, autumn.

EDIBILITY Uncertain. Some have reported it as poisonous/indigestible. SIMILAR The **SILVERY VIOLET WEBCAP** (p. 240) has violet gills, violet marbling in the sliced stem, and a more silver sheen in the cap. *Cortinarius camphoratus* also differs by having touches of violet in the gills, violet marbling in the upper stem, and a rancid smell somewhat like that of rotting potatoes. COMMENTS FRUITY LILAC WEBCAP appears to be widespread in BC. ◦ "Traganus" means "pertaining to goats," referring to a smell detected on European specimens. BC sniffers do not report the smell.

Violet Webcap   *Cortinarius violaceus*

CAP To 12 cm across; hemispheric or more shallowly convex, becoming flat or broadly umbonate, margins incurved or curved down, sometimes ragged; deep, dark violet to almost black, lighter in age; dry; when young, densely covered with upright scales that give the cap a distinctive velvety appearance, the scales later flattening out and an almost metallic sheen developing; flesh thick (5 mm–1.2 cm), violet. GILLS Broadly or narrowly attached, and notched; coloured like cap, taking on rusty brown hues as spores mature; becoming moderately well spaced. ODOUR Not distinctive, but sometimes faintly of cedar/pencils. TASTE Not distinctive. SPORE PRINT Rusty brown. STEM To 16 cm tall × 2.5 cm wide; widening downward, sometimes bulbous; sliced stem showing violet marbled with white; violet surface, base sometimes lighter, darkening where handled; dry; surface has silky fibres; sometimes with blue mycelium at base. RING Cobwebby; purple; disappearing but sometimes leaving a zone on the stem that becomes spore-coloured. FRUITING Single to scattered; on the ground; under conifers and hardwoods; late summer, autumn.

EDIBILITY Edible. But somewhat risky for beginners because of the many toxic and possibly toxic *Cortinarius* species with significant violet tints. SIMILAR Some *Leptonia* species (p. 226) can have a deep purple colour, but these are smaller, have pink spores, and do not have a cobwebby veil. COMMENTS The VIOLET WEBCAP occurs worldwide, but it seems to be more common in the US Pacific Northwest and southern BC than in other places. ◦ The VIOLET WEBCAP does not make a good dyeing mushroom, despite its royal purple hues. ◦ "Violaceus" means "violet-coloured."

Red-banded Webcap   *Cortinarius armillatus*

CAP To 12 cm across; bell-shaped or convex becoming flat, often broadly umbonate, sometimes with veil remnants on the margin; yellow-brown to orange-brown or red-brown, often with a darker centre; dry; smooth or minutely hairy/scaly in age; flesh thick, white, or pale brown. GILLS Broadly to narrowly attached; deep; pale cinnamon, becoming rusty brown; somewhat widely spaced. ODOUR Slightly of radish. TASTE Bitter or not distinctive. SPORE PRINT Rusty brown. STEM To 15 cm tall × 2 cm wide; base swollen; white to pale brown, with 1–4 dull to bright red bands (universal veil remnants) on stem; smooth, silky. RING Cobwebby; white; disappearing but leaving hairs on upper stem. FRUITING Single or scattered; on the ground; with birch; summer, autumn.

EDIBILITY Poisonous. SIMILAR The smaller *Cortinarius boulderensis*, which grows under conifers, has an orange-banded stem with muted violet tints at the top, greyish lilac gills, and a hygrophanous cap that sometimes has striations. *Cortinarius paragaudis* (whose BC representatives may actually be *C. luteo-ornatus*, if these 2 are not the same species) has a darker cap, stem rings that are more reddish brown, and a habitat with conifers rather than birches. COMMENTS The RED-BANDED WEBCAP contains a small but detectable amount of the compound orellanine, which has caused poisonings and death from *Cortinarius* species that contain higher concentrations of it. ◦ The RED-BANDED WEBCAP belongs, both by character grouping and genetic analysis, to the huge *Telamonia* subgenus of *Cortinarius*. Species in this subgenus have brownish hues and dry caps and stems, and are typically hygrophanous. ◦ *Cortinarius armillatus* is found worldwide, but we may also have one or more cryptic species hiding under this name in BC. ◦ Because of its association with birches, this is a species of Interior BC. ◦ "Armillatus" means "with a bracelet" in Latin.

Granny's Nightcap   *Cortinarius caperatus*

CAP To 15 cm across; egg-shaped or bell-shaped becoming convex or nearly flat, sometimes umbonate; tan at first, becoming yellow-brown or orange-brown; dry; often with a frosted look when young, at maturity dull and usually radially wrinkled; flesh somewhat thick, white. GILLS Broadly or narrowly attached; wavy when young; pale, becoming brown as spores mature; closely spaced to crowded; intermittent subgills. ODOUR Not distinctive. TASTE Not distinctive. SPORE PRINT Rusty brown. STEM To 13 cm tall × 2.5 cm wide; equal, often widening toward base; whitish to pale yellow-brown; dry; with longitudinal striations that may appear shaggy near base; the universal veil sometimes leaving a volva-like zone on the base. RING Membranous; on the middle of the stem; white, sometimes with purple tinge; persistent. FRUITING Scattered or in groups; on the ground; usually with conifers; late summer, autumn.

EDIBILITY Edible. SIMILAR The SPRING AGROCYBE (p. 279) is visually similar, but it lacks the frosted/wrinkled cap and it is a decomposer that is found on lawns, wood chips, and other built environments. It also tends to be smaller and have a slimmer (often less than 1 cm) stem. ALASKAN GOLD (p. 280), though usually larger, shares GRANNY'S NIGHTCAP's habitat and overall appearance, but it has a granular surface on the cap and stem. COMMENTS *Cortinarius caperatus* is called GYPSY MUSHROOM in most other field guides. Since "gypsy" is considered a racial slur, we are using another (much less common) name. ☙ GRANNY'S NIGHTCAP is tasty, widespread in BC, and often available in large quantities. But be aware of harvest context: it has been shown to bioaccumulate mercury and radioactive cesium. ☙ In the 19th century, *Cortinarius* species with persistent membranous rings, including GRANNY'S NIGHTCAP, were moved into a new genus, *Rozites*. Genetic sequencing at the end of the 20th century proved that the unusual rings did not define a different genus but were the result of convergent evolution, so almost all *Rozites* species were moved back into *Cortinarius*. ☙ "Caperatus" means "wrinkled," a reference to the cap texture.

Bitter Brown Webcap   *Cortinarius vibratilis* group

CAP To 5 cm across; bell-shaped or convex, sometimes becoming flat, occasionally with an umbo; yellow-brown or orange-brown, margins paler, drying paler; slimy; smooth; hygrophanous; flesh thin, whitish, sometimes with a yellow-brown tinge. GILLS Broadly to narrowly attached, notched to slightly decurrent; whitish at first, then taking on spore coloration; closely spaced. ODOUR Not distinctive. TASTE Intensely bitter (best experienced by licking the cap). SPORE PRINT Rusty brown. STEM To 7 cm tall × 1 cm wide; equal or widening downward, sometimes rooting; intensely white, fading in age; slimy when young from the glutinous universal veil, when older slimy only at base; smooth. RING Cobwebby; clear; disappearing but sometimes leaving a few fibrils on the stem that take on the spore colour. FRUITING Single to scattered; on the ground; under conifers; autumn.

EDIBILITY Unknown. Too *bitter* to *consitter*. SIMILAR ***Cortinarius causticus*** is quite similar (and the picture above could be this species), but its caps tend to be darker. Two tests that may distinguish the species: licking the stem—supposedly only the BITTER BROWN WEBCAP has a bitter stem—and rubbing the top—the surface of the *C. causticus* cap is more granular and pebbled, like curling-rink ice. COMMENTS The BITTER BROWN WEBCAP is a common mushroom in BC forests, but frequently misidentified, to judge by the variety of names associated with the DNA sequences that have been registered for it. ◦ With the slimy cap and stem, the BITTER BROWN WEBCAP looks like it should belong to the classical *Myxacium* subgenus, but genetic tests indicate that it and other bitter-tasting mushrooms are part of an ancient subgroup of *Cortinarius* that is distinct from the modern *Myxacium* subgenus. ◦ "Vibratilis," which means "vibrating, scintillating," was probably attached to this species because of the way light reflected from the slimy cap or because of the way the slime on the cap quivered. It could equally well refer to the tongue's reaction to contacting this intensely bitter mushroom!

Blood-red Webcap   *Cortinarius neosanguineus*

CAP To 5 cm across; conical to convex to flat, the margins inrolled at first; deep red to blood red; dry; smooth or with fine radial lines; flesh thin, blood red or paler. **GILLS** Broadly to narrowly attached; cap-coloured, becoming rusty brown as spores mature; medium-spaced; with 1–3 subgills between neighbouring main gills. **ODOUR** Mild to cedar-like. **TASTE** Not distinctive. **SPORE PRINT** Rusty brown. **STEM** To 8 cm tall × 5 mm wide; equal or widening slightly below; coloured like cap or paler, sometimes streaky; dry; often with silky longitudinal fibres; with yellow to red mycelium at base. **RING** Cobwebby; reddish; disappearing but may leave a few fibrils on stem. **FRUITING** Single to scattered; on the ground; in conifer forests; autumn.

    EDIBILITY Unknown. **SIMILAR** A number of *Cortinarius* species with intense yellow, orange, and red caps and gills have traditionally been placed in the *Dermocybe* subgenus, sometimes even assigned to the (no longer recognized) genus *Dermocybe*. One of these species, the ***Cortinarius californicus* group** (which, unlike the others in this section, has a hygrophanous cap and actually belongs to the *Telamonia* subgenus of *Cortinarius*), tends to be larger, the gills more brownish orange, and the gill edges more ragged than the same fruiting body parts in the BLOOD-RED WEBCAP. It does, however, have the same streaky red-orange stem. ***Cortinarius smithii*** (photo next page), previously called *C. phoeniceus* var. *occidentalis*, also has the same rich red cap and gills as the BLOOD-RED WEBCAP, but it has a yellow stem with (sometimes) a red-brown base. A yellow stem may also indicate another mushroom, *C. ominosus* (photo next page), formerly *C. semisanguineus*. Though the cap of *C. ominosus* is more typically yellow or olive-brown, there are local populations with more reddish caps and gills to match. The lower stem (of the reddish-capped versions, at least) fluoresces a rich orange-yellow under 360 nm UV light, while that of *C. smithii* does not. ***Cortinarius cinnamomeus*** has a yellow-brown stem with red-brown to grey-brown veil fibrils. Its cap ranges from yellow-brown (especially toward the margins) to red-brown. The gills are persistently bright

Cortinarius smithii.

orange to yellow-orange. ***Cortinarius croceus*** can also have yellow-brown or red-brown caps, but the gills, at least on younger specimens, have a distinct mustard-yellow tone (sometimes greenish in the gills of the youngest specimens) that sets them apart from *C. cinnamomeus*. ***Cortinarius idahoensis***, though its cap may start off reddish brown, tends to have an olive-brown cap in maturity. Its rusty brown stem, with a covering of similarly coloured fibrils, turns a darker hue from the base up, and its gills are orange-brown rather than the mustard yellow of *C. croceus*. COMMENTS The BLOOD-RED WEBCAP and many of the other *Cortinarius* species in the section above can be used for dyeing cloth (see essay on p. 342). ✒ BC's BLOOD-RED WEBCAP was known as *C. sanguineus* until a 2013 publication definitively separated it into a western North American and an eastern North American/European pair of species—the "neo" (new) in "neosanguineus" flags this change in the North American species.

Cortinarius ominosus.

Goldband Webcap *Cortinarius gentilis* group

CAP To 5 cm across; bell- or cone-shaped, becoming convex to flat, usually with a prominent umbo; reddish brown, fading to yellow, but often remaining darker on disc; dry; smooth, sometimes appearing silky; margins striate when wet and sometimes with yellow universal veil remnants; hygrophanous; flesh thin, brownish yellow or red-brown. **GILLS** Broadly or narrowly attached; light yellow or yellow-brown or brownish orange, becoming reddish brown as spores develop; well spaced. **ODOUR** Not distinctive, or of radishes or raw potatoes, also described as rubber-like. **TASTE** Not distinctive. **SPORE PRINT** Rusty brown. **STEM** To 12 cm tall × 5 mm wide; equal and often narrowing at base and rooting; light yellow at first, then brownish orange, sometimes with bands of yellow universal veil remnants when young; dry. **RING** Cobwebby; pale yellow; quickly disappearing. **FRUITING** Scattered or in groups; on the ground, or from rotten woody debris; under conifers; late summer, autumn.

EDIBILITY Potentially very poisonous. One member of this group has been shown to cause kidney damage in rats. **SIMILAR** *Cortinarius kroegeri*, a species described in 2016 and named after Vancouver mycologist Paul Kroeger, might be confused with a mature GOLDBAND WEBCAP whose universal veil has faded. *Cortinarius kroegeri* has no significant odour and has a moist, hygrophanous cap with a broader umbo. The cap is orange-brown mixed with reddish brown, with scattered yellow fibrils and small scales. **COMMENTS** Molecular studies of GOLDBAND WEBCAP specimens hint that we may have several related species grouped under one name. ☙ "Gentilis" is a Latin word meaning "native, of the same house." The Latin word is also the source of the word "gentile," so it could also mean just the opposite: "foreigner, non-Jewish." In any case, the connection between this species epithet and the mushroom features has been lost.

Bluefoot Webcap

Cortinarius glaucopus group

CAP To 12 cm across; convex becoming flat, often lumpy and lobed in age, margins incurved when young and sometimes remaining curved down; colour variable, sometimes including olive greens and bluish greys, becoming reddish brown from the centre outward with age; slimy/sticky; smooth but with silky radial fibrils, especially toward the margins; flesh thick, pale or violet, often with darker violet mottling, becoming yellow-brown. GILLS Broadly to narrowly attached; bluish grey, becoming brown; closely spaced. ODOUR Usually not distinctive, sometimes farinaceous. TASTE Not distinctive. SPORE PRINT Rusty brown. STEM To 10 cm tall × 3 cm wide; equal but with an abrupt, tapered basal bulb (to 6 cm across) when young; solid; surface bluish or blue-green near top, paler below with occasional yellowish tints, aging brown; stem flesh is violet, becoming yellow-brown, especially in the base; dry. RING Cobwebby; bluish or paler; usually leaving fibrils on stem that take on the brown spore colour. FRUITING Scattered or in groups or clusters; on the ground; in conifers or hardwood forests; spring, autumn, winter.

EDIBILITY Uncertain. There are wide variations within the group, and the similarity with other *Cortinarius* species and species groups make consumption risky. SIMILAR *Cortinarius occidentalis* **group** (also known as *C. mutabilis*) mushrooms also have slimy caps and abrupt bulbs, but their caps are more purple/violet and have dark purple radial streaking, and the flesh stains purplish when injured. *Cortinarius olympianus* is like *C. occidentalis*, but without the dramatic purple staining, and a drop of KOH turns the cap and flesh a bright red. The coloration of BLUEFOOT WEBCAP somewhat resembles that of the BLEWIT (p. 130), but the BLEWIT has pinkish spores, a citrusy odour, and a greasy rather than a slimy cap that usually has lilac tones. COMMENTS The critical features of the BLUEFOOT WEBCAP—a slimy brownish cap, a dry violet stem with an abrupt bulb—are shared by about 2 dozen species that have been collected in BC, so identification with certainty is a job for experts. ❧ "Glaucopus" means "with blue-grey foot," presumably a reference to the stem colour.

Woolly Webcap   *Cortinarius laniger*

CAP To 10 cm across; nearly hemispheric becoming more shallowly convex or nearly flat, often broadly umbonate; dark reddish brown when moist, beige when dry, often with a white band at the margin when young; dry; smooth or wrinkled, finely hairy or silky when young; hygrophanous; flesh firm, coloured as cap or whitish and bruising yellow-brown. GILLS Broadly to narrowly attached, often notched; orange-brown when young, then rusty brown as the spores fall; closely spaced. ODOUR Of radish or geranium. TASTE Not distinctive. SPORE PRINT Rusty brown. STEM To 10 cm tall × 2 cm wide; equal, often with bulbous base when young; firm; white to brownish with white patches of universal veil material below the ring zone; dry. RING Cobwebby; white; disappearing but often leaving a zone of fibrils. FRUITING Scattered or in groups; on the ground; under conifers; autumn.

EDIBILITY Not edible. SIMILAR It is difficult to know where to begin in listing similar species. Hundreds of *Cortinarius* species, most of them in the *Telamonia* part of *Cortinarius*, have a dry, hygrophanous cap and a dry stem. WOOLLY WEBCAP differs from many of these by having no hint of violet colour in the cap, gills, or stem, but adding this characteristic only narrows the list down to several dozen, many of which have the same bulbous base as the WOOLLY WEBCAP. If the young cap has fine hairs and the gills smell of radish, the WOOLLY WEBCAP identification becomes more certain, but these 2 characteristics can be difficult to observe. *Cortinarius solis-occasus* supposedly has a cap that is less hairy/silky and a grey-lilac veil that hangs around on the margin; however, it is possible that it and WOOLLY WEBCAP are the same species. COMMENTS "Laniger" means "bearing wool," a Latin descriptor of the hairy young caps.

Olive Webcap   *Cortinarius clandestinus* group

CAP To 10 cm across; bell-shaped becoming convex or nearly flat, umbonate when young, margins incurved when young and sometimes hung with yellowish partial veil remnants; young caps are olive-brown to dark brown from pressed-down fibrils, the background golden colour emerging at the margin and between the fibrils as the cap expands, producing a black-on-gold pointillist effect, the disc centre remaining darker; dry; flesh thin, firm, yellowish olive. GILLS Broadly or narrowly attached, often notched; usually somewhat shallow; at first pale, then yellow with olive tints and, in age, yellow-brown; somewhat closely spaced. ODOUR Usually of radish. TASTE Not distinctive. SPORE PRINT Rusty brown. STEM To 10 cm tall × 2 cm wide; equal or slightly enlarged below or sometimes tapered to base; stuffed becoming hollow; yellow to yellow-brown; dry; smooth or with longitudinal fibres and veil remnants. RING Cobwebby but sparse; yellow to olive; rapidly disappearing but sometimes remaining as a zone of fibrils that take on the spore colour. FRUITING Single or scattered; on the ground; usually with conifers; spring, summer, autumn.

EDIBILITY Unknown. SIMILAR *Cortinarius parkeri* is another yellow-olive (but sometimes yellow-brown without the olive), dry-capped *Cortinarius* species. It appears in the spring rather than the autumn, however, and its pale yellow universal veil persists on the base as a volva-like sheath. The white-spored PRUNES AND CUSTARD (p. 166) has a pale yellow stem, and it fruits on rotting conifer logs rather than the forest floor. COMMENTS The OLIVE WEBCAP belongs to a group within the *Cortinarius* genus that is often noted as subgenus *Leprocybe*, which holds species with scaly dry caps, generally dry stems, and yellow and brown colours. Like many members of this *Leprocybe* group, the tissues of the OLIVE WEBCAP fluoresce a bright yellow under UV light. ◦ Genetic tests indicate that some cryptic species may be clumped under the name of *C. clandestinus*. ◦ "Clandestinus" means "hidden," perhaps named for the way the young caps nestle into the forest duff.

Slimy Brown Webcap   *Cortinarius seidliae*

CAP To 8 cm across; hemispheric becoming more shallowly convex to flat, broadly umbonate, the margins radially wrinkled; yellow-brown with an olive tinge, or darker brown, the disc and striations darker than the background, the margin often whitish when young; extraordinarily glutinous; hygrophanous; flesh brown. GILLS Narrowly attached, notched; pale brown, later darker brown, sometimes with purplish tinge. ODOUR Often not distinctive, but stem base may sometimes smell like hospital antiseptic or sweetish. TASTE Not distinctive. SPORE PRINT Rusty brown. STEM To 15 cm tall × 2 cm wide; equal; flesh in the main part a very pale brown, but yellow-brown in the base; surface white, but adhering veil remnants in young specimens may have violet tints; glutinous, the slime on the stem, like that on the cap, being the remnant of a pale violet, almost white, universal veil; smooth. RING Disappearing. FRUITING Scattered or in groups; on the ground; under conifers; late summer, autumn.

EDIBILITY Unknown. SIMILAR *Cortinarius collinitus* group (which would also include *C. muscigenus*), found in higher-elevation BC forests and often near sphagnum moss, has an orange-brown cap, dingy white flesh that is sometimes tinged yellow, and no particular odour. COMMENTS At one time, all *Cortinarius* species with slimy caps and slimy stems were placed in the *Myxacium* subgenus. Genetic testing has redistributed many of these species. The SLIMY BROWN WEBCAP now lives in the *Defibulati* section. ⌖ This species seems to be confined to BC's coast. ⌖ You may still hear *C. seidliae* described as *C. vanduzerensis* group mushrooms, a name that was widely used before we discovered that few if any of our local SLIMY BROWN WEBCAPS were a genetic match for *C. vanduzerensis*. ⌖ The SLIMY BROWN WEBCAP is so slippery that it can be difficult to pick up and hold on to. ⌖ "Seidliae" honours Washington mycologist Michelle T. Seidl.

Inocybe and Similar

Mushrooms in the genus *Inocybe*, commonly called "fibreheads" (a direct translation of the Greek compound "Inocybe"), are classic LBMs (little brown mushrooms). They stipple the floors of BC forests in the autumn, their abundance exceeded only by their anonymity and their ecological importance.

Our BC species tend to be small- to medium-sized with muted colours that range from white to yellow-brown to brown. Mushrooms in this genus are mycorrhizal, so they grow around trees, especially conifers. Inocybe caps may be smooth, silky, or dense with raised fibrils, and the cap surfaces often show radial lines. When they first poke out of the ground, the caps tend to be conical or bell-shaped. In age they become more flattened, but they often retain a central bump, an umbo. Their gills tend to start out white or cream, but they eventually take on the dull brown hue of the spores. Inocybe gills usually have interesting crystal-studded sterile cells (cystidia) between the spore-bearing basidia. While a compound microscope is the best way to see these sterile cells, they can sometimes be observed with a hand lens as pale fringes on the edge of the darkening gills. Stems of inocybes are smooth or covered with fibrils and seldom have any sign of a ring—the partial veils are, like those of cortinariuses, cobwebby, so the best they can manage is to leave tatters on the cap margins or to leave obscure ring zones on the stems. Many inocybes have strong odours, the most common one being a persistent musky smell that is usually described as having the odour of semen, or as spermatic.

Many fibreheads contain muscarine, a substance that is toxic and even deadly in high doses. A recent review of Chinese mushrooms classified over 1,600 species by edibility, toxicity, and medicinal uses. Not surprisingly, *every* inocybe they catalogued was listed as poisonous. A glance at mushroom-poisoning records, however, shows relatively few cases involving humans—fibreheads are too small and odd-smelling to hold the interest of most foragers. A large number of animals, however, are drawn by the smells. Young puppies and very small dog breeds are especially at risk of severe and sometimes fatal poisoning.

No one knows how many species of *Inocybe* there are. The estimate of a thousand worldwide may be low or may be high, depending on what is moved out of the genus by current research. In comparison to other large mushroom-bearing genera of fungi, fibreheads are somewhat understudied. Attempts to divide them into subgenera have been frustrated by the difficulty of matching specimens to species descriptions—in most cases, chemical work and careful microscopic study is necessary. Genetic studies are helping to clarify the muddled picture.

In this book we present only four common BC fibreheads as main entries. These four are species that we believe beginning students have some chance of adding to their arsenal of easily recognizable mushrooms. Those wanting to go further with inocybes will have to turn to books and online resources with greater coverage of these LBMs.

White Fibrehead   *Inocybe geophylla* group

CAP To 3 cm across; conical expanding to convex or almost flat, but usually retaining a sharp umbo, margins incurved at first and then lifting; whitish, sometimes aging a buff colour; somewhat slimy/sticky when wet; smooth over umbo, silky/glossy and finely fibrillose elsewhere; flesh thin, white. **GILLS** Broadly to narrowly attached to free; whitish, becoming grey and eventually brown as spores develop, but edges often remaining paler; closely spaced; with 1–3 subgills between neighbouring gills. **ODOUR** Of semen. **TASTE** Not distinctive. **SPORE PRINT** Dull brown. **STEM** To 5 cm tall × 5 mm wide; equal but often with a slightly bulbous base; whitish, or whitish grey; dry; finely fibrillose or almost smooth, often minutely dusted at top. **RING** Cobwebby; white; disappearing. **FRUITING** Single or in small groups; on the ground, sometimes on rotting wood; under conifer or in hardwood forests; late summer, autumn.

    EDIBILITY Poisonous. Contains muscarine. **SIMILAR** The **WHITE FIBREHEAD** often grows around *Hebeloma* species that have a similar colour and stature (p. 275), but most of these are a bit larger, have slimier tops, and give off a radishy odour. *Inocybe pudica* (also known as *I. whitei*) may start out white, but it develops a pinkish or salmon colour on its cap, gills, flesh, and/or stem. It also tends to have a broader umbo. The **WESTERN LILAC FIBREHEAD** (p. 255) starts off with lilac tones on its cap and stem, but these important features may disappear with age and the cap and stem take on yellow-brown hues. **COMMENTS** What we currently call *I. geophylla* probably comprises several distinct BC species, but the molecular work to separate these has not been done. ✱ "Geophylla" means "earth gills," presumably a reference to the brown colour of the mature gills.

Western Lilac Fibrehead   *Inocybe pallidicremea*

CAP To 4 cm across; bell-shaped to conical expanding to convex but usually retaining a sharp umbo, the margins downcurved; lilac when young but fading, the umbo becoming yellow-brown with the colour creeping toward the margin, the cap sometimes keeping greyish lilac streaks; dry to tacky; centre smooth around umbo, elsewhere silky; flesh thin (up to 4 mm under umbo), white. GILLS Broadly to narrowly attached; pale grey or whitish, becoming brown as spores develop, the edges often paler; closely spaced; several tiers of subgills. ODOUR Of semen. TASTE Not distinctive. SPORE PRINT Dull brown. STEM To 6 cm tall × 6 mm wide; equal with a slightly bulbous base; solid; coloured as cap, the base sometimes with yellow tones; dry; smooth, but sometimes minutely dusted at top, or with fine longitudinal striations. RING Cobwebby; white; disappearing or leaving a ring zone. FRUITING Single or in small groups; on the ground; in conifer or hardwood forests; late summer, autumn.

EDIBILITY Poisonous. Probably contains muscarine. SIMILAR The lilac tones call to mind some of the lilac members of the *Cortinarius* genus, such as the SILVERY VIOLET WEBCAP (p. 240), but the latter is much larger (cap to 9 cm across, stem to 12 cm tall). The lilac colours might also lead to a confusion with a mycena, particularly the LILAC BONNET (p. 177), but the mycena has white spores and a smooth, almost greasy, hygrophanous cap. *Inocybe griseolilacina* also has lilac colours, but the cap is covered with uplifted (and sometimes pressed-down) yellow-brown fibrils. See the entry for the WHITE FIBREHEAD (p. 254) for other comparisons. COMMENTS Until recently, the WESTERN LILAC FIBREHEAD was recorded in BC species surveys as *I. lilacina*. A 2018 study of mushrooms with this designation showed BC specimens matched the genetic signature of *I. pallidicremea*, a mushroom first described in the 1970s. ☞ "Pallidicremea" is a reference to the pale cream colour of faded specimens.

Mushroom Poisons

Anyone collecting and eating wild mushrooms should obviously become familiar with BC's best edibles. They should also, however, get to know BC's poisonous mushrooms, especially those that can be confused with choice edibles. The list of mushrooms that are good edibles and the list of mushrooms that are poisonous are, when compared with the number of mushrooms found in BC, surprisingly small. Most BC mushrooms, like most BC plants, are neither delicious nor poisonous.

The great majority of mushroom poisonings are probably due not to eating poisonous mushrooms, but to eating edible species under the wrong circumstances. Consuming decayed and infected mushrooms, improper storage, incomplete cooking, overeating, ingesting mushrooms growing in contaminated sites, and food allergies can all contribute to bad experiences with otherwise edible mushrooms. Cases in which people are directly poisoned by the toxins contained in some mushrooms, however, though less common than the incidental cases, tend to receive the most media attention.

The toxins involved and the effect of ingesting these toxins vary widely. The most serious mushroom poisonings involve amatoxins (such as those found in DEATH CAP, p. 112, FUNERAL BELL, p. 286, and DEADLY PARASOL, p. 103), amino-hexadienoic acid (found in SMITH'S AMANITA, p. 117), and orellanine (found in some *Cortinarius* species). These poisonings can lead to liver and kidney failure and sometimes to death. Almost all fatal mushroom poisonings involve these species.

Some mushroom poisonings are characterized by rhabdomyolysis, the rapid breakdown of skeletal muscle and consequent leakage of the muscle protein myoglobin into the urine. Rhabdomyolysis can be caused by the carboxylic acid found in the Asian species *Russula subnigricans*. We don't have this species in BC, but a cautious approach would suggest not eating its close BC relative, the BLACKENING RUSSULA (p. 58). Rhabdomyolysis has also been associated with compounds found in MAN ON HORSEBACK (p. 148) and perhaps in the MOUSE TRICH (p. 156), though these two species have been eaten regularly by some in our province without obvious effect.

A number of other BC mushrooms contain a variety of compounds with different, but still serious, effects on human metabolism. The gyromitrins found in the FALSE MOREL (p. 444) and COMMON CUDONIA (p. 366), for example, decompose in the stomach into hydrazines, which can cause vomiting, diarrhea, and in some cases death. The muscarines in some of the inocybes (p. 253) and clitocybes (p. 125) can also lead to vomiting and diarrhea within a few hours of consumption. The coprines in INKY CAP (p. 292) cause unpleasant effects if alcohol is consumed with, or sometimes several days before or after, the mushroom. Serious autoimmune reactions are sometimes seen in those who have been eating POISON PAX (p. 273) for a long time. ANGEL WINGS (p. 211) have been responsible for fatal poisonings in Japan.

If you suspect mushroom poisoning, contact the BC Poison Control Centre at 1-800-567-8911. If possible, save the mushrooms or some of the leftover food containing the mushrooms to help confirm identification.

Amanita phalloides illustrated by Frank L. Beebe, in George A. Hardy's *Some Mushrooms and Other Fungi of British Columbia* (1946), part of the BC Provincial Museum's handbook series, a predecessor to this guide.

Corn-silk Fibrehead   *Pseudosperma sororium*

CAP To 8 cm across; conical or bell-shaped expanding to convex or almost flat but usually retaining an umbo, margins initially curved under but eventually upturned and splitting, often hung with veil remnants; whitish or pale yellow, darkening with age; dry; silky, often with prominent radial fibres; flesh thin, white but sometimes with pale yellow tints. GILLS Broadly to narrowly attached, sometimes almost free; shallow (to 3 mm); whitish or pale yellow, with darker yellow and olive tones in age; closely spaced. ODOUR Corn silk. TASTE Not distinctive. SPORE PRINT Dull brown. STEM To 12 cm tall × 1 cm wide; equal or slightly wider below; white or cream, yellowing with age; dry; silky or scurfy, becoming smooth in age. RING Absent. FRUITING Single or in small groups; on the ground; in conifer or hardwood forests; late summer, autumn, winter.

EDIBILITY Poisonous. Contains muscarine. SIMILAR Three other fairly common *Inocybe* species resemble CORN-SILK FIBREHEAD but smell more of semen. *Pseudosperma rimosum* (previously known as *Inocybe fastigiata*) has more brown hues in the cap. *Inocybe ceskae*, a variant of the European *I. mixtilis* that was named for BC's inocybe queen, Oluna Ceska, has a honey-brown, often greasy cap that has less prominent radial fibres than the CORN-SILK FIBREHEAD, does not readily split at the margins, and has a white stem minutely dusted for its entire length and a small, abrupt bulb at the base. *Inocybe albodisca* (possibly the same species as the one traditionally called *I. grammata*) also has less prominent radial fibres on the cap and a white stem dusted for its entire length, but the cap tends to split at the margins and the centre of the disc is covered with a white to cream layer that looks like a melted dollop of vanilla ice cream. COMMENTS *Pseudosperma sororium*, previously known as *Inocybe sororia*, is largely restricted to coastal areas of our province. ☙ "Sororium" means "of a sister," perhaps because the split yellow caps with radial lines reminded early mycologists of the flaxen tresses of young women.

Green-foot Fibrehead   *Inosperma calamistratum*

CAP To 4 cm across; bell-shaped or convex; dark brown; dry; densely covered with fine, lifted-up scales, especially in the cap centre, but sometimes over the whole cap; flesh thin, pale brown, becoming reddish where cut, bruising a darker brown. GILLS Broadly to narrowly attached or nearly free; deep; brown, with whitish edges, at least when young; closely spaced. ODOUR Variously described. Said to be like pine resin combined with fresh raw fish, or the odour of crushed geranium leaves, or just sweetish. TASTE Not distinctive. SPORE PRINT Brown to yellowish brown. STEM To 10 cm tall × 5 mm wide; equal or slightly wider below; colour same as the cap, with blue-green or greenish colours on the lower part; dry; sprinkled with fine, lifted-up scales, the scales wearing away exposing a longitudinally striate surface. RING Cobwebby; may or may not be evident on stem. FRUITING Single or in small groups; on the ground; usually under conifers, but also under hardwoods; late summer, autumn.

EDIBILITY Unknown. May contain muscarine, which can trigger serious reactions. SIMILAR Two variants of *Inocybe* species that have recently been raised to species status also have blue-green colours on the lower part of their stems. One is *Inosperma mucidiolens*, formerly a variety of the GREEN-FOOT FIBREHEAD. It is said to have a corn-silk odour. The other, *Inosperma maximum*, was once a variety of *Inocybe hirsuta*. It has the raw fish/resin odour of the GREEN-FOOT FIBREHEAD, but its cap is reddish brown and its flesh shows a stronger reddish staining. *Inocybe lacera* also has cap scales, but the odour is faint, the cap becomes cracked as it dries, and the overall-whitish stem lacks scales, especially in the upper half, and isn't green at the base. COMMENTS This species appears to be restricted to coastal areas in our province. ❧ *Inosperma calamistratum* is also known as *Inocybe calamistrata*. ❧ "Calamistratum" means "crisped" or "curled."

GOLDEN PHOLIOTA (*Pholiota limonella* group), p. 268.

Gymnopilus and Pholiota

Mushrooms in the genera *Gymnopilus* and *Pholiota* are medium to large wood decomposers that are usually attached to dead or dying trees or logs, though some can be terrestrial, feeding on wood buried in the ground. They generally have rusty brown spores, though those of *Pholiota* can tend toward dirty brown in some species, and they tend to wear yellow-brown to reddish brown colours on their caps and stems. Caps of *Gymnopilus* species are usually smooth ("gymnopilus" means "naked cap"), and those of *Pholiota* usually scaly ("pholiota" comes from the Greek word for "scale"). Both species have partial veils, with those of *Pholiota* species usually disappearing quickly and leaving few remnants and those of *Gymnopilus* often displaying remnants of this veil as tatters on the cap and as stem rings. Most *Gymnopilus* species have a bitter taste; most *Pholiota* species do not.

Genetic analysis suggests that species in *Gymnopilus* and *Pholiota* are related, though the nature of this relationship is still under debate. Some mycologists group them, along with several other genera of brown- and dark-spored mushrooms, in the Strophariaceae family. BC has about a dozen species of *Gymnopilus* (of 200 species described worldwide) and approximately 30 species of *Pholiota* (of more than 400 worldwide).

We have sparse information on the edibility of most species in this section. A couple of the gymnopiluses may be hallucinogenic, but no edibles are flagged among them. The pholiotas are not much better fare. BRISTLY PHOLIOTA (p. 266) often produces gastrointestinal distress, and even pholiotas that are supposedly edible may produce bad reactions in certain people and/or develop strong unpleasant smells and tastes when cooked.

For more brown-spored, medium to large wood-rotting mushrooms, see the entries in the "Other Big Brown-spored" (p. 271) section.

Jumbo Gym
Gymnopilus ventricosus group

CAP To 40 cm across; convex to nearly flat, margins at first incurved, later wavy, often festooned with veil remnants; yellow to yellow-orange can dominate young caps, later reddish brown to orange-brown or tawny gold, margins often darker; dry; smooth to silky, sometimes with fine, pressed-down scales outside of central area; flesh thick, firm, yellowish. GILLS Broadly attached, sometimes notched or with a decurrent tooth; deep; pale yellow, becoming rusty brown as spores mature; crowded. ODOUR Not distinctive. TASTE Bitter. SPORE PRINT Rusty orange. STEM To 25 cm tall × 6 cm wide; wider in middle, often curved; firm; solid; coloured as cap, often paler at top and with red-brown streaking below; dry; longitudinally striate. RING Membranous, and lifted up but soon drooping to skirt-like; pale yellow, then taking on the spore colour; persistent or (more rarely) disappearing. FRUITING In groups or clustered; on rotting logs, tree bases or higher on trees, usually conifers; autumn.

EDIBILITY Not edible. SIMILAR ALASKAN GOLD (p. 280) is also large, has some of the same golden tints, and wears a drooping ring, but it fruits in the soil. COMMENTS *Gymnopilus ventricosus* is the most common member of the group in BC, but we also have *G. voitkii*, first described in 2020 and currently only differentiated from *G. ventricosus* by DNA or by close microscopic work. *Gymnopilus junonius* specimens from Asia are reportedly hallucinogenic (hence its common name BIG LAUGHING GYM), and the specific hallucinogenic chemicals derived from them have been studied in Japan. The Asian reputation as a hallucinogen spills over to our JUMBO GYM and the other species in the *G. ventricosus* group, but local user experience does not support this transfer. ◦ "Ventricosus" means "wider in the middle," a description of the stem.

Fir Flamecap

Gymnopilus sapineus group

CAP To 6 cm across; hemispheric to more shallowly convex, in age becoming flat and sometimes cracked; yellow-brown to orange-brown, margins sometimes paler; dry; with fine pressed-down scales; flesh firm, yellowish. **GILLS** Broadly attached; deep; often finely sawtoothed and irregular in age; yellow, developing red-brown spots, becoming cinnamon as spores mature; closely spaced. **ODOUR** Not distinctive. **TASTE** Often bitter. **SPORE PRINT** Rusty orange. **STEM** To 7 cm tall × 1 cm wide; equal or slightly narrowed below; yellow or yellowish brown, becoming brown in lower part where handled; dry; smooth or finely scaly; often with white mycelium at the base. **RING** Flimsy; yellow; disappearing or leaving fibrils near stem top that take on the spore colour. **FRUITING** Single or scattered or clustered; on decaying wood, usually coniferous, or in wood-rich substrates; summer, autumn.

    EDIBILITY Unknown. **SIMILAR** *Gymnopilus penetrans*, if not the same species as FIR FLAMECAP, differs mainly by having a white ring and a smooth cap. *Gymnopilus picreus* is about half the size of the FIR FLAMECAP and has no ring. *Gymnopilus bellulus* is also half the size and also has no ring (in North America, at least). It has smaller spores than *G. picreus*. The **OLIVE-GOLD LOGLOVER** (p. 203) shares the habitat and overall look of FIR FLAMECAP, but the former has no ring or ring remnants and its yellow-brown cap usually has tints of olive green. **COMMENTS** *Gymnopilus sapineus* and the 3 similar *Gymnopilus* species we just mentioned (and several other small *Gymnopilus* species not mentioned here because most BC collectors are not in the habit of reporting them on species lists) are all quite similar and in need of closer morphological and genetic study. ● "Sapineus" is from a Late Latin word referring to different kinds of conifers.

Yellow-gilled Gym   *Gymnopilus luteofolius*

CAP To 10 cm across; convex becoming nearly flat, margins inrolled when young and often hung with veil remnants; covered with dark red or reddish brown scales when young, the scales fading eventually to pink-red or yellow-red and then falling off, leaving a yellowish base colour that is occasionally spotted or bruised blue-green; dry; flesh thick, reddish or light purple, fading to yellowish. **GILLS** Broadly or narrowly attached, sometimes notched or slightly decurrent; deep; edges ragged; yellow, becoming rusty orange as spores mature; somewhat closely spaced. **ODOUR** Not distinctive. **TASTE** Bitter. **SPORE PRINT** Rusty orange. **STEM** To 8 cm tall × 2 cm wide; equal or widening downward (single mushrooms) or narrowing downward (clusters), often curved; purplish pink above the ring, below coloured as the cap, the base sometimes bruising bluish; dry; surface has longitudinal striations. **RING** Cobwebby to membranous; posed near the top of the stem; yellowish; sometimes disappearing or becoming a ring zone that takes on the colour of the spores. **FRUITING** In groups or (usually) clustered; on decaying wood (usually conifer), wood chips, or wood-rich soil; late autumn, winter.

EDIBILITY Unknown. **SIMILAR** *Gymnopilus aeruginosus* (if it's a different species) is supposed to display more green staining. **BLUE-GREEN FLAMECAP** (p. 265) has pinky brown and lilac tints at first, which develop into widespread dull green colours. **PLUMS AND CUSTARD** (p. 167) has white spores and lacks a partial veil. **COMMENTS** Paul Stamets, the omnibus mycologist and founder of Fungi Perfecti, first pointed out the blue-green bruising and spotting of the YELLOW-GILLED GYM (the original description of *G. luteofolius* did not mention it). He believes that the mushroom may be mildly hallucinogenic. YELLOW-GILLED GYM is known (so far) only from southwestern BC. ◦ "Luteofolius" means "yellow-gilled."

Blue-green Flamecap

Gymnopilus punctifolius

CAP To 10 cm across; convex becoming flat, margins inrolled, sometimes wavy; pinkish brown or lilac when very young, then dull greenish with a bluish green bloom, sometimes with yellow hues in the mix, and becoming olive-brown or brown in age; dry; finely silky/scaly near centre, becoming smooth; flesh thin, firm, greenish yellow. GILLS Broadly attached to deeply notched; deep; edges often ragged; olive-yellow, with yellow or rusty spots with age, becoming browner as the spores mature; closely spaced. ODOUR Not distinctive. TASTE Bitter. SPORE PRINT Rusty orange. STEM To 15 cm tall × 2 cm wide; equal, often curvy, sometimes narrow and rooting at base; same colour as the cap; dry; longitudinally striate; sometimes with lilac mycelium at base. RING Absent. FRUITING Single or scattered; on wood, usually coniferous, or in rich humus; summer, autumn, winter.

EDIBILITY Not edible. SIMILAR *Gymnopilus aeruginosus* (which may be the same as the YELLOW-GILLED GYM, p. 264) also has green hues and bruising, but it has a ring or ring zone. When still green, smaller specimens of the BLUE-GREEN FLAMECAP might resemble another wood rotter, SULPHUR TUFT (p. 300), but SULPHUR TUFT has purple-brown spores. In the later olive-brown stages of the BLUE-GREEN FLAMECAP, specimens might resemble some of the olive-brown *Cortinarius* species, such as the OLIVE WEBCAP (p. 251). COMMENTS The BLUE-GREEN FLAMECAP seems to be primarily a western North America species that has, to date, only been recorded in our province from coastal BC. Numerous collections of it have been made from Haida Gwaii. ❧ "Punctifolius" means "dotted gills," a reference to the rusty-spotted gills.

Bristly Pholiota   *Pholiota squarrosa*

CAP To 10 cm across; almost spherical, hemispheric, or more shallowly convex becoming bell-shaped to nearly flat, sometimes with a small umbo, the margins curved in initially and usually with veil remnants; light tan to pale yellow or pale yellow-brown, in age darker and sometimes with yellow-green tints at the margin; dry; densely covered with conspicuous yellowish brown or brown upturned scales; flesh moderately thick, pale yellow. GILLS Broadly to narrowly attached, sometimes slightly decurrent; shallow; yellow or greenish yellow, becoming rusty brown as spores develop; closely spaced. ODOUR Usually unpleasant (garlic, radish, skunk), but some specimens seem to have no smell. TASTE Rancid or not distinctive. SPORE PRINT Rusty brown. STEM To 12 cm tall × 1.5 cm wide; equal or narrowing downward; solid; coloured as cap, sometimes becoming a darker red-brown below; dry; smooth above, with scales that jut out and curve back along the lower stem. RING Membranous; whitish to yellowish; persistent or disappearing. FRUITING In groups or densely clustered; on dead wood or at the base of live trees, both conifers and hardwoods; summer, autumn.

EDIBILITY Poisonous. Causes severe stomach upset in some cases. SIMILAR *Pholiota squarrosoides* has a slimy/sticky and paler cap background, gills that don't take on a greenish hue, a cinnamony odour, and a preference for hardwoods. The GOLDEN PHOLIOTA (p. 268) has a slimy, dark yellow to orange cap. TERRESTRIAL PHOLIOTA (p. 269) has flatter scales and grows on the ground in open areas. When the caps of BRISTLY PHOLIOTA darken and the scales become flatter and less prominent, they can start to resemble caps of HONEY MUSHROOMS (p. 164). HONEY MUSHROOMS, however, have white spores, white fibrils on their stems, and black rhizomorphs. COMMENTS The BRISTLY PHOLIOTA is the type species chosen to represent the entire *Pholiota* genus. ❧ "Squarrosa" means "scurfy," a reference to the upturned scales on the caps and stems.

Poplar Pholiota   *Pholiota populnea*

CAP To 20 cm across; convex, sometimes becoming nearly flat, margins inrolled or downcurved and often hung with veil remnants; white or cream, sometimes developing brown colours, especially over the disc, with white or buff patches and scales that may wash off in age; slightly slimy/sticky when moist; flesh dense, thick, firm, white. GILLS Broadly attached, notched; deep; white becoming rusty cinnamon as spores mature; closely spaced. ODOUR Not distinctive. TASTE Not distinctive, or sometimes slightly bitter. SPORE PRINT Cinnamon brown. STEM To 15 cm tall × 3 cm wide; equal or widening downward; hard; solid; central or off-centre; white, then later brownish below; dry; above ring smooth or silky, below ring white- or buff-scaly. RING Thick and cottony; slightly above the middle of the stem; white; sometimes disappearing. FRUITING Single or in groups or in clusters; on live trees and the dead wood (stems, logs) of poplars (most commonly BLACK COTTONWOOD); autumn.

EDIBILITY Edible. But tough and not tasty. SIMILAR BRISTLY PHOLIOTA (p. 266), which does not restrict itself to poplars, has more yellow hues in the flesh and cap, and the scales on the cap are a yellowish brown or brown colour. COMMENTS POPLAR PHOLIOTA causes a yellow laminated butt rot on poplars (see essay on the different kinds of rots on p. 394). The fungus is most active in living trees, only remaining alive for a couple of years after the tree has died. ✦ The flesh of this mushroom is notably tough. Young specimens can be as hard as lacrosse balls. ✦ The name of this species may also be listed as *Hemipholiota populnea*. ✦ POPLAR PHOLIOTA is a species found (like poplars) mostly in the BC Interior. ✦ "Populnea" means "pertaining to poplar."

Golden Pholiota   *Pholiota limonella* group

CAP To 16 cm across; bell-shaped to convex or nearly flat, with a broad umbo, the margins curved down and often hung with veil remnants; dark yellowish or shades of orange; gelatinous or sticky, especially when wet; covered with dark, flattened, sometimes triangular scales that may wash off; flesh thick, pale yellow. GILLS Broadly attached to notched; deep (0.5–1 cm); pale yellow, becoming brown as spores develop; closely spaced. ODOUR Not distinctive or sometimes sweet and fruity. TASTE Not distinctive. SPORE PRINT Rusty brown. STEM To 8 cm tall × 1.5 cm wide; equal; central or off-centre; yellow or yellowish brown; dry; cottony above the ring, with often uplifted scales below ring. RING Pale or yellowish; vanishing, but sometimes leaving a slight ring of fibres or ring zone. FRUITING In groups or clustered; on wood (logs, stumps, buried wood); summer, autumn.

EDIBILITY Not edible. SIMILAR *Pholiota flammans* has a bright yellow cap with yellow scales that is usually drier (or at least less slimy) than the GOLDEN PHOLIOTA. It also has a bright yellow stem and young gills. *Pholiota squarrosoides* has a cap that is paler, sometimes with just hints of dark yellow or orange, and the scales are more upright. BRISTLY PHOLIOTA (p. 266) has a paler yellow-brown cap that is dry. COMMENTS Mating tests have determined that there are several apparently non-interbreeding *Pholiota* species (e.g., *P. aurivella*, *P. limonella*, and *P. adiposa*) that look so much alike they can only be reliably separated by measuring spore size. Depending on the outcome of DNA studies, they could end up being considered varieties of the same species. ◆ Young GOLDEN PHOLIOTAS can form beautiful clusters on standing or fallen dead trees, impressive and photogenic. ◆ "Limonella" means "little lemon," referring to the yellow colour of the cap, stem, and young gills.

Terrestrial Pholiota

Pholiota terrestris

CAP To 8 cm across; hemispheric-conical or more shallowly convex becoming flat, sometimes with a small umbo, margins incurved or curved down and often with a fringe of veil remnants; brown, grey-brown, yellow-brown, or dull red-brown, at first darker because of merged pressed-down fibrils/scales, in maturity the scales spreading to show a lighter background dotted with raised darker brown scales (that sometimes wash off); slimy/sticky when wet; flesh moderately thick (to 4 mm), pale yellowish brown, darkening with age. **GILLS** Broadly attached; shallow; pale, becoming greyish brown to cinnamon brown as spores develop; closely spaced. **ODOUR** Not distinctive. **TASTE** Not distinctive. **SPORE PRINT** Brown. **STEM** To 8 cm tall × 1 cm wide; equal or narrowing downward; coloured as cap, darker brown below; dry; finely hairy above the ring/ring zone, with brown scales or patches like those on the cap below the ring zone. **RING** Membranous, thin; near the top of stem; white; persistent or disappearing. **FRUITING** In groups or clustered; on the ground; in open areas (trail edges, along roads, lawns); late summer, autumn, winter.

 EDIBILITY Edible. But not tasty. **SIMILAR** *Pholiota squarrosoides* has the slimy-when-wet cap and pale to brown gills. It grows in closed forest habitats, however, and the cap background and stem scales are a lighter brown than those of the TERRESTRIAL PHOLIOTA. With its upright brown scales washed off, the TERRESTRIAL PHOLIOTA might be confused with *P. decorata*, but *P. decorata* has a pale beige (though often brown at the centre) cap, a non-clustered growth habit, and a preference for forest habitats where there are buried twigs. **COMMENTS** The TERRESTRIAL PHOLIOTA, as the common and scientific names indicate, is the only *Pholiota* species in this guide with a ground habitat. (On occasion, wood-growing species may appear to be terrestrial because of buried wood.) ◆ It can occasionally be found inland, but it seems to be much more frequent in southwestern BC coastal areas. ◆ "Terrestris" means "growing on the ground."

Sheathed Woodtuft

Kuehneromyces mutabilis

CAP To 6 cm across but typically smaller; convex, becoming bell-shaped or nearly flat, with a broad umbo, the margins inrolled and tending to remain downcurved; orange-brown or reddish brown, fading yellow-brown from the centre out as it dries; with a peelable skin; sticky or greasy before the skin is peeled or washed off by rain; smooth or with fine white fibrils from the veil when very young; translucent-striate when wet; hygrophanous; flesh thin, whitish, sometimes tinged brown. GILLS Broadly attached to slightly decurrent; deep; whitish, becoming cinnamon-coloured as spores develop; crowded. ODOUR Not distinctive. TASTE Not usually distinctive. SPORE PRINT Cinnamon brown. STEM To 10 cm tall × 1.2 cm wide; equal or narrowed toward base; whitish when young, then later brown to blackish from the base up; silky to finely striate, then later bald above ring; with upright, pale-brown scales below ring; lower base sometimes with white mycelium. RING Membranous; whitish; sometimes vanishing and leaving remnant fibrils on stem. FRUITING Usually in clusters, sometimes quite large ones; on wood (logs, stumps, buried wood); most common in autumn, but fruiting in all seasons.

EDIBILITY Edible. But with dangerous look-alikes. SIMILAR The deadly poisonous FUNERAL BELL (p. 286), which does not form the mass clusters that the SHEATHED WOODTUFT does, has a farinaceous odour and lacks the prominent pale-brown scales below the ring. *Kuehneromyces lignicola* (inset photo) also tends to gather in large clusters, usually fruits in the spring at higher elevations near melting snow, and tends to have neither a ring nor raised scales on the lower stem. The HONEY MUSHROOM (p. 164), especially the *Armillaria nabsnona* version, can be quite similar in look and habitat, but it has white spores and a less hygrophanous cap. COMMENTS *Kuehneromyces mutabilis* was once known as *Pholiota mutabilis*. ✤ "Mutabilis" means "changeable," possibly a reference to the distinctly hygrophanous cap.

Other Big Brown-spored

This section and the next ("Other Little Brown-spored," p. 281) pull together a motley group of brown-spored mushrooms. We've separated the remaining bigger brown-spored mushrooms—with caps generally larger than five centimetres across—from the next section, which contains many of the LBMs, or little brown mushrooms.

In dividing by cap size, we have also created a rough partition between mycorrhizal and decomposer species. This is not an accident: fruiting bodies of mycorrhizal species are usually larger than fruiting bodies of decomposers. While there are exceptions—small mycorrhizal species and large decomposers—the general rule holds. One reason for this is probably that mycorrhizal species are better poised to take advantage of the huge nutrient bonus offered by the larger and living plant partners. In this section, four of the seven genera represented in the main entries are known to be mycorrhizal.

The mycorrhizal genus *Hebeloma* contains, worldwide and in BC, many species that are difficult to separate without a good microscope and a lot of patience. A research project on North American *Hebeloma* species, not published yet, has so far confirmed about 20 species in BC. We've included *H. crustuliniforme* group (POISON PIE, p. 275) to represent this important and challenging genus. The genus *Phaeocollybia* comprises about two dozen species in the Pacific Northwest, of which 10, including the KAUFFMAN'S ROOTSHANK (p. 278), have been reported in BC studies. They are important mycorrhizal partners of the giant trees of old-growth forests. *Phylloporus rhodoxanthus* group (GILLED BOLETE, p. 274) species are members of a curious and relatively large genus (about 70 named species, only a few of which are in BC) of mycorrhizal mushrooms that, in spite of their gills, are closely related to pored boletes. *Paxillus involutus* (POISON PAX, p. 273) and *Tapinella atrotomentosa* (VELVET ROLLRIM, p. 272), both also related to boletes, share a superficial similarity and were once thought to belong to the same genus. *Paxillus* species, however, are mycorrhizal mushrooms, and *Tapinella* species are decomposers. Another genus of decomposer mushrooms, *Agrocybe*, has one extremely common BC species group, which we include here (SPRING AGROCYBE, p. 279). It is unknown whether *Phaeolepiota* (ALASKAN GOLD, p. 280) is a decomposer or is mycorrhizal.

Those looking for table mushrooms will not find much of interest in this section.

Velvet Rollrim — *Tapinella atrotomentosa*

CAP To 15 cm across; convex becoming flat or depressed and vase-shaped, sometimes cracking, the margins inrolled when young, wavy and often lobed in age; brown or dark brown, margins sometimes yellowish; dry; velvety with matted hairs, becoming smooth at the margin; flesh thick, tough, pale yellowish brown. **GILLS** Decurrent; shallow; often forked, sometimes resembling pores near stem; cream to yellow or yellowish brown, bruising darker brown; closely spaced. **ODOUR** Not distinctive. **TASTE** Bitter or not distinctive. **SPORE PRINT** Yellowish brown. **STEM** To 9 cm tall × 3 cm wide; short and stout; solid; often off-centre; dark brown, sometimes paler near top; dry; surface velvety with densely matted dark brown or blackish hairs. **RING** Absent. **FRUITING** Single or in groups, sometimes clustered; on conifer wood (logs, stumps); summer, autumn.

EDIBILITY Unknown. **SIMILAR** The VELVET ROLLRIM was once known as *Paxillus atrotomentosus* because of its morphological similarity to *Paxillus involutus* (**POISON PAX**, p. 273). The latter has a central, smooth (or finely striate) stem and grows on the ground near its mycorrhizal partners. The smaller *Tapinella panuoides*, another mushroom that resembles the VELVET ROLLRIM, has no stem, or else a very small lateral one. **SMELLY OYSTER** (p. 213) caps, when they have a rudimentary stem, can also be similar, but the caps of smelly oysters are pale orange to buff rather than brown, and their gills do not fork. **COMMENTS** VELVET ROLLRIM, a brown-rot wood decomposer, is common in southern BC. ◆ It is used by dyers to give cloth a dark purple, green, or blue colour. ◆ The mushroom tissue stains a bright purple with common household ammonia. ◆ "Atrotomentosa" means "with black hair," a reference to the velvety cap and stem.

Poison Pax

Paxillus involutus

CAP To 12 cm across; convex becoming flat and centrally depressed, but often retaining a broad umbo in the depression, the margins inrolled; grey-brown to yellow-brown, sometimes light reddish brown; slimy/sticky when moist; felted when young, becoming smooth; flesh thick, yellowish, slowly bruising brown. GILLS Decurrent; often forking near stem and with cross-veins, sometimes forming structures resembling pores; yellow to pale yellow-brown, bruising brown or reddish brown; crowded. ODOUR Acid to fruity or not distinctive. TASTE Usually sour. SPORE PRINT Brown to yellow-brown, sometimes slightly reddish. STEM To 8 cm tall × 2 cm wide; equal, often curved; quickly bruising reddish brown when cut; pale at first, darkening red-brown from the base up with age; dry; smooth or finely striate. RING Absent. FRUITING Single or in groups; on the ground; in forests; autumn.

EDIBILITY Poisonous. POISON PAX was at one time brought to the table, but no longer—undercooked caps can cause stomach upset within an hour or two, and extended consumption of even well-cooked caps can lead to eventual autoimmune reactions and kidney failure. POISON PAX has the dubious distinction of being the only known mushroom to have killed a professional mycologist (Julius Schäffer, in 1944). SIMILAR *Paxillus cuprinus* develops a coppery top that can become cracked in dry weather, usually has no umbo, and can have a thinner stem than the POISON PAX. It grows in lawns and boulevards around birch trees and is typically found in the urban areas of southwestern BC. See the entry for the VELVET ROLLRIM (p. 272) for other look-alikes. COMMENTS POISON PAX is one of a complex of species, several of which were originally designated as *P. involutus*. The whole complex has been extensively studied, however, and in recent decades we have been able to separate it into discrete species, several of which occur in our province. ◆ "Involutus" means "inrolled," a reference to the cap margin.

Gilled Bolete — *Phylloporus rhodoxanthus* group

CAP To 8 cm across; convex becoming flat or sometimes depressed, in age sometimes developing cracks and the margins lifting up; usually red or reddish brown, sometimes olive-brown, sometimes yellowish in the cracks; dry; velvety or smooth; flesh thick, whitish or pale yellow. GILLS Broadly attached to decurrent; deep; sometimes forked or with cross-veins, sometimes even forming pores near the stem; bright yellow, becoming mustard yellow, sometimes slowly bruising blue; widely spaced. ODOUR Not distinctive. TASTE Not distinctive. SPORE PRINT Yellow-brown or orange-brown. STEM To 10 cm tall × 1.5 cm wide; usually equal; yellow, with reddish tints, often staining reddish brown; dry; smooth or with reddish brown dots; often with yellow basal mycelium. RING Absent. FRUITING Single or in small groups; on the ground; under trees; spring, summer, autumn.

EDIBILITY Edible. SIMILAR Red-brown caps, yellow gills, and stems with red and yellow tones may call to mind the similar (but white-spored) PLUMS AND CUSTARD (p. 167). COMMENTS *Phylloporus rhodoxanthus* is found in the eastern US. Similar mushrooms in the US Pacific Northwest are usually identified as *P. arenicola*. *Phylloporus arenicola* fruiting bodies, however, do not stain blue, and some of our West Coast specimens do—a puzzle that needs to be solved. ❧ The GILLED BOLETE is genetically a bolete: almost every morphological feature matches that of the boletes, except for the gills, and even these may take on a pore-like look near the stem. ❧ Artisan dyers value the GILLED BOLETE for its beige or gold mushroom-dye colour. ❧ "Rhodoxanthus" means "red-yellow," a good description of the top and bottom cap colours.

Poison Pie — *Hebeloma crustuliniforme* group

CAP To 10 cm across; convex becoming flat, sometimes umbonate, margins inrolled when young and sometimes lifted up and lobed in age; cream, becoming tan (the colour of a well-cooked pie), often paler toward the margin; slimy/sticky and often picking up debris, shiny when dry; smooth; flesh thick, white. GILLS Broadly attached, becoming narrowly attached or notched; edges sometimes beaded with water drops that dry into brown spots; whitish, becoming dull brown as spores mature, edges sometimes white; crowded. ODOUR Strongly of radishes. TASTE Bitter or not distinctive. SPORE PRINT Milk-chocolate brown. STEM To 12 cm tall × 1.5 cm wide; equal or base abruptly widened; whitish, or pale shade of the cap colour, sometimes with stains from spores; dry; longitudinally striate or smooth, the top often covered in powder-like granules. RING Absent. FRUITING Scattered or in groups, often in fairy rings; on the ground; in forests, pastures, and open woods; usually autumn, sometimes spring.

EDIBILITY Poisonous. Can cause stomach upset within a couple of hours. SIMILAR We have 2 other fairly common *Hebeloma* groups in BC. The *H. mesophaeum* **group** includes the many species with a fibrillose veil, often scanty, that when broken usually leaves remnants on the cap margin or stem. These species tend to be smaller than POISON PIE and have darker brown caps. The *H. sacchariolens* **group** species have a strong, sweet odour, somewhat like caramel or fruit candy. COMMENTS When we append the word "group" to a species name in this guide, we normally mean that there are 2 or more closely related species. In this case, the appended word actually designates a not-so-closely-related gumbo of *Hebeloma* species that don't have fibrillose veils, lack strong sweet odours, and have masqueraded under the *H. crustuliniforme* name. The current best-guess candidate for the actual *Hebeloma* species that we most commonly encounter in BC is *H. velutipes*, which is quite similar to *H. crustuliniforme* morphologically but not genetically. ◆ "Crustuliniforme" means "crust-like, cookie-like."

Corpse Mushrooms

Throughout this guide, we've specified the habitats where you may expect to find certain mushrooms. Some mushrooms, we have noted, appear in fields, others in forests. A few types of mushrooms, it turns out, prefer to grow on or around corpses.

We know of approximately 40 species of fungi that fruit more vigorously in the presence of ammonia. In natural systems, ammonia is released as a byproduct of the decomposition of organic matter containing nitrogen compounds, and animal remains are an important source of this natural nitrogen. Fungi that benefit from the decomposition of (usually buried) animal corpses are sometimes termed post-putrefaction fungi. Or, more simply, corpse mushrooms.

Corpse mushrooms process the nitrogen in animal remains in an orderly succession, the stages perhaps regulated by what forms of nitrogen are available. Proteins in corpses are initially broken down into amino acids and ammonia, and early-stage corpse fungi may be those best adapted to using these forms of nitrogen. Later-stage corpse fungi may be those better adapted to using nitrates and nitrites.

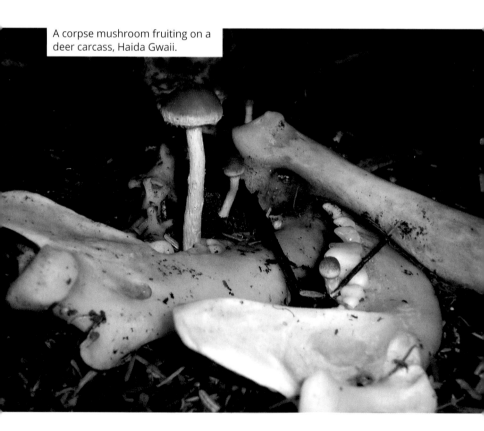

A corpse mushroom fruiting on a deer carcass, Haida Gwaii.

Common BC fungi associated with first-year corpses are the imperfect fungi (ones with no known sexual stage), ascomycetes (including *Peziza* species, p. 450), and decomposer basidiomycetes, especially those in the genera *Coprinellus* and *Coprinopsis* (pp. 291–293). After this first year, and up to the fourth year, corpse mushrooms are predominantly mycorrhizal basidiomycetes, including species of *Hebeloma* (p. 275), *Laccaria* (pp. 126–128), and *Suillus* (pp. 326–331), and the BLEWIT (p. 130).

Recognition of the role of corpse fungi is not new. Their association with death made them a source of concern in folk traditions. Naohiko Sagara of Kyoto University, a Japanese scientist whose research includes these mushrooms, cites a Chinese work, the *Tàipíng Guǎngjì*, written more than a millennium ago (with his annotations in parentheses):

As a custom in Lǐngnán (Guǎngdōng and southern provinces), people… make old slaves eat Yěgé (*Gelsemium elegans*, a poisonous plant) and die. After the dead are buried, a fungus grows on the mounds. If one eats the fruit bodies occurring right above the abdomen (of the corpse), he will die at once. If one eats those occurring above the hands, feet, or forehead, he will die within the day. Those occurring within the vicinity (of the corpse) cause death in several days. Those occurring a little away cause death in one or two months. One who eats the fruit bodies occurring quite far (from the corpse) may survive another two or three years but will never recover.

Modern researchers put a more positive spin on corpse mushrooms. It is possible, for example, that corpse mushroom succession might prove useful to forensic scientists, serving as some sort of fungal CSI.

One project designed to encourage mushrooms to decay human corpses is what Jae Rhim Lee calls her "mushroom death suit." Artist Lee has created an Infinity Mushroom strain, developed by feeding different fungi her skin, hair, and nails and selecting colonies that thrived on them. Impregnate the mushroom death suit with the Infinity Mushroom, insert human corpse, and decomposition and detoxification begin. For more on Lee's mushroom death suit, check out her suitably creepy TED Talk. Death suit or not, mycophiles may take comfort in knowing that their own corpses, buried in the ground, will eventually feed members of their favourite kingdom of organisms.

Kauffman's Rootshank
Phaeocollybia kauffmanii

CAP To 15 cm across or more; conical or convex becoming bell-shaped with a broad umbo, the margins inrolled, sometimes uplifted (but remaining inrolled), and often wavy; often zonate with orange-brown on disc, sometimes with a pale to bright brown-orange margin, dark brown or black where damaged; sticky when dry and slimy to glutinous when wet, shiny; smooth; flesh somewhat thick (to 1 cm), firm, yellow cream to smoky pink when young, darkening when wet or old. GILLS Narrowly attached or free; deep; sometimes forking, edges toothed or uneven; buff when young, becoming dull smoky golden brown as spores mature; closely spaced; with 2–6 tiered subgills. ODOUR Usually farinaceous, sometimes not distinctive. TASTE Occasionally bitter. SPORE PRINT Cinnamon brown. STEM To 11 cm tall (above ground) × 2.5 cm wide at top; widening downward up to 3.7 cm at ground level, then tapering downward as a rooting stem up to 30 cm or more long; cartilaginous; buff, light orange, or pale yellow-brown at top when young, aging to cinnamon above and deep orange-brown below; moist or dry; smooth or with pressed-down fibres, finely longitudinally striate. RING None, but with veil sometimes leaving remnant fibrils near stem top. FRUITING Single, scattered, or in groups; in rich humus under conifers, especially old-growth forests; autumn.

EDIBILITY Unknown. SIMILAR A team that travelled to Carmanah valley in the early 1990s, which included Lorelei Norvell and one of the authors of this guide, found the first *Phaeocollybia* in Western Canada. They had trouble picking it out from the multitude of HONEY MUSHROOMS (p. 164) in the old-growth forest—which is a good clue that the white-spored HONEY MUSHROOM resembles, at least superficially and from above, some of the *Phaeocollybia* species. COMMENTS For those wanting to study *Phaeocollybia* species, a copy of Lorelei Norvell and Ronald Exeter's *Phaeocollybia of Pacific Northwest North America* (US Department of the Interior, 2010) is essential. ☙ "Kauffmanii" honours Calvin Henry Kauffman (1869–1931), professor of botany at the University of Michigan.

Spring Agrocybe
Agrocybe praecox group

CAP To 10 cm across; convex to flat, sometimes broadly umbonate or depressed, often wrinkled, typically cracked in age, margins at first incurved and sometimes with veil remnants, sometimes splitting in age; tan or cream, often yellow-brown at centre; mostly dry; smooth; flesh thin, white or pale yellow-brown. **GILLS** Broadly to narrowly attached to notched; deep (to 8 mm); whitish, becoming pale brown to darker brown; closely spaced. **ODOUR** Sometimes farinaceous. **TASTE** Sometimes bitter. **SPORE PRINT** Dark brown or rusty brown. **STEM** To 12 cm tall × 1 cm or larger wide; equal or widening at base; white to tan, the bottom often staining brownish when older; smooth or longitudinally striate; sometimes with white mycelium at base. **RING** Membranous, thin, skirt-like; high on stem; whitish; sometimes disappearing and leaving a ring zone. **FRUITING** Single, scattered, or in groups, sometimes clustered; on the ground; in grassy areas, gardens, and wood chips; usually in spring, but also summer and autumn.

EDIBILITY Uncertain. The difficulty of doing exact identification within the *Agrocybe praecox* group of species suggests caution. **SIMILAR** *Agrocybe pediades* **group** mushrooms, though similar in most respects, are usually smaller (the largest have caps to 3.5 cm across and stems to 2.5 cm tall × 5 mm wide), have more widely spaced gills, have rings that often disappear without leaving a trace, and prefer fields and dung-infested areas. **GRANNY'S NIGHTCAP** (p. 244) grows in forests, does not have a cracked cap, has thicker flesh under the cap, and has a more persistent ring that is in the middle of (rather than in the upper part of) the stem. **COMMENTS** The SPRING AGROCYBE is common in BC and has a worldwide distribution. ☙ Mating studies have established that there are at least 4 distinct species in the *A. praecox* group. They can usually be distinguished by microscopic details and by habitat. ☙ The Latin word "praecox" (which also gave us the English word "precocious") means "early," a reference to the typical springtime appearance.

Alaskan Gold *Phaeolepiota aurea*

CAP To 20 cm across, sometimes larger; widely conical, becoming shallowly convex or nearly flat, with a broad umbo, the margin often with hanging veil remnants; orange-brown when young, fading to golden brown; dry; covered with golden granules when young that wash off with age; flesh thick, whitish to yellow or orange. GILLS Broadly to narrowly attached or free, sometimes with a decurrent tooth; moderately deep; pale at first, soon coloured as cap; closely spaced. ODOUR Sweetish or not distinctive. TASTE Sometimes bitter and/or astringent. SPORE PRINT Yellow-brown to orange-buff. STEM To 15 cm tall × 5 cm wide; widening downward; coloured as cap, sometimes a bit darker at top; dry; smooth above ring, below the ring covered with granular material as on cap. RING Membranous, flaring upward and then hanging, smooth above and granular below; coloured as cap; persistent. FRUITING Small groups or clusters; on the ground; in compost-rich soils, often under deciduous-tree regrowth (alder or poplar) along old country roads and trails; autumn.

EDIBILITY A significant number of consumers experience gastrointestinal distress. Notwithstanding, one of the authors consumes it with gusto. SIMILAR Easily mistaken for JUMBO GYM (p. 262) if the habitat is not taken into account—JUMBO GYM grows on trees rather than on the soil. GRANNY'S NIGHTCAP (p. 244) does grow on the ground, but its spore print is more rusty brown and the top of its stem is striate rather than smooth and does not have granules when young. COMMENTS The genus *Phaeolepiota* is closely related to *Cystoderma* (pp. 100–101). More complete studies may one day turn this species into *C. aureum*. • ALASKAN GOLD is most common in montane areas of western North America. In BC, this is largely an Interior species. • Chemical tests have shown that the caps from certain locations can contain significant amounts of cadmium as well as cyanide compounds, both of which appear to be only partially removed by cooking. • "Aurea" means "golden."

Other Little Brown-spored

As discussed previously, we've separated the rest of the brown-spored mushrooms into two groups: a collection of bigger brown-spored mushrooms (p. 271) and a collection of littler ones (caps generally less than five centimetres in diameter, this section). The division also highlights a difference in ecological roles—*most* of the species in the previous section are mycorrhizal, and *all* of the smaller ones in this section are decomposers. These smaller ones are a core component of the typically ignored mushrooms that we sometimes label with the derisory term "LBM," little brown mushrooms.

The genera *Bolbitius* and *Tubaria* are each home to one really common species that far outnumbers, in BC counts, the other species in the genera. All students of BC mushrooms should familiarize themselves with *B. titubans* (SUNNY SIDE UP, p. 282) and the *T. furfuracea* group (SCURFY TWIGLET, p. 284).

Unlike the two genera that contain one really common species, the genera *Conocybe* and *Galerina* contain several common species that show up in BC counts. We were forced to select just one of these to represent each genus—not an easy task. The *C. tenera* group (BROWN DUNCE CAP, p. 283) that we chose for *Conocybe* is perhaps atypical of the genus as a whole, since *C. tenera* group mushrooms grow in lawns and pastures, while the other *Conocybe* species prefer such diverse habitats as dung and houseplant pots. Our choice for *Galerina* is also a bit atypical. Most of the 50 species of *Galerina* that have been identified in our province are tiny little mushrooms found in moss beds. We chose a slightly larger wood-decomposing species, *G. marginata* (FUNERAL BELL, p. 286), because of its toxic nature.

Since the mushrooms in this section are small and often challenging to identify, and count among their numbers some seriously poisonous LBMs, they are justifiably ignored by foragers in search of edibles.

Conocybe filaris (RINGED CONOCYBE), another of the little brown mushrooms that befuddle beginning mushroomers.

Sunny Side Up   *Bolbitius titubans*

CAP To 6 cm across when expanded; ovoid or bell-shaped, becoming shallowly convex or flat; bright yellow, fading with age to tan, grey, or white, but often retaining some yellow in centre, making it look like an unflipped fried egg; slimy/sticky when moist; smooth; margins striate when older and often becoming radially pleated; flesh thin, yellow. GILLS Variably attached or free; shallow; fragile, collapsing or dissolving in moist conditions; pale yellow, becoming rusty brown as spores mature; closely spaced. ODOUR Not distinctive. TASTE Not distinctive. SPORE PRINT Rusty brown. STEM To 10 cm tall × 1 cm wide; equal or widening below; fragile, sometimes collapsing; hollow; whitish or pale yellow; finely scurfy. RING Absent. FRUITING Single or scattered or in groups; on dung, straw, or compost or in grass; cultivated open areas; spring, summer, autumn.

EDIBILITY Edible. But one is *un oeuf.* SIMILAR The pale-spored FLOWERPOT PARASOL (p. 104) also has a bright yellow cap and is about the same size, but its cap is dry, its gills are free, and it has a ring. COMMENTS This small decomposer is a highly variable species, tempting taxon specialists to split it into different species. When the features that the specialists traditionally rely on to define species—mostly microscopic and chemical features—are examined, however, the species-level differences fade away. The one genetic study done, in contrast, suggests that we may really have multiple species. Because of all this taxonomic thrashing about, you may see SUNNY SIDE UP associated with other scientific names, such as *Bolbitius vitellinus.* The description above is for the variety currently known as *B. titubans* var. *titubans.* ✴ "Bolbitius" probably means "of cow dung," and "titubans" means "staggering," making it an appropriate binomial, since SUNNY SIDE UP is often found near composted manure and has been known to poke out of the ground, expand, and collapse in a single day.

Brown Dunce Cap   *Conocybe tenera* group

CAP To 2.5 cm across; conical or bell-shaped; brown, yellow-brown, or orange-brown, fading to tan; usually dry; smooth; translucent-striate when moist; hygrophanous; flesh thin, cream to brown. GILLS Broadly attached to narrowly attached to free; whitish to cream becoming rusty brown as spores mature; closely spaced; with 3 subgills in 2 tiers between gills. ODOUR Not distinctive. TASTE Not distinctive. SPORE PRINT Rusty brown. STEM To 9 cm tall × 4 mm wide; equal or with a swollen base; fragile; becoming hollow; coloured as the cap or paler, darkening with age; smooth but often covered with fine powder when young. RING Absent. FRUITING Scattered or in groups; on dung, straw, or compost, or in grass; cultivated or grassy open areas, often abundant in newly installed landscaping and in lawns with rich composted soil mixes; summer mainly, also spring or autumn.

EDIBILITY Unknown. Close relatives, though, are seriously poisonous. SIMILAR The HAYMAKER'S MUSHROOM (p. 312) has a more chestnut-brown cap with a darker marginal band and sometimes a sour taste. The BROWN BONNET (p. 181) is similar in colour, shape, and size, but it has white spores and a pale stem and grows in forest duff under conifers. COMMENTS *Conocybe* species, some poisonous, can fruit in the same habitat as *Psilocybe* species (pp. 310–311), and magic mushroom pickers should learn to tell them apart (a spore print will help). ✦ The group of small *Conocybe* species closely matching the description of the BROWN DUNCE CAP is difficult to sort out. ✦ This is a worldwide species. Records for the BROWN DUNCE CAP cluster around the coastal areas of southwestern BC, but it occurs in inland mountainous areas of Washington, so the lack of BC inland records may reflect the locations of people able to put a name to this uncharismatic LBM. ✦ "Conocybe" means "cone head," and "tenera" means "fragile, slender," both appropriate descriptions of the BROWN DUNCE CAP.

Scurfy Twiglet   *Tubaria furfuracea* group

CAP To 3 cm across; convex becoming flat or depressed, sometimes with a small umbo, margins curved down at first and then lifted up and sometimes wavy; reddish brown or cinnamon brown, drying buff and eventually whitish, sometimes with white patches or flecks left over from the veil when young, especially near the margin; dry; minutely hairy or smooth; translucent-striate when moist; hygrophanous; flesh thin, brown or pinkish brown. **GILLS** Broadly attached or slightly decurrent; shallow (2–4 mm); creamy at first, taking on the yellow-brown or cinnamon brown of the spores; closely spaced. **ODOUR** Not distinctive. **TASTE** Not distinctive. **SPORE PRINT** Yellow-brown or cinnamon brown. **STEM** To 6 cm tall × 4 mm wide; equal or widening slightly downward; fragile; colour of the cap or paler and with or without white flecks; dry; smooth or silky; often with white mycelium at the base. **RING** Silky; white; quickly disappearing, sometimes leaving a small ring zone. **FRUITING** Single or in groups, sometimes clustered; on sticks, wood chips, and woody debris; mostly autumn and winter, but any season with enough moisture.

EDIBILITY Unknown. **SIMILAR** *Alnicola escharioides* **group** mushrooms have caps that tend to be more of a beige colour. They have a slightly bitter taste, and because they are mycorrhizal with alders, they fruit on the forest floor. The somewhat similar **FUNERAL BELL** (p. 286) usually grows on wood. It lacks the white flecks on the caps and develops darker brown colours on the lower base. **COMMENTS** SCURFY TWIGLET is sometimes abundant on wood-chip landscaping. It is also found in nutrient-dense materials such as fallen and decaying holly and hawthorn fruits or spilled seeds under bird feeders. ✿ Also in the group with *Tubaria furfuracea* is the hard-to-differentiate *T. hiemalis*. *Tubaria hiemalis* tends to appear in spring and summer, *T. furfuracea* almost anytime. ✿ "Furfuracea" means "scaly," perhaps a way of describing the white flecks from the veil.

Christmas Tubaria

In extreme southwestern BC, finding the CHRISTMAS TUBARIA (*Tubaria punicea*) can be a seasonal treat.

Oluna and Adolf Ceska found an unusual small red mushroom at the base of an ARBUTUS (*Arbutus menziesii*) for the first time in December 2001, and then not again until December 2005. The Ceskas identified the mushroom as *Naucoria vinicolor*. Because these first two collections were in December, and because Oluna recognized the mushroom as something close to a *Naucoria*, it quickly acquired the nickname CHRISTMAS NAUCORIA.

The Ceskas' southern Vancouver Island collections eventually contributed to a larger study of the wine-red species of the related genus *Tubaria*. The results of this study by P. Brandon Matheny, Oluna, and others were published in a scholarly journal in 2007. This article identified the Vancouver Island collections as *T. punicea*. CHRISTMAS NAUCORIA became CHRISTMAS TUBARIA.

CHRISTMAS TUBARIA has a cap up to five centimetres across (but usually half this size) that is wine red to blood red. The surface of the cap is shiny and dry. The gills are attached to slightly decurrent, coloured as the cap at first but aging brown. The stem of the mushroom, which can be up to eight centimetres long (usually much shorter), is also wine red and often has white veil remnants in a ring zone. The spore deposit is cinnamon brown.

CHRISTMAS TUBARIA is one of BC's rarer mushrooms, for several reasons. First of all, it is found on rotten (and sometimes burned) ARBUTUS bases and stumps. This limits it to the range of a tree that in BC is only found in southeastern Vancouver Island, the southern Gulf Islands, and a thin strip along the drier mainland's south coast. Second, mature ARBUTUS trees that have rotten bases are rarer still. Third, having the right habitat doesn't guarantee that the mushroom will be there—on one

Vancouver Island site where a hundred large ARBUTUS were surveyed, only two populations of the mushroom were found. Rare as it is, however, a number of BC people have found it. If you want to clap eyes on this rare beauty, check the right habitat at the right time. The best time is between late October and early January, though fruitings as late as March have been documented.

For more on this fascinating fungus, check out the article "Distribution of a Mushroom *Tubaria punicea* on Southern Vancouver Island" by Oluna and Adolf Ceska in the May 2008 edition of the online *Botanical Electronic News*.

Funeral Bell   *Galerina marginata*

CAP To 6.5 cm across, but often smaller; domed or more shallowly convex to flat, sometimes slightly umbonate; yellow-brown or orange-brown to occasionally dark brown, often lighter at the margin, becoming paler when dry; moist to sticky, but not usually slimy; smooth; hygrophanous; translucent-striate when moist; flesh thin, pale yellowish brown. GILLS Broadly attached to slightly decurrent, sometimes becoming free; fairly shallow; pale brown or coloured about like the cap, darkening as spores mature, sometimes retaining whitish edges; crowded. ODOUR Slightly to strongly farinaceous. TASTE Usually not distinctive. SPORE PRINT Reddish brown. STEM To 9 cm tall × 1 cm wide; equal or slightly widened downward; becoming hollow; yellowish brown above, darker brown below; dry; powdery above ring, silky below and sometimes with covering of pale fibrils below when young. RING Usually of cobwebby fibrils, but sometimes membranous; brown; typically short-lived, often leaving a ring zone on the stem that picks up spore colours. FRUITING Single, scattered, or clustered; on or near wood (which may be buried), especially conifers; late summer, autumn, early winter, occasionally spring.

EDIBILITY Poisonous. SIMILAR It is important to distinguish between the deadly FUNERAL BELL and *Psilocybe* species (pp. 310–311), since the latter are sometimes picked and eaten for recreational purposes. The *Psilocybe* species yield purplish brown or purplish black spore prints and have tissues that stain blue. The SHEATHED WOODTUFT (p. 270; see the entry for other look-alikes), though similar in many respects to the FUNERAL BELL, differs from it by usually growing in clusters, lacking a farinaceous odour, and having prominent pale brown scales below the ring. COMMENTS We are treating *Galerina autumnalis* as a synonym. ◆ The FUNERAL BELL and certain other *Galerina* species can contain more deadly amatoxin per gram of fresh weight than even the DEATH CAP. ◆ "Galerina" means "helmet-like" (in reference to the domed cap), and "marginata" means "with a border"—marginate gills are ones that have differently coloured edges.

The mushroom world is full of little brown mushrooms, often referred to as LBMs, which can be difficult to identify. Among them are many small and toxic galerinas such as FUNERAL BELL (*Galerina marginata*).

Dark-spored Gilled

The dark-spored group of mushrooms contains some good edible mushrooms, some poisonous species, and our best-known hallucinogenic mushrooms (see the essay on magic mushrooms, p. 308). Mushrooms in this group have black or purplish black spore prints. As with other spore colour groups, these dark-spored gilled mushrooms are not necessarily related to each other.

There are fewer mushrooms in this category than in the pale-spored and brown-spored sections, so we've divided these mushrooms into just three groups:

- If your field or forest mushroom has closely spaced purplish black or black gills that digest themselves into black goo, look in "**Coprinus and Similar**" (p. 289).
- If your black-spored forest mushroom has thick, white to pale orange, widely spaced and decurrent gills, check out "**Gomphidius and Similar**" (p. 295).
- And if your dark-spored mushroom doesn't match either of the above descriptions, look in "**Other Dark-spored**" (p. 299).

SULPHUR TUFT (*Hypholoma fasciculare*), p. 300.

Coprinus and Similar

One morning, at the edge of a copse, Jill finds a group of large, pale mushrooms. She picks one up. The cap and stem, she discovers, are strangely fragile. The closely spaced gills under the cap look like they might be turning a dark black or purple-black. Wanting to study the mushroom further, she wraps it in a piece of waxed paper and puts it in a bag. Later that day, at home, she remembers her morning find. When she unwraps the paper, all that is left is a stem marinating in a pool of oil-dark liquid.

What Jill has found is an inkcap mushroom. Many species that were traditionally grouped in the dark-spored genus *Coprinus* have gills that digest themselves at maturity, turning themselves into black goo. This process, called "autodigestion" or "deliquescence," helps these species to spread their spores. While some spores may drop to the ground in the goo, a large number are spread the way other gilled mushrooms distribute their spores—by launching them on wind currents. The crowded gills that are found in many inkcap species, however, do not allow the spores ready access to the open air. By liquefying and removing gill sections that have already shed their spores, inkcap mushrooms open up new air channels for the later-maturing sections of their gills.

This gills-to-goo feature is so unusual in the world of mushrooms that early taxonomists made the natural assumption that deliquescing species and their relatives belonged to the same genus. They lumped them into the genus *Coprinus*. The assumption, though, turned out to be a hasty one: evolution has invented deliquescence more than once. Molecular studies in the late 1990s and early 2000s revealed that some of the deliquescing species in *Coprinus* were more closely related to species in *Agaricus* and *Lepiota* and that others were more closely related to *Psathyrella* species. Over the next decade, taxonomists broke apart the old *Coprinus* genus and redistributed its mushrooms into new genera. Today, only a handful of species remain in the *Agaricus*-related *Coprinus* genus. A couple of hundred other species, the ones more closely related to *Psathyrella*, were moved into the genera *Coprinellus* ("little Coprinus"), *Coprinopsis* ("looking like Coprinus"), and *Parasola*.

Parasola species are not included here—they are either overlooked or rare in BC. On these pages you will find, however, one *Coprinus* species, two *Coprinopsis* species, and one *Coprinellus* species. All four have the characteristic deliquescing gills of the inkcaps. All of them except the WOOLLY INKY CAP (p. 291) are collected for the table. Of the three that are eaten, one comes with a big gotcha—consuming alcohol with INKY CAP mushrooms (p. 292) can make tipplers ill.

Shaggy Mane

Coprinus comatus

CAP To 12 cm high when young before it expands, to 10 cm across when expanded; ovoid or bullet-shaped when young, expanding to conical, eventually becoming bell-shaped with edges curled up, the margin often splitting in age; brownish at disc, elsewhere white beneath brown-edged scales; dry; the disc smooth, the rest of cap covered by fibrils that group themselves into coarse (and sometimes lifted-up) scales; flesh thin (to 3 mm), soft, white. GILLS From very free to narrowly attached; deep (to 1 cm); deliquescing; white, becoming rose pink, then grey-black, and eventually turning sooty black as spores mature; very crowded. ODOUR Not distinctive. TASTE Not distinctive. SPORE PRINT Black. STEM To 20 cm tall × 2 cm wide; even or widening downward, base often ending in a pointed bulb; hollow or stuffed with fibres or a vertical cord; white; dry; smooth. RING Membranous; white; often becoming free and dropping to the bottom of the stem or disappearing. FRUITING Single or in dense groups; on disturbed areas (lawns, roadsides, mulched areas), rarely in open forest; summer, autumn.

EDIBILITY Choice. But use before the gills turn to black goo. SIMILAR The INKY CAP (p. 292) tends to grow in clusters and has a greyish cap that (except when very young) lacks fibrils and scales. COMMENTS Deliquescing clumps of SHAGGY MANE caps may be parasitized by *Psathyrella epimyces*, a medium-sized white mushroom that has an ovoid-to-conical cap, a white, volva-like ring, and pale to blackish gills with white edges. ☙ SHAGGY MANE is a common decomposer that is found throughout BC, and worldwide in urban spaces. ☙ SHAGGY MANE is a known bioaccumulator of metals, especially mercury, and may possibly pick up lawn pesticides, so picking habitat is important. ☙ The mycelium has spines (and possibly toxins) that can kill nematode worms. ☙ "Coprinus" means "living on dung," a habitat for some species formerly in this genus. "Comatus" means "long-haired," presumably a description of the dense fibrils on the cap.

Woolly Inky Cap *Coprinopsis lagopus* group

CAP To 6 cm across when expanded; ovoid to conical, eventually flat, margins often upturned and splitting but later ragged and droopy from deliquescing; grey, becoming blackish grey with age, sometimes with buff on disc; dry; pleated, especially at the margins, and with white or grey fibrils (remnants of the universal veil) that drop off in age; striate; flesh thin, soft, greyish white. **GILLS** Free; shallow; deliquescing; whitish, becoming grey and eventually black as spores mature; closely spaced. **ODOUR** Not distinctive. **TASTE** Not distinctive. **SPORE PRINT** Black. **STEM** To 12 cm tall × 5 mm wide; equal or widening downward; fragile; hollow; white; dry; dotted with fine white fibrils when young, smooth with age. **RING** Absent. **FRUITING** Single or in dense groups or clusters; on a variety of substrates (wood, wood chips, manure, leaf litter); autumn, winter, spring.

EDIBILITY Unknown. **SIMILAR** Because of the thin stem and pleated, striate cap, the WOOLLY INKY CAP is unlikely to be confused with other mushrooms in this section. **COMMENTS** The most recent genetic studies suggest that there are several distinct species of WOOLLY INKY CAPS instead of just one, but the genetic groupings do not correspond well to previous attempts to subdivide the species. ◦ The WOOLLY INKY CAP is a short-lived decomposer species, often popping out of wood chips, opening, and deliquescing in the course of a single day, or even a few hours. ◦ A cluster of these can show a huge variation in mature cap size, with the ratio between the smallest and the largest being 1:100. ◦ "Lagopus" means "rabbit's foot," which is exactly what the hairy, ovoid, unopened caps look like.

Inky Cap   *Coprinopsis atramentaria* group

CAP To 8 cm across when expanded; ovoid, sometimes lobed, expanding to conical or bell-shaped, margins often upturned and split in age; deliquescing from the margin inward; greyish brown, becoming blackish grey with age; dry; with fibrils or scales from the universal veil when very young, then smooth or finely silky; sometimes striate; flesh thin, soft, whitish to grey. **GILLS** Free; deliquescing; white, becoming grey (often with pink or purple tints) and eventually black as spores mature; crowded. **ODOUR** Not distinctive. **TASTE** Not distinctive. **SPORE PRINT** Brownish black to black. **STEM** To 15 cm tall × 1.5 cm wide; equal, but sometimes broader in the middle and tapering below; fragile; hollow; white; dry; smooth, but sometimes with small brown scales from the universal veil on the lower part. **RING** Partial veil absent, but universal veil may leave basal ring or ring-like remnants. **FRUITING** Single or in dense groups or clustered; on the ground; on disturbed areas (lawns, roadsides, mulched areas) and soils rich in woody material; summer, autumn, occasionally spring.

EDIBILITY Edible. But consuming alcohol before or after (in rare cases, up to several days before or after) eating INKY CAP mushrooms can lead to almost immediate negative reactions, including sweating, headaches, dizziness, and nausea. This is because INKY CAP mushrooms contain a compound that inhibits an enzyme the body uses to metabolize alcohol. **SIMILAR** The **MICA CAP** (p. 293) is similar, but it is smaller and thinner stemmed. It has caps that sport more brownish tones and (when young) glistening mica-like scales. **SHAGGY MANE** (p. 290) is typically taller (to 20 cm), has a cap with coarse scales, and does not grow in clusters. **COMMENTS** INKY CAP is common and widespread in our province. ◆ Recent genetic analysis shows that specimens identified as INKY CAPS include a number of other hard-to-differentiate species. ◆ "Atramentaria" means "pertaining to ink," no doubt in reference (like the common name) to the deliquescing gills.

Mica Cap   *Coprinellus micaceus* group

CAP To 4 cm across; ovoid, expanding to bell-shaped and then convex, margins grooved/pleated most of the way to the disc and often curling up and splitting in age; yellowish brown to cinnamon brown, greyer with age, especially toward the margins; moist or dry; smooth but covered with glistening particles of the universal veil that often wash away in the rain; flesh thin, soft, white to pale yellow-brown. **GILLS** Narrowly attached to free; medium-deep (3–5 mm); deliquescing; whitish at first, becoming grey-brown and quickly becoming black as spores mature; crowded. **ODOUR** Not distinctive. **TASTE** Not distinctive. **SPORE PRINT** Black. **STEM** To 8 cm tall × 6 mm wide; equal or enlarging slightly downward; fragile; hollow; whitish or discolouring to cream from the base up; dry; smooth or with small hairs. **RING** Absent. **FRUITING** Usually in groups or clustered; on wood or substrates rich in woody material (e.g., bark mulch); in both forests and urban areas; all seasons but rarer in dry summer heat.

EDIBILITY Edible. **SIMILAR** The INKY CAP (p. 292) is much larger, with thicker flesh and stems, and the upper surfaces of its caps are missing the mica-like particles and have fewer yellow-brown tones. **COMMENTS** MICA CAP is too fragile for many culinary uses, but at least it lacks the alcohol-digestion issues of the INKY CAP. It is a known bioaccumulator of heavy metals, however, so be aware of picking locales. ⬥ MICA CAP is a cosmopolitan decomposer that is common and widespread in BC. DNA analysis suggests that we may have multiple species of MICA CAP with few clear morphological differences among them. ⬥ MICA CAP has also been identified as a fungal endophyte, growing inside the wood of living trees of PAPER MULBERRY and COMMON HACKBERRY in Argentina. ⬥ "Micaceus" may be a reference to mica, a glittery silicate whose name has been influenced by the Latin words for "crumb, grain of salt" and for "glistening."

Climate Change and Mushrooms

As the global climate changes, British Columbia's climate is changing also. The direction of change is clear: our BC climate is warming. Over the last century, our province's mean annual temperature has increased more than one degree Celsius. In many regions, summer precipitation has decreased, winter precipitation increased. And these trends are projected to continue—with the caveat that, over such a climatically diverse province, the changes will probably not be evenly applied.

Since many of the mushrooms in this field guide form mycorrhizal associations (p. 74) with trees, the fate of trees and fungi are often linked. Sometimes the climatic effect on trees and their partners is short-term. For example, BC experienced extended summertime droughts in the 2010s. This was likely one factor contributing to below-average mushroom fruitings in the autumns of that decade. When trees photosynthesize less, they have less sugars to share with their fungal partners. Less food for the fungi means less energy available for producing the fruiting bodies we call mushrooms.

Climate change can also have long-term effects on trees and fungi. Some parts of the province—especially in southwestern BC—have seen increased tree death due in part to increasing summertime droughts. WESTERN REDCEDAR, ARBUTUS, DOUGLAS-FIR, and (most recently) SITKA SPRUCE have been particularly hard hit. In some of these cases, the drought killed the trees outright. In other cases, stressed trees were more susceptible to attack by parasitic fungi (the likely case with ARBUTUS and various leaf blights). Also, warmer winters were a factor contributing to the MOUNTAIN PINE BEETLE epidemic in BC that, beginning in the early 1990s, killed LODGEPOLE PINE in over 18 million hectares of forest in BC's Interior. Regardless of the mechanism, the death of a tree means that the tree's mycorrhizal fungi also perish.

Changes to climate will affect BC's fungi in other ways. The treeline, the level below which trees can grow, is increasing in elevation, leading to more tree-associated fungi and less habitat for alpine fungi. Warmer summers and winters open BC up to invasion by fungi from the US Pacific Northwest. The area burned annually by forest fires is increasing, which means more trees—and more of their mycorrhizal fungi—killed, but also more habitat for morels (p. 436) in the springtime.

The most certain prediction about the effects of a changing climate on BC's mushrooms is that the future is uncertain—there will be many changes that surprise us.

Warmer, drier summers are expected to increase forest-fire frequency and intensity, increasing habitat for phoenicoid mushrooms, such as these GREY FIRE MORELS (p. 440).

Gomphidius and Similar

In the 1950s, all of the species in this section belonged to the genus *Gomphidius*. In the 1960s, mycologists started to recognize the differences—differences that were supported by later genetic analysis—between classical *Gomphidius* species and the ones we now know as *Chroogomphus*, pine spikes.

The most important field difference between *Chroogomphus* and *Gomphidius* species is the flesh colour—almost all *Gomphidius* species have whitish flesh, while the flesh of *Chroogomphus* species is more darkly coloured and usually turns purple when exposed to heat or certain chemicals. In addition, the young gills of *Gomphidius* species are white or pale, while those of *Chroogomphus* species usually have a pale orange to yellow-brown colour. What the two genera have in common, however, is much more extensive than their differences. Both *Gomphidius* and *Chroogomphus* species leave blackish spore deposits. Their gills, which are thick, waxy-looking, and well spaced, often extend down the stem. Both groups have partial veils when young, but their veils, insubstantial and cobwebby, usually end up—if they don't disappear—as vague ring zones. The two genera also share a number of microscopic features that set them apart from other species of mushrooms.

Because mushrooms in both *Gomphidius* and *Chroogomphus* are usually found in conifer forests, the traditional assumption has been that they were mycorrhizal with conifers. Evidence is accumulating, however, that more may be going on: species in these two genera may also be parasitizing other mycorrhizal species, especially species that are in or closely related to the *Suillus* genus (pp. 326–331). From an evolutionary point of view, *Gomphidius* and *Chroogomphus* species are much more closely related to the pored species in the bolete family than to other families of gilled mushrooms, so their parasitic relationships may be more like family arguments than all-out war. The next time you see a gomphidius in a BC forest, look around and see whether you can find a *Suillus* species nearby—you may be witnessing thieves at work.

The name "Gomphidius" comes from "gomphos," a Greek word for a nail with a large head (i.e., a spike), in reference to the overall shape of the fruiting bodies. And since the "chroo-" prefix is from the Greek word for "colour," "Chroogomphus" means "coloured spike."

All of the species described in this section are reported as edible. None of them, however, are the sort of edibles that most foragers would go out of their way to find and cook.

Rosy Gomphidius   *Gomphidius subroseus*

CAP To 7 cm across; peg- or top-like, becoming convex, flat, or depressed, with an incurved margin when young that is later uplifted and wavy; pink to red, sometimes paler at the margins, spotted greyish in age; glutinous or slimy/sticky, the slime layer often completely peelable as a distinct skin; smooth; flesh thick (to 1 cm) near disc, soft, white but taking on cap colours in the layer nearest the cap. GILLS Strongly decurrent; deep (to 6 mm); waxy-looking; whitish at first, becoming grey, then black as the spores mature; moderately spaced. ODOUR Not distinctive. TASTE Not distinctive. SPORE PRINT Blackish grey to black. STEM To 7 cm tall × 1.5 cm wide; equal or narrowing downward; white above ring, vivid yellow near base (both on the surface and in the flesh), blackening where handled or with age; dry above ring, glutinous below; smooth. RING Slimy, cobwebby; clear, leaving a glutinous ring zone on the stem that turns black from spores. FRUITING Single or scattered in a group; on the ground; under conifers, usually near *Suillus*, often the MATTE JACK (p. 327); autumn, winter.

   EDIBILITY Edible. But not usually harvested in BC. SIMILAR *Gomphidius smithii*'s pink cap has more buff tones in it, and its stem often lacks (or has only a touch of) the yellow colours of other *Gomphidius* species. See the entry on the HIDEOUS GOMPHIDIUS (p. 297) for other similar species. COMMENTS ROSY GOMPHIDIUS is abundant in BC. In some ways, this species is *our Gomphidius*: distribution maps show it primarily occurring in western North America, with only a few records from eastern North America and elsewhere, unlike the more widely reported HIDEOUS GOMPHIDIUS. ◦ "Subroseus" means "nearly *roseus*," a taxonomically coded distinction separating it from the European *G. roseus*.

Hideous Gomphidius · *Gomphidius glutinosus*

CAP To 10 cm across; peg- or top-like, becoming convex or flat, margins initially incurved, later upturned and wavy; brownish grey to purple-brown to reddish brown, lighter-hued in age, sometimes mottled to streaked, staining black; sticky when dry and slimy to glutinous when wet, the slime layer often completely peelable as a distinct skin; smooth; flesh thick, soft, whitish, occasionally with pink tinge. **GILLS** Strongly decurrent; deep (to 8 mm); thick and waxy-looking; whitish, then greyish, staining black and becoming entirely black as spores mature; widely spaced. **ODOUR** Not distinctive. **TASTE** Not distinctive or slightly sour. **SPORE PRINT** Black or blackish grey. **STEM** To 10 cm tall × 3 cm wide; narrowing to base; solid; white, usually with a vivid yellow base (both on the surface and in the flesh), sometimes spotting black; slimy below ring; smooth. **RING** Slimy, cobwebby; clear, leaving a glutinous ring zone on the stem that turns black from spores. **FRUITING** Single or in small groups; on the ground; in conifer forests, usually near *Suillus* species; autumn, winter.

EDIBILITY Edible. But not usually harvested in BC. **SIMILAR** *Gomphidius oregonensis* has a cap that is more beige than purple, has shorter spores, and almost always grows in fused clusters. See also the **ROSY GOMPHIDIUS** (p. 296) entry for other look-alikes. From the top, the HIDEOUS GOMPHIDIUS can resemble the pored **SLIPPERY JACK** (p. 331). The **OLIVE-BROWN WAXY CAP** (p. 89), besides having white spores, has yellow at the top of the stem rather than at the bottom. **COMMENTS** HIDEOUS GOMPHIDIUS is known to concentrate toxins from the environment, which may explain why some people (including one of the authors) has experienced gastrointestinal distress after consumption. In a Ukraine study done in the decade after the Chernobyl disaster, HIDEOUS GOMPHIDIUS was found to harbour radioactive cesium at levels a thousand times stronger than the safest per-kilo dosage. ◆ Appropriately, "glutinosus" means "glutinous, very slimy."

Woolly Pine Spike   *Chroogomphus tomentosus*

CAP To 8 cm across; ovoid when young, becoming conical to convex, then flat, sometimes with a broad umbo, the margins at first incurved, later stretched out and ragged; dull orange to yellowish brown, sometimes staining purple with age; dry; covered with pressed-down, felt-like woolly fibrils; flesh thick, orange. GILLS Decurrent, occasionally broadly attached; deep (to 7 mm) in the middle but shallower at ends; coloured as the cap, becoming black as spores mature; moderately spaced. ODOUR Not distinctive. TASTE Not distinctive. SPORE PRINT Dark grey to black. STEM To 18 cm tall × 1.5 cm wide; equal or narrowing toward a root-like base; solid; coloured as the cap, darkening where handled; dry; with sparse, pressed-down fibres. RING Dull orange; disappearing, leaving hairy remnants. FRUITING Single, scattered groups, or in small groups, sometimes clustered; on the ground; under conifers, sometimes near the ADMIRABLE BOLETE (p. 322); late summer, autumn, early winter.

EDIBILITY Edible. When cooked, however, the caps and stems turn a vivid, non-food-looking purple. SIMILAR The cap of *Chroogomphus ochraceus* is smooth, sometimes with an almost metallic sheen, typically slimy/sticky, and often with a pointed umbo. It can display tones of yellowish orange, yellowish brown, reddish brown, olive-brown, greyish brown, or dark brown. Dark red-brown specimens of *C. ochraceus* used to be regarded as *C. rutilus*, but that is a European species. *Chroogomphus vinicolor* also has a smooth, lustrous, often slimy/sticky cap with a broad umbo, but the cap tends to have strong mahogany-brown tones. Beginning mushroom students have also been known to confuse WOOLLY PINE SPIKES with PACIFIC GOLDEN CHANTERELLES (p. 34) because the 2 species grow in the same habitats and have similar cap colours. The woolly cap, orange flesh, and dark spore print of the PINE SPIKE, though, should signal the correct species. One other quick way to tell them apart: touch a flame to the stem. *Chroogomphus* species, unlike *Chanterelle* species, turn a dark purple when burned. COMMENTS "Tomentosus" means "densely hairy."

Other Dark-spored

The collection of dark-spored species in this section have spores that have enough purple or black hues to grab the attention of those learning to identify mushrooms. They are also, one and all, decomposer mushrooms—many can be found in grassy areas, on dung, on duff and wood chips, and on logs, busy at their recycling work.

As with many other sections of this book, species in the "Other Dark-spored" section are included for ease of identification—they may not be closely related to each other. In this section, for example, the dark-spored genera *Stropharia*, *Psilocybe*, *Deconica*, and *Hypholoma* are closely related to the brown-spored *Pholiota* species. *Psathyrella* is not a near relative of the other genera—it's more closely connected to the INKY CAP (p. 292).

The genus *Stropharia* is represented in this section by four species. This odd genus name is derived from a Greek word for "belt," and the four medium-sized species covered here have significant (though sometimes disappearing) belt-like rings on their stems. Although large enough to think about harvesting, they do not get invited to our dinner tables, with one exception (the cultivated WINE CAP STROPHARIA, p. 305). The *Protostropharia* species described in this section was once a *Stropharia*.

The two closely related species of *Hypholoma* discussed here are not comestible equals—CONIFER TUFT (p. 301) is edible (though not incredible), but SULPHUR TUFT (p. 300) can give those who eat it a couple of days of misery. "Hypholoma" means "mushrooms with threads," a possible reference to cobwebby veils on many of the *Hypholoma* species.

We have about two dozen *Psilocybe* species in Canada, perhaps 10 per cent of the worldwide total, and most of these Canadian species can be found in BC. *Psilocybe* species get a lot of attention because many of them contain psychoactive substances (p. 308). These species tend to be small and have brownish caps that change colour when they go from wet to dry. Many show significant blue staining in their tissues, a colour change caused by the same substances that make them psychoactive. The CHIP CHERRY (p. 316) and the MOUNTAIN MOSS MUSHROOM (p. 306) in this section were both considered *Psilocybe* species at one time.

The two BC *Psathyrella* species in this section are tokens of a rather large genus (many hundreds of species worldwide) of brown-spored and dark-spored LBMs (little brown mushrooms). The word "psathyrella" comes from a Greek word that means "little crumbling thing," and the caps of these species are far from robust—it can be difficult to get picked samples home to look more closely at them. The genus *Panaeolus*—represented in this section by the HAYMAKER'S MUSHROOM (p. 312)—is also related to *Psathyrella* and most of the inkcap genera.

Sulphur Tuft

Hypholoma fasciculare

CAP To 6 cm across; conical or hemispheric, becoming less hemispheric to nearly flat with a small umbo, the margins when young incurved and sometimes hung with yellow veil remnants; yellowish orange when young, becoming bright yellow or greenish yellow, the centre typically darker (orange-brown); moist or dry; smooth; flesh thin (to 4 mm), pale yellow. GILLS Broadly to narrowly attached; shallow (to 3 mm); yellow, becoming greenish yellow and finally purple-brown as spores mature; closely spaced, 50–55 reaching the stem; up to 7 subgills between neighbouring gills. ODOUR Not distinctive. TASTE Very bitter. SPORE PRINT Purple-brown. STEM To 10 cm tall × 1 cm wide; roughly equal; yellow, the lower part reddish brown in age and sometimes with a whitish and/or fuzzy base; dry; finely longitudinally striate. RING Cobwebby; yellow; disappearing but sometimes leaving a spore-coloured ring zone high on the stem. FRUITING In groups, usually in clumps; on decaying wood (sometimes buried) of coniferous or deciduous trees; all seasons, but most common in late summer, autumn.

EDIBILITY Poisonous. Can cause severe gastrointestinal distress. SIMILAR CONIFER TUFT (p. 301), which grows only on conifers, has gills that are smoky grey and a mild taste. See the CONIFER TUFT entry for more look-alikes. *Pholiota spumosa* **group** species have brown spores and are more typically found on the ground, and the caps are sticky when dry and slimy to glutinous when wet. A small, older BLUE-GREEN FLAMECAP (p. 265) might be mistaken for SULPHUR TUFT, but the former has rusty orange spores and (usually) a greenish, curvy, rooting stem. COMMENTS SULPHUR TUFT is a prolific and widespread decomposer in BC, seen mostly around stumps and logs but also on the ground. It grows so readily on decaying wood that it has been shown, in one BC study, to displace slower-growing and parasitic species of *Armillaria*. • "Fasciculare" means "bundled," a reference to the clumped growth habit of this species.

Conifer Tuft   *Hypholoma capnoides*

CAP To 6 cm across; hemispheric, conical, or more shallowly convex, sometimes umbonate, becoming flat, the margins inrolled at first and sometimes with hanging veil remnants; yellow to orange-brown or reddish brown, the margins often pale yellow; dry or occasionally moist; smooth; flesh thin, whitish to pale yellow. GILLS Broadly attached; shallow (to 5 mm); cream or pale grey becoming greyish brown, then purple-brown as spores mature; closely spaced, 34–40 reaching the stem; up to 7 subgills between neighbouring gills. ODOUR Not distinctive. TASTE Not distinctive. SPORE PRINT Purple-brown. STEM To 8 cm tall × 1.5 cm wide; equal or slightly widened below; often curved; pale yellow in the top part, the apex sometimes whitish, the bottom usually reddish brown; dry; finely longitudinally striate, sometimes with whitish chevron-shaped fibrils. RING Cobwebby; white; disappearing but sometimes leaving a spore-coloured ring zone. FRUITING In groups or (usually) clusters; on conifer logs; late summer, autumn, winter.

 EDIBILITY Edible. But not tasty. SIMILAR SULPHUR TUFT (p. 300) has yellowish green gills and a bitter taste. *Hypholoma dispersum* has a smaller cap (usually to 3 cm across) that remains conical or convex in age rather than flattening out and a taller, narrower stem which is usually not curved. It more commonly grows on the ground (buried wood) rather than on logs. If a mushroom find looks like CONIFER TUFT but it has a cinnamon-brown rather than a purple-brown spore print, it may be one of the species in the *Flammula malicola* **group** (once known as the *Pholiota malicola* **group**) or perhaps a SHEATHED WOODTUFT (p. 270). The *Flammula* has more narrowly attached/notched gills. SHEATHED WOODTUFT usually has a stem ring and upright brownish scales below the ring. The bog-dwelling *Hypholoma elongatum* has caps that are smaller (to 2 cm across) and stems that are thinner (to 3 mm) than CONIFER TUFT. COMMENTS "Capnoides" means "smoky," a probable reference to the gill colour.

Ambiguous Stropharia
Stropharia ambigua

CAP To 12 cm or more across; convex becoming flat, the margins, which are inrolled at first and then often uplifted, are typically hung with white, cottony veil remnants; amber to yellowish brown, becoming pale yellow to almost white, sometimes brownish; slimy/sticky when wet; smooth, but veil remnants can ascend the margin in young caps; flesh moderately thick (to 1 cm), soft, white. GILLS Often broadly attached, sometimes narrowly attached or with a decurrent tooth; moderately deep (5 mm); whitish becoming grey and then dark purplish brown as spores mature; closely spaced to crowded; numerous subgills. ODOUR Not distinctive. TASTE Somewhat radishy or not distinctive. SPORE PRINT Dark purplish brown or purplish black. STEM To 16 cm tall × 2 cm wide; equal or sometimes enlarged below; stuffed to hollow; whitish to grey; dry; silky or longitudinally striate above ring, cottony white scales below, usually smooth in age; with white rhizomorphs at base. RING Membranous; white; disappearing, but sometimes leaving ring zone on stem. FRUITING Single or (usually) in groups; on rich soil under conifers or hardwoods, also on wood chips; usually autumn, sometimes spring.

EDIBILITY Unknown. SIMILAR The related CONIFER ROUNDHEAD (p. 303) usually has a darker reddish brown cap and a persistent ring. When the warts have washed off of its cap, the JONQUIL AMANITA (p. 109) can resemble the AMBIGUOUS STROPHARIA in colour and stature, but the amanita has a white spore print, a more flaring (but also disappearing) ring, and a collar line where the volva attaches to the base of the stem. COMMENTS The AMBIGUOUS STROPHARIA is a wood decomposer found primarily on the West Coast of North America, from California to BC. ⬧ It is a favourite mushroom of spore print fans because it is abundant and can quickly produce large and colourful spore prints. ⬧ "Ambigua" means "changeable, uncertain."

Conifer Roundhead
Stropharia hornemannii

CAP To 10 cm across; convex becoming broadly umbonate to flat, the margins inrolled when young and often hung with white veil remnants that can rise fairly high on the margins; reddish brown to brown, sometimes with purple tints, fading to yellow-brown or tan, sometimes with radial streaking; slimy/sticky when wet; smooth; flesh thick, soft, white. GILLS Usually broadly attached, sometimes with a decurrent tooth; deep; light grey with paler edges, becoming purplish brown to black as spores mature; closely spaced or crowded; numerous subgills. ODOUR Not distinctive. TASTE Disagreeable or not distinctive. SPORE PRINT Purple-black. STEM To 15 cm tall × 2 cm wide; equal or base widened, often curved near base; white above ring, cream to yellowish below; dry; smooth to longitudinally striate above ring, with thick white scales below that may disappear in age; with white mycelium at base. RING Membranous, skirt-like, slightly grooved above; high on stem; white, but becoming darker as spores fall on it; usually persistent. FRUITING Single, scattered, in groups, or in small clusters; on the ground or on rotting wood; under conifers; late summer, autumn.

EDIBILITY Unknown. SIMILAR The AMBIGUOUS STROPHARIA (p. 302) has a more yellow-brown cap and a disappearing ring that can leave a ring zone. The WINE CAP STROPHARIA (p. 305), likely an introduced species, is considerably larger, has a drier, wine-red cap, a stiffer ring that is radially split underneath, and grows primarily on wood chips. COMMENTS "Hornemannii" honours Danish botanist Jens Wilken Hornemann (1770–1841).

Blue-green Stropharia
Stropharia aeruginosa

CAP To 8 cm across; convex or bell-shaped, becoming nearly flat, often with a broad umbo; bluish green when young, becoming yellowish to yellow-brown with age, especially near centre; with a gelatinous, peelable skin; slimy/sticky when wet; smooth but often with white flecks near the margin and a white curtain at the margin from the veils; flesh thin, whitish, sometimes partly tinged blue-green. GILLS Broadly attached; deep; whitish becoming dark purplish brown as spores mature, edges remaining whitish; closely spaced, 32–38 reaching the stem; subgills in multiple tiers. ODOUR Not distinctive. TASTE Not usually distinctive, but sometimes with a bitter aftertaste. SPORE PRINT Dark purplish brown or purplish black. STEM To 8 cm tall × 1 cm wide; roughly equal; cap-coloured or paler, to whitish above ring; dry but often slimy/sticky below the ring; smooth or finely striate above the ring and with erect cottony white scales below the ring that disappear in age; white rhizomorphs at the base. RING Membranous, fragile; white above and cap-coloured underneath; disappearing with age. FRUITING Single or in small groups; on bark mulch or soils rich in buried wood; conifer forest edges, parklands; usually late summer and autumn, sometimes also spring.

EDIBILITY Uncertain. SIMILAR The BLUE-GREEN STROPHARIA is not the only *Stropharia* with strong blue or green colours. The others, however, though they have been documented in western North America, have rarely been noted by BC mycologists. Nor are the lines between the various blue and green *Stropharia* species clearly drawn—the whole complex needs closer morphological and molecular analysis. COMMENTS Finding a mushroom of such beauty and rarity can make your whole year—*if* you are lucky enough to find young caps that are still at the brilliant blue-green stage. ❧ "Aeruginosa" means "copper rust," a reference to verdigris, the blue-green coating of oxidized copper.

Wine Cap Stropharia   *Stropharia rugosoannulata*

CAP To 15 cm or more across, sometimes much larger; convex or bell-shaped becoming flat or broadly umbonate, margins incurved for a long time and hung with white veil remnants when young; deep wine red or reddish brown, especially when young, fading to pale yellow-brown or grey; glossy when dry, slightly sticky when wet; smooth, sometimes cracking with age; flesh thick, firm, white. GILLS Broadly to narrowly attached, sometimes free when older; shallow near the margin; edges often rough, irregular; whitish or pale grey becoming dark purplish brown as spores mature, edges sometimes remaining whitish; crowded; with several tiers of subgills. ODOUR Pleasant, radish-like, or not distinctive. TASTE Not distinctive. SPORE PRINT Dark purplish brown or purplish black. STEM To 12 cm tall × 3 cm wide, sometimes much larger; widened at base; solid; white, sometimes discolouring yellow or brown in age; dry; longitudinally striate; with white rhizomorphs at base. RING Membranous, striate above and radially split under; high on the stem; white, but soon darkened by falling spores; usually persistent. FRUITING Single or in groups; on the ground; in cultivated areas (bark mulch, gardens, lawns); spring, summer, autumn.

EDIBILITY Choice. SIMILAR When large and wine red, nothing growing in gardens and lawns looks much like WINE CAP STROPHARIA. A look-alike in forest habitats is the CONIFER ROUNDHEAD (p. 303). COMMENTS The mushroom is readily cultivatable, preferring buried beds of hardwood chips, and it can continue to bloom for years without renewal. Spawn for this mushroom is sold to gardeners under the common name GARDEN GIANT. • The mycelium of the WINE CAP STROPHARIA has spiny cells that can immobilize nematode worms and allow the mycelium to digest them, making it a good companion plant for crops attacked by nematodes, such as corn. • The WINE CAP STROPHARIA is probably a species introduced to BC for cultivation purposes. • "Rugosoannulata" is a compound of words for "wrinkled" and "ringed," referring to the radially grooved ring.

Mountain Moss Mushroom   *Deconica montana*

CAP To 2 cm across; hemispheric, becoming more shallowly convex and eventually flattening, sometimes slightly umbonate, the margin sometimes with hanging veil remnants; dark reddish brown, becoming yellowish brown to beige; dry to slimy/sticky when moist; with a separable gelatinous skin; smooth, shiny; strongly hygrophanous; translucent-striate to half the cap radius when moist; flesh thin, whitish. GILLS Broadly attached, sometimes slightly decurrent; greyish brown, becoming dark reddish brown or purple-brown as spores mature, edges somewhat lighter; somewhat widely spaced; 2–3 tiers of subgills. ODOUR Not distinctive. TASTE Not distinctive. SPORE PRINT Purple-brown or dark greyish brown. STEM To 4 cm tall × 2 mm wide; equal or slightly enlarged below; often curved; stuffed to hollow; usually reddish brown or cap-coloured, darkening from the base up with age; dry; smooth or longitudinally striate, with chevron-shaped patches from veil. RING Web-like; white; soon disappearing but sometimes leaving ring zone on the stem. FRUITING Usually in groups; often in dense moss mats in open sites, with a preference for higher elevations; spring, summer, autumn.

EDIBILITY Unknown. SIMILAR The deadly FUNERAL BELL (p. 286) is similar, but it has a brown spore print and tends to grow on wood. See the entry for the SHEATHED WOODTUFT (p. 270) for further look-alikes. Two other *Deconica* species are commonly found in BC: *Deconica inquilina* closely resembles the MOUNTAIN MOSS MUSHROOM, but it commonly grows on rotting grass bases or on twigs and sticks. *Deconica horizontalis* has (often) a kidney-shaped cap and a curved off-centre stem, and it grows on old fabrics (mattresses, seat covers, rugs) or on wood. COMMENTS MOUNTAIN MOSS MUSHROOM, once widely known as *Psilocybe montana*, was moved into the genus *Deconica* when genetic sequencing revealed that it and most of the other non-psychoactive species traditionally included in *Psilocybe* were not closely related to the psychoactive species. ✚ "Montana" means "pertaining to mountains," referring to this species' preference for lofty habitats.

MOUNTAIN MOSS MUSHROOM
(*Deconica montana*).

Magic Mushrooms in BC

A small number of BC mushroom species contain hallucinogenic compounds. They are sometimes called magic mushrooms or, more colloquially, "shrooms." These shrooms include psychoactive *Psilocybe* species such as LIBERTY CAP (p. 310) and WAVY CAP (p. 311). Magic mushrooms contain the compound psilocybin, which when eaten is rapidly converted into psilocin, a chemical similar to both the neurotransmitter serotonin and also to LSD (lysergic acid diethylamide). Common effects of ingesting magic mushrooms include pupil dilation, audio and visual distortions, changes in perception of time and space, uncontrollable laughter, euphoria, and a general inability to concentrate.

Algerian and Spanish cave paintings hint that magic mushrooms may have been in use thousands of years ago. The earliest Spanish chroniclers in Mesoamerica documented the ritual use of these mushrooms by Indigenous peoples. The modern era of magic mushroom use seems to have been launched by a 1957 article in *Life* magazine by R. Gordon Wasson about traditional religious use of magic mushrooms. In the 1960s, people began travelling to Mexico to experience these magic mushrooms. Reports were soon filed about *Psilocybe* species elsewhere in the Americas, including North America's West Coast, that also contained

psychoactive compounds. One of the first documented cases of collection and use of magic mushrooms outside of Mexico was when the RCMP confiscated LIBERTY CAP mushrooms from some University of British Columbia students in Vancouver in 1965.

By the 1970s, people from across Canada were travelling to BC to pick LIBERTY CAP from BC agricultural fields, particularly in the Lower Mainland and Haida Gwaii. Conflicts ensued, with charges from concerned locals of trespassing and property damage. In 1974, possession of psilocybin was prohibited under Canada's Food and Drugs Act. However, in late 1979 the BC Court of Appeal ruled that possession of magic mushrooms in their natural state did not constitute possession of the restricted compound, and so from 1979 to 1982, possession of magic mushrooms was not illegal in our province. This changed in 1982 when Canada's Supreme Court confirmed that possession of the dried mushrooms was equivalent to possession of psilocybin.

The law and court ruling remain in effect to this day, though much of the conflict generated by the initial rulings seems to have subsided and enforcement seems to have relaxed. Those wanting to experiment with magic mushrooms often turn to home cultivation of the subtropical species *Psilocybe cubensis*. Wild harvest of native species, however, continues to be important in certain regions of BC. Researchers are once again experimenting with psilocybin to treat conditions such as depression and PTSD (post-traumatic stress disorder) and to support terminal-cancer patients dealing with anxiety over death and dying.

People considering picking and eating magic mushrooms should keep in mind that our native *Psilocybe* species are LBMs (little brown mushrooms) and that they can be similar in appearance—and, disconcertingly, often grow alongside—deadly poisonous and potentially poisonous LBMs such as *Galerina* (p. 286) and *Conocybe* (p. 283) species. For more information about magic mushrooms, check out the excellent articles by Paul Kroeger on the Vancouver Mycological Society's website.

Liberty Cap   *Psilocybe semilanceata*

CAP To 2 cm across; conical or bell-shaped with a pronounced tall, pointy, nipple-like umbo and rarely flattening; chestnut brown to olive-brown when wet, drying to whitish or pale yellowish white, at times with olive tints and in age occasionally with bluish stains, the margin sometimes paler; with a gelatinous skin that is slimy/sticky when wet, can sometimes be peeled, and becomes opaque whitish when drier (hygrophanous); smooth; margins translucent-striate when wet and often becoming purplish from spores; flesh thin, whitish to cap-coloured, bruising slightly blue. **GILLS** Broadly to narrowly attached; moderately shallow; white becoming grey and eventually purplish brown as spores mature, edges remaining whitish; closely spaced. **ODOUR** Slightly farinaceous, or not distinctive. **TASTE** Not distinctive. **SPORE PRINT** Purplish brown. **STEM** To 10 cm tall × 2 mm wide; equal; often wavy; white, browner at base, bruising blue in age or with handling; dry; sometimes finely hairy at top when young, becoming smooth or longitudinally striate. **RING** Cobwebby; soon disappearing, often not even leaving a ring zone. **FRUITING** Scattered or in groups; grassy areas (pastures, lawns), especially abundant on well-manured fields, but usually not directly on dung; most common and abundant in late summer and autumn.

    EDIBILITY Edible, hallucinogenic. **SIMILAR** *Psilocybe pelliculosa* has a broad rather than pointy umbo and prefers decayed conifer duff, so it is usually found in forest habitats. *Hypholoma dispersum*, which shares the broader umbo of *Psilocybe pelliculosa*, is also found in forest habitats, but it has a somewhat bitter taste, (often) a yellow to brownish yellow stem, and a cap margin that is white-fringed from the veil remnants. **COMMENTS** If you find dozens of psychonauts on their knees in a pasture, the small LIBERTY CAP is probably the shroom they are looking for. • The common name LIBERTY CAP is based on a pointed cap worn by liberty-loving French and American revolutionaries in the 18th century. • "Semilanceata" means "half spear-shaped," from the spear-like shape of cap.

Wavy Cap   *Psilocybe cyanescens*

CAP To 5 cm across; conical becoming convex and eventually flat, sometimes with a broad umbo, the margins wavy and usually extending beyond the gill edges; chestnut brown becoming caramel-coloured, sometimes fading to beige as it dries, often bruising blue or blue-green; with a gelatinous skin that is slimy/sticky when wet and can sometimes be peeled; smooth; hygrophanous; translucent-striate when wet; flesh thin (to 3 mm), cap-coloured, bruising blue. **GILLS** Broadly attached; deepest in middle (to 6 mm); cinnamon brown, becoming purplish black as spores mature, edges often eroded and/or paler, sometimes mottled, sometimes bruising blue; somewhat closely spaced; subgills in 3–4 tiers. **ODOUR** Not distinctive, or farinaceous. **TASTE** Not usually distinctive, but sometimes bitter. **SPORE PRINT** Purplish brown or purplish black. **STEM** To 8 cm tall × 5 mm wide; roughly equal, sometimes with a slightly widened base and/or top; whitish, bruising blue; dry; finely longitudinally striate; with white rhizomorphs at base. **RING** Cobwebby; white; usually disappearing but sometimes leaving a slight ring zone on stem. **FRUITING** Usually in groups, sometimes dense or clustered; on wood-chip mulch or soils rich in woody debris; gardens, paths, mixedwood forest edges; late autumn, winter.

EDIBILITY Edible, hallucinogenic. **SIMILAR** Be careful to differentiate between WAVY CAP mushrooms and toxic species in the brown-spored genera *Conocybe* and *Galerina* (such as the **FUNERAL BELL**, p. 286, which is often distinguishable by its dark brown stem base and growth on logs). The slightly smaller *Psilocybe stuntzii*, which has a persistent membranous ring, favours woody debris and coastal-area lawns, has olive-brown hues on the cap (especially the margin), and has dingy yellowish hues on the stem. **COMMENTS** WAVY CAP is BC's most potent magic mushroom. Users often experience difficulty in coordinating movement (so-called rubbery legs), a temporary condition not usual in other magic mushrooms such as the LIBERTY CAP (p. 310) ● "Cyanescens" means "becoming blue," referring to the staining characteristics of this species.

Haymaker's Mushroom · *Panaeolus foenisecii*

CAP To 3 cm across; conical or bell-shaped or hemispheric, later more shallowly convex to nearly flat, margins inrolled; dark brown or reddish brown when wet, drying to tan or greyish brown but often retaining a darker band near the margin; dry; smooth but sometimes with fine cracks when dry; hygrophanous; flesh thin (to 2 mm), fragile, pale brown (wet) to whitish (dry). GILLS Broadly to narrowly attached; moderately deep (to 5 mm); whitish, becoming dark brown as spores mature, the edges paler, the faces often mottled; moderately spaced. ODOUR Not distinctive. TASTE Not distinctive, or sometimes sour. SPORE PRINT Dark brown or purplish brown. STEM To 8 cm tall × 4 mm wide; equal, sometimes twisted near apex; fragile; becoming hollow; whitish, later becoming brownish from base upward or where handled; dry; smooth to finely longitudinally striate to finely hairy. RING Absent. FRUITING Single or in groups; on the ground; in grassy areas; late spring, summer (most common), autumn.

EDIBILITY Uncertain. Some sources cite the HAYMAKER'S MUSHROOM as psychoactive, but efforts to find the relevant chemical compounds have not been successful. SIMILAR The larger, truly psychoactive *Panaeolus subbalteatus* **group** mushrooms, whose cap and stems may bruise bluish, grow in clusters on dung and have a black spore print and black gills in age. They often have a darker marginal band on the cap. The common *P. papilionaceus* also prefers dung and has veil remnants that form white, tooth-like projections around the cap. *Psathyrella gracilis* **group** mushrooms are quite similar to the HAYMAKER'S MUSHROOM, but they tend to grow on wood chips rather than grass. COMMENTS You may see the genus of HAYMAKER'S MUSHROOM cited in some sources as *Panaeolina* rather than *Panaeolus*, a switch promoted because the HAYMAKER'S MUSHROOM is not a typical *Panaeolus*. More typical *Panaeolus* species are dung-loving, have a blackish spore print, and can be trip-inducing psychedelic mushrooms. ☙ "Foenisecii" comes from a Latin compound meaning "hay mower."

Dung Dome   *Protostropharia semiglobata*

CAP To 5 cm across; hemispheric or bell-shaped becoming more shallowly convex, sometimes with an umbo, the margins curved down; pale yellow to pale yellowish brown in centre, paler toward the margin; with a gelatinous skin, slimy to glutinous when wet, shiny when dry; smooth; flesh thin (to 5 mm), pale yellow. **GILLS** Broadly attached; deep (to 8 mm); grey, becoming purplish black as spores mature, often mottled, edges paler; moderately spaced; subgills in 2–4 tiers. **ODOUR** Not distinctive. **TASTE** Not distinctive. **SPORE PRINT** Purplish brown or purplish black. **STEM** To 8 cm tall × 5 mm wide; equal or widening toward base; becoming hollow; whitish to pale yellow, sometimes yellow-brown below; dry above the ring zone, often with fine hairs, and sticky when dry and slimy to glutinous when wet from the ring zone downward. **RING** Membranous, glutinous; sometimes disappearing, leaving ring zone of fibres near the top of stem. **FRUITING** Scattered or in small groups; on dung, or soils rich in organic matter; spring, summer, autumn.

    EDIBILITY Edible. But how many fecal pies are you willing to rummage through to collect enough small DUNG DOMES for a meal? **SIMILAR** On moose dung in BC's Interior, look for ***Protostropharia alcis*** (which differs from the DUNG DOME in mostly microscopic features) and ***Panaeolus alcis*** (which has a cap not more than 1 cm across). ***Panaeolus semiovatus***, a dung mushroom with a preference for horse excrement, has an ivory-white to straw-coloured cap, a dry stem, a white (but soon blackening) ring, and sometimes a white fringe at the cap margins. ***Deconica coprophila*** has a hygrophanous orange-brown to reddish brown cap, a whitish to yellow-brown stem, and no ring (though sometimes with a poorly developed ring zone). For other dung mushrooms, see **HAYMAKER'S MUSHROOM** (p. 312). **COMMENTS** Many field guides still list DUNG DOME as *Stropharia semiglobata*. ⚬ "Semiglobata" means "hemispheric," a description of the shape of the young caps.

Suburban Psathyrella   *Psathyrella candolleana* group

CAP To 7 cm across; ovoid before cap opens, then conical or convex, sometimes becoming flat with a broad umbo, margins with white partial veil remnants when young, sometimes splitting in age; dotted when young with white fibrils from the universal veil; pale yellowish brown when moist, drying paler or whitish, usually darker in centre; dry; smooth; hygrophanous; slightly translucent-striate when moist; flesh thin (to 2 mm), fragile, and the colour of the cap. **GILLS** Broadly attached; shallow (2–5 mm deep); whitish, becoming grey and then dark purplish brown as spores mature, the edges paler; crowded, 54–57 reaching the stem; 2–3 tiers of subgills. **ODOUR** Not distinctive. **TASTE** Not distinctive. **SPORE PRINT** Dark brown or purplish brown. **STEM** To 10 cm tall × 8 mm wide; equal; hollow; whitish; dry; silky and longitudinally striate, sometimes scurfy, especially in the lower part. **RING** Absent normally, but the partial veil can sometimes leave a faint zone on stem. **FRUITING** Scattered, in groups, or clustered; on the ground; around hardwood stumps or buried wood, in lawns, gardens and open forest; year-round.

    EDIBILITY Edible. Difficult to identify, however, and quite similar to species that may be toxic. **SIMILAR** A reddish brown young cap, gills that start off brown, and a darkening stem on what otherwise appears to be SUBURBAN PSATHYRELLA may indicate *Psathyrella piluliformis* or, if found along coastal dunes with a stem buried in the sand, *P. ammophila*. **COMMENTS** SUBURBAN PSATHYRELLA, though frequent in BC, is a species that must be encountered many times to see the full array of physical presentations. Noting the usually wide cap for such a narrow stem can be a connecting clue. • Over the years this highly variable mushroom has spun off several new species with definitions that differ in only microscopic ways. In addition, a recent proposal would see SUBURBAN PSATHYRELLA moved to a new genus as *Candolleomyces candolleanus*. • "Candolleana" honours Swiss botanist Augustin Pyramus de Candolle (1778–1841).

Ringed Psathyrella   *Psathyrella longistriata*

CAP To 8 cm across; conical or convex, becoming shallowly convex to flat, sometimes broadly umbonate; various shades of brown, paler with age; dry; with flecks/hairs of white veil remnants when young, later smooth, sometimes wrinkled in age; hygrophanous; translucent-striate when moist; flesh thin (to 5 mm), fragile, coloured as the cap. GILLS Broadly to narrowly attached; moderately deep (5–7 mm); whitish or pale brown, becoming dark red-brown, then purplish brown as spores mature, the edges paler; closely spaced, 46–54 reaching the stem; subgills in 3–4 tiers. ODOUR Not distinctive. TASTE Not distinctive. SPORE PRINT Dark purplish brown to nearly black. STEM To 10 cm tall × 1 cm wide; equal or slightly widened below; hollow; white; dry; often white-scurfy and finely longitudinally striate or silky. RING Membranous, silky to striate on top, woolly on the bottom; white; usually persistent. FRUITING Scattered or in groups; on the ground; in conifer and mixedwood forests; autumn, winter, more rarely spring.

  EDIBILITY Unknown. SIMILAR The presence of a ring sets the RINGED PSATHYRELLA apart from most other *Psathyrella* species. *Panaeolus semiovatus* and **DUNG DOME** (p. 313) can look similar and often have rings, but they grow in grassy areas or on dung. COMMENTS First described by Alexander H. Smith in the mid-20th century from Washington, the RINGED PSATHYRELLA is confined to states and provinces along the North American Pacific coast. ◦ "Longistrata" means "long-striate," a reference to the striations on the cap or perhaps the stem.

Chip Cherry   *Leratiomyces ceres*

CAP To 6 cm across; hemispheric to convex becoming nearly flat or broadly umbonate, the margins incurved when young and hung with whitish veil remnants; bright scarlet or reddish orange, sometimes paler at the margin; slightly slimy/sticky when moist, soon dry; smooth; flesh thin, whitish or pale yellow or red-brown. **GILLS** Broadly attached, notched; moderately deep (to 1 cm); cream to pale yellow, becoming greyish brown or greyish olive and finally purple-brown, sometimes with paler edges; somewhat closely spaced. **ODOUR** Not distinctive. **TASTE** Not distinctive. **SPORE PRINT** Purple-brown. **STEM** To 8 cm tall × 1 cm wide; equal, often widening a bit downward; white, later pale yellow, especially at the top, in the lower part often acquiring orange-brown stains; dry; longitudinally striate; with white mycelium at the base. **RING** Cottony; white; disappearing and leaving a thin ring zone. **FRUITING** Scattered or in groups, sometimes in clusters; in bark mulch or gardens or lawns rich in decaying wood; autumn, winter.

EDIBILITY Unknown. **SIMILAR** *Pyrrhulomyces astragalinus* (formerly *Pholiota astragalina*) has a slimier pink-orange cap that ages or bruises blackish, a brown spore print, gills that are a brighter yellow, and a preference for logs. The cap colour, says one of our poetic mycologists, is reminiscent of the colour of the sun obscured by forest-fire smoke. Young caps of the chip-loving *Hypholoma tuberosum* have more of an orange-brown than reddish orange colour, and their stems are connected to a large underground sclerotium. **COMMENTS** Until recently, *Leratiomyces ceres* went under other names, such as *Stropharia aurantiaca*, *Hypholoma aurantiacum*, and *Psilocybe ceres*. ◆ Supposedly this is an invasive, brought to BC on landscaping chips, but research in Britain, where CHIP CHERRY also seems to be a recent arrival, suggests that the mycelium resides deep in the soil and can be found where there have been no applications of imported chips. Possibly wood chips, rather than being infected agents, provide an essential nutrient/habitat that triggers fruiting.

Boletes

Almost all the mushrooms in the bolete family bear their spores on an underside pocked with tiny tubes. Spore-bearing bodies (basidia) line the inside of the tubes, allowing the mushrooms to produce more spores per square centimetre of cap size. Boletes, though, are not the only group of mushrooms to make use of tubes—many of the polypores (p. 378) have tubes. The tube holes on boletes, however, tend to be wider than those on polypores. Also, unlike polypores, the whole spore-bearing surface of boletes is fleshy and can usually be peeled from the cap with just a push of the thumb.

Worldwide, there are at least 800 species in the bolete family, and they are currently divided into more than 60 genera. We know of about 75 bolete species in BC, and these are usually arranged into three large groups: the traditional boletes (here represented by the genera *Boletus*, *Aureoboletus*, *Caloboletus*, *Chalciporus*, and *Xerocomellus*), the jacks (genus *Suillus*), and the scaberstalks (genus *Leccinum*). In general, boletes often have dry caps, jacks have slimy/sticky caps, and scaberstalks have small, rigid projections (scabers) on their stems.

In recent decades, boletes have been the subjects of intense research, and this research has overturned many traditional ideas about the genetic and morphological differences among members of this family. Those of us who have lived through this period have had to learn a lot of new names for the mushrooms we know. You will see some of these changes on the following pages. And the research goes on: revisit this book in 20 years, and you will no doubt find that more names have been replaced.

Boletes have reputations as ectomycorrhizal species, and the ones found in BC—with the possible exception of the PEPPERY BOLETE (p. 324)—will probably turn out to be ectomycorrhizal when the plant associations are more fully studied. They form these associations with many kinds of trees, but they prefer trees in the pine family, such as true firs and DOUGLAS-FIRS, pines, larches, spruces, and hemlocks. Many are also associated with birches and aspens and related catkin-forming broadleaf trees. Boletes often have preferences for certain tree partners, so knowing the tree can help identify the bolete.

As a general rule, boletes are edible, though there are a few that can make you ill (some of the *Rubroboletus* species, for example) and some that are too bitter (the BITTER BOLETE, p. 323) to even think about consuming. Experience has also shown that some boletes long thought to be good edibles, such as the rough-stemmed leccinums, can cause gastrointestinal problems for some people. The sovereign among the many edible boletes is the aptly named KING BOLETE (p. 318), which vies with chanterelles for the coveted title of "world's most popular wild edible mushroom."

King Bolete
Boletus edulis

CAP To 25 cm across (occasionally much larger); hemispheric to more shallowly convex becoming nearly flat, often uneven, the margins incurved at first and then curved down, later lifted up and wavy; pale/medium brown or yellowish brown or reddish brown, often paler at edge; dry, becoming slightly slippery when wet or older; smooth, sometimes becoming wrinkled with age; flesh 2–4 cm thick, white, not staining. PORES White, appearing stuffed with cotton (mycelium) when young, becoming yellow or eventually brown with age or bruising; round, 2–3 per mm, to 3 cm deep. ODOUR Not distinctive. TASTE Pleasant, nutty. SPORE PRINT Olive-brown. STEM To 25 cm × 3 cm at apex, 7 cm at base; usually enlarging downward to rounded base when mature, but when young can appear entirely rounded like a ball, making the mushroom look like BB-8 in the later *Star Wars* movies; flesh white and firm; surface white or pale brown; dry to moist; reticulate (see photo on the next page), especially near the top. RING Absent. FRUITING Single, scattered, or in groups; under conifers; on the ground, sometimes partly buried in the duff; late summer or autumn.

EDIBILITY Choice. Sweetly nutty. A single cap can get big enough to feed a crew, but at this late stage the caps are usually slug-eaten and maggoty—table collectors prefer smaller caps. SIMILAR *Boletus fibrillosus* has a cap that is often velvety, dry, and a darker red-brown, a pore layer that starts off cream to light yellow rather than white, and a darker brown stem, especially in the lower part. The SPRING KING (*Boletus rex-veris*), which is found at higher elevations in the spring, has a more consistently reddish brown cap. Its white pore layer tends toward greenish in age, and its stem can be curved and tapered. Beginning mushroomers have been known to confuse the KING BOLETE with the BITTER BOLETE (p. 323). The blue-staining gills and bitter taste of the latter will quickly resolve any ambiguity. COMMENTS The KING BOLETE is native to Northern Hemisphere forests and has been introduced on the roots of trees to the Southern

Hemisphere land masses. The work has not been done that would tell us whether or not this widely spread mushroom is a single species or a collection of similar species. ❧ The KING BOLETE, a mycorrhizal species, has resisted cultivation, so the harvest is entirely wild-collected. In spite of this restriction, it is one of the world's most economically important mushrooms, with yearly harvests estimated to be as high as a hundred thousand tonnes. ❧ Perhaps no other mushroom in modern mycology has accumulated such a deep lore around its collection and culinary use. One can travel to Italy and procure the services of a *fungaiolo* who will—properly recompensed—play the role of PORCINI guide, leading you into the countryside and initiating you into the art of hunting these elusive mushrooms. Those in BC who have found their "spots" where KING BOLETES come up year after year often keep the location information a closely guarded secret and visit their patches only after making sure that they're not followed by competing collectors. ❧ KING BOLETES can be easily preserved via several methods, including pickling and freezing, but the preferred method is drying—the dried flesh of this mushroom keeps its flavour and readily reconstitutes. ❧ There are many common names for this popular mushroom in other languages. To Italians, it is PORCINI ("little pig," for its fat stem), a name often used in English-based cuisine (hint: pronounce the word "porcini" with the "c" as a *ch* and with broad gesticulations followed by a smack of the lips). French speakers call it CÈPES ("stalk," again a reference to the fat stem), and German speakers call it STEINPILZ ("stone mushroom," for its firm flesh). ❧ "Edulis" means "edible."

Red-cracked Bolete   *Xerocomellus diffractus*

CAP To 10 cm across; almost spherical to hemispheric to more shallowly convex, becoming nearly flat; dark brown to olive-grey, sometimes with reddish margins, in age with pale to yellow to reddish cracks; dry; woolly to velvety; flesh to 1.5 cm deep, firm, white becoming yellow with age, slowly and irregularly bruising blue-green. PORES Yellow and in age yellow-brown to yellow-green, bruising blue; irregular, large (to 1.5 mm across) and moderately deep (to 1 cm) in mature caps. ODOUR Not distinctive. TASTE Not distinctive. SPORE PRINT Olive-brown. STEM To 10 cm tall × 1.5 cm wide; equal or enlarging downward; solid; flesh yellow but sometimes with reddish colours, especially near base, in age becoming more red from base upward, and staining blue-green; surface yellow, punctuated with reddish hues and streaks below the small region at the top of stem; dry; smooth but sometimes with longitudinal striations and/ or scurfy; with white mycelium at the base. RING Absent. FRUITING Single or in groups; on the ground; under hardwoods and conifers; spring to autumn. EDIBILITY Edible. SIMILAR ZELLER'S BOLETE (p. 321) caps generally have a much darker brownish black to reddish black tone and tend to have less cracking than the RED-CRACKED BOLETE cap. The PEPPERY BOLETE (p. 324) is much smaller, does not stain blue in any of its tissues, has a peppery taste, and has a yellow mycelium at the stem base. COMMENTS Until the current millennium, the RED-CRACKED BOLETE was known as *Boletus chrysenteron*. It was moved to *Xerocomellus*, its current home, in 2008. The *X. chrysenteron* group, however, is a European complex that comprises a group of related species. The recently described *X. diffractus* is one of the western North American species in this group and is perhaps the one most often encountered by BC foragers. ◆ Caps of older RED-CRACKED BOLETES can often be found infected by the white or gold mould of *Hypomyces chrysospermus*. ◆ "Diffractus" means "shattered," a reference to the cracked cap.

Zeller's Bolete   *Xerocomellus zelleri*

CAP To 10 cm across; convex becoming nearly flat, margins incurved and often remaining curved down, rarely with cracks; blackish to dark olive-brown, rarely deep red-black, with a white to yellowish band around the margin, often with a white bloom when young; dry; when young, often wrinkled, velvety, in age matted or smooth and sometimes slightly cracked; flesh to 1.5 cm deep, firm, white to pale yellow, unchanging when cut or sometimes staining blue. PORES Sometimes slightly decurrent; pale yellow to olive-yellow, darker in age and sometimes reddish, at times bruising slightly blue; irregular, large (1–2 mm across), moderately deep (to 1.5 cm). ODOUR Not distinctive. TASTE Not distinctive. SPORE PRINT Olive-brown. STEM To 8 cm tall × 2 cm wide; equal or nearly so, sometimes widening and then tapering at base; solid; flesh yellow, turning red in parts, sometimes turning blue when cut; surface yellow punctuated with red granules, in age becoming mostly dark red; dry; smooth, with longitudinal striations; with white to pale yellow mycelium at base. RING Absent. FRUITING Single or clustered; on the ground or on rotting wood; under conifers; all seasons.

    EDIBILITY Edible. SIMILAR See the RED-CRACKED BOLETE (p. 320) entry for a comparison with that species. We also have the newly described *Xerocomellus atropurpureus* in BC. Its cap is more reddish purple, lacks the white band around the margin, and is smooth even when young. In our experience, beginners may have trouble telling ZELLER'S BOLETE from the ADMIRABLE BOLETE (p. 322). The latter has a reddish brown, sometimes mottled cap that keeps its velvety look and feel in age and a stem that widens down and is often bent. COMMENTS "Zelleri" is in honour of American mycologist Sanford Myron Zeller (1885–1948).

Admirable Bolete   *Aureoboletus mirabilis*

CAP To 15 cm across; hemispheric or more shallowly convex becoming somewhat flat, margins incurved at first and often extending beyond pores and hung with veil fragments; dark reddish brown to chocolate brown, sometimes mottled with buff in age, margins often lighter; moist when young, dry with age; scaly to plush; flesh somewhat thick (to 2.5 cm), soft, white to yellow, occasionally reddish near the cap skin and rarely staining blue. PORES Pale yellow becoming greenish yellow, sometimes a deeper yellow where bruised; round to angular, 1–2 mm across and up to 2 cm deep. ODOUR Not distinctive. TASTE Usually not distinctive, but on occasion lemony. SPORE PRINT Olive-brown. STEM To 15 cm or more × 3 cm or more; expanding downward, often curved; flesh firm; solid; pale red-brown, sometimes with yellow streaks; surface same colour as cap but with yellow or buff streaks; moist to dry; with longitudinal ridges, often somewhat reticulate near the top; with yellow mycelium at base. RING Absent. FRUITING Single or scattered; on or near rotting conifer (often hemlock) logs; summer or autumn.

EDIBILITY Choice. At times with a delightful citrus/lemony taste. SIMILAR *Boletus smithii* differs by having tissues that always stain blue and a stem that is 2-toned, with red toward the top changing to yellow at the base. See also the comparison notes at ZELLER'S BOLETE (p. 321). COMMENTS You may see this species listed as *Boletus mirabilis*. Its recent placement in *Aureoboletus*, a genus with some other golden- or yellow-pored species ("aureo" = golden), is supported by low-volume DNA sequencing. ❧ The ADMIRABLE BOLETE is believed to be mycorrhizal, but it always seems to be growing around decomposing logs. These nurse logs and stumps are densely infiltrated with hemlock tree roots—the mycelium may be colonizing the wood as a brown rot and reverting to being mycorrhizal upon contact with the hemlock roots. ❧ "Mirabilis" means "wonderful," which this species certainly is.

Bitter Bolete
Caloboletus conifericola

CAP To 30 cm across; hemispheric, expanding to more shallowly convex, cracking in age, margins initially incurved and often remaining downcurved; olive-grey becoming greyish brown, sometimes with reddish or black streaks, darkening where handled; dry; matte and smooth to velvety; flesh thick, white to pale yellow, bruising instantly blue. **PORES** Pale yellow or olive green, becoming dingy yellow, bruising immediately blue and eventually brown or yellow-brown; round to angular, 2–3 per mm. **ODOUR** Not distinctive. **TASTE** Very bitter. **SPORE PRINT** Olive-brown. **STEM** To 12 cm tall × 5 cm wide; equal or widening downward to a rounded base; yellow at first, later darker (often an olive-brown) from the base up, bruising blue; dry; smooth, sometimes finely reticulate near the top. **RING** Absent. **FRUITING** Single or scattered; on the ground; under conifers; autumn.

   EDIBILITY Not edible. Much too bitter. **SIMILAR** The BITTER BOLETE is the only common BC species with a bitter taste, a brown cap, a yellow stem (at least at the top), yellow pores, and flesh and pores that turn an immediate blue. The BITTER BOLETE has less common *Caloboletus* cousins in our area, such as **C. rubripes**, which, though similar in most other respects, have some red on the stems, the amount of red increasing with age. **COMMENTS** Could also be called Big Disappointment—mycological neophytes who find a huge, yellow-pored, blue-staining forest bolete may think at first that they have found dinner. A small taste corrects this first impression. ✎ Until recently, this species was called *Boletus coniferarum*. The new genus name, "caloboletus," means "beautiful bolete," described this way because of the fetching red tinges on the stems of some *Caloboletus* species (but not this one). "Conifericola" means "living around conifers."

Peppery Bolete   *Chalciporus piperatus*

CAP To 8 cm across, usually smaller; hemispheric or more shallowly convex becoming flat, occasionally with a slight umbo, margins often extending beyond gills; yellow-brown to reddish brown, margins sometimes paler; moist and sticky at first, then dry; smooth, but sometimes with pressed-down fibres when young, often cracked with age; flesh to 1.5 cm deep, pale yellow, sometimes with reddish tints. PORES Cinnamon becoming reddish brown, sometimes slight darkening on bruising; angular, 0.5–2 mm wide, to 1 cm deep. ODOUR Not distinctive. TASTE Quickly peppery. SPORE PRINT Cinnamon brown. STEM Slender, to 8 cm tall × 1 cm wide; equal or narrowing downward; solid; flesh yellow-brown above and lemon-yellow in base; surface coloured like cap; dry; smooth to slightly hairy; with bright yellow mycelium at the base. RING Absent. FRUITING Single, scattered, or in groups; with coniferous and broadleaf trees; summer or autumn.

EDIBILITY Unknown. There are some reports of it being eaten. SIMILAR A not-well-researched distinction is sometimes made between the PEPPERY BOLETE and *Chalciporus piperatoides*, with the latter being less peppery and having a blue-staining pore layer. This blue-stainer occurs in BC. Other than this close look-alike, however, no other BC species closely resembles this small, narrow-stemmed, red-pored, hot-tasting species. Beginners, though, might confuse it with the RED-CRACKED BOLETE (p. 320) or the RED-PORED BOLETE (p. 325)—see the detailed comparisons on these species' pages. COMMENTS The PEPPERY BOLETE was historically assumed to be mycorrhizal, like almost all other boletes, but attempts to find traces of this relationship have been inconclusive. Genetic evidence strongly suggests that it is a parasite on other mushrooms, perhaps the FLY AGARIC (p. 106), which is often found in the vicinity of PEPPERY BOLETES. ◆ "Piperatus" means "peppery."

Red-pored Bolete

Rubroboletus pulcherrimus

CAP To 20 cm across; almost spherical to hemispheric or more shallowly convex, expanding to flat, sometimes cracked in age, the margins incurved and then curved down, often extending beyond the pores underneath; reddish brown, the scales becoming olive-brown to greyish, more reddish near the margin; dry; smooth or somewhat velvety when young, then with pressed-down scales; flesh thick (to 4 cm), yellow, and when cut or bruised quickly staining blue. PORES Dark red becoming reddish brown in age, bruising dark blue instantly; angular or irregular, 2–3 or more per mm and to 1.5 cm deep. ODOUR Not distinctive. TASTE Not distinctive. SPORE PRINT Brown or olive-brown. STEM To 16 cm tall × 5 cm wide; with non-abrupt bulbous or rounded base; solid; flesh pale yellow, staining blue; surface is pale reddish brown, with dark red reticulations, bruising blue; dry. RING Absent. FRUITING Single or scattered; on the ground; under conifers or hardwoods; summer, autumn, winter.

EDIBILITY Poisonous. At least one person is known to have died from eating this species. SIMILAR The much smaller PEPPERY BOLETE (p. 324) also has a red-brown cap and pores, but it has a yellow-brown stem that often narrows downward, yellow mycelium at the stem base, and a peppery taste. Compare also the red-stemmed *Caloboletus rubripes* (discussed on p. 323). COMMENTS Boletes with red pores that stain blue have been responsible for serious poisonings. They are considered a bad bunch—one European species even goes by the tendentious name *Rubroboletus satanas* ("satan")! So far, the RED-PORED BOLETE is the only member of this lethal crew reported from BC, and it does not seem to be very common. ✿ "Pulcherrimus" means "very beautiful" in Latin.

Fat Jack   *Suillus caerulescens*

CAP To 14 cm across; convex to nearly flat, margins inrolled when young, often with hanging veil remnants when first expanded; dull reddish brown or orangish brown to cinnamon or yellowish brown; slimy/sticky; smooth, with streaks of darker, pressed-down fibrils that sometimes clump into scales that can uplift a bit; flesh 1–2 cm thick, pale yellow, sometimes taking on pinkish hues. PORES Sometimes decurrent; yellow to yellow-brown, bruising dingy red-brown or orange-brown; angular to irregular, large (about 1 mm across to 1.5 cm deep), often arrayed radially. ODOUR Not distinctive. TASTE Slightly sour or not distinctive. SPORE PRINT Cinnamon brown. STEM To 8 cm tall × 3 cm wide; equal or narrowing at the top and/or bottom; flesh staining blue-green, especially at the base, and/or red-brown or orange-brown; surface is yellow above ring, dull yellow-brown below it; dry above, sometimes tacky below; smooth to hairy below ring, often weakly reticulate at top, but lacking glandular dots. RING Membranous, thin, band-like; white, aging to the cap colour; somewhat persistent. FRUITING Scattered or in groups; on the ground; under conifers, most commonly DOUGLAS-FIR; summer, autumn, winter.

EDIBILITY Edible. Reportedly with a citrus flavour, but slimy. SIMILAR The cap of MATTE JACK (p. 327) is usually covered with erect scales (though these can wash off), and the flesh in the stem base does not turn blue or blues only slightly. COMMENTS The FAT JACK, some speculate, may act as a host for *Gomphidius oregonensis*. ◦ First described in the 1960s, FAT JACK is a mostly (if not exclusively) western North American species. ◦ A friend's comments on eating *Suillus* species deserves repetition: "First peel the slimy skin from the cap. Next take a spoon and carefully scoop out the mushy tube layer. Finally, discard the stems, as they have probably fallen off by now anyway. This leaves virtually nothing left to cook so you may as well throw that away as well." ◦ "Caerulescens" means "becoming sky blue."

Matte Jack   *Suillus lakei*

CAP To 15 cm across; convex, becoming nearly flat and sometimes lumpy/ irregular in age, margins inrolled when young and with hanging veil remnants when it first opens; reddish brown to yellow-brown; often dry, but can be slimy/ sticky when wet; when young somewhat felty/woolly from darker, dense, erect fibrils that clump into scales, in age the fibrils flattening and becoming smooth; flesh thick (to 2 cm), yellowish, sometimes staining pinkish. PORES Sometimes decurrent; yellow to yellow-brown, staining brownish or reddish when bruised; angular and often radially elongated, large (1–2.5 mm across), somewhat shallow (to 1 cm). ODOUR Not distinctive. TASTE Not distinctive. SPORE PRINT Dull cinnamon brown. STEM To 12 cm tall × 3 cm wide; usually equal, sometimes widening downward and tapering at the extreme base; solid, but occasionally hollowed in age; flesh may stain weakly blue-green at the stem base in young specimens; surface yellowish above the ring, yellowish to brownish-streaked below it; dry; sometimes obscurely reticulate at the top, but lacks glandular dots. RING Membranous, thin, woolly, band-like; white to yellow; sometimes disappearing. FRUITING Scattered or in groups; on the ground; under conifers, most commonly DOUGLAS-FIR; spring, summer, autumn.

EDIBILITY Edible. Reportedly tasty, but also slimy. SIMILAR See comparison with FAT JACK (p. 326) in the entry for that mushroom. The TAMARACK JACK (p. 328) grows around larch trees and has a hollow lower stem. The WOOLLY JACK (p. 329) favours 2-needle pines as an associate, has a pore layer that bruises blue, and has dark orange glandular dots on the stem. COMMENTS The mycelium of ROSY GOMPHIDIUS (p. 296) is thought to be a parasite on the MATTE JACK mycelium, stealing the nutrients that the *Suillus* gets from its DOUGLAS-FIR associates. ᴥ MATTE JACK is primarily a western North American species, but it has accompanied DOUGLAS-FIR, one of the world's most common forestry plantation trees, on its intercontinental travels. ᴥ "Lakei" is in honour of American botanist Edward Ralph Lake.

Tamarack Jack   *Suillus ampliporus*

CAP To 10 cm across; almost spherical to hemispheric or more shallowly convex, expanding to nearly flat or broadly umbonate, the margins often with hanging white veil remnants; orange-brown or reddish brown, sometimes yellowish brown; dry; densely hairy or finely scaly, often with a suede-like texture; flesh soft, whitish to yellow, and not changing colour when cut or bruised. PORES Sometimes decurrent; pale yellow to greenish yellow, not changing colour when cut or bruised; angular, sometimes elongated, fairly large (0.5–1.5 mm or more across), sometimes arrayed in radial lines. ODOUR Not distinctive. TASTE Not distinctive. SPORE PRINT Brown or olive-brown. STEM To 9 cm tall × 2 cm wide; usually equal; upper half solid, lower half typically hollow; coloured as cap but paler, upper part sometimes yellow; dry; often with reticulation on upper parts. RING Cottony, fragile; often disappearing. FRUITING Single or scattered; on the ground; under larch (*Larix*); late summer, autumn.

EDIBILITY Edible. SIMILAR Habitat can serve to separate TAMARACK JACK from MATTE JACK (p. 327), the other BC *Suillus* species with a suede-like brown cap—the latter grows around DOUGLAS-FIR. It also lacks the hollow lower stem of TAMARACK JACK. *Suillus ochraceoroseus*, another larch lover, has a bitter taste, a solid stem, and a cap that is covered with rosy pink to dark red scales and that often has a yellow margin. COMMENTS BC has 3 larch species—WESTERN LARCH (*Larix occidentalis*), SUBALPINE LARCH (*L. lyallii*), and TAMARACK (*L. laricina*). *Suillus ampliporus* grows with TAMARACK and WESTERN LARCH and probably with SUBALPINE LARCH. ☙ Until 2016, *S. ampliporus* was known as *S. cavipes*. That name has since been identified more closely with the European species, leaving the North American species free to pick up the name *S. ampliporus* from an earlier description. ☙ "Suillus" is from "sus," the word in Latin for "pig," and "ampliporus" means "large-pored."

Woolly Jack   *Suillus tomentosus*

CAP To 15 cm across; almost spherical to hemispheric to more shallowly convex, becoming nearly flat, margins incurved when young, often extending past the underlying pore layer; yellow to orange undertint with pinkish buff to greyish yellow to reddish brown scales; usually slimy/sticky, but sometimes appearing dry; with fine uplifted scales when young, then with scales pressed down, then losing the scales to become smooth in age; flesh deep (to 2.5 cm), soft, white or yellow, slowly staining blue-green when cut. PORES Sometimes slightly decurrent; brown to reddish brown at first, becoming yellow to olive-yellow, bruising blue; angular, 1–2 per mm, to 2 cm deep. ODOUR Not distinctive. TASTE Not distinctive. SPORE PRINT Brown to dull cinnamon brown. STEM To 10 cm tall × 2.5 cm wide; equal or widening downward; flesh yellow, sometimes slightly blue-staining; surface yellow to a muted orange, sometimes reddish tints on base; dry to sticky; with dark orange to brown glandular dots. RING Absent. FRUITING Scattered or in groups; on the ground; usually under 2-needle pines; summer, autumn.

EDIBILITY Edible. SIMILAR WOOLLY JACK is the only blue-staining *Suillus* in this guide that doesn't have a veil. Two of the veiled species that can stain blue are the FAT JACK (p. 326) and the MATTE JACK (p. 327). They favour DOUGLAS-FIR, and their blue staining, if present, is in the lower stem but not in the cap or pores. COMMENTS WOOLLY JACKS can sometimes stain fingers blue. ◦ Though technically edible, this mushroom is the king of blandland. It has reportedly caused gastric distress in certain consumers. ◦ "Tomentosus" means "densely hairy," presumably a description of the scaly cap.

Short-stemmed Slippery Jack *Suillus brevipes*

CAP To 10 cm across; hemispheric to more shallowly convex or nearly flat in age, margins initially incurved or curved down; dark purplish brown fading to a cinnamon brown or a streaky and pale yellowish brown; peelable; slimy to glutinous when wet; smooth; flesh thick (to 2 cm), soft, white. PORES White to yellow, sometimes becoming olive-yellow, no colour change on bruising; roundish, 1–2 per mm, to 1 cm deep. ODOUR Not distinctive. TASTE Not distinctive. SPORE PRINT Dull brown to cinnamon. STEM To 5 cm tall × 2 cm wide, often appearing short in relation to cap width; usually equal, sometimes thicker in the middle; solid; flesh white but becoming yellowish, especially at the stem top; surface white becoming pale yellow; dry; smooth, sometimes with inconspicuous glandular dots in age. RING Absent. FRUITING Scattered or densely clustered; on the ground; under 2- and 3-needle pines; summer, autumn.

EDIBILITY Edible. SIMILAR *Suillus granulatus*, which prefers to associate with 5-needle pines, differs by having a slimy and light brown to cinnamon cap, pinkish to brown glandular dots over the stem, and pores that are sometimes elongated and/or radially arrayed. (*Suillus granulatus* is a European species. North American species are genetically quite different and may inherit the name *S. weaverae*.) *Suillus punctatipes* resembles *S. granulatus* and *S. brevipes*, but it has a darker brown cap and prefers to partner with DOUGLAS-FIR and hemlocks. COMMENTS In forests, the SHORT-STEMMED SLIPPERY JACK appears to associate only with hard (2- and 3-needle) pines, such as LODGEPOLE PINE. It's also common in urban settings, where introduced 2-needle pines are often planted as landscaping trees. ❧ A 2002 study of Yellowstone GRIZZLY BEAR diets revealed that they consumed large numbers of mushrooms, including quantities of the SHORT-STEMMED SLIPPERY JACK. This is likely the case in parts of BC. ❧ *Suillus* species are often collectively known as slippery jacks, since many of them (including this species) are slimy or glutinous. ❧ "Brevipes" means "short-footed," a characterization of the stem length.

Slippery Jack   *Suillus luteus*

CAP To 12 cm across; almost spherical to hemispheric becoming more shallowly convex to nearly flat, margins often hung with veil remnants; red-brown to yellow-brown, often with darker radial streaking in age; with a peelable cap; slimy/sticky to glutinous when wet, shiny when dry; smooth; flesh white or pale yellow, not staining. PORES White to pale yellow, becoming yellow-brown with age, not staining; angular, 1–3 per mm, shallow (to 7 mm deep). ODOUR Not distinctive. TASTE Not distinctive. SPORE PRINT Brown to dull cinnamon brown. STEM To 8 cm tall × 2.5 cm wide; usually equal or expanding downward; solid; white at first, later pale yellow above the ring and having purplish to brown tones layered over yellow below; often slimy below the ring; prominent glandular dots during all stages, at least above the ring. RING Large, membranous, sheathing and flaring, gelatinous when moist; white with purplish tones; usually persistent. FRUITING Single or in small groups; on the ground; around conifers, especially pines of all types; summer, autumn, occasionally spring.

EDIBILITY Edible. But slimy. SIMILAR *Suillus flavidus* (was *S. umbonatus*), usually found with LODGEPOLE PINE and SHORE PINE in BC, has a slimy/sticky, somewhat umbonate cap that is more yellow-brown to yellow-olive, flesh that turns a light cinnamon when cut, and larger pores (to 1.5 mm) that stain pinkish cinnamon when bruised. *Suillus clintonianus*, the name now being given to BC specimens that were known as *S. grevillei*, grows with larch (*Larix*). It has a glutinous cap that is a duller red-brown than the SLIPPERY JACK's cap, and its stem does not have glandular dots. COMMENTS A recent genetic study of *Suillus* species suggests that SLIPPERY JACK, because of its ability to adapt to multiple conifer hosts, is the most widespread *Suillus* in the world. It was originally described in Europe, however, and though it is known to occur in eastern North America, its relationship to our western North American SLIPPERY JACKS needs further study. ◦ "Luteus" means "yellow," perhaps a reference to the pore layer.

Orange-capped Scaberstalk *Leccinum aurantiacum* group

CAP To 20 cm across; convex becoming nearly flat; orange-brown to brick red; dry; with pressed-down fibres when young, smooth in age; flesh thick (to 3 cm), white, but when cut or bruised, slowly staining pinkish to dark red and then darkening to bluish grey and eventually black. **PORES** Whitish, staining greyish to olive-brown in age or when bruised; angular, small (2–3 per mm). **ODOUR** Not distinctive. **TASTE** Not distinctive. **SPORE PRINT** Yellow-brown or cinnamon. **STEM** To 16 cm tall × 3 cm wide; equal or sometimes with expanded base; solid; whitish, the base sometimes bruising pinkish to wine red and then later turning greenish blue to blue; dry; smooth but dotted with blackish scabers. **RING** Absent. **FRUITING** Scattered or in groups; on the ground; usually under conifers; summer, autumn.

EDIBILITY Edible. But with caution—poisonings have been reported for similar orange-capped boletes. **SIMILAR ASPEN SCABERSTALK** (p. 333), which grows under **TREMBLING ASPEN**, has tissues that stain blue without an intervening pinkish stage and a cap that often has a more orange-brown hue than a dark red. **BIRCH SCABERSTALK** (p. 334), which grows under birch, has a lighter, yellow-brown cap, and the white flesh in its stem may slowly turn pinkish buff. *Leccinum manzanitae*, which grows with manzanita bushes and ARBUTUS trees, also has flesh that bruises blue without an intervening pinkish stage. **COMMENTS** We have a mushroom species in the BC Interior that fits the above description and that has often been identified by researchers and foragers as *L. aurantiacum*. However, the European *L. aurantiacum* differs in several small ways from what we have in BC, especially by growing with hardwoods rather than conifers. The DNA of one of our *L. aurantiacum* specimens from the BC Interior closely matches *L. vulpinum*, a European-defined species that *does* grow under conifers. ➤ "Aurantiacum" means "orange-coloured."

Aspen Scaberstalk   *Leccinum insigne*

CAP To 16 cm across; convex becoming broad and almost flat, the skin at the margin overhanging the edge and splitting in age; usually reddish orange to reddish brown, often paler and sometimes mottled and/or pitted in age; dry to moist; velvety or finely scaly; flesh thick (to 3 cm), white, soft in age, when cut or bruised staining purplish grey (but not reddish) and eventually black, often staining irregularly and slowly. PORES Whitish becoming yellowish to brown in age or when bruised, not turning blue; round to angular, 1–3 per mm. ODOUR Not distinctive. TASTE Not distinctive. SPORE PRINT Yellow-brown to olive-brown. STEM To 12 cm tall × 2 cm wide; equal or widening downward; solid; whitish, with pale scabers that darken to brown and eventually blacken with age, the base sometimes bruising blue on the surface and in the flesh; dry. RING Absent. FRUITING Scattered or in groups; on the ground, under TREMBLING ASPEN; spring, summer, autumn.

EDIBILITY Edible. But there have been occasional poisonings associated with this and similar orange- or red-capped boletes. SIMILAR See the ORANGE-CAPPED SCABERSTALK (p. 332) for comparisons. *Leccinum* species with reddish brown caps show wide variations in colour and can be difficult to tell apart. They are, however, host specialists, forming mycorrhizal associations with only certain plants, so the trees in the vicinity are often the best clues. COMMENTS TREMBLING ASPEN in BC is largely an Interior species, and so is the ASPEN SCABERSTALK. There are a few outlier TREMBLING ASPEN populations along the coast on southeastern Vancouver Island, but so far this stately leccinum has not been found in them. ✸ "Insigne" means "remarkable, distinguished."

Birch Scaberstalk   *Leccinum scabrum*

CAP To 10 cm across; hemispheric to shallowly convex; pale yellow-brown or dull brown, sometimes with olive tones in age; dry to moist, to sometimes slimy when wet; smooth, sometimes with lumps and depressions and some cracking in age; flesh thick (to 2 cm), white, occasionally turning brownish. PORES White becoming brown as spores mature, colour changing (if at all) to an olive-buff on bruising; round to irregular, 2–3 per mm and up to 2 cm deep. ODOUR Not distinctive. TASTE Not distinctive. SPORE PRINT Brown. STEM To 14 cm tall × 1.5 cm wide; usually widening downward; solid; flesh in stem white, but may slowly turn pinkish buff when exposed or bruised; surface whitish; dry; smooth, with longitudinal striations and with dark brown or black scabers. RING Absent. FRUITING Single, scattered, or in groups; on the ground; almost always with birches; summer, autumn.

EDIBILITY Edible. Stomach upsets have been widely reported, however. SIMILAR *Leccinum* species are usually easy to separate from other boletes because of their stem scabers. Separating the various *Leccinum* species from each other can be more of a problem. Fortunately, *Leccinum* species (unlike most other boletes) are fairly specific in their preferences for hosts, and so noting the trees around *Leccinum* species can provide important clues. As a general rule, the yellow-brown capped BIRCH SCABERSTALK grows with birches, the ORANGE-CAPPED SCABERSTALK (p. 332) grows with conifers, and ASPEN SCABERSTALK (p. 333), also with an orange cap, grows with TREMBLING ASPEN. COMMENTS BIRCH SCABERSTALK is reported from stands of native PAPER BIRCH that grow in BC's Interior. It is also found in southwestern BC with birches introduced into urban landscapes. ◆ In Tolstoy's *Anna Karenina*, Sergei Ivanovich Koznyshev describes scabers: "The birch mushroom's stalk suggests a dark man's chin after two days without shaving." ◆ "Scabrum" means "rough," presumably a reference to the stem scabers.

Toothed

Species in this section share one major trait: the spore-bearing surface under their caps is populated by closely spaced teeth (also called spines). Sharing this feature, however, does not mean that all the mushrooms in this section are closely related—fungal evolution has invented teeth more than once.

The mushrooms in the genera *Phellodon*, *Hydnellum*, and *Sarcodon* are ectomycorrhizal mushrooms that live in our BC forests. *Phellodon* is white-spored; *Hydnellum* and *Sarcodon* are brown-spored. None of these three genera are well populated with species. There are perhaps 18 *Phellodon* species around the world, and we have only a handful in BC. They have thin, leathery flesh, and the clustered caps often fuse together, incorporating sticks and needles from the forest floor into their expanding tissues. Though inedible because of their tough flesh, they are still foraged by those seeking natural dyes for fabrics.

Species in the genera *Hydnellum* and *Sarcodon* are being reordered by mushroom taxonomists, with some *Sarcodon* species moving into *Hydnellum*. BC is blessed with about a quarter of the world's 50 or so *Hydnellum* species. Hydnellums are slow-growing mushrooms with corky and woody flesh, and they sometimes contain bitter-tasting compounds that discourage eaters. The same compounds, however, make them attractive to cloth dyers and medical researchers. There are about 40 *Sarcodon* species worldwide, and we have found less than a quarter of them in BC. They can have softer flesh and lower levels of bitterness—one important edible, the HAWK'S WING mushroom (p. 340), is a *Sarcodon*.

The other toothed fungi in this section are all white-spored. The mycorrhizal *Hydnum* species are related to the chanterelles and, like the chanterelles, are often foraged by mycophagists. *Hydnum* has historically been a small genus, but genetic studies now suggest that it contains many cryptic species with only tiny morphological differences. A number of new species have been defined in the last decade, and we have been able to identify (so far) at least a half dozen of them in BC.

We have four of the white-spored *Hericium* species in BC, which is a substantial portion of the whole genus. *Hericium* species, now placed in the same order as the russulas, are sought as choice edibles. They are not found as frequently, however, as foragers would like.

The CONIFER-CONE TOOTH (p. 347), also in the same order as the russulas, is a small decomposer. Only a few species belong to the *Auriscalpium* genus.

Other species in this book have teeth, but their overall look made them a better fit for other sections. One of these is the SPIRIT GUMMY BEAR (p. 416), a toothed fungus in the "Jelly Fungi" section.

Hedgehog   *Hydnum washingtonianum*

CAP To 11 cm across; convex becoming flat or slightly depressed, margins inrolled when young, then uplifted; cream to pale orange; usually dry; smooth; flesh thick, firm, white staining yellow-brown. **TEETH** Often decurrent; white when fresh, later pale yellow, crowded; to 5 mm long. **ODOUR** Not distinctive. **TASTE** Not distinctive. **SPORE PRINT** White. **STEM** To 5 cm tall × 1.5 cm wide; usually equal, sometimes widening downward and/or tapering at the lower base; central or off-centre; cream, staining yellow-brown; dry; smooth. **RING** Absent. **FRUITING** Single or in groups, sometimes clustered; on the ground; in conifer forests; late summer, autumn, and (on the coast at least) mild winters.

    EDIBILITY Choice. **SIMILAR** The **BELLYBUTTON HEDGEHOG** (p. 337) has a smaller cap that is darker orange and has a distinct navel (as opposed to just being depressed), a slender stem in relation to the cap size, and larger spores. **COMMENTS** In simpler days, hedgehog mushrooms that were small and orange-brown and had a navel were all *Hydnum umbilicatum* (p. 337), and the larger, lighter-capped ones that had no distinct navel were all *H. repandum* (or *Dentinum repandum*). Recent genetic and morphological studies, however, have shown that the simple days were, alas, too simple to be true. We have many cryptic *Hydnum* species, and they often lack definitive features that can separate them in the field. The name *H. repandum* is now identified with a European species that is probably not in North America. One western North American species, now equated with *H. washingtonianum*, a species first described from the Olympic Mountains in Washington in the 1890s, has been confirmed in BC through DNA analysis. Others will probably be documented.

Bellybutton Hedgehog   *Hydnum umbilicatum* group

CAP To 7 cm across; convex to flat to shallowly depressed, often with a distinct central navel, margins inrolled when young, wavy; pale orange becoming brownish orange, often slowly bruising a darker orange, margins often paler and separated from the disc by a line or lines; dry; smooth and matte or slightly hairy or scurfy; flesh somewhat thin (about 5 mm thick), whitish or pale orange and bruising darker orange. **TEETH** Sometimes slightly decurrent; cream, bruising darker; to 8 mm long. **ODOUR** Not distinctive. **TASTE** Not distinctive. **SPORE PRINT** White. **STEM** To 8 cm tall × 1.5 cm wide; equal or slightly enlarged downward, often bent; central or slightly off-centre; cream or yellowish or peach, bruising orange to orange-brown; dry; smooth or slightly hairy or scurfy. **RING** Absent. **FRUITING** Single or in groups; on the ground; under conifers; autumn, winter.

EDIBILITY Choice. **SIMILAR** The **HEDGEHOG** (p. 336), with a larger, paler top that usually does not have a navel, with a wider stem, and with smaller spores, has enough variability that it could at times be mistaken for the **BELLYBUTTON HEDGEHOG**, even by skilled identifiers. Fortunately for foragers, the mistake is not serious—both are good edibles. **COMMENTS** The small, orange, navelled, ectomycorrhizal *Hydnum* that can be found in BC forests is not one species, but many. How many is not clear yet. A number of once–*H. umbilicatum* species have already been described, and of the new batch of species, we have at least 3 in BC and nearby US states, one of which has a genetic signature that is similar to the eastern North American species with the *H. umbilicatum* name. ☙ The **BELLYBUTTON HEDGEHOG** tends to appear at the end of the autumn season, overlapping with the **WINTER CHANTERELLE** (p. 38). ☙ "Umbilicatum" means "with a navel." In this species group, the bellybutton is always an innie.

Bear's Head   *Hericium abietis*

CAP To 75 cm or more across and high; many branches from a common rooting base, often rebranching, open or compact, teeth hanging in clumps from the ends of both short and long branches; white, cream, or yellowish or pinkish buff, often bruising yellow or yellow-brown; dry; smooth; flesh firm, white. TEETH White to cream to pinkish; to 1 cm long, sometimes longer. ODOUR Not distinctive. TASTE Not distinctive. SPORE PRINT White. STEM A massive knob-like structure that is attached to cracks in the substrate; tough. RING Absent. FRUITING Usually single, occasionally in small groups; on dead wood of conifers, usually on true fir (*Abies* spp.), WESTERN HEMLOCK, and DOUGLAS-FIR logs; autumn.

    EDIBILITY Choice. Delicious and widely sought by foragers. SIMILAR If the mass of white teeth is growing on a hardwood, it may be either *Hericium coralloides* or LION'S MANE (p. 339). Like BEAR'S HEAD, *H. coralloides* has a branched fruiting body, but it has a more open, sparse structure and smaller teeth (3–8 mm) that are arrayed along the branches like teeth on a comb. The LION'S MANE has an unbranched fruiting body, with long (2–6 cm) teeth. COMMENTS A mature specimen of BEAR'S HEAD is a sublime vision. It resembles a cascade of white rapids paused in time. Another name for it, in fact, is FROZEN WATERFALL. ❧ Heads of this white-rot decomposer will often reappear year after year on the same log until the nutrient base is exhausted. The mycelium excavates small cavities (pockets) in the wood. ❧ "Abietis" means "of true fir," a reference to its growth on *Abies* species.

Lion's Mane   *Hericium erinaceus*

CAP To 40 cm or more across and high, but typically more softball-sized or soccer-ball-sized; somewhat spherical or ovoid, unbranched, with many long teeth hanging from a coarse, spongy, rooted upper surface; white becoming yellowish or eventually brown; dry; flesh stringy, white. TEETH White; smooth; to 6 cm long or longer. ODOUR Not distinctive or slightly acidic. TASTE Not distinctive. SPORE PRINT White. STEM Solid structure, ropy on top; laterally attached to substrate; tough. RING Absent. FRUITING Usually single; on living or dead hardwood trunks or hardwood logs; late summer or autumn.

EDIBILITY Choice. Delicious when young, but sometimes less tasty with age. SIMILAR When mature, LION'S MANE has no look-alikes, but when very young it can be confused with other *Hericium* species (see BEAR'S HEAD, p. 338, for comparison details). COMMENTS The unique appearance of LION'S MANE makes it a relatively safe forage edible for beginners. It can grow high on tree trunks, though, so perhaps the danger of balancing on wobbly ladders should be added to the risk factor. ⚮ The potent polysaccharides found in LION'S MANE have attracted the attention of modern researchers (see the essay on medicinal fungi, p. 400). ⚮ LION'S MANE is not found in great abundance in BC, but it is not rare. Many countries in Europe, however, record it as an endangered species. In recent years, a domesticated strain of this decomposer has been sold by mushroom growers. ⚮ *Hericium* is classed in the russula order (Russulales), which means that these toothed species have relatives that are gilled (e.g., *Russula*) or are polypores (e.g., *Bondarzewia*), coral fungi (*Artomyces*), crusts (e.g., *Stereum*), and truffles (e.g., *Zelleromyces*). ⚮ "Erinaceus" means "hedgehog" in Latin—the long LION'S MANE teeth apparently reminded people of the spines of a hedgehog.

Hawk's Wing   *Sarcodon imbricatus*

CAP To 15 cm across typically, but giant specimens have been reported; convex becoming flat and then funnel-shaped, sometimes the centre depressing into the top of the stem, occasionally cracking with age, the margins at first inrolled, then irregular and wavy; tan to reddish brown, darker brown with age; dry; with large (to 1.5 cm long) dark brown to blackish scales, often upturned, that may wear off in age, especially around their edges; flesh thick (to 3 cm), firm, whitish or grey or tan. **TEETH** Somewhat decurrent; pale brown or greyish and becoming darker brown with age; to 7 mm long or longer. **ODOUR** Not distinctive or somewhat disagreeable. **TASTE** Slightly bitter or not distinctive. **SPORE PRINT** Brown. **STEM** To 8 cm tall × 3 cm wide; usually equal, but sometimes tapering downward or enlarging; central or off-centre; cinnamon brown, lighter at base, bruising darker brown; dry. **RING** Absent. **FRUITING** Single or in groups, sometimes in fairy rings; on the ground; usually under conifers, but also reported from hardwoods; spring, summer, or autumn.

    EDIBILITY Edible. Especially when harvested young. When older, it can be tough and bitter. **SIMILAR** Taxonomists now separate *Sarcodon squamosus* from *S. imbricatus*. The 2 sarcodons look much alike, the main differences being that the cap of *S. imbricatus* is often paler, has larger scales, and is more depressed. Also, *S. squamosus* prefers pines as tree partners, but *S. imbricatus* seems to prefer spruce. Though our BC field reports usually mention *S. imbricatus* rather than *S. squamosus*, we have both (and possibly other quite similar) species in BC. ***Hydnellum scabrosum*** (previously known as *S. scabrosus*) has paler teeth, a cap whose scales develop later and are not as upturned, and a bluish green to dark olive stem base. **COMMENTS** The sarcodons are ectomycorrhizal species. • HAWK'S WING is used to dye wool various shades of green and blue. • "Imbricatus" means "covered with tiles," a reference to the cap appearing to be composed of overlapping roof tiles.

Strawberries and Cream   *Hydnellum peckii*

CAP To 10 cm or more across; convex or irregularly shaped like a top, becoming flat or depressed to funnel-shaped, the margins wavy, often incorporating small twigs or conifer needles; tough; white, quickly becoming reddish brown and eventually blackish brown starting from the centre; dry; the surface plush-like, often with blood-red droplets when actively growing and moist, becoming nearly bald with age, knobbly and scaly or roughened with age; flesh tough, fibrous, pinkish brown to reddish brown, concentrically zoned. TEETH Whitish to pink, becoming reddish brown with paler tips; to 5 mm long. ODOUR Pleasant, sour, or not distinctive. TASTE Intensely and unpleasantly peppery. SPORE PRINT Brown. STEM To 5 cm tall × 3 cm wide; usually equal; central or off-centre; tough; surface is cap-coloured or darker; flesh is coloured as flesh in cap; dry; densely hairy, often with forest-floor materials sticking to the base. RING Absent. FRUITING Single or in groups or small clusters, the caps sometimes fused; on the ground; in conifer forests; late summer or autumn.

EDIBILITY Not edible. SIMILAR Mushrooms in the *Hydnellum scrobiculatum* **group** can appear similar, even including having red droplets, but they do not usually have the same intensely peppery taste and they often have a swollen base at or under the soil line. These distinguishing characteristics can, however, fall within the natural variations found in specimens of STRAWBERRIES AND CREAM. COMMENTS Coming across a fresh specimen of this mycorrhizal species with its spectacular drops of burgundy "blood" can be a defining experience for the new mycologist. If he or she applies the taste test, by licking or chewing and spitting out a bit of the flesh, the experience can become defining in another way—the nasty, nauseating taste can persist in the mouth for a long time, making a mockery of the common name, STRAWBERRIES AND CREAM. ◆ "Peckii" is in honour of Charles Horton Peck (1833–1917), who collected the type.

Dyeing with Fungi

Prior to the discovery of synthetic (petrochemical) dyes in the mid-19th century, all dyes were natural dyes derived from plants, fungi, lichens, invertebrates, and minerals. The synthetic dyes largely displaced natural dyes because they were easier to brew up in the large amounts needed by the fabric industry. Additionally, the new dyes proved to be more effective than natural dyes in colouring fabrics woven from synthetic fibres (also concocted from petrochemical sources).

With the decline in the use of natural dyes, there was a corresponding loss of knowledge about which species were good sources for dyes. In recent decades,

Alissa Allen (mycopigments.com), displaying wool dyed with mushrooms and lichens.

however, there has been a resurgence of interest, both artisanal and industrial, in the use of mushrooms and other natural sources as dyestuffs. The movement reflects both a longing to reconnect with the natural world and a desire to reduce the use of, and contact with, petrochemicals.

A rainbow of colours are available from BC's mushroom species. Reds and oranges are often derived from species in the *Dermocybe* part of *Cortinarius* (see p. 246) and the DEAD MAN'S FOOT (p. 430). Purples come from some ramarias (pp. 372–375). Several important BC edibles also yield dye colours. The KING BOLETE (p. 318) and LOBSTER CRUST (p. 39) produce various yellows and may leave mushroom foragers wondering whether to toss them in the dyeing pot or the cooking pot.

While most mushroom dyes can be effectively processed in boiling water, pigments from some species are better extracted by other solvents, such as vinegar or ammonia (traditionally sourced from aged urine in a pee pot on the back porch, for those who want the full artisanal effect!). The extraction process affects the colour obtained from mushroom dyes, as does the choice of mordants, the mineral salts that are sometimes used to fix colours to the fabrics. The DYER'S CONK (p. 390), a favourite choice of BC mushroom dyers, yields hues ranging from green to gold to yellow and sometimes orange and brown, depending on the pH modifier, mordant selection, and processing procedures. Fabrics dyed with STRAWBERRIES AND CREAM (p. 341), another common BC mushroom, produce elusive greens and greys.

As with mushroom identification, the best way to learn how to dye with mushrooms is to meet up with like-minded folks who have been using natural dyes for a while. A good place to locate such people might be your local mycological or natural history society. Those wishing to consult written references usually find their way to Arleen and Alan Bessette's *The Rainbow Beneath My Feet* (Syracuse University Press, 2001). A number of websites also have pictures, videos, and instructions that can help beginners get started. Alissa Allen's mycopigments.com and the Facebook group Mushroom and Lichen Dyers United are two good places to start.

KING BOLETE (*Boletus edulis*), p. 318.

Orange Tooth

Hydnellum aurantiacum

CAP To 12 cm across; convex or shaped like a top, becoming flat or depressed, margins wedge-shaped but rounded and often wavy; white, quickly becoming orange to cinnamon brown but often keeping whitish margins; typically dry; the surface plush-like, becoming knobbly and roughened with age, often incorporating small twigs or conifer needles; flesh thick (to 1.5 cm), fibrous, and woody, except spongy on cap top, orange to rusty cinnamon, often horizontally zoned. **TEETH** Sometimes flowing down and gradually merging into base; white, aging orange to brown; to 4 mm, longest near stem. **ODOUR** Usually not distinctive, but sometimes pungent. **TASTE** Slightly bitter. **SPORE PRINT** Brown. **STEM** To 5 cm tall × 2 cm wide; usually equal or narrowing downward; firm; central to off-centre; flesh usually a deeper orange than cap flesh; surface is orange, becoming cinnamon to darker brown; dry; finely hairy, often with forest debris sticking to the base. **RING** Absent. **FRUITING** Single or scattered or in small groups, the bases and/or caps sometimes fused into clusters; on the ground; in conifer forests; summer or autumn.

EDIBILITY Not edible. **SIMILAR** The polypore **DYER'S CONK** (p. 390), from the top at least, can resemble ORANGE TOOTH. From the bottom, the difference is obvious: the polypore has pores rather than teeth (look closely: the pores can be quite ragged). **COMMENTS** ORANGE TOOTH is part of a complex of similar, highly variable mushrooms. Variations may include bulbous stems, smoother caps, and thinner, fan-like lobes. ◆ ORANGE TOOTH and STRAWBERRIES AND CREAM (p. 341) form mycorrhizal associations with a vascular plant, the achlorophyllous GNOME PLANT (*Hemitomes congestum*). These 2 *Hydnellum* species transfer sugars from nearby conifers to the GNOME PLANT (see the discussion of mycoheterotrophy on p. 54). ◆ ORANGE TOOTH can be used to dye cloth a grey to grey-green colour. ◆ "Aurantiacum" means "orange-coloured."

Violet Tooth   *Hydnellum fuscoindicum*

CAP To 15 cm across; convex becoming flat or depressed, the margins wavy; dark violet to dark blue to nearly black, the growing margin often paler; dry; smooth becoming cracked and scaly in age, scales roughest at the disc and often pressed down toward the margin, flesh thick, firm, brittle, deep violet. **TEETH** Decurrent, sometimes far down the stem; deep violet (the tips paler) becoming brown; brittle; to 5 mm long. **ODOUR** Not distinctive, or cinnamon and/or somewhat farinaceous. **TASTE** Usually not distinctive, but by one report it can cause a burning sensation in the throat. **SPORE PRINT** Brown. **STEM** To 10 cm tall × 3 cm wide; usually narrowing downward, often to a rounded point; solid; central or off-centre; flesh violet; surface deep violet; dry; smooth. **RING** Absent. **FRUITING** Single or in groups, sometimes clustered; on the ground; under conifers; autumn.

EDIBILITY Edible. **SIMILAR** *Hydnellum scabrosum* (was *Sarcodon scabrosus*), also a fleshy, medium-to-large toothed species, has a pinkish to reddish brown cap, but it can occasionally have violet tints. The teeth under the cap are usually buff to brown, but they can also be purplish brown. The stem base is usually dominated by olive or bluish green colours and the taste is extremely bitter. *Hydnellum suaveolens* could be confused with VIOLET TOOTH. The former has a whitish to yellow-brown cap that can have violet tints, light to deep blue flesh, and a grey-blue stem. Apart from its lighter blues, what most sets it apart from VIOLET TOOTH is its powerful, fragrant, sickly sweet odour. **COMMENTS** We have been aware for some time that species in the genera *Sarcodon* and *Hydnellum* are not well divided. The North American endemic species that we have been calling *Sarcodon fuscoindicus* belongs, it turns out, to the *Hydnellum* genus. ◆ Some years VIOLET TOOTH is uncommon, other years it fruits abundantly. ◆ This mushroom gives a blue colour to dyed fabrics. ◆ "Fuscoindicum" means "dark indigo."

Owl Eyes
Phellodon tomentosus

CAP To 6 cm across; flat to depressed or funnel-shaped, the margins thick, wavy, and upturned, multiple caps often fused; whitish becoming concentrically zoned with shades of orange-brown or reddish brown, the margin often staying white, surface sometimes a darker brown where bruised; usually dry; finely hairy to felted, sometimes later becoming smooth in centre; flesh thin (to 2 mm thick), leathery, brown, zoned. TEETH Somewhat decurrent; white, becoming brown with age, staining red-brown; to 3 mm long. ODOUR Slightly sweet-spicy, molasses-like, especially when dried, but not always distinctive. TASTE Variable, ranging from not distinctive to sweet to bitter. SPORE PRINT White. STEM To 5 cm tall × 5 mm wide; usually equal or tapering downward, flattened, not fused even when the caps are; central to off-centre; flesh in stem red-brown or darker with corky outer layer; surface has the colours of the darker parts of cap; dry; arising from a mycelial pad in humus. RING Absent. FRUITING In groups or clustered, sometimes in fairy rings; on the ground; under conifers; late summer or autumn.

EDIBILITY Unknown. SIMILAR OWL EYES can resemble the zoned polypore TIGER'S EYE (p. 384) from above, but underneath, the polypore has pores rather than teeth. The related *Phellodon atratus*, though similar in most other respects, has a quite different coloration—its cap, teeth, and stem are bluish black to black (or sometimes purple-tinged), with the teeth and cap margin paler than other parts. *Phellodon melaleucus* also has a white-margined cap, but the cap is darker (greyish brown) and less zonate than OWL EYES, its stem is sometimes rooting, and its flesh stains dark olive in KOH. COMMENTS "Tomentosus" means "densely hairy."

Conifer-cone Tooth

Auriscalpium vulgare

CAP To 2 cm across; convex becoming nearly flat or slightly depressed, often showing a bump above the point of stem attachment, kidney-shaped to nearly round; brown, usually a dark chocolate brown, often paler at the margin but darkening with age; dry; densely hairy, including a fringe on the margin; flesh thin (to 1 mm thick), leathery, white to tan. TEETH White to yellowish, sometimes darkening to brown with age; to 3 mm long. ODOUR Not distinctive. TASTE Slightly peppery. SPORE PRINT White. STEM To 8 cm tall × 3 mm wide; roughly equal but sometimes widening at the base, occasionally branched; almost always lateral; rusty to dark brown; dry; covered in densely matted grey to brown hairs. RING Absent. FRUITING Single or in groups of 2 or 3; on fallen conifer cones, most commonly DOUGLAS-FIR; summer or autumn.

EDIBILITY Unknown. SIMILAR The teeth, the lateral attachment of the cap, and the cone habitat render the CONIFER-CONE TOOTH an unmistakable mushroom. COMMENTS A decomposer that can be grown on standard lab media, the CONIFER-CONE TOOTH has been extensively researched. ◆ Another curious place to find CONIFER-CONE TOOTH is on squirrel middens. Helene Schalkwijk-Barendsen (*Mushrooms of Western Canada*, 1994) reports finding this mushroom "on spruce needles on top of squirrel dens; cone bracts were present in the duff." ◆ Modern molecular studies have shown that it is closely related to *Lentinellus* (p. 218) and that it resides in the same order as species in the genus *Russula*. ◆ Only a few species belong to the *Auriscalpium* genus, and the CONIFER-CONE TOOTH is the only one of these inhabiting the temperate zones of the Northern Hemisphere. Within this zone, though, it is found worldwide. ◆ Another common name for this mushroom, the EAR PICK FUNGUS, is a translation of the word "auriscalpium," a name that Linnaeus applied to this species. He noted the resemblance of this odd-shaped mushroom to the small metal scoops used in his day to remove wax from ears. ◆ "Vulgare" means "common, ordinary."

VELVETY EARTH TONGUE, *Trichoglossum hirsutum.*

Clubs

The mushroom species in this section, though grouped here, are not a natural group—that is, they're not all closely related. One of the most ancient evolutionary forks in the road to modern fungi is the one that led on the one side to basidiomycetes, the fungi that bear their spores on top of basidia, and on the other side to ascomycetes, fungi that bear their spores inside long sacs called "asci" (p. 5). We think that this split may have happened more than a half billion years ago. This ancient division has remained a clean break—no basidiomycete has evolved asci, and no ascomycete has ever evolved basidia. However, branches of both of these ancient groups, in spite of using radically different spore-production mechanisms, have evolved similar shapes to their fruiting bodies. One of these co-evolved shapes is that of the simple and (usually) unbranched club with the reproductive bodies lining the outside.

Among the basidiomycete clubs landing in this artificial grouping are fungi that are—or were—part of the genus *Clavaria*. These are represented in this section by species in the genera *Clavaria*, *Clavariadelphus*, *Clavulinopsis*, *Alloclavaria*, and *Mucronella*. Species in the stinkhorn genera *Phallus* and *Mutinus* are also basidiomycetes. Many of the clubbed basidiomycetes are now thought to be mycorrhizal.

All of the other species in this section are ascomycete clubs. They are all presumed to be parasites or decomposers. The ascomycete clubs include species in the genera *Cudonia* and *Vibrissea*, whose heads resemble the caps found on gilled mushrooms. Our representative cordyceps in this section, *Tolypocladium*, is also an ascomycete with a distinct cap. The spore-bearing bodies are arrayed over the upper surfaces of these ascomycete caps, not clumped under the cap in spore-bearing structures such as gills, pores, and teeth.

The species in this section that are in the genera *Spathularia*, *Geoglossum*, and *Mitrula* have heads that contain the fertile tissues, but the heads are not well defined—they seem to be swellings of the stems, rather than caps. *Spathularia* species are closely related to *Cudonia* mushrooms, despite the difference in their fertile heads. And both *Spathularia* and *Cudonia* are closely related to *Rhytisma* species, such as the SPECKLED TAR SPOT (p. 475), which looks nothing like clubs.

The *Xylaria* in this section is our sole example of a really large worldwide genus—it contains about 500 different species. *Xylaria* are of special interest because many of them have both a sexual stage and an asexual stage. During the asexual stage, some of them live and reproduce inside tissues of healthy plants without (apparently) harming them.

Fairy fingers
Clavaria fragilis group

FRUITING BODY To 5 mm wide × 15 cm tall; upright, sometimes wavy, unbranched (or occasionally once-branched at top), cylindrical but sometimes narrowing at the top and/or bottom, solid becoming hollow, tip constricted and typically with a point, often grooved longitudinally; white, at times partly translucent, aging yellowish at the tip; flesh brittle, white. **ODOUR** Not distinctive. **TASTE** Not distinctive. **SPORE PRINT** White. **FRUITING** In large groups, usually clustered; on the ground, in wet areas; in forests and fields; spring, summer, autumn.

EDIBILITY Edible. But inconsequential. **SIMILAR** The clubs in genus *Typhula* can be white, but they are much smaller and usually grow directly on decomposing leaves and stems. **COMMENTS** *Clavaria vermicularis* is a synonym. ◦ Genetic signatures and spore sizes of this worldwide mushroom vary greatly—it is likely that a number of cryptic species lurk inside the current name. ◦ "Clavaria" is from the Latin "clava" meaning "club, cudgel"; "fragilis" means "fragile," and it deserves the name—the thin clubs often break apart when they are picked up.

Purple Fairy Club
Alloclavaria purpurea

FRUITING BODY To 6 mm wide × 12 cm tall; upright, unbranched (though on rare occasion forking near the base), cylindrical or somewhat flattened, hollow, with a pointed top and sometimes narrowed base, often grooved longitudinally; various shades of purple, or pale brown, aging lilac-grey to pinkish buff, not staining; smooth; flesh brittle, white to pale purple. ODOUR Not distinctive to slightly unpleasant, fishy. TASTE Not distinctive to slightly fishy. SPORE PRINT White. FRUITING Usually in groups and clustered; on the ground, in wet areas; often under or near conifers; spring, summer, early autumn. EDIBILITY Edible. Or supposedly edible—too small to have much of a track record. SIMILAR Because of its colour, the PURPLE FAIRY CLUB is distinctive among the club mushrooms found in BC, but if the clubs are faded and brown, they might be confused with STRAP CLUB (p. 353). The rare *Clavariadelphus subfastigiatus* is also found clustered, but is pinkish brown to reddish in colour, is not brittle, and stains green in KOH. The extremely rare *Clavaria rosea*, which has rose-pink colours, has been reported from BC and Washington. COMMENTS PURPLE FAIRY CLUB, the only species in the genus *Alloclavaria*, belongs to a different genetic lineage than the other *Clavaria* species. ➤ The PURPLE FAIRY CLUB may be a decomposer, or it may be mycorrhizal with its associated conifers. ➤ "Alloclavaria" means "other clavaria," and "purpurea" means "purple."

Flat-topped Candy Club
Clavariadelphus truncatus

FRUITING BODY To 4 cm wide at top × 15 cm tall; upright, unbranched (or occasionally forked), like a baseball club held upright, but with the top flattened or slightly depressed and the margin sometimes lifted up, lumpy; yellow or orange becoming cinnamon brown or light brown, the top often lighter (yellow or orange), staining light brown to cinnamon brown when bruised; dry; smooth, becoming longitudinally wrinkled in age to the point that it can resemble a veined mushroom, such as a chanterelle; flesh solid, becoming soft and spongy in age, white or red-brown, staining light brown to cinnamon brown. **ODOUR** Not distinctive. **TASTE** Sweet. To check this, taste a little bit of the outer skin. **SPORE PRINT** Whitish. **FRUITING** Scattered or in groups; on the ground; in conifer and mixedwood forests; summer, autumn.

EDIBILITY Edible. Delicious and sweet. **SIMILAR** A mature FLAT-TOPPED CANDY CLUB whose top is depressed and whose sides are well wrinkled can resemble a very young PIG'S EAR (p. 41), but the latter has cross-veining and does not have a sweet taste. **COMMENTS** One of the chemicals that makes the FLAT-TOPPED CANDY CLUB sweet is mannitol. Mannitol is commonly used as a sugar substitute and as a medical ingredient. Its low digestibility may account for some reports of the laxative effect of consuming quantities of this mushroom. ◦ Most edible mushrooms in this book are best served as appetizers or main courses. FLAT-TOPPED CANDY CLUB, sautéed, makes a sweet dessert to finish off a fungal feast. ◦ *Clavariadelphus* species are mycorrhizal. ◦ "Truncatus" is a Latin word for "cut or broken off," a reference to the flat head.

Strap Club *Clavariadelphus ligula*

FRUITING BODY To 1.2 cm wide (wider at top) × 10 cm tall; upright, unbranched (or occasionally forked), somewhat cylindrical becoming shaped like a baseball bat with the hand grip at the bottom, top generally rounded but sometimes with a broad point and sometimes flattening and spreading slightly; pale yellow or orange becoming buff or light brown, staining yellow when bruised, tips sometimes with green tints; dry; smooth, becoming longitudinally wrinkled in age; with white mycelium at the base gathered into rhizomorphs; flesh solid, becoming softer in age and toward the top, white, slowly staining brown, buff or cinnamon. **ODOUR** Not distinctive. **TASTE** Not distinctive or slightly bitter. **SPORE PRINT** White or buff. **FRUITING** Scattered or (more commonly) in dense groups, sometimes clustered; on the ground, in humus; in conifer forests; summer, autumn.

    EDIBILITY Unknown. **SIMILAR** *Clavariadelphus sachalinensis* (if not the same species) differs only microscopically, having spores that are up to twice as long. *Clavariadelphus mucronatus* is quite similar, except that it has a narrow, sharp point at the top of a flattened or rounded head. Aged clubs of **GOLDEN FAIRY CLUB** (p. 354) can resemble **STRAP CLUB**, but when young they are a bright orange or yellow. *Macrotyphula juncea* can be just as tall as **STRAP CLUB**, but its fruiting bodies are very narrow (to 2 mm wide), and in age they become bent, twisted, and floppy. **PURPLE FAIRY CLUB** (p. 351), normally a shade of purple, can sometimes fade and become pale brown. When it does, the fact that it is more cylindrical (not as club-shaped) and has a pointed top can be important differences with **STRAP CLUB**. **COMMENTS** *Clavariadelphus* species are mycorrhizal. ✦ "Clavariadelphus" means "brother of *Clavaria*," and "ligula" means "shoe strap, small tongue."

Golden Fairy Club
Clavulinopsis laeticolor

FRUITING BODY Usually to 5 mm wide × 7 cm tall; upright, unbranched (or occasionally forked), cylindrical but with top or bottom sometimes smaller, occasionally flattened in the upper part, the top either pointed, rounded, or squared off; bright yellow or orange, fading in age, the tip sometimes becoming brown; dry; smooth, often longitudinally wrinkled or grooved; flesh solid, whitish. ODOUR Not distinctive. TASTE Not distinctive. SPORE PRINT White. FRUITING Single, scattered, or in groups, sometimes clustered; on the ground, in wet areas; in conifer and mixedwood forests; autumn, winter, spring.

EDIBILITY Unknown. SIMILAR The GOLDEN FAIRY CLUB is our only common club species that has prominent golden yellow colours. *Calocera* species such as SMALL STAGHORN (p. 415), which also have this colour, are usually smaller, have firm-gelatinous fruiting bodies, and grow on decaying wood. COMMENTS *Clavulinopsis* species are related to *Clavaria* species, and both are related more distantly to the brown-spored *Gymnopilus* species. ☙ Michael Kuo (mushroomexpert.com) offers some self-help advice regarding GOLDEN FAIRY CLUB: "This tiny club fungus is easily overlooked, and can be quite a challenge to collect, unless you happen to carry tweezers with you when you go collecting. And, to be honest, if you do carry tweezers on your woodland mushroom outings, you probably need help." ☙ "Clavulinopsis" means "looking like a clavulina" (see CRESTED CORAL, p. 371, for an example of a clavulina). "Laeticolor" is based on the Latin word "laetus," so as a compound it means "of a bright or joyful colour"—which this mushroom certainly is, especially when backlit and poking out of dark duff.

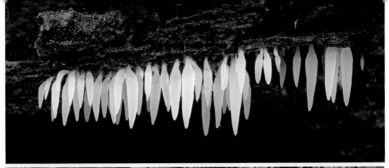

White Icicle

Mucronella pendula

FRUITING BODY To 3 mm wide × 8 mm long; from a short stem, the stem base growing briefly upward or sideways but then the fruiting body is mostly hanging down, conical; white; not slimy; fleshy and watery. **STEM** To 3 mm long × 1.5 mm wide; yellow-brown to yellow; rooted in an almost invisible white mycelium. **ODOUR** Not distinctive. **TASTE** Not distinctive. **FRUITING** Single or in groups, not often clustered; on conifer wood; autumn.

EDIBILITY Unknown. **SIMILAR** Another short-stemmed *Mucronella* reported from BC forays, *M. fusiformis*, may turn out to be the same species. When the fruiting body has no stem and is highly clustered, it may be **M. calva**. We also have another stemless *Mucronella* species in western North America that has a yellow to orange-yellow fruiting body, which (for now) is called **M. pulchra** (lower photo). *Mucronella pulchra* and *M. pendula* can sometimes be found growing in side-by-side clumps. In our experience, the white and especially the yellow-orange *Mucronella* species are sometimes mistaken for slime moulds. **COMMENTS** *Mucronella* species are brown-rot fungi that grow on well-decayed wood. ⮞ The work that would clarify how *Mucronella* names and descriptions apply to the situation in BC and the rest of western North America has not been done. *Mucronella pendula* was described using a BC specimen in 1980, so we know that we at least have this species in the BC mix—though the name itself may not survive a more thorough study. ⮞ "Mucronella" means "a small, sharp point." "Pendula" means "hanging," a reference to how the fungi grow.

Common Stinkhorn   *Phallus impudicus*

FRUITING BODY Begins as a buried or partly buried egg (inset photo) that is up to 4 cm wide × 6 cm tall; the egg's outer layer is white, sometimes tinted yellow, and rupturing to expose a gelatinous inner layer covering the fruiting body; swollen head of the fruiting body to 4 cm wide, typically 2–4 cm tall; head white, when young covered with a foul-smelling, olive-brown, spore-bearing slime, except for the sometimes perforated white tip; surface of the head roughened, pitted; flesh spongy. **STEM** To 20 cm (or more) tall × 3 cm wide; roughly equal or narrowed at top and bottom; fragile; hollow; white; moist to slippery; roughened and pitted. **VOLVA** Outer layer of the buried egg remaining as a cup at the base when the stem shoots up; attached to the substrate by white mycelial strands. **ODOUR** Cap slime is obnoxious-smelling, putrid. **TASTE** Not distinctive. **SPORE PRINT** Spores in the olive-brown slime are colourless. **FRUITING** Single or in small groups; on the ground; often in disturbed habitats rich in humus (trail edges, gardens); spring, summer, autumn.

EDIBILITY Edible. But only at the egg stage. Those who have tried it at this stage show little enthusiasm about repeating the experience. If you do eat them at the egg stage, beware of mistaking amanita buttons for stinkhorn eggs (see inset photo for the distinctive interior of a stinkhorn egg). **SIMILAR** The mature heads and stems of the COMMON STINKHORN have been mistaken for morels (p. 436). They also bear a curious resemblance to certain human body parts. **COMMENTS** Stinkhorns, including the COMMON STINKHORN, smell as they do in order to attract flies. Some flies carry away spores on their feet. Blowflies eat the spore-laden slime. The flies then deposit the spores elsewhere, either rubbed off their feet or in their feces. ✒ The COMMON STINKHORN is one of several mushrooms with a reputation for breaking through asphalt and pavement. The full stem can push up quickly, in only an hour or two, and a mere 3 fruiting bodies, one study calculated, could raise a 400 kg weight. ✒ John Gerard's 1597 *Herball*, or *Generall Historie of Plantes* gives the English name of the plant as the "pricke mushrum" and the Latin name as *Fungus virilis penis arecti*. ✒ The meaning of "phallus" is obvious; "impudicus" is a Latin word for "shameless."

Gwen Raverat (1885–1957) was Charles Darwin's granddaughter. She was a founding member of the Society of Wood Engravers in Britain. The engraving below is hers, from her delightful 1952 memoir *Period Piece: A Cambridge Childhood*. In this book, Raverat describes the stinkhorn adventures of Aunt Etty (who was Darwin's daughter Henrietta Emma Darwin [1843–1927]) in these words:

This little wood was also the scene of a form of sport, of which Aunt Etty can claim to be the inventor; and which certainly deserves to be more widely known. In our native woods there grows a kind of toadstool, called in the vernacular *The Stinkhorn*, though in Latin it bears a grosser name. The name is justified, for the fungus can be hunted by the scent alone; and this was Aunt Etty's great invention. Armed with a basket and a pointed stick, and wearing special hunting cloak and gloves, she would sniff her way round the wood, pausing here and there, her nostrils twitching, when she caught a whiff of her prey; then at last, with a deadly pounce, she would fall upon her victim, and poke his putrid carcass into her basket. At the end of the day's sport, the catch was brought back and burnt in the deepest secrecy on the drawing-room fire, with the doors locked; *because of the morals of the maids.*

Stinkhorn hunter in full cry.

Dog Stinkhorn
Mutinus caninus

FRUITING BODY Starts out as a buried or partly buried egg that is up to 2.5 cm wide × 4 cm tall; the egg covered by a white outer layer, often tinted yellow or pinkish, surrounding an inner jelly-like layer; mature body upright or drooping, cylindrical, unbranched, sometimes curved; the head 2–3 cm tall × 1 cm wide, orange-red or pink (rarely white), and when young covered with a foul-smelling, olive-brown, spore-bearing slime, except for the bluntly pointed tip; surface of the head roughened and pitted; flesh spongy. **STEM** To 10 cm tall × 1.2 cm wide, typically wider than top but sometimes narrower; roughly equal; fragile; sometimes hollow; colour about the same as cap but generally paler, sometimes white at the base; moist to slightly slippery; roughened. **VOLVA** Outer layer of the buried egg remaining as a cup at the base when the stem shoots up; attached to the substrate by white mycelial strands. **ODOUR** Cap slime is obnoxious-smelling, redolent of predator feces. **TASTE** Not distinctive. **SPORE PRINT** Spores in the olive-brown slime are yellow. **FRUITING** Single or in small groups; on the ground; often in disturbed habitats (trail edges, gardens, lawns), also in flowerpots; summer, autumn.

EDIBILITY Uncertain. The smell would probably keep anything but a carrion insect from attempting to eat the mature mushroom, but at the egg stage it has apparently been consumed by humans. (Beware, though, of mistaking amanita buttons for stinkhorn eggs.) **SIMILAR** Michael Kuo, the creator of mushroomexpert.com, says, "Unlike *Phallus* species, which mimic human anatomy, *Mutinus* species have more of a canine thrust." **COMMENTS** The DOG STINKHORN can be rare in BC—count yourself lucky if you have found it. ๑ "Mutinus" is the Latin diminutive for "penis," and "caninus" is an adjective for "of a dog," earning it the evocative epithet DOGGY DICK.

Carbon Antlers   *Xylaria hypoxylon*

FRUITING BODY To 6 mm wide × 8 cm tall; erect, oval or flattened in cross-section, twisted and bent, unbranched when young and the top often forked or branched at maturity like antlers; black overall, but when fresh covered with a whitish or grey powder in upper parts, eventually all black; roughened, warty in age, somewhat hairy, especially toward base; flesh tough, whitish when young. ODOUR Not distinctive. TASTE Not distinctive. SPORE PRINT Blackish. FRUITING Single or in groups, sometimes clustered; on rotting wood, often on RED ALDER, though sometimes the wood is buried and the fungus is not immediately visible; usually in forests; year-round.

EDIBILITY Unknown. Too tough to care. SIMILAR Not much out there looks like CARBON ANTLERS. COMMENTS CARBON ANTLERS are ascomycetes and late-stage decomposers of wood and plant materials. ❧ The fine white granules on the tips of younger stems are asexual reproductive bodies. These disperse early in the season and are replaced by sexual reproductive bodies that take the form of warts on the black stems (use a hand lens to see the openings for spore dispersal). ❧ CARBON ANTLERS contain a number of chemical compounds that attract the interest of medical researchers. ❧ Recent molecular studies suggest that the *Xylaria hypoxylon* concept may contain cryptic species. We do, however, have an exact DNA match in BC for some of the European species that will retain the name *X. hypoxylon*. ❧ CARBON ANTLERS are usually associated with RED ALDER (and perhaps other alder species). It is most common on the coast, with collections eastward along the Fraser River (to Hope) and Skeena River (to Terrace)—matching the range of RED ALDER. ❧ This species is also known by the common name CANDLESNUFF. ❧ "Xylaria" is derived from a word for "wood," and "hypoxylon" is a Greek compound for "almost ligneous or wooden," a name bestowed for the woody texture.

Zombie Ants and Other Horrors

The ascomycete genus *Cordyceps* (and various genera split from it, such as *Ophiocordyceps* and *Tolypocladium*) contains about 400 species of fungi that are parasitic on insects and, more rarely, on other fungi. Members of this genus are most abundant and best known from tropical forests, but there are temperate-zone species and a handful of them have been found in BC.

Cordyceps species and their near relatives are typically choosy about their hosts. BC's TRUFFLE EATER (p. 362) and its close relative *Tolypocladium ophioglossoides* are both parasitic on the COMMON DEER TRUFFLE (p. 465). Among BC's insect-parasitizing species, *Ophiocordyceps myrmecophila* parasitizes mostly ants, *O. ravenelii* parasitizes beetle larvae, and *O. variabilis* parasitizes a family of flies. *Cordyceps militaris*, a parasite found in BC and widespread throughout the Northern Hemisphere, attacks a much broader range of insect species.

These fungi grow into the live host's tissues, gradually replacing them with fungal tissues. The host is eventually killed, and a cylindrical or branched fruiting structure grows out of the host. It produces spores that settle on new hosts, and the cycle begins anew.

Certain *Cordyceps* species are particularly skilled at manipulating the behaviour of their insect hosts and keeping the insect alive as the fungus gradually eats them from inside. In the case of what are called "zombie ants," a cordyceps-infected

ant leaves its nest, climbs to the underside of a highly placed leaf, and locks its mandibles onto a piece of vegetation. Some days later, the fungus kills the ant and fruits through its head. Such odd behaviour is of no benefit to the ant, but it allows the *Cordyceps* species to distribute its spores from a high, dry place.

TRUFFLE EATER and *C. militaris* appear to be BC's most abundant and widespread *Cordyceps* species. However, if you're on the sand dunes near Ucluelet or Tofino (see photos), keep an eye out for dried-up larvae of JUNE BUGS (*Polyphylla*), which are sometimes parasitized by *O. ravenelii* (pictured in this essay). This fungus has a disconcerting habit of fruiting out through the eyes of its dead host.

Cordyceps species, especially the caterpillar parasite *O. sinensis*, are widely employed in traditional Chinese medicine for a variety of medical issues. Fruiting bodies of the caterpillar host with its attached fungal fruiting bodies can be (and are widely) wild-harvested, but the mycelium can also be laboratory-grown. This fungus is recommended by some people for, among other things, increasing energy, slowing aging, reducing cardiovascular disease, taming cancers, and curing Type 2 diabetes. As with other phallic fungi, it is also prescribed for male sexual problems. Collection of this *Ophiocordyceps* and its host is economically important in some parts of Tibet and the Sichuan Province of China, where its price by weight can be three times that of gold. Extensive harvesting there has led to concerns about sustainability.

Truffle Eater   *Tolypocladium capitatum*

FRUITING BODY Head to 1.5 cm across; ovoid to convex or conical; red-brown to brownish yellow to green-black; dry; minutely pimply on top from clumped reproductive bodies (the smoother tissue underneath the cap is sterile); flesh white. **STEM** To 8 cm tall × 1.5 cm wide; roughly equal, sometimes forked into 2 heads, sometimes flattened; yellow or brownish yellow to olive-brown, darkening with age; dry; smooth or finely scurfy with longitudinal striations. **ODOUR** Not distinctive. **TASTE** Not distinctive. **SPORE PRINT** Colourless. **FRUITING** Single or clustered; on the ground, growing on underground fruiting bodies of COMMON DEER TRUFFLE (p. 465); autumn.

    EDIBILITY Unknown. **SIMILAR** The TRUFFLE EATER can resemble several gilled LBMs (little brown mushrooms), but looking under the cap and seeing no gills and then digging up the base to find a COMMON DEER TRUFFLE (p. 465) host soon resolves the confusion. *Tolypocladium ophioglossoides*, another parasite of *Elaphomyces* truffle species that is found in BC, is smaller, has cylindrical black heads, and has yellow cords reaching into the soil. **COMMENTS** Until recently, the ascomycete TRUFFLE EATER was known as *Elaphocordyceps capitata* or *Cordyceps capitata*. Certain species in *Elaphocordyceps*, however, have both a decomposer asexual stage and a parasitic sexual stage, and in the 1990s one of the *Elaphocordyceps* was found to have a decomposing, mould-like asexual stage that had already been identified as a species in the genus *Tolypocladium*. ("Tolype" is the Greek word for an unspun clump of wool, and "cladium" is from the word for a small branch—not a bad compound to describe an asexual mycelium.) Since the name for the asexual stage (*Tolypocladium*) was coined before the name for the sexual stage (*Elaphocordyceps*), and a fungus can't have two names, *Tolypocladium* takes precedence over *Elaphocordyceps*, and all of the *Elaphocordyceps* species become *Tolypocladium*. ⚬ The TRUFFLE EATER is a parasite on another fungus. More commonly, however, cordyceps are parasites on insects (see essay on p. 360). ⚬ "Capitatum" means "with a head," presumably named to underline the fact that, unlike most other cordyceps, TRUFFLE EATER's head looks like a cap.

Swamp Beacon   *Mitrula elegans*

FRUITING BODY Head to 1.2 cm across × 2 cm high; upright, cucumber- or pear-shaped or irregular; bright yellow to orange, somewhat translucent, dull orange in age; smooth or slightly wrinkled, shiny; flesh jelly-like. STEM To 4 cm tall × 3 mm wide; equal or slightly wider below; whitish to beige, translucent, sometimes with pink tints; smooth, shiny, and slightly slippery, especially near the top, sometimes slightly hairy near base. ODOUR Not distinctive. TASTE Not distinctive. SPORE PRINT Colourless. FRUITING Single or in small to large groups; often in standing water, sprouting from rotting vegetation on the ground or in the water; habitat variable; spring, summer, early autumn.

EDIBILITY Unknown. SIMILAR The WATER CLUB (p. 364), a similarly coloured (but smaller) mushroom typically found in or near flowing streams, has an almost spherical to hemispheric cap with turned-under margins. The FAIRY FAN (p. 365) has a cream to pale yellow head that is often flattened and hand-fan-shaped. *Mitrula borealis*, which differs from the SWAMP BEACON mainly by spore size and shape, has been reported from the BC Interior. COMMENTS SWAMP BEACON is an important decomposer of plant material in swamps, bogs, and lakeshores. ◆ It is the most widely distributed of the several *Mitrula* species found in North America and the most common in BC. ◆ SWAMP BEACON's fruiting body is the sexual stage of an ascomycete. In the early 2000s, mycologists were able to grow the mycelium on lab media and discovered the less obvious asexual form of this mushroom. ◆ "Mitrula" means "a small mitre" (a bishop's hat), referring to the shape of the fertile head. "Elegans" means "choice, elegant," which this winsome wetland wonder certainly is.

Water Club   *Vibrissea truncorum*

FRUITING BODY Cap to 5 mm across and high; hemispheric; margins inrolled; pale yellow or orange to pinkish buff; smooth; flesh somewhat jelly-like. **STEM** To 1.5 cm tall × 2 mm wide; cylindrical, sometimes narrowing downward; hollow; whitish to grey-white to pale brown, darker below; at times dark-hairy or minutely scaly, especially near the base; anchored to the substrate by a mat of dense brown mycelial threads. **ODOUR** Not distinctive. **TASTE** Not distinctive. **SPORE PRINT** Colourless. **FRUITING** Single or (usually) in groups, sometimes in clusters of 2 or 3; on rotting vegetation and wood, or in wet places, often in standing or running water; spring, summer.

    EDIBILITY Unknown. **SIMILAR** The WATER CLUB can look like a tiny **SWAMP BEACON** (p. 363) and can occupy the same watery habitat. The head of the latter, however, is larger and less regular and hemispheric. *Cudoniella clavus* also likes to grow on submerged wood. It lacks the yellow or orange colours and can be mistaken for old washed-out WATER CLUBS. WATER CLUB can also look like the fruiting bodies of some slime moulds. **COMMENTS** WATER CLUB is an ascomycete and a decomposer. ⚬ The spore-bearing bodies (asci) are packed onto the surface of the cap; the tissue under the cap is sterile. ⚬ It is not unusual to see the head of this mushroom completely submerged in water. Running water may play some role in the dispersion of the spores. ⚬ "Vibrissea" is from the Latin "to tremble, vibrate"—perhaps an allusion to the motion of WATER CLUBS in flowing water. "Truncorum" means "of stems," underlining the presence of stems in this genus.

Fairy Fan
Spathularia flavida

FRUITING BODY Fertile head to 2.5 cm across × 4 cm high; spatulate or hand-fan-shaped, flattened, sometimes lobed, edges of head running down stem; cream to pale yellow, developing brownish colours in age; smooth or slightly wrinkled; flesh somewhat rubbery, whitish to yellowish. STEM To 8 cm tall × 1 cm wide; variable, often equal or slightly wider below, cylindrical, or upper part slightly flattened; hollow; coloured as cap but often with a paler version of the colour; smooth or mealy; white to pale yellow mycelium at base. ODOUR Not distinctive. TASTE Not distinctive. SPORE PRINT Colourless to yellow-brown.
FRUITING Single or in groups or clustered, sometimes in fairy rings; on the ground or on rotting wood, around moss; in coniferous and mixedwood forests; summer, autumn.
EDIBILITY Uncertain. SIMILAR The SWAMP BEACON (p. 363) is a brighter orange-yellow, has a more cylindrical head, and prefers water or water-soaked environs. *Neolecta vitellina*, an ascomycete, has a fertile head that is a brighter yellow. Its shape, while sometimes spatulate, is usually more irregular.
COMMENTS The FAIRY FAN is an ascomycete, probably a decomposer. ⋆ Injured heads of FAIRY FAN appear to give off a chemical that repels fungus-feeding springtails. ⋆ *Spathularia flavida* is a European-defined species, and a number of North American varieties have been described—closer study might one day turn some of these varieties into western North American species. ⋆ "Spathularia" comes from a Latin word for "kitchen spatula" or "broadsword," and "flavida" is a Latin word for "blond, golden yellow."

Common Cudonia   *Cudonia circinans*

CAP To 2 cm across; convex often with a central depression and somewhat irregular in shape, margins rolled under, underside often with radial veins that extend to stem; cream to yellow or pale brown, often with pinkish to lilac tint; dry; smooth or wrinkled; flesh thin, leathery when dry, coloured as cap surface. STEM To 7 cm tall × 6 mm wide; equal but sometimes wider below, somewhat flattened, furrowed; solid when young, hollow in age; same colour as cap, but darker, sometimes with lilac tints; dry; sometimes longitudinally ridged at top. ODOUR Not distinctive. TASTE Not distinctive. SPORE PRINT Spores viewed under a microscope are colourless. FRUITING Scattered or in groups, sometimes clustered; on the ground or on rotten wood; usually in conifer forests; spring, summer, autumn.

EDIBILITY Poisonous. SIMILAR *Cudoniella clavus* has a smaller, beige to grey-white cap and grows on rotting cones, twigs, and stems, often in places where there is standing water. COMMON CUDONIA bears some resemblance to species in *Helvella* and to the COMPRESSED ELFIN SADDLE (p. 446) in particular. The elfin saddle, though, has a cap with more clearly defined double lobes, a stem that is whitish and lighter than the cap, and a more solitary habitat. COMMENTS Chemical tests show that COMMON CUDONIA contains the same volatile chemicals as the FALSE MOREL (p. 444) and at the same concentrations. ◆ COMMON CUDONIA, an ascomycete, is probably a duff decomposer. ◆ "Cudonia" may be a reference to "Cydonia," a name for the Greek goddess Athena, whose images show her wearing a helmet. "Circinans" comes from a Latin word that is used in botanical nomenclature to mean "coiled." Both names, then, may be references to the convoluted cap with curved-under margins.

Black Earth Tongue   *Geoglossum umbratile*

FRUITING BODY To 4 mm wide × 8 cm tall; like an upright baseball bat, unbranched, the fertile part (approximately the upper half to the upper third) often somewhat lance-shaped, sometimes flattened and/or with a longitudinal groove; dark brown or black; dry, but the lower part can be slightly slimy/sticky; smooth, sometimes with pressed-down scales on the part below the fertile head; flesh thin, usually black. **ODOUR** Not distinctive. **TASTE** Not distinctive. **SPORE PRINT** Brownish, but hard to obtain. **FRUITING** Single or in small groups; on the ground; habitat variable, usually in wet areas, often among mosses; spring, autumn.

EDIBILITY Unknown. **SIMILAR** Microscopic work is required for secure identification of the various earth tongues. We also lack a comprehensive study of the western North American earth tongues. If the upper, fertile part and stem of a dark-coloured earth tongue are slimy/sticky, you may have found *Glutinoglossum glutinosum*. **VELVETY EARTH TONGUE**, *Trichoglossum hirsutum* (p. 348), is finely hairy/velvety (use hand lens) on both the fertile upper part and the lower stem part, and the fertile part is short (often just a fifth of the length of the whole club) and more defined from the stem. **COMMENTS** "Geoglossum" means the same as the common name: "earth tongue." "Umbratile" means "shaded, shadowy," named this for its dark colour.

Corals

The coral fungi—named for their resemblance to marine corals—are club-like fungi in which the upright fruiting bodies branch into multiple shafts. As we might expect, the line between clubs and corals is not an easy one to maintain. There are clubs, for example, that have some branching. But at the far ends of the spectrum of shapes between clubs and corals, the fruiting bodies in the two groups look quite different.

Of the six main entries in this section, four belong to the genus *Ramaria*. The hundreds of species of *Ramaria*—about 40 of these have been recorded in BC—are often large, brightly coloured masses of smaller upright branches that grow in the soil. They are found around the trees that they have mycorrhizal relationships with.

Ramaria specimens, readily recognizable as part of the genus, are notoriously hard to identify to the species level. Most ramaria discoveries require work with microscopes and chemicals to have any certainty about the species. As a result, BC inventories of mushrooms often resort to "*Ramaria* sp." as the name. This uncertainty about exact species identification factors into their edibility. While some species are reported to be delicious, others can make consumers ill. In North America, caution seems to regulate their table use. This is not the case in other places—in Central America and Asia, *Ramaria* species seem to be widely and almost indiscriminately consumed.

Ramaria species, it turns out, are related to species in *Gomphus* and *Turbinellus*. In this section we have also included the coral-shaped mushrooms in *Clavulina*, which are related to chanterelles. The 75 known species of *Clavulina* are mycorrhizal mushrooms. They are mostly found in the tropics—at this point, only a handful of *Clavulina* species have been noted in BC records.

The lone *Sparassis* in this section is the odd mushroom out. While it is arguably coral-like, with its flat branching slabs, it is actually more closely related to polypores and, like the polypores, is a decomposer or parasite rather than a mycorrhizal fungus. *Sparassis* species are delicious and can be grown commercially, as many other decomposers can. Cultivated heads are starting to appear in local specialty markets.

Western Cauliflower Mushroom · *Sparassis radicata*

FRUITING BODY To 50 cm (or more) across and high; a many-branched mass of thin, flat, wide (to 2.5 cm) lobes with frilly edges; cream or yellowish, pale brown in age; the individual lobes smooth; the flesh substantial and pliant, white. **STEM** To 13 cm tall × 5 cm wide; merging with the lobes above, narrower downward, sometimes deeply buried in tree or soil; flesh tough. **ODOUR** Spicy, pleasant. **TASTE** Almost sweet. **SPORE PRINT** White. **FRUITING** Usually single; on or near the base of conifer stumps and trees; autumn, winter.

    EDIBILITY Choice. A few have reported stomach upsets. Getting the dirt out from between the lobes can be a challenge. **SIMILAR** Nothing looks much like the WESTERN CAULIFLOWER MUSHROOM except another *Sparassis* mushroom—of which there are about a dozen species around the world. None of these others, however, occur in BC. **COMMENTS** You may see the WESTERN CAULIFLOWER MUSHROOM listed as *S. crispa*, the name of the European species. Though some taxonomists think the 2 species are the same, DNA studies suggest our western North American species differs from *S. crispa* enough to deserve its own species name. ❧ Calling this species a CAULIFLOWER MUSHROOM is a bit misleading—many ramarias with tightly packed heads, such as the PINK-TIPPED CORAL (p. 372), look more like a cauliflower. This mushroom looks more like a tight mass of wide, whitish egg noodles. ❧ Because the WESTERN CAULIFLOWER MUSHROOM often occurs at the base of living trees (often DOUGLAS-FIR), it is presumed to be a brown-rot or butt-rot parasite that contributes to the demise of its hosts. ❧ This mushroom will often come up many years in the same place, feeding at the same tree. ❧ "Sparassis" comes from a Greek word meaning "rip, tear." "Radicata" means "rooted," a name presumably bestowed because of its deeply buried stem.

Crested Coral   *Clavulina coralloides* group

FRUITING BODY To 4 cm across × 8 cm high; upright, often densely but irregularly branched from base, the branches cylindrical or flattened, knobbly or longitudinally wrinkled, the tips either simply pointed, crested, fringed, or jagged; whitish, often with yellow, yellow-brown, or pale brown tints in age; dry; smooth; flesh tough to brittle, white. **STEM** Absent, or to 3 cm tall × 5 mm wide, white. **ODOUR** Not distinctive. **TASTE** Not distinctive. **SPORE PRINT** White. **FRUITING** Single or scattered; on the ground or less commonly on well-rotted wood; usually in forests; summer, autumn, early winter.

EDIBILITY Edible. Some collectors even prize it. But avoid infected fruiting bodies (see below). **SIMILAR** *Clavulina cristata* is usually considered a synonym of *C. coralloides*. Currently, a CRESTED CORAL that is not highly branched and whose vertical shafts are wrinkled and blunt is sometimes assigned to *C. rugosa*, although this species may simply be a variant of *C. coralloides*. If the coral has wrinkled and blunt tips with lilac-grey tints, it may be recorded as *C. cinerea*. Mushrooms in the *Lentaria pinicola* (also known as *Ramaria pinicola*) **group** have more buff to brown colours, but the tips—which usually have simple points rather than crests and fringes—can be white. *Tremellodendropsis tuberosa*, a relative of jelly fungi, has flattened and wavy, barely branching, whitish to buff shafts that arise from a common base, and tips that lack fringes. **COMMENTS** The CRESTED CORAL and other clavulinas are often infected, from the base up, with the ascomycete crust fungus *Helminthosphaeria clavariarum*. The fungus has grey to black colours on its surface and is dotted with tiny black bumps (use a hand lens) that are its reproductive bodies. ⟡ CRESTED CORAL is probably mycorrhizal, mostly with conifers, even though it sometimes grows on rotten wood. ⟡ "Clavulina" is based on "clava," the Latin word for "club, cudgel"; "coralloides" means "like a coral."

Pink-tipped Coral   *Ramaria botrytis*

FRUITING BODY To 12 cm across and high; upright, densely branched with short branches when young, like a cauliflower, the branches lengthening in age but often retaining many finger-like projections at the tip; white, sometimes with pink tints when young, bruising pale yellow or pale brown, the tips pink, red, or purple; surface smooth; flesh thick, solid, fibrous, white. **STEM** To 5 cm tall × 3 cm wide; cylindrical, often festooned with stubby branches; white, bruising pale yellow or pale brown. **ODOUR** Not distinctive or slightly sweet. **TASTE** Not distinctive. **SPORE PRINT** Pale orange-brown. **FRUITING** Single or scattered; on the ground; under conifers; late summer, autumn.

EDIBILITY Edible. Some even say choice. But easy to confuse with less palatable ramarias and having a laxative effect on some eaters. **SIMILAR** Because the BC ramarias that most resemble PINK-TIPPED CORAL have mostly microscopic differences from it and from one another, they are almost impossible to separate in the field. **COMMENTS** When young and displaying many short and red- or pink-tipped branches, the PINK-TIPPED CORAL can be one of the easier ramarias to identify to species (with the exception, of course, of its microscope-differentiated look-alikes). ● It is a worldwide mushroom and relatively abundant in most of western North America, though not widely reported yet from BC. ● As is the case with many other *Ramaria* species, the PINK-TIPPED CORAL is probably mycorrhizal with nearby trees. ● "Ramaria" means "furnished with many branches," a good descriptor for this genus and especially for this species. "Botrytis" means "like a bunch of grapes," a name perhaps occasioned by the reddish tips.

Upright Coral

Ramaria stricta

FRUITING BODY To 10 cm across × 14 cm high; much-branched and the branches long, compact, straight, slender (to 5 mm across), and cylindrical (but sometimes flattened or grooved), branch tips pointy and often divided near the point; colour variable, pale yellow to pinkish tan to pale brown, often with a darker to lighter gradient from bottom to top of the fruiting body, readily bruising brownish or purple-brown, branch tips often pale yellow with greenish yellow tints when young; smooth; flesh leathery, drying brittle, white with brown tints. **STEM** Absent and branched from base or, if present, to 2 cm tall and cylindrical; dull yellow-brown to pale brown, bruising purplish brown; often covered with felty mycelium. **ODOUR** Sweet, faintly of anise (when detectable). **TASTE** Bitter. **SPORE PRINT** Pale yellow to yellowish brown. **FRUITING** Single or scattered; on rotting conifer or hardwood wood; in conifer and mixedwood forests; spring, summer, autumn.

EDIBILITY Uncertain. **SIMILAR** *Lentaria pinicola* is a smaller mushroom (less than 5 cm tall) without the sweet odour and with rounder, wavier shafts arising from the branch points. *Ramaria apiculata* has branch tips that are more persistently yellow-green (though there are specimens without the green). *Phaeoclavulina abietina* can have a yellow-brown fruiting body, but it often has green tints and the whole fruiting body turns blue-green after picking or where handled. *Phaeoclavulina myceliosa* can have olive tones on its branches, especially when older, and its base is attached to the soil by conspicuous rhizomorphs that are slender and whitish. **COMMENTS** UPRIGHT CORAL is common in Europe and in western North America. Our western North American specimens are often labelled *R. stricta* var. *stricta*. ☙ We would expect UPRIGHT CORAL to be mycorrhizal, but its habit of growing on wood (sometimes submerged beneath the soil) hints at a decomposing lifestyle. ☙ "Stricta" comes from a Latin word meaning "straight," probably a reference to the long, non-wavy branches.

Yellow Mountain Coral   *Ramaria rasilispora*

FRUITING BODY To 15 cm across and high; rather spherical in overall shape; often partly buried in soil; ascending, multi-forking branches packed together in a cauliflower-like head for a long time but lengthening a little and opening up in age, shafts somewhat circular in cross-section, large branches up to 3 cm across, small upper branches to 1.5 cm, tips rounded to bluntly pointed; lower branches whitish, especially if buried, rest of the branch surfaces pale yellow or pale orange, tips pale yellow or yellow-green when young, and in age, sometimes the extreme tips blushing pale pink or brownish; surface smooth; flesh fibrous, white. STEM To 6 cm tall × 5 cm wide; conical to cylindrical, often rounded at the base, sometimes with a few branch stubs in addition to branches; whitish, not bruising; smooth, sometimes finely hairy where it contacts soil; flesh in stem fibrous or spongy-fibrous and sometimes with watery spots. ODOUR Not distinctive. TASTE Not distinctive. SPORE PRINT Yellow-brown to yellow-orange. FRUITING Single or scattered; on the ground; under montane conifers; spring, early summer.

EDIBILITY Edible. But often dirty and hard to clean from being buried. Some eaters report mild adverse reactions. SIMILAR Another yellow ramaria, ***Ramaria cystidiophora***, has a thick white mass of basal mycelium, may have a strong citrus or strong anise odour, and usually appears in autumn rather than spring. COMMENTS YELLOW MOUNTAIN CORAL is considered a primarily North American West Coast species. It is harvested and sold in markets in some areas of Mexico. ◦ "Rasilispora" means "with smooth spores."

Orange-red Coral   *Ramaria stuntzii*

FRUITING BODY To 14 cm across × 16 cm high; erect and much-branched, in a dense cauliflower form when young but branches extending with age and the top spreading, the first branches from the base up to 4 cm across, the smaller shafts circular or somewhat flattened in cross-section, branch tips rounded; pinkish red to scarlet, fading to pale orange-red or pale orange, branch tips often remaining scarlet; smooth; flesh in branches leathery, drying brittle, greyish red to orange. **STEM** Massive, to 7 cm tall × 7 cm wide; conical to cylindrical, partly buried, often bearing small white branch stubs; white on base, pale orange above; flesh spongy or fibrous, whitish to pale yellow. **ODOUR** Not distinctive. **TASTE** Slightly bitter. **SPORE PRINT** Apricot yellow. **FRUITING** Scattered or in groups, sometimes in a fairy ring; on the ground; in conifer forests (especially with WESTERN HEMLOCK); autumn.

EDIBILITY Uncertain. **SIMILAR** *Ramaria araiospora* is similar but has a slightly bulbous but not massive base (up to 3 cm × 1.5 cm). In the central part, its colour is more deep red to magenta than orange-red, and its branch tips are sometimes pale yellow. **COMMENTS** Not exactly a common BC mushroom, but the patience it takes to find this stunning ramaria is well rewarded. ⚬ Species of *Ramaria* can sometimes be challenging to identify, requiring careful microscopy and chemical tests. For those up to the challenge, we recommend *Ramaria of the Pacific Northwestern United States* (US Department of the Interior, 2006) by Ronald Exeter, Lorelei Norvell, and Efrén Cázares. ⚬ "Stuntzii" is in honour of Daniel Elliot Stuntz (1909–83), an important West Coast mycologist who was based at University of Washington.

Crusts

Have you come across thin, parchment-like sheets on decaying tree trunks, stumps, leaves, twigs, and logs and wondered what they were? Many of them turn out to be the fruiting bodies of fungal mycelia that are decomposing their substrates. These fungi have not bothered with any of the more complex tricks for spreading their spores abroad—the basidia and asci are simply arrayed on a flat and either smooth or wrinkled surface that exposes them to the wind currents.

In some ways, crust mushrooms are the black holes of mycology. Not because they are rare—kick over any rotting log and you might find one—but because they are so hard to put names to. While a few of them have outstanding features that make them recognizable, the vast majority don't. Sometimes they are nothing more than drab, often-whitish parchments hiding along the edges of logs. Even good fungal scientists can find it challenging to tell one of these pale crusts from another.

For all their physical similarities, crusts do not make up a natural group. They trace back through many different branches on the fungal family tree. Most crusts are basidiomycetes, but a few, such as the *Hypomyces* species, are ascomycetes. Most crusts are decomposers, but some are parasites and a rare few are mycorrhizal.

A few of the mushrooms covered in various categories in this guide might be considered crusts. The polypores NETTED CRUST (p. 410) and JELLY ROT (p. 409), though they can extend their fruiting bodies into shelf-like extensions, often appear as flat fruiting surfaces. Many very young conks can look crust-like—immature RED-BELTED CONKS (p. 398), for example, can be hard to place as polypores when they first

form. FALSE TURKEY TAIL (p. 387) is more likely to present itself as layered shelves, but if you look closely, you may see crust-like sections scattered among the shelves.

Some crust-like fungi, instead of feeding on wood, parasitize other fungi and slime moulds. The ascomycete that makes LOBSTER MUSHROOMS (p. 39), *Hypomyces lactifluorum*, could be classified as a crust. There are other *Hypomyces* species that also attack mushrooms. *Hypomyces cervinigenus*, for example, appears as a whitish fuzz that turns pinkish brown, on caps of FLUTED BLACK ELFIN SADDLE (see p. 447 for more details). *Hypomyces rosellus* appears as beautiful rose-red dots on a white, cottony mycelium that is in the process of decomposing some gilled, veined, and toothed mushrooms. *Hypomyces aurantius* is a cottony orange growth on polypores and other fungi. *Hypomyces luteovirens* (pictured on the facing page) deforms the gills and caps of russulas as it displaces the cells of its host with its own, creating what are called GREEN LOBSTER MUSHROOMS. Crusts in the *H. chrysospermus* group engulf boletes, such as the RED-CRACKED BOLETE (p. 320), with layers of white to bright yellow, mould-like mycelial mats.

Hypomyces species are not our only parasitic crusts. *Nectriopsis violacea* (pictured below) produces a layer of thick violet dots on masses of the yellow slime mould *Fuligo septica* (for more on slime moulds, see p. 205). *Hypocrea pulvinata* forms small blobs on conks, especially the RED-BELTED CONK (p. 398). These hairy blobs, which often run together into larger sheets, are yellow-orange to grey to brown and have small holes in them.

Polypores

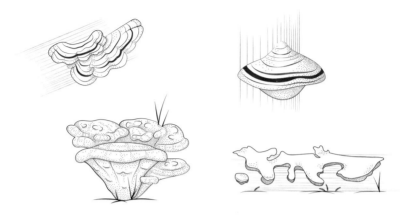

The polypore species in this section have their basidia arrayed inside of small vertical tubes that are open on the bottom end as pores. Boletes (p. 317) also have these tubes, but boletes are fleshy and the pore layer, which is typically thicker in boletes, usually peels away easily from the cap. Polypores are usually leathery or woody, and the pore layer and the cap almost always bind tightly together. But it is difficult to generalize about polypores—they can assume many different shapes and features. We have organized the polymorphous polypores in this large section into stemmed polypores, shelf mushrooms, ground-dwelling polypores, conks, and crust-like polypores.

Several of the polypore species on these pages—the ones in the genera *Albatrellus*, *Coltricia*, *Boletopsis*, *Picipes*, and *Jahnoporus*—have stems and caps. Species of *Albatrellus* and *Boletopsis*—and *Coltricia*, at least some species, some of the time—are mycorrhizal. The other two genera, like all of the other mushrooms in the main entries of this polypore section, are parasites or decomposers.

A few of the pored species here are shelf mushrooms. They have caps that are somewhat flexible, and they grow in rows—sometimes in overlapping, shingled rows—along decaying trunks and logs that they are decomposing. Shelf mushrooms can be found in *Gloeophyllum*, *Trametes*, *Pycnoporus*, and *Postia*.

The species that are in the genera *Phaeolus* and *Bondarzewia*, even though they are wood parasites and decomposers, usually appear on or near the ground, with the wood being consumed by their mycelial mats hidden below the soil. Their fruiting bodies are, at least when young, somewhat soft and pliable. The clustered arrays of their fruiting bodies tend to grow in circles or rosettes.

Most of the species here fall into the conk category. These are the ones in the genera *Laetiporus*, *Cryptoporus*, *Inonotus*, *Echinodontium*, *Fomes*, *Rhodofomes*, *Fomitopsis*, *Laricifomes*, *Ganoderma*, and *Porodaedalea*. Conks are typically woody. They grow on living or dead trees, sometimes while the trees are still standing. They are widely known among foresters because their mycelia, feasting on the heartwood and sapwood of their host trees, can render the wood unfit for commercial purposes. Three of the conks—the BIRCH CONK (p. 399), the WESTERN VARNISHED CONK (p. 392), and the CONIFER SULPHUR SHELF (p. 403)—produce annual conks that may last over the winter, but they do not start growing again the next year. The rest of the conks are perennial. Each season the perennial conks add a new fertile layer to the bottom of the conk. Some perennial conks can attain great age and size.

We have included in this section two mushrooms that do not have pores—the sometimes-stemmed EARTH FAN (p. 408) and the shelf-like crust that is FALSE TURKEY TAIL (p. 387)—in order to compare them to their pored look-alikes.

Two of the polypores covered in this section—*Byssomerulius* and *Phlebia*—form crust-like fruiting bodies, with the fertile surface hardly more than an exposed sheet. The surfaces, however, can be wrinkled in a way that creates pit-like depressions that can resemble shallow pores. For more on crusts, see the essay on p. 376.

For those wanting to know more about BC's polypores, we highly recommend *Polypores of British Columbia* (Government of BC, 2017) by James Ginns. It is available online.

ARTIST'S CONK (p. 393) etched by an artist.

Sheep Polypore   *Albatrellus ovinus*

CAP To 15 cm across; circular to kidney-shaped, convex becoming flat or depressed, margins becoming wavy; white, cream, tan, or greyish, staining yellow, especially in the cracks; dry; smooth but dull, becoming cracked and often wrinkled with age; flesh to 2 cm thick, firm at maturity, cream to yellow or pinkish brown. PORES Decurrent; cream or pale yellow, drying darker yellow or sometimes pinkish buff or olive; tiny, 2–4 per mm, to 3 mm deep. ODOUR Not distinctive, or somewhat fruity. TASTE Can be almondy, sometimes slightly bitter. SPORE PRINT White. STEM To 8 cm tall × 4 cm wide; equal or enlarged, then narrowed below; firm; solid; central or slightly off-centre; cream, sometimes staining pinkish brown; finely hairy or smooth, sometimes wrinkled when dry. FRUITING Single, scattered, or in groups, often in clusters with stem bases fused; on the ground; in coniferous or mixedwood forests; late summer, autumn.

EDIBILITY Edible. But large amounts can act as a laxative. SIMILAR *Albatrellopsis flettii* starts off with a distinctive grey-blue cap, though in age it can become pinkish brown to orange-brown. Its pore layer is white and develops salmon-coloured stains. *Neoalbatrellus subcaeruleoporus* also has bluish grey on its fresh caps, but unlike *A. flettii*, its pore layer is also bluish grey. *Albatrellus avellaneus* is quite similar to the SHEEP POLYPORE, but it has larger spores, the cap tends to be scurfy with dark scales, and yellow hues tend to be more extensive. It is most common along the Pacific coast, found with SITKA SPRUCE and WESTERN HEMLOCK. The less common *Scutiger ellisii* (formerly known as *Albatrellus ellisii*) has a yellow-green to yellow-brown and hairy to scaly cap, white pores that stain greenish, and flesh that turns lavender to green when cut. COMMENTS The SHEEP POLYPORE is mycorrhizal and found throughout BC. ◆ "Ovinus" means "pertaining to sheep" in Latin.

Bitter Brown Polypore
Jahnoporus hirtus

CAP To 15 cm across; circular, semicircular, or tongue-shaped, convex to flat to depressed, sometimes wrinkled and wavy, margins curved down, sometimes multiple-lobed; tan to grey-brown to purple-brown to dark brown; dry; hairy or bristly-hairy; flesh to 1.5 cm thick, firm, sometimes corky, white. PORES Often decurrent; white or cream, drying yellowish; angular, edges eroded in age, 1–2 per mm, to 8 mm deep. ODOUR Some report an iodine odour when specimens first picked, others nothing. TASTE Intensely and lingeringly bitter, but sometimes after a short pause. SPORE PRINT White. STEM To 10 cm tall × 4 cm wide; equal or narrowing downward; solid; simple or branched, usually off-centre or lateral; coloured as the cap; velvety. FRUITING Single or in groups, sometimes clustered; on the ground near the base of conifer trees or stumps; autumn, winter.

EDIBILITY Not edible. Too bitter. SIMILAR The WESTERN MOUNTAIN POLYPORE (p. 391) typically has numerous caps and indistinct stems on a single base, the caps sometimes forming a rosette. It also has thinner (to 7 mm) flesh and a less bitter taste. *Ischnoderma benzoinum* (*I. resinosum*, which favours hardwoods, may or may not be the same species), a conifer conk that can also have a dark brown, velvety surface, imparts an almond odour to the wood it rots and has a white underside that quickly darkens when bruised. A BITTER BROWN POLYPORE with a pale tan cap might be mistaken for the SHEEP POLYPORE (p. 380), but the latter has a much shallower pore layer with denser, rounder pores, and if bitter at all, it lacks the intense bitter taste of the BITTER BROWN POLYPORE. COMMENTS This is a fairly common species in older BC forests. ❧ The BITTER BROWN POLYPORE was once called *Polyporus hirtus*. ❧ "Hirtus" means "hairy, rough."

Grey False Bolete
Boletopsis grisea group

CAP To 15 cm across; circular but at times irregular, convex to flat or slightly depressed, sometimes lumpy, margins inrolled at first, becoming wavy and/or lobed; colour variable, whitish to grey or blackish, often with blue or purple tints, becoming darker or olive-brown to brown, sometimes appearing streaked; dry; smooth at first to finely scaly in age, dull; flesh to 3 cm thick, firm, white, sometimes tinged with the cap colour, darkening where cut or handled. PORES Decurrent; intense white when young, drying grey to brown; 1–4 per mm. ODOUR Farinaceous or not distinctive. TASTE Bitter or not distinctive. SPORE PRINT Pale brown. STEM To 10 cm tall × 3 cm wide; roughly equal; flesh firm; solid; central or off-centre; surface whitish or grey, generally coloured as cap; smooth to finely scaly, wrinkled when dry. FRUITING Single, scattered, or in groups, sometimes clustered; on the ground; usually in conifer, sometimes hardwood, forests; summer, early autumn.

EDIBILITY Edible. Sometimes bitter. SIMILAR As the common name indicates, the GREY FALSE BOLETE could at first glance be mistaken for a bolete. Its pore layer, however, is generally thinner and harder to remove than the pore layers of most boletes. The SHEEP POLYPORE (p. 380) is similar but is white-spored and has more yellowish tones, especially on its pore layer. COMMENTS The GREY FALSE BOLETE is a widespread mycorrhizal species in conifer zones, especially in the Northern Hemisphere. The group includes *Boletopsis grisea* in the strict sense (which has a preference for pines), *B. leucomelaena* (which is generally a spruce associate), and possibly other cryptic species in our province. ๑ BC foragers, though not always valuing this mushroom as an edible, consider it a good indicator for the widely harvested PINE MUSHROOM (p. 146). ๑ You may see this mushroom listed in some guides by the older (and probably mistaken) name *B. subsquamosa*. ๑ "Boletopsis" means "looking like a bolete," and "grisea" means "grey."

Blackleg   *Picipes badius*

CAP To 15 cm across; roughly circular, convex to flat to depressed, sometimes with a sunken middle, leathery to stiff, margins sharp, sometimes wavy and lobed; whitish to light brown to dark or reddish brown, darker in the centre, sometimes becoming fully blackish, sometimes with radial striping; dry; smooth, sometimes becoming wrinkled; flesh to 5 mm thick or more, tough, white becoming brown in age. PORES Decurrent; whitish aging pale brown to pale yellow-brown; round to angular, dense (6–10 per mm), and shallow (to 3 mm). ODOUR Not distinctive. TASTE Not distinctive. SPORE PRINT White. STEM To 6 cm tall × 1.5 cm wide; equal or narrowing downward; flesh tough; solid; central to off-centre; black at base, pale brown, later black, above; dry; smooth above, finely hairy at base. FRUITING Single or in groups, sometimes clustered; on rotting wood of hardwoods, occasionally conifers; year-round.

EDIBILITY Unknown. Too tough to eat. SIMILAR *Picipes badius* is also called *Polyporus badius*. There are a number of closely related *Polyporus* species that are hard to tell apart. The most likely of these to appear on BC inventory lists, besides BLACKLEG, are ***Polyporus elegans*** and ***P. varius***. Both have buff to tan caps and are usually smaller than BLACKLEG (caps generally to 10 cm diameter). *Polyporus elegans* has 5–7 pores per mm; *P. varius* has 7–9 per mm. The cap of *P. varius* is often radially streaked. COMMENTS BLACKLEG, a white-rot decomposer, is found in the temperate belts of the Northern Hemisphere and is common throughout BC. ◆ "Badius," which means "chestnut-coloured, brown," is the Latin term from which English gets its word "bay" (as in bay horse). The alternate common name for BLACKLEG, the BAY POLYPORE, is based on this connection.

Tiger's Eye   *Coltricia perennis*

CAP To 10 cm across; circular, flat to funnel-shaped, radially wrinkled in age, cap edges often fused with adjacent cap edges and incorporating debris, margins wavy and often irregular; cinnamon or rusty colours that are darker when wet and lighter when dry, strongly zoned, the growing margin becoming paler; dry; velvety but often smooth in age; flesh to 2 mm thick, leathery, cinnamon brown. **PORES** Often somewhat decurrent; to 3 mm thick, thinned or missing near the margin; cream, then pale yellow or golden brown, bruising or aging darker; 2–4 per mm. **ODOUR** Not distinctive. **TASTE** Sometimes pucker-inducing. **SPORE PRINT** Pale yellow-brown. **STEM** To 7 cm tall × 1 cm wide; cylindrical; usually central; dark brown to reddish brown; velvety. **FRUITING** Single or in groups; on the ground or occasionally on rotting wood; in coniferous or hardwood forests, often in disturbed sites (e.g., trail edges, burns); summer, autumn, winter.

EDIBILITY Not edible. Too leathery. **SIMILAR** The **FAIRY STOOL** (*Coltricia cinnamomea*) is smaller (cap to 4 mm across, stem to 6 mm wide), prefers hardwood forests, and has a silky/shiny cap with less distinct zones, and its pore layer is not usually decurrent. *Onnia tomentosa* has a yellow-brown cap with indistinct zoning, and its flesh is thicker (to 4 mm) and spongy. Two toothed fungi, the *Hydnellum scrobiculatum* **group** (see STRAWBERRIES AND CREAM, p. 341, under SIMILAR) and **OWL EYES** (p. 346), can look like TIGER'S EYE from above, but under the cap they have teeth rather than pores. The **EARTH FAN** (p. 408) also has a from-the-top similarity, but its margins are more uneven and it has no pores or teeth underneath. **COMMENTS** Members of the *Coltricia* genus, though in a genetic line that consists largely of wood-decay fungi, have somehow managed to evolve mycorrhizal habits. ❧ "Coltricia" derives from an Italian word that referred to a small feather bed. "Perennis" means "long-lasting." If TIGER'S EYE is a bed, it's only for the wee folk.

Blue Cheese Polypore   *Postia caesia* group

CAP To 6 cm across and projecting 4 cm from substrate; shelf-like, roughly semicircular, convex or flat, margins sometimes wavy from radial wrinkling, usually sharp; soft when young, harder in age; whitish or greyish, usually with blue tinges, especially around margins; dry; finely to coarsely hairy but sometimes smooth in age; flesh to 1 cm thick, soft and spongy when young, white at first and then becoming grey or yellowish. PORES White or bluish; angular or maze-like, sometimes ragged, tooth-like, 2–4 per mm, to 8 mm deep. ODOUR Pleasant, sweet. TASTE Soapy or sweet. SPORE PRINT Pale blue or bluish white. STEM Absent. FRUITING Usually single; on rotting wood of conifers and (less frequently) hardwoods; year-round, but especially in summer or autumn.

EDIBILITY Unknown. Sadly, it only *looks* like blue cheese. SIMILAR *Fuscopostia fragilis* (also called *Postia fragilis*), instead of blue tints, has reddish stains in age or where bruised. The larger *Tyromyces chioneus* (cap to 8 cm, flesh to 2 cm deep), which causes a white rot in hardwoods, is whitish to cream, bruises or ages a pale yellow, has white flesh that becomes chalky and crumbly in age, and gives off a spicy, citrusy smell. COMMENTS Earlier names for this widespread BC species were *Tyromyces caesius* and *Oligoporus caesius*. Recent genetic studies, however, indicate that a number of different US Pacific Northwest species are encompassed in the *Postia caesia* complex and that most of these species are difficult to differentiate in the field. In Washington State, and probably also in BC, BLUE CHEESE POLYPORE as described above, with some blue on the cap, growing on conifer wood, and coarsely hairy when young, is likely to be *P. simulans*. ❧ The mycelium of the BLUE CHEESE POLYPORE produces a brown rot. ❧ "Postia" is probably a Latin-derived term for "of a place." "Caesia" means "blue-grey" in Latin.

Turkey Tail

Trametes versicolor

CAP To 10 cm across; semicircular or tongue-shaped, growing shelf-like or in rosettes, sometimes fused, leathery at first but becoming tougher and less flexible, margins sometimes wavy; various colours in strongly contrasting concentric zones, sometimes greenish when covered in algae; dry; very hairy, alternating silky or velvety from zone to zone; flesh to 3 mm thick, tough, white or cream. PORES Cream to yellowish; 3–6 per mm, to 2 mm deep. ODOUR Not distinctive. TASTE Not distinctive. SPORE PRINT White or pale yellowish. STEM Absent. FRUITING Usually in groups or shingled clusters; on dead wood of hardwoods, rarely on conifers; perennial, year-round.

EDIBILITY Not edible. Too tough. SIMILAR The species most commonly confused with TURKEY TAIL is probably FALSE TURKEY TAIL (p. 387). To see the difference, look underneath: FALSE TURKEY TAIL, a crust fungus, has no pores (a hand lens may be needed). *Trichaptum abietinum*, a smaller and very common zoned shelf mushroom that is almost always found on dead conifer wood, has a pore layer that is purplish or violet when fresh (especially toward the margins) and the tubes in the pore layer are often ragged. Its upper surface is whitish to greyish and does not have the strongly contrasting colours seen on fresh TURKEY TAIL. The similar but much rarer *Trichaptum biforme*, also with purplish to violet pores, grows on hardwoods. *Trametes hirsuta* has a whitish to greyish cap with low-contrast zones, somewhat thicker (to 5 mm) flesh, and (often) an anise odour. COMMENTS TURKEY TAIL is perhaps BC's most common and widespread polypore. It is a white-rot decomposer found almost everywhere in the world. ◆ This shelf mushroom is widely used in folk medicine, typically by being ground up and drunk as a tea. It is often billed as an immune system booster and cancer-fighting agent (see the discussion of medicinal mushrooms on p. 400). ◆ "Trametes" means "one who is thin," and "versicolor" means "varying in colour."

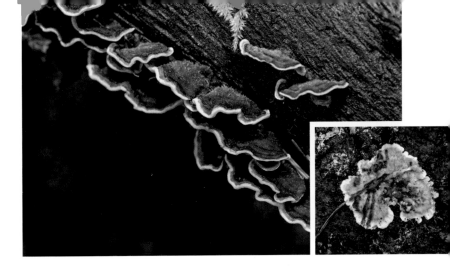

False Turkey Tail

Stereum hirsutum

FRUITING BODY Sometimes spread out under rotting branches as a crust with wing-like edges reaching away from the substrate, but more often on the edge of logs and stumps as thin (to 2 mm), semicircular, sometimes lobed shelves (projecting up to 3 cm), with the shelves often in closely spaced rows and the adjacent shelves sometimes fused; upper surface of shelves various shades from yellow-orange to reddish brown, becoming greyer in age, zoned, often with whitish edges when young; dry; densely hairy, becoming smooth in age; flesh tough, pliant when young, yellow to red-brown; underside ranges from yellow or orange to brown or grey, without pores, aging buff. **ODOUR** Not distinctive. **TASTE** Not distinctive. **SPORE PRINT** White. **FRUITING** Usually in dense, overlapping, and run-together groups; on branches and trunks of hardwoods and occasionally conifers; year-round, sending out spores in the autumn.

EDIBILITY Not edible. Too tough. **SIMILAR** FALSE TURKEY TAIL and TURKEY TAIL (p. 386) can look remarkably alike, with their shelf-like growth on rotting wood and their zonate caps. It's easy, however, to be certain which is which by examining the fertile surface under the shelves. Only TURKEY TAIL has visible pores. (You may need a hand lens to see this.) The crust *Chondrostereum purpureum* has a purplish spore-bearing surface under its shelf-like projections. The tops are buff and often hairy, and when the cap is sliced, a black line is visible in the flesh. *Stereum sanguinolentum* (inset photo) grows on conifer wood, most commonly as a spread-out brown crust, and quickly bleeds red when cut. *Hydnoporia* (was *Hymenochaetopsis*) *tabacina* also appears more often as a spread-out brown crust. Its zoned caps, when they form, are small (projecting about 1 cm), and the upper surface is golden brown when young and darker grey-brown when old. **COMMENTS** FALSE TURKEY TAIL is a highly variable, extremely common white-rot decomposer. ◦ "Stereum" means "tough, rigid" (which this species is generally not), and "hirsutum" means "hairy."

Conifer Mazegill

Gloeophyllum sepiarium

CAP To 12 cm across and projecting 8 cm; bracket- or shelf-like, semicircular or in fused rosettes, shallowly convex, leathery becoming woody, margins thinner; orangey to yellow-brown when young, becoming reddish brown to greyish brown and eventually black from the centre outward, often zoned concentrically with different colours and textures, growing margin white, yellow, or orangish; dry; finely hairy becoming smooth but sometimes keeping hair tufts in age, often radially wrinkled; flesh to 5 mm thick, yellow-brown to red-brown. PORES Formed by maze-like reproductive structures that resemble blunt-edged gills (to 7 mm deep) with cross-walls, gills eroding and becoming sawtoothed in age; golden brown aging to dark brown. ODOUR Not distinctive. TASTE Not distinctive. SPORE PRINT White. STEM Absent. FRUITING Single or in shingled groups; on dead wood (trees, stumps, logs, lumber), usually conifers but also hardwoods; annual or perennial, year-round.

EDIBILITY Unknown. Too leathery to consider. SIMILAR The CONIFER MAZE CONK (p. 404) also has a brown, maze-like pore layer, but it has pale brown spores and a cap that is crusty, rough, and cracked, and it tends to grow on living (or recently fallen) conifers. Another shelf-like mushroom with maze gills, the polypore *Lenzites betulina* (also called *Trametes betulina*) has white flesh and a whitish pore layer and almost always grows on hardwood logs and stumps. COMMENTS CONIFER MAZEGILL is closely related to gilled mushrooms in the genus *Neolentinus* (pp. 216–217), but the gills of CONIFER MAZEGILL form pore-like shapes reminiscent of polypores. ◄ The mycelium of CONIFER MAZEGILL produces a brown rot in wood. ◄ "Gloeophyllum" means "sticky gills," perhaps referring to the cross-walls that stick the gills together. "Sepiarium" is based on a botanical Latin term for "hedge, fence," either an allusion to its habit of growing on structural wood or a reference to the fence-like meandering of the mazed gills.

Cinnabar Polypore   *Pycnoporus cinnabarinus*

CAP To 10 cm across and 7 cm out from tree; fertile surface often flat against the substrate and bending outward to form elongated or semicircular or kidney-shaped caps, tops convex to flat, leathery becoming woody; bright orangish red to red, but sometimes fading in age; dry; slightly roughened and often wrinkled and warty, may be slightly hairy when young but smooth with age; flesh to 1.5 cm thick, leathery or corky, orange or red. PORES Sometimes in multiple layers; orange-red to blood red; 3–4 per mm, to 5 mm deep, walls thinning and tearing with age. ODOUR Not distinctive. TASTE Not distinctive. SPORE PRINT White. STEM Absent. FRUITING Single or several growing together; on usually hardwood logs; summer or autumn.

EDIBILITY Unknown. Too leathery to eat. SIMILAR *Pycnoporellus fulgens* is perhaps even more common in BC than the CINNABAR POLYPORE, especially in the BC Interior. It favours conifer logs as a substrate, its caps are pale orange to rusty, and its pore layer is pale orange. *Pycnoporellus alboluteus*, another close look-alike to the CINNABAR POLYPORE, is somewhat similar to *P. fulgens*, but it has larger pores (1–3 mm wide instead of 2–3 per mm) and tends to stay flat against the substrate, not bending outward to form caps. Its tubes are longer (up to 20 mm instead of up to 6 mm) and are often white at the ends (hence the "albo," meaning "white," in "alboluteus"). COMMENTS CINNABAR POLYPORE is common across the southern half of our province. It is an early-stage, white-rot decomposer that favours freshly dead wood. ◖ Not only is the cap and fertile surface a vivid orange-red, the mycelium in the wood host can also be this colour. ◖ The genus *Pycnoporus* is quite closely related to *Trametes* (p. 386)—in fact, the correct name for the CINNABAR POLYPORE may turn out to be *T. cinnabarina*. ◖ "Pycnoporus" means "densely pored." "Cinnabarinus" is from the Greek word for "cinnabar," a toxic red ore from which mercury was mined and which was also used to make red pigments.

Dyer's Conk   *Phaeolus schweinitzii*

CAP To 30 cm or more across; sometimes growing as a shelf-like conk, but more typically appearing as a clump/rosette of multiple, overlapping, flat or depressed, partly circular caps that arise from a common base attached either to the bottom of a tree or to the tree's roots, the margins often roughened, wavy; yellow-brown, greenish yellow, or orangey, becoming reddish brown to dark brown or black in age, often concentrically zoned with a mix of these colours; dry; densely hairy and sometimes lumpy, and spongy and flexible when young but becoming leathery and eventually dry and brittle in age; flesh in caps to 1.5 cm thick, fibrous, yellowish brown to rusty brown. PORES Decurrent on the stem; yellow or green, sometimes with orange tints, bruising or aging grey, brown, or black; angular, with eroding walls, 1–3 per mm, to 1.5 cm deep. ODOUR Not distinctive. TASTE Somewhat sour. SPORE PRINT White. STEM Present or absent; if present, to 10 cm tall × 5 cm wide; narrowing downward, often rooted; central or off-centre, simple or branched; coloured as cap; hairy. FRUITING Single or in groups (often tiered); usually on the ground at the base of conifer trees and stumps; summer or autumn, the dried fruiting body persisting into the winter or spring.

EDIBILITY Unknown. Perhaps poisonous. SIMILAR The smaller (cap to 12 cm across) **Onnia tomentosa** does not have the array of overlapping caps, its caps are more velvety, and the pore surface is greyish to brown, even when young. COMMENTS DYER'S CONK, widespread throughout our province, is a tree pathogen that causes a red-brown rot that attacks tree heartwood and roots—foresters call it SCHWEINITZII BUTT ROT. ✦ Artisanal dyers eagerly seek out this mushroom, especially younger fruiting bodies. Depending on the pH modifier, mordant, and type of processing, the resulting colours range from green to gold to yellow and sometimes orange and brown. ✦ "Phaeolus" is based on a Greek word for "dark." "Schweinitzii" is in honour of the early American mycologist Lewis David de Schweinitz (1780–1834).

Western Mountain Polypore   *Bondarzewia occidentalis*

CAP Each cap to 20 cm across and 10 cm out from base or substrate; irregular or shaped like a hand fan, convex to flat to concave, caps often clustered into rosettes; yellowish brown to orange-brown when fresh, grey to reddish brown when dry, zoned; dry; smooth; flesh to 7 mm thick at base, corky and watery when fresh, corky and hard when dry, white or cream. **PORES** Cream-coloured, darkening slightly to grey-buff or pink-buff with age; irregular, angular, 1–3 per mm, with thin edges that become eroded. **ODOUR** Uncertain, possibly slightly sweet or nut-like. **TASTE** Uncertain, perhaps bitter in age. **SPORE PRINT** White. **STEM** Sometimes absent with the caps attached to substrate mycelium; if present, to 5 cm tall; colour continuous with caps. **FRUITING** Usually a single compound fruiting body with many caps; on the ground, near the base of a conifer tree or stump; annual, durable, autumn but lasting into winter.

EDIBILITY Edible. Though typically tough and bitter, it has been advertised and sold as "wild MAITAKE." **SIMILAR** *Grifola frondosa*, the real MAITAKE (also called HEN OF THE WOODS), is similar to the WESTERN MOUNTAIN POLYPORE. Rarely found in BC, true MAITAKE has a mass of smaller, thinner, non-zoned, overlapping, laterally attached caps arising from a repeatedly branching base. The BITTER BROWN POLYPORE (p. 381) has an intensely bitter taste and usually has a single velvety cap attached to its stem. **COMMENTS** The WESTERN MOUNTAIN POLYPORE is a white-rot decomposer. ◆ WESTERN MOUNTAIN POLYPORE is not a particularly apt name for this species in our province, where it has been collected mostly near sea level. ◆ Until recently, this species was known as *Bondarzewia mesenterica*. A 2016 study of worldwide species that are lumped under this name broke the one concept into a number of new species. ◆ "Bondarzewia" is in honour of Apollinaris Semenovich Bondartsev (1877–1968), a Russian researcher of wood-decay fungi. "Occidentalis" means "western."

Western Varnished Conk   *Ganoderma oregonense*

CAP To 100 cm across × 20 cm high and projecting up to 40 cm from the substrate, but mostly smaller; shelf-like, semicircular, lobed, convex, concentrically ridged, with a waxy, cracking crust; upper surface dark reddish brown, often with bands of colour (including yellow, white) toward the margins; dry; surface smooth, crust appearing lacquered (though sheen often dulled by spore deposition); flesh to 15 cm thick, soft-fibrous, cream to pale brown. PORES Cream, aging brownish, bruising brown or purplish brown; 2–3 per mm, up to 3 cm deep. ODOUR Not distinctive. TASTE Not distinctive. SPORE PRINT Rusty brown. STEM Usually absent, sometimes with a short lateral stem. FRUITING Single or with conjoined caps or in overlapping groups; on dead conifer trees, logs, and stumps; annual conk, late spring, summer, or autumn.

EDIBILITY Unknown. Too woody. SIMILAR The European and Chinese *Ganoderma lucidum*, sold under the names REISHI and LINGZHI, is considered an important medicinal mushroom. This conk appears now and then in western North America, perhaps as an escapee from mushroom cultivation. It is a hardwood associate and grows like a long tube with an asymmetric flared cap at the end. The RED-BELTED CONK (p. 398) may appear somewhat varnished when young, but it lacks a waxy, cracking crust. COMMENTS The conifer associate *G. tsugae*, which is almost identical except for having a stem (typically, but not always) and perhaps having smaller spores, may be the same species. It is known primarily from eastern North America. ◆ Genetic tests show that the WESTERN VARNISHED CONK that we have in BC is only a distant relative of the REISHI mentioned above. It differs in its chemical signature and may not have the same medicinal properties. ◆ The mycelium of the WESTERN VARNISHED CONK causes a white rot in the conifer it infects. ◆ "Oregonense" means "from Oregon."

Artist's Conk
Ganoderma applanatum

CAP To 50 cm or more across, projecting to 40 cm from substrate; usually semicircular and plate-like, as though a flying saucer had crashed into a tree, convex or depressed, margins thinner; whitish to light brown when young, later dark brown, greyish brown, sometimes black, typically with a whitish margin when still growing, often with a dusting of chocolate-brown spores that resemble cocoa powder; dry; concentrically ridged and sometimes zoned, surface smooth but becoming warty, furrowed, and/or cracked; flesh to 5 cm thick, corky and tough, reddish brown to dark brown. PORES Fertile layer 1–2 cm deep, stratified with red-brown bands between yearly growth; surface white to cream, aging to tan, bruising instantly brown and keeping the bruise; circular, 4–6 per mm. ODOUR Not distinctive. TASTE Not distinctive. SPORE PRINT Brown or rusty brown. STEM Usually absent. FRUITING Single, scattered, or in groups; on living and dead trees, stumps, and logs, most commonly on hardwoods but also on conifers; perennial conk, year-round.

EDIBILITY Edible. But only when ground up as a food additive. SIMILAR The RED-BELTED CONK (p. 398) has pale flesh, a pore layer that does not accept dark marks, and differently coloured bands on its upper surface. The WESTERN VARNISHED CONK (p. 392), a closely related *Ganoderma* that grows on conifers, has a lacquered red-brown crust. COMMENTS ARTIST'S CONK is used in a variety of medicinal compounds and as a flavour enhancer in cooked dishes. ◆ This parasite and decomposer is common throughout BC. The mycelium causes heartwood rot. ◆ The common name ARTIST'S CONK is based on the fact that it is possible to draw on the fertile surface with a fingernail or stylus (as on p. 379). The region darkened by the hard object can remain darker for many years. ◆ The ARTIST'S CONK is one of the world's champion spore producers. It has been estimated that a single conk can, over a 6-month fruiting season, send out 5 trillion spores. Laid end to end, these microscopic spores would circle the globe. ◆ "Ganoderma" means "shining skin," and "applanatum" means "flattened."

White Rot, Brown Rot, and Butt Rot

Some common fungi are parasites on BC trees—they attack and often kill them. Others are decomposers, deriving their nutrition from the dying and dead parts of trees. The distinction between parasite and decomposer roles is not always clear. Certain fungi, for example, will attack live hosts and continue to decompose them after the host dies.

Fungi that interact with trees have been widely studied in BC, mostly because they have important economic effects on trees that might one day be logged for timber. The field that these researchers, surveyors, and foresters work in is usually called "forest health," and their work is designed to reduce the effect of these pathogens on our forests. Of course, a healthy forest requires these parasites and decomposers.

Most of the fungi studied in forest health are polypores, and their fruiting bodies are usually conks or brackets. Others, such as the HONEY MUSHROOM (p. 164) and the RAGGED SPRUCE ROT MUSHROOM (p. 216), are gilled.

Foresters often give these fungi common names that either reflect the damage they cause to trees or the place on the trees where they cause that damage. Some fungi, for example, attack the roots and sometimes lower bole (called the "butt") of trees. A few examples: *Armillaria ostoyae*, which we have called HONEY MUSHROOM in this book, foresters call ARMILLARIA ROOT DISEASE; *Coniferiporia sulphurascens*,

a relatively inconspicuous crust fungus, foresters call LAMINATED ROOT ROT; and *Phaeolus schweinitzii* (facing page), which we call DYER'S CONK (p. 390), foresters call SCHWEINITZII BUTT ROT (though mycologists talking to school groups have been known to use the foresters' name, purely for effect).

Fungi that rot the main trunk of trees are generally divided into "white rots" and "brown rots." Brown-rot fungi decay the white cellulose and hemicellulose, but not the lignin, leaving behind brown wood (pictured below). As the wood is broken down, the lignin component often dries and shrinks into stacked cubical structures. White-rot fungi break down the other major structural component of trees, the brown lignin (and varying amounts of cellulose), leaving the remaining wood white. These two kinds of rot are reflected in the names that foresters use. The fungus we call RED-BELTED CONK (p. 398) is known to foresters as BROWN CRUMBLY ROT, CONIFER SULPHUR SHELF (p. 403) is BROWN CUBICAL ROT, AGARIKON (p. 396) is BROWN TRUNK ROT, and the ARTIST'S CONK (p. 393) is WHITE MOTTLED ROT.

Forest managers may struggle with the activities of these fungi, but they recognize that fungi are important for decaying wood in BC's forests, creating habitat for other organisms, and eventually returning tree nutrients to forest soils to be recycled. For more information, see *Common Tree Diseases of British Columbia* (Natural Resources Canada, 1996) by Eric Allen, Duncan Morrison, and Gordon Wallis (the pdf of the book is available online).

Brown rot.

Agarikon   *Laricifomes officinalis*

CAP To 25 cm across × 40 cm or more high; hoof-shaped becoming columnar, margins rounded; pale yellowish at first, then chalky white, sometimes becoming grey, often with a covering of green algae; dry; smooth becoming cracked and/ or furrowed with age; flesh to 10 cm thick, white, when young the texture of cheese, crumbly with age. PORES Individual layers to 2 cm thick, stratified; fertile surface white, aging pale brown; 1–4 per mm. ODOUR Farinaceous. TASTE Very bitter. SPORE PRINT White. STEM Absent. FRUITING Single to a few; on conifer trees (living and dead) and stumps, usually in old-growth forests; perennial conk, year-round.

EDIBILITY Not edible. Possibly somewhat poisonous. SIMILAR While still hoof-shaped, AGARIKON can resemble the RED-BELTED CONK (p. 398). When it becomes columnar, it can resemble the columnar form of the TINDER CONK (p. 402). AGARIKON's chalky-white surface and flesh and its extremely bitter taste (the source of its alternate common name, QUININE CONK) set it apart. COMMENTS AGARIKON has a long history of use as a religious and medicinal mushroom in Asia, Europe, and North America. First Nations groups in BC and the US Pacific Northwest, some of whom called it "ghost bread," carved the conks and used them in shamanistic rites. ⬥ AGARIKON has traditionally been used to treat asthma, cough, and stomach and lung ailments. ⬥ Conks of this polypore are found in southern BC and Haida Gwaii. The old giants, which can live for up to 75 years, are becoming increasingly rare—if you find one, please do not harvest it. ⬥ The mycelium causes a brown rot in standing trees. ⬥ *Laricifomes officinalis* was previously called *Fomitopsis officinalis*, but genetic studies show that it belongs to a separate and more ancient lineage of polypores. ⬥ "Laricifomes" means "larch *Fomes*" (a genus of conks), and 2 BC references do report this species as most common on WESTERN LARCH, though it is also found on other conifers. "Officinalis" means "used in medicine."

Rosy Conk   *Rhodofomes cajanderi*

CAP To 15 cm across and projecting to 7 cm; hoof- to plate-shaped with a wavy margin, or sometimes flattened against a log or tree trunk; shades of pink, becoming pinkish brown and eventually black (but margins remaining pink while still growing), often concentrically zonate; dry; hairy, becoming smooth with age; flesh thin (to 1 cm), pink to pinkish brown, soft at first and then becoming corky. PORES To 2 cm deep, stratified; rosy pink becoming reddish brown in age; 3–5 per mm. ODOUR Not distinctive. TASTE Not distinctive. SPORE PRINT White. STEM Absent. FRUITING Single or in groups, sometimes stacked like shelves; on dead trees, usually conifers, but occasionally on hardwoods, often on the cut ends of logs; perennial conk, year-round.

   EDIBILITY Not edible. Too tough. SIMILAR The smaller (to 6 cm across) *Leptoporus mollis* conk has a fleshier, softer pink cap and a maze-like pore layer that is white to purplish. COMMENTS The ROSY CONK is one of the most colourful and beautiful of our tree conks, though the intense rosy pink colours may fade a bit in age. To ROSY CONK's natural beauty, nature has added jewels—young, wet conks can be bedecked with glistening red-brown drops of exuded liquid. ☙ ROSY CONK is widespread in southern BC. ☙ This conk is listed as *Fomitopsis cajanderi* in most references. The 2013 genetic study that moved it to *Rhodofomes* noted that it and the *Fomitopsis* species are too distantly related to be placed in the same genus without disturbing a lot of other established genus names. ☙ The ROSY CONK is a parasite and brown-rot decomposer. ☙ "Rhodofomes" means "red *Fomes*" (a traditional genus name for conks), and "cajanderi" honours Aimo Kaarlo Cajander (1879–1943), botanist, forester, and prime minister of Finland before and at the start of WWII.

Red-belted Conk   *Fomitopsis mounceae*

CAP To 40 cm across and 20 cm out from the tree; knob-like or tube-like when very young, becoming hoof-shaped or plate-shaped, hard, and tough, margins rounded; cream to yellowish when young, developing orange or reddish colours over the upper surface that become reddish brown or even black, with a typical colour banding (from the substrate outward) of black with greyish patches, then grey and black and red-brown interspersed, then a red-brown belt (the source of the common name), then a yellow band, then whitish at the margin; dry; smooth but becoming concentrically ridged with age, sometimes appearing slightly varnished; flesh to 12 cm thick, woody, cream or pinkish or yellowish, sometimes bruising pink when fresh. PORES Cream or pale yellow, aging light brown but not bruising dark brown when scratched; tiny, circular, 3–5 per mm. ODOUR Often notable, a sharp smell described with words such as tobaccoish, lemon-like, acidic. TASTE Bitter or sour or not distinctive. SPORE PRINT Pale yellow or cream. STEM Absent. FRUITING Single or in groups; occasionally on living trees, but mostly on dead trees and stumps and logs, usually conifers, but also TREMBLING ASPEN and birch; perennial conk, year-round.

EDIBILITY Not edible. SIMILAR The cap of *Fomitopsis ochracea* has duller grey to brown bands and occasionally a dark orange-brown band at the margin. Its pore layer often recedes from the edges and is surrounded by an extended cap margin. COMMENTS Until recently, these widespread, common brown-rot pathogens/decomposers went under the name *Fomitopsis pinicola*. This name, however, is now known to embrace at least 4 distinct species, 2 of which occur in BC. • "Mounceae" honours Irene Mounce (1894–1987), who in the 1930s studied the fungal decomposers of airplane-grade SITKA SPRUCE on Haida Gwaii. Following this, she worked at Saanichton's Dominion Laboratory of Plant Pathology from 1942 to 1945, resigning at age 50 because she got married—employment of married women in federal public service was forbidden in Canada until 1955.

Birch Conk   *Fomitopsis betulina*

CAP To 25 cm across and 15 cm out from the tree; ovoid at first, then hoof-shaped or like a semicircular or kidney-shaped plate, convex to more or less flat, hard to the touch when dry, margins rounded, inrolled, and projecting below the pore surface in parts; whitish to light brown or greyish brown or light reddish brown; dry; covered with a smooth, suede-like surface that fractures into patches to reveal the white flesh underneath; flesh to 5 cm thick, tough becoming corky, white. PORES To 1 cm thick; white aging pale brown; with pore sides splitting and clumping to give a tooth-like appearance, 2–4 per mm. ODOUR Pleasant. TASTE Somewhat sour or bitter. SPORE PRINT White. STEM Present or absent; if present, to 6 cm tall × 5 cm wide; lateral, as an extension of the cap; white to brown; smooth. FRUITING Single or in small groups; on trunks of birch trees; annual, spring, summer, autumn, old conks at times persisting to the next season.

EDIBILITY Not edible. Too tough to bother with. SIMILAR If it grows on birch and it is large, whitish, and rounded, it can only be a BIRCH CONK. COMMENTS The BIRCH CONK is a brown-rot fungus that probably kills living birch and certainly decomposes dead and fallen birch wood. It infects living trees through wounds such as broken branch stubs and may lie dormant for years, until stresses such as drought or shading weaken the birch, allowing the BIRCH CONK to overcome the tree's defences and kill it. ● Within its BC range, which corresponds to the range of PAPER BIRCH, it is a common mushroom. ● The BIRCH CONK has a long history as a folk medicine, being employed as an anti-inflammatory, a pain reliever, an antiseptic, and a dewormer. Ötzi the Iceman's 5,400-year-old stash of survival gear included 2 BIRCH CONKS, possibly as a medication (see essay on p. 400). ● Studies indicate that the BIRCH CONK serves as a major host for insects and arthropods, providing food and breeding sites for hundreds of species. ● *Fomitopsis betulina* is also known as *Piptoporus betulinus*. ● "Betulina" means "pertaining to birch."

Medicinal Mushrooms

The nature-embalmed mummy of Iceman Ötzi was found on the Italian-Austrian border of the Alps in September 1991. He had been dead for some time—perhaps as long as 5,400 years. Among his preserved possessions were a pair of polypores: tinder material from the TINDER CONK (p. 402) and two BIRCH CONKS (p. 399) with thongs through them (pictured below). Ötzi probably carried tinder from TINDER CONK as part of his elaborate fire-starting kit. The BIRCH CONK, which has a long history of use in Europe for treating worms, cancer, and stomach ailments, may have served the Iceman as a medicine.

Members of the kingdom Fungi, under continual attack from bacteria, viruses, protists, other fungi, plants, and animals, have developed an arsenal of compounds to defend themselves. Some of these fungal weapons, when applied to the war against human diseases, have been employed as immunosuppressants, antibiotics, anticancer drugs, psychedelics, and cholesterol inhibitors. Other compounds derived from fungi may help us avoid illness in the first place by strengthening our natural immune systems.

Western medical practice has tended to hold treatments using mushrooms at arm's length. Broad, peer-reviewed, controlled studies of the medical effects of fungi are thin on the ground in mainstream biomedical journals. Non-Western health and healing practices, such as traditional Chinese medicine, make more use of mushrooms, employing them fresh, dried, powdered (sometimes in capsules), and in teas and tinctures.

Two BC polypores are commonly employed to enhance the human immune system and to provide adjuvant therapy for cancer patients. Their most effective

Iceman Ötzi's BIRCH CONKS.

ingredients are believed to be complex beta-glucan polysaccharides. The REISHI or LINGZHI mushroom (the Japanese and Chinese names for polypores in the *Ganoderma lucidum* complex) has a long Asian history as a cancer treatment, energy enhancer, and aging antagonist. Though *G. lucidum* may not be present in BC, its more common relative, the WESTERN VARNISHED CONK (p. 392), has been employed in a similar fashion. TURKEY TAIL (p. 386), referred to in Japanese as KAWARATAKE and in Chinese as YUN ZHI, is also used to strengthen the immune system in cancer patients, and it can be found throughout BC. In both cases, these polypores can be made into teas or extracts that are taken orally.

A number of other BC species have Western traditions as medicinal mushrooms. LION'S MANE (p. 339), in addition to its role as a delicious edible, has been promoted for many medical uses, including as an antioxidant, an immune system booster, and a brain neuron growth factor. CHAGA (p. 405) has been used for centuries to boost immune system health. AGARIKON (p. 396) has been used to treat asthma, cough, and stomach and lung ailments. Species in the *Psilocybe* genus of magic mushrooms (pp. 310 and 311) are currently under clinical investigation for their use in treating depression, addictions, OCD (obsessive-compulsive disorder), and PTSD (post-traumatic stress disorder).

If you are considering using these or other mushrooms as medicines, you should familiarize yourself with their potential risks as well as benefits. For more information on medicinal use of mushrooms and contraindications, you could also check out *The Fungal Pharmacy* by Robert Rogers (North Atlantic Books, 2011) and *Healing Mushrooms* by Tero Isokauppila (Avery, 2017).

LION'S MANE (*Hericium erinaceus*), p. 339.

Tinder Conk
Fomes fomentarius

CAP To 15 cm across × 15 cm high, projecting to 20 cm from substrate, occasionally larger; hoof-shaped, bumpy, and woody; silvery grey to grey-brown to grey-black, the margins cream to light brown; dry; minutely hairy when young, but developing a smooth, hard crust in age that is horizontally grooved in concentric rings (representing growth years) and that often hangs lower than the pore layer; flesh to 2 cm thick, corky and spongy, brown to yellow-brown but sometimes white-mottled. PORES Tube layer thick (to 7 cm), stratified; pale brown to golden brown, bruising darker; pores round, small with thick edges, and dense (4–5 per mm), sometimes packed with white mycelium. ODOUR Pleasantly fungal, some say like bananas. TASTE Bitter. SPORE PRINT White to pale yellow. STEM Absent. Conk broadly attached to its substrate. FRUITING Single to a few; on hardwoods (living and dead), most commonly birches; perennial conk, present year-round and with new growth in the autumn.

EDIBILITY Not edible. Too woody. SIMILAR Mushrooms in the ***Phellinus igniarius* group**, which are also hardwood-infecting, white-rot conks that can be used as tinder, are more shelf-like. Their caps are typically black and cracked, and their flesh is dark brown with whitish streaks. RED-BELTED CONK (p. 398) and AGARIKON (p. 396) and *Fomitopsis ochracea* (discussed on p. 398) might also be compared. COMMENTS The spongy inner tissue of TINDER CONK, called "amadou," makes an excellent medium for catching the spark from flint and steel, especially after being soaked in saltpetre and dried. The use of this conk as a fire starter goes back many thousands of years (see essay on medicinal mushrooms, p. 400). Amadou can also be hammered into a felt to make handsome bags and hats. ◦ Acting as both a parasite and a decomposer, the mycelium of the TINDER CONK produces a white rot in wood. ◦ The genus name and the species epithet are somewhat redundant: "fomes" means "tinder," and "fomentarius" means "used for tinder."

Conifer Sulphur Shelf — *Laetiporus conifericola*

CAP To 40 cm across; roughly semicircular shelves, sometimes shaped like a hand fan, flat to concave, the margins somewhat rounded and wavy, sometimes lobed; bright yellow to orange or salmon, sometimes faintly zoned, margins often yellow and in age fading to whitish; dry to moist; smooth or finely hairy, often wrinkled or radially furrowed; flesh to 2 cm thick, soft and often watery when young, crumbly with age, whitish to pale yellow, becoming yellow. PORES Bright yellow, bruising darker, tan in age; round, 2–4 per mm. ODOUR Often pleasant, nut-like. TASTE Pleasant, but sometimes sour with age. SPORE PRINT White. STEM Absent, or with a lateral, stem-like narrowed base. FRUITING Occasionally single but usually in overlapping shelves; on conifer trunks, stumps, and logs; annual, summer or autumn.

EDIBILITY Edible. Tasty when young; when older, somewhat tough and bitter. A few eaters have had bad allergic reactions to western North American *Laetiporus* species, especially to *L. gilbertsonii*. SIMILAR If the conk is growing on hardwood, you may have found the almost identical *L. gilbertsonii*, which is not common in BC. COMMENTS The CONIFER SULPHUR SHELF, certainly one of our most strikingly beautiful polypores, is a brown-rot fungus that probably acts as both a parasite and a decomposer. DNA analysis shows that it has close genetic relationships to *Fomitopsis*, *Pycnoporellus*, and *Phaeolus* species. ◆ Later in the season you may find corpses—rotten, whitish, chalky remnants of the fruiting body—on the ground at the tree base. ◆ The texture and taste of CONIFER SULPHUR SHELF have inspired its other common name, CHICKEN OF THE WOODS. The scientific name was once thought to be *L. sulphureus*, but this older name was found to harbour several distinct species. ◆ "Laetiporus" means "bright-pored," and "conifericola" means "living around conifers," both excellent descriptors.

Conifer Maze Conk *Porodaedalea pini* group

CAP To 20 cm across and 15 cm out from tree; roughly semicircular, plate-like to hoof-shaped, convex to flat, with a sharp margin; reddish brown becoming blackish in age, the margin usually paler; dry; surface roughened and somewhat hairy, concentrically grooved in age, sometimes cracked; flesh to 1 cm thick, tough, yellowish brown to reddish brown. **PORES** Stratified, each layer to 6 mm; yellow-brown or rusty brown, aging brown; angular or maze-like, 2–4 per mm. **ODOUR** Not distinctive. **TASTE** Not distinctive. **SPORE PRINT** Pale brown. **STEM** Absent. **FRUITING** Single or in a shingled array; on trunks of living conifers and recently fallen conifer logs; perennial, year-round.

EDIBILITY Not edible. Too woody. **SIMILAR** The pores of mushrooms in the *Heterobasidion annosum* **group** can be somewhat maze-like, but the pore surface is cream-coloured and often spreads out over the substrate like a crust. The caps are a roughened brown to blackish, but smaller (projecting to 9 cm). **COMMENTS** CONIFER MAZE CONK and its close relatives—among the world's most significant wood-decay fungi—were at one time included in the genus *Phellinus*. The genus name *Phellinus* was eventually reserved for hardwood rotters, and the conifer decomposers were assigned to *Porodaedalea* and other genera, turning the BC species into *Porodaedalea pini*. The name changes may not be over: we seem to have a number of cryptic species in BC, none of which appear to be the European *P. pini*. ◆ We call *P. pini* CONIFER MAZE CONK, but foresters refer to it as RED RING ROT because a cross-section of infected heartwood taken in the early stages of decay can feature a well-defined ring of red staining. ◆ "Porodaedalea" means "with maze-like pores." In Greek mythology, Daedelus was the architect and builder of the labyrinth constructed to house the minotaur. "Pini" means "on pine."

Chaga   *Inonotus obliquus*

CAP Sterile portion to 30 cm across and high, extending to 10 cm from trunk, developing under the bark and bursting through the bark; irregular in shape, deeply cracked, and black, giving it the look of charcoal, the surface easily flaking off; the seldom-observed fertile stage to 5 mm thick, crust-like, dark brown, and growing under bark near the sterile portion or sometimes, after the tree falls, on the ground; dry; flesh in sterile portion thick, corky, yellowish brown, faintly zoned. **PORES** White becoming dark brown or reddish brown; often angular and elongated, slanting obliquely, 6–8 per mm. **ODOUR** Not distinctive. **TASTE** Not distinctive. **SPORE PRINT** White. **STEM** Absent.

FRUITING Single usually, or small groups; on bark of living and recently dead PAPER BIRCH, rarely on BLACK COTTONWOOD; usually perennial; year-round.

EDIBILITY Edible. But only as an infusion or ground up as a food additive. **SIMILAR** Mushrooms in the *Phellinus igniarius* **group** can also be black and also grow on birch and other hardwoods, but they form more distinct shelves and have a brown pore layer on the underside. **COMMENTS** The obvious cankers on birch trunks are sterile structures formed of fungal and tree tissues. The actual fruiting structure is a crustose layer of pores, produced under the bark of recently dead trees. These pore layers are consumed by beetles, who may disperse CHAGA spores by flying away and burrowing through the bark of other trees, carrying the spores with them. ☙ It is both a parasite and decomposer—even a single CHAGA conk indicates extensive heartwood decay. ☙ The sterile conks of this mushroom have a long history of use as a folk medicine (often prepared as a tea) and are studied by modern researchers for anticancer and immunotherapy potential. ☙ The common name CHAGA is borrowed from a Russian word for the conk. "Inonotus" is a compound of Greek words for "fibre, sinew" and "ear." "Obliquus" means "slanting sideways," referring to the pores on the fertile portion.

Veiled Polypore *Cryptoporus volvatus*

CAP To 8 cm across; spherical to ovoid and often slightly flattened or hoof-like, margins extended to cover the pore surface, in age with (usually) a single hole on the underside; white or pale yellow or tan, drying reddish brown; dry; with a thin glazed coating that breaks up into plates; flesh thick (to 2 cm), rubbery, tough, white. **PORES** White becoming pinkish or brown; 3–4 per mm, 3–5 mm deep; enclosed within the cap, not visible externally. **ODOUR** Slightly fragrant or not distinctive. **TASTE** Slightly bitter. **SPORE PRINT** White to cream or pinkish. **STEM** Absent. Basal mycelium often rooted in insect tunnels. **FRUITING** Single, scattered, or in large groups; on dying or recently dead conifer trunks; annual conk with long-lasting caps, late spring, summer, or autumn.

EDIBILITY Not edible. Too tough. **SIMILAR** Young caps of the VEILED POLYPORE can resemble puffballs, such as the **GEMMED PUFFBALL** (p. 423), even to the extent of developing holes for dispersing the enclosed spores. No puffballs, however, grow on trees. **COMMENTS** The mycelium of the VEILED POLYPORE causes a soft rot in the sapwood of conifers. This rotter, common and widespread throughout BC, often shows up while the trees are still alive and continues its work of decay after the tree's death. ◆ The thick, uninterrupted covering over the bottom of the conk prevents the pore layer from drying out. The hole that allows the spores to exit is often chewed open by insects, especially by bark beetles, who take up residence in the polypore, using it as a food source and mating chamber. VEILED POLYPORES and bark beetles have a mutualistic relationship: in return for food and shelter, the beetles carry the spores with them when they burrow into new trees to create brood tunnels. The bark beetles, in turn, kill new trees, which are then decayed by the VEILED POLYPORE. ◆ "Cryptoporus" is a Greek compound for "hidden pore." "Volvatus" means "with a covering, wrapped," probably a reference to the way the pores are initially covered.

Red Paint Fungus
Echinodontium tinctorium

CAP To 30 cm across, 15 cm thick; hoof- to plate-shaped, typically growing on trunks beneath large branches, upper surface hard, crusty, often cracked, and hairy; blackish unless the brick-red flesh is showing through; dry; flesh to 5 cm thick, woody, orange-red to (usually) brick red. **PORES** Splitting (except at the margin) into long (to 2 cm), flat or cylindrical, and blunt teeth; brittle; buff becoming greyish or black. **ODOUR** Not distinctive. **TASTE** Not distinctive. **SPORE PRINT** White. **STEM** Absent. **FRUITING** Single to a few; on living or recently dead conifers (especially hemlocks and true firs); perennial conk, year-round.

EDIBILITY Not edible. Too woody. **SIMILAR** From a distance, the conk bears a distinct resemblance to body parts of a Sasquatch sticking out from behind a tree. **COMMENTS** RED PAINT FUNGUS, most commonly found in BC's inland temperate rainforest, is also found at higher elevations on the coast. ◆ Though the fruiting body is not a common find, the mycelium of this conk is one of the major sources of heart rot in BC true firs (*Abies* spp.) and hemlocks. It enters trees through small branches and can remain dormant for decades. ◆ Burned and powdered RED PAINT FUNGUS has been used as a red pigment for paint by a number of First Nations in BC, including the Haida, Secwépemc, and Kwakwaka'wakw. The conk itself does not grow in Haida Gwaii—the Haida apparently imported it from the Tsimshian. The powdered conk was mixed with other media such as pitch, grease, or salmon eggs before being applied to wood, hides, or faces. It is still valued by modern artisanal dyers for its orange and brown tints. ◆ RED PAINT FUNGUS traces its evolutionary roots back to the ancestors of russulas. ◆ "Echinodontium" means "spiny-toothed," and "tinctorium" means "used for dyeing."

Earth Fan
Thelephora terrestris group

CAP To 5 cm across; vase-shaped or like overlapping folding fans, sometimes in large clusters with partially fused caps to 10 cm or more across and sometimes shelf-like, the margin smooth when young but fringed and splitting in age; brown, reddish brown, greyish brown, to chocolate brown, with sometimes-indistinct concentric bands, margins often whitish, the whole surface darkening with age; dry; finely hairy or scaly above, the fertile underside smooth or irregularly wrinkled, sometimes with irregular nipple-like bumps; flesh thin (3 mm thick), tough, coloured as surface. ODOUR Not distinctive. TASTE Not distinctive. SPORE PRINT Purple-brown. STEM Absent or, if present, to 7 cm tall; central or lateral; flesh tough; coloured as cap; dry. FRUITING Usually in clusters; on the ground, on rotting wood, on woody stems, or directly on tree roots; usually under forest conifers, but also found in pots and greenhouse soil where conifer seedlings are grown; fruiting mainly in summer and autumn, but can be present year-round.

EDIBILITY Not edible. SIMILAR STINKING EARTH FAN (*Thelephora palmata*) is almost as common in BC as the EARTH FAN and has a fruiting body composed of branching, flattened, brown to purplish fronds with white tips. When fresh, it typically has a much stronger odour than the EARTH FAN, the smell fetid, like rotting cabbage or garlic. COMMENTS In BC, we have a common *Thelephora*, found in young forest stands and disturbed soils, that we currently call *T. terrestris*, but it is not the same as the European species with that name. We also have an unknown number of less common *Thelephora* species, typically found in mature forest stands, that may one day need new names. ● Even though EARTH FAN favours habitats that have rotting wood, such as old stumps, it is mycorrhizal and has been tested as an inoculant to promote the growth of conifer seedlings. ● "Thelephora" means "having a nipple" (referring to nipple-like outgrowths on the fruiting surface), and "terrestris" means "growing on the ground."

Jelly Rot

Phlebia tremellosa

FRUITING BODY Somewhat circular (to 5 cm), spread-out patches on wood substrates, the patches joining together to cover large (to 25 cm × 10 cm) areas; part of the patches sometimes bent away from the substrate to form shelves that may be 5 cm across, 2.5 cm out from the substrate, and 3 mm thick; white to yellowish or pinkish orange, sometimes lightly zoned, and with translucent or whitish or yellowish edges; the upper surface of shelves densely hairy, the edges of the shelves waxy and wavy; the flesh in the caps gelatinous to cartilaginous; the fertile surfaces facing outward from the wood surface and under the caps gelatinous, soft, and waxy, pale orange to orange-red but aging/drying blood red, with narrow radiating folds and ridges that can form shallow, long-rectangular, radially aligned depressions ("false pores") (1–2 per mm). **ODOUR** Not distinctive. **TASTE** Not distinctive. **SPORE PRINT** Whitish. **FRUITING** Single or in groups (often run together); on stumps, branches, and trunks of trees, usually hardwoods, occasionally conifers; year-round, but producing spores in late summer, autumn, winter.

    EDIBILITY Unknown. **SIMILAR** *Phlebia radiata* (inset photo) resembles JELLY ROT in its spread-out stage, but it does not go on to form caps, and its radiating, bumpy, furrowed ridges do not usually create structures that resemble false pores. **NETTED CRUST** (p. 410) does share JELLY ROT's habit of forming caps, but NETTED CRUST is usually a lighter colour (white to nearer pink or yellow or orange) and it grows more consistently on the undersides of branches. **COMMENTS** JELLY ROT and other *Phlebia* species are white-rot fungi. They have been found to be effective decomposers that may one day play a role in mycoremediation, cleaning up polluted environments by using fungi to break down toxic biochemicals. ☙ "Phlebia" means "veined" (referring to the fertile underside). "Tremellosa" means "trembling"—the caps can vibrate like jelly if struck.

Netted Crust
Byssomerulius corium

FRUITING BODY On horizontal surfaces, spread out like paint (typically as a sheet up to 10 cm × 5 cm), and often attached to the underside of twigs and branches, in maturity growing away from the substrate to form narrow shelf-like caps that project up to 2 cm and are up to 5 mm thick, the upper surfaces of the caps often zoned and/or woolly and the outer edges of the caps often fringed, the undersides of the caps (the spread-out surface) smoother at first, then later warty, with the bumps growing into each other to form distinctive reticulations and shallow pore-like pits; the spread-out surface white at first and then often pinkish tan, sometimes yellowish or orange, the caps white or grey or green (from algae) above and cream or coloured like the spread-out surface below; the flesh of the spread-out surface very thin (less than 1 mm), soft to firm, pliant, whitish. **ODOUR** Not distinctive. **TASTE** Not distinctive. **SPORE PRINT** White. **FRUITING** Single or in groups that sometimes run together; on bark or wood of hardwood (and sometimes conifer) branches and twigs; year-round, but producing spores in late summer, autumn.

EDIBILITY Unknown. **SIMILAR** The top surfaces of **JELLY ROT** (p. 409) tend to be a deeper orange, and the underside of the caps has larger, radiating, pink-orange false pores. **COMMENTS** The **NETTED CRUST** is a common and widespread white-rot fungus, known from every continent except Antarctica. ◦ "Bysso" derives from the name in Greek of a type of fine linen cloth, possibly a reference to the wrinkled and ridged surfaces of the species. "Merulius" is a closely related genus of crust fungus and was once the genus name of the **NETTED CRUST**. "Corium" means "skin, hide, leather," perhaps a description of the thin fruiting body.

Jelly Fungi

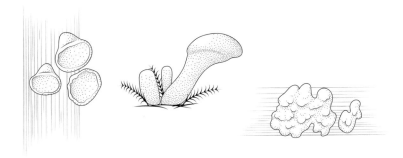

Whoever spends time with mushrooms eventually becomes a bit jaded to strangeness—there is so much of it in the kingdom Fungi. The jelly fungi, however, are beyond strange and can usually awaken a sense of wonder. What are we to make of fungal bodies that have the consistency of jelly? That dry out and reconstitute like mosses? That have the shape of brains and blobs?

On the fungal family tree, the groups to which almost all the jellies belong are early offshoots from the basidiomycete branch. For more than a century, taxonomists laboured to put them into a single evolutionary branch, calling them heterobasidiomycetes. Through genetic studies, we have learned that jelly fungi belong to several independent branches: the orders Auriculariales (*Auricularia*, *Guepinia*, *Pseudohydnum*), Dacrymycetales (*Calocera*, *Dacrymyces*, *Heterotextus*), and Tremellales (*Tremella*). We also include here a member of the genus *Ascocoryne*, a representative of the comparatively few ascomycetes that have evolved jelly-like characteristics.

Our jelly fungi are for the most part wood decomposers, but jelly fungi in the genus *Tremella* parasitize other fungi. The jelly-like fruiting bodies are almost always organs of sexual reproduction. A number of these species have significant and widely studied asexual phases, but these are usually too small to note in the field.

Above all, jelly fungi can be fun—fun to poke, fun to flick with your finger, fun to rub on your skin, fun to discover with a group of children. It's almost as though these mushrooms invite us to set the science aside, step back, and think about what it is that attracts so many of us to the world of fungi.

In this section, you may note, we have omitted the EDIBILITY category. With the possible exception of the WESTERN JELLY EAR (but see anticoagulant warning on p. 417), the eating story is the same for all of the jelly fungi discussed here: they are not toxic, but neither are they interesting. They have no flavour and they take up no flavours from what they are cooked with. Some of them are so watery, in fact, that they turn to liquid when cooked.

Witch's Butter   *Dacrymyces chrysospermus*

FRUITING BODY Masses to 6 cm across × 4 cm high; individuals are initially cup-, lens-, plate-, or hand-fan-shaped bodies that are clustered, stemless or with a stem, coalescing into brain-like blobs; orange to yellow, drying orange-red; sometimes with hairs on stem and cap base; usually moist; flesh firm-gelatinous, sometimes liquefying in age, same colour as the surface. **STEM** Present or absent; arising from a whitish rooting base. **ODOUR** Not distinctive. **TASTE** Not distinctive. **SPORE PRINT** Orange. **FRUITING** Single, in groups, or in clustered masses; on decaying wood (logs, stumps) of conifers, but occasionally on hardwood; year-round, whenever it is wet enough.

SIMILAR See **HARDWOOD WITCH'S BUTTER** (p. 413) for a look-alike in the genus *Tremella*. There are also a number of small *Dacrymyces* species that might be confused with **WITCH'S BUTTER**. The one most often reported in BC is **D. stillatus.** When growing individually, specimens of *D. stillatus* are up to 4 mm across, sometimes have a small stem (not a white rooting base), and are cushion-shaped but occasionally disc- or cup-shaped. They can merge into amorphous brain-shaped masses up to 2 cm across, however, making them resemble a smaller **WITCH'S BUTTER**. **COMMENTS** Folk traditions have given the name "witch's butter" to different brain-shaped and blob-like fungi, ranging in colour from black to gold. The English natural philosopher John Glanvill (1636–80), in his posthumous collection of folk tales about witches and the supernatural, recounts how certain witches have cat-like companions that, when fetching food for their owners, "fill themselves so full, sometimes, that they are forced to spew by the way, which spewing is found… not far from the house of those Witches. It is of a yellow colour like Gold, and is called *Butter of Witches*." ◆ You may find *D. chrysospermus* listed as *D. palmatus* in older guides. ◆ **WITCH'S BUTTER** causes a brown rot in decaying wood. ◆ "Dacrymyces" means "weeping mushroom," and "chrysospermus" means "golden-spored."

Hardwood Witch's Butter   *Tremella mesenterica*

FRUITING BODY Masses to 10 cm across × 4 cm high; brain-like when young, becoming more like clusters of folded leaves in age; usually bright orange to golden yellow, paler in age, drying darker; smooth, shiny; flesh is soft-gelatinous, hardening somewhat when dry. **STEM** Absent. **ODOUR** Not distinctive. **TASTE** Not distinctive. **SPORE PRINT** Colourless to yellow or orange. **FRUITING** Single or in small groups; usually on or around species of the crust fungus *Peniophora* that are growing on decaying hardwood logs and sticks, especially alder; spring, summer, autumn.

    SIMILAR *Tremella mesenterica* and the closely related *T. mesenterella* (the main difference between them being spore shape) look quite similar to WITCH'S BUTTER (p. 412). There are clear indications which is which under a microscope—the *Dacrymyces* has tuning-fork-like basidia and spores divided into sections, and the *Tremella* has basidia divided into sections and non-sectioned spores. In the field, it helps to know that the tremellas do not have white rooting bases and are always found on hardwoods. *Dacrymyces* species decay wood, but the mycelia of *Tremella* species are parasites on other fungi. In the case of HARDWOOD WITCH'S BUTTER, the host is an inconspicuous crust fungus (genus *Peniophora*) on the same wood. If the tremella is parasitizing *Stereum* species (such as FALSE TURKEY TAIL, p. 387), it is ***Naematelia aurantia*** (the new name for *T. aurantia*) when it is bright yellow to pale yellow to yellow-orange and *N. encephala* (the new name for *T. encephala*) when it is yellow-brown to cinnamon. **COMMENTS** Basidiospores of HARDWOOD WITCH'S BUTTER germinate to produce a budding yeast phase. When mating hormones encourage yeasts of compatible mating types to come together, the conjoined yeasts form a primordium beneath the bark that produces the conspicuous orange fruiting bodies. "Tremella" is based on a Latin word for "trembling." "Mesenterica" means "middle intestine," presumably an interpretation of what the fruiting body resembles.

Alpine Jelly Cone   *Heterotextus alpinus*

FRUITING BODY To 1 cm across and high; cup- or cone-shaped, top concave or convex, orientation sometimes upright, sometimes sideways or hanging; yellow to orange, drying reddish orange; gelatinous; spore-bearing surface above smooth and sometimes with small folds and undulations, sterile surface below ribbed and/or bumpy on sides, margins sometimes with scalloping corresponding to the ribs. STEM Short, just a narrowing where base is attached to the substrate; central rather than off-centre. ODOUR Not distinctive. TASTE Not distinctive. SPORE PRINT Yellowish. FRUITING Scattered or in dense groups; on barkless conifer wood (sticks, logs, stumps); most common in spring, also in summer and autumn.

SIMILAR The less common *Heterotextus luteus* tends to be a little smaller (to 8 mm); otherwise, the main difference is in the number of sections that the spores are divided into. WITCH'S BUTTER and its similar species (p. 412), though gelatinous and yellow, do not have the distinct cone shape with ribbed/bumpy outer surfaces. YELLOW FAIRY CUPS (p. 462) are much smaller (to 3 mm) and not gelatinous. COMMENTS You may find this mushroom listed as *Guepiniopsis alpina* in some guides. • ALPINE JELLY CONE, a basidiomycete and wood rotter, is sometimes abundant near melting snowbanks at high elevations—hence the "alpinus" in the scientific name—but it can be found right down to sea level. • Although occasionally found in Europe and Asia, this mushroom is primarily a species of western North and South America. It is common over most of BC. • "Heterotextus" means "differently woven or textured," possibly a reference to the contrast between the smooth upper surface and the ribbed lower surface.

Small Staghorn

Calocera cornea

FRUITING BODY Short, to 2 cm high × 2 mm across; simple and cylindrical, sometimes bulbous at the base, circular in cross-section, the tips blunt or pointed or (very rarely) forking; yellow to orange-yellow, drying a reddish brown; smooth; flesh firm-gelatinous, same colour as surface. **STEM** Absent or rudimentary (see below). **ODOUR** Not distinctive. **TASTE** Not distinctive. **SPORE PRINT** White. **FRUITING** Single, in groups, or clustered; usually on barkless hardwood logs, occasionally on conifers; mainly late summer and autumn, but any time it is wet enough.

SIMILAR If the mushroom looks like SMALL STAGHORN but is taller (to 10 cm), is more branched (often 2–3 times), and grows on conifer wood, it is probably *Calocera viscosa* (inset photo). The GOLDEN FAIRY CLUB (p. 354) is also taller (to 7 cm), is non-gelatinous, and grows in soil/duff. **COMMENTS** The mycelium of this wood decomposer causes a brown rot. ◦ With its upright, single-shaft growth, SMALL STAGHORN could equally well be described as a club mushroom. It belongs, however, to the same family as many of the jelly fungi. ◦ The spore-bearing basidia line the surface of the upper section of the shaft. It is not always easy to see where the basidia region transitions into a non-fertile surface, but sometimes the line is distinct, dividing the shaft into a lighter head and a somewhat darker stem. ◦ "Calocera" is a compound of Greek words for "beautiful" and "waxy," and "cornea" means "horn-like." This is one of those times when the binomial absolutely nails it.

Spirit Gummy Bear   *Pseudohydnum gelatinosum* group

FRUITING BODY Cap to 6 cm across; tongue- to spoon-shaped, often with a wavy margin; translucent white or grey or bluish grey, darkening with age and taking on brownish hues, underside often paler than top and stem; roughened to bumpy above, toothed on the fertile surface underneath, the teeth to 3 mm long and pointy and often running partway down the stem; flesh rubbery, gelatinous, same colour as surface. **STEM** To 5 cm tall × 1.5 cm wide, a cylindrical extension of the cap rather than a true stem, but occasionally missing; laterally attached to cap; same colour and texture as the cap; surface roughened to bumpy/hairy. **ODOUR** Not distinctive. **TASTE** Not distinctive. **SPORE PRINT** White. **FRUITING** Scattered or in groups, sometimes clustered; on conifer wood (sticks, logs, stumps); year-round.

    SIMILAR The number of other rubbery, white-translucent, toothed fungi in BC? Exactly none. **COMMENTS** SPIRIT GUMMY BEAR is found worldwide and varies significantly in physical expressions and DNA signatures. Since the scientific name *Pseudohydnum gelatinosum* properly belongs to the European species that was first described with this name, it is likely that we will one day have a new name (or names) for our BC species. It is closely related to the WESTERN JELLY EAR (p. 417). ◦ SPIRIT GUMMY BEAR is a basidiomycete and wood-decay fungus. ◦ This species goes by several other common names, including JELLY TOOTH and CAT'S TONGUE. The latter phrase refers to the way the underside of the cap feels when rubbed across the skin. SPIRIT GUMMY BEAR is a made-in-BC common name that recognizes the resemblance of this fungus to a gummy bear (size, texture) and to the SPIRIT BEAR (colour), BC's iconic white-coloured BLACK BEAR. ◦ "Pseudohydnum" means "false *Hydnum*" (a genus of toothed fungi), and "gelatinosum" means "gelatinous, very slimy." Beginners may twist their tongues over this long binomial, but it does capture the essence of the species.

Western Jelly Ear *Auricularia americana* group

FRUITING BODY To 10 cm across and often reaching out several centimetres from the substrate; ear-shaped or cup-shaped but often irregular, margins sharp; if stemmed, usually laterally attached; yellow-brown to red-brown, drying blackish; elastic and gelatinous, drying tough and hard but softening when wetted; upper (sterile) surface hairy, often wrinkled, lower (fertile) surface ribbed or wrinkled, sometimes with a whitish bloom. **STEM** Present (rudimentary) or absent. **ODOUR** Not distinctive. **TASTE** Not distinctive. **SPORE PRINT** White. **FRUITING** Single, in groups, or clustered; on montane conifer logs and also on hardwoods; year-round.

SIMILAR Nothing else in this book closely resembles this species group. **COMMENTS** For many years, this white-rot species was called *Auricularia auricula*, a correction of the older (and curious) name of *A. auricula-judae*. More careful studies of morphology, mating types, and DNA sequences have revealed that our BC "species" is a closely related *group* of species. One of these species, *A. americana*, which grows on conifers rather than on hardwoods, was originally described from Quebec. At least some of the conifer-based BC species in this complex (a specimen from Whistler, for example) match the DNA signature of *A. americana*, so we have chosen to describe our western North American group under this name. There is probably more than one species in BC, however. ◆ Members of this group that are found in Asia have been cultivated as table mushrooms for millennia. Selling under the commercial common name of WOOD EAR MUSHROOMS and often used to add mouthfeel to soups, the Asian domestic and external markets for this fungus are currently a multibillion-dollar business. Recent biochemical research, however, has shown that mushrooms in the *A. americana* group exhibit a strong anticoagulant effect that people with certain medical conditions should keep in mind before consuming. ◆ "Auricularia" means "relating to the ears," and "americana" is, of course, derived from "America," a reminder that the type species was found in North America.

Purple Jelly-drops   *Ascocoryne sarcoides*

FRUITING BODY To 1 cm across; spherical at first, then typically brain-like or blob-like in its asexual phase and often cup-shaped or disc-shaped (flattened or slightly concave) in its sexual phase; fertile upper surface is purplish pink to reddish purple, smooth to wrinkled, outside of the cup is smooth or slightly wrinkled, scurfy; flesh rubbery, gelatinous. **STEM** Usually absent. **ODOUR** Not distinctive. **TASTE** Not distinctive. **FRUITING** Typically in groups or in dense, fused clusters; on stumps and logs (often on the cut or broken end), primarily on hardwood, but also on conifers; autumn.

SIMILAR Mycologists also identify *Ascocoryne cylichnium* in BC. It appears to differ from PURPLE JELLY-DROPS in microscopic features (mainly by having larger spores). *Phaeotremella foliacea* (previously known as *Tremella foliacea*), which grows on conifers as a parasite of *Stereum sanguinolentum* (p. 387), forms a mass of wavy, reddish brown to purplish lobes. COMMENTS Unlike the other jelly fungi in this section, PURPLE JELLY-DROPS are ascomycetes. They are related to cup fungi such as YELLOW FAIRY CUPS (p. 462) and some of the clubs. ✦ When young, PURPLE JELLY-DROPS produce asexual spores (conidia) on their surfaces, but in maturity the mushrooms transition into producing sexual spores (ascospores) in asci. ✦ The mycelium of PURPLE JELLY-DROPS is a wood decomposer and has attracted attention as a potential biofuel producer. Almost the entire genome has been sequenced. ✦ *Ascocoryne sarcoides* was at one time called *Coryne sarcoides*. Scientific naming conventions forced the genus into a new name, which was compounded out of "ascomycete" and "coryne" (a word that may be based on the Greek word for "club, cudgel"). "Sarcoides" means "like flesh."

Apricot Jelly   *Guepinia helvelloides*

FRUITING BODY To 5 cm across × 10 cm high; spatulate to tongue- to funnel-shaped, split down one side, the margins often lobed; translucent pinkish orange, sometimes described as apricot-coloured; smooth or finely bumpy, outer surface (the upper part of which is the fertile surface) often veined in age; flesh elastic, firm-gelatinous, same colour as the surface. STEM The top usually tapers down to a cylindrical section that might be described as a stem or tall base; sometimes off-centre; sometimes grooved or overlapped as an extension of the cap split; often paler than the top of the fruiting body, sometimes whitish at the base from the mycelium. ODOUR Not distinctive. TASTE Not distinctive. SPORE PRINT White. FRUITING Single or clustered; on the ground (presumably on buried wood) or, more commonly, on very rotten decaying wood; in wet areas in forests, on trailsides, and in bark mulch gardens; usually late summer, autumn.

SIMILAR With its funnel shape and pinkish orange colour, APRICOT JELLY is hard to mistake for any other mushroom. Michael Kuo (mushroomexpert.com) suggests helpfully, "If you are worried about look-alikes, yank your putative [APRICOT JELLY] hard as you pick it; if you hear screaming, you have pulled someone's tongue, and a little searching will probably reveal a human being concealed in the substrate." COMMENTS There is unresolved confusion over the correct genus for this species. You may find *Guepinia helvelloides* listed as *Tremiscus helvelloides* or *Phlogiotis helvelloides*. ◆ In one BC study, APRICOT JELLY extracts from Haida Gwaii showed strong immunostimulatory and anti-inflammatory activity. ◆ APRICOT JELLY is a basidiomycete and a wood decomposer. ◆ "Guepinia" honours Jean Pierre Guépin (1779–1858), an early French mycologist and botanist, and "helvelloides" means "like *Helvella*" (a genus of mushrooms).

Mushrooms, Thunder, and Lightning

Thunder and lightning have a long history with mushrooms and fairy rings. The Greeks and Romans speculated that mushrooms were produced by thunder. Erasmus Darwin (Charles Darwin's grandfather) made the connection between lightning and fairy rings in his 1790 poetic epic, *The Botanic Garden*: "So from dark clouds the playful lightning springs, / Rives the firm oak, or prints the Fairy-rings."

The connection is not implausible: mushrooms often mysteriously appear overnight in long, curved lines running through open fields, accompanied by what looks a bit like charred ground, especially after a rain that might have been accompanied by lightning. Current understanding would describe these mushrooms as large fairy ring arcs (see essay on p. 188), with the scorching interpretation based on the contrast between the colonized vegetation inside the ring and the more verdant grass surrounding the ring.

Among the mushrooms eaten by the Nlaka'pamux (Thompson) First Nation people of southern Interior British Columbia (see essay on p. 471) was a mushroom called "thunderstorm head" or "lightning" or "thunder" mushroom, which seems to have some association with electrical storms. This mushroom may be *Lepista praemagna*, or THUNDER MUSHROOM (see photo), a relative of the BLEWIT (p. 130).

The THUNDER MUSHROOM emerges in BC grasslands at mid-elevations (500 to 1,000 metres) and ranges at least as far north as the Chilcotin. It's a springtime mushroom, and in BC the mushroom usually appears in May and June, often in large fairy rings. One BC naturalist, Gary Hunt of the Kamloops Naturalist Club, proposes a regionally apt calendar rule. You might start looking for THUNDER MUSHROOM in BC, he says, "when the ARROW-LEAVED BALSAMROOT flowers are out." This delicious edible has a long history of collection by southern Interior First Nations and continues to be harvested for personal consumption and for sale at local farmers' markets.

Puffballs

The mushrooms in this section are united by a curious method of spore dispersal. Their spores, when they mature, find themselves encased inside an ovoid skin. To get the spores lifted into the air, the skins must break apart or develop holes. When compared to the clever methods that other types of mushrooms employ to send their spores abroad—gills, pores, teeth—spore dispersal in the puffballs feels a little, well, underplanned. We do find some imagination, however, in the *Lycoperdon* puffballs—they have thin skins and small holes in the top that allow raindrops to push the spores, bellows-like, out of the spore sacs and into the moving air.

The spore masses in all of these mushrooms progress through spore-production stages in a similar way. They start out with the spore-bearing bodies developing inside a well-packed, whitish flesh. The flesh then begins to self-dissolve, often turning a green-yellow colour. Finally, the captive moisture leaks out of the mass, leaving behind a dry heap of dark spores.

You may sometimes see the mushrooms in this section listed as "gasteromycetes," a name that means "stomach mushroom," which is a reference to their enclosed spore masses. The name, however, is a flag of convenience—the mushrooms that have adopted this lifestyle come from many parts of the fungal tree of life. Mushrooms in the genera *Calvatia*, *Bovista*, *Calbovista*, *Apioperdon*, and *Lycoperdon* are decomposer fungi that are related to gilled decomposer fungi in the *Lepiota* and *Agaricus* genera. The *Geastrum* earthstars belong to the branch of the fungal family tree that contains ramarias. Species in *Scleroderma* and *Pisolithus* are mycorrhizal and are related to boletes, which are also mycorrhizal.

When the young flesh of puffballs is firm and white, almost all are edible (notable exceptions: earthballs in the *Scleroderma* genus and possibly *Pisolithus*). Any thoughts about cooking and eating these mushrooms after the white stage should be strongly suppressed. Even at the white stage, care in harvesting is needed—*Amanita* species, some of which are seriously poisonous, can in their button stages resemble puffballs. All puffballs headed to the table should be vertically sliced and examined for the immature gills and/or stem that signal an amanita.

While the authors of this book believe that all mushrooms are beautiful, one of them in this section, the DEAD MAN'S FOOT (p. 430), sorely tests our faith.

Pear Puffball
Apioperdon pyriforme

OUTER SURFACE To 5 cm across × 5 cm high; upside-down-pear-shaped to nearly spherical; whitish when young to chestnut brown in age, the pore-hole region at the top sometimes raised or depressed and/or lighter or darker; smooth when young with a few small spines (rub with finger to detect) that wear off, then later often coarsely granular from fine cracking. **INNER LAYER** Papery; whitish to tan, darker brown in age with a pore at the top. **SPORE MASS** Firm and white when young, becoming powdery and olive-brown. **STEM** Sterile base half or less of the total height of puffball; white, unchanging in age; spongy with small chambers; the base appearing pinched and with white rhizomorphs. **ODOUR** Unique and hard to describe. The words "fungal" and "gasoline" are sometimes applied. **TASTE** Not distinctive. **FRUITING** Usually in groups or clustered; on rotten wood, on the ground in soils with lots of wood in them, or near wood and attached to it by rhizomorphs; in conifer and mixedwood forests; late summer, autumn.

EDIBILITY Edible. But only when young and pure white with a firm texture. **SIMILAR** PEAR PUFFBALL closely resembles the **GEMMED PUFFBALL** (p. 423)—see comparisons under that entry. ● **COMMENTS** PEAR PUFFBALL was formerly known as *Lycoperdon pyriforme*. Genetic tests suggest, however, that it is not closely related to other *Lycoperdon* species. ● The BC town of Popkum, near Chilliwack, is derived from the Halkomelem name for a puffball (pópkw'em). ● The new *Apioperdon* genus ("apio" from the Greek word for "pear") was invented just to hold this one puffball. "Pyriforme" means "pear-shaped."

Gemmed Puffball

Lycoperdon perlatum

OUTER SURFACE To 6 cm across × 8 cm high; spherical or upside-down-pear-shaped or shaped like a top; whitish when young to olive-brown in age; with conical white or grey (sometimes brown-tipped) spines surrounded by smaller spines, the larger spines falling off and their scars often leaving behind a netted pattern. **INNER LAYER** Membranous, tough, with a net-like pattern once the spines have fallen; whitish to tan, darker brown in age; a pore at top through which spores escape when the outer surface tears and flakes off. **SPORE MASS** Firm and white when young, becoming powdery and olive-brown in age. **STEM** Sterile base to 3 cm wide, about two-thirds of the total height of the puffball; surface white, later olive-brown to chocolate brown; flesh chambered and going through the same colour phases as the spores; the surface sometimes with spines when young, becoming spineless with age. **ODOUR** Not distinctive. **TASTE** Not distinctive. **FRUITING** Usually in groups or clustered; on the ground, in a variety of forested and non-forested habitats; summer, autumn, winter.

EDIBILITY Edible when young. **SIMILAR** The **PEAR PUFFBALL** (p. 422), another common BC mushroom, grows on wood (though the wood it connects to may be hidden by a soil layer), and it has white tissue in the sterile base at maturity that connects to white rhizomorphs. The outer surface can have a few spines, but they do not leave behind a network pattern. *Lycoperdon nigrescens* (inset photo) also grows in soil and can be studded with spines, but the spines are dark brown to black on a light to dark brown outer layer. **COMMENTS** *Lycoperdon* species are also known to bioaccumulate heavy metals. ⬩ "Lycoperdon" is a Greek compound meaning "wolf fart," a reference to the dark cloud of puffed spores. Delightfully, the French-Canadian name for puffball, "vesse-de-loup," means the same thing. "Perlatum" means "very broad"—this cosmopolitan species can be found on all continents except Antarctica.

Sculptured Giant Puffball — *Calbovista subsculpta*

OUTER SURFACE To 16 cm across; spherical to upside-down-pear-shaped; whitish to cream, aging pale yellow-brown; thick and leathery, broken up into 3- to 6-sided, flat-topped pyramidal warts that are up to 8 mm high on the top of the puffball, somewhat shorter on the puffball sides. **INNER LAYER** Thin, fragile; sometimes shiny; drying and breaking up as the spores dry. **SPORE MASS** Firm and white when young, becoming yellowish and eventually powdery and dark brown or purplish brown. **STEM** The lower third or quarter of this puffball (cut it in half to see this) is a sterile base that remains behind after spore dispersal; mycelial fibres at the base attach the puffball to soil. **ODOUR** Not distinctive. **TASTE** Not distinctive. **FRUITING** Single, in groups, or clustered; in open conifer forests, at higher (usually more than 900 m) elevations; spring, summer.

EDIBILITY Edible when young. **SIMILAR** Because of its crocodile-like skin, the **SCULPTURED GIANT PUFFBALL** is likely to be mistaken for only 2 other mushrooms: ***Calvatia sculpta***, of western North America (but not, so far, known from BC), which has taller (to 3 cm tall), pointier warts, as well as microscopic differences; and the **WESTERN GIANT PUFFBALL** (p. 425), which is usually much larger (to 60 cm across), lacks a significant sterile base under the spore mass, and is attached to the ground by a cord-like rhizomorph. **COMMENTS** The genus *Calbovista* was created to hold the **SCULPTURED GIANT PUFFBALL**, and it is still the only species in it. ♠ The scientific name is a set of references to other puffballs. "Calbovista," the genus name, is compounded out of *Calvatia* (p. 425) and *Bovista* (p. 426). "Subsculpta" means "nearly (*Calvatia*) sculpta," the even spinier mountain puffball mentioned above.

Western Giant Puffball
Calvatia booniana

OUTER SURFACE To 60 cm across, 30 cm or more high; spherical to (more commonly) flattened and pillow-like, generally circular when viewed from above, but sometimes oval, irregular, or lobed; whitish to cream, aging to tan; cottony when young, soon broken up into 4- to 6-sided, sometimes raised (but always flat-topped) plates that eventually fall off exposing the inner layer or spore mass; outer layer to 5 mm thick. **INNER LAYER** Thin (to 2 mm thick), attached to outer layer; felt-like; whitish, eventually disintegrating. **SPORE MASS** Firm and white when young, becoming greenish yellow and eventually powdery and olive-brown. **STEM** Absent. The thin sterile base is attached to the ground by a white, cord-like rhizomorph. **ODOUR** Not distinctive. **TASTE** Not distinctive. **FRUITING** Single or widely scattered; on the ground, sometimes in large fairy rings; in open grasslands and shrublands; late spring, summer.

    EDIBILITY Edible when young. **SIMILAR** When the fruiting body is small, the WESTERN GIANT PUFFBALL can resemble the SCULPTURED GIANT PUFFBALL (p. 424), but the WESTERN GIANT PUFFBALL lacks a significant sterile base under the spore mass and is attached to the ground by a cord-like rhizomorph. West Coast specimens that are more ovoid and have smooth skins in maturity are occasionally identified as *Calvatia gigantea*, a mushroom known in Europe and in North America east of the Rockies, but whether these are really *C. gigantea* or *C. booniana* or some other *Calvatia* species is unknown. **COMMENTS** The WESTERN GIANT PUFFBALL is a decomposer species of the alpine meadows in the BC Rockies and of the BC Interior plateau grasslands, but one turned up recently in a grazing field in coastal Metchosin, BC, likely an introduction. ▲ "Calvatia" is perhaps adapted from Latin words meaning "skull" or "bald"; "booniana" is in honour of William Judson Boone, first president of the College of Idaho, who showed the mycologist Alexander H. Smith some specimens of this mushroom in 1935.

Lead-coloured Puffball
Bovista plumbea

OUTER SURFACE To 4 cm across; spherical, sometimes slightly flattened; white; outer layer smooth or with flattened scales when young, sometimes cracked, then breaking into pieces and/or peeling away with age. **INNER LAYER** Greyish white to blue-grey, with a metallic lustre, becoming black with age; smooth, like parchment, rupturing to form an opening up to 1 cm across where the dry spores can be released. **SPORE MASS** Firm and white when young, becoming mushy and olive-yellow, and eventually powdery and olive-brown to darker browns. **STEM** No real stem, but mycelial fibres at the base attach the puffball to soil. **ODOUR** Not distinctive. **TASTE** Slightly peppery. **FRUITING** Single, scattered, or in groups; in grass (lawns, fields, pastures) and disturbed areas; spring, summer, autumn.

EDIBILITY Edible when young. **SIMILAR** *Bovista pila*, not as common, is somewhat larger (to 9 cm across), has a bronze rather than greyish inner layer, and attaches itself to the soil via a small cord. **COMMENTS** The fibres attaching this puffball to the soil break at maturity, allowing the wind to move the mushroom and its spores to new locations. ❧ Names for puffballs in First Nations languages sometimes refer to ghosts: "ghost's or corpse's face powder" (Nlaka'pamux), "ghost smoke" (Haisla), and "ghost fart" (Gitxsan). "Bovista" appears to come from a German word that means "fox fart"—for the curious link between canine flatulence and puffballs, see also the page for the GEMMED PUFFBALL (p. 423). "Plumbea" means "lead-like" in Latin, named for the blue-grey metallic sheen of the inner layer.

Hot, Dry, and Lovin' It

One of the reasons that BC has so many different types of mushrooms is that it has so many different climates, ranging from sea level to alpine, from rainforests to near-desert. BC's warmest, driest climates can be found in the southern Interior, in the rain shadow of the Coast and Cascade Mountains, along valleys of the Okanagan, the Similkameen, the Thompson, the Nicola, the middle Fraser, and the lower Chilcotin Rivers. At elevations below 900 metres in these valleys, summertime droughts make it difficult for trees to survive. Instead, landscapes are covered by bunchgrasses, sagebrush, and a soil crust of lichens and bryophytes—and, as visitors soon discover, plantations of grapevines with their attached wineries.

Most of us associate mushrooms with moist climates rather than with the near-deserts, the shrub-steppes, in BC's southern Interior. The fungi whose mycelia form mycorrhizal associations with trees will certainly be absent in a landscape without trees. There are, however, a few mushrooms that flourish in these dry ecosystems and that are rarely found elsewhere.

Mushrooms specifically adapted to these dry habitats have usually found a way to protect their spore-producing surfaces. Standard-issue gills can be a problem in a dry environment: they are designed to maximize surface area for spore production, but that means that they are also maximizing surface area for evaporation. Mushrooms that are adapted to these habitats either produce masses of spores enclosed within an outer skin (e.g., puffballs, or truffles, p. 463), or they feature poorly formed gills or pores that huddle inside unexpanded caps. The former are often called "gasteroid fungi," the latter "secotioid fungi."

DESERT SHAGGY MANE.

Five species of *Tulostoma*, a genus of stalked puffballs, have been collected in BC (of the more than a hundred species described worldwide). While they are not entirely restricted to desert environments, these gasteroid fungi seem to occur most abundantly there. In structure, the stalked puffballs are very much like other puffballs, but the small spore-bearing structure (usually just several centimetres across) is elevated on a short (usually less than five centimetres tall) stalk. Another distinctive stalked puffball of our southern BC near-deserts is the DESERT DRUMSTICK (*Battarrea phalloides*). It's much larger than *Tulostoma* species, with a spore case to 10 centimetres or more across and a tough, often hairy, long-lasting stalk up to 50 centimetres tall.

A distinctive secotioid mushroom that is found in BC primarily in near-desert regions is the DESERT SHAGGY MANE (*Podaxis pistillaris*, pictured), which closely resembles the SHAGGY MANE mushroom (p. 290). Instead of having regular gills that deliquesce, as the SHAGGY MANE does, this species has contorted gill-like plates that are eventually converted into a mass of dark brown to black spores. Despite its resemblance to SHAGGY MANE mushrooms, DESERT SHAGGY MANE is instead related to species in *Lepiota* and relatives.

Bowl Earthstar
Geastrum saccatum

OUTER SURFACE When young, spherical to bulb-shaped and resembling a small puffball to 2 cm across, with a small beak at the top and rhizomorphs at the bottom; the thick yellow-brown to tan outer layer soon splitting into 4–10 rays, the rays bending back to make the whole mushroom up to 5 cm wide; the inner (now top) surface of rays tan to chestnut brown; rays fleshy, not incorporating debris, sometimes finely cracked. **INNER LAYER** Thin, papery; whitish to dull brown; forming an ovoid spore sac to 2 cm across sitting in the depression at the centre of the rays, developing a beaked spore-release opening at the top that is usually slightly paler or darker than surrounding tissue and delimited by a raised or depressed circular line. **SPORE MASS** Firm and white when young, becoming powdery and brown or purplish brown. **STEM** None. **ODOUR** Not distinctive. **TASTE** Not distinctive. **FRUITING** Single, scattered, or in groups; on the ground, in rich humus; most commonly in conifer forests, also in mixedwood forests and open areas; late summer, autumn.

EDIBILITY Uncertain. Not edible when mature, for sure. **SIMILAR** Nothing looks like an earthstar except another earthstar. Besides the BOWL EARTHSTAR, BC foragers might come across *Geastrum fimbriatum* (like the BOWL EARTHSTAR, but the pore at the top is not delimited by a paler or darker circle, and the outer, splitting layer incorporates surrounding debris), *G. triplex* (typically larger than the BOWL EARTHSTAR, to 10 cm or more across when expanded, and with an outer layer that divides, part of it forming rays and part of it making a ragged saucer for the spore case to sit in), or *G. quadrifidum* (with a spore case sitting on a small stem that raises the case 1–2 mm above the splayed outer surface). **COMMENTS** The BOWL EARTHSTAR, like other *Geastrum* species, is a forest-floor decomposer. ◆ A cosmopolitan species, it seems to be relatively common in BC forests. ◆ "Saccatum" comes from a word meaning "sac."

Lemon Earthball *Scleroderma citrinum*

OUTER SURFACE To 10 cm across; spherical or somewhat flattened; whitish becoming yellow or yellow-brown, turning pinkish when rubbed; thick (to 3 mm), rubbery, smooth, cracking into coarse brown scales, each scale a central prominence surrounded by a lighter polygonal background. **SPORE MASS** At first, fleshy, solid, and white, then quickly becoming (from the inside out) violet or purple-grey and eventually powdery purple-black, often with whitish veins in the darkening mass. **STEM** Absent, but sometimes with a buried, thick, stem-like base of ridges and white mycelial fibres. **ODOUR** Bread-like or strong and pungent, also sometimes described as rubber-like or fish-like. **TASTE** Bitter. **FRUITING** Usually in groups or clustered; on the ground or rotting wood, sometimes partly buried; in forests or in gardens; usually late summer or autumn, sometimes spring.

EDIBILITY Poisonous. **SIMILAR** Those who eat puffballs must take special care not to accidentally consume the thicker-skinned, poisonous *Scleroderma* species. *Scleroderma cepa*, which appears to be at least as common as the LEMON EARTHBALL, has a smoother skin when young, and later, as the skin cracks, does not develop the rosette warts that give the LEMON EARTHBALL a pigskin appearance. *Gastropila fumosa* (was *Calvatia fumosa*) has an exceptionally thick, fused skin for a puffball and can be mistaken for a *Scleroderma*. It has a smoke-grey, cracked cap, has no whitish veins in the spore mass, grows under mountain conifers in the spring and summer, and smells like sour milk or a pit toilet. **COMMENTS** The LEMON EARTHBALL and other *Scleroderma* species lack the distinct spore-release pore found on some puffballs, preferring to free their spores upon the collapse of their outer skin. They do, however, sometimes develop splits or tears (often star-shaped) along their top surfaces that can resemble and imitate the release mechanism of puffballs. ◦ "Scleroderma" means "hard skinned." "Citrinum" means "lemon-like," presumably from the colour of the outer skin.

Dead Man's Foot   *Pisolithus arhizus* group

OUTER SURFACE To 20 cm across × 30 cm high; initially spherical to upside-down-pear-shaped, then elongating toward a cylindrical shape; whitish to yellow-brown, becoming purplish or black in age; thin (about 1 mm), fragile, and cracking and peeling away in maturity to expose the spore mass. **SPORE MASS** Initially containing hundreds of pea-like (2–4 mm) spore compartments that are whitish, greenish yellow, yellow, brown, or red-brown and are embedded in a moist, blackish flesh, both the flesh and the peas breaking up (starting from the top down) and crumbling into a dusty mass of dark brown spores. **STEM** Sterile base to 10 cm wide; fibrous, sturdy, often buried; yellowish or brownish, sometimes marbled; commonly with brown or greenish yellow mycelium at base. **ODOUR** Not distinctive when young, becoming unpleasant with age. **TASTE** Reportedly sweet. **FRUITING** Usually single or in a small group; on the ground; typically along roads, trails, and driveways, also around gardens; mycorrhizal with a number of different trees and shrubs; late summer, autumn.

EDIBILITY Not edible. Though it is collected and eaten in certain areas of Europe, where it is sometimes referred to as BOHEMIAN TRUFFLE. **SIMILAR** The most similar thing to DEAD MAN'S FOOT is a big hunk of fresh horse doo-doo. **COMMENTS** Chances are that we have several species of *Pisolithus* in BC, especially given that some multi-host *Pisolithus* species have been imported and used as inoculants to promote the growth of forest trees. ☙ DEAD MAN'S FOOT, now generally known as *P. arhizus*, was called (and still is called by some) *P. tinctorius*, the "tinctorius" reflecting its use as a natural dye. The underdeveloped peridioles (spore cases) contain a mucus that imparts red and orange colours to fabrics. ☙ "Pisolithus" means "pea stone," and "arhizus" means "rootless."

Bird's Nest Fungi

Bird's nest mushrooms rank among the strangest visual echoes in the fungal world—they look like small avian nests, complete with eggs. What appear to be eggs are spore cases called "peridioles." Basidia inside the peridioles produce the spores in vast numbers—up to 50 million spores per peridiole. The nests holding the eggs serve as splash cups. When drops of water hit these cups, the egg cases are propelled  from the cups at high speeds, sometimes travelling up to a metre from the nest. The cases, made of waxy, sticky material, can attach themselves to nearby vegetation, dry out, and release the spores. Some of the bird's nest species have cords that attach the eggs to the inside of the cups. When the eggs fly out, the cords, which break away from the nest and accompany the spore case, wrap around support structures, suspending the eggs in the drying air.

The bird's nest fungi are decomposers. They fall into about half a dozen genera, all in the same family. The family is closely related to some of the gilled mushrooms and to puffballs. We cover in our main entries only two genera, *Nidula* and *Crucibulum*, the two that are most common in BC. We mention species from the less common *Cyathus* genus in the comparison sections.

The spore prints and spore colours that are so important in other groups of mushrooms are omitted here. The spore masses inside the peridioles are often white, but the spores themselves are typically colourless or a light yellow-brown when looked at under a microscope.

With a little effort, beginners can learn to distinguish among the various species of bird's nest fungi. The nests themselves, the splash cups, can hang around long after the eggs have flown the coop, becoming worn and thin. At this late stage, even experts sometimes confuse them. When the fruiting bodies are young and still have their spore cases, however, there are a number of clues available. Two of the most significant clues are the colour of the spore cases and the presence/absence of cords on the cases. Whitish eggs and cords suggest a species in *Crucibulum*. Greyish brown to blackish eggs and cords are usually *Cyathus* species. No cords suggest *Nidula* species, with ones having darker brown eggs usually being WHITE BARREL BIRD'S NEST (p. 433) and ones with pale grey or pale brown eggs being FLOWERPOT BIRD'S NEST (p. 432).

The Canadian mycologist Harold J. Brodie (1907–89), who was born in Winnipeg and who taught for many years at the University of Alberta, spent much of his professional life working on bird's nest fungi. His book *The Bird's Nest Fungi* (University of Toronto Press, 1975) is an important resource for those wanting to know more about this fascinating group.

Flowerpot Bird's Nest   *Nidula candida*

NEST To 8 mm across × 1.5 cm high; short-cylindrical, the top usually rounded when still capped, and after the cap is removed flared margins are exposed giving the mushroom the look of a tiny flowerpot; nest sides tough, persistent; outer surface grey to light brown, shaggy and forming a fringe around the open mouth; inner surface whitish to yellow-brown, paler toward rim, shiny when wet, smooth; mouth of nest initially covered by a hairy lid that is whitish to greyish to yellow-brown. **EGGS** To 2 mm across; flattened or lens-like discs; smooth when moist, wrinkled when dry; numerous, initially in a gelatinous liquid, not attached to the nest by a cord; light grey to light brown. **ODOUR** Not distinctive. **TASTE** Not distinctive. **FRUITING** In groups; on twigs and decaying wood, especially berry canes and plant remains, or on the ground; nests found year-round, but eggs mostly in autumn.

EDIBILITY Not edible. **SIMILAR** The **WHITE BARREL BIRD'S NEST** (p. 433), the other *Nidula* in this section, has smaller, mug-shaped cups, a shaggier, snow-white exterior (sometimes with brown tints in age, though), and smaller (to 1 mm across), darker brown eggs. See the **WHITE-EGG BIRD'S NEST** entry (p. 434) for more comparisons. **COMMENTS** The 2 *Nidula* species in this section are mainly found on the West Coast of North America. ◦ "Nidula" means "little nest." "Candida" means "white," a strange species epithet for a bird's nest fungus whose outer surface and eggs are darker than those in some other BC bird's nest fungi.

White Barrel Bird's Nest — *Nidula niveotomentosa*

NEST Small, to 6 mm across × 6 mm high; short-cylindrical, forming a mug with parallel sides that flares slightly at the mouth; walls tough, persistent; outer surface snowy white and shaggy and forming a fringe around the open mouth, sometimes tinged with yellowish brown in age and in advanced age becoming smooth; inner surface yellow-brown, shiny, smooth, paler toward rim; mouth of nest initially covered by a white-hairy lid. **EGGS** To 1 mm across; flattened discs, sometimes lens-shaped, smooth when moist, wrinkled when dry; numerous, initially in a gelatinous liquid, not attached to nest by a cord; dark chestnut brown. **ODOUR** Not distinctive. **TASTE** Not distinctive. **FRUITING** Scattered or clustered; on twigs, stumps, or on woody debris on the ground, often in the vicinity of bracken fern and typically nested among mosses; nests present year-round, eggs mainly in autumn and early winter.

    EDIBILITY Not edible. **SIMILAR** See the entry for **FLOWERPOT BIRD'S NEST** (p. 432) for a close look-alike. Consult also the entry for **WHITE-EGG BIRD'S NEST** (p. 434) for wider comparisons. **COMMENTS** The WHITE BARREL BIRD'S NEST and the WHITE-EGG BIRD'S NEST sometimes exhibit twinning—cups next to each other will grow into one another and form tops and margins that resemble a figure eight. ❧ "Nidula" means "small nest." "Niveotomentosa" is a compound that means "snowy and densely hairy," a reference to the shaggy white outer surface.

White-egg Bird's Nest
Crucibulum crucibuliforme

NEST To 1 cm across × 1 cm high; spherical at first, becoming short-cylindrical, sometimes narrowed below, the top forming a deep cup that is exposed when the lid is removed; the nest walls are tough, persistent; outer surface yellowish brown, velvety-hairy to shaggy, smooth in age; inner surface whitish to silvery grey to pale cinnamon, smooth, shiny; mouth of nest initially covered by a yellow-orange (but aging white) hairy lid. **EGGS** To 2 mm across; variable in size, lens-shaped, 5–12 per nest; initially in a gelatinous liquid that soon dries out; attached to the inner surface of nest by a thin cord (disappearing with age) that is fastened to a nipple-like bump (not disappearing) on the bottom of the egg; whitish to buff. **ODOUR** Not distinctive. **TASTE** Not distinctive. **FRUITING** Scattered or in dense groups; usually on twigs, sometimes also on buried wood or on manure, not on larger logs or directly on soil; nests can persist year-round, and eggs appear in spring, summer, autumn.

EDIBILITY Not edible. **SIMILAR** The eggs of the 2 *Nidula* species in this guide (pp. 432 and 433) are darker and lack the attaching cords. *Cyathus olla* (large grey to black eggs to 5 mm across, thick walls, dark brown exterior, interior grey-brown, wide cup) and **FLUTED BIRD'S NEST**, *Cyathus striatus* (greyish brown eggs to 2 mm across, inner walls radially ribbed, flaring cup; see photo on facing page), do have cords, but the eggs don't have nipples/bumps on the bottom where the cord attaches. **COMMENTS** *Crucibulum laeve* is a synonym and is still used in many guides. ✦ The WHITE-EGG BIRD'S NEST is found worldwide in the earth's temperate zones. ✦ "Crucibulum" means "earthen pot," so "crucibuliforme" means "in the shape of a pot."

FLUTED BIRD'S NEST (*Cyathus striatus*).

Morels and Similar

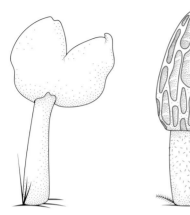

Mushrooms in this section cluster into three related groups of stemmed ascomycetes: morels, false morels, and elfin saddles. In addition to these three groups, we include one mushroom from *Verpa*, a genus connected to the morels.

The term "morel" is these days usually restricted to members of *Morchella*, a genus whose name may derive from an old German word for "carrot, parsnip." The false morels are in *Gyromitra*, a genus that takes its name from a Greek compound composed of "gyro" (meaning "round, convoluted") and "mitra" (meaning "headband, turban"). The elfin saddles described in this section are all in *Helvella*. The genus name *Helvella* has an obscure etymology, though it is worth noting that Linnaeus, who included a couple of elfin saddles in his *Systema Naturae*, referred to the genus as *Elvella*, which might hint at a connection to "elf."

Morels, because of their culinary role, are among the most famous mushrooms in the world. They have caps with vertical and horizontal ridges surrounding deep pits, which contain the asci, the spore-bearing bodies. BC morels are sometimes divided into yellow (or blond) morels—morels with yellow to pale brown ridges and more common under deciduous trees; and black morels—with brown to black ridges (at least when mature) and common not only in deciduous forests, but also on disturbed ground and on forest lands that have recently been burned. In recent years, genetic studies have reconfigured a lot of what we thought we knew about morels. Our best guess is that, when the smoke clears, we will end up with about 50 to 80 worldwide species. A number of these species are found in BC.

Morels, it is thought, include both mycorrhizal and decomposer species. The fact that some of them have mycorrhizal associations may be one of the reasons why they have proved difficult to cultivate. Until a few decades ago, all morels that came to the table were wild-harvested. Morels famously appear in forest areas in the springtime following a fire, and there may be smaller fruitings in the same spot for another year or two. They can appear on these burns in great abundance—on one site in Austria, a burned half-hectare yielded almost 20 tonnes of morels. Wild harvesting, however, is no longer the only source of morels. Currently, Chinese producers grow and sell more than 900 tonnes of cultivated and dried morels each year. Whether you forage and collect wild morels or whether you buy them at a market, you should thoroughly cook them before they are consumed. There are numerous reports of poisonings from undercooked morels, and occasionally reactions have been reported even from cooked morels.

We have about 10 species of false morels (*Gyromitra*) in North America, and almost all of these species have been found in BC. In many places and times, the false morels have been foraged for and eaten, but they have more toxic compounds than in morels and the toxins are not always removed by cooking. Of all mushroom fatalities, 2 to 4 per cent come from mishandled or misjudged false morels.

Of the hundred or so elfin saddles, about a dozen have been reported in BC. Older texts sometimes report them as poisonous, but a consensus seems to be developing that they are not very dangerous and chemical tests have not turned up much evidence of toxins.

Our two species of *Verpa* (of a handful known globally) are good edibles. As with all morels and morel relatives, remember to cook them well.

Laddered Landscape Morel
Morchella importuna

CAP To 9 cm across × 15 cm high; usually cone-shaped, sometimes ovoid, with 12–20 main vertical ridges and numerous horizontal ridges, creating a ladder-like appearance with vertically elongated pits between the rungs of the ladders; pale to dark grey when young, developing brownish to blackish colours in age, especially along the ridges; dry; ridges and pits smooth or finely hairy; flesh relatively thin (1–3 mm in cap), whitish to pale tan. ODOUR Not distinctive. TASTE Not distinctive. SPORE PRINT Light yellow-brown. STEM To 10 cm tall × 6 cm wide; often with a widened base and at the top having a groove (to 5 mm) between stem and cap; hollow; whitish or pale brown; dry; sometimes mealy with whitish particles, with longitudinal ridges (at least near the base). FRUITING Single to scattered or in groups; on the ground; in gardens, greenhouses, and bark-mulched areas, also sometimes in thinned forests; spring.

EDIBILITY Choice. SIMILAR With the combination of its distinct habitat and morphology, the LADDERED LANDSCAPE MOREL is one of the few BC morels that can be identified in the field with some confidence. COMMENTS Recent genetic work has placed the LADDERED LANDSCAPE MOREL with other morels in the black-morel section. Until recently, some BC inventories identified this mushroom as *Morchella elata*. LADDERED LANDSCAPE MOREL is distributed in western North America and in Europe. European populations may represent introductions from North America. ● This species is commercially cultivated in China, with annual exports of up to 900 tonnes. ● "Importuna" means "assertive, inconsiderate." Gardeners may complain about this in-your-face mushroom, but most people wish that it were *more* importunate than it is.

Snyder's Morel *Morchella snyderi*

CAP To 5 cm across × 8 cm high; usually cone-shaped, with 16–22 main vertical ridges, often with secondary vertical ridges and some (sunken) horizontal ridges, creating a series of vertically elongated pits, the ridges sometimes eroding in age; ridges pale yellow, becoming tan, greyish brown and in age or with drying nearly black, the pits similar but paler, not blackening; dry; ridges smooth or finely hairy, pits finely hairy; flesh thin (1–2 mm in cap), whitish. **ODOUR** Not distinctive. **TASTE** Not distinctive. **STEM** To 7 cm tall × 4 cm wide; equal or somewhat widened at base; whitish or pale brown; dry; white-mealy at first, then longitudinally ridged and with holes and hollows at maturity, especially at the base. **FRUITING** Usually in clusters; on the ground; in non-burned montane conifer forests; spring, early summer.

EDIBILITY Choice. **SIMILAR** Growing in the forest, having a granulated and ridged stem when young, and having yellow/tan ridges that later blacken set SNYDER'S MOREL apart. *Morchella brunnea*, another mushroom from the black-morel section that we probably have in BC, matches most features of the description in the paragraph above, but its stem is more slender, and when young, its cap is browner and its stem is not as ridged. It is also less clustered, and it tends to grow around hardwoods. Young specimens of SNYDER'S MOREL can resemble yellow morels such as AMERICAN YELLOW MOREL (*M. americana*, lower photo, what we used to call *M. esculenta*), but mushrooms in the yellow section generally do not go on to develop blackened ridges. **COMMENTS** SNYDER'S MOREL, in the black section of the morels, is a natural morel, one that we would expect to see in the woods rather than in landscaped areas or burn sites. • "Snyderi" honours the American botanist Leon Carleton Snyder (1908–87).

Grey Fire Morel   *Morchella tomentosa*

CAP To 5 cm across × 10 cm high; cone-shaped to almost cylindrical or ovoid, with 18–26 main vertical ridges, also with secondary vertical ridges and horizontal ridges that interweave to create a series of often vertically elongated pits, the ridges blunt/rounded when young, in age flattened and/or eroded to the extent that the white flesh shows through; ridges pale black or silvery grey or brown when young, becoming grey or pale tan in age, the pits similar in colour; dry; ridges densely hairy when young, pits smooth; flesh thin to thick (1–5 mm in cap), whitish. **ODOUR** Not distinctive. **TASTE** Not distinctive. **STEM** To 6 cm tall × 4 cm wide; equal or enlarged at base; grey to black when young, grey to pale tan in age; dry; densely hairy when young, somewhat hairy to nearly hairless in age. **FRUITING** Single to scattered; on the ground; in higher-elevation (generally above 1,000 m) burned conifer forests, fruiting abundantly the year after forest fires, sometimes smaller crops 2 and 3 years after; spring, summer.

    EDIBILITY Choice. **SIMILAR** *Morchella eximia* is another morel that comes up on recently burned sites. Its genetic signature has been identified in BC under the synonyms of **M. carbonaria** and **M. anthracophila**. The cap of *M. eximia* can assume a range of colours, from brown to grey to pinkish brown, even white or nearly black, and it lacks the hairs found on the ridges and stem of the GREY FIRE MOREL. In addition, GREY FIRE MOREL is a species of western North America; *M. eximia* has a worldwide distribution. **COMMENTS** Like the other 2 main-entry morels in this book, the GREY FIRE MOREL is part of the black-morel section of morels. ☙ This species develops sclerotia in the soil under the fruiting body. The thickened white (when the dirt is scraped off) sclerotial mass branches 2 or 3 times before joining up with the rest of the mycelium. ☙ "Tomentosa" means "densely hairy."

Thimble Cap
Verpa conica group

CAP To 4 cm across × 4 cm high; thimble-shaped to bell-shaped, occasionally lobed and convoluted, sometimes with a depression on top in age, margins inrolled when young, rolled out in age, and not attached to stem; yellow-brown to reddish brown, both on fertile surface on top and the sterile surface underneath; dry; smooth or with fine ridging; flesh thin, fragile, white. **ODOUR** Not distinctive. **TASTE** Not distinctive. **SPORE PRINT** Yellow to pale orange. **STEM** To 12 cm tall × 1.5 cm wide; equal or sometimes widening or narrowing below; round in cross-section; with cottony pith inside when young, becoming hollow; white to yellowish brown; smooth or with fine, darker scales in bands around the stem. **FRUITING** Single, scattered, or in groups; on the ground; in open forests and forest edges; spring.

EDIBILITY Choice. Some negative reactions reported. **SIMILAR** The lobed and convoluted version of the THIMBLE CAP can make it look like a spring *Gyromitra* such as the **FALSE MOREL** (p. 444). The free cap margins and pithy stem (when young) of the THIMBLE CAP set it apart. *Verpa bohemica* (lower photo) can also resemble the lobed and convoluted version of the THIMBLE CAP, but its convolutions take the form of wavy, vertically aligned ridges, making it look more like the cap of a morel. Unlike a morel, however, the *V. bohemica* cap is only attached at the top of the stem. **COMMENTS** Certain morphological variations among specimens of *V. conica* hint that we may have several species clumped under the one name and that our western North American species may not be the same as the European species that the name was originally assigned to. ◦ The ancient Romans used the word "verpa" as one of their words for "penis." "Conica" means "cone-shaped."

Commercial Mushroom Harvesting in BC

Most of those who head to the forests and fields to collect BC's delicious, nutritious wild mushrooms do it for their own consumption. Some, however, do it for money. When mushroom picking is a business, it is part of BC's commercial mushroom harvest.

We aren't sure how big BC's current commercial mushroom harvest is, since it's largely unregulated and no provincial agency has been tasked with pulling together the figures. There was a report on the harvest compiled in 1999, but the numbers in the report—even if they are correct—may not reflect the situation today. At the time of this report, the PINE MUSHROOM (p. 146) was BC's most important commercial mushroom species, with export volumes of 250,000 to 400,000 kilograms annually and before-tax revenues of $25 million to $45 million. Other exports at that time were (in good years) chanterelles (750,000 kilograms), the KING BOLETE (100,000 kilograms), morels (225,000 kilograms), and a number of less significant species, including LOBSTER MUSHROOMS, WESTERN CAULIFLOWER MUSHROOMS, HEDGEHOGS and BELLYBUTTON HEDGEHOGS, and a variety of other boletes. And of course BC has a storied history of picking magic mushrooms (see essay on p. 308), mostly for personal consumption, but occasionally for sale.

The mushroom species in this 1999 report represent only mushrooms that might be marketed for food. As the authors of the report note, the market for medicinal mushrooms (see p. 400) dwarfs the market for edible wild mushrooms, both in BC and worldwide. We have no account of what this segment of the commercial

Dan Freeman at his and Jan Dahlen's mushroom-buying station in Nakusp, BC.

mushroom harvest means to the BC economy. Nor do we have a good handle on how the wild mushroom harvest affects the economic health of the province and its residents. Forestry in BC is largely the activity of big corporations; the monetary transactions around wild mushrooms represent small businesses and supplemental incomes that impact many thousands of BC workers.

Most of BC's commercially important wild mushrooms are the fruiting bodies of mycorrhizal fungi, and they usually associate with trees. If the trees are killed, the fungi and their mushrooms disappear with them. Even if the trees are replanted and the fungi return, it can take 30 to 40 years or more before the mycelial mats of mycorrhizal fungi become robust enough to produce mushrooms. This loss of potentially harvestable mushrooms and the revenue from them is significant, but it passes under the radar of government accountants. Only the trees are pegged with a monetary value—the BC government receives revenue, called "stumpage," when trees on provincial Crown land are logged. Since the province receives almost nothing from the mushroom crop that is available from uncut trees, the pressure to increase government revenue translates into pressure to reduce the number of mature trees and therefore the number of wild mushrooms available for harvest. Only a few small areas around the province have been set aside for mushroom picking. BC's land-use planning needs to do a better job of identifying and protecting commercially productive and valuable mushroom habitat, both for the mushrooms and also for all of the other values associated with those forests.

False Morel
Gyromitra esculenta

CAP To 10 cm across; irregularly 3- to 5-lobed, and sometimes saddle-shaped but usually convoluted and brain-like in maturity, the margins curving toward the stem, either free or attaching; the outer surface occasionally yellow-brown but usually reddish brown and drying even darker; flesh thin, brittle, whitish. **ODOUR** Not distinctive. **TASTE** Not distinctive. **SPORE PRINT** White to yellow-brown. **STEM** To 12 cm tall × 2.5 cm wide; equal or widened at base; irregular, round, or compressed in cross-section, often longitudinally furrowed; stuffed to hollow; whitish to cream, sometimes with pale brown, pink, or purple tints; dry; smooth to finely hairy. **FRUITING** Single or in groups, occasionally clustered; on the ground or on well-rotted wood; in conifer and mixedwood forests, occasionally in lawns; spring, early summer.

EDIBILITY Poisonous. **SIMILAR** The **SADDLE-SHAPED FALSE MOREL** (p. 445, see this entry for further look-alikes), which appears in late summer and autumn, has a lighter, yellow-brown or orange-brown head that is less convoluted, making the saddle shape more apparent. **COMMENTS** Even though the FALSE MOREL has been harvested and consumed for many years, accumulating evidence of its potential toxicity, including several fatalities, has led to a ban on its harvest and marketing in some regions of Europe. ◦ The FALSE MOREL contains gyromitrin, a water-soluble hydrazine that can metabolize into other hydrazines that are carcinogenic and that can damage livers, kidneys, and the central nervous system. FALSE MORELS may be the only BC mushrooms that can poison collectors without ingestion—simply cooking them in a closed-in space and breathing the volatile compounds can be dangerous. ◦ In a recent biomedical study, FALSE MORELS from northern BC showed potent immunostimulatory activity. ◦ This species may be a decomposer, a parasite, and/or a mycorrhizal species. ◦ "Esculenta" means "edible."

Saddle-shaped False Morel   *Gyromitra infula*

CAP To 12 cm across × 8 cm high; usually 2-lobed, rarely 3-lobed, typically saddle-shaped, with opposite sides of the cap rising and the margins curving downward and attaching to the stem and/or the opposite margin; pale yellowish brown or orange-brown when young, later dark reddish brown, underside paler than top and finely hairy; smooth, often wavy and wrinkled, but not convoluted and brain-like; flesh thin, brittle, whitish. ODOUR Not distinctive. TASTE Not distinctive. SPORE PRINT White to slightly yellowish. STEM To 12 cm tall (including the part enclosed by the cap) × 2.5 cm wide; equal or widened at base; round in cross-section, sometimes compressed and furrowed longitudinally; hollowed by chambers; surface whitish to cream, sometimes with pink, lilac, or pale brown tints; dry; smooth or finely hairy; white mycelium at the base. FRUITING Single or in groups, sometimes clustered; on the ground or commonly on well-rotted wood; in conifer and mixedwood forests; late summer, autumn.

EDIBILITY Poisonous. It has the same toxins as the FALSE MOREL. SIMILAR The FALSE MOREL (p. 444), a spring mushroom, has a larger, more convoluted head that is red-brown, even when young. The COMPRESSED ELFIN SADDLE (p. 446) and *Helvella elastica* (see inset photo on that page) have caps that are less wavy and wrinkled, smaller (to 5 cm across), and more greyish brown. COMMENTS The SADDLE-SHAPED FALSE MOREL is an ascomycete. The asci line the upper surface of the cap. ◆ An "infula" is a white head cover worn by early and medieval priests and bishops. The cap of the SADDLE-SHAPED FALSE MOREL apparently reminded 18th-century mycologists of this piece of apparel.

Compressed Elfin Saddle   *Helvella compressa*

CAP To 5 cm across × 4 cm high; 2-lobed or (rarely) 3-lobed, typically saddle-shaped with a deep central cleft, the margins curved up slightly, at least initially, and then opposite parts of the cap rising almost to touch each other while the rest of the cap bends downward toward the stem; upper surface grey-brown to brown to dark brown, smooth to wrinkled, lower sterile surface whitish to greyish brown and with longish, soft, white hairs; flesh thin, brittle, pale grey. ODOUR Not distinctive. TASTE Not distinctive. STEM To 10 cm tall × 1 cm wide; equal or widened at base; round or slightly flattened in cross-section; usually solid; whitish to cream; dry; smooth to finely hairy, sometimes pitted near base. FRUITING Single, scattered, or in groups, sometimes clustered; on the ground; in conifer and mixedwood forests; mainly spring, also summer, autumn.

EDIBILITY Unknown. SIMILAR *Helvella elastica* (inset photo) has a hollow stem, the cap underside is smooth (no long hairs), and the cap margin is not initially rolled up. The SADDLE-SHAPED FALSE MOREL (p. 445) has a cap that is much larger, up to 12 cm across, and is wavy and wrinkled. It also fruits most typically on wood. COMMENTS The COMPRESSED ELFIN SADDLE is a species known only from North America, and mainly from western North America. Some western North American specimens identified as *H. compressa* are the same species as the European *H. corbierei*, which has also been identified in western North America. ✑Genetic material from *Helvella* species isolated from root tips and from archived collections in BC seems a poor match for any published genetic sequences. This suggests that a number of new *Helvella* species await discovery and description in our province. ✑ "Compressa" means "pressed together," perhaps referring to the way the opposite margins meet at the bottom of the cap and flatten against each other.

Fluted Black Elfin Saddle

Helvella vespertina

CAP Usually to 5 cm across × 5 cm high, sometimes much larger; occasionally saddle-shaped with 2 or 3 lobes, more commonly irregularly lobed and brain-like, margins usually attached to stem; black or grey to greyish black on the top fertile surface, the sterile underside greyish to greyish brown; smooth to wrinkled on top, the underside smooth, sometimes ribbed; flesh in cap thin, brittle, white to grey. ODOUR Not distinctive. TASTE Not distinctive. STEM To 15 cm tall × 5 cm wide, or larger; equal or widened at base; usually whitish to grey, sometimes black; dry; surface with deep longitudinal, sometimes sharpish double-edged ridges that separate and rejoin to form elongated pockets; flesh cartilaginous, with internal chambers. FRUITING Single or in groups, sometimes clustered; usually on the ground; in conifer and mixedwood forests; usually summer, autumn.

EDIBILITY Edible. Close kinship with more dangerous *Gyromitra* species suggests caution. Avoid infected specimens, such as those attacked by *Hypomyces cervinigenus* (see inset photo). SIMILAR *Helvella crispa* starts off with a rolled-up margin and tends to have a whitish cap, and the underside of the cap is darker and more downy than the top. *Helvella maculata* has a brown to grey-brown cap that is rolled up when young and remains free from the stem. Its underside is white to grey with longish white hairs. COMMENTS This may be the best BC mushroom to listen to. Place the fruiting surface of a fresh cap deep into your ear canal, and enjoy the crackle of ascospores being forcibly ejected. ⬥ Probably a mycorrhizal species, but the FLUTED BLACK ELFIN SADDLE may also dabble in decomposing lifestyles. ⬥ FLUTED BLACK ELFIN SADDLE was once known as *Helvella lacunosa*, a name now restricted to a species common in Europe and eastern North America. ⬥ Caps are often infected by a whitish fuzz that turns pinkish brown—the mould *Hypomyces cervinigenus* (inset photo). ⬥ "Vespertina" means "evening" and by extension "western," the direction of the evening sun.

Cups

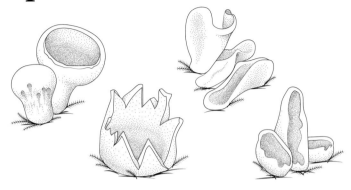

At one time, the cup fungi were lumped into a single class, Discomycetes, along with a few non-cup ascomycetes. This is a dated approach—today the fungi that produce cups are spread over a variety of classes and orders within the phylum Ascomycota—but you may still hear cup fungi referred to informally as discomycetes or simply "discos."

Most of the cups fall inside the order Pezizales, and taxonomists have been busy reorganizing the families of this order. The cup fungi in this order fall into four broad groups. *Peziza* and *Sarcosphaera* are in the Pezizaceae family. This family has mostly cup-shaped fruiting bodies, though a few of them are underground, truffle-like fungi. *Gyromitra* and *Caloscypha* have ended up in a pair of families that are, surprisingly, closely related to the morels (p. 436). *Plectania* and *Urnula* are in the Sarcosomataceae family, a family whose species almost all sport cup-shaped fruiting bodies. *Otidea*, *Scutellinia*, *Aleuria*, and *Humaria* are members of a large, diverse family that has about 80 genera and more than 600 species. In addition to the order Pezizales cups, we also present here species from *Chlorociboria* and *Bisporella*, two genera now placed in a rich and ancient lineage of ascomycetes—mostly found in the tropics—that include some small cups.

You may notice that the descriptions in this section do not contain the category SPORE PRINT. Because these mushrooms are ascomycete cups that have their asci arrayed on their upper surfaces, they typically shoot their spores upward. If you disturb a cup fungus or warm it up (with your hand or your breath), you may see a sudden cloud of spores expelled (facing page). Getting a spore print under these conditions would take some trickery. And even if you did a print, you might not learn much—when viewed under a microscope, the spores of many of the cup fungi in this section are colourless.

BC's cup fungi are largely decomposers, though a few are mycorrhizal or parasites. Most are too small and/or too tasteless to be treated as comestibles.

Brown Cup   *Peziza varia* group

FRUITING BODY To 6 cm across; initially cup-shaped, then expanding to flat or even convex, often with wavy, irregular margins that are initially curved in and then later bent outward; pale brown inside cup, darkening with age or when wet (i.e., hygrophanous), whitish to pale brown outside; dry; smooth or wrinkled and convoluted above, underside slightly scurfy; flesh to 0.7 mm, whitish to greyish brown, sometimes with layers or a black line visible (hand lens or stronger magnification needed). **ODOUR** Not distinctive. **TASTE** Not distinctive. **STEM** Very short or absent. **FRUITING** Single, in groups, or fused in clusters; usually on rotting wood (logs, lumber), sometimes indoors on wood tiles, paper residues, textiles, or in cellars, sometimes outside on the ground or on dung; year-round.

EDIBILITY Uncertain. **SIMILAR** The more than 100 worldwide species in the genus *Peziza* can be difficult to tell apart—they often end up on foray lists as "*Peziza* sp." What sets the *Peziza varia* group apart is the large size of the cups and the multiple layers in the flesh of the cup (up to 5 layers; cut the flesh to see this). *Peziza domiciliana*, which resembles the BROWN CUP, can also grow indoors. When young, it can be whitish inside the cup before turning brown. It lacks the flesh layers, and its spores are finely warted. **COMMENTS** *Peziza* species are decomposers. They belong to a different and older evolutionary branch of the ascomycete cups than the one inhabited by many of the other cup fungi in this section. ◦ Genetic tests suggest that what has traditionally been called *P. varia* is a number of different species, some fitting already assigned names, some cryptic. Specimens labelled *P. repanda* by BC mycologists often (but not always) belong to this group. ◦ The genus name "peziza" may come from the Latin word for "foot"; "varia" means "different, variable."

Crown Fungus
Sarcosphaera coronaria

FRUITING BODY Initially spherical or flat-spherical and hollow, to 10 cm across, and growing under or at the soil line, later opening at the top and exposing its fertile surfaces to the air by splitting into 6–10 rays to form a large, deep, crown-like cup up to 20 cm across from side to side; inner surface of cup whitish when young, becoming lilac, and eventually pale purple-brown, outside surface whitish, sometimes with purple tints, incorporating dirt; dry; smooth inside, outside usually scurfy; flesh thick (to 3 mm), brittle, whitish. **ODOUR** Not distinctive. **TASTE** Not distinctive. **STEM** Short (to 2 cm) or absent.

FRUITING Single or in groups, sometimes clustered; on or slightly below the ground; usually in conifer forests, sometimes along path edges or near melting snow; most common in spring, also summer, autumn.

EDIBILITY Poisonous. **SIMILAR** Could be mistaken for a truffle or puffball of some kind (e.g., the **LEMON EARTHBALL**, p. 429) when young, but the hollow interior will always distinguish the **CROWN FUNGUS**. *Neournula pouchetii* has a whitish outside, but is smaller, with thinner, less brittle flesh, and the interior is pinkish to grey. **COMMENTS** Once thought edible (but blah), **CROWN FUNGUS** is now known to bioaccumulate arsenic and other metals and is believed to contain toxins. ✦ The **CROWN FUNGUS** is called *Sarcosphaera crassa* in some older texts. ✦ Genetic evidence points to a close relationship with *Peziza* species. ✦ Sources sometimes list the **CROWN FUNGUS** as a decomposer, but evidence is accumulating that the **CROWN FUNGUS** has a mycorrhizal role with surrounding bushes and trees. ✦ The **CROWN FUNGUS** is found in both hemispheres, but it is primarily a species of western North America. ✦ The scientific name covers its development: "sarcosphaera" means "fleshy ball," which is a good description of the young stage, and "coronaria" means "pertaining to a crown," a reference to the opened-out, star-like shape of the mature fruiting body.

Thick Cup

Gyromitra ancilis

FRUITING BODY To 10 cm across; cup-shaped at first and with the margins rolled in, becoming flattened to convex and irregular and with margins rolled down; upper (fertile) surface tan, yellowish brown, or reddish brown, lower surface whitish to pale brown; upper surface usually wrinkled, wavy, or convoluted, lower surface smooth or with fine hairs; flesh to 3 mm thick, brittle, whitish. **ODOUR** Not distinctive. **TASTE** Not distinctive. **STEM** Absent, or to 2 cm tall; a thickened base; often strongly fluted or pitted; whitish to pale brown. **FRUITING** Single or in groups, sometimes clustered; usually on the ground, less commonly on rotten wood; in conifer forests, especially common at higher elevations, near melting snow; spring, early summer.

EDIBILITY Uncertain. **SIMILAR** Specimens of THICK CUP might be mistaken for one of the *Peziza* species, such as **BROWN CUP** (p. 450), but the latter is not as wrinkled on the inside of the cup and its flesh is thinner. **COMMENTS** Some BC foragers collect and eat this species. Its placement in the *Gyromitra* genus, however, argues for caution. The possible presence of hydrazines, thought to be carcinogenic, is also a concern. ◆ The most popular common name for this mushroom is PIG'S EAR, but that is also the name for *Gomphus clavatus* (p. 41), so we have decided for this guide to use the name THICK CUP. ◆ In most texts, you will still find the scientific name of THICK CUP listed as *Discina perlata*. Genetic studies, however, place it squarely in the genus *Gyromitra*. ◆ "Ancilis" echoes the name of a mythological shield, "ancile." The huge spores of THICK CUP, oblong bodies with knobs at each end and festooned with oil drops, look like ornate shields.

Snowbank Orange Peel *Caloscypha fulgens*

FRUITING BODY To 4 cm across; initially spherical, becoming cup-shaped (sometimes with a constricted mouth) or saucer-shaped, the margin often lobed or split; orange-yellow inside the cup with some blue-green spotting, yellowish brown outside the cup, often with green or blue-green tinting and bruising; dry; smooth to minutely bumpy inside, smooth to mealy outside; flesh quite thin (to 1 mm thick), brittle, yellow. **ODOUR** Not distinctive. **TASTE** Not distinctive. **STEM** Usually absent, with attachment of the cup to the soil by the mycelium; if present, very short and whitish. **FRUITING** Single, scattered, or in groups, sometimes clustered; on the ground; in conifer forests, often at higher elevations; generally fruiting immediately following the snowmelt in spring.

EDIBILITY Uncertain. Apparently poisonous to some. **SIMILAR** See the page for the **ORANGE PEEL FUNGUS** (p. 456) for further comparisons. **COMMENTS** The asexual form of the SNOWBANK ORANGE PEEL, which is a cold-loving fungal parasite on certain types of conifer seeds, causes extensive losses in greenhouses and plant nurseries. The presence of the sexual cup fungus is often a signal that the mycelium has been feeding on seeds in fallen conifer cones, often in caches of cones that have been collected by squirrels. ❧ The SNOWBANK ORANGE PEEL has been used by foragers as an indicator species for morels. And it may well be an indicator of good morel habitat: despite its outward similarity to the ORANGE PEEL FUNGUS, genetic studies suggest that the SNOWBANK ORANGE PEEL is more closely related to morels. ❧ "Caloscypha" means "beautiful goblet," and "fulgens" means "shining."

Orange-dusted Cup   *Plectania melastoma*

FRUITING BODY To 2 cm across × 3 cm high; initially spherical, becoming shaped like a brandy snifter with margins incurved, only in later stages margins expanding to make the fruiting body look like a cup or saucer, margins sometimes splitting in age; the interior is black to brownish black, glistening when moist, the exterior also black but with orange granules that are often concentrated around the top rim; dry; inside surface sometimes wrinkled, underside wrinkled and finely hairy when young; flesh tough, with a gelatinous (when wet) inner layer. **ODOUR** Not distinctive. **TASTE** Not distinctive. **STEM** Absent, or short (to 1 cm), black, with wiry black mycelia at base. **FRUITING** Single, and often in groups or clustered; on twigs and other duff materials; usually in conifer forests; spring.

EDIBILITY Unknown. **SIMILAR** *Plectania milleri* looks like the ORANGE-DUSTED CUP, but without the orange granules and with a margin that often appears to be arrayed with small teeth. *Donadinia nigrella* (new name for *Plectania nannfeldtii*) has a long (to 3.5 cm) stem and a more spreading cup. It grows near the snow line and has no orange granules. Two spring wood-decaying species that have the black surfaces and the outer hairiness of ORANGE-DUSTED CUP but lack the orange granules are *Pseudoplectania melaena* (stem to 2–3 cm tall, straight or wavy hairs on the outside) and *Pseudoplectania nigrella* (short or no stem and coiled hairs). See also the entry for **STARVING MAN'S LICORICE** (p. 455) for another look-alike. **COMMENTS** "Plectania" is from a Greek word meaning "wreath, coil," and "melastoma" means "with a black mouth."

Starving Man's Licorice   *Urnula padeniana*

FRUITING BODY To 10 cm across × 10 cm high; shaped like an inverted cone, top hollowed into a cup, margins incurved and then expanding and sometimes irregular; dark brown to black inside, outside dark grey to black; dry; smooth inside, and also shiny when wet on the inside, mealy or with dark hairs on the outside; flesh thick, rubbery, gelatinous, glistening when cut, brownish or grey or shiny black (resembling, some think, black licorice), filling the base and around the cup. ODOUR Not distinctive. TASTE Not distinctive. STEM Body narrows downward into a stem that is often ribbed and gouged with hollowed-out pockets. FRUITING Single to scattered or in groups; on the ground or on rotten wood; under conifers; late winter, spring, summer, early autumn.

EDIBILITY Unknown. SIMILAR *Pseudosarcosoma latahense*, a generally smaller (to 7.5 cm across) species that prefers higher elevations, has flesh that is less gelatinous, especially when older. The key difference, however, is microscopic—its spores have no oil droplets, while those of STARVING MAN'S LICORICE have 1–3 drops. See also the comparisons in the entry for ORANGE-DUSTED CUP (p. 454). COMMENTS A somewhat rare mushroom, but where it occurs it can be locally abundant. ◆ STARVING MAN'S LICORICE shows up on many BC lists as *Sarcosoma mexicana* or *S. mexicanum*. Genetic analysis done in the 2010s showed that the species is firmly nested in the *Urnula* genus. ◆ "Padeniana" honours mycologist John Wilburn Paden, who contributed to the study of this species. John Paden taught in the Biology Department at the University of Victoria from 1966 until his death in 1990.

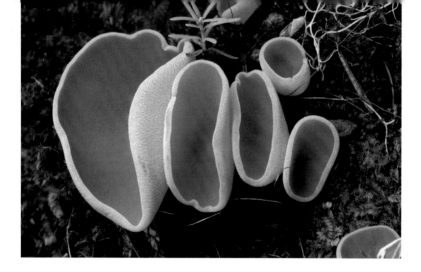

Orange Peel Fungus   *Aleuria aurantia*

FRUITING BODY To 8 cm across; initially spherical, then cup-shaped, expanding and flattening to a saucer shape, but often distorted from growing in tight clusters, the margins sometimes lobed or split; bright orange inside the cup, fading somewhat with age, paler (to white) under the cup; dry; smooth inside, downy/white-mealy outside; flesh thin, fragile, white or orange. **ODOUR** Not distinctive. **TASTE** Not distinctive. **STEM** Usually absent. **FRUITING** Scattered or in groups, often in dense clusters; on the ground, especially on hard-packed soils (e.g., trail edges, roadsides, and gravel paths); spring, summer, autumn.

    EDIBILITY Edible. Nothing to write home about, though. **SIMILAR** The **SNOWBANK ORANGE PEEL** (p. 453) has a more orange-yellow hue inside the cup and is tinted with green or blue-green on the outside. It grows at higher elevations in the spring, often beside melting snowbanks, and usually near conifers. ***Sowerbyella rhenana***, which is found in mature conifer forests, resembles an ORANGE PEEL FUNGUS on a short pole—it has a stem up to 2 cm tall. **COMMENTS** The ORANGE PEEL FUNGUS is quite a common sight on BC paths and roadsides. It sometimes looks so much like a discarded orange peel that some hikers do not initially recognize it as a mushroom. ◦ Given its habitat, ORANGE PEEL FUNGUS is presumably a decomposer, but an isotope study found some evidence that it may also play mycorrhizal roles. ◦ An ascomycete, it sometimes discharges its spores in thick clouds from the fertile surface inside the cup when triggered by a warm breath or by handling. ◦ "Aleuria" means "flour" in Greek, possibly a reference to the white-mealy dusting on the underside of young caps. "Aurantia" means "orange-coloured."

Eyelash Cup   *Scutellinia scutellata* group

FRUITING BODY Small, to 1.5 cm across; teacup-shaped to saucer-shaped; bright orange or red inside/above, pale brown to brown-orange outside/below; dry; upper surface smooth, but the margin and underside having stiff dark brown or black hairs with the longest hairs on the margin, making the cup resemble a red eye with dark eyelashes; flesh thin. **ODOUR** Not distinctive. **TASTE** Not distinctive. **STEM** Absent. **FRUITING** Scattered or in groups, sometimes clustered; on rotten wood or soil, or occasionally on rotting vegetation; spring, summer, autumn.

EDIBILITY Unknown. **SIMILAR** *Cytidia salicina* also starts off as tiny red discs, but the discs soon coalesce into bands many centimetres long. It does not have dark hairs around the discs and prefers to grow on willow, RED ALDER, and PAPER BIRCH branches 1–2 m off the ground. *Sarcoscypha coccinea*, a much rarer and larger (to 5 cm) cup fungus, has a scarlet upper surface and a white to pinkish lower surface. It lacks the long eyelash-like hairs at the margin. **COMMENTS** A large number of less common *Scutellinia* species have been described in the technical literature, and some can look distressingly alike. ☙ EYELASH CUP makes its living by decomposing woody materials. ☙ Researchers have found that, as spores are formed in EYELASH CUP's asci, certain strains of bacteria invade the asci and assemble on the surfaces of the spores. The purpose of this invasion is uncertain. The bacteria may be just hitching a ride, but they may also play some role in spore germination—a good reminder that, while mushrooms participate in larger ecosystems, they can also *be* miniature ecosystems. ☙ Both "scutellinia" and "scutellata" are derived from Latin words that can refer to a small, flat shield or a flat dish. A mushroom so beautiful they named it twice.

Phoenicoid Fungi

The phoenix, as described in ancient Greek legends, is a bird that lives for centuries. At the end of its long life, it bursts into flames and a new phoenix is born from its ashes. Phoenicoid fungi are specialized fungi that, like the phoenix for which they are named, seem to rise magically from burned wood, soil, or ashes.

In BC, most phoenicoid fungi are ascomycetes, usually morels (p. 436) or cup fungi (p. 449). In the near-desert ecosystems of southern Interior BC, species belonging to the class Sordariomycetes (also called Pyrenomycetes), ascomycetes with mostly flask-shaped fruiting bodies, may predominate. A few basidiomycete mushroom species are also considered phoenicoid fungi, such as certain *Pholiota* species, including *P. highlandensis* (also known as *P. carbonaria*, the BURNT-GROUND PHOLIOTA), *Bonomyces sinopicus* (the BRICK-RED CLITOCYBE), and *Myxomphalia maura* (the BURN SITE MYCENA), all of which are usually found in late summer and fall on burn sites.

Morels, BC's best-known phoenicoid fungi, fruit in many habitats, and often turn up in unexpected places. Those fruiting in unburned habitats are sometimes referred to as natural morels. Several species, including the GREY FIRE MOREL (p. 440), fruit most commonly and abundantly in the spring that follows the previous year's forest fires. Mushroom pickers often use forest-fire maps to guide them to good harvesting areas. The BC commercial morel harvest—currently unregulated—is worth millions of dollars each year.

A succession of BC cup fungi may fruit abundantly following fires. Several months following a fire, some *Peziza* cups and the red-brown, convoluted lumps of *Rhizina undulata* may show up. Other species, such as the stalked *Peziza* relative *Geopyxis carbonaria* (see photo), tend to show up from 4 to 16 months following a fire. The timing of fruiting of these species seems to depend more on the time of burning than on the season.

Why do phoenicoid mushrooms fruit on burn sites? For most species we're not certain, but we have a few guesses. Some morels, we know, form symbiotic

associations with trees—when fire kills their partner trees, they may decide that it is their last chance to reproduce. Decomposer phoenicoid mushrooms could be responding to the physical and nutrient effects of fire on soils and wood, including the clearance of competing vegetation, the warming of soils, the concentration of nutrients, and ash-induced increase in alkalinity. These, however, are only informed guesses—we really don't know the whole story behind the partnership between fire and phoenicoid mushrooms.

Hairy Fairy Cup
Humaria hemisphaerica

FRUITING BODY To 3 cm across × 1.5 cm high; roughly spherical at first, becoming cup-shaped; inside whitish to grey with a brown margin above merging into a brown outside; dry; smooth inside, the margin and outside covered with stiff, sharp-pointed brown hairs; flesh thin, wax-like, greyish white. **ODOUR** Not distinctive. **TASTE** Not distinctive. **STEM** Absent. **FRUITING** Single or in groups; on the ground or on well-decayed wood; in coniferous and hardwood forests; summer, autumn.

EDIBILITY Unknown. **SIMILAR** Except for some species rarely (if ever) seen in BC, there aren't cup fungi this size and colour that have hairy outer surfaces. **COMMENTS** Most cup fungi in the family to which the *Humaria* species belong are decomposers. The HAIRY FAIRY CUP and other members of its genus are unusual in this family because they assume mycorrhizal roles with surrounding vegetation. HAIRY FAIRY CUP is noted for forming mycorrhizal associations both with mixotrophic BC wintergreens (*Orthilia secunda* and *Pyrola* species; see essay on p. 54) and also with nearby trees, permitting the wintergreens to steal sugars from the trees with the fungus as an intermediary. ● "Hemisphaerica" means "half of a sphere."

Donkey Ears

Otidea onotica

FRUITING BODY To 6 cm across × 10 cm high; spoon-shaped or shaped like a rabbit or donkey ear, with one side open to the base, often irregular, margins sometimes bent inward, especially when young; yellow-brown, orange-brown, or cinnamon, occasionally with pinkish tints inside, outside a hygrophanous orangey brown that dries to a paler shade or to yellowish brown, lacking pink tints; dry; smooth inside, outside sometimes slightly scurfy; flesh thin, brittle, white or yellowish. **ODOUR** Not distinctive. **TASTE** Not distinctive. **STEM** Fruiting body usually arising from debris held together by white mycelia, but occasionally a short, hairy, yellowish to whitish base (to 2.5 cm). **FRUITING** Usually in groups or clustered; on the ground; usually under conifers; summer, autumn.

EDIBILITY Uncertain. **SIMILAR DONKEY EARS** are the most commonly reported *Otidea* in BC, but several others are found here, and they can be quite difficult to tell apart in the field. Mushrooms in the **Otidea alutacea group** (inset photo), which are about as common as DONKEY EARS, have a squatter shape (to 4 cm across × 6 cm high and more like cropped donkey ears) and tan to greyish brown or yellowish brown surfaces. *Otidea smithii*, somewhat rarer, is dark brown to deep purple on the inside and sometimes even darker outside. Also rarer, but perhaps the most similar to DONKEY EARS, is **O. leporina**, which is smaller (to 2.5 cm across × 5 cm tall) and has duller cream-yellow to yellow-brown colours with fewer pink tints. All of the *Otidea* species might be mistaken for pezizas such as the **BROWN CUP** (p. 450), but *Peziza* species generally lack the split cap. **COMMENTS** *Otidea* species, like the *Humaria* species, are unusual in the world of ascomycete cup fungi because they appear to form mycorrhizal relationships with nearby plants and trees. ● "Otidea" probably comes from the Greek word for "ear"; "onotica" means "pertaining to a donkey."

Green Cups   *Chlorociboria aeruginascens*

FRUITING BODY To 7 mm across; cup-shaped or spoon-shaped, becoming funnel-shaped; green to bluish green inside and outside the cup, darkening somewhat on drying; dry; smooth to finely hairy or bumpy; flesh thin, same colour as exterior. ODOUR Not distinctive. TASTE Not distinctive. STEM To 5 mm tall; often several stems rising from one hyphal mass; off-centre or more rarely central; coloured as cup. FRUITING Single or in groups; on decayed barkless wood and rotten logs, most commonly hardwood but sometimes conifers; year-round when wet enough, the fruiting bodies most commonly appearing in the autumn.

EDIBILITY Not edible. SIMILAR *Chlorociboria* is mostly a Southern Hemisphere genus, but we have 2 common members of the genus in Europe and North America and both species are in BC. *Chlorociboria aeruginosa* (note the small spelling change in the species epithet) is usually smaller, has a centrally attached stem, and has larger spores. COMMENTS The mycelium of the ascomycete decomposer GREEN CUPS is common throughout BC. Its pigment, xylindein, stains well-decayed wood bluish green. The cups, the sexual fruiting bodies, are much less common. GREEN CUPS has a vigorous asexual stage and seems to prefer that mode of reproduction. ◦ At least since the Italian Renaissance, wood infused with GREEN CUPS has been used as small inlay pieces for decoration. Wood stained by this fungus is still sought after by woodcrafters. ◦ "Chlorociboria" means "green drinking cup," and "aeruginascens" means "becoming blue-green."

Yellow Fairy Cups   *Bisporella citrina*

FRUITING BODY Tiny, to 3 mm across × 1 mm high; taking the form of a shallow cup or plate, but sometimes distorted by close neighbours; yellow, becoming orange-yellow with age inside the cup, similar but slightly paler outside; dry; smooth. **ODOUR** Not distinctive. **TASTE** Not distinctive. **STEM** Usually absent, or very short and tapering downward. **FRUITING** In groups, sometimes clustered; on hardwood branches, especially ones without bark, but sometimes bursting through the bark; autumn, winter.

EDIBILITY Unknown. **SIMILAR** *Lachnellula agassizii* also has small orange-yellow cups on short stems, but the cups have wavy white hairs on the outside and on the margins. It grows on conifer wood. *Chloroscypha flavida* is jelly-like and slightly larger (to 5 mm across with a stem to 5 mm long), and has a convex, translucent-yellow top in maturity. It grows at higher altitude, often near snowbanks, on the decaying cones, twigs, and needles of YELLOW-CEDAR. Two yellow jelly fungi might also, at quick glance, be confused with YELLOW FAIRY CUPS. *Dacrymyces stillatus* has small yellow to orange to red-brown heads that are gelatinous and translucent and that can assume the shape of cups, plates, or lenses. It prefers conifer wood and construction wood. The gelatinous ALPINE JELLY CONE (p. 414) and the similar *Heterotextus luteus* are usually larger (with the biggest caps to 1 cm across), and they fruit on conifer wood. **COMMENTS** YELLOW FAIRY CUPS are common decomposers in BC forests. They can appear on logs in great masses. ◦ "Bisporella" means "little double-spored"; spores of YELLOW FAIRY CUPS are divided by a cross-wall. "Citrina" means "lemon-like" in Latin.

Truffles

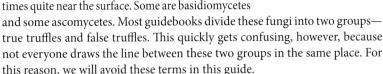

The mushrooms in this section grow underground, sometimes tens of centimetres down, but at other times quite near the surface. Some are basidiomycetes and some ascomycetes. Most guidebooks divide these fungi into two groups— true truffles and false truffles. This quickly gets confusing, however, because not everyone draws the line between these two groups in the same place. For this reason, we will avoid these terms in this guide.

In BC and the US Pacific Northwest, we have about 350 different species of truffles, grouped into 50 to 60 different genera. The fruiting bodies are usually less than four centimetres long, and often look like small potatoes when dug up. They typically do not show up as frequently on BC inventories as other kinds of mushrooms, for the simple reason that they can be difficult to find.

Evolution favours organisms that can disperse new generations to fresh territories. Growing a spore mass underground, while it protects the spores during development, raises the question of how the spores disperse. At least some of the truffles achieve this through animal intervention—they produce potent smells that animals can detect. The animals dig the mushrooms out of the ground and carry them to more distant locations. We know of several dozen species of local mammals that provide this service, with the NORTHERN FLYING SQUIRREL and the RED-BACKED VOLE among the most observed. When the truffles are fruiting, some small mammals eat little but truffles.

Taxonomists once lumped the truffle-like genera and species together, but the era of genetic sequencing has made it obvious that many of the groups of underground fungi are more closely related to above-ground fungi than to one another. The ascomycete truffles *Tuber* and *Leucangium* are related to cup fungi, and *Elaphomyces* to green and blue moulds. All of the basidiomycete truffles in this section are related to boletes.

Truffles in the genera *Tuber* and *Leucangium* are highly favoured edibles. (See the essay on p. 466 for more on these truffles in BC.) The rest of the underground mushrooms are not usually sought out by mycophagists, even though relatively few of them seem to be poisonous. The issue of collecting for the table is compounded by the issue of identifiability—beginners can sometimes confuse edibles with poisonous *Scleroderma* species.

The truffles seem to be mostly mycorrhizal fungi. They form associations with many different plant species. Researchers aligned with Oregon State University documented over 120 different BC and US Pacific Northwest species of plants from 19 different families that enter into these compacts with underground fungi. If you want to know more about truffles, consult a publication that emerged from this Oregon research: Matt Trappe, Frank Evans, and James Trappe's *Field Guide to North American Truffles* (Ten Speed Press, 2007).

Fall Western White Truffle *Tuber oregonense*

FRUITING BODY To 5 cm across; smaller specimens spherical, larger specimens irregular, sometimes lobed and furrowed; whitish when young, developing patches of yellow-brown or reddish brown, then reddish brown all over when mature; smooth to slightly hairy (especially in furrows) and roughened; outer skin very thin (to 0.4 mm). **INTERIOR** Firm and white when young and becoming brown as spores mature, with a marbling of white hyphal veins, giving it the look of fat-marbled beef, the whitish interior veins sometimes punching through to the outer surface. **ODOUR** Not always distinctive when young but with the unique truffle scent (described at times as garlicky, spicy, and cheesy, but not exactly like any of these) when mature. **TASTE** Not distinctive. **FRUITING** Single or scattered; maturing underground; usually under younger (less than a hundred years old) DOUGLAS-FIR and less commonly other conifers; autumn, winter.

EDIBILITY Choice. Collected commercially. **SIMILAR** The FALL WESTERN WHITE TRUFFLE is part of a complex of at least 4 native white truffles that associate with the abundant DOUGLAS-FIRS in BC and the US Pacific Northwest. Another member of this complex, the **SPRING WESTERN WHITE TRUFFLE** (*Tuber gibbosum*), mainly differs from the FALL WESTERN WHITE TRUFFLE by appearing in the late winter and spring rather than the autumn. *Tuber gibbosum* usually does not develop the same reddish brown hues, remaining more yellow-brown to olive-brown. In addition to the white truffles, there are edible native black truffles in BC that also have the unique truffly smell. The most common of these, the **WESTERN BLACK TRUFFLE** (*Leucangium carthusianum*, p. 467), is usually larger (to 8 cm) and has a finely warted outer surface that is dark grey to dark brown to black. Its interior transitions from white to greyish green and exudes a clear latex. **COMMENTS** "Tuber" is a Latin word for "lump," and "oregonense" means "from Oregon," named this because western Oregon is the region typically associated with this truffle.

Common Deer Truffle   *Elaphomyces granulatus* group

FRUITING BODY To 4 cm across; ovoid to spherical; surface finely warty, whitish, becoming yellow-brown; rind thick (to 5 mm), firm, with a yellowish outer layer and a thicker white to greyish inner layer; often with yellow mycelium attached. **INTERIOR** White and firm when young, becoming grey to purplish and eventually becoming a powdery dark brown to black mass. **ODOUR** Not distinctive or faintly metallic. **TASTE** Not distinctive. **FRUITING** Single, scattered, or in groups; typically buried (to 8 cm), but often on the surface dug up by animals; usually under conifers, less commonly hardwoods; summer, autumn.

EDIBILITY Reported to be edible by some, but it is a serious arsenic accumulator and should be treated with great caution. **SIMILAR** With its powdery black spore mass and thick outer skin, the COMMON DEER TRUFFLE can resemble the basidiomycete earthballs in the *Scleroderma* genus such as the LEMON EARTHBALL (p. 429), but the earthballs are at most partly buried, show a distinct point of attachment to the substrate, and do not have the warty outer skin of the truffle. **COMMENTS** The COMMON DEER TRUFFLE is easiest to find when it has been parasitized by TRUFFLE EATER (p. 362), an above-ground mushroom whose stem serves as a flag to mark the truffle buried below. ⬥ The COMMON DEER TRUFFLE is a mycorrhizal ascomycete that is found throughout BC. ⬥ Preliminary studies indicate that the COMMON DEER TRUFFLE of the West Coast of North America is really a collection of cryptic species, probably none of which is the same as the European-defined *Elaphomyces granulatus*. ⬥ The "deer" in the common name is based on observations of deer mycophagy, but the main consumers of this truffle in BC forests seem to be squirrels and voles. ⬥ "Elaphomyces" is a compound word for "deer mushroom." "Granulatus" means "granular," a reference to the warty outer skin.

Truffle Adventures

Truffles command a special place among the edible fungi of BC. Their presence on tables of haute cuisine, the difficulty of finding them, their potent smells, their unique tastes, their well-known properties as aphrodisiacs—all weave a story of fungal adventure that more mundane edibles find hard to match.

Truffles are ectomycorrhizal species, living in symbiosis with plants. In south coastal BC, DOUGLAS-FIR hosts all three of the renowned native culinary truffles—two species of western white truffles and one species of western black (see FALL WESTERN WHITE TRUFFLE, p. 464). The DOUGLAS-FIR is also home to an array of lesser-known native truffles that appeal more to small mammals than to humans. Using molecular assessments of ectomycorrhizae and focused searches near small-mammal digs in south central BC, mycologists and their students have discovered that DEER MICE, YELLOW-PINE CHIPMUNKS, RED-BACKED VOLES, RED SQUIRRELS, and NORTHERN FLYING SQUIRRELS have a taste for truffles. These researchers counted 18 species of native truffles, some of them undescribed species in the *Tuber* and *Leucangium* genera.

BC has exotic as well as native truffles. Three of the famous Mediterranean truffle species (*Tuber melanosporum*, *T. aestivum*, and *T. borchii*) are currently being harvested from oak and hazelnut truffle orchards on Vancouver Island and the

BC truffle-dog extraordinaire Dexter and his handler, Brooke Page.

lower Fraser Valley. Truffle orchards are being installed in Okanagan Valley as well. To find these cultivated (and wild) truffles, trained dogs are now employed, replacing the historic use of pigs in Europe. But not always: At one commercial truffle orchard on Vancouver Island, Annabelle the VIETNAMESE POT-BELLIED PIG is regularly sent in search of truffles.

The introduction of Mediterranean truffles into the province might be a concern if the fungi were to escape cultivation and displace native ectomycorrhizal fungi in native forests. So far there is no evidence of the escape of these Mediterranean species from places where their cultivation has been introduced. There is, however, evidence that other truffle-like species have been moved into BC inadvertently. *Hydnangium carneum*, for example, has hitchhiked to BC from Australia on the roots of eucalyptus trees and can fruit in abundance in the autumn. Thus far it has been found only with planted eucalyptus and not with any of our native trees. *Tuber rapaeodorum*, which is associated with horticultural trees, is another European species that is now found in BC and around the world.

Truffle adventures in BC, it is safe to say, are only beginning. In coming years, further genetic study and a more concerted effort with trained truffle dogs will undoubtedly reveal a wealth of new truffles and new ranges for known truffles.

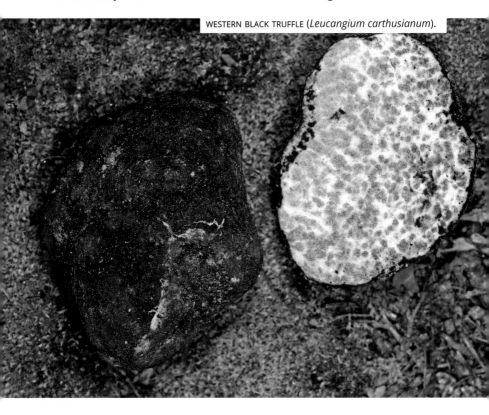

WESTERN BLACK TRUFFLE (*Leucangium carthusianum*).

Red Gravel   *Alpova diplophloeus*

FRUITING BODY To 4 cm across; oval to spherical, sometimes with irregular lobes; rind thin (about 1 mm thick), one-layered; surface reddish brown, deep reddish brown where bruised, sometimes drying black; rhizomorphs few or absent, but when present pressed tightly to the surface, fine, and darker than the surface; flesh of the rind brownish but sometimes darker near the surface. INTERIOR Chambered, the chambers to 2.5 mm across, gel-filled, and separated by whitish veins; chambers reddish brown but reddish black in age or where exposed; the gel sticky when young, hard and waxy in age. ODOUR Not distinctive. One researcher, however, says that after freezing and thawing, a collection of RED GRAVEL had the smell of Baileys Irish Cream. TASTE Not distinctive. FRUITING Single, scattered, or in groups; buried in the soil but often breaking the surface when mature; under alder; late summer, autumn.

EDIBILITY Uncertain. Some sources report it as edible. SIMILAR The red-brown exterior and the marbled interior of this truffle may lead to confusion with the FALL WESTERN WHITE TRUFFLE (p. 464). The FALL WESTERN WHITE TRUFFLE grows with conifers (usually DOUGLAS-FIR), has whitish to brownish, non-gelatinous interior tissue, and emits the famous truffly odour. Two similar alder-associated *Alpova* species have long been referred to as *A. diplophloeus*. Both produce smaller spores and have rinds with 2 structurally distinct layers. One of them, *A. concolor*, has been documented from BC. COMMENTS RED GRAVEL is mycorrhizal with alders. ✦ "Alpova" is a portmanteau based on the names of Alfred H. Povah, a botanist and collector of the specimens on which the genus is based. "Diplophloeus" is from Greek "diplo," meaning "double," and "phloeus," meaning "rind," a reference to the 2-layered outer rind (though this double layering does not hold for *A. diplophloeus* itself, only for another species once confused with it).

Dark Pogie   *Rhizopogon parksii*

FRUITING BODY To 3 cm across; spherical to somewhat irregular; while still young whitish but staining pink or violet when bruised and overlain with dense dark hyphae, the surface later becoming dark grey, brown, or dark olive, the outer layer separating in portions to expose a pinkish underlying layer that turns blue and eventually black; firm, rubbery. **INTERIOR** Whitish and firm when young, becoming grey to olive or tan, darkening with age, sometimes parts staining purple. **ODOUR** Not distinctive, or slightly garlicky/spicy. **TASTE** Not distinctive. **FRUITING** Scattered or in groups; growing under the soil line but sometimes erupting to the surface; under DOUGLAS-FIR and pines; late summer, autumn, winter.

    EDIBILITY Not edible. **SIMILAR** The 2 *Rhizopogon* species that most consistently show up in BC mushroom inventories are the DARK POGIE and *R. vinicolor*. The latter differs from the DARK POGIE mainly by having an outer surface that, starting off whitish, soon turns to wine red or lilac-rose. **COMMENTS** We may have several dozen *Rhizopogon* species in BC and more than a hundred species in the Pacific Northwest. *Rhizopogon* species are important mycorrhizal associates of pines and DOUGLAS-FIR. ☙ Species in the *Rhizopogon* genus are related to boletes in the genus *Suillus*. ☙ All 7 fungal species in the *Rhizopogon* subgenus *Amylopogon* form mycorrhizal associations with plant species in the Monotrope family. In BC, *R. arctostaphyli* and *R. salebrosus* form mycorrhizal connections to PINEDROPS (*Pterospora andromedea*), a mycoheterotrophic plant (see essay on p. 54) that lacks chlorophyll. The 2 *Rhizopogon* species also form mycorrhizae with nearby conifers and transfer sugars from the trees to the PINEDROPS. ☙ "Rhizopogon" is a compound meaning "root beard," referring to the dense hyphal mats that overlay the fruiting bodies. "Parksii" is in honour of American mycologist Harold Ernest Parks (1880–1967), who collected the type species.

Lemon Truffle   *Truncocolumella citrina*

FRUITING BODY To 5 cm across × 5 cm high; spherical to irregular or lobed, sometimes heart- or kidney-shaped; briefly whitish when young, quickly becoming yellowish gold, then greenish yellow and greyish olive; dry; smooth or with a few cracks; rind very thin (to 1 mm). **INTERIOR** With numerous small chambers; white to grey, becoming yellow-brown to nearly black; firm, rubbery, interior sometimes gelatinous in age and maggot-infested. **STEM** A short, narrowing, pinched base on the outside is attached to rhizomorphs; inside a yellowish columella (a mass of dense sterile tissue) often sends branches into the interior spore mass. **ODOUR** Not distinctive. **TASTE** Not distinctive. **FRUITING** Single or scattered or in groups; usually found in the humus, just below or projecting slightly above the soil line; under DOUGLAS-FIR (and less commonly other conifers); late summer, autumn.

EDIBILITY Edible. But apparently flavourless. **SIMILAR** *Rhizopogon occidentalis* has a lemon-yellow exterior, but the surface is often streaked with brown rhizomorphs. Its interior starts off pale orange-yellow, becoming greenish grey, and it lacks the LEMON TRUFFLE's columella of sterile tissue branching into the spore mass. **COMMENTS** The LEMON TRUFFLE, a basidiomycete, is a common truffle in southern BC. It is more frequently reported in BC inventories than other truffle-like fruiting bodies in this section, perhaps because it is easy to identify and more likely to emerge on its own from under the ground or to be dug up by animals. ❧ The LEMON TRUFFLE, like *Rhizopogon* species, is closely related to boletes in the genus *Suillus*. ❧ *Truncocolumella*, a genus defined in the late 1930s, has a name that is probably a botanical term for a tree trunk ("trunco") compounded with "columella," the technical term for the mass of sterile tissue inside the base of certain puffballs and truffles. "Citrina" means "lemon-like," probably more in reference to its surface colour than to its shape or odour.

First Nations and Fungi

Indigenous peoples in BC have used fungi for various purposes for millennia. The Nlaka'pamux, Stl'atl'imx, and other Interior Salish people in the past consumed many of the same mushrooms that Indigenous and non-Indigenous folks forage for today—including CHANTERELLES (p. 34 and image below), PINE MUSHROOMS (p. 146), and a mushroom known by the Nlaka'pamux as "thunderstorm head" or "lightning" mushroom (p. 420). Interior Salish Nations collect POPLAR TRICH (p. 152) in early autumn from around BLACK COTTONWOOD growing on alluvial sands—the mushrooms are eaten dried, fried, and in stews.

Indigenous peoples both on the coast and in the Interior use various polypore conks for technical, medicinal, and spiritual purposes. TINDER CONK (p. 402), RED-BELTED CONK (p. 398), and other conks were once, and in some cases still are, used for tinder, for tanning animal hides, and as smudges for repelling biting insects. RED PAINT FUNGUS (p. 407) is used as a red pigment. RED-BELTED CONK, CHAGA (p. 405), and other polypores are employed as medicines by the Nlaka'pamux, Secwépemc, and others. The Nuxalk have been known to dust puffball spores on wounds to hasten healing. The W̱SÁNEĆ (Saanich) name for tree fungus, TU,TU,ÁLEḴEP (TUʔTUʔÉLƏQƏP), means "echo" and is also used for "telephone." These fungi are associated with the echoes heard when one calls out in the woods.

The Haida, Tlingit, Tsimshian, and other coastal First Nations employ conks of AGARIKON (p. 396), not just for medicine but also for carving spirit figures. The Nuxalk paint faces on bracket fungi to be used in their kusiut ceremonies, which celebrate the canoe journey of supernatural beings up the Bella Coola River. For the Haida, Tree Fungus Man was the steadfast steersman of Yáahl's (Raven's) canoe when Yáahl paddled out to retrieve the first female genitalia from the intertidal. On previous voyages, Junco and Steller's Jay had proved not up to the task, so Yáahl drew an image on a bracket fungus—perhaps an ARTIST'S CONK (p. 393)—and set it in the stern of his canoe.

Other Fungi

The fungi in this section are a miscellany that do not fit neatly into other sections in this book. They include some basidiomycetes, some ascomycetes, and even one zygomycete (YELLOW MOUNTAIN PEA, p. 476). They are parasites and decomposers that are referred to by names such as rusts, spots, knots, and curls. Several of them are noticed in the field by the changes they induce in their plant hosts, not by their fruiting bodies.

While many of the fungi here are small, their impact on British Columbians can be great. Some have a serious economic impact on plants that we value, especially on the coniferous trees that we use for timber and on the fruit trees and shrubs whose fruit we harvest. As a result, they are often studied more than the charismatic mushrooms in the other parts of this text. In fact, the great majority of the professional mycologists who have worked in BC over the last century have spent their careers investigating them.

Fir-blueberry Rust
Pucciniastrum goeppertianum

The plant diseases that are known as rusts are caused by basidiomycete pathogens. The FIR-BLUEBERRY RUST fungus has 2 hosts and multiple spore types. Its hosts are any blueberry/huckleberry (*Vaccinium*) species and any species of true fir (*Abies*). The most obvious symptoms of this infection appear on the *Vaccinium* species: infected plants produce a so-called "witch's broom," a clump of thickened, spongy branches with few leaves. The life cycle of FIR-BLUEBERRY RUST as it moves between hosts is quite complex in comparison with the mushrooms described in the other sections of this guide. When it lives on *Vaccinium* branches, small fruiting bodies called "telia" produce teliospores. These in turn produce basidiospores, which are transferred by rain to the *Abies* host. Tube-like bodies called "aecia," found on the underside of fir needles, generate aeciospores that then infect *Vaccinium* species. Contemplating this complex arrangement should make us thankful that the human reproductive cycle mimics the birds and the bees!

Saskatoon-juniper Rust
Gymnosporangium nelsonii

Just as blueberry pickers may encounter FIR-BLUEBERRY RUST, pickers of SASKATOON BERRIES (the tasty fruit of *Amelanchier alnifolia*) may encounter SASKATOON-JUNIPER RUST. This rust produces spherical galls on the stems of junipers (*Juniperus*). The reproductive cycle is similar to that of FIR-BLUEBERRY RUST, only with different hosts. The galls on the junipers produce teliospores, which germinate and produce basidiospores. The basidiospores are then dispersed by wind or rain splash to plants in the rose family, in BC most commonly to SASKATOON BERRY, where the spores produce orange-yellow spots on the leaves. Later, cylindrical aecia 3–4 mm long develop on the underside of the SASKATOON BERRY leaves. These aecia produce aeciospores in the late summer or autumn, which are dispersed by wind and complete the cycle by infecting junipers. This rust has 2 places it can be easily noted in the field: on SASKATOON BERRY leaves and on juniper branches.

White Pine Blister Rust
Cronartium ribicola

WHITE PINE BLISTER RUST is native to Siberia. It was accidentally introduced to BC—perhaps several times—around 1910. WHITE PINE BLISTER RUST produces 5 different spore types on 2 unrelated plant hosts. White (5-needle) pines are one host. In BC, this means WESTERN WHITE PINE (*Pinus monticola*), WHITEBARK PINE (*P. albicaulis*), and LIMBER PINE (*P. flexilis*). The other host is usually a species of currant or gooseberry, members of the genus *Ribes*. Evidence of the rust on the currant can be subtle, sometimes no more than small pustules under the plant's leaves that bear rusty-coloured spores. On the pines, the rust causes perennial cankers on the stem and branches. If the branches or stem are small enough, the cankers can encircle them, girdling and killing the branch or the entire tree. WESTERN WHITE PINE, once so common that it was an important lumber species in BC, is now threatened by this rust throughout its range—the southern half of the province. Efforts are underway in BC and elsewhere to identify rust-resistant WESTERN WHITE PINES so that this magnificent tree can be grown more widely. Just as significant is the effect of WHITE PINE BLISTER RUST on the ecologically important WHITEBARK PINE. This pine species, which only grows at high elevations in the southern half of

Interior BC, has been decimated by a combination of threats, including WHITE PINE BLISTER RUST, MOUNTAIN PINE BEETLES, and the effects of climate change.

When checking the 5-needled white pines for the deadly rust cankers, hikers in BC should also check the 2-needled LODGEPOLE PINE (*P. contorta*) and 3-needled PONDEROSA PINE (*P. ponderosa*), for WESTERN GALL RUST (*Cronartium harknessii*, formerly *Endocronartium harknessii*). It is a native rust, and the pines are its only host. The characteristic cankers and galls, which occur on the branches or main stems, release orange spores in the spring. As with WHITE PINE BLISTER RUST, large galls can girdle and kill their hosts.

Rose Rusts   *Phragmidium* spp.

Phragmidium species are rust fungi that parasitize plants in the rose family. Common symptoms of infection include stem swelling, formation of galls, and, in the late spring and summer, bright (almost phosphorescent) clumps of orange spores on leaf undersides and other plant parts. One of BC's native species, *Phragmidium mucronatum*, a rust that is found on most continents, attacks rose species (genus *Rosa*). In southwestern BC, the introduced *Phragmidium violaceum* infects 2 introduced berry species, HIMALAYAN BLACKBERRY (*Rubus armeniacus*) and CUT-LEAF BLACKBERRY (*R. laciniatus*). It produces purple leaf spots that have tan and yellow centres on the top of the leaf and yellow to orange pustules on the lower surface.

Red Leaf Spot
Exobasidium vaccinii

RED LEAF SPOT is a basidiomycete parasite of heather-family plants, including (in BC) species in *Vaccinium*, *Arctostaphylos*, *Arbutus*, and *Rhododendron*. The primary symptom of a RED LEAF SPOT infection is the development of thickened gall-like structures on the leaves. These structures are red above, often with a yellow border; below, they eventually become whitish from the spores. The infection reduces leaf and fruit production, and branches can die. RED LEAF SPOT is common and widespread across BC. At least 6 other BC *Exobasidium* species, differentiated largely on spore characters, parasitize heather-family plants in BC. Where they take, however, they also give: *Exobasidium* galls on FALSE AZALEA (*Rhododendron menziesii*, previously known as *Menziesia ferruginea*, pictured above) were eaten by 9 BC coastal First Nations and had mythological importance among at least 3 Nations—the Henaaksiala, Heiltsuk, and Tsimshian (see also the essay on First Nations and fungi, p. 471).

Speckled Tar Spot
Rhytisma punctatum

SPECKLED TAR SPOT is an ascomycete that infects maple leaves. The black blots that supposedly resemble tar spots are stromata, hard mycelial masses that protect the fungus's asci. The spots are most evident in the autumn, when maple leaves fall. Before dropping their leaves in the autumn, maples and other deciduous trees withdraw as much of the nutrients from the leaves as they can. The leaves lose their dominant green colours when these nutrients disappear and the other colours of the leaves begin to show through. SPECKLED TAR SPOT somehow hijacks this process, forcing the maple to retain chlorophyll (and presumably some photosynthetic ability) in green islands around the stromata. The retained nutrients feed the fungus over the winter, and in the springtime, when new maple leaves are emerging, the asci in the old leaves release their ascospores into the wind to swirl upward and infect the young maple leaves. WILLOW TAR SPOT (*Rhytisma salicinum*), which causes black spots on BC's willow species, has a life cycle similar to that of SPECKLED TAR SPOT.

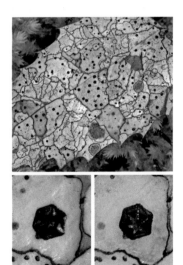

Hexagonal Spot
Coccomyces dentatus

HEXAGONAL SPOT, a close relative of SPECKLED TAR SPOT, also feeds on leaves. It prefers to grow on the leaves of Oregon-grapes (*Berberis*, as in the top photo), SALAL (*Gaultheria shallon*), ARBUTUS (*Arbutus menziesii*), oaks (*Quercus*), and rhododendrons (*Rhododendron*). The black fruiting bodies are hexagonal and are covered by 6 flaps that open in the springtime when ascospores are released (lower photos). The black lines that sometimes form a spectacular jigsaw pattern on the infected leaves mark the borders where the mycelia of 2 sexually incompatible individuals interact. This species is found worldwide at temperate latitudes.

Yellow Mountain Pea
Endogone pisiformis

The YELLOW MOUNTAIN PEA is a zygomycete, and its sexual spores are zygospores, making it one of only 2 species mentioned in this book that is not a basidiomycete or an ascomycete (the other is the pin mould *Spinellus fusiger*, discussed on p. 173). The fruiting bodies that bear the zygospores are yellow to orange, thick, waxy, and spherical or lobed. They are generally 2–5 mm across, but occasionally larger, and usually feature a basal indentation. The YELLOW MOUNTAIN PEA is a wood decomposer that is typically found in conifer forests at higher elevations, on the ground, under the ground, or on decaying wood, during any time of the year that's warm enough and wet enough to support fruiting.

Alder Tongue
Taphrina occidentalis

Taphrina species are ascomycete parasites that cause leaf curls in a wide variety of plants. ALDER TONGUE is a parasite on all 3 of BC's native alder species: SPECKLED ALDER (*Alnus incana*), RED ALDER (*A. rubra*), and GREEN ALDER (*A. alnobetula*, previously known as *A. viridis*). The most obvious symptom of infection by ALDER TONGUE is the elongated, tongue-shaped growth of the bracts of female alder catkins. The tongues are long and twisted, yellowish green (later becoming reddish to purple), and brown when dry. Two other common *Taphrina* species in our province are PEACH LEAF CURL (*T. deformans*), which causes the leaves of peach trees to thicken and curl, and TAPHRINA LEAF BLISTER (*T. populina*), which causes golden leaf spots on TREMBLING ASPEN and BLACK COTTONWOOD.

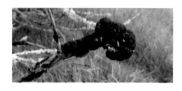

Black Knot
Apiosporina morbosa

BLACK KNOT is an ascomycete parasite, primarily of cherries and plums (*Prunus* species). The fungus produces black, knobbly, perennial structures on branches of infected trees. Michael Kuo of mushroomexpert.com aptly describes these structures as resembling "dried cat poop on a stick." Ascospores produced on the surface of these overwintering structures can infect the next year's young green twigs. When a knot encircles a branch, it can girdle the branch and kill it. To control this infection, orchardists keep a close eye on their trees and prune the knots whenever they find them.

Acknowledgements

We are grateful to the many wonderful people who contributed their time and talents to this handbook. Where names are in lists, those lists are alphabetical.

A number of friends and colleagues edited the text on these pages. Ian Gibson helped us in the organizing and list-making phase and stayed with us throughout the project, providing detailed comments on the whole text. Paul Kroeger reviewed all the species descriptions and picture selections and brought his valuable field experience to bear on our many questions. Dan Durall, Keith Egger, Tyson Ehlers, and Hugues Massicotte also edited the descriptions and provided valuable regional insights from Interior BC. Marty Kranabetter shared his field insights and provided us with specimen sequences. Others reviewed sections for which they have specific expertise: Shannon Adams (*Cortinarius*); Anna Bazzicalupo (*Russula*); Henry Beker (*Hebeloma*); Emma Harrower (*Cortinarius*); Buck McAdoo (*Marasmius*); Danny Miller (*Amanita, Cortinarius, Russula*); Steve Ness (*Hygrophorus*); Thom O'Dell (*Cantharellus*); Fred Rhoades (*Mycena*); and Steve Trudell (*Tricholoma*). Joe Ammirati gave us valuable advice on *Cortinarius* pictures. Jacob Kalichman, Brandon Matheny, Danny Miller, and Noah Siegel answered some sticky taxonomic questions for us. Shannon Berch wrote the first draft of the truffles essay and helped to draft some of the descriptions. Helpful reviews of the essays came from Ian Gibson (all of the essays), as well as Alissa Allen (mushroom dyes), Trevor Goward (lichens), Paul Kroeger (magic mushrooms, DEATH CAPS, and rare mushrooms), Robert Rogers (medicinal mushrooms), and Nancy Turner (First Nations mushrooms). In the end, of course, all decisions about text were made by us, and so responsibility for errors (whether errors in fact or errors in taste) rests with us.

Cara Gibson produced the wonderful line drawings that accompany the text.

Very few of the approximately 450 photographs in this book were taken by the authors. We owe a great debt of gratitude to the 70 or so people who allowed us to use their photographs in the book. Several of them, in order to supply us with photographs that they had taken over many years, went to great trouble to organize and label their collections for us. To see a full list of these generous people, we refer you to the image credits (p. 482).

We would also like to thank the people at the Royal BC Museum who helped us put this book together: Eve Rickert (the publisher who ably guided the book from beginning to end), Jeff Werner (cover and interior design), Grace Yaginuma (copy editing), Lana Okerlund (proofreading), and Catherine Plear (index).

And finally, we would like to thank the two extraordinarily kind and patient women who put up with us while we produced this book, Mairi MacKinnon and Jeanne Luther.

Andy MacKinnon & Kem Luther
Metchosin, BC

Glossary

Terms in italics have not been used in the species descriptions.

acrid—Burning or peppery taste.

adnate—*See* **broadly attached**.

adnexed—*See* **narrowly attached**.

anastomosing—Forming a closed network; the lines formed by the pattern diverge and converge.

apex (of stem)—The top or highest part of something, typically the top of a mushroom stem. *See also* **base**.

ascomycete—A fungus that produces its spores in sacs called **asci** (see p. 5).

ascus (pl. asci)—A microscopic spore-producing body found on the fertile surfaces of **ascomycetes** (see p. 5). It is a sac-like container that on most ascomycete mushrooms holds eight spores.

astringent—Causing a contraction or pucker of the mouth membranes.

base (of stem)—The lowest part of the stem. *See also* **apex**.

basidiomycete—A fungus that produces its spores on club-shaped **basidia** (see p. 5).

basidium (pl. basidia)—A microscopic spore-producing body found on the fertile surfaces of **basidiomycetes** (see p. 5). They produce from two to eight spores, commonly four.

binomial—Scientific name consisting of the genus and species name, based broadly on Latin syntax and usually employing Greek- or Latin-based terms.

broadly attached (gills)—Much or all of the depth of the **gill** is attached to the stem. Also called "adnate."

buff—A light yellowish brown or very pale tan.

bulbous—Enlarged and bulb-like, often referring to the stem **base**.

caespitose (cespitose)—*See* **clustered**.

cartilaginous—Tissue that is tough, like cartilage.

chevron—A line or stripe in the shape of a shallow letter "V."

clavate (stems)—Club-shaped, with a shaft small at one end and widening at the other.

close (gills)—*See* **closely spaced**.

closely spaced (gills)—**Gills** that are nearly touching, but with some small space between them. Also called "close."

clustered—Growing together, either very close or with stems from a common **base**. Also called "caespitose" or "tufted."

concave—Surface regularly rounded like a bowl, with the centre below the **margins**. Most often used to describe mushroom caps.

convex—Surface regularly rounded like an inverted bowl. Most often used to describe mushroom caps.

cortina—A web-like, silky **veil**, which often disappears leaving remnants on the stem or cap **margin**.

cross-veined—**Gills** or **veins** connected by ridges that run between them. Also called "interveined."

crowded (gills)—**Gills** that are very **closely spaced**, sometimes touching, with almost no space between them.

cryptic species—Species that are **morphologically** indistinct but pass other tests for being separate species, such as genetic tests.

cuticle—The skin of a mushroom cap, but sometimes just the surface layer of cells.

cystidia (sing. cystidium)—Sterile cells that separate the **basidia** in **basidiomycete** fungi.

decurrent—Refers to **gills**, **veins**, **teeth**, or **pores** that run down the stem.

decurrent tooth—A small portion of the lower edge of a **gill** curving sharply downward when it reaches the stem.

deep (gills)—Gills where the distance from the bottom edge to where it attaches to the cap at the top is relatively large. Also called "broad."

deliquescing—Dissolving into liquid, usually referring to the **gills** and cap of *Coprinus*, *Coprinellus*, or *Coprinopsis* species.

disc—Central part of the top of the cap.

distant (gills)—*See* **widely spaced**.

duff—Decaying organic matter on the forest floor.

ectomycorrhiza (pl. ectomycorrhizae)—A type of **mycorrhiza** in which the fungal **hyphae** reside between the root cells of the host plant without penetrating the cells.

endemic—Native only to a certain country or region.

fairy ring—A circle or part of a circle that is made up of mushroom fruiting bodies (see essay on p. 188).

farinaceous—The odour of fresh ground meal from whole grain, especially ground wheat.

fibrillose—With a cover or dusting of **fibrils**; used to describe the surface of a mushroom.

fibrils—Small tufts or thread-like fibres on the surface of a mushroom cap or on the stem or its **ring** zone. *See also* **fibrillose**.

fibrous—Mushroom flesh (usually stem flesh) in which the tissues can be separated into long fibres.

floccose—With easily removed cottony or woolly tufts.

forking (gills)—**Gills** that divide into two or more branches as they go away from stem.

free (gills)—**Gills** that are not attached to stem.

fungal endophyte—A fungus that lives within plant tissues, usually without causing any symptoms.

fusoid—*See* **spindle-shaped**.

gills—Thin, radially aligned, vertically arrayed plates that are found on the underside of mushroom caps and that hold the spore-bearing **basidia**.

glutinous—Very slimy.

hygrophanous—With a surface that changes colour markedly as it dries, usually having a darker appearance when wet and turning a lighter opaque colour on drying.

hymenium—Fertile area of fruiting body where spores are produced.

hypha (pl. hyphae)—A microscopic thread-like fungal structure.

inferior (ring)—A **ring** located below the middle of the stem.

inrolled (margin)—A cap **margin** that is rolled inward so that the edge of the margin points toward the stem. Also, the margin of a cup fungus that is rolled inward toward the spore-bearing surface.

interveined—*See* **cross-veined**.

KOH—Potassium hydroxide, a chemical agent causing colour changes. It is occasionally used in mushroom identification.

lateral (stem)—A stem that is attached to the side of a cap.

latex—Liquid exuded from the **gills** or other mushroom tissues; the liquid found in milky cap (*Lactarius* species) and certain other mushrooms. Also called "milk."

long-decurrent—**Decurrent gills, veins, teeth**, or **pores** that run a long way down the stem.

macrofungus—a fungus whose fruiting body is visible without a microscope or hand lens.

margin—The edge of the cap.

membranous (ring)—Like a thin membrane, skin-like, or somewhat like tissue paper.

milk—*See* **latex**.

mixedwood—A forest with hardwood and conifer trees.

morphology—Form or structure.

mycelium (pl. mycelia)—Network of **hyphae** that may or may not mass together and form a mushroom.

mycophagists—People who eat fungi. Are those who eat a lot of fungi "megamycophagists"?

mycorrhiza (pl. mycorrhizae)—A symbiotic association between plants and fungi in which the fungi attach themselves to plants via the plant's root system (see p. 74).

narrowly attached (gills)—A small portion of the depth of the **gill** is attached to the stem. The rise of the gill's bottom edge to the lower end of the narrow attachment point may be gradual or sudden. Also called "adnexed."

narrowly spaced (gills)—**Gills** that are close together at the end near the **margin**, sometimes with just the width of a gill between them.

notched (gills)—**Gills** that take a small leap upward as they near the stem, sometimes coming back down slightly at the stem.

off-centre (stem)—Attachment of a stem to somewhere other than the centre of a cap.

ovoid—Literally egg-shaped, but it can informally refer to any spheroid with dimensions that are not all the same length.

partial veil—Inner **veil** of tissue that joins the stem to the cap **margin** and often breaks to leave a **ring** on stem and/or remnants on the cap margin.

pendant (ring)—A **ring** that is hanging down, like a skirt or kilt.

peridiole—A capsule containing spores.

pileus—Cap of a mushroom.

pores—Small encased tubes or depressions that increase the area for spore-bearing **basidia**. Pore layers that are on the undersides of mushroom caps can be removable or fixed tightly to the caps.

pruinose—Appearing finely powdered or finely granular; a condition also described as frosted, dusted, or speckled with powder.

radial—Diverging in lines from a common centre (e.g., lines running from a cap centre to its **margins**).

reticulate—Covered with a network of interlacing lines or ridges.

rhizomorph—A cord-like strand of **hyphae** twisted together.

ridges—*See* **veins**.

ring—A collar of tissue on the stem formed by the rupture of the **partial veil**.

saprobic—Fungi that are decomposers, which get their nutrition from decaying organic matter. Also called "saprotrophic."

scabers—Short projections of tufted fibres or hairs, typically seen on the stems of *Leccinum* mushrooms.

sclerotium (pl. sclerotia)—An encased mass of nutrients and **mycelia** that provides the growing mushroom with food reserves.

scrobiculate—Pitted with conspicuous and slightly depressed areas.

scurfy—Having a surface covered with bran-like particles.

serrated (gills)—Sawtoothed or ragged.

shallow (gills)—**Gills** where the distance from the bottom edge to where it attaches to the cap at the top is relatively small. Also called "narrow."

short-decurrent—**Decurrent gills, veins, teeth,** or **pores** that run a short way down the stem.

spatulate—Small at one end and wider at the other, like some wooden spatulas.

spindle-shaped—Relatively wide in the middle and tapering evenly to both ends. Also called "fusoid."

stipe—Mushroom stem.

striations (adj. striate)—Delicate lines, ridges, or grooves.

stroma (pl. stromata)—A mass of fungal vegetative **hyphae**, often combined with the tissue of the plant host.

subdistant (gills)—**Gills** spaced quite far apart, but not as far apart as those described as distant or **widely spaced**.

subgills—Short **gills** that do not reach all the way from the cap **margin** to the stem.

superior (ring)—A **ring** located above the middle of the stem.

tawny—An orange-brown or yellowish brown colour, a light gold colour.

teeth—Long, thin spines that hang down from the caps of toothed fungi (p. 335), their surfaces covered with **basidia**.

tomentose—Covered with soft hairs, sometimes matted.

translucent-striate—A condition where the **gills** show through a translucent mushroom cap, appearing as **striations** on the surface of the cap.

tufted—*See* **clustered**.

type species—The species on which the description of a genus is based.

umbilicate—A narrowish and moderate to deep depression in the centre of a cap.

umbo—A raised knob or mound at the centre of a mushroom cap.

umbonate—With an **umbo**.

universal veil—An enveloping **veil** initially covering the whole mushroom, including the top of the cap, and sometimes leaving behind fragments on the cap or the stem and/or leaving a **volva** at the **base** of the stem.

veil—A protective membrane either joining the stem to the cap edge (**partial veil**) or covering the entire fruiting body including the top of the cap (**universal veil**).

veins—**Basidia**-bearing wrinkles on the fruiting surface of some fungi (see veined mushrooms, p. 33), sometimes called "ridges." Also lines of differently coloured or textured material inside of certain fruiting bodies.

vinaceous—Colour of red wine in a glass, a reddish purple with some brown tones.

viscid—Sticky/slimy. The cap or stem of a viscid mushroom usually feels somewhat slimy or slippery when wet but when drier feels sticky (may need to be wetted slightly to feel sticky).

volva—The remains of the **universal veil** found at the **base** of the stem, usually in the form of a sac, collar, or concentric rings.

widely spaced (gills)—**Gills** that have spaces between them at the **margin** that are equivalent to the width of several gills. Also called "distant."

zonate, zoned—Having differing colours or textures that form rings or stripes.

Credits

Cover and interior design by Jeff Werner
Illustrations by Cara Gibson (© Cara Gibson)
Illustration on p. 471 by Agnes Seaweed Wisden, Kwakwa̱ka̱'wakw
Copy editing by Grace Yaginuma
Proofreading by Lana Okerlund
Index by Catherine Plear

All photographs, illustrations, and watercolours are printed by permission. Photographers retain copyright to their works. Numbers refer to pages; letters indicate the photograph's relative position on the page.

Cover photographs: Richard Morrison (front cover) and Jessica Wolf and Rich Mably (back cover).

Shannon Adams: 240, 241, 245, 246, 247a, 248, 249, 252.
Anonymous 19th-century woodcut: 188.
Chris Ashurst: 107, 276.
Aaron Baldwin: 474b.
Edward Barge: 196.
Harley Barnhart, used with permission from Michael Beug: 111, 358, 468.
Frank L. Beebe: 257.
Beentree: 395 (CC BY-SA 3.0, commons.wikimedia.org/wiki/File:Cubical_rot_checked_quercus_bialowieza_1_beentree.jpg).
Shannon Berch: 420.
Michael Beug: 68, 120, 150, 157, 183, 233, 329, 352, 375, 385, 388, 426, 429, 433.
Danielle Brady: 360, 361.
Bob Brett: 8, 21.
Kent Brothers: 82, 93, 100, 128, 166, 237, 274, 284, 323, 337, 345, 365, 371, 432, 434, 457.

Caleb Brown: 39 (CC BY-SA 3.0, mushroomobserver.org/image/show_image/359126), 139, 264, 265 (CC BY-SA 3.0, mushroomobserver.org/image/show_image/456985), 310, 311, 316.
Adam Bryant: 83a, 99, 154, 242.
Britt Bunyard: 382.
Byrain: 153 (CC BY-SA 3.0, mushroomobserver.org/image/show_image/401318), 236 (CC BY-SA 3.0, mushroomobserver.org/image/show_image/199587), 314 (CC BY-SA 3.0, mushroomobserver.org/image/show_image/298643).
Federico Calledda: 57.
Alan J. Cann: 17 (CC BY-SA 2.0, commons.wikimedia.org/wiki/File:Spore_Print_of_the_Week_(37475625491).jpg).
Stan Czolowski: 161, 308, 309.
Paul Dawson: 226.
Yves Deneyer: 92.
Darwin DeShazer: 103a, 198.
Connor Dooley: 201, 246, 366, 465.

Richard Droker: 55a, 138, 390, 413, 475b, 475c, 475d.

Tyson Ehlers: 34, 42, 55b, 63, 84, 88, 101, 117, 131, 144a, 146, 152, 155, 159, 168, 169, 199, 200, 206, 217, 218, 232, 235, 251, 279, 291b, 294, 301, 306, 307, 319, 322, 325, 328, 334, 364, 367, 374, 376, 402, 437, 439a, 441b, 442, 443, 445, 448, 452.

Daniel Henslowe: 455 (CC BY-SA 3.0, mushroomobserver.org/image/show_image/629039).

Chris Herrera: 127.

Jeff Hitchcock: 70.

Megan Hodde: 342.

Christopher Hodge: 176a (CC BY-SA 3.0, mushroomobserver.org/image/show_image/407516).

Jason Hollinger: 129, 243, 328, 389a, 389b, 399a, 399b, 444.

James Holkko: vi, 32, 37, 46, 110, 112, 142b, 191, 204, 211, 266, 272, 275, 288, 346, 350, 384, 387a, 387b, 393, 409a, 415a, 416, 423a, 435, 470, 472, 475a.

Dominic Janus: 474a.

Josimda: 189 (CC BY-SA 3.0, commons.wikimedia.org/wiki/File:Hexenring_Nebelgrauer_Trichterling.jpg).

Gerry Kahrmann, used with permission from the Vancouver Sun: 114. May Kald: 40a, 52, 119b, 141b, 209, 210, 214b, 260, 262, 268, 287, 290b, 291a, 292, 347a, 347b, 359, 381, 383, 392, 401, 412, 438, 441a, 446a, 447b, 460a.

Jacob Kalichman: 98, 219, 406.

Bryan Kelly-McArthur: 405.

John Kirkpatrick: 372.

Kiwibirdman: 94 (CC BY-SA 3.0, commons.wikimedia.org/wiki/File:Royal_Oak_Burial_Park_and_Little_Saanich_Mountain_-_panoramio.jpg).

Paul Kroeger: 106, 108, 113, 115, 202.

Ruzica and Sava Krstic: 66, 104, 140, 167, 177a, 178, 180, 181, 184, 194, 223, 238, 340, 348, 368, 380.

Michael Kuo: 67.

T. Abe Lloyd: 473b.

Taylor Lockwood: 81, 90, 177b, 212, 213, 293, 304, 456.

Randy Longnecker: 79, 224.

Kem Luther: 95, 377, 476c.

Rich Mably: 40b, 41, 60, 76, 87, 96, 174a, 175, 205, 208, 285, 290a, 318, 339, 341, 344, 354, 355a, 370, 386, 391, 394, 398, 408, 414, 417, 428, 454.

Andy MacKinnon: 54a, 64, 163, 425.

James MacKinnon: 124.

Hugues Massicotte: 473a.

Diane and Mike McIvor: 86, 327.

Luke Mikler: 58, 73, 89, 103b, 123, 126, 130, 136, 147, 160, 162, 171, 244, 247b, 313, 343, 466.

Amber Miner: 356b.

Dan Molter: 332 (CC BY-SA 3.0, mushroomobserver.org/image/show_image/439611).

Richard Morrison: 59, 137a, 141a, 142a, 164, 165, 190, 195, 197, 230, 296, 320, 324, 351, 415b, 423b, 424, 446b, 447a, 450, 458, 461, 462.

Steve Ness: 80.

Danny Newman: 156, 407.

NRC Research Press: 74 (Marty Kranabetter), 75.

Dana Nygard: 379.

Ron Pastorino: 35, 65, 71, 72, 109, 119a, 135, 203, 216, 231, 234, 245, 250, 258, 300, 459.

John Plischke: 467.

Todd Ramsden: 476b.

Britney Ramsey: 149, 263.

Gwen Raverat, used with permission from Faber and Faber: 357.

Scott Redhead: 36, 192, 278.

Fred M. Rhoades: 38, 47a, 47b, 50, 54b, 132, 133, 137b, 144b, 151, 170, 173, 176b, 179a, 179b, 193, 225, 270a, 270b, 273, 281, 286, 297, 298, 315, 326, 330, 355b, 396, 409b, 430, 460b.

Alan Rockefeller: 91a, 116, 148, 222, 282, 283.

Tim Sage: 62, 172, 186, 269, 302, 312, 331, 397, 410.

Kit Scates Barnhart, used with permission from Michael Beug: 48, 56, 118, 121, 122, 134, 158, 215, 254, 255, 259, 280a, 305, 333, 451, 453.

Christian Schwarz: 69, 85, 469, 476a.

Noah Siegel: 321.

Ryane Snow: 303 (CC BY-SA 2.0, mushroomobserver.org/image/show_image/169756).

South Tyrol Museum of Archaeology (www.iceman.it): 400.

Rosemary Taylor: 214a.

Richard M. Tehan: 182, 336, 362, 403.

Jen Tompkins: 227, 419, 439b.

Matt Trappe: 464.

Kevin Trim: 356a.

Cindy Trubovitz: 220.

Steve Trudell: 440.

Daryl Thompson: 78, 83b, 91b, 102, 143, 174b, 187, 267, 280b, 338, 353, 363, 373, 418.

US Forest Service: 404.

Glen van Niekerk: 427 (CC BY-SA 3.0, mushroomobserver.org/image/show_image/579339).

We Must Make A Better Planet Than We Now Possess: 53 (CC BY-SA 3.0, mushroomobserver.org/image/show_image/471084).

Ben Woo, used with permission from the University of Washington Herbarium, Burke Museum: 49, 51.

Rand Workman: 422.

Index

*Note: Page numbers in **bold** indicate a photograph or illustration.*

acute conic waxy cap, 78, 79, **79**, 80
admirable bolete, 321, 322, **322**
agaricales, 43
agaricus: diminutive, 238, **238**; felt-ringed, 230, 231, **231**, 237; flat-top, 230, 231, 236, 237, **237**; meadow, 229, 232, 236, **236**; red-staining, 116, 234, **234**; woodland, 231, 232, 233, **233**
Agaricus, 28, 97, 189, 228, 229, 232, 238, 421; *abruptibulbus*, 233, **233**; *albolutescens*, 233; *arvensis* group, 232, **232**, 233, 236; *augustus*, 230, **230**, 231; *bisporus*, 229, 236; *buckmacadooi*, 237; *campestris*, 229, 232, 236, **236**; *crocodilinus*, 232; *deardorffensis* group, 230, 231, 236, 237, **237**; *diminutivus* group, 238, **238**; *fissuratus*, 232; *hondensis*, 230, 231, **231**, 237; *kerriganii*, 238; *micromegethus*, 238; *moelleri*, 237; *moronii*, 233; *praeclaresquamosus*, 237; *semotus*, 238; *sylvaticus* group, 116, 234, **234**; *sylvicola* group, 231, 232, 233, **233**
Agaricus of North America (Kerrigan), 229
agarikon, 395, 396, **396**, 401, 402, 471
Agrocybe, 271; *pediades* group, 279; *praecox* group, 244, 271, 279, **279**
Alaskan gold, 244, 262, 271, 280, **280**
Albatrellopsis flettii, 380
Albatrellus, 378; *avellaneus*, 380; *ellisii*, 380; *ovinus*, 380, **380**, 381, 382
alder: green, 476; red, 94, 457, 476; speckled, 476
alder tongue, 476, **476**
Aleuria, 449; *aurantia* 453, 456, **456**
All That the Rain Promises (Arora), 27
Allen, Eric, 395
Alloclavaria, 349, 351; *purpurea*, 351, **351**, 353
Allotropa virgata, 55, **55**, 147
Alnicola escharioides group, 284
Alnus, 476
alpine jelly cone, 414, **414**, 462
Alpova: *concolor*, 468; *diplophloeus*, 468, **468**
amanita: jonquil, 106, 108, 109, **109**, 110, 111, 120, 302; purple-brown, 120, **120**; Smith's, 117, **117**, 118, 123, 146, 163, 256; sunshine, 106, 109, 110, **110**, 111; western woodland, 118, **118**; western yellow-veil, 111, **111**
Amanita, 13, 19, 24, 44, 105, 121, 123, 145, 221, 356, 358, 421; *aprica*, 106, 109, 110, **110**, 111; *aspera*, 111; *augusta*, 111, **111**; *bisporigera*, 113; *constricta*, 119, 120; *franchetii*, 111; *gemmata* group, 106, 108, 109, **109**, 110, 111, 120, 302; *muscaria* group, 106, 106–7, **107**, 108, 109, 110, 324; *ocreata*, 113; *novinupta*, 116, **116**, 234; *pachycolea* group, 119; *pantherina* group, 106, 108, **108**, 109, 111, 120;

pantherinoides, 108; *phalloides*, 105, **112**, 112–15, **113**, **114**, **115**, 123, 148, 233, 256, **257**; *porphyria*, 120, **120**; *princeps*, 112; *rubescens*, 116; *silvicola*, 118, **118**; *smithiana*, 117, **117**, 118, 123, 146, 163, 256; *vaginata* group, 119; *verna*, 113; *virosa*, 105, 113
Amanitas of North America (Bunyard & Justice), 105
ambiguous stropharia, 302, **302**, 303
American parasol, 122
amethyst laccaria, 126, **126**, 127, 177
Ammirati, Joe, 27, 28
Ampulloclitocybe, 77, 125; *avellaneialba*, 137; *clavipes*, 133, 137, **137**
angel wings, 191, 208–9, 211, **211**, 214, 256
anise clitocybe, 132, **132**, 221
Aphroditeola olida, 136, **136**
Apioperdon, 421, 422; *pyriforme*, 422, **422**, 423
Apiosporina morbosa, 476, **476**
apricot jelly, 419, **419**
arbutus, 94, 285, 294, 300, 332, 474, 475
Ariolimax columbianus, 223
Armillaria, 145, 154, 164–65, 300; *altimontana*, 165; *cepistipes*, 165; *gallica*, 165; *nabsnona*, 165, 270; *ostoyae*, **164**, 164–65, **165**, 170, 266, 270, 278, 394; *sinapina*, 164–65, **165**
armillaria root disease, 165, 394
Arora, David, 27
Arrhenia, 77; *chlorocyanea*, 142, **142**; *epichysium*, 139, 142, **142**
Arrhenius, Johan Peter, 142
artist's conk, 393, **393**, 395, 471
asci, 5, **5**, 6
Ascocoryne, 77; *cylichnium*, 418; *sarcoides*, 418, **418**
ascomycetes, 6, 138, 349, 360–61, 376, 458, 463
ashen trich, 156, 157, 158, **158**, 159
aspen scaberstalk, 332, 333, **333**, 334
Aspropaxillus giganteus, 133
Asterophora parasitica, 59
Atheniella, 173; *adonis*, 174, **174**, 175; *aurantiidisca*, 175, **175**
Aureoboletus, 317; *mirabilis*, 321, 322, **322**
Auricularia, 411, 417; *americana* group, 411, 416, 417, **417**; *auricula*, 417; *auricula-judae*, 417
Auriscalpium, 335, 347; *vulgare*, 335, 347, **347**

Baeospora myosura, 204
basidia, 5, **5**, 6
basidiomycetes, 6, 349, 463
bay polypore, 383
BC Poison Control Centre, 256
bear lentinellus, 218, **218**
bear's head, 338, **338**, 339

Beebe, Frank L., 257
bellybutton hedgehog, 336, 337, **337**, 442
Berberis, 475, **475**
Berch, Shannon, 115
Bessette, Alan and Arleen, 343
big brown cat, 146, 163, **163**
big laughing gym, 262
bigleaf maple, 94
birch conk, 379, 399, **399**, 400, **400**
birch scaberstalk, 332, 334, **334**
bird's nest: flowerpot, 431, 432, **432**, 433; fluted, 434, **435**; white barrel, 431, 432, 433, **433**; white-egg, 432, 433, 434, **434**
The Bird's Nest Fungi (Brodie), 431
Bisporella, 449; *citrina*, 414, 418, 462, **462**
biting russula, 46, 49, **49**
bitter bolete, 317, 318, 323, **323**
bitter brown polypore, 381, **381**, 391
bitter brown webcap, 245, **245**
black cottonwood: and alder tongue, 476; and bear lentinellus, 218; and chaga, 405; and fly agaric, 106, 107; and hyp pop, 215; and mycorrhizae, 75; and oyster mushroom, 209; and poplar pholiota, 267; and poplar trich, 152, 471; and red-brown trich 151; smell, 53
black earth tongue, 367, **367**
black knot, 476, **476**
blackberry: cut-leaf, 474; Himalayan, 474
blackening lyophyllum, 170, 171, **171**
blackening russula, 58, **58**, 59, 116, 256
blackleg, 383, **383**
bleach bonnet, 179, 180, **180**, 181, 182
bleeding milk cap, 62, 63, **63**
bleeding mycena, 173, 176, **176**
blewit, 125, 130, **130**, 189, 221, 240, 249, 277, 420
blood-red webcap, **246**, 246–47
blue chanterelle, 41, 42, **42**
blue cheese polypore, 385, **385**
blue-edge pinkgill, 226, **226**
bluefoot bonnet, 177, 182, **182**
bluefoot webcap, 189, 249, **249**
blue-green flamecap, 264, 265, **265**, 300
blue-green stropharia, 304, **304**
blusher, 116, **116**, 234
blushing waxy cap, 91, **91**
Bolbitius, 281; *titubans*, 104, 281, 282, **282**; *vitellinus*, 282
bolete: admirable, 321, 322, **322**; bitter, 317, 318, 323, **323**; gilled, 167, 271, 274, **274**; grey false, 382, **382**; king, 107, 223, 317, **318**, 318–19, **319**, 343, **343**, 442; peppery, 317, 320, 324, **324**, 325; red-cracked, 320, **320**, 321, 324, 377; red-pored, 325, **325**; Zeller's, 320, 321, **321**, 322
Boletopsis, 378, 382; *grisea* group, 382, **382**; *leucomelaena*, 382; *subsquamosa*, 382
Boletus, 317; *chrysenteron*, 320; *coniferarum*, 323; *edulis*, 107, 223, 317, **318**, 318–19, **319**, 343, **343**, 442; *fibrillosus*, 318; *mirabilis*, 318; *rex-veris*, 24, 318; *smithii*, 322

Bondartsev, Apollinaris Semenovich, 391
Bondarzewia, 339, 378, 391; *mesenterica*, 391; *occidentalis*, 381, 391, **391**
bonnet: bleach, 179, 180, **180**, 181, 182; bluefoot, 177, 182, **182**; brown, 181, **181**, 182, 283; lilac, 126, 173, 177, **177**, 182, 255; orange-yellow, 175, **175**; scarlet, 174, **174**, 175; yellowleg, 140, 173, 178, **178**. *See also* mycena
Bonomyces sinopicus, 137, 458
boot-lace fungus, 164, **164**, 165
The Botanic Garden (Darwin), 420
Bovista, 421, 424, 426; *pila*, 391; *plumbea*, 426, **426**
bowl earthstar, 428, **428**
branched collybia, 56, 195, 201, **201**
bristly pholiota, 261, 266, **266**, 267, 268
Brodie, Harold J., 431
brown almond waxy cap, 88, **88**, 199
brown bonnet, 181, **181**, 182, 283
brown crumbly rot, 395
brown cubical rot, 395
brown cup, 450, **450**, 452, 460
brown dunce cap, 281, 283, **283**
brown trunk rot, 395
bunapi-shimeji, 215
buna-shimeji, 215
Bunyard, Britt, 105
Burlingham, Gertrude, 49
burn site mycena, 458
burnt-ground pholiota, 458
buttery collybia, 186, 192, 197, 198, **198**, 221
button mushroom, 229, 236
Byssomerulius, 379; *corium*, 376, 409, 410, **410**

Cajander, Aimo Kaarlo, 397
Calbovista, 421, 424; *subsculpta*, 424, **424**, 425
California oaks, 115
Callistosporium luteo-olivaceum, 166, 203, **203**, 263
Caloboletus, 317, 323; *conifericola*, 317, 318, 323, **323**; *rubripes*, 323, 325
Calocera, 354, 411, 415; *cornea*, 354, 415, **415**; *viscosa*, 415, **415**
Caloscypha, 449; *fulgens*, 453, **453**, 456
Calvatia, 421, 424, 425, 429; *booniana*, 424, 425, **425**; *fumosa*, 429; *gigantea*, 425; *sculpta*, 424
Camarophyllus, 92
candlesnuff, 359
Candolleomyces candolleanus, 314
candy cap, 64
candystick, 55, **55**, 147
Cantharellula umbonata, 143, **143**, 189
Cantharellus, 33, 40; *albidus*, 37; *cascadensis*, 34, 35; *cibarius*, 35, 36, 37; *formosus*, **34**, 34–35, **35**, 36, 37, 40, 129, 298; *roseocanus*, 34, 36, **36**; *subalbidus*, 37, **37**
caps, **13**, 13–14, **14**
carbon antlers, 359, **359**
cascade chanterelle, 34, 35
Catathelasma, 146, 163; *imperiale* group, 146, 163, **163**; *ventricosum*, 146, 163

cat's tongue, 416
cauliflower mushroom, 370, **370**, 442
Cázares, Efrén, 375
cedar waxy cap, 85
celery-scented trich, 160, **160**, 161, 169
Ceska, Adolf, 94–95, 285
Ceska, Oluna, 13, 27, 94–95, 258, 285
chaga, 401, 405, **405**, 471
Chalciporus, 317; *piperatoides*, 324; *piperatus*, 317, 320, 324, **324**, 325
chanterelle: blue, 41, 42, **42**; cascade, 34, 35; false, 35, 129, **129**, 136; Pacific golden, **34**, 34–35, **35**, 36, 37, 40, 129, 298; rainbow, 34, 36, **36**; white, 37, **37**; winter, 38, **38**, 141, 337; woolly, **32**, 34, 40, **40**, 41
chicken of the woods, 403
Chimaphila, 55
chip cherry, 299, 316, **316**
Chlorociboria, 449, 461; *aeruginascens*, 461, **461**; *aeruginosa*, 461
Chlorophyllum: *brunneum*, 97, 98, **98**, 99, 116, 123; *molybdites*, 98; *olivieri*, 98, 99, **99**; *rhacodes*, 98
Chloroscypha flavida, 462
Chondrostereum purpureum, 387
Christmas naucoria, 285, **285**
Christmas tubaria, 285, **285**
Chromosera, 77; *cyanophylla*, 140, **140**, 178
Chroogomphus, 43, 295, 298; *ochraceus*, 298; *rutilus*, 298; *tomentosus*, 34–35, 298, **298**; *vinicolor*, 298
Chrysomphalina, 77, 125, 141; *aurantiaca*, 140, 141, **141**, 183; *chrysophylla*, 38, 129, 141, **141**, 166
cinnabar polypore, 389, **389**
citizen science, 25–26
Clavaria, 349, 350, 351, 354; *fragilis* group, 350, **350**; *rosea*, 351; *vermicularis*, 350
Clavariadelphus, 349, 351, 352, 353; *ligula*, 351, 353, **353**; *mucronatus*, 353; *sachalinensis*, 353; *subfastigiatus*, 351; *truncatus*, 352, **352**
Clavulina, 369, 371; *cinerea*, 371; *coralloides* group, 354, 371, **371**; *cristata*, 371; *rugosa*, 371
Clavulinopsis, 349, 354; *laeticolor*, 353, 354, **354**, 415
climate: change, 294; hot and dry, 427
clitocybe: anise, 132, **132**, 221; cloudy, 133, **133**, 168; crowded white, 134, **134**, 135, 170; snowmelt, 131, **131**; sweat-producing, 85, 134, 135, **135**, 186, 189, 223
Clitocybe, 44, 125, 134, 256; *albirhiza*, 131, **131**; *connata*, 134; *dealbata*, 135; *deceptiva*, 132, **132**, 221; *dilatata*, 134, **134**, 135, 170; *elegantula*, 132; *fragrans*, 132; *gigantea*, 133; *glacialis*, 131; *nebularis*, 133, **133**, 168; *nuda*, 130; *odora*, 132; *rivulosa*, 85, 134, 135, **135**, 186, 189, 223; *sinopica*, 137
Clitocybula, 125; *atrialba*, 137
Clitopilus, 221; *cystidiatus*, 223; *prunulus* group, 221, 223, **223**
cloudy clitocybe, 133, **133**, 168
club: flat-topped candy, 352, **352**; golden fairy, 353, 354, **354**, 415; purple fairy, 351, **351**, 353; strap, 351, 353, **353**; water, 363, 364, **364**

club-foot, 133, 137, **137**
clustered collybia, 192, 200, **200**
Coccomyces dentatus, 475, **475**
coconut milk cap, 66, **66**
collecting. *See* foraging
collybia: branched, 56, 192, 201, **201**; buttery, 186, 192, 197, 198, **198**, 221; clustered, 192, 200, **200**; fragrant, 88, 199, **199**; oak-loving, 192, 197, **197**, 198; tuberous, 185, 195, **195**, 201; tufted, 192, **192**, 193, 197, 198, 200
Collybia, 185, 195; *acervata*, 200; *cirrhata*, 195; *cookei*, 195; *tuberosa*, 185, 195, **195**, 201
Collybiopsis: *confluens*, 192, **192**; *peronatus*, 193, **193**
Coltricia, 378, 384; *cinnamomea*, 384; *perennis*, 346, 384, **384**
comb russula, 53, **53**
common cudonia, 366, **366**
common deer truffle, 360, 362, 465, **465**
Common Mushrooms of the Northwest (Sept), 27
common stinkhorn, **356**, 356–57
Common Tree Diseases of British Columbia (Allen, Morrison & Wallis), 395
compressed elfin saddle, 366, 445, 446, **446**
conifer maze conk, 388, 404, **404**
conifer mazegill, 388, **388**
conifer roundhead, 302, 303, **303**, 305
conifer sulphur shelf, 379, 395, 403, **403**
conifer tuft, **95**, 299, 300, 301, **301**
conifer-cone tooth, 335, 347, **347**
Coniferiporia sulphurascens, 394–95
conk: artist's, 393, **393**, 395, 471; birch, 379, 399, **399**, 400, **400**; conifer maze, 388, 404, **404**; dyer's, 343, 344, 390, **390**, **394**, 395; quinine, 396, **396**; red-belted, 376, 392, 393, 395, 396, 398, **398**, 402, 471; rosy, 397, **397**; tinder, 396, 400, 402, **402**, 471; western varnished, 379, 392, **392**, 393, 401
Connopus acervatus, 192, 200, **200**
Conocybe, 281, 283, 309, 311; *filaris*, **281**; *tenera* group, 281, 283, **283**
constricted grisette, 119, **119**, 120
Coprinellus, 277, 289; *micaceus* group, 292, 293, **293**
Coprinopsis, 277, 289; *atramentaria* group, 137, 256, 289, 290, 292, **292**, 293; *lagopus* group, 289, 291, **291**
Coprinus, 97, 289, 289; *comatus*, 290, **290**, 292, 427
coral: crested, 354, 371, **371**; orange-red, 375, **375**; pink-tipped, 370, 372, **372**; upright, 373, **373**; yellow mountain, 374, **374**
Cordyceps, 349, 360–61, 362; *capitata*, 362; *militaris*, 277, 289, 361
Corner, E.J.H., 35
corn-silk fibrehead, 258, **258**
corpse mushrooms, **276**, 276–77
Cortinarius, 95, 126, 130, 161, 228, 239, 242, 243, 244, 246, 250, 256; *alboviolaceus*, 240, **240**, 241, 255; *armillatus*, 243, **243**; *boulderensis*, 243; *californicus* group, 246; *camphoratus*, 240, 241; *caperatus*, 239, 244, **244**, 279, 280;

Cortinarius (continued)
causticus, 245; *ceskae*, 95; *cinnamomeus*, 246–47; *clandestinus* group, 166, 251, **251**, 265; *collinitus* group, 252; *croceus*, 247; *gentilis* group, 248, **248**; *glaucopus* group, 189, 249, **249**; *griseoviolaceus*, 240; *idahoensis*, 247; *kroegeri*, 248; *laniger*, 250, **250**; *Leprocybe* subgenus, 251; *luteo-ornatus*, 243; *muscigenus*, 252; *mutabilis*, 240, 249; *Myxacium* subgenus, 239, 245, 252; *neosanguineus*, **246**, 246–47; *occidentalis* group, 240, 249; *olympianus*, 249; *ominosus*, 246, **247**; *paragaudis*, 243; *parkeri*, 251; *phoeniceus* var. *occidentalis*, 246; *sanguineus*, **246**, 247; *seidliae*, 252, **252**; *semisanguineus*, 246; *smithii*, 246, **247**; *solis-occasus*, 250; *Telamonia* subgenus, 239, 243, 250; *traganus*, 240, 241, **241**; *vanduzerensis* group, 252; *vibratilis* group, 245, **245**; *violaceus*, 239, 242, **242**
Coryne sarcoides, 418
cowboy's handkerchief, 84, **84**, 85, 86, 121
Craterellus, 33; *calicornucopioides*, 42; *tubaeformis* group, 38, **38**, 141, 337
cremini mushrooms, 229
crep: flat, 209, 211, 214, **214**, 218, 220; jelly, 214, **214**; snowy, 214
Crepidotus, 214; *applanatus*, 209, 211, 214, **214**, 218, 220; *epibryus*, 214; *mollis*, 214, **214**
crested coral, 354, 371, **371**
Cronartium: *harknessii*, 474; *ribicola*, 473, **473**
crowded white clitocybe, 134, **134**, 135, 170
crown fungus, 451, **451**
Crucibulum, 431, 434; *crucibuliforme*, 432, 433, 434, **434**; *laeve*, 434
crusts: lobster, 33, 39, **39**, 45, 46, 52, 69, 343, 377, 442; netted, 376, 409, 410, **410**
Cryptoporus, 378, 406; *volvatus*, 406, **406**
Cudonia, 253, 349, 366; *circinans*, 366, **366**
Cudoniella clavus, 364, 366
cup: brown, 450, **450**, 452, 460; eyelash, 457, **457**; green, 461, **461**; hairy fairy, 459, **459**; orange-dusted, 454, **454**, 455; thick, 41, 452, **452**; yellow fairy, 414, 418, 462, **462**
Cuphophyllus, 85; *pratensis* group, 81, 91; *russocoriaceus*, 85
cut-leaf blackberry, 474
cyanobacteria, 138
Cyathus, 431; *olla*, 434; *striatus*, 434, **435**
Cystoderma, 96, 97, 280; *amianthinum* group, 100, **100**, 101; *aureum*, 280; *carcharias*, 101; *fallax*, **96**, 100, 101, **101**
Cystodermella: *cinnabarina*, 100; *granulosa*, 100
Cystolepiota seminuda group, 194
Cytidia salicina, 457

Dacrymyces, 411, 412, 413, 462; *chrysospermus*, 412, **412**, 413, 414; *palmatus*, 412; *stillatus*, 412, 462
Dahlen, Jan, 442
dark funnel, 139, 142, **142**
dark melanoleuca, 172, **172**

dark pogie, 469, **469**
Darwin, Charles, 357, 420
Darwin, Erasmus, 420
de Candolle, Augustin Pyramus, 314
de Schweinitz, Lewis David, 390
dead man's foot, 343, 421, 430, **430**
deadly parasol, 97, 102, 103, **103**, 256
death cap, 105, **112**, 112–15, **113**, **114**, **115**, 123, 148, 233, 256, **257**
deaths, from poisonous mushrooms, 22, 113, 114, 148, 211, 243, 256, 273, 325
the deceiver, 128
Deconica, 299; *coprophila*, 313; *horizontalis*, 306; *inquilina*, 306; *montana*, 306, **306**, **307**
deer mushroom, 221, 222, **222**
The Deerholme Mushroom Book: From Foraging to Feasting (Jones), 25
delicious milk cap, 61, 62, **62**, 63
Dendrocollybia racemosa, 56, 195, 201, **201**
Dentinum repandum, 336
desert climate (near), and mushrooms, 427
desert shaggy mane, 427, **427**
destroying angel: all species, 113; *Amanita virosa*, 105, 113
diminutive agaricus, 238, **238**
Discina perlata, 452
disclaimer, edibility, 20
discomycetes, 449
dog stinkhorn, 358, **358**
doggy dick, 358
Dominion Astrophysical Observatory, 94, **94**
Donadinia nigrella, 454
donkey ears, 460, **460**
Douglas-fir: and blusher, 116; and boletes, 317; and chanterelles, 37, 38; and climate change, 294; and conifer-cone tooth, 347; and Douglas-fir cone mushroom, 204; and fall western white truffle, 464; and fat jack, 326; and lemon truffle, 470; and matte jack, 327; mycorrhizae, 75, 469; on Observatory Hill, 94; and orange-yellow bonnet, 175; and Pacific golden chanterelle, 35; and phoenix russula, 51; and *Rhizopogon* genus, 469; *Suillus* species associated with, 330; and sunshine amanita, 110; and tamarack jack, 328; and truffles, 466, 468; and western cauliflower mushroom, 370; and woolly jack, 329
Douglas-fir cone mushroom, 204, **204**
Doyle, Arthur Conan, 60
dripping slimecap, 84, 121, **121**
Dryas, 161
dung dome, 313, **313**, 315
dwarf willows, 161
dyer's conk, 343, 344, 390, **390**, **394**, 395
dyes, from mushrooms: about, 27, **342**, 342–43; blue chanterelle, 42; dyer's conk, 390; gilled bolete, 274; hawk's wing, 340; *Hydnellum* species, 335; lichens, 138; red paint fungus, 407; violet webcap, 242

ear pick fungus, 347
earth fan, 33, 379, 384, 408, **408**
earth tongue: black, 367, **367**; velvety, **348**, 367
earthy powdercap, 100, **100**, 101
Echinoderma asperum, 103, **103**
Echinodontium, 378, 407; *tinctorium*, 407, **407**, 471
edibility. *See* mushrooms, as food
E-Flora BC, 28
Ehlers, Tyson, 27
Elaphocordyceps, 362; *capitata*, 362
Elaphomyces, 362, 463, 465; *granulatus* group, 360, 362, 465, **465**
An Elementary Text-book of British Fungi (Hay), 22
elfin saddle: compressed, 366, 445, 446, **446**; fluted black, 377, 447, **447**
Endocronartium harknessii, 474
Endogone pisiformis, 476, **476**
enoki, 202
entoloma: midnight, 157, 224, **224**; rosy, 225, **225**
Entoloma, 221, 222, 224, 225; *bloxamii*, 224; *holoconiotum*, 227; *madidum*, 224; *medianox* group, 157, 224, **224**; *rhodopolium* group 225, **225**; *serrulatum*, 225, 226
Eukaryota (domain), 3
eukaryotes, 3, 205
Evans, Frank, 463
Exeter, Ronald, 278, 375
Exobasidium vaccinii, 474, **474**
eyelash cup, 457, **457**

fairy fan, 363, 365, **365**
fairy fingers, 350, **350**
fairy ring mushroom, 135, 185, 186, **186**, 198
fairy rings, 100, **188**, 188–89, **189**, 420
fairy stool, 384
fall western white truffle, 464, **464**, 466, 468
false azalea, 474
false chanterelle, 35, 129, **129**, 136
false morel, 366, 441, 444, **444**, 445
false turkey tail, 377, 386, 387, **387**
fan: earth, 33, 379, 384, 408, **408**; fairy, 363, 365, **365**; stinking earth, 408
fat jack, 326, **326**, 327, 329
felt-ringed agaricus, 230, 231, **231**, 237
fibrehead: corn-silk, 258, **258**; green-foot, 259, **259**; western lilac, 177, 240, 254, 255, **255**; white, 254, **254**, 255
Field Guide to North American Truffles (Trappe, Evans & Trappe), 463
Finston, Terrie, 115
fir flamecap, 203, 263, **263**
fir-blueberry rust, 472, **472**
First Nations, 152, 407, 420, 426, 471
flamecap: blue-green, 264, 265, **265**, 300; fir, 203, 263, **263**
Flammula malicola group, 301
Flammulina velutipes, 25, 190, 202, **202**
flat crep, 209, 211, 214, **214**, 218, 220
flat-top agaricus, 230, 231, 236, 237, **237**

flat-topped candy club, 352, **352**
flowerpot bird's nest, 431, 432, **432**, 433
flowerpot parasol, 104, **104**, 282
fluted bird's nest, 434, **435**
fluted black elfin saddle, 377, 447, **447**
fly agaric, **106**, 106–7, **107**, 108, 109, 324
Fomes fomentarius, 396, 400, 402, **402**, 471
Fomitopsis, 378, 397, 403; *betulina*, 379, 399, **399**, 400, **400**; *cajanderi*, 397; *mounceae*, 376, 392, 393, 395, 396, 398, **398**, 402, 471; *ochracea*, 398, 402; *officinalis*, 396; *pinicola*, 398
foraging, 22–25, 26, 33, 61, 147
fragrant collybia, 88, 199, **199**
Freeman, Dan, **442**
fried chicken mushroom, 164, 170, **170**, 171, 189
Fries, Elias M., 92, 97
frozen waterfall, 338
fruity lilac webcap, 240, 241, **241**
Fuligo septica, 377
funeral bell, 202, 256, 270, 281, 284, 286, **286**, 287, 306, 311
The Fungal Pharmacy (Rogers), 401
fungi: decomposer, 6–7, 25, 104, 125, 141, 166, 173, 180, 185, 229, 232, 261, 271, 394–95, 411, 431, 436, 449; definition, 3; diversity, 3–4; evolution, 3, 11, 33, 43, 207, 349; fungal mantles, **74**, **75**; fungophobia, 22; and lichen, 138; and mycoheterotrophs, 54–55; phoenicoid, 458, **458**; structure, 4; taxonomy, 11. *See also* mushrooms
Fuscopostia fragilis, 385
fuzztop, 151, 153, **153**, 169
fuzzyfoot, 141, 144, **144**

Galerina, 202, 281, 286, **287**, 309, 311; *autumnalis*, 286; *marginata*, 202, 256, 270, 281, 284, 286, **286**, **287**, 311
Ganoderma, 378, 393; *applanatum*, 393, **393**, 395, 471; *lucidum*, 392, 401; *oregonense*, 379, 392, **392**, 393, 401; *tsugae*, 392
garden giant, 305
Garry oak, 52, 94, 112, 115, 116, 210
Gastropila fumosa, 429
Gaultheria shallon, 475
Geastrum, 421; *fimbriatum*, 428; *quadrifidum*, 428; *saccatum*, 428, **428**; *triplex*, 428
gemmed puffball, 406, 422, 423, **423**, 426
Generall Historie of Plantes (Gerard), 357
Geoglossum, 349; *umbratile*, 367, **367**
Geopyxis carbonaria, 458, **458**
Gerard, John, 357
Gerronema atrialbum, 137, **137**
ghost pipe, 52, **54**, 54–55, 74
Gibson, Ian, 28
gilled bolete, 167, 271, 274, **274**
gills, 14–15, **15**
Ginns, James, 379
Glanvill, John, 412
Gliophorus, 77, 87; *laetus* group, 80, 87, 90, **90**; *psittacinus*, 87, **87**, 90

Gloeophyllum, 378; *sepiarium*, 388, **388**
glossary, 478–81. *See also* terminology,
  mycological
Glutinoglossum glutinosum, 367
gnome plant, 344
the goblet, 142, 143
goldband webcap, 248, **248**
golden edge bonnet, 173
golden fairy club, 353, 354, **354**, 415
golden pholiota, **260**, 268, **268**
golden-fringed waxy cap, 84, 86, **86**
goldgill navelcap, 38, 129, 141, **141**, 166
gomphidius: hideous, 89, 93, 296, 297, **297**; rosy,
  296, **296**, 297, 327
Gomphidius, 77, 288, 295; *glutinosus*, 89, 93, 296,
  297, **297**; *oregonensis*, 297, 326; *smithii*, 296;
  subroseus, 296, **296**, 297, 327
Gomphus, 33, 40, 369; *clavatus*, 41, **41**, 42, 352, 452
Goward, Trevor, 138
grand fir, 94
granny's nightcap, 239, 244, **244**, 279, 280
grass green russula, 57, **57**
green alder, 476
green cups, 461, **461**
green lobster mushrooms, 377
green-foot fibrehead, 259, **259**
grey false bolete, 382, **382**
grey fire morel, **294**, 440, **440**, 458
greyling, 72, 143, **143**, 189
Grifola frondosa, 391
Guépin, Jean Pierre, 419
Guepinia, 411; *helvelloides*, 419, **419**
Guepiniopsis alpina, 414
"Guide to Mushroom Groups," 2, 9, 30–31
gym: big laughing, 262; jumbo, 262, **262**, 280;
  yellow-gilled, 167, 264, **264**
Gymnopilus, 228, 261, 263, 354; *aeruginosus*, 264,
  265; *bellulus*, 263; *junonius*, 262; *luteofolius*,
  167, 264, **264**; *penetrans*, 263; *picreus*, 263;
  punctifolius, 264, 265, **265**, 300; *sapineus* group,
  203, 263, **263**; *ventricosus* group, 262, **262**, 280;
  voitkii, 262
Gymnopus, 185; *acervatus*, 200; *androsaceus*,
  196, **196**; *confluens*, 192; *dryophilus*, 192, 197,
  197, 198; *fuscopurpureus*, 200; *perforans*, 196;
  peronatus, 193
Gymnosporangium nelsonii, 473, **473**
gypsy mushroom, 244
Gyromitra, 436, 437, 447, 449; *ancilis*, 41, 452, **452**;
  esculenta, 366, 441, 444, **444**, 445; *infula*, 444,
  445, **445**, 446

hairy fairy cup, 459, **459**
hardwood witch's butter, 412, 413, **413**
Hardy, George A., 257
hawk's wing, 335, 340, **340**
Hay, William Delisle, 22
haymaker's mushroom, 283, 312, **312**
Healing Mushrooms (Isokauppila), 401

Hebeloma, 95, 161, 254, 271, 277; *crustuliniforme*
  group, 189, 275, **275**, 277; *mesophaeum* group,
  275; *sacchariolens* group, 275; *velutipes*, 275
hedgehog, 38, 336, **336**, 337, 442; bellybutton,
  336, 337, **337**, 442
Heimiomyces fulvipes, 144
Helminthosphaeria clavariarum, 371
Helvella, 366, 419, 436, 447; *compressa*, 366, 445,
  446, **446**; *corbierei*, 446; *crispa*, 447; *elastica*,
  445, 446, **446**; *lacunosa*, 447; *maculata*, 447;
  vespertina, 377, 447, **447**
Hemimycena, 184, 191; *delectabilis*, 184
Hemipholiota populnea, 267
Hemitomes congestum, 344
hen of the woods, 391
herald of winter, 89
Herball (Gerard), 357
Hericium, 335, 339; *abietis*, 338, **338**, 339; *coralloides*,
  338; *erinaceus*, 338, 339, **339**, 401, **401**
Heterotextus, 411; *alpinus*, 414, **414**, 462; *luteus*,
  414, 462
Heufler zu Rasen und Perdonegg, Ludwig Samuel
  Joseph David Alexander, 219
hexagonal spot, 475, **475**
hideous gomphidius, 89, 93, 296, 297, **297**
Himalayan blackberry, 474
Hodophilus paupertinus, 139
Hohenbuehelia, 209, 219; *petaloides*, 210, 219,
  219; *serotina*, 212
honey mushroom, **164**, 164–65, 170, 266, 270,
  278, 394
horn of plenty, 42
Hornemann, Jens Wilken, 303
horse mushroom, 232, **232**, 233, 236
horsehair mushroom, 196, **196**
Humaria, 449, 459, 460; *hemisphaerica*, 459, **459**
Hunt, Gary, 420
Hussey, Anna Maria, 57
Hydnangium carneum, 467
Hydnellum, 55, 335, 345; *aurantiacum*, 344, **344**;
  fuscoindicum, 345, **345**; *peckii*, 341, **341**, 343,
  344, 384; *scabrosum*, 340, 345; *scrobiculatum*
  group, 341, 384; *suaveolens*, 345
Hydnoporia tabacina, 387
Hydnum, 335, 336, 337; *repandum*, 336; *umbilicatum*
  group, 336, 337, **337**; *washingtonianum*, 336,
  336, 337, 442
Hygrocybe, 77; *acutoconica* group, 78, 79, **79**, 80;
  chlorophana, 80; *coccinea*, 83, **83**; *conica*, 78;
  flavescens group, 79, 80, **80**; *miniata* group, **76**,
  82, **82**, 83; *pratensis*, 91; *psittacina*, 87; *punicea*,
  81, 82, 83, **83**; *russocoriacea*, 85; *singeri* group,
  78, **78**, 79
Hygrophoropsis, 43, 77; *aurantiaca* group, 35, 129,
  129, 136
Hygrophorus, 44, 77, 129; *agathosmus*, 88, 92;
  bakerensis, 88, **88**, 199; *boyeri*, 89, **89**, 93;
  calophyllus, 92; *camarophyllus*, 92, **92**; *chrysodon*
  group, 84, 86, **86**; *conica*, 78; *eburneus* group,

84, **84**, 85, 86, 121; *erubescens*, 91, **91**; *hypothejus*, 89; *marzuolus*, 92; *olivaceoalbus* group, 89, 93, **93**; *piceae*, 84, 85, **85**, 86, 121; *pudorinus*, 91, **91**; *saxatilis*, 91; *speciosus*, 81, **81**, 83; *subalpinus*, 52
Hymenochaetopsis tabacina, 387
hyp pop, **206**, 210, 215, **215**
Hypholoma, 299; *aurantiacum*, 316; *capnoides*, **95**, 299, 300, 301, **301**; *dispersum*, 301, 310; *elongatum*, 301; *fasciculare*, 265, **288**, 299, 300, **300**, 301; *tuberosum*, 316
Hypocrea pulvinata, 377
Hypomyces, 376, 377; *aurantius*, 377; *cervinigenus*, 377, 447, **447**; *chrysospermus* group, 320, 377; *lactifluorum*, 33, 39, **39**, 45, 46, 52, 69, 343, 377, 442; *luteovirens*, 377; *rosellus*, 377; *torminosus*, 377
Hypsizygus tessulatus, **206**, 210, 215, **215**

Iceman Ötzi, 57, 399, 400
Illustrations of British Mycology (Hussey), 57
iNaturalist.org, 26
Infundibulicybe, 125
inky cap, 137, 256, 289, 290, 292, **292**, 293; woolly, 289, 291, **291**
Inocybe, 95, 161, 228, 253, 256, 259; *albodisca*, 258; *calamistrata*, 259; *ceskae*, 95, 258; *fastigiata*, 258; *geophylla* group, 254, **254**, 255; *grammata*, 258; *griseolilacina*, 255; *hirsuta*, 259; *lacera*, 259; *lilacina*, 255; *mixtilis*, 258; *pallidicremea*, 177, 240, 254, 255, **255**; *pudica*, 254; *sororia*, 258; *whitei*, 254
Inonotus, 378; *obliquus*, 401, 405, **405**, 471
Inosperma: *calamistratum*, 259, **259**; *maximum*, 259; *mucidiolens*, 259
Ischnoderma: *benzoinum*, 381; *resinosum*, 381
Isokauppila, Tero, 401

jack: fat, 326, **326**, 327, 329; matte, 326, 327, **327**, 328, 329; slippery, 331, **331**; tamarack, 327, 328, **328**; woolly, 327, 329, **329**
Jahnoporus, 378; *hirtus*, 381, **381**, 391
jelly crep, 214, **214**
jelly ear 411, 416, 417, **417**
jelly rot, 376, 409, **409**, 410
jelly tooth, 416
Jones, Bill, 25
jonquil amanita, 106, 108, 109, **109**, 110, 111, 120, 302
jumbo gym, 262, **262**, 280
Justice, Jay, 105

Kauffman, Calvin Henry, 71, 216, 278
Kauffman's milk cap, 71, **71**, 72
Kauffman's rootshank, 71, 161, 271, 278, **278**
Kendrick, Bryce, 27
Kerrigan, Richard, 229
king bolete, 107, 223, 317, **318**, 318–19, **319**, 343, **343**, 442
Kroeger, Paul, **114**, 115, 154, 248, 309
Kuehneromyces: *lignicola*, 270, **270**; *mutabilis*, 165, 202, 270, **270**, 286, 301, 306

Kühner, Robert, 85
Kuo, Michael, 354, 358, 419, 476

laccaria: amethyst, 126, **126**, 127, 177; lacklustre, 127, 128, **128**; two-coloured, 126, 127, **127**, 128
Laccaria, 77, 126, 277; *amethysteo-occidentalis*, 126, **126**, 127, 177; *bicolor*, 126, 127, **127**, 128; *laccata* group, 127, 128, **128**
Lachnellula agassizii, 462
lacklustre laccaria, 127, 128, **128**
Lactarius, 15, 39, 43, 44, 45, 61; *controversus*, 68; *deliciosus* group, 61, 62, **62**, 63; *fallax* group, 70, **70**; *glyciosmus*, 66, **66**; *hepaticus*, 65; *kauffmanii*, 71, **71**, 72; *luculentus*, 64, **64**; *montanus*, 66, 67, **67**; *mucidus*, 72; *necator*, 73; *occidentalis*, 65; *olivaceoumbrinus*, 73, **73**; *olympianus*, 62; *pallescens*, 67; *payettensis*, 68; *plumbeus*, 73; *pseudomucidus*, 70, 71, 72, **72**, 143; *repraesentaneus*, 68; *rubidus*, 64; *rubrilacteus*, 62, 63, **63**; *rufus*, 64, 65, **65**; *scrobiculatus*, 68, **68**, 69; *subflammeus*, 64; *substriatus*, 64; *subviscidus*, 64; *torminosus*, 39, 66, 68, 69, **69**; *turpis*, 73; *uvidus*, 67
laddered landscape morel, 438, **438**
Laetiporus, 378, 403; *conifericola*, 379, 395, 403, **403**; *gilbertsonii*, 403; *sulphureus*, 403
laminated root rot, 395
larch, 81, 328, 331
larch waxy cap, 81, **81**, 83
large white leucopax, 133, 146, 168, **168**
Laricifomes, 378; *officinalis*, 395, 396, **396**, 401, 402, 471
Larix, 81, 328, 331; *laricina*, 328; *lyallii*, 328; *occidentalis*, 328, 396
latex, 15
lead-coloured puffball, 426, **426**
Leccinum, 172, 277, 317, 333, 334; *aurantiacum* group, 332, **332**, 333, 334; *insigne*, 332, 333, **333**, 334; *manzanitae*, 332; *scabrum*, 332, 334, **334**; *vulpinum*, 332
Lee, Jae Rhim, 277
lemon earthball, 429, **429**, 451, 465
lemon truffle, 470, **470**
Lentaria pinicola, 371, 373
Lentinellus, 43, 347; *flabelliformis*, 218; *micheneri*, 218; *ursinus* group, 218, **218**
Lentinus, 216, 218; *ponderosus*, 217
Lenzites betulina, 388
leopard trich, 146, 155, 156, 157, 158, 159, **159**, 168
Lepiota, 44, 97, 289, 421, 427; *aspera* group, 103, **103**; *castanea*, 100, 103; *clypeolaria*, 102; *cristata*, 102; *flammeotincta*, 103, 122; *josserandii*, 103; *magnispora*, 102, **102**; *rubrotinctoides*, 122; *subincarnata*, 97, 102, 103, **103**, 256
Lepista, 130; *flaccida*, 198; *inversa*, 198; *irina*, 133; *nuda*, 125, 130, **130**, 189, 221, 240, 249, 277, 420; *praemagna*, 420; *tarda*, 130
Leprocybe subgenus, 251
Leptonia, 221, 226, 242; *serrulata*, 226, **226**

Leptoporus mollis, 397
Leratiomyces ceres, 299, 316, **316**
Leucangium, 463, 466; *carthusianum*, 464, **467**
Leucoagaricus, 97; *americanus*, 122; *leucothites*, 113, 123, **123**, 236; *rubrotinctus* group, 122, **122**
Leucocoprinus, 97; *birnbaumii*, 104, **104**, 282
Leucocybe connata, 134
leucopax, large white, 168, **168**
Leucopaxillus, 145, 168; *albissimus* group, 133, 146, 168, **168**; *amarus*, 169; *gentianeus*, 153, 160, 169, **169**; *giganteus*, 133
liberty cap, 308, 309, 310, **310**, 311
lichen, 9, 60, 138, 139, 147, 342, 427
lichen agaric, 9, 138, 139, **139**, 142, 183
Lichenomphalia, 77; *umbellifera*, 9, 138, 139, **139**, 142, 183
life cycles, 4–6, 24
lilac bonnet, 126, 173, 177, **177**, 182, 255
lilac-gilled umbrella, 140, **140**, 178
Limacella, 121; *delicata*, 121; *glioderma* group, 121; *illinita*, 121
Limacium, 92
limber pine, 473
Linnaeus, 436
lion's mane, 338, 339, **339**, 401, **401**
little brown mushrooms (LBMS), 228, 253, 271, 281, **287**, 309, 362
lobster crust / lobster mushroom, 33, 39, **39**, 45, 46, 52, 69, 343, 377, 442
lodgepole pine, 294, 330, 331, 474
Lycoperdon, 59, 421, 422, 423; *nigrescens*, 423; *perlatum*, 406, 422, 423, **423**, 426; *pyriforme*, 422
Lyophyllum, 145, 171; *decastes* group, 164, 170, **170**, 171, 189; *semitale*, 170, 171, **171**

Macrocystidia cucumis, 187, 190, **190**, 221
Macrotyphula juncea, 353
magic mushrooms, 26–27, 262, 264, 288, 299, 308–9, 442
maitake, 391
man on horseback, 113, 145, 148, **148**, 149, 150, 166
Marasmiellus: candidus, 191, **191**; *confluens*, 192, 193, 197, 198, 200; *peronatus*, 192, 193
Marasmius, 44, 185, 186; *androsaceus*, 196; *oreades*, 135, 185, 186, **186**, 198; *plicatulus*, 187, **187**, 190; *salalis*, 194
Marrone, Teresa, 28
matsutake, 147
matte jack, 326, 327, **327**, 328, 329
McBride, Doug, 27
McIlvaine, Charles, 105
McKenny, Margaret, 28
meadow agaricus, 229, 232, 236, **236**
medicinal uses. *See* mushrooms, as medicine
Megacollybia fallax, 172
Melanoleuca, 145, 172; *cognata*, 172; *melaleuca* group, 172, **172**; *verrucipes*, 172
Menziesia ferruginea, 474
mica cap, 292, 293, **293**

midnight entoloma, 157, 224, **224**
milk cap: bleeding, 62, 63, **63**; coconut, 66, **66**; delicious, 61, 62, **62**, 63; Kauffman's, 71, **71**, 72; orange, 64, **64**; pitted, 68, **68**, 69; purple-staining, 66, 67, **67**; red hot, 64, 65, **65**; slimy, 70, 71, 72, **72**, 143; toadskin, 73, **73**; velvety, 70, **70**; woolly, 39, 66, 68, 69, **69**
Miller, Danny, 28
Mitrula, 349, 363; *borealis*, 363; *elegans*, 363, **363**, 364, 365
mixotrophs, 55
Monotropa uniflora, 52, **54**, 54–55, 74
Morchella, 436; *americana*, 439, **439**; *anthracophila*, 440; *brunnea*, 439; *carbonaria*, 440; *elata*, 438; *esculenta*, 439; *eximia*, 440; *importuna*, 438, **438**; *snyderi*, 439, **439**; *tomentosa*, 294, 440, **440**, 458
morel: false, 366, 441, 444, **444**, 445; grey fire, 294, 440, **440**, 458; laddered landscape, 438, **438**; saddle-shaped false, 444, 445, **445**, 446; Snyder's, 439, **439**
Morrison, Duncan, 395
Morse, Elizabeth, 37
Moser, Meinhard, 140
Mounce, Irene, 398
Mount Elphinstone Provincial Park, 161
mountain caribou, 138
mountain moss mushroom, 299, 306, **306**, **307**
mountain pine beetles, 294, 474
mountain-avens, 161
mouse trich, 156, **156**, 158, 159
Mucronella, 30, 349, 355; *calva*, 355; *fusiformis*, 355; *pendula*, 355, **355**; *pulchra*, 355, **355**
Murrill, William Alphonso, 47, 147
mushroomobserver.org, 26
mushrooms: carnivorous, 127, 208, 220; commercial, 35, 147, 202, 229, 442–43; cultivation, 25, 437; defined, 4; diversity, 10, 45, 95; dry habitats, 427; ecological roles, 6–9, 207; enjoying, 25; as fruiting bodies, 4; life cycles, 4–6, 24; magic, 26–27, 262, 264, 288, 299, 308–9, 442; medicinal uses, 27, 33, 42, 215, 352, 359, 361, 386, 393, 399, 400–401, 405, 442, 444; mushroom clubs, 25, 26, 28, 114; names, 3, 4, 10, 11–12, 147; odour, 16; poisons, 39, 253, 256, 286, 437, 444, 465; as psychedelics, 26–27, 308–9; rare, 161; taste, 16; thunder and lightning, 420
mushrooms, anatomy: about, 12–13, **13**; caps, **13**, 13–14, **14**; fertile surface, 14–15; fruiting bodies, 14; latex, 15; ring, 18, **18**; stem, **17**, 17–18; structure, 4; volva, 19, **19**
mushrooms, as food, 3, 20, 437; for animals, 6; avoiding, 67; cap meat, 13; chanterelles, 33; collecting and eating, 22–25; disclaimer, 20; First Nations, 152, 420, 471; poisons, 256; raw vs. cooked, 25; taste-test, 16
mushrooms, as medicine: about, 27, 400–401; artist's conk, 393; birch conk, 399; carbon antlers, 359; chaga, 405; *Cordyceps* species, 361;

false morels, 444; flat-topped candy club, 352; hyp pop, 215; market for, 442–43; *Polyozellus* species, 33, 42; turkey tail, 386
Mushrooms, Russia and History (Wasson & Wasson), 235
Mushrooms Demystified (Arora), 27
Mushrooms of the Northwest (Marrone & Parker), 28
Mushrooms of the Pacific Northwest (Trudell & Ammirati), 27
Mushrooms of the Redwood Coast (Siegel & Schwarz), 27
Mushrooms of Western Canada (Schalkwijk-Barendsen), 28, 347
Mushrooms to Look for in the Kootenays (McBride & Ehlers), 27
Mushrooms Up! Edible and Poisonous Species of Coastal BC and the Pacific Northwest (website), 28
Mutinus, 349; *caninus*, 358, **358**
mycena: bleeding, 173, 176, **176**; burn site, 458; slippery, 184, **184**; toque mycena, 179, **179**. *See also* bonnet
Mycena, 44, 173, 187, 191, 255; *acicula*, 175; *aciculata*, 184; *alcalina*, 180; *amicta*, 177, 182, **182**; *aurantiomarginata*, **173**, 175; *capillaripes*, 180; *citrinomarginata*, 175; *epipterygia*, 140, 173, 178, **178**; *filopes*, 181; *galericulata*, 179, **179**; *haematopus*, 173, 176, **176**; *leptocephala*, 179, 180, **180**, 181, 182; *maculata*, 176, 179, **179**; *metata*, 181, **181**, 182, 283; *monticola*, 174; *overholtsii*, 181; *pura* group, 126, 173, **177**, 182, 255; *purpureofusca*, 177, **177**; *robusta*, 179; *rorida*, 184; *rosella*, 174; *sanguinolenta*, 176, **176**; *strobilinoidea*, 174, **174**; *tenax*, 184
Mycetinis: copelandii, 194; *salalis*, 194, **194**, 204
mycoheterotrophs, **54**, 54–55, **55**
MycoMatch: Mushrooms of the Pacific Northwest (mycomatch.com), 10, 28
mycophobia (fear of mushrooms), 22
mycoremediation, 207, 209
mycorrhizae, 7, **74**, 74–75, **75**; vs. decomposer fungi, 271; and trees, 244, 443
Myxacium subgenus, 239, 245, 252
Myxogastria, 205

Naematelia: aurantia, 413; *encephala*, 413
Naucoria vinicolor, 285, **285**
Nectriopsis violacea, 377, **377**
Neoalbatrellus subcaeruleoporus, 380
Neolecta vitellina, 365
Neolentinus, 388; *kauffmanii*, 71, 216, **216**, 217, 394; *lepideus*, 216, 217, **217**, *ponderosus*, 217
netted crust, 376, 409, 410, **410**
The New Savory Wild Mushroom (McKenny & Stuntz), 28
Nidula, 431, 432, 434; *candida*, 431, 432, **432**, 433; *niveotomentosa*, 431, 432, 433, **433**
nippled brown pinkgill, 227, **227**

Nolanea, 221; *holoconiota*, 227, **227**; *sericea*, 227; *verna*, 227
Norvell, Lorelei, 278, 375

oak: California, 115; Garry, 52, 94, 112, 115, 116, 210
oak-loving collybia, 192, 197, **197**, 198
Observatory Hill mushrooms, 94–95
Oligoporus caesius, 385
olive shaggy parasol, 98, 99, **99**
olive webcap, 166, 251, **251**, 265
olive-brown waxy cap, 89, **89**, 93
olive-gold loglover, 166, 203, **203**, 263
omphalinas, 125, 141, 142, 144
One Thousand American Fungi (McIlvaine), 105
Onnia tomentosa, 384, 390
Ophiocordyceps, 360; *myrmecophila*, 360; *ravenelii*, 360; *sinensis*, 361; *variabilis*, 360
orange milk cap, 64, **64**
orange mosscap, 139, 183, **183**
orange peel fungus, 453, 456, **456**
orange tooth, 344, **344**
orange-brown waxy cap, 80, 87, 90, **90**
orange-capped scaberstalk, 332, **332**, 333, 334
orange-dusted cup, 454, **454**, 455
orange-red coral, 375, **375**
orange-yellow bonnet, 175, **175**
Oregon Mycological Society, 24
Oregon-grapes, 194, 475, **475**
Otidea, 449, 460; *alutacea* group, 460, **460**; *leporina*, 460; *onotica*, 460, **460**; *smithii*, 460
Ötzi (Iceman), 57, 399, 400
The Outer Spores: Mushrooms of Haida Gwaii (Kroeger, Kendrick, Ceska & Roberts), 27
owl eyes, 346, **346**, 384
oyster, 207, **208**, 208–9, **209**, 210, 211, 212, 218, 219; shoehorn, 210, 219, **219**; smelly, 213, **213**; veiled, 209, 210, **210**, 215, 217, 219; winter, 209, 212, **212**

Pacific banana slug, 223
Pacific golden chanterelle, **34**, 34–35, **35**, 36, 37, 40, 129, 298
paddy straw mushroom, 112
Paden, John Wilburn, 455
Panaeolus, 299, 312; *alcis*, 313; *foenisecii*, 283, 312, **312**; *papilionaceus*, 312; *semiovatus*, 313, 315; *subbalteatus* group, 312
pancake mushroom, 153, 160, 169, **169**
Panellus: longinquus, 213, 214; *mitis*, 211; *serotinus*, 212; *stipticus*, 214
panther cap, 106, 108, **108**, 109, 111, 120
paper birch, 334, 339, 405, 457
Paragymnopus perforans, 196
Paralepista flaccida, 198
parasites: ascomycete, 33, 39; *Asterophora parasitica*, 59; *Chroogomphus*, 295; *Gomphidius*, 295; jelly fungi, 411; mushrooms as, 7; peppery bolete, 324; *Pleurotus* and similar as, 207; *Psathyrella epimyces*, 290; rot, 394–95; slime moulds as, 205; woolly milk cap, 69

parasol: American, 122; deadly, 97, 102, 103, **103**, 256; flowerpot, 104, **104**, 282; olive shaggy, 98, 99, **99**; ruby, 122, **122**; shaggy, 97, 98, **98**, 99, 116, 123; white, 113, 123, **123**, 236
Parasola, 289
Parker, Drew, 28
Parks, Harold Ernest, 469
parrot waxy cap, 87, **87**, 90
Paxillus, 271; *atrotomentosus*, 272; *cuprinus*, 273; *involutus*, **75**, 256, 271, 272, 273, **273**
peach leaf curl, 476
pear puffball, 422, **422**, 423
Peck, Charles Horton, 341
peppery bolete, 317, 320, 324, **324**, 325
Period Piece: A Cambridge Childhood (Raverat), 357
Peziza, 277, 449, 450, 451, 452, 458, 460; *domiciliana*, 450; *repanda*, 450; *varia* group, 450, **450**, 452, 460
Phaeoclavulina: abietina, 373; *myceliosa*, 373
Phaeocollybia, 271, 278; *kauffmanii*, 71, 161, 271, 278, **278**
Phaeocollybia of Pacific Northwest North America (Norvell & Exeter), 278
Phaeolepiota, 271, 280; *aurea*, 244, 262, 271, 280, **280**
Phaeolus, 378, 403; *schweinitzii*, 343, 344, 390, **390**, **394**, 395
Phaeotremella foliacea, 418
Phallus, 113, 349, 358; *impudicus*, **356**, 356–57
Phellinus, 404; *igniarius* group, 402, 405
Phellodon, 335; *atratus*, 346; *melaleucus*, 346; *tomentosus*, 346, **346**, 384
Phlebia, 379, 409; *radiata*, 409, **409**; *tremellosa*, 376, 409, **409**, 410
Phloeomana speirea, 184
Phlogiotis helvelloides, 419
phoenicoid fungi, 458, **458**
phoenix russula, 51, **51**
pholiota: bristly, 261, 266, **266**, 267, 268; burnt-ground, 458; golden, **260**, 268, **268**; poplar, 267, **267**; terrestrial, 266, 269, **269**
Pholiota, 228, 261, 458; *adiposa*, 268; *astragalina*, 316; *carbonaria*, 458; *decorata*, 269; *flammans*, 268; *highlandensis*, 458; *limonella* group, **260**, 268, **268**; *malicola* group, 301; *mutabilis*, 270; *populnea*, 267, **267**; *spumosa* group, 300; *squarrosa*, 261, 266, **266**, 267, 268; *squarrosoides*, 266, 268, 269; *terrestris*, 266, 269, **269**
Phragmidium, 474, **474**; *mucronatum*, 474; *violaceum*, 474
Phylloporus, 43; *arenicola*, 274; *rhodoxanthus* group, 167, 271, 274, **274**
Phyllotopsis nidulans, 213, **213**
Picipes, 378, 383; *badius*, 383, **383**
pig's ear, 41, **41**, 42, 352, 452
pine: limber, 473; lodgepole, 294, 330, 331, 474; ponderosa, 217; western white, 473; whitebark, 473

pine mushroom: about, **146**, 146–47, **147**, 154, 442; edibility of, 145; and First Nations, 471; and grey false bolete, 382; identifying, 117, 160, 163, 168; and leopard trich, 159; and mycoheterotrophs, 55, **55**
pinedrops, 469
pink bubble gum mushroom, 136, **136**
pinkgill: blue-edge, 226, **226**; nippled brown, 227, **227**
pink-tipped coral, 370, 372, **372**
pipsissewas, 55
Piptoporus betulinus, 399
Pisolithus, 421, 430; *arhizus* group, 343, 421, 430, **430**; *tinctorius*, 430
pitted milk cap, 68, **68**, 69
Plectania, 449; *melastoma*, 454, **454**, 455; *milleri*, 454; *nannfeldtii*, 454
Pleurocybella porrigens, 191, 208–9, 211, **211**, 214, 256
Pleurotus, 44, 207, 209; *dryinus*, 209, 210, **210**, 215, 217, 219; *ostreatus* group, 207, **208**, 208–9, **209**, 210, 211, 212, 218, 219; *populinus*, 209; *pulmonarius*, 209
plums and custard, 167, **167**, 264, 274
Pluteus, 221, 222; *atromarginatus*, 222; *cervinus* group, 221, 222, **222**; *exilis*, 222
Podaxis pistillaris, 427, **427**
poison pax, **75**, 256, 271, 272, 273, **273**
poison pie, 189, 275, **275**, 277
Polyozellus, 33; *atrolazulinus*, 41, 42, **42**; *marymargaretae*, 42; *multiplex*, 42
polypore: bay, 383; bitter brown, 381, **381**, 391; blue cheese, 385, **385**; cinnabar, 389, **389**; sheep, 380, **380**, 381, 382; veiled, 406, **406**; western mountain, 381, 391, **391**
Polypores of British Columbia (Ginns), 379
Polyporus: badius, 383; *elegans*, 383; *hirtus*, 381; *varius*, 383
poplar pholiota, 267, **267**
poplar trich, 151, 152, **152**, 471
Porodaedalea, 378, 404; *pini* group, 388, 404, **404**
portobellos, 229
Postia, 378; *caesia* group, 385, **385**; *fragilis*, 385; *simulans*, 385
powdercap: earthy, 100, **100**, 101; sheathed, **96**, 100, 101, **101**
the prince, 230, **230**, 231
Protostropharia, 299; *alcis*, 313; *semiglobata*, 313, **313**, 315
prunes and custard, 166, **166**, 203
psathyrella: ringed, 315, **315**; suburban, 314, **314**
Psathyrella, 289, 299; *ammophila*, 314; *candolleana* group, 314, **314**; *epimyces*, 290; *gracilis* group, 312; *longistriata*, 315, **315**; *piluliformis*, 314
Pseudoarmillariella ectypoides, 141
Pseudoclitocybe cyathiformis, 142, 143
Pseudohydnum, 411, 416; *gelatinosum* group, 335, 416, **416**
Pseudoplectania: melaena, 454; *nigrella*, 454

Pseudosarcosoma latahense, 455
Pseudosperma: *rimosum*, 258; *sororium*, 258, **258**
Psilocybe, 283, 286, 299, 306, 308–9, 310, 311, 316, 401; *ceres*, 316; *cubensis*, 306; *cyanescens*, 308, 311, **311**; *montana*, 306; *pelliculosa*, 310; *semilanceata*, 308, 310, **310**, 311, 390; *stuntzii*, 311
psychedelics, 26–27, 262, 264, 288, 299, 308–9, 442
Pterospora andromedea, 469
Pucciniastrum goeppertianum, 472, **472**
puffball: gemmed, 406, 422, 423, **423**, 426; lead-coloured, 426, **426**; pear, 422, **422**, 423; sculptured giant, 424, **424**, 425; western giant, 424, 425, **425**
purple fairy club, 351, **351**, 353
purple jelly-drops, 418, **418**
purple-brown amanita, 120, **120**
purple-staining milk cap, 66, 67, **67**
Pycnoporellus, 403; *alboluteus*, 389; *fulgens*, 389
Pycnoporus, 378, 389; *cinnabarinus*, 389, **389**
Pyrrhulomyces astragalinus, 316

quinine conk, 396, **396**

ragged spruce rot mushroom, 71, 216, **216**, 217, 394
The Rainbow Beneath My Feet (Bessette & Bessette), 343
rainbow chanterelle, 34, 36, **36**
Ramaria, 41, 239, 343, 369, 372, 375; *apiculata*, 373; *araiospora*, 375; *botrytis*, 370, 372, **372**; *cystidiophora*, 374; *pinicola*, 371; *rasilispora*, 374, **374**; *stricta*, 373, **373**; *stuntzii*, 375, **375**
Ramaria araiospora, 375
Ramaria of the Pacific Northwestern United States (Exeter, Novell & Cázares), 375
Raverat, Gwen, 357
red alder, 94, 457, 476
red gravel, 468, **468**
red hot milk cap, 64, 65, **65**
red hot russula, 46, 49, 50, **50**
red leaf spot, 474, **474**
red paint fungus, 407, **407**, 471
red ring rot, 404
red-banded webcap, 243, **243**
red-belted conk, 376, 392, 393, 395, 396, 398, **398**, 402, 471
red-brown trich, 145, 151, **151**, 152, 153
red-cracked bolete, 320, **320**, 321, 324, 377
Redhead, Scott, 36, 161
red-pored bolete, 325, **325**
red-staining agaricus, 116, 234, **234**
reproduction, 4–6, 24
resources, 27–28
Rhizina undulata, 458
Rhizopogon, 55, 469, 470; *Amylopogon* subgenus, 469; *arctostaphyli*, 469; *occidentalis*, 470; *parksii*, 469, **469**; *salebrosus*, 469; *vinicolor*, 469
Rhodocollybia, 185, 199; *badiialba*, 198, 199; *butyracea*, 186, 192, 197, 198, **198**, 221; *maculata*, 199; *oregonensis*, 88, 199, **199**

Rhodocybe nitellina, 197, 198
Rhododendron menziesii, 474
rhododendrons, 475
Rhodofomes, 378, 397; *cajanderi*, 397, **397**
Rhodophana nitellina, 197, 198
Rhytisma, 349; *punctatum*, 349, 475, **475**; *salicinum*, 475
Ribes, 473
Rickenella, 183; *fibula*, 139, 183, **183**; *swartzii*, 139, 183
ring, 18, **18**
ringed conocybe, 281
ringed psathyrella, 315, **315**
Rogers, Maggie (Mary Margaret), 42
Rogers, Robert, 401
roles, ecological, 6–9
Roridomyces roridus, 184, **184**
rose rusts, 474, **474**
rosy conk, 397, **397**
rosy entoloma, 225, **225**
rosy gomphidius, 296, **296**, 297, 327
rot: brown crumbly, 395; brown cubical, 395; brown trunk, 395; jelly, 376, 409, **409**, 410; laminated root, 395; ragged spruce, 71, 216, **216**, 217, 394; red ring, 404
Rozites, 244
Rubroboletus, 317; *pulcherrimus*, 325, **325**; *satanas*, 325
Rubus: *armeniacus*, 474; *laciniatus*, 474
ruby parasol, 122, **122**
russula: biting, 46, 49, **49**; blackening, 58, **58**, 59, 116, 256; comb, 53, **53**; grass green, 57, **57**; phoenix, 51, **51**; red hot, 46, 49, 50, **50**; short-stemmed, 39, 45, 52, **52**, **54**, 54–55, 56, 146; shrimp, 45, 46, **46**, 49, 50; thick-skinned, 56, **56**; violet, 47, **47**
Russula, 39, 43, 44, 45, 239, 339; *adusta*, 58; *aeruginea*, 57; *albonigra*, 58; *americana*, 50; *benwooii*, 46; *bicolor*, 48; *brevipes* group, 39, 45, 52, **52**, **54**, 54–55, 56, 146; *cascadensis*, 52; *cerolens*, 53, **53**; *crassotunicata*, 56, **56**; *decolorans*, 58; *densifolia*, 58; *dissimulans*, 58; *emetica*, 45, 48, **48**, 50; *favrei*, 46; *fragilis*, 51; *fragrantissima* group, 53; *graminea*, 57, **57**; *hypofragilis*, 51; *lutea*, 57; *montana*, 48; *mordax*, 46, 49, **49**; *murrillii* group, 47, **47**; *nigricans* group, 58, **58**, 59, 116, 256; *olivina*, 57; *phoenicea*, 51, **51**; *queletii* group, 47, **47**; *rhodocephala*, 46, 49, 50, **50**; *rosacea*, 50; *sanguinaria*, 50; *sanguinea*, 50; *silvicola*, 48; *sororia*, 53; *stuntzii*, 51, 56, **56**; *subnigricans*, 256; *versicolor*, 51; *veternosa*, 49; *viridofusca*, 46; *xerampelina* group, 45, 46, **46**, 49, 50; *zelleri*, 47
rust: fir-blueberry, 472, **472**; rose, 474, **474**; Saskatoon-juniper, 473, **473**; western gall, 474; white pine blister, 473, **473**

saddle-shaped false morel, 444, 445, **445**, 446
Sagara, Naohiko, 277

salal, 194, 475
salal garlic mushroom, 194, **194**, 204
Salix, 161
Sarcodon, 335, 340, 345; *fuscoindicus*, 345; *imbricatus*, 335, 340, **340**; *scabrosus*, 340, 345; *squamosus*, 340
Sarcomyxa serotina, 209, 212, **212**
Sarcoscypha coccinea, 457
Sarcosoma: *mexicana*, 455; *mexicanum*, 455
Sarcosphaera, 449, 451; *coronaria*, 451, **451**; *crassa*, 451
Saskatoon berry, 473
Saskatoon-juniper rust, 473, **473**
scaberstalk: aspen, 332, 333, **333**, 334; birch, 332, 334, **334**; orange-capped, 332, **332**, 333, 334
scarlet bonnet, 174, **174**, 175
scarlet waxy cap, 81, 82, 83, **83**
Schäffer, Julius, 273
Schalkwijk-Barendsen, Helene, 347
Schizophyllum commune group, 220, **220**
Scleroderma, 421, 429, 463, 465; *cepa*, 429; *citrinum*, 429, **429**, 451, 465
scrambled egg slime mould, **205**
sculptured giant puffball, 424, **424**, 425
scurfy twiglet, 281, 284, **284**
Scutellinia, 449, 457; *scutellata* group, 457, **457**
Scutiger ellisii, 380
Scytinotus longinquus, 213, 214
seasons, 24
Seidl, Michelle T., 252
separating trich, 148, 149, **149**, 157
Sept, Duane, 27
shaggy mane, 290, **290**, 292, 427; desert, 427, **427**
shaggy parasol, 97, 98, **98**, 99, 116, 123
Shakespeare, 188
sheathed powdercap, **96**, 100, 101, **101**
sheathed waxy cap, 89, 93, **93**
sheathed woodtuft, 165, 202, 270, **270**, 286, 301, 306
sheep polypore, 380, **380**, 381, 382
shoehorn oyster, 210, 219, **219**
shore pine, 331
short-stemmed russula, 39, 45, 52, **52**, **54**, 54–55, 56, 146
short-stemmed slippery jack, 330, **330**
shrimp russula, 45, 46, **46**, 49, 50
the sickener, 45, 48, **48**, 50
Siegel, Noah, 27
silvery violet webcap, 240, **240**, 241, 255
Singer, Rolf, 78
Sir Nigel (Doyle), 60
Sitka spruce, 35, 38, 73, 204, 216, 294, 380, 398
slime moulds, 205, **205**, 355, 364, 377
slimy brown webcap, 252, **252**
slimy milk cap, 70, 71, 72, **72**, 143
slippery jack, 331, **331**
slippery mycena, 184, **184**
small staghorn, 354, 415, **415**
smelly oyster, 213, **213**

smelly trich, 150, 162, **162**
Smith, Alexander H., 37, 67, 71, 425
Smith's amanita, 117, **117**, 118, 123, 146, 163, 256
snowbank orange peel, 453, **453**, 456
snowmelt clitocybe, 131, **131**
snowy crep, 214
Snyder, Leon Carleton, 439
Snyder's morel, 439, **439**
soapy trich, 155, **155**, 159
Some Mushrooms and Other Fungi of British Columbia (Hardy), 257
sooty brown waxy cap, 92, **92**
South Vancouver Island Mycological Society (SVIMS), 114
Sowerbyella rhenana, 456
Sparassis, 369, 370; *crispa*, 370; *radicata*, 370, **370**, 442
Spathularia, 349, 365; *flavida*, 363, 365, **365**
species, cryptic, 12, 177, 220, 229, 243, 251, 336, 350, 404
species, descriptions, 10–20
speckled alder, 476
speckled tar spot, 349, 475, **475**
Spinellus fusiger mould, 173, 476
spirit gummy bear, 335, 416, **416**
split gill, 220, **220**
spore print, 16–17, **17**
spot: hexagonal, 475, **475**; red leaf, 474, **474**; speckled tar, 349, 475, **475**; willow tar, 475
spring agrocybe, 244, 271, 279, **279**
spring king, 24, 318
spring western white truffle, 464
spruce waxy cap, 84, 85, **85**, 86, 121
St. George's mushroom, **420**
Stamets, Paul, 264
starving man's licorice, 454, 455, **455**
stems, **17**, 17–18
Stereum, 339, 413; *hirsutum*, 377, 386, 387, **387**; *sanguinolentum*, 387, **387**, 418
the stinker, 148, 150, **150**, 162
stinkhorn: common, **356**, 356–57; dog, 358, **358**
stinking earth fan, 408
strap club, 351, 353, **353**
strawberries and cream, 341, **341**, 343, 344, 384
streaked trich, 145, 149, 157, **157**, 158, 159, 224
Strobilurus: *albipilatus*, 204; *occidentalis*, 204; *trullisatus*, 204, **204**
stropharia: ambiguous, 302, **302**, 303; blue-green, 304, **304**; wine cap, 299, 303, 305, **305**
Stropharia, 299, 304; *aeruginosa*, 304, **304**; *ambigua*, 302, **302**, 303; *aurantiaca*, 316; *hornemannii*, 302, 303, **303**, 305; *rugosoannulata*, 299, 303, 305, **305**; *semiglobata*, 313
Stuntz, Daniel E., 28, 375
subalpine larch, 328
suburban psathyrella, 314, **314**
Suillus, 277, 295, 296, 297, 317, 326, 327, 328, 330, 469, 470; *ampliporus*, 327, 328, **328**; *brevipes*, 330, **330**; *caerulescens*, 326, **326**, 327, 329; *cavipes*,

328; *clintonianus*, 331; *flavidus*, 331; *granulatus*, 330; *grevillei*, 331; *lakei*, 326, 327, **327**, 328, 329; *luteus*, 331, **331**; *ochraceoroseus*, 328; *punctatipes*, 330; *tomentosus*, 327, 329, **329**; *umbonatus*, 331; *weaverae*, 330
sulphur tuft, 265, **288**, 300, **300**, 301
sunny side up, 104, 281, 282, **282**
sunshine amanita, 106, 109, 110, **110**, 111
surface, fertile, 14–15
sushi mushroom, 187, 190, **190**, 221
swamp beacon, 363, **363**, 364, 365
sweat-producing clitocybe, 85, 134, 135, **135**, 186, 189, 223
sweetbread mushroom, 221, 223, **223**
Swift, Jonathan, 213
Systema Naturae (Linnaeus), 436
Tàipíng Guǎngjì, 277
tamarack, 328
tamarack jack, 327, 328, **328**
Taphrina: deformans, 476; *occidentalis*, 476, **476**; *populina*, 476
taphrina leaf blister, 476
Tapinella, 271; *atrotomentosa*, 271, 272, **272**, 273; *panuoides*, 212, 213, 272
taxonomy, fungal, 11
Telamonia subgenus, 239, 243, 250
The Tempest (Shakespeare), 188
terminology, mycological, 3; basidiomycetes vs. ascomycetes, 6; "group," 12; mushroom, as term, 4. *See also* glossary
terrestrial pholiota, 266, 269, **269**
Tetrapyrgos subdendrophora, 191
Thelephora, 33, 55, 408; *palmata*, 408; *terrestris* group, 33, 379, 384, 408, **408**
thick cup, 41, 452, **452**
thick-skinned russula, 56, **56**
thimble cap, 441, **441**
tiger's eye, 346, 384, **384**
tinder conk, 396, 400, 402, **402**, 471
toadskin milk cap, 73, **73**
Tolypocladium, 349, 360, 362; *capitatum*, 360, 361, 362, **362**, 465; *ophioglossoides*, 360, 362
tooth: conifer-cone, 335, 347, **347**; jelly, 416; orange, 344, **344**; violet, 345, **345**
toque mycena, 179, **179**
train wrecker, 216, 217, **217**
Trametes, 378, 389; *betulina*, 388; *cinnabarina*, 389; *hirsuta*, 386; *versicolor*, **379**, 386, **386**, 387, 401, 413
Trappe, James, 463
Trappe, Matt, 463
trembling aspen, 75, 152, 209, 215, 332, 333, 334, 398, 476
Tremella, 411, 412, 413, 418; *aurantia*, 413; *encephala*, 413; *foliacea*, 418; *mesenterica*, 412, 413, **413**
Tremellodendropsis tuberosa, 371
Tremiscus helvelloides, 419

trich: ashen, 156, 157, 158, **158**, 159; celery-scented, 160, **160**, 161, 169; leopard, 146, 155, 156, 157, 158, 159, **159**, 168; mouse, 156, **156**, 158, 159; poplar, 151, 152, **152**, 471; red-brown, 145, 151, **151**, 152, 153; separating, 148, 149, **149**, 157; smelly, 150, 162, **162**; soapy, 155, **155**, 159; streaked, 145, 149, 157, **157**, 158, 159, 224; veiled orange, 146, 154, **154**
Trichaptum: abietinum, 386; *biforme*, 386
Trichoglossum hirsutum, **348**, 367
Tricholoma, 44, 145, 189; *apium*, 160, **160**, 161, 169; *atroviolaceum*, 159; *caligatum*, 146; *davisiae*, 149; *dulciolens*, 146; *equestre* group, 113, 145, 148, **148**, 149, 150, 166; *flavovirens*, 148; *focale* group, 146, 154, **154**; *imbricatum*, 151, 153, 169; *inamoenum*, 150, 162, **162**; *intermedium*, 148, 149; *magnivelare*, 147; *murrillianum*, 55, **55**, 117, 145, **146**, 146–47, **147**, 154, 159, 160, 163, 168, 382, 442, 471; *pardinum*, 146, 155, 156, 157, 158, 159, **159**, 168; *pessundatum* group, 145, 151, **151**, 152, 153; *populinum*, 151, 152, **152**, 471; *portentosum*, 145, 149, 157, **157**, 158, 159, 224; *robustum*, 154; *saponaceum* group, 155, **155**, 159; *sejunctum* group, 148, 149, **149**, 157; *sulphurescens*, 162; *sulphureum* group, 148, 150, **150**, 162; *terreum* group, 156, **156**, 158, 159; *vaccinum*, 151, 153, **153**, 169; *virgatum*, 156, 157, 158, **158**, 159; *zelleri*, 154
Tricholomas of North America (Bessette et al.), 145
Tricholomopsis, 145, 167; *decora*, 166, **166**, 203; *rutilans*, 166, 167, **167**, 264, 274
Trudell, Steve, 27, 147
truffle: common deer, 360, 362, 465, **465**; fall western white, 464, **464**, 466, 468; western black, 464, **467**
truffle eater, 360, 361, 362, **362**, 465
Truncocolumella, 470; *citrina*, 470, **470**
Tubaria, 281; *furfuracea* group, 281, 284, **284**; *hiemalis*, 284; *punicea*, 285, **285**
Tuber, 463, 466; *aestivum*, 466; *borchii*, 466; *gibbosum*, 464; *melanosporum*, 466; *oregonense*, 464, **464**, 466, 468; *rapaeodorum*, 467
tuberous collybia, 185, 195, **195**, 201
tufted collybia, 192, **192**, 193, 197, 198, 200
Tulostoma, 427
Turbinellus, 33, 40, 41, 369; *floccosus*, **32**, 34, 40, **40**, 41; *kauffmanii*, 40, **40**, 41
turkey tail, **379**, 386, **386**, 387, 401, 413
two-coloured laccaria, 126, 127, **127**, 128
Tyromyces: caesius, 385; *chioneus*, 385

upright coral, 373, **373**
Urnula, 449; *padeniana*, 454, 455, **455**

Vancouver Mycological Society (VMS), 114, 115
varnished conk 379, 392, **392**, 393, 401
veiled orange trich, 146, 154, **154**
veiled oyster mushroom, 209, 210, **210**, 215, 217, 219
veiled polypore, 406, **406**
velvet foot, 25, 190, 202, **202**
velvet pinwheel, 187, **187**, 190

velvet rollrim, 271, 272, **272**, 273
velvety earth tongue, **348**, 367
velvety milk cap, 70, **70**
vermilion waxy cap, **76**, 82, **82**, 83
Verpa, 436, 437; *bohemica*, 441, **441**; *conica* group, 441, **441**
Vibrissea, 349; *truncorum*, 363, 364, **364**
violet russula, 47, **47**
violet tooth, 345, **345**
violet webcap, 239, 242, **242**
vocabulary. *See* terminology, mycological

Wallis, Gordon, 395
Wasson, R. Gordon, 235, 308
Wasson, Valentina Pavlovna, 235
water club, 363, 364, **364**
wavy cap, 308, 311, **311**
waxy cap: acute conic, 78, 79, **79**, 80; blushing, 91, **91**; brown almond, 88, **88**, 199; cedar, 85; golden-fringed, 84, 86, **86**; larch, 81, **81**, 83; olive-brown, 89, **89**, 93; orange-brown, 80, 87, 90, **90**; parrot, 87, **87**, 90; scarlet, 81, 82, 83, **83**; sheathed, 89, 93, **93**; sooty brown, 92, **92**; spruce, 84, 85, **85**, 86, 121; vermilion, **76**, 82, **82**, 83
webcap: bitter brown, 245, **245**; blood-red, **246**, 246–47; bluefoot, 189, 249, **249**; fruity lilac, 240, 241, **241**; goldband, 248, **248**; olive, 166, 251, **251**, 265; red-banded, 243, **243**; silvery violet, 240, **240**, 241, 255; slimy brown, 252, **252**; violet, 239, 242, **242**; woolly, 250, **250**
western black truffle, 464, **467**
western cauliflower mushroom, 370, **370**, 442
western gall rust, 474
western giant puffball, 424, 425, **425**
western hemlock, 35, 37, 38, 74, 338, 375, 380
western jelly ear, 411, 416, 417, **417**
western larch, 328, 396
western lilac fibrehead, 177, 240, 254, 255, **255**
western mountain polypore, 381, 391, **391**
western redcedar, 94, 294
western varnished conk, 379, 392, **392**, 393, 401
western white pine, 473
western woodland amanita, 118, **118**
western yellow-veil amanita, 111, **111**
white barrel bird's nest, 431, 432, 433, **433**
white caesar, 112
white chanterelle, 37, **37**
white fibrehead, 254, **254**, 255
white icicle, 355, **355**
white marasmius, 191, **191**
white parasol, 113, 123, **123**, 236
white pine blister rust, 473, **473**
whitebark pine, 473
white-egg bird's nest, 432, 433, 434, **434**
willow tar spot, 475
wine cap stropharia, 299, 303, 305, **305**
winter chanterelle, 38, **38**, 141, 337
winter oyster, 209, 212, **212**

wintergreens, 55, 459
witch's butter, 412, **412**, 413, 414; hardwood, 412, 413, **413**
witch's hat, 78, **78**, 79
wood ear mushrooms, 417, **417**
wood woollyfoot, 192, 193, **193**
woodland agaricus, 231, 232, 233, **233**
woolly chanterelle, **32**, 34, 40, **40**, 41
woolly inky cap, 289, 291, **291**
woolly jack, 327, 329, **329**
woolly milk cap, 39, 66, 68, 69, **69**
woolly pine spike, 34–35, 298, **298**
woolly webcap, 250, **250**
Xerocomellus, 317; *atropurpureus*, 321; *chrysenteron*, 320; *diffractus*, 320, **320**, 321, 324, 377; *zelleri*, 320, 321, **321**, 322
Xeromphalina, 144; *campanella* group, 141, 144, **144**; *cauticinalis*, 144; *cornui*, 144; *fulvipes*, 144, **144**
Xylaria, 349; *hypoxylon*, 359, **359**

yellow fairy cups, 414, 418, 462, **462**
yellow mountain coral, 374, **374**
yellow mountain pea, 476, **476**
yellow waxy cap, 79, 80, **80**
yellowfoot (chanterelle), 38
yellowfoot dapperling, 102, **102**
yellow-gilled gym, 167, 264, **264**
yellowleg bonnet, 140, 173, 178, **178**

Zeller, Myron, 321
Zeller's bolete, 320, 321, **321**, 322
Zhu-Liang Yang, 121
Zhuliangomyces, 121; *illinitus*, 84, 121, **121**
zombie ants, 360–61, **361**